A Fire You Can't Put Out

Religion and American Culture

Series Editors   David Edwin Harrell

Wayne Flynt

Edith L. Blumhofer

A Fire You Can't Put Out

The Civil Rights Life of Birmingham's Reverend Fred Shuttlesworth

Andrew M. Manis

To Bill Madges,
With appreciation & my best
wishes,
Andrew M. Manis

To: Bill
Sincerely and Best Wishes,
Rev. F. L. Shuttlesworth

The University of Alabama Press ▪ Tuscaloosa and London

∞

The paper on which this book is printed meets the minimum requirements of
American National Standard for Information Science-Permanence of Paper for
Printed Library Materials, ANSI z39.48-1984.

Library of Congress Cataloging-in-Publication Data

Manis, Andrew Michael.
    A fire you can't put out : the civil rights life of
Birmingham's Reverend Fred Shuttlesworth / Andrew M. Manis.
        p.   cm. — (Religion and American culture)
    Includes bibliographical references (p.   ) and index.

    ISBN 0–8173–0968–3 (alk. paper)
    1. Shuttlesworth, Fred L., 1922–   2. Civil rights
movements—Alabama—Birmingham—History—20th century.
3. Afro-Americans—Civil rights—Alabama—Birmingham—History—20th
century.   4. Birmingham (Ala.)—Race relations.   5. Civil rights
workers—Alabama—Birmingham—Biography.   I. Title.   II. Series:
Religion and American culture (Tuscaloosa, Ala.)
    E334.B69 N448 1999
    305.8′960730761781—dc21
                                    99–6033
                                    CIP

British Library Cataloguing-in-Publication data available

Jacket design by Mary Frances Burt. Text design by Shari DeGraw.

To Meigan

Contents

Preface

Somewhere in these pages the reader will find a mature Fred Shuttlesworth looking back over what he called a "vagabond life." Such has been the case for me in the twelve years that I have worked on the book you now—finally—have in your hands. Since beginning the research I have changed jobs and cities and life situations. My acknowledgments will mention helpful colleagues in four cities where I have lived and many others that I have visited. Still, one element has remained a constant—"the Shuttlesworth book."

One is tempted to ask why anyone would spend such a large part of one's life reading, thinking, talking, and writing about a person of whom no one but participants in the civil rights movement and a few historians has ever heard. The most obvious answer is so that the story can get out to the wider public. There are other answers, some historical, some personal.

This is the story of probably the most unsung of the many heroes of the American civil rights movement. Put very bluntly, without Fred Shuttlesworth the 1963 Birmingham protests could not have happened, and without those demonstrations Congress would have ended racial segregation in public accommodations later than it did. That notable contribution makes Shuttlesworth's story worth spending time on. Another reason is the story's compelling drama, to which I hope I have done justice.

A few historians have written about Shuttlesworth on their way to telling the story of Martin Luther King Jr. Stephen Oates, David Levering Lewis, David Garrow, Adam Fairclough, and Taylor Branch fall into this category. In their collective work they have produced incidental vignettes of Fred Shuttlesworth's involvement in civil rights and, to a much lesser degree, of his life as an African American minister. Their works show varying degrees of appreciation for and understanding of Shuttlesworth. These historians have quite appropriately kept their "cameras" on King and only discuss Shuttlesworth when he came into the frame with King.

More recently, Glenn T. Eskew has focused on events in Birmingham and the persons central to the action there. No one was more central to the action than Fred Shuttlesworth. Eskew, more than anyone to date, has kept his camera on the firebrand minister from Birmingham. I have greatly profited from his insights, both from conversations and from the reading of his fine book. My story differs from his in that my camera has followed Shuttlesworth into his churches and into his home both as a child and as an adult. Eskew and the others recognize the religious and pastoral background of Shuttlesworth's civil rights life. I *emphasize* it because it is indispensable for understanding the persona of Fred Shuttlesworth.

I also emphasize it because of my own background. As a southern white boy who grew up in Birmingham, I remember the times depicted here. I remember the feeling that something out of the ordinary had happened the day my mother called me in from a Southside playground with the grim warning that African Americans in our town were "causing trouble again." I also remember the morning I came out of Sunday school and learned that some little girls just a few years my senior had been killed in a bombing at another church not very far away.

Years later I read about those events in King's book *Why We Can't Wait* for my seminary ethics class. At that crucial point in my education, while I was writing a paper on white Southern Baptists' reactions to King, I happened to visit my uncle in Cincinnati, Ohio. As we talked, I offhandedly mentioned my research topic, and he asked if I had ever heard of Fred Shuttlesworth. In his construction business, it turned out, my uncle had only recently built the sanctuary of the Greater New Light Baptist Church, where Shuttlesworth was pastor. After a quick call and an hour's wait, Shuttlesworth appeared in my uncle's living room where we began the first of many conversations about his life. I interviewed him later while researching my doctoral dissertation, which became my first book, *Southern Civil Religions in Conflict: Black and White Baptists and Civil Rights, 1947–1957*. After finishing that book, as a professor at the historically black Xavier University of Louisiana, I decided that "the Shuttlesworth book" would be my next project.

Thus I come to this story as a former Birminghamian who grew up to be a historian of southern and African American religion. From this vantage point I try to place Shuttlesworth's story within the context of the religious experience of black people in the American South. I believe Shuttlesworth personified a significant essence of African American spirituality and the black way of being Christian. I give attention to Shuttlesworth's ministerial career, which was of course the platform from which he launched his civil rights life. Nevertheless, to a great extent his ministerial career (just to phrase it in this manner is to secularize it—Shuttlesworth, like most ministers, would simply say his "ministry") and his civil rights activism were different sides of the same coin. I also give attention to his theological views and how they shaped his actions in civil rights and in what are nowadays called "justice issues." As a historian of religion, I am best able to evaluate certain religious aspects of his life and work. I do so within the social, political, and legal contexts of these events, but I acknowledge that I do not address these concerns with as much attention or clarity as some readers might like. Finally, my narrative gives the reader a peek into the minister's family life and how it was affected by his religious and social perspectives and his civil rights involvement.

Of course, I could not have painted this picture without the aid of Fred Shuttlesworth himself. As he often quipped, he was "a fighter, not a writer." He produced no great body of writings for scholars to analyze. This biography therefore is based largely, though certainly not solely, on my interviews with the subject. In several lengthy sessions that amounted to some seventy-five hours of conversation, I gathered oral information with which to supplement my written sources, of which there are very many. Some readers will take this as a sign that this is an "as told to" book and an apology for Shuttlesworth's interpretation of the events.

Naturally, no historian is free of bias, and biographers are often said to love or hate their subjects. Admittedly, I am sympathetic to Fred Shuttlesworth, still living as of this writing, as a person and to his role in the civil rights movement. Yet I strongly disagree with many of his views and criticize him at a number of points in this narrative. I should also note that despite his giving me extensive blocks of his time for interviews, he did not attempt nor would I have allowed him to exercise any editorial control over what appears here. I have attempted to be evenhanded in my analysis of Fred Shuttlesworth; whether I have succeeded, others can and will judge.

Having thus made the transition to acknowledgment, I now proceed with my words of thanks to the many other persons who have aided me along this journey. In addition to Fred Shuttlesworth himself, to whom I owe my greatest debt, I am grateful to the many other colleagues of the movement, church members, fellow ministers, and family members who granted me interviews. Audiotapes for all and transcripts for most of these interviews will eventually be available for other scholars in the Department of Archives and Manuscripts at the Birmingham Public Library. In that context, Marvin Y. Whiting, recently retired from his role as archivist there, has given me great help and cheered me on as much as anyone. His successor, Jim Baggett, has helped me obtain some of the photographs that appear in this volume, and his assistant, Don Veazey, has always helped make my many research trips to Birmingham more productive.

Many other archivists and librarians have helped me along the way, not all of whose names I had the presence of mind to record. To those whom I have neglected, I extend my thanks and beg their indulgence. Among these are the staffs of the John F. Kennedy Presidential Library in Boston and the Mugar Library at Boston University; the library of the Department of History at the University of Alabama in Birmingham; the library of Selma University; and the library of the University of Pennsylvania in Philadelphia.

I do note the assistance of Esme Bahn at the Moorland-Spingarn Research Center of Howard University, Washington, D.C.; Diane Ware of the Martin Luther King Jr. Center for Nonviolent Social Change in Atlanta; Wilma Musholder of the Peace Collection at the library of Swarthmore College, Swarthmore, Pennsylvania; and Colleen Phillips of the Public Library of Cincinnati and Hamilton County, Ohio. Jack Mendelsohn, president of the Blackside Civil Rights Project, Inc. helped me procure a copy of Shuttlesworth's interview from the prize-winning documentary *Eyes on the Prize*.

The research and writing of this book has happily been aided by the financial support of a number of charitable foundations. During the 1988–1989 academic year the Andrew W. Mellon Foundation supported my research through its Fellowship in the Humanities program at the University of Pennsylvania. While at Penn I profited greatly from conversations with and encouragement from Jack Reese, Evelyn Brooks Higginbotham (now of the Harvard Divinity School), Mary Frances Berry, and Drew Gilpin Faust. For the academic year 1994–1995 the work was underwritten by the Pew Evangelical Scholars Program, University of Notre Dame. I am grateful for the encouragement provided by Nathan Hatch, director of the program, as well as by fellow recipients Jim Bradley, Alan Jacobs, and Charles Marsh. The United Negro College Fund also aided this effort through a 1988 Strengthening the Humanities grant, as did a 1988 Travel to Collections grant from the National Endowment for the Humanities.

In 1992 and 1993 my research and my teaching were enhanced by a Fellowship for Young Scholars in American Religion sponsored by the Center for the Study of Religion and American Culture, Indiana University/Purdue University at Indianapolis. The junior scholars who were my colleagues and the senior scholars who were our leaders deserve my thanks. All of them read the first draft of my first chapter and gave me good suggestions for improving it. They have faithfully pulled for me to get the work done. I especially thank Tony Fels, Gerry McDermott, Tom Tweed, and Valarie Ziegler for their input. Thanks also to Conrad Cherry, director of the program, and Catherine Albanese and William Hutchison, who served as seminar leaders.

Probably as significant in my conceiving this project was the opportunity to be part of a 1986 NEH Summer Institute on African-American Religious History at Princeton University. Led by Albert Raboteau and David Wills, this gathering of devotees of African American studies inspired me to pursue this subject. Over the years since we spent summer camp together these scholars have helped me think about Fred Shuttlesworth and convinced me that his story was important. I especially thank Sandy D. Martin for his encouragement and Robert Hall, who put me up in his home during a research trip to Washington. In addition I thank Harriet Amos Doss, Randall Burkett, and the late James Melvin Washington for their insights and their urging me to continue.

Another NEH Summer Seminar on Southern Religion in 1992 took me to the University of Mississippi, where I bounced some of these ideas off my colleagues there. Charles Reagan Wilson, David Chappell, and Stephen Ward Angell have cheered for me ever since, and our conversations have helped me avoid errors I might otherwise have made. In the same category I would put John B. Boles, professor of history at Rice University and editor of the *Journal of Southern History.*

Special thanks is due David J. Garrow, whose work on the life of Martin Luther King Jr. was a high standard toward which to aim. He graciously encouraged a young researcher whom he did not previously know, opening to me both his home and his voluminous files on the civil rights movement. He also read the manuscript and offered many helpful suggestions, not all of which I had the good sense to follow but for which I remain very grateful. Wayne Flynt, my mentor from college days, has prodded me along and has never failed to believe in me and in this project, as has Bill J. Leonard, my doctoral supervisor and friend.

I would also thank many former and current colleagues who have nursed me through the low points along the way and have rejoiced with me at the high points: Gordon Wilson; Bill Lindsey; Kathleen Gaffney; Bernice Guillaume; the late Sister Rosemary Kleinhaus; John Laughlin; Richard Vinson; Bill Trimyer; Barbara Clark; Ann Garbett; Sue Rogers; and Rebecca Clark. Marc Jolley suggested ways to improve the manuscript. Shana Foster read the first half of the manuscript and pestered me every day for a year to finish the rest of it, always telling me it was worth the effort. Thanks should also go to Sonja Grube for the money clip she gave me two Christmases ago—to hold all the money I will make from this book. Amelia Barclay and Diane Wudel expertly helped me clean up my writing, making the manuscript much more readable and more than anyone convinced me the final product was worth reading. My friend and talented graphic designer Mary Frances Burt showed interest in the project and designed the jacket cover for the book.

I would also like to thank the staff at the University of Alabama Press. Director Nicole Mitchell has been a consummate professional through the publication process, offering encouragement and helpful guidance; Mindy Wilson helped me iron out difficulties over permissions; Priscilla McWilliams and Michelle Sellers were unfailingly enthusiastic about the book and have worked diligently to market the book; Kathy Swain expertly served as copyeditor and brought the work to a more publishable form.

On a more personal note, let me express my appreciation to Bill and Christine Chronis for introducing me to Fred Shuttlesworth and for opening their home to me on numerous and lengthy occasions when I visited Cincinnati on research trips. My cousin Valerie Chronis Bickett always offered hospitality and encouragement. My sister, Kalliope Manis Findley, and her husband, Fred, have supported and encouraged me in this effort and through life struggles with love and great devotion. My brother, Pete, and cousin Ann Katros have also given me important support and friendship. Of course, my wife, Linda, has cheered me on and cheered me up over the last part of the writing. She is the sort of life companion about whom most people dream and, if so inclined, pray for.

Finally, my daughter, Meigan. She is an extraordinary young woman who has always lit up her daddy's eyes. She has often wanted her dad to come to her classes to tell some of the stories in this book, especially the ones about Fred Shuttlesworth's children. She graciously forgives my failures and my absences. Somehow, even at fifteen, she still seems to believe in her dad. For that, more than anything else, I am very grateful. And so to her I dedicate this book.

Abbreviations

ACMHR	Alabama Christian Movement for Human Rights
AIC	Anti-Injustice Committee
AME	African Methodist Episcopal
B.D.	Bachelor of Divinity
CMBCA	Colored Missionary Baptist Convention of Alabama
CORE	Congress of Racial Equality
FEPC	Fair Employment Practices Commission
FOR	Fellowship of Reconciliation
ICC	Inter-Citizens Committee
IMA	Interdenominational Ministerial Alliance
JCBA	Jefferson County Betterment Association
MIA	Montgomery Improvement Association
NAACP	National Association for the Advancement of Colored People
NBC	National Baptist Convention of the United States of America, Incorporated
SCEF	Southern Conference Educational Fund
SCHW	Southern Conference for Human Welfare
SCLC	Southern Christian Leadership Conference
SNCC	Student Nonviolent Coordinating Committee
SOC	Southern Organizing Committee for Economic and Social Justice
TCA	Tuskegee Civil Association
YMBC	Young Men's Business Club

Chronology of the Life
of Fred Lee Shuttlesworth

Mid-1870s	Birth of March Robinson, maternal grandfather of Fred Shuttlesworth.
Late 1890s	March Robinson marries Martha Carpenter, Montgomery County, Alabama.
August 25, 1900	Birth of Alberta Robinson, mother of Fred Shuttlesworth.
March 18, 1922	Birth of Freddie Lee Robinson, Mt. Meigs, Montgomery County, Alabama. The baby was the offspring of an unmarried relationship between Alberta Robinson and Vedder Greene. The couple never married, although they did give birth to another child, a girl named Cleola.
1925	Robinson family moves to Oxmoor, Jefferson County, Alabama.
January 22, 1927	Alberta Robinson marries William Nathan Shuttlesworth (born Tuscaloosa County, Alabama, 1877); Alberta's children are given their stepfather's name.
May 1940	Shuttlesworth graduates from Rosedale High School.
August 4, 1940	Shuttlesworth arrested for distilling; sentenced to two years probation.
October 20, 1941	Shuttlesworth marries Ruby Lanette Keeler (born Birmingham, Alabama, May 30, 1922).
1943	Birth of daughter Patricia.
April 1943	Shuttlesworth and family move to Mobile; Fred goes to work at Brookley Air Force Base as a truck driver.
June 1943	Shuttlesworth, an African Methodist, becomes a Baptist by joining Corinthian Baptist Church. Within a few

months, Shuttlesworth begins occasional preaching at the invitation of the Reverend E. A. Palmer. Attends Cedar Grove Academy Bible College in Pritchard, Alabama.

1945   Birth of daughter Ruby Fredericka.

1947   Birth of son Fred Jr.

September 1947   Begins work on A.B. degree at Selma University.

1948   Begins pastoral ministry: Everdale Baptist Church, Selma (July 1948); Mt. Zion Baptist Church, Potter Station, Alabama (October 1948). Ordained to the Baptist ministry August 10, 1948, Corinthian Baptist Church, Mobile, Alabama.

September 1949   Shuttlesworth decides to attend Alabama State College; family moves to Montgomery, Alabama.

October 1949   Shuttlesworth becomes interim pastor of the First (African) Baptist Church, Selma, Alabama; birth of daughter Carolyn.

May 1950   Shuttlesworth accepts full-time pastorate at First Baptist Church, Selma.

December 1952   After months of conflict with church lay leaders, Shuttlesworth leaves the pastorate of First Baptist Church, Selma; lives with wife's family in Birmingham.

March 1, 1953   Shuttlesworth begins pastorate of Bethel Baptist Church in the North Birmingham section known as Collegeville.

June 18–25, 1953   Baton Rouge, Louisiana, bus boycott.

November 1953   After four terms in office, Commissioner of Public Safety Eugene T. "Bull" Connor opts not to run for reelection in the wake of a sex scandal. He is succeeded by Robert Lindbergh.

May 17, 1954	U.S. Supreme Court outlaws racial segregation in the *Brown v. Board of Education* ruling.
May 31, 1955	U.S. Supreme Court orders states with segregated public schools to begin desegregating "with all deliberate speed."
July 25, 1955	Shuttlesworth petitions Birmingham City Commission for black police officers. Issues a statement, endorsed by seventy-six ministers, called "Crime, Delinquency, and Lawlessness." Leads a second delegation to city hall on September 1. Pleas rejected.
December 1, 1955	Rosa Parks refuses to give up seat on Montgomery bus; Montgomery bus boycott begins four days later; Shuttlesworth attends meetings of the Montgomery Improvement Association (MIA).

1956

February 29	Shuttlesworth and attorney Arthur Shores accompany Autherine Lucy in her attempt to become the first African American student at the University of Alabama.
June 1	Alabama circuit judge Walter B. Jones issues an injunction against the National Association for the Advancement of Colored People in Alabama barring all activities of the organization within the state.
June 5	Shuttlesworth founds the Alabama Christian Movement for Human Rights (ACMHR).
July 7	Shuttlesworth, N. H. Smith, and C. H. George request the removal of segregation signs and the establishment of a "first come, first served" seating policy on buses. They also seek the hiring of black drivers. Both requests are rejected.
August 20	Shuttlesworth accompanies two African Americans to take civil service exams. Applications are denied twice, leading to an ACMHR suit.

November 13	U.S. Supreme Court outlaws segregated bus seating in Montgomery, giving the bus boycott and the civil rights movement a major victory. Decision sparks a Shuttlesworth announcement that ACMHR members would ignore segregated seating on Birmingham buses.
December 20	MIA ends the Montgomery boycott, with buses desegregated the next day; Shuttlesworth and N. H. Smith send an ultimatum to the city commission calling for the desegregation of bus seating by December 26. Noncompliance would cause ACMHR members to ride buses on an integrated basis on that date.
December 25	Shuttlesworth's home bombed. His survival convinces Shuttlesworth and his followers that "God saved him to lead the fight."
December 26	Shuttlesworth and other African Americans ride buses and ignore segregated seating, an action that results in twenty-one riders being arrested.

1957

January 10–11	King, Abernathy, Shuttlesworth, and other African American ministers meet at Atlanta's Ebenezer Baptist Church; plan the founding of the Southern Leadership Conference on Transportation and Nonviolent Integration.
February 14	In a meeting in New Orleans, Shuttlesworth participates in the founding of the Southern Christian Leadership Conference (SCLC). Martin Luther King Jr. serves as president; by August Shuttlesworth replaces the Reverend T. J. Jemison as SCLC secretary.
March 6	Fred and Ruby Shuttlesworth take seats in the segregated terminal station waiting room. A mob of some fifty young toughs greet them with verbal abuse but no violence. White union worker and lay minister Lamar

Weaver joins the Shuttlesworths in the waiting room and is beaten by the mob as he attempts to leave the station.

May 17   On the third anniversary of *Brown,* an estimated eighteen thousand African Americans engage in a prayer pilgrimage to Washington, D.C. King gives his "Give Us the Ballot" speech; Shuttlesworth tells of his "miraculous" survival of the Christmas bombing.

June   Aided by Shuttlesworth's agitation and segregationist reaction to it, Connor defeats Lindbergh in the primary election for commissioner of public safety, virtually assuring his return to office in November.

August 22   Shuttlesworth petitions the Birmingham Board of Education to enroll daughters Pat and Ricky at the all-white Phillips High School.

September 2   Six Klan members castrate a young black man, Judge Aaron, warning that the same will happen to African American schoolchildren if Shuttlesworth continues with plans to integrate white schools.

September 9   Shuttlesworth attempts to enroll his daughters at Phillips High and is beaten by a mob with bicycle chains and baseball bats. Suffers only a slight concussion. His wife and daughter Ricky incur slight injuries. The same day President Eisenhower signs the 1957 Civil Rights Act; lawyers seek a writ to force Arkansas governor Orval Faubus to permit school integration in Little Rock.

1958

January 1   The *Birmingham World* names Shuttlesworth "Newsmaker of the Year" for 1957. Begins a "year of utter harassment" for the ACMHR by Connor.

June 2–3   Shuttlesworth renews call for the hiring of black police officers before the city commission. Connor invites

Shuttlesworth to take a polygraph test regarding the Christmas bombing; Shuttlesworth agrees if Connor will also submit to the test. Connor declines.

June 21   Connor's detectives meet with white supremacist J. B. Stoner to plan another bombing of Shuttlesworth's church, with hopes of killing the minister.

June 29   Bethel Baptist Church is bombed a second time.

July 25–27   Shuttlesworth and Connor engage in a war of words over Shuttlesworth's "dangerous leadership." Police intimidate and arrest ACMHR members who guard Bethel Baptist Church.

October 14   City commission passes an ordinance allowing the Birmingham Transit Company to set its own seating policies; transit company announces a "new" policy: whites board from the front and blacks from the rear. Denouncing "an unholy conspiracy" between city officials and the transit company, Shuttlesworth calls on African Americans to violate the new policy.

October 20–21   Connor calls for Shuttlesworth's arrest; Shuttlesworth turns himself in. Thirteen others arrested. Incarcerated for the first time, Shuttlesworth serves five days in jail.

October 28   Shuttlesworth calls for a limited boycott; gets little support from Birmingham ministers.

November 22   Connor tells a reporter from the *Baltimore Afro-American*, "Damn the law. Down here we make our own law." ACMHR member Reverend Calvin Woods is arrested, and ministers lodge a protest.

1959

January–June   Shuttlesworth has disputes with local black attorneys regarding legal fees; Birmingham's African American middle class holds Shuttlesworth and ACMHR at arm's length. Black press criticizes Birmingham's "leadership stalemate."

April 24   Shuttlesworth begins lobbying King to increase his pressure on segregationist forces, particularly in Birmingham. Writes King strong letters that call for more than "flowery speeches."

October 26   Representing eighty black families, Shuttlesworth renews an old request and petitions new school superintendent Theo Wright to desegregate city school. Also renews a suit to desegregate Birmingham parks.

November 23   U.S. district judge H. H. Grooms rules that the Birmingham Transit Company has the right to set its own seating policies and that blacks are "not entitled to injunctive or declaratory relief." At the same time, however, he rules that refusal to move to the rear of a bus does not of itself constitute a breach of the peace. Shuttlesworth claims a partial victory.

November 30   King resigns pastorate of Dexter Avenue Baptist Church, effective January 31, 1960, to give his full attention to the SCLC.

1960

February 1   Black students stage first sit-in in Greensboro, North Carolina.

February 11   Shuttlesworth observes student sit-ins at High Point, North Carolina, department stores; advises SCLC: "We have to get with this right away."

February 29   Simultaneous sit-ins by students in Montgomery and Birmingham; Shuttlesworth chides MIA president Ralph Abernathy for weak support of the sit-ins.

March 30	Shuttlesworth advises Birmingham students to sit in at five Birmingham stores; Shuttlesworth arrested for aiding and abetting.
April 19	Shuttlesworth named with Abernathy, Joseph Lowery, and Solomon S. Seay in libel case against the New York Times *(Sullivan v. New York Times)*.
August 16	Shuttlesworth's children Pat, Ricky, and Fred Jr. arrested in Gadsden, Alabama, for allegedly causing a disturbance on a Greyhound bus.
November 3	Shuttlesworth and the others are convicted in the *Sullivan* case; damages assessed at $500,000. Shuttlesworth's car is confiscated by law enforcement officials.
November 8	John F. Kennedy is elected president of the United States.
November 22	Shuttlesworth and the Reverend Charles Billups's suit against Connor and police chief Jamie Moore for harassment of the ACMHR comes to trial. For effect Shuttlesworth acts as his own attorney in order to question Connor directly.

1961

January 20	John F. Kennedy is inaugurated president of the United States.
March 13	CBS films the documentary *Who Speaks for Birmingham?* in which newsman Howard K. Smith calls Shuttlesworth "the man most feared by southern racists and the voice of the new militancy among Birmingham Negroes."
Spring	Fred and Ruby Shuttlesworth increasingly quarrel over money, civil rights activities, and church responsibilities. Shuttlesworth is courted by the Revelation Baptist Church, a larger congregation in Cincinnati, Ohio.

May 14–22   Shuttlesworth involved in aiding the Freedom Rides in
                 Alabama.

June 2   Shuttlesworth announces his acceptance of the pastorate
                 of Revelation Baptist Church effective August 20.

November 8   U.S. district judge H. H. Grooms orders the desegregation
                 of Birmingham parks by January 15, 1962.

December 11–18   Demonstrations in Albany, Georgia.

1962

January 1   Connor closes Birmingham's parks rather than
                 desegregate them.

January 8   U.S. Supreme Court refuses to review Shuttlesworth and
                 Billups's 1958 convictions for nonsegregated bus riding.

January 26   Shuttlesworth and Billups surrender to police, begin
                 serving their jail sentences.

March 1   After exhausting all state remedies, Shuttlesworth's
                 attorneys take requests for bail to Judge Grooms, who
                 immediately orders their client's release after thirty-six
                 days in jail.

March 6   With Shuttlesworth's encouragement students at Miles
                 College form the Anti-Injustice League, call for a selective
                 buying campaign (boycott) against downtown
                 department stores.

April 4   While observing downtown boycotts Shuttlesworth and
                 the Reverend J. S. Phifer are arrested and charged with
                 obstructing a sidewalk and refusing to obey an officer.
                 The next day they are convicted and sentenced to
                 eighteen days in jail.

April 9   Shuttlesworth accompanies King and others to a
                 Washington meeting with Robert Kennedy and Vice

President Lyndon Johnson, hoping to convince the president to end segregation with a second Emancipation Proclamation.

April 13–14 At Shuttlesworth's insistence the SCLC, Southern Conference Educational Fund (SCEF), and Student Nonviolent Coordinating Committee join the ACMHR for a civil rights conference and workshop in Birmingham.

May 16 At an SCLC board meeting Shuttlesworth convinces King to hold SCLC's annual convention in Birmingham as a way of threatening major demonstrations.

May 28 Judge George C. Wallace outpolls state senator Ryan deGraffenreid in a primary runoff election for governor, assuring his victory in the November general election.

August 28 Jefferson County Democratic Campaign Committee garners enough support to change Birmingham's municipal government from a commission to a mayor-council system.

Early September Birmingham Chamber of Commerce president Sidney Smyer forms the Senior Citizens Committee, which includes black business leaders but not Shuttlesworth.

September 24 Shuttlesworth meets with Smyer, who hopes to stave off demonstrations during the SCLC convention; negotiations yield token desegregation in some downtown stores. Shuttlesworth anticipates segregation signs will reappear after SCLC leaves town.

September 25–28 SCLC convention meets in Birmingham.

October 1 James Meredith enrolls at the University of Mississippi.

Early October Jim Crow signs reappear; Shuttlesworth renews pressure for ACMHR and SCLC to combine forces for major demonstrations.

November 6	Wallace is elected governor of Alabama; Birmingham voters approve change in city government; mayoral elections set for March 5, 1963.
December 13	Bethel Baptist Church is bombed for the third time.

1963

January 10–11	Shuttlesworth attends meeting in Dorchester, Georgia, where King commits the SCLC to major demonstrations in Birmingham; plan is nicknamed Project C (Confrontation).
January 16	Wallace inaugurated as governor of Alabama; calls for "segregation today, segregation tomorrow, segregation forever."
February 6	Shuttlesworth and ACMHR board confer with King and Wyatt T. Walker.
March 5	Mayoral vote necessitates an April 2 runoff election between Albert Boutwell and Bull Connor; ACMHR-SCLC forces postpone demonstrations until after the election.
April 2	Boutwell elected over Connor, but city commission refuses to vacate offices; Boutwell sues, and eventually the Alabama Supreme Court rules in his favor (May 23).
April 3	Project C is launched with Miles College students holding sit-ins at five department stores.
April 6	Shuttlesworth personally leads first mass marches toward city hall.
April 7	King leads second march on city hall; police use billy clubs; movement grows.
April 9	King meets with black bourgeoisie, ministers to enlist support.

April 10	State circuit court judge William A. Jenkins issues a temporary injunction against the demonstrations; King decides to violate the injunction and go to jail.
April 12	King, Abernathy, and Shuttlesworth lead demonstrations on Good Friday; King and Abernathy arrested and jailed; Shuttlesworth deliberately avoids arrest in order to continue fund-raising efforts while King is in jail.
April 13	White ministers publish open letter to King, calling the demonstrations "unwise and untimely."
April 18	In response to the ministers, King writes "Letter from Birmingham Jail"; released on bail two days later.
April 29	James Bevel suggests using schoolchildren in the marches.
May 2	"D-Day": teenagers march for the first time; more than one thousand arrests made.
May 3	"Double D-Day": more mass marches; police use dogs and fire hoses; negotiations move into high gear.
May 4	Assistant Attorney General Burke Marshall and Assistant Deputy Attorney General Joseph Dolan arrive in Birmingham to help with negotiations; Shuttlesworth objects to segregated negotiations.
May 5	Large march led by Charles Billups proceeds from New Pilgrim Baptist Church to downtown area; advisory committee of black bourgeoisie meet with white leaders; suggest Four Points for Progress.
May 6	An estimated two thousand young people march to downtown area.
May 7	With Birmingham's jail's overflowing with young demonstrators, two thousand more young people march

downtown; Shuttlesworth is hit by a fire hose, bruises a rib, and is hospitalized.

May 8	Advisory committee recommends that the SCLC call off demonstrations for twenty-four hours; King agrees; Shuttlesworth privately blasts King for calling off demonstrations without consulting him and without gaining definite concessions for desegregating local stores.

May 10   Mollified, Shuttlesworth agrees to truce agreement; King, Abernathy, and Shuttlesworth face reporters and declare the end of the demonstrations.

May 12   The Gaston Motel and home of A. D. Williams King, Martin's brother, are bombed; some twenty-five hundred enraged blacks riot near the downtown area.

May 17   Still recovering from his injuries Shuttlesworth returns to Cincinnati after the Birmingham demonstrations.

June 9   Shuttlesworth accused of Communist associations after being named president of SCEF.

June 11   Governor George Wallace stands "in the schoolhouse door" to prevent the integration of the University of Alabama; that night President Kennedy speaks to the nation, announcing new legislation to ban segregation of public facilities.

August 23   March on Washington occurs. Shuttlesworth originally left off the speaker list; King delivers his "I Have a Dream" speech.

September 4 Birmingham schools are integrated; Shuttlesworth accompanies two students to their first day of classes; the home of black attorney Arthur Shores is bombed; during ensuing riot armed whites shoot and kill army veteran John Coley, mistakenly believing him to be Shuttlesworth.

September 15 — Sixteenth Street Baptist Church is bombed, killing four young girls. Fifteen years later Klan member Robert E. "Dynamite Bob" Chambliss convicted of the murders.

September 17 — Shuttlesworth threatens to renew demonstrations in Birmingham; speaks at the funeral of Carole Robertson, one of the victims of the bombing.

September 18 — Funeral of the other victims, Cynthia Wesley, Denise McNair, and Addie Mae Collins; King delivers the main eulogy; Shuttlesworth makes incidental remarks.

September 24 — Army General Kenneth Royall and Colonel Earl ("Red") Blaik, personal representatives of President Kennedy, arrive in Birmingham to help mediate racial tensions. They remain until October 4.

November 7 — Shuttlesworth writes King, pressing him to refocus the SCLC's attention on the lack of progress in Birmingham since the spring demonstrations.

November 22 — President Kennedy is assassinated in Dallas.

1964

March 9 — In what becomes a landmark free speech case, *Sullivan v. New York Times* is reversed by the U.S. Supreme Court. In addition, the Court reverses Shuttlesworth's convictions related to the Freedom Rides.

March–June — Shuttlesworth continues to threaten renewed demonstrations unless Boutwell hires African Americans for police or civil servant jobs; complains that King, looking at St. Augustine, Florida, will not return to Birmingham.

June 18 — Shuttlesworth arrested in demonstrations in St. Augustine, Florida. Within a week, he and C. T. Vivian lead a wade-in at a previously all-white beach.

July 2	President Johnson signs the 1964 Civil Rights Act; that night Shuttlesworth and ACMHR contingents test the new law by patronizing formerly segregated establishments in Birmingham.

1965

February 4	Shuttlesworth speaks at rally in Selma with Malcolm X.
March 7	"Bloody Sunday" in Selma. Six hundred demonstrators begin a march from Selma to Montgomery. They are halted at the Edmund Pettus Bridge by state troopers and local police who are using tear gas and billy clubs. King calls for a second march with protesters from across the country for March 9.
March 9	Shuttlesworth joins fifteen hundred marchers who kneel in prayer with King just across the bridge, making a symbolic statement. That night the Reverend James Reeb is severely beaten and later dies. Shuttlesworth organizes and leads sympathy marches for Reeb in Birmingham and Cincinnati.
March 25	An estimated twenty-five thousand marchers reach Montgomery, rally for voting rights.
August 15	A contingent of members of Revelation Baptist Church complain of Shuttlesworth's dictatorial leadership and question his handling of church finances; interrupt a worship service with protests against their pastor.
August 15–22	The dissidents file suit against Shuttlesworth for misappropriation of funds; Shuttlesworth calls the effort a "right-wing conspiracy" to discredit him. Common pleas court judge Otis R. Hess calls for an audit of church's finances. On September 28 the audit exonerates Shuttlesworth. Controversy continues.

November 5	Church votes 284 to 276 to retain Shuttlesworth as pastor; despite the narrow margin, Shuttlesworth claims victory. Dissidents continue to disrupt services.

1966

January 2	Shuttlesworth announces his resignation from Revelation Baptist Church, effective in May.
January 16	A group of 150 Shuttlesworth supporters withdraw from Revelation Baptist Church to form a new congregation, ask Shuttlesworth to become their pastor; Shuttlesworth agrees and makes his resignation effective immediately.
June 24	Shuttlesworth announces resignation as president of the ACMHR; members prevail on him to remain in office. He continues to push Birmingham officials to hire black police officers and to reform police brutality against blacks. Protests in Birmingham gradually peter out over next three years.
June–July	Shuttlesworth participates in protests against discriminatory hiring practices at Cincinnati's Drake Memorial Hospital.
March 1967	Shuttlesworth protests Birmingham police killings of ten African Americans over fourteen-month period.
June 15–25, 1967	Riots erupt in Cincinnati after a young black male is sentenced to death after a murder conviction. Nonviolent demonstrations turn violent; Shuttlesworth and other ministers try to quell the rioters by preaching non-violence and attempt to convince city officials to listen to black complaints of injustice.
June 1969	Shuttlesworth steps down as president of the ACMHR.
April 20, 1970	After twenty-nine years of marriage, Fred and Ruby Shuttlesworth divorce.

February 1, 1971   Ruby Shuttlesworth dies of heart failure.

September 1978   The city of Birmingham renames Huntsville Road in Shuttlesworth's honor.

June 1979   Shuttlesworth leads protests at the Ohio statehouse against unfair utility practices.

July 1979   As chair of Direct Action for the Coalition Concerned for Justice and Equality, Shuttlesworth leads protests against granting police .357 Magnum handguns and hollow-point–controlled expansion bullets.

August 1979   Shuttlesworth calls for a boycott of Cincinnati's downtown businesses to help increase African American representation on the police force.

June 19, 1981   Shuttlesworth and seven others leave a White House tour to protest President Reagan's budget cuts.

August 1988   After a May 10 bond issue is defeated, Birmingham mayor Richard Arrington calls on Shuttlesworth and local ministers to help petition the city council to support the building of a civil rights museum.

March 1989   Shuttlesworth establishes the Shuttlesworth Housing Foundation to provide low-cost housing for poor families.

1988–1992   Shuttlesworth raises money for the civil rights museum project and serves on the board of directors.

November 1992   The Birmingham Civil Rights Institute and Museum is opened to the public; officials unveil a statue of Shuttlesworth in front of the institute.

A Fire You Can't Put Out

Introduction

Fred Shuttlesworth was back in Birmingham, but this time in unaccustomed fashion—welcomed back. Gloating only slightly, the preacher read the editorial headline "Welcome, Jailbirds" in the same newspaper that had once called for his prosecution. Over the intervening years, on return trips to his boyhood home Shuttlesworth had often joked about being another criminal returning to the scene of the crime. Now, however, attending a reunion of civil rights activists, the aging warhorse of Birmingham's civil rights movement basked in the spotlight. City officials, former church members, friends, and erstwhile followers in the movement gathered on Huntsville Road to honor Shuttlesworth. Waiting for the ceremony to begin, the sixty-six-year-old preacher and his daughter Ricky could not help reminding each other what had once happened on that same Birmingham street almost thirty years earlier.

In those days of more turbulent race relations, city bus drivers deliberately inconvenienced the Shuttlesworth children in retaliation for their father's civil rights agitation. As an attempt at intimidation, the driver of Bus 23—North Birmingham often drove past the stop nearest the Shuttlesworth home, leaving the Shuttlesworths and other black children without a ride to school. On the return trip from school, the driver ignored their drop-off point, forcing them to walk home from a more distant stop. One afternoon, aware of this tactic and purposely waiting at the stop, Shuttlesworth spotted his teenagers on the bus as it rumbled past. He quickly fired up his Plymouth and sped down Twentieth-ninth Avenue and caught up with and cut off the bus, which had narrowly missed crashing into his car. Blocking the bus at the end of Huntsville Road, Shuttlesworth refused to move the car until the driver made amends. When a police officer arrived, Shuttlesworth sermonized him and the driver for harassing his children and the others. Before long, the bus dispatcher arrived and offered to break the impasse by taking the teenagers home in his car. "They didn't pay to ride in your car," insisted Shuttlesworth. "They paid to ride the bus. So the bus will carry them back." When the police officer insisted that he move his car, Shuttlesworth again refused, saying, "The bus driver had no right to take my kids by my home. You arrest him or make him turn the bus around and carry them back." In time the dispatcher acceded to the minister's demands and ordered the driver to turn the bus around and deposit the young people at their proper destination.[1]

Now, on a warm June afternoon in 1988, the Shuttlesworth family smiled at the irony. Before the day passed and the ceremony concluded, Birmingham city officials would give a new name to the street where the bus incident occurred: F. L. Shuttlesworth Drive. The city whose slogan in the 1960s was "It's Nice to Have You in Birmingham" now officially embraced its pioneer civil rights leader. What a difference a quarter century made. Given the number of times that Shuttlesworth had placed himself in harm's way in the town many African Americans called "Bombingham," few would have predicted at the outset of the civil rights movement that Shuttlesworth's life would even last into senior adulthood. As lawyer Charles Morgan, one of Birmingham's few white liberals at the time said, "There was no rational reason for a Fred Shuttlesworth to exist in Birmingham. For him to exist in Birmingham and stay alive, for him to do the things that he did, there's nothing rational about it." What was needed among Birmingham's blacks was a leader who, as one Birmingham minister suggested, "couldn't lose nothing but his life." Shuttlesworth inspired support for "the struggle" in Birmingham and the South by his almost legendary willingness, even eagerness, to sacrifice his life in reckless defiance of Jim Crow laws. For this reason Martin Luther King Jr. called him "one of the nation's most courageous freedom fighters," a testimonial echoed by virtually all veterans of the civil rights movement.[2]

Telling the story of his life in Birmingham and beyond is reason enough for this biography. There are other justifications as well. Fred Shuttlesworth represents many important themes in civil rights and African American religious history, not the least of which is his role as pastor or, perhaps better, as "civil rights preacher." This less-than-perfect term has the virtue of keeping together the concepts of preaching the Christian gospel and preaching civil rights. The typical sermons and civil rights addresses of King, Shuttlesworth, Ralph David Abernathy, and others to a great degree melded into one genre. In a similar vein, these preachers understood their activism as part of their responsibilities as Christian ministers in the African American community. Shuttlesworth differs from King in that his primary identifying role throughout his career remained that of a local pastor. After the founding of the Southern Christian Leadership Conference (SCLC) in 1957, King served only as the copastor of Atlanta's Ebenezer Baptist Church and held almost exclusively homiletical responsibilities. In contrast, Shuttlesworth conducted his civil rights activities with his hands still tightly grasping the pastoral reins of his local churches. His pastoral ministry provided the context for his civil rights activities; his concern for social justice was central to his "care of souls" and his prophetic proclamation. His role always remained that of pastor-preacher rather than that of "civil rights leader," as white journalists and politicians preferred to think of him. Yet his efforts to bear full pastoral responsibilities alongside his civil rights activities created significant tensions in both his church and his community. Over the years his authoritarian leadership style alienated many persons in his larger black communities, contributing to conflict and schism in each of his congregations. How Shuttlesworth balanced these roles and how laypersons in the local black churches interacted with him thus became an important aspect of his civil rights life. Furthermore, his dual roles as pastor and civil rights leader, each with a different set of problems and expectations, poignantly brought certain pressures to bear on his personal life. Members of his family, as well as Shuttlesworth himself, bore the scars of his involvement "on the inside," as one of Shuttlesworth's followers once observed.[3]

Related to his blended role as civil rights preacher was his often stormy relationship with an older generation of African American ministers in Birmingham whose civil rights commitments were less public and whose preaching to "this-worldly" concerns was less direct than Shuttlesworth's. Much of this rivalry had to do with ministerial jealousies similar to those between King and Joseph H. Jackson, president of the National Baptist Convention of the United States of America, Incorporated (NBC). Once events had convinced Shuttlesworth that God was directing his involvement in civil rights, his certainty fostered a forthright insistence that other ministers join the fight—in his typical mode of expression, that they act as well as talk. His willingness to sacrifice his own life and even the lives of his family translated into a visceral impatience, implied and expressed in pointed fashion, with anyone (particularly other ministers) who did not share his commitment or his timetable. His actions thus pushed him to the head of the line of older clergy vying for leadership in the African American community and produced considerable controversy.

The situation in Birmingham also included class tensions. Unlike the middle-class, urban, and increasingly urbane Martin Luther King, Shuttlesworth emerged from a relatively impoverished southern rural working-class family. He possessed neither the high-caliber education nor the rhetorical polish of King. Shuttlesworth better exemplified the poorer backgrounds of most southern blacks in the civil rights era, which helps explain the long-lasting loyalty Shuttlesworth won from his followers in Birmingham. Although some pastors and laypersons in the silk-stocking, middle-class black churches disliked his "demonstrate now, work out the details later" style, his charisma and confrontational personality attracted working-class blacks in large numbers. He often aroused his supporters at church or mass meetings with the unpolished rhetoric of the black folk pulpit, but he primarily appealed to them through daring acts of defiance against his principal antagonist, Theophilus Eugene "Bull" Connor, Birmingham's commissioner of public safety. His actions inspired the courage and confidence of ordinary blacks who loved and adored him.

An activist professor at Birmingham's Miles College thus argued: "The rank and file, they were the ones who believed strongly. They were the ones who adored, they were the ones who just loved the man, because he could articulate the innermost feelings of the rank and file." In blunt, unembellished terms, his expression of raw emotionality captured their feelings in ways that even King, with his oratorical polish, sometimes did not. More important, however, his bold confrontations fundamentally embodied the feelings of poor and working-class blacks. Longtime friend James Armstrong compared Shuttlesworth to King, noting: "I would follow Shuttlesworth quicker than I would Martin Luther King because, to me, he was a much stronger man. Now Martin knew how to say it; Fred know how to do it. . . . I've had good preachers to preach to me, but Fred has preached to me in action." Colonel Stone Johnson, who served for many years as Shuttlesworth's bodyguard, asserted that "no other man would dare to try to take Shuttlesworth's place back then, not even Martin Luther King. . . . And I've seen times that Martin showed a little fear, and Fred *never* showed *none*." To note such testimony is not to celebrate Shuttlesworth's contribution to the civil rights movement at the expense of King's but rather to indicate his followers' fervent devotion to him and the reasons for it.[4]

Shuttlesworth's experience also takes the story of the civil rights movement beyond the circle of Martin Luther King and his "lieutenants." Local and lesser-known figures in the civil rights movement rarely escape King's shadow. Because of his own blunt and unpolished manner, a leader such as Shuttlesworth often suffers by comparison to King's mythic image. Attention to the contributions of Shuttlesworth and others like him, however, enables the civil rights movement to be understood without viewing King as its single superhero. Local campaigns and organizations, studied from indigenous points of view, reveal as much if not more about the civil rights movement and African American religion as studies of King. Moreover, their leaders deserve historical attention in their own right, perhaps none more than the leader of the Alabama Christian Movement for Human Rights (ACMHR), which King considered the SCLC's strongest local affiliate.

Beyond the pure drama of his life, which alone makes the story worth telling, one should not overlook Shuttlesworth's central role in a Birmingham campaign that was crucial to the success of the civil rights movement. Although historians may debate whether the demonstrations actually *were* successful (in terms of what actually was desegregated in Birmingham itself) and how success in the movement might be accurately measured, some realities are clear. From the perspective of America's collective memory, few episodes of the struggle for African American civil rights were as seared into the American consciousness as the images of the Birmingham demonstrations. Granted, most Americans have grown to associate the movement with the familiar footage of King's "I Have a Dream" speech, aided since 1986 by the annual television replays on Martin Luther King Day. Yet the sight of dogs and fire hoses remains a powerful visual image of the extremes to which Americans were prepared to go in support of and in opposition to the struggle for civil rights.[5]

Moreover, the impact of those images on the nation's collective, or at least congressional, will in 1963 cannot be gainsaid. The televised scenes of the dramatic events of the 1963 demonstrations in large measure convinced President Kennedy, the Congress, and millions of American voters that major legislation in the area of civil rights should and could be passed. Earlier, in January 1963, believing Congress was unlikely to pass civil rights legislation, Kennedy had shied away from introducing such a bill. One month after the Birmingham demonstrations, however, Kennedy introduced into Congress legislation that eventually became the Civil Rights Act of 1964. In his speech, he specifically referred to the events in Birmingham and privately told supporters that "but for Birmingham, we would not be here today." Robert Kennedy later corroborated this series of events, noting that his brother saw the Civil Rights Act as politically viable only after Birmingham. Wyatt Tee Walker, then executive director of the SCLC, referring to journalists' and historians' phrases such as "before Birmingham" and "since Birmingham," insisted that the demonstrations made the critical difference. Calling those events "a major watershed in the history of the Negro in America," Walker pointed out Kennedy's change of strategy between January and June: "In six months, the plight of Negroes had not changed substantively," he said, "but there had been a Birmingham." If not the high-water mark of the civil rights movement, the "battle of Birmingham" certainly set the stage for it in the Selma-to-Montgomery march two years later. Shuttlesworth and his indigenous organization were at least as indispensable to winning that battle as the forces who came to the city from Atlanta and the SCLC. Journalistic references at the time ordinarily designated King as the leader of the demonstrations, but the activities of the SCLC were built on the foundation laid by Shuttlesworth and the ACMHR. Although sometimes viewed as an outgrowth of King's work with the Montgomery Improvement Association, in reality Shuttlesworth's organization was of independent origin, and Shuttlesworth's civic work in Birmingham as pastor of the Bethel Baptist Church predated King's arrival in Montgomery. Beginning in 1956, Shuttlesworth built an organization that provided consistent agitation and confrontation with the Magic City's Jim Crow system. At times his followers numbered in the thousands, and very early in the movement Shuttlesworth recognized Birmingham's symbolic importance to the success of the civil rights movement. The end of segregation in Birmingham, he argued, would signal a rapid demise of the racial caste system throughout the South. He urged King to throw a national spotlight on the Magic City through a massive direct action campaign.[6]

King and the SCLC decided to go to Birmingham because of Shuttlesworth's direct invitation and because of a cadre of available demonstrators Shuttlesworth's organization had developed during the previous seven years. Close observers emphasized this aspect of his preparatory work. James T. Montgomery, a longtime supporter of the ACMHR and former physician to the Shuttlesworth family, argued that Shuttlesworth contributed most significantly by developing a following in Birmingham that was large enough and loyal enough to fill the streets and the jails, as had been attempted unsuccessfully in the SCLC's earlier campaign in Albany, Georgia. He believed that the size and fervor of the protests first led by Shuttlesworth's adult troops inspired larger numbers of young people to volunteer to be jailed in the Birmingham demonstrations. He argued: "At that time it [was] kind of easy to jump onto a moving train. But there would have been no train to move or get started. . . . There was no doubt about Martin's magnetism. . . . But it was Fred's organization that allowed the thing to get to this point. If it had not been for the Alabama Christian Movement, there would have been no big demonstrations. . . . Martin would not have been successful. If he had come by himself to do what Fred did, he could not have done that. There was no organization strong enough to get him to the point where he needed to get."[7]

In large measure, however, the ACMHR constituted the organizational extension of Fred Shuttlesworth's personality. Birmingham and Bull Connor's intransigence were directly proportional to Fred Shuttlesworth's militancy. The contest between Connor and Shuttlesworth is legendary, providing this biography much of its drama. For this reason, Joseph Lowery, one of King's successors as SCLC president, suggested that Connor and Shuttlesworth were made for each other. The reality, as Selma lawyer J. L. Chestnut rightly pointed out, was that "there was Bull Connors all over Alabama." Virulent racism and the violent defense of segregation were virtually ubiquitous in the Deep South, as the unfolding events of the civil rights movement made clear. The presence of a Fred Shuttlesworth made the crucial difference in Birmingham. Wyatt T. Walker argued: "I'm absolutely convinced without any reservation [that] Birmingham never would have been without a Fred Shuttlesworth. You could not have come to Birmingham if there hadn't been a Fred Shuttlesworth there. He was not just a preacher in Birmingham with some people who were interested in human rights. It was the very nature of his persona—his doggedness, his tenacity, his courage, his craziness. I mean all of that congealed to make Birmingham fertile for what we needed to do."[8]

An incident typifying not only Fred Shuttlesworth's role in Birmingham's civil rights struggles but also in many ways his life and ministry occurred at a mass meeting one Monday night in 1959. For several consecutive weeks the Birmingham Fire Department had served as the city's instrument of harassment and intimidation, regularly interrupting ACMHR mass meetings. On this occasion again, the wail of sirens drowned out the voices from the pulpit of the St. James Baptist Church. Moments later, firefighters rushed into the church sanctuary, wielding hoses and axes and ostensibly searching for a fire. Standing up and interrupting a speech by ACMHR treasurer William E. Shortridge, Shuttlesworth asked the firefighters, "Gentlemen, what are you looking for?" Apprising Shuttlesworth that he had received a "report" of a fire in the building, the fire chief asked Shuttlesworth to clear the aisle of people. Suspecting that the real purpose of the fire department's arrival lay in stampeding the meeting and feeling exasperated by the repeated interruptions, Shuttlesworth agitatedly replied, "Now, Chief, we're just tired as hell of Bull Connor harassing us, and we are about ready to just all of us go to jail. If Bull's got room enough to arrest all the thousands of us, okay. We are just tired! We are not going to move!" "This is no trick, Reverend," the chief pleaded with the preacher, beginning an explanation of the operative fire codes. Knowing he would eventually be forced to give in but wishing to encourage his onlooking followers, Shuttlesworth used the situation to fullest advantage. "Chief," he demanded, "can you assure me that this isn't Bull Connor harassing us? Because if this is Bull, we are staying! You will have to drag us out!" Receiving the chief's promise, the leader ordered the meeting moved to another church a few blocks away. Before leaving the premises, however, Shuttlesworth slipped in one last zinger: "Y'all think it's a fire in here? You know there ain't no fire here. The kind of fire we have in here you can't put out with hoses and axes!"[9]

Perhaps there *was* no fire in St. James Baptist Church that night, but in the persona of Fred Shuttlesworth there burned a fire that persisted throughout a lifetime of ministry to African Americans, both in the church and in the streets. As Shuttlesworth moved from anonymity as a young pastor to national notoriety as a civil rights leader and finally to status as an icon of the movement, "a fire you can't put out" has burned in him brightly. In time this "old soldier" of the movement was forced to adjust to a declining national leadership role as events moved him out of the limelight and into the shadow of Martin Luther King Jr. Nonetheless, the fire of his youth remained unextinguished throughout his life, burning prophetically in both his churchly and in his more secular ministries. Theologian James H. Evans Jr. recently wrote of the "heavenly fire" of black Christianity. Similarly, social critic Cornel West has drawn attention to what he calls a "combative spirituality," by which he means an eager, joyful spirituality that preserves meaning by fighting against claims of inferiority. West says that this combative spirituality is a subversive joy that in the midst of political struggle transforms tears into laughter. "Fiery glad" instead of "fiery mad," this distinctively African American spirituality looks disappointment and despair and death in the face and declares that beyond all these there is hope. Perhaps more than anyone else in the entire civil rights movement, Fred Shuttlesworth embodied in undiluted fashion the fiery, "combative spirituality" at the heart of African American religion.[10]

In Shuttlesworth's life one may thus see a prototype, combining these two components—heavenly fire and combative spirituality—that form a central characteristic of African American religion. More particularly, his life reveals the development of a charismatic and confrontational personality who withstood and often created considerable conflict in all his important relationships and contexts—family, southern society, his churches, and the civil rights movement. Shuttlesworth's combustible persona waxed hot against perceived enemies of righteousness and justice, attracting true believers to its incandescence. His life reveals in very clear form something about the nature of African American religion. Lit in an impoverished and rural southern home and fueled in the hearth of the African American church, Fred Shuttlesworth's fiery and combative spirituality flamed dramatically in its encounter with Birmingham and Bull Connor. In 1992, Benno Schmidt, the former president of Yale University, made a speech to the National Press Club. In the question-and-answer period that followed, he made an offhand reference to Bull Connor. That he could invoke Connor's name without feeling the need to identify him, while the name of the drama's protagonist has dropped from America's historical consciousness, may be the best reason of all to attend to Fred Shuttlesworth's story.

Alberta

There have been many times I wanted to try Mama,
but one thing I know, Alberta didn't play.
— Fred L. Shuttlesworth

According to an old southern story, a young boy once asked, "Daddy, what makes a lightning bug light?" Hoping not to appear stumped and thus preserve the mystique of parental omniscience, the father offered a long and purposely bewildering explanation. After several moments, the bemused lad cut through the verbiage, insisting, "C'mon, Daddy, for real. How come the lightning bug lights?" "Well, Son," the father sheepishly replied, "the stuff is just in him!" So one might say about Fred Shuttlesworth's spirited, confrontational personality. His character was a natural outgrowth of the situations and personalities around him. More than anyone else, however, his mother, Alberta Robinson Shuttlesworth, shaped Fred's resolute disposition. To recognize his mother's hard-bitten ways and the extent to which Fred adopted them is to understand how the "stuff" of his character got in him. This chapter covers Shuttlesworth's family background and early life up through his graduation from high school. It highlights how his upbringing in the shadow of the volatile and often violent relationship between his mother and stepfather shaped a combative personality that eventually expressed itself in all of Shuttlesworth's relationships. In particular, this part of the story details the ways the personality of his mother influenced that of her eldest child, preparing him in part for his later role as a hard-nosed minister and civil rights agitator.

Fred's determination and combativeness came naturally. Family and friends remembered Alberta's earthy piety and fabled strength of character. Eventually enfeebled, blind, and bedridden, she displayed an indomitable constitution by living to age ninety-four on the same hill where her nine children grew up. The civil rights preacher later called "a hard man for a hard town" shared this feistiness. Reminiscing about her father and grandmother, Patricia Shuttlesworth Massengill described an image that epitomized their spirited nature—Saturday night visits when both generations sat bobbing on a sofa, jabbing the air as they watched boxing matches on television. As Shuttlesworth's son, Fred Jr. further testified, "My old man don't kick butts no better than she do. . . . He looks like her; he talks like her. He has all of her mannerisms." Fred Sr.'s younger brother Clifton went one generation better by pointing to Alberta's father, March Robinson, as the source of this trait: "Fred . . . just won't let nothin' stop him until he accomplishes what he started, and that's the way it was with my mother, and that's the way it was with my grandfather." The combative and at times earthy spirituality that marked the life of Fred Shuttlesworth thus persisted through generations on his mother's side of the family.[1]

Born in the mid-1870s in Montgomery County, Alabama, March Robinson married Martha Carpenter just before the turn of the century in a small rural community known as McGhee Switch near the small town of Mt. Meigs. A devout Methodist, March became a steward and a trustee in the St. Matthew African Methodist Episcopal (AME) Church after moving to the community near Birmingham known as Oxmoor. Both before and after his family's move, he earned a modest living as a tenant farmer, primarily raising corn and cotton. When fatigued from working the fields, he often asked his wife to sing "Amazing Grace" to him. He ordinarily owned livestock, especially chickens, a cow, and a very recalcitrant mule, which he sometimes beat with a chain. Although he had lost an eye in an accident, he was renowned as a sharpshooter with his twenty-two caliber rifle. He had very little formal schooling, although he had learned enough to read newspapers. He also prized education, and he insisted that his daughter get as much education as possible. One colorful family tale has him announcing his intention to avoid catching the measles, which had laid low most of the children. Declaring, "No, I'm not gon' catch those devilish things," he took up his blanket and slept in the barn. March and Martha, however, seldom used these sleeping arrangements, for they became the parents of eight children.[2]

The first arrival, born August 25, 1900, was a daughter named Alberta, who became the apple of her father's protective eye. Later, the family remembered the affectionate and exaggerated manner by which March pronounced his daughter's name: "A-l-l-l-l-l-berta," with six syllables instead of three. Father and daughter were very close emotionally and lived near each other until March's death in 1945. As the first born, Alberta kept house for her parents while they worked the fields together, and as siblings arrived she participated in their rearing. She finished elementary school and took some courses at Alabama State Normal School (later called Alabama State College and still later Alabama State University), but never graduated. For a while she worked as a teacher's aide in the public schools, but by age twenty-one, circumstances ended her formal education and her opportunities for a teaching career.[3]

She became involved with a young man named Vetter Greene, who had grown up in the area and developed a reputation for his easygoing manner. Greene lived in a dilapidated shack in an alley in Montgomery, making his meager living keeping dogs and repairing watches and guns. Although expert at his craft, he had neither much education nor any perceptible ambition to advance to any higher station in life. To March Robinson these traits marked him as less than suitable as a prospective son-in-law. Exhibiting a trait his daughter and grandson eventually shared, March aspired to a higher state for his children and took a dislike to young Greene. Although the couple was very much in love, March refused them permission to marry. Showing her own independence of mind, however, Alberta defied her father's wishes and continued the relationship. She became pregnant by Greene, and on March 18, 1922, gave birth to a son, whom she named Fred after a brother who had died some years earlier. Even after the arrival of an illegitimate son, and against her father's wishes, Alberta continued her relationship with Vetter Greene, becoming pregnant again in 1923. By this time, March Robinson had decided to move his large family, including the pregnant Alberta and her infant son, to the rapidly growing industrial county of Jefferson, ending Alberta's relationship with Vetter Greene.[4]

Like thousands of other migrants settling in Jefferson County, March Robinson made the move for economic reasons. The city of Birmingham, founded in 1871 by railroad developers and land speculators of the Elyton Land Company and blessed with large deposits of coal, limestone, and iron ore, grew quickly into a New South industrial center. Through annexation in 1910, Birmingham grew into the third largest city in the former Confederacy. With a population of 132,685, it earned the nicknames the "Magic City" for its rapid growth and the "Pittsburgh of the South" for its importance as a steel producer. Combining the worst elements and excesses of both the Old South and the new, industry gradually created an atmosphere of exploitation in the city, especially for African Americans. In the 1920s, most new residents overlooked these matters, however, contenting themselves with the area's economic opportunities. Nonetheless, as the industry developed, exploitation of workers and poor working conditions in the mines kept pace with Birmingham's industrial reputation. The incomes of coal miners remained uncertain while their typical workdays lasted twelve to fourteen hours without overtime pay.[5]

Even before Emancipation, the area, cursed with poor soil, had not been conducive to large plantations. Birmingham's community of freed slaves in the post-Emancipation era thus numbered only about twenty-five hundred. The developing industry of Jefferson County, however, attracted thousands of blacks from cotton farms downstate, most of whom were sharecroppers or tenant farmers like March Robinson. By 1880 the black population had doubled, and it increased by six times in the next decade. When the Robinsons arrived, they joined a black community of more than 130,000, which was 39 percent of the city's total population. This percentage of black residency marked the highest of any American city with more than one hundred thousand in population. As the number of African Americans grew between 1900 and 1920, whites pressed for the passage of legislation to control blacks' availability as cheap sources of labor. Most blacks became coal miners or steelworkers, relegated to menial and unskilled jobs. Other positions were deemed "white folks's jobs." Coal mines, requiring a great deal of heavy lifting and moving, employed blacks as virtual "beasts of burden." As in March Robinson's case, blacks were also hired to tend the animals that pulled the carts. In addition to working occasionally for the mines, Robinson rented a parcel of land in the former coal-mining community called Oxmoor, ten miles south of Birmingham proper, near the Wenonah and Ishkooda Mines.

After the mines were depleted, the companies dismantled their smelting plants. By the 1930s, Birmingham industrialists had been hit hard by the depression and were remembering a saying from the city's earliest days: "Hard times come here first and stay longest." The dire situation portended even worse results for the city's black workers, who by this time comprised half the coal miners and 65 percent of the steelworkers in the state. Tighter competition resulted in a declining number of jobs for blacks as white workers and managers often colluded to wrest their positions from them. The mines' departure gradually ended the townlike amenities, reducing Oxmoor to two segregated communities four miles apart. While some blacks supported themselves by farming and by working in what remained of mining operations, others in Birmingham served as domestics, yardmen, and chauffeurs. According to historian Robert J. Norrell, patterns of industrial race relations in Birmingham matched those in South Africa, where job competition became a powerful incentive for maintaining segregation. This situation suggests one reason why by the 1960s the city had earned the name the "Johannesburg of the South." Prejudice and economic necessity thus forced blacks to accept lower-paying jobs outside heavy industry or to move to the North.[6]

Blacks generally settled in the less attractive land left vacant by industry and by white residential areas, usually along creek beds or railroad lines. "Negro" sections such as Smithfield, Collegeville, and "Tuxedo Junction" remained unlighted, unpaved, and untouched by city services. The housing of most blacks barely improved on the ramshackle sharecropper cabins these migrants had left behind in their former rural districts. Many lived in rows of "company houses," three- to four-room rental dwellings owned by the coal and steel companies. Alberta lived with her family in such an arrangement in Oxmoor until she entered into a short-lived marriage to a man named Satterfield. The surroundings were less than commodious, and in later years her children often heard her remark about the old days on "Rat Row."[7]

By the time her son turned five, Alberta had divorced Satterfield and had met William Nathan Shuttlesworth, reputed to be among the community's most eligible men. Born in Tuscaloosa County in 1877, Will Shuttlesworth was abandoned by his mother and reared by an aunt. Not much younger than March Robinson, he learned to read but acquired little education beyond the third grade. Sometime early in the century, Shuttlesworth migrated to Detroit to work in the automobile industry. He married a woman named Mayberry and raised two sons, Preston and Lawrence. After the marriage soured and the couple divorced, Will moved back to Alabama, settling in Oxmoor. He worked in the mines until silicosis, a disease of the lungs resulting from breathing ore dust, cost him his job. After retiring from the mines, Will supported himself by farming the three acres he had been able to buy with money he had earned in Detroit. Later, he also rented fifteen acres of land from another farmer near Edgewood Lake. On these parcels of land, Shuttlesworth primarily raised corn, which he used to feed his livestock and to distill liquor. His small-time bootlegging operation continued until his death in 1940, but it never produced more than a weekly five-gallon barrel of liquor. He primarily served the miners who found their way to his operation after drawing their paychecks on weekends. This activity, coupled with his almost "religious" avoidance of churchgoing, made him as unlikely to win pious March Robinson's approval as Alberta's earlier suitors. Alberta asserted her will again, however, marrying Will Shuttlesworth on January 22, 1927. By this time, she had given birth to her second child by Vetter Greene, a girl named Cleola. Soon after the wedding Alberta changed the names of her children to Shuttlesworth. She later taught her children by Greene that "the man who takes care of you and brings you up is your father." Such a flexible view of paternity, in both the mother and her children, reflects an attitude typical among rural African Americans, who, in sociologist Lewis W. Jones's words, "accept the fact of having been born with a simplicity that more sophisticated people find difficult to appreciate." In this and other ways, Freddie Lee Shuttlesworth would grow up identifying with the common folk.[8]

Alberta, Fred, and Cleo moved into the house that Will Shuttlesworth built with help from his friend, Morris Haygood. Eventually, the large house would be filled with seven other children from the union of Alberta and Will—Eugene, Eula Mae, Ernestine, Awilda, Clifton, Truzella, and Betty. In addition, the household often included the sons of Will's previous marriage, who came for extended visits. Photographs of Booker T. Washington, Abraham Lincoln, and Jesus decorated the living room. These figures rarely became the objects of teaching sessions, although the parents as well as the children looked up to them as important parts of the black heritage. The Shuttlesworth home did not have running water or electric power; candles and kerosene lamps provided the illumination. The boys hauled water—drinking water from the well at the nearby schoolyard and wash water from a favorite spring—in two fifty-five gallon drums. This house, along with the red house where his grandmother Martha Robinson died, became the significant settings for Fred's first childhood memories.[9]

Like most of the families in the community, the Shuttlesworths were poor. Fred was eleven or twelve before he acquired a pair of long pants. Wearing them proudly, Fred walked to school the next morning concerned that his creases not wrinkle. (This was apparently the beginning of his attention to his dapper appearance—later during his civil rights career, a relatively hostile Birmingham police officer would concede that "Shuttlesworth always looked good in his clothes."[10]) Their poverty notwithstanding, the family managed by ingenuity and teamwork to avoid the most extreme forms of deprivation. Both parents, but especially Alberta, enforced their expectations that each of the children, as they grew old enough, would contribute to the family's well-being. Like many of their neighbors, the family benefited from the New Deal welfare programs and often expressed the popular slogan, "Let Roosevelt feed you and the good Lord lead you." At twelve Fred often rode his bicycle to the food distribution office on Second Avenue South and Twenty-fourth Street. His stepfather drove his Model-T Ford into Birmingham to buy day-old bread from a bakery. In addition, their diet consisted of beans, peas, greens of various sorts, welfare flour, wheat, and lard, with occasional opportunities for meat.

Life in the Shuttlesworth home, however, periodically deteriorated to a less than harmonious state. With strong personalities and hot tempers, the parents frequently engaged in spirited arguments, sometimes in vitriolic language. Twenty-three years older than his wife, Will was jealous of her attractiveness to younger men. Similarly concerned about her husband's wandering eye, Alberta had good reason to worry. Will had been known in Oxmoor as "one of the catches of the area." Eugene Shuttlesworth, the first of Alberta's children by Will, speculated that his father had likely "stepped out on" Alberta. For his part, Fred remembered that his stepfather had had a liaison with a woman in the community named Louise, a sister of one of Will's friends. Will's extramarital affairs were no secret to Alberta. As a black woman with several children, Alberta knew her precarious financial situation precluded any serious consideration of divorce. Moreover, she did not wish to be rid of Will. If the couple ever spoke of divorce, they never did so within earshot of their children. Nevertheless, Alberta's anger at her husband's sexual indiscretions at times bubbled vigorously to the surface in forceful complaints, and, as their conflicts escalated, so did the violence of their conflicts. The frequency and intensity of physical confrontations between their parents convinced daughters Cleo and Eula that serious harm might come to Alberta. This led Cleo to suggest that they intervene in one of their parents' fights, saying to Eula, "They fightin'. Let's get him. Here, you take this," as she handed her a large rock.[11]

During another fight, Will slapped Alberta across the face as they tangled on the front porch. Infuriated, Alberta chased him down the stairs and into the yard. As he tried to distance himself from her, Alberta clawed his face, and both loudly cursed at one another. Will noticed neighbor Maggie Tolbert watching the proceedings from across the road. Trying to shame his wife into retreat, he cried out, "Look at Maggie!! She's watching you." Alberta shot back, "Damn Maggie! You slapped me, you son of a bitch!!" In their home the instance of domestic violence with the most severe and irreparable consequences occurred one day when an angry Alberta attacked her husband with a broom handle. Attempting to defend himself, he raised a chair to block her blows. As she swung at him she hit the chair, however, and her broomstick splintered. One of the shards struck her in the face and gouged her eye. Fred blamed his stepfather for Alberta's permanent injury and convinced his siblings of Will's responsibility. Over the next few years, Fred periodically mumbled accusations under his breath and nurtured the determination to avenge his mother. When he was fifteen, he hatched a plot with Eugene and Cleo to beat up his stepfather. On the predetermined day, as Fred served on kitchen duty, he deliberately picked a fight with Will, accusing him of hurting his mother. "You knocked Mama's eye out," he said defiantly, "and you ain't gon' get away with it." Meanwhile, a broom-wielding Cleo and the heavy-set Gene were ready to enter the kitchen on cue from opposite doors. Fred and Gene would hold him while Cleo administered his punishment. Somehow alert to the developing plot, Will waited until the trio converged. When Fred's accomplices entered the room, he stamped his foot, shouting loudly at Cleo, "What the hell you gon' do with that broom?!!" The wide-eyed brother and sister straightaway bolted, leaving Fred staring his would-be victim square in the face. Defeated and silent, Fred sullenly left the room, ending the failed attempt to avenge his mother's injury. Cleo later admitted, "I don't guess we even had the nerve to do it."[12]

Thinking back on their home, the children of this marriage generally did not view the violence they witnessed as unusual. Fred Shuttlesworth grew up in an era and culture much less sensitive to family violence than contemporary times. Will and Alberta Shuttlesworth's relationship was at best stormy. Yet the children observed times of tenderness between them. Despite his parents' intermittent battles, Fred became convinced that "that old man really loved Mama." His brother Eugene saw evidence of this affection in their having seven children together in fifteen years of marriage. He further thought that although Alberta and Will had an abusive relationship, the abuse went in both directions. In their confrontations, Alberta clearly delivered almost as much as she received, and now and then she, in Eugene's words, "might have gloated because she had gotten the best of him." Unquestionably, however, these hard-edged situations built into Fred Shuttlesworth an essential toughness that would later manifest itself in overt ways.[13]

The Shuttlesworths' lack of concern with family violence was attributable to several factors. This concern is of relatively recent provenance, arising in American society only in the late 1960s or 1970s. Discussions of corporal punishment of children or domestic violence played little part in American life in the early twentieth century. In addition, the South has had a reputation for violence, typically expressed in greater support for the military, corporal punishment of children, gun ownership, and recreational fighting. Although these tendencies have been most pronounced in white southerners, blacks have shared their region's comparatively violent ethos. This larger culture influenced the Shuttlesworth family and lent to their home life a hard-nosed character. Furthermore, as members of the agricultural working class, Will and Alberta Shuttlesworth were unlikely to conform to what E. Franklin Frazier called "bourgeois ideals and standards of behavior." They lacked the smooth, educated savoir faire of the black middle class, which generally sought to avoid the traditional folk culture of "common" blacks. Beyond this aspect, regardless of race, families of lower economic status experience more frustrations and have fewer resources for coping with them. As a result, such families resort to violence more often than those in higher status groups. Although the Shuttlesworths did exhibit the piety, thrift, respectability, and other traits Frazier associated with the "black bourgeoisie," they lacked the social heritage, formal education, and professional status of the upper or middle classes. They showed middle-class traits not because they enjoyed middle-class status but because they aspired to it. Such aspirations typified what sociologist Charles Johnson called the "upper lower" or, preferably, the agricultural working class. In the 1930s this orientation characterized most rural blacks in Alabama and expressed itself in certain distinguishing marks: the renting of land, less-than-comfortable income level, little education coupled with high ambitions for children, church membership as an indication of respectability, concern for "staying out of trouble," and both emulating and ridiculing the pretenses of the upper classes. Fred Shuttlesworth was the product of a family that bore most of these marks, which in large measure illuminate his developing character.[14]

The same tough family setting that created a penchant for family violence also made for an unsentimental home life. Although Fred and the other children never felt unloved, their parents rarely demonstrated their affection for them. Fred in particular sometimes received harsh treatment from his stepfather in their somewhat tense relationship. The children's difficulties did not result from Will's disciplinary measures; Alberta filled that role. As Fred's sister Eula recalled, her father seldom participated in disciplining the children, although he once gave her a switching for directly disobeying him. In other situations, however, Fred saw his stepfather as cruel and abusive, especially toward him and Cleo, the stepchildren: "When I was young I thought he was a cruel man, much more cruel than he should have been. He didn't have any reason to be mean to us but he was. I and my older sister were his stepchildren. He was really strict and hard on us."[15]

Fred's desires to retaliate against his stepfather are understandable in light of an emotionally debilitating ritual to which William Shuttlesworth subjected his children. He often used profane but, to Will's mind, playful name-calling with the children as he "helped the plates." He characteristically distributed to Cleo the wing of the chicken because, as he would say, "that little heifer likes to fly" from her parents. He often poked fun at Gene as a "big-headed hound." At Fred he often pointed a crooked finger, adding a threatening tone to his verbal abuse: "You white-eyed hound, I'm going to beat hell out of you" or "I got hell up my sleeve for you." Good-natured though such actions and words may have been to Will, they were not interpreted in that way by Fred. To him they seemed serious and left him with little recourse but silent acquiescence. The stepson admitted, however, "I wish I could have grabbed him," and he wondered how they as children managed to avoid digestive problems (not to mention problems of self-image) from such hurtful incidents at the table.[16]

In characteristic fashion, Gene Shuttlesworth remembered his father more charitably than Fred. The younger brother disagreed about Will's cruelty, seeing him as a caring father, at least insofar as he provided for the family and insisted that his children receive the education he never attained. He insisted on their "getting their lessons," expressing pride in their accomplishments. Nonetheless, Fred saw "Papa" as far from a positive example for him, later lamenting that he had to look elsewhere for more positive role models.[17]

Will's mistreatment of his stepchildren caused almost as many problems as his infidelities. For example, after Will's death Alberta refused to marry again until all of her children had left home, not wishing, she later told her son Clifton, to "put any man over" her children. Although she eventually did remarry after her children were grown, her reticence partly reflected an effort to avoid making the same mistake twice—subjecting her remaining children to a stepfather's potential abuse. The conflict Fred observed between his parents, however, loomed even larger. He occasionally heard his mother blame Will for the loss of her eye. Fred of course shared his mother's view and took his mother's part when he perceived her as suffering unjustly by her husband's hand. These experiences may have exacerbated a kind of oedipal struggle between Fred and his stepfather, for male children in violent marriages often become allied with their mothers as protectors against their fathers.[18]

Fred and the other children had a more positive male role model in their grandfather, who continued to live nearby in Oxmoor. March Robinson disapproved of Will Shuttlesworth's amoral lifestyle. He objected to his son-in-law's profane temperament and his lack of church attendance. He particularly disliked Will's bootlegging operation and womanizing. Given his history of rejecting his daughter's suitors, March probably had impossibly high standards, and no one Alberta chose would have passed muster. His moralistic and devout demeanor, however, suggested a particular coolness toward William Shuttlesworth. Until his death in 1952, March lived near his daughter's family, first with his wife, Martha, and later with occasional visits from his mother, Sarah Robinson. "Grandma Sarah" had the same feistiness as March and Alberta, insisting that her great-grandchildren earn their keep by sweeping the yard. Both Sarah and her son earned reverential respect from all the Shuttlesworth children. A tall, imposing man weighing almost three hundred pounds, March Robinson demanded obedience from his grandchildren without having to say things twice.[19]

By age fourteen, however, Fred's developing spirit of independence overcame his awe of his grandfather—at least once. As March ambled through a nearby cotton field with his grandsons, he issued an order that won an impudent reply from Fred. March took up a cotton stalk to administer corporal discipline. Fred scampered away, but was surprised when his grandfather gave chase until the youthful fugitive caught his shirt trying escape through a barbed-wire fence. Reaching through the fence, March effectively applied his punishment, and Fred never challenged him again. Beyond his intimidating size and strict bearing, March Robinson provided Fred and the others a kindly and pious example. His punctilious attendance and respected involvement in the St. Matthew AME Church impressed them. His warmheartedness attracted them when they visited him after church each Sunday. He often told them ghost stories and parched peanuts for them, and he regularly brought oranges to Eula, who was often ill and confined to the house. March Robinson thus largely countered the example of Fred Shuttlesworth's stepfather and provided Fred a proud role model. The elder Robinson's greatest legacy, however, lay in the traits of character he and Alberta helped shape in his grandson.[20]

Like many sons, Fred Shuttlesworth views his mother rather uncritically and hails her as the dominant influence in his life. "I have nothing but praise for Mama," he has said, "except for [her] using vile and intemperate language," which fairly often bubbled up in her battles with her husband. The family marveled at her strength of character and her integrity. Fred recalled her always working assiduously to add to the family's coffers, yet never owning more than two dresses. She adjusted to her meager possessions with a spartan demeanor. Once when she lost a twenty dollar bill, Fred, expecting his mother to be upset by what he viewed as a major financial setback, asked her, "Don't you feel like crying?" "Son," she explained, "you can't miss what you never had. But you can be yourself with or without it. This doesn't stop me from being what I am. It's better to have a little with principle than to have much with no principle." In similar fashion, as he grew older, Clifton Shuttlesworth discovered that the entire community respected her integrity, knowing that she could be trusted to pay her debts.[21]

Alberta was a no-nonsense mother who worked hard and demanded that her children do the same, as was commonly the case in poor rural families in which both parents contributed to the family income. She did occasional day labor as a domestic or worked with her children for fifty cents a day in a neighbor's field. Later, Alberta had a long-term job as a housekeeper for the family of R. B. Kent, a well-to-do dairyman in the Oak Grove section of Jefferson County. The Kents treated her kindly, never displaying any extreme racist attitudes. Alberta ordinarily returned home by four o'clock in the afternoon, and then she would prepare the evening meal.[22]

Alberta made her most vivid impressions on her brood with her hard-nosed discipline. Fred often confessed to toeing the line dutifully at his imperious mother's commands. He declared, "There have been many times I wanted to try Mama, but one thing I know, Alberta didn't play. And I didn't play with her." Indeed, all of her children knew not to play with Alberta. Just before their mother returned from work, they all scurried around the house, frantically making sure their responsibilities had been met by the time she arrived and called them into account. Speaking to a college audience later, Fred told of her proficiency at not sparing the rod: "She was an expert in applying either the switch or the 'board of education' to the 'seat of knowledge,' which caused a burning without and some sensations within." She often whipped the children in a row, from the oldest to the youngest, when generally displeased with the level of discipline around the house. Her whippings were frequent and severe. One of Alberta's switchings left a permanent scar on Fred's hip. On another occasion, she slapped him near his eyes, causing him literally to see stars. She had little time or inclination to discuss matters of disagreement with her children, often using corporal discipline as a first resort. At times the children were bothered by this stern approach. Her fourth child, Eula, once told her, "Mama, I think you whup me just 'cause you can." Apparently conscience stricken, Alberta caught herself and laid down the strap. Observing the felicitous results of Eula's words, younger brother Clifton filed them away, later using them himself while suffering the wrath of Alberta—this time, however, to no avail. The line worked only once.[23]

Fred's parents required the firstborn to act in their absence as surrogate parent. Assigning firstborn children a responsible role indicated a high positive valuation placed on "mothering," regardless of gender. Alberta expected Fred to wash, boil, scrub, and iron the clothes, all of which he considered "a girl's thing." His indifference toward this chore led him to accomplish it rarely to Alberta's satisfaction. Fred occasionally allowed his overseeing responsibilities to go to his head, applying discipline to his siblings almost as vigorously as did his mother. Eula often complained about her older brother being too bossy in exercising his "parental" privileges. But Alberta held him responsible for making sure the other children's chores and lessons were done. Beyond these duties, the boys usually worked in the fields with their father or grandfather. They arose at five A.M., taking care of some light chores before school, such as cutting wood and gathering coal. The boys learned at a young age how to plow, hoe, care for livestock, and milk the cows every morning before school. The girls helped haul water from the well in large washtubs, which were used both for washing and for boiling the clothes. The girls also took care of the house. After they completed their appointed jobs, Fred and the others settled in to do their homework by the light of kerosene lamps. Later, Alberta checked over the children's school assignments and then enforced her rule of lights out at 10 P.M.[24]

Alberta insisted on certain behaviors as correct because they conformed to a rule or regulation. In Alberta's domain, the children dared not challenge her rules. Some would characterize this mode of instruction as "authoritarian," considering the norms or rules over the preferences of the child. As an adult, Fred clearly used this child-rearing style. Studies of the "authoritarian personality" have consistently shown connections between exhibiting this style and having experienced severe parental punishment, and Fred Shuttlesworth fits this profile. In both his pastoral and his civil rights work, he reflected a robust authoritarian style. He always took care to adhere above all to "principle"—another name for a rule from which one may not deviate. Shuttlesworth willingly, even brazenly, disregarded the rule of Birmingham's segregated society, but only out of his conviction that Jim Crow laws violated the principles of divine law and human dignity. He could thus paradoxically flout the authoritarian norms of segregation from within his own authoritarian view of the world.[25]

Along with her demanding nature, which perhaps dominated her personality, Alberta also displayed a softer, nurturing side, a traditional role among African American mothers. Despite her unbending, hyper-disciplinary approach to child rearing, or perhaps because of it, Alberta communicated to her children a close emotional family attachment. Alberta's occasional violence notwithstanding, this family, centered on the rule (and rules) of their mother, became their source of connection and self-respect. In her rough-edged manner, Alberta provided her children a legitimation of being. Without syrupy or overly sentimental expressions of her love, she instilled in Fred and the others a sense of validation and worth—in themselves as individuals and as a family—by demonstrating a strong protectiveness. She kept her children close to home, making certain each contributed to the family's needs. While Fred picked up odd jobs away from home as he moved into his teens, Alberta kept the other children nearby. Cleola often recalled her mother's unwavering vow: "If we eat bread and drink water, we are going to be together." Within a tight family circle, the mother whom Fred said never did much talking nevertheless underscored for her children a basic dignity and persevering strength. Cleola recalled: "Mama would talk to us. If anybody talked you down, if anybody do such and such, you don't have to pay any attention to that. You go forward. Don't look back so much. You've got to look up. Keep your head up. Don't hold your head down."[26] From his mother's efforts to build up her children's self-esteem and from other quiet affirmations, Fred developed a definite sense of his own personal security, which naturally contributed to his responding confidently to more unfamiliar experiences outside the home.

The most obvious of such experiences would eventually be his confrontations with Birmingham's Jim Crow system. Yet in the strongly segregated rural setting of Oxmoor, such experiences were relatively unfamiliar, at least during Fred Shuttlesworth's childhood. In spite of Birmingham's segregated housing patterns, black and white neighborhoods within the city limits lay in relative proximity to each other. Such was not the case on the outskirts of the city, however. Only one white family lived in the Shuttlesworths' immediate vicinity in Oxmoor, and Fred was not provided with any defining incident for confronting the harsher aspects of segregation. Furthermore, black citizens of Oxmoor rarely encountered whites, and thus neither Fred nor his siblings testify to much instruction in the racial facts of life—no direct recitations of the appropriate conventions, no overarching explanations of why, as Martin Luther King's daughter would later ask, "white people treat Negroes so mean." Alberta occasionally made indirect references to slavery, but primarily encouraged them to ignore its significance, as Cleo again indicated: "No, they [Will and Alberta] didn't talk very much, but Mama would tell us, 'You don't pay any attention to that [slavery] because what already has happened, it's gone. God said love everybody, and you will love everybody before you see His face.'" Although he and his siblings gradually perceived the meaning of the White Only signs, Clifton similarly remembered no direct or distinct teaching on how to get along with whites. Instead, Alberta included such advice within her general demand that the children respect all their elders. Clifton noted: "I don't ever remember my mother say [anything like] that [explanations of how to behave around whites] because it was something that I just automatically adopted myself to. My mother always taught us, whether you were black or white, I had to give you respect. It was always a 'Mr.' or a 'Mrs.'"[27]

Fred's mother responded to racial matters without explicit instruction in her determination to keep her children out of trouble—a concern typical of blacks who aspired to middle-class status. Black children who ran afoul of white strictures were often placed in reformatories or detention homes away from their parents. Thus, Alberta declared to her children unequivocally, "You're mine. I'm gon' raise you. I'm not gon' let white folks raise my children." This concern accounted in part for her strong, even harsh, child-rearing practices. A woman of her age and traditions, Alberta unquestionably viewed physical punishment as the most effective means of disciplining her children. She seemed to have shared in what sociologist Ruby F. Lassiter called "the legacy" of harsh discipline among African American parents. In order to teach the danger of transgressing white expectations, many black parents since the time of slavery have employed harsh disciplinary methods and have passed on that parental style well into the twentieth century. Even if this motivation for harsh discipline never entered her mind, Alberta easily might have followed such practices as a cultural inheritance. Her concern that *she*, rather than white folks, raise her children, however, suggests a conscious motivation. In addition, Alberta customarily sought divine aid in her effort to rear and protect her children. Both Fred and Cleola remembered hearing their mother often mumble prayers, as she walked about the house doing her own chores, for strength and help in rearing the children right. She also importuned God to take care of them and to "let her see her baby get grown." Such piety made a powerful impression on Fred, who eventually developed a similar kind of "combative spirituality."[28]

Even in her piety, Alberta revealed her strong authoritarian personality. Like her father, she held membership in the St. Matthew AME Church. (Will

Shuttlesworth had come from a Baptist background, but Fred remembered his attending services only twice.) Alberta did not give extensive religious training to her children. Just as she hazarded few explanations of the Jim Crow world around them, similarly she gave her children little specific religious instruction beyond occasional Bible reading. She did require her children to attend Sunday school and worship services regularly. Fred later commented that on Sunday mornings his mother never asked, "Are you going to church?" but rather, "How soon can you get there?" She inclined toward the classic parental ultimatum: "If you live in *this* house, you're gonna serve God by getting up there to Sunday school." Alberta at least partially set the example by her faithful attendance at worship services, though she rarely made it to Sunday school. Rather cool and not given to demonstrative expressions, Alberta never rose to the emotional level of shouting in church. St. Matthew's AME typified southern rural black churches in the area. One could expect three worshippers or so to express themselves in the form of the shout; one could expect Alberta Shuttlesworth not to. Occasionally, when moved by the spirit, she might weep quietly in her pew, once prompting Clifton to ask why she cried in church. "If you have God in you, you're gonna feel it," she answered, "and I felt God."[29]

Fred Shuttlesworth learned his lessons from a faculty larger than one, however. Alberta naturally served as his "major professor," but other adults in Oxmoor also taught him by precept and example. Although his early life was dominated by his mother, Fred was brought up in an atmosphere that vividly illustrated the well-known African saying, "It takes a whole village to raise a child." Adults in Oxmoor commonly functioned in loco parentis for all the children in the community. Alberta Shuttlesworth operated by this principle with her own children and the children of others. Alberta encouraged other adults to keep a watchful eye on and even to apply a disciplinary hand to her children—and especially Fred, who became known for his mischievous ways. "She knew that if she didn't control my devilish tendencies," he later acknowledged, "I could be a rat and turn the wrong way." Alberta duplicated at home any "whippin'" Fred received in school or in the community and returned the favor for other mothers. At home with the babies, Alberta more than once spotted youngsters from the neighborhood sneaking away to play hooky. Picking up her child and assuming the role of sentry, she quickly "captured" the escapees and marched them back to school. "So all of the kids respected her," Eugene Shuttlesworth noted, "especially when she got the strap or the switch and started working on us."[30]

Aside from his mother, Fred was influenced by the church communities in Oxmoor more than anything else. Neither St. Matthew's AME nor Shady Grove Baptist Church, both attended by the Shuttlesworth family, gave evidence of any strong denominational consciousness. These "half-time" churches met on alternate Sundays, and most members regularly attended services at both sites. Both played important nurturing roles in Fred's youth, though the AME background dominated in the family's life. And in a fair turnabout, the Robinson and Shuttlesworth families dominated the small congregation at St. Matthew's. Because they did not have air conditioning, worshippers typically cooled themselves with fans provided by a local funeral home, though at times some were overcome by the heat, if not the religious fervor. Ushers often revived them with smelling salts and then carried them out of the sanctuary to sit under a tree. Occasionally, the church sent young people to an annual Sunday school convention in Philadelphia. Along with lay leaders and various Sunday school teachers, a succession of ministers made significant impressions on Fred. The Reverends W. D. Travel and L. A. Hubbard particularly distinguished themselves by working with the youth of the church and community, providing them affirmation and leisure-time activities. "They made the young feel like they were somebody," said Cleola Willis. One minister, the Reverend W. P. Driver, impressed Fred with his quotations of scripture and his emphasis on the sanctity of communion. He often prayed, "Lord, we do not presume to come to your table professing that we are holy." Another minister, the Reverend Andrew Morrisett, visited the Shuttlesworth family often. Morrisett stood out in Fred's memory as the only minister who ever managed to persuade his stepfather to go to services. Ministers of the Baptist church also made positive impressions on Fred, particularly Reverends S. D. Martin and S. B. Brown. At Shady Grove Baptist Church, deacon Jack Hawthorne captured Fred's verbal imagination with his eloquent stock conclusion to his prayers: "Lord, do thou have mercy for Jesus' sake."[31]

Characteristic of that era, the generally uneducated ministers who first modeled the ministry for Fred took a moderate stance on the issue of race. None explicitly supported segregation but rather veiled their criticisms of whites or expressed them in subdued tones. Shuttlesworth noted that any minister who outwardly defended segregation would quickly see his congregation's support evaporate: "Everybody would be against him." As a young member, Fred heard his ministers assume the sinfulness of segregation while typically expressing confidence that "the Lord is going to straighten out this world and make the white man do right. God knows where you are, and He has his own time set." Early on, Fred uncritically accepted the philosophy that although Jim Crow laws were unjust, in God's providence matters of race eventually would be put right. Fred accepted the realities of segregation while believing that the racial status quo demanded improvement. None of his ministers, however, directly attacked segregation, believing that such efforts would accomplish little. Fred later explained that such ministers were "not moved in any extraordinary way to do anything about it. You see nothing around you that would, if you move, move with you."[32]

Largely for this reason, Fred never faulted the ministers of his youth for failing to attack Jim Crow laws actively. Later, during the civil rights movement, he would strongly reproach older ministers who held similar views. A simple but significant distinction explains the apparent disparity. The former ministerial group, living earlier in the century, saw little or no promise in attacking segregation; such a strategy seemed futile. In contrast, after World War II these older ministers, as Shuttlesworth might have analyzed matters, clung to their passive "wait on the Lord" approach in spite of signs that with determined attacks segregation's walls might indeed "come a-tumbling down."

Thus, the good impressions left by his ministers created for Fred a positive image of the ministry. As a result, he gravitated early toward the ministry as a possible vocation. Only two callings—the ministry and the practice of medicine—ever interested young Fred Shuttlesworth. Gradually, however, his activities within the church, coupled possibly with the absence of medical role models nearby, turned him more definitely toward a life in the ministry. Fred's spiritual development proceeded gradually as part of his nurturing within the African American church. Fred was always a son of the church, and his "conversion experience" resembled more the culmination of a natural religious development than a dramatic cataclysm. Sometime between ages eight and twelve, Fred "accepted Christ" during an early morning revival service conducted by the Reverend W. P. Driver. The sermon that day focused on the scripture passage "Be thou faithful unto death, and I will give thee a crown of life" (Rev. 2:10). At the altar call, the boy experienced no traumatic paroxysm or spirit possession, no extreme expression of emotion. He felt a definite emotion, however—that he was being divinely and extraordinarily drawn to make a spiritual commitment. He needed no "praying through" to salvation, nor did he evidence a deep need for any supernatural experience of forgiveness. He later explained: "[It was] a gradual conversion. . . . I didn't think I would have to yearn for help. I had done nothing so bad that I was broken and contrite like David. For me it was a growing into and accepting God."[33]

This meaningful confirmatory experience solidified his sense of calling to work in the church. Between that time and his high school commencement, he was graduated from Sunday school pupil to teacher of the primary children at St. Matthew's. He also rose to the position of Sunday school superintendent while still a teenager. Such a leadership position was not unusual for the small congregation—all the Shuttlesworth children eventually served in similar capacities. Fred, however, kept private his leanings toward the ministry. Although active in the life of the church, he scarcely made a name for himself as a person of unusual piety. (In light of his mother's demands and demeanor, one could say all the children participated in church activities in self-defense.) No one expected Fred to enter the clergy. He surprised even his siblings Clifton and Eula when he opted for the ministry. Clifton testified that he "showed nothing that he would be a minister. . . . I didn't see it in him." His church activities possibly provided some camouflage, but in school he displayed a distinct playfulness—or "devilishness," as his family called it. Such mischief making hinted at the down-to-earth (and occasionally earthy) spirituality he eventually developed.[34]

Typical of the South in the early twentieth century, Birmingham moved slowly to equalize the educational facilities and opportunities for its white and black students. General public education in the city lagged behind that in other major southern cities. Birmingham paid for new school buildings at a rate of only $24.27 per pupil, compared with $41.17 in Memphis, $42.93 in Atlanta, and Richmond's $77.66. Early in the century, allocations displayed discrimination, with $8.04 appropriated per black child compared with $24.13 for every white child. White teachers averaged thirty-six students in their classes compared with fifty-eight for black teachers. In 1911, the property of white schools was valued at $97.84 per pupil compared with $20.22 per pupil for black schools. In 1922, the year of Fred Shuttlesworth's birth, schools were overcrowded for all students, but more so for black students. White school enrollment was 131 percent of the buildings' normal capacity compared with 264 percent for black school buildings. By the time Fred reached high school, little had changed. In the 1937–1938 school year, the state of Alabama spent $49.37 for every white pupil but only $14.75 for each black child. The school system paid white teachers an average annual salary of $827 but only $393 for black teachers. Although the illiteracy rate for blacks in Birmingham had fallen from the 40 percent seen in 1900, the rate during Fred's early childhood still hovered around 18 percent.[35]

Until 1935 Fred and his older siblings attended Oxmoor School, a two-room schoolhouse where two teachers taught all children up to the eighth grade. After 1935 a new school, Oxmoor-Reading Junior High, replaced the old building. The new, slightly enlarged school doubled the number of rooms and teachers—one instructing the first and second grades, another teaching grades three through five, a third for grades six and seven, and a fourth for grades seven and eight. Fred especially liked two teachers at Oxmoor, Miss Worth and Miss Windham. Miss Windham was legendary among all the Shuttlesworth children. In his schoolwork, Fred not only dealt with a demanding mother who accepted no grades less than a C but also was put through his paces by a woman after Alberta's own heart. A strict disciplinarian who pushed her students to excel, Miss Windham took personally her responsibility to prepare her charges for work at Rosedale High School. She often said, "My profession is teaching, and if you don't know, you don't go. You're not going to Rosedale and make me look bad, as if I'm not doing my job down here."[36]

The principal of Oxmoor School, Israel L. Ramsey, however, influenced Fred most profoundly. Providing the positive male role model that Fred's stepfather did not, Ramsey impressed Fred with his piety and sensitivity to the needs of students. A smallish, impeccably dressed man of dignity, he exuded a sense of self-confidence and pride and taught his students to take pride in themselves. Fred observed him carefully and sought to emulate him in his basic carriage. The young Shuttlesworth detected in him a demonstrable and effectual Christian faith and a charismatic presence that attracted Fred in spite of Ramsey's stern discipline. Fred took particular notice of Ramsey's physical courage in disciplining boys who towered over him. More important to Fred, however, was Ramsey's piety: "You felt like you knew God through him. You knew he was conscious of God and his fellow man by the way he conducted his school." A particular incident that generated a profound respect in Fred occurred on a day when Ramsey was teaching. Generally quick to pick up his lessons, Fred sat with his hand raised, clamoring to be recognized and to give the answer. Ramsey held Fred off, however, not wanting to embarrass the older pupils by calling on the younger student. In time Ramsey Socratically guided them into discovering the answer and led Fred into understanding his gentle pedagogy that stroked the ego and built the self-confidence of his students.[37]

Fred later credited these mentors with teaching him how to analyze persons and size them up. He took to heart their advice—"Pay attention to what people do, not what they say." Through their example, he developed a talent that became helpful in dealing with southern politicians and other black ministers in the civil rights movement. More important, however, teachers such as Miss Windham stirred the sparks of interest in students such as Fred and cultivated in them an ambition to make something of themselves. Although Fred's practical education would never give him the sophistication or polish of some other black leaders of his era, his teachers were greatly impressed with his ability, particularly his powerful photographic memory. In the seventh grade, he was assigned a seven-page oration, which he recited after reading it over only three or four times. Later, during the civil rights movement his memory enabled him to retain a hundred phone numbers without use of a directory.[38]

Fred also made a name for himself as one of Oxmoor School's head mischief makers. His playful sense of humor once ran him afoul of another teacher, Mrs. Owens. She put him in a corner for talking in class and then momentarily left the room. Exploiting the opportunity, Fred moved the classroom clock up forty-five minutes until it indicated the time for dismissal. After ringing the bell for general dismissal, Mrs. Owens discovered both the "crime" and the culprit. With some embarrassment, she called the students back to their seats, and with much exasperation she called Fred to the cloakroom, where she administered corporal punishment. Emerging with a smile, Fred antagonized his teacher all the more. "Oh, it's funny to you?" she asked as she escorted him back for a second paddling. Fred stoically accepted the punishments, not wanting his classmates to see him give in. After replaying this scene several times, and as the strap began to take its toll, he ended the drama, feigning tears by placing saliva on his cheeks. He often played the role of a happy-go-lucky prankster, both at school and around the house. On one occasion he put pepper in his sister's mouth while she was asleep. His biggest caper involved brother Eugene and young friend Thomas Milton. Masterminding a scheme to sell meat in the neighborhood, Fred led the trio in putting up a small mud clay building beside the Shuttlesworth home to serve as a makeshift butcher shop. Some days later Fred and Thomas spotted a pig in the fields, ran it down, caught it, and took it to their "establishment." With no idea how to raise the pig undetected, Fred sent the animal home with Thomas. Soon Alberta discovered the whole operation and immediately marched over to Thomas's house to get to the bottom of things. The boys defended themselves, saying they had found the pig unattended and had only claimed it for themselves. Alberta vigorously explained to the boys that even if they had found it out in the forest, "you know it wasn't your pig." Punctuating her moral lesson with a spanking, she took the boys along as she sought out the pig's rightful owner.[39]

Both at home and at school, Fred exhibited a mildly contentious nature and an attraction for fights, playful and otherwise. His home environment, with the stormy relationship of his parents, produced early manifestations of Fred's combative personality. His role as surrogate parent engendered in him a bossy demeanor toward his siblings. He frequently barked orders and served as enforcer. In addition, he often playfully slapped his sister Cleo, whose own feisty nature escalated such encounters into more serious fracases. In addition to home life, developments outside the world of Oxmoor contributed to Fred's pugnacious propensities. The ascent of Joe Louis as world heavyweight champion (1937–1949) generated great interest in the sport, and Louis's legendary presence created large numbers of idolizing fans, particularly among rural blacks. Fred participated enthusiastically in his school's boxing club and quickly became the champion in his weight division. Older boys were impressed by his vigor and his abilities, often spurring him to take on virtually any opponent, regardless of size or reputation. Hearing them say "I bet Fred can beat him" almost always inspired him to enter the ring and show his stuff. Coupling his friskiness with his pugilism, he regularly engaged in good-natured sparring with one of his friends. On other occasions his skirmishes took on a more serious tone, as when he battled with Sadie Dukes and her sister, who were by his account "some of the worst kids in the school." More inclined to goofing off than met Fred's approval, Sadie also had the "disadvantage" of being of lighter complexion than Fred. For no particular reason that he could pinpoint, the very dark-skinned Fred developed a dislike for lighter-skinned African Americans. Searching for an explanation, he later said, "I didn't like light-skinned girls for some reason. . . . I guess I figured they would call me black, and I'd have to do something [in retaliation]."[40]

After negotiating his way through Miss Windham's and Mr. Ramsey's classes at Oxmoor, Fred moved on to high school. For part of a year he was assigned to Wenonah High School, several miles away from home. Later he transferred to Rosedale, a smaller school with less than fifty students in each class. The faculty at Rosedale was of high quality, and graduates often advanced into college and then into successful careers. Several alumni became lawyers and physicians, including James T. Montgomery, who went from Rosedale to Morehouse College and then to Harvard Medical School. Later, Montgomery returned to practice in Birmingham and served as Fred Shuttlesworth's doctor. Montgomery's uncle, D. M. Montgomery, served as Rosedale's principal for forty-eight years, during which he built its reputation for academic excellence under limited conditions. At Rosedale, Fred's reputation as an athlete grew, particularly on the football field. Early in his playing career, he was a reserve, without even a jersey. Later, however, an injury necessitated Fred's taking another player's jersey off his back and entering the game as a tackle despite his smallish size. His athletic abilities improved rapidly, and he developed an impressive shoestring tackle. Alongside his athletic prowess, Fred distinguished himself as a student, graduating in 1940 as class valedictorian.[41]

Despite his high school achievements, Fred also encountered racial discrimination for the first time. As a pre-teenager, Fred seldom noticed the racial world around him. His jobs distributing newspapers and working as a delivery boy for a drugstore left him untouched. While they attended school in Oxmoor, Fred's family had few contacts with whites and made few comparisons with white school facilities. After riding the bus to Rosedale, however, Fred noticed the dilapidated condition of the buses for black schools. White schools typically garnered new-model vehicles, whereas black students rode buses discarded by the white schools. Often Fred and the others missed whole days of school because buses broke down on the way to Rosedale. The qualitative difference in the buses introduced Fred Shuttlesworth to a Jim Crow world he would learn to despise. His growing maturity as a student also clarified his vision of the numerous distinctions between whites and blacks in Birmingham.

Like most American cities with large black populations, and particularly southern cities in the segregation era, Birmingham worked tensely to control its "Negro problem." In the first two decades of the twentieth century, Birmingham underwent a series of reform efforts to reshape its policies toward blacks. White groups such as industrial corporations, commercial and professional organizations, organized labor, both sides of the prohibition struggle, and local law enforcement contended with one another to control the supposed dangers of the black population in ways beneficial to their own interests. These white groups generally shared a fearfulness of "the Negro menace" founded on race-based stereotypes. Whites called for government control of blacks to counter their alleged unreliability as workers and their criminality, but to do so in ways that would keep them available as sources of cheap labor.[42]

Birmingham whites particularly concerned themselves with the regulation of saloons and the enforcement of vagrancy laws. Whites criticized what they called "these Negro dives," which dated back to the latter years of the nineteenth century, as "deep, dark, damnable dens of degradation." They attacked them by raising license taxes (which squeezed some out of business) and by creating well-policed "saloon districts." Black saloons, however, continued without supervision. Later, Mayor George B. Ward used police power to restrict prostitution to "red light districts" that had been relocated near black residential sections. Such discriminatory law enforcement practices effectively cleaned up the problem for white areas of the city but exacerbated the situation in black areas. In addition, complaining about what they perceived as blacks' irregular work habits, white Birmingham pressed for stricter laws and the stricter enforcement of vagrancy laws, which were not usually applied to whites. A week of effort to clean out the saloons in 1913 resulted in some two hundred vagrancy arrests that included very few whites. During this and other waves of such activity, officials operated according to the slogan "Go to work or go to jail" and regularly arrested anyone who could not verify employment. By the time of Fred's youth, these law enforcement efforts had placed blacks more completely under the dominance of powerful white group interests. Moreover, the problems they generated in the black community remained in effect throughout Fred's youth, persisting even into his adulthood when he became a pastor in the city.[43]

In high school Fred Shuttlesworth encountered this wider world of discriminatory law enforcement that was customary in Birmingham and uncritically accepted by most whites. One egregious example was that Birmingham courts as a matter of course accepted the testimony of whites over that of any black witness—a practice rarely if ever questioned by whites. Fred observed such an instance in Oxmoor. Most members of the black community became aware that a black bus driver had killed a man but had managed to be exonerated in two ways. He had killed another black man, which generally won more lenient attention from the all-white justice system. More important to Fred's thinking, the defendant used the time-honored tactic of having a white man testify for him in court, vouching for his character as "a good nigger." Commenting on this, Fred later admitted, "I guess you store all these things in your mind. But there was nothing you could do about it."[44]

The world of white justice came closer to home for Fred after his graduation from high school. His stepfather's bootlegging operation was the source of his first brush with the law. Will Shuttlesworth had required his older sons, Fred and Eugene, to assist with his distilling efforts. At times Fred sought to beg off, but his stepfather prevailed. Often they began activities before dawn in order to evade the watchful eye of authorities, particularly an Oxmoor deputy sheriff named Newton Hubbard. Fred suspected that a neighboring family named Satterfield, who competed with Will for Oxmoor's small-time clientele, turned them in. After Will died, his bootlegging concern fell into disuse because the sons were uninterested in continuing the "family business." Unfortunately, they were late in dismantling and discarding their still. On August 4, 1940, acting on a tip from the Satterfields, who hoped to make certain the Shuttlesworth boys did not reenter the market, the deputy sheriff appeared at the Shuttlesworth place demanding to see their condenser. Arrested by the Jefferson County Sheriff's Office, the eighteen-year-old Fred received two years' probation when the case came to court in February 1941. (Eugene, still a juvenile, was released into his mother's custody.) Fred thus encountered what he saw as an unjust system for blacks in his native Birmingham. There is some question about the level of injustice in this case, however. Fred had admittedly participated in Will's bootlegging activities, and the apparatus remained intact, though not in operation, at the time of the arrest. Also, two years later Fred was arrested again for violating probation.[45]

Fred's graduation from high school marked a passage between the carefree days of childhood and youthfulness and the responsibilities of adulthood. Soon he would be leaving the nurturing community of Oxmoor and Alberta Shuttlesworth's tough-minded school of literal hard knocks. Her hard-edged lessons and toughness of character took firm root in her oldest son. In later adulthood, Fred would reflect on the origin of his traits of combativeness, forthrightness, and directness, saying, "It's just been part of my disposition. I guess in times where it's needed, innate things that are in people come out."[46] As Fred moved out of his mother's shadow and into a very independent adulthood, he would find many occasions for the "stuff that was in him"—mostly instilled by Alberta—to come out.

Ready

Fix me so I don't worry so much.
— Fred L. Shuttlesworth

In 1941, much like an America not yet ready to fight Hitler or Jim Crow, Fred Shuttlesworth was not yet prepared for a preaching or a civil rights life. By his lights God took care of that process over the next thirteen years. During this time Fred led a "vagabond life." He left his mother and his mother church to move slowly—and at first uncertainly—toward what ultimately became an unshakable conviction of a call to the Baptist ministry. Unlike many of his fellow ministers, he had no dramatic call experience to prepare and steel him for eventual confrontations. Events gradually became his trainers. Through them the confidence planted by Alberta Shuttlesworth in Oxmoor came to fruition, preparing him for Birmingham. This chapter describes the pivotal events that trained him for the pastorate of Birmingham's Bethel Baptist Church, where other circumstances led him into civil rights and away from the anonymous ministry that might otherwise have been his lot. Beginning in 1941 his training at Mobile's Cedar Grove Bible Academy, Selma University, and, most important, his first difficult pastorate at Selma's First (Colored) Baptist Church built on what Alberta Shuttlesworth had begun. By 1953 his experiences had "fixed him where he didn't worry so much" and hardened his persona into one that was ready to take on both Jim Crow and Bull Connor—or so Fred came to believe.[1]

Not quite ready for the ministry or to become a major player in events that would change black life in America, Fred did soon believe himself ready for marriage. Within a year of his graduation from Rosedale High School, he went to work at the Southern Club in downtown Birmingham. Hired as an orderly for physicians who examined welfare applicants, Fred became romantically interested in a fellow worker named Ruby Keeler. He began a short courtship by walking her home, pushing his bicycle along the way. Before long he was visiting at her home and taking her to an occasional movie or to church. Not temperamentally given to philosophical discussions, particularly with women, Fred engaged in superficial conversation with Ruby, barely learning the details of her life before their meeting. Attracted to her looks and enjoying her company, he developed with Ruby a sturdy, affable relationship that moved steadily toward marriage.[2]

Heavyset, with long wavy hair and a lighter complexion than Fred, Ruby had a more advantaged background than did her new suitor. Born in Birmingham on May 30, 1922, she grew up in the home of her uncle and aunt, Augustus U. Morris and Adell Morris. In his well-kept home in the West End section of town, Augustus Morris provided well for his niece. As a result, Ruby never knew the relative deprivation experienced in Oxmoor by her future husband. The Morrises struck others in the Birmingham black community as very cultured and religious. Fred Shuttlesworth Jr. remembered "Uncle Josh" (Augustus) as dressing like a preacher and keeping his car spotless. Augustus had worked as a clerk for the Louisville and Nashville Railroad, and for a time he served as president of the Brotherhood of Railway Clerks Union. He also moonlighted as an undertaker, a profession that moved him up to the black middle class and afforded him higher status in the community.[3]

With no children of their own, Augustus and Adell treated Ruby as their daughter. Their financial means provided virtually for her every whim, and Adell always kidded her about being a "spoiled brat." As quiet, dignified, middle-class "parents," the Morrises insisted that Ruby advance her education. After graduating from Parker High School, she studied nursing at Tuskegee Institute. Her academic ability gave her a well-spoken confidence and a quiet assertiveness. Later, Ruby's daughter Ricky (Ruby Fredericka) noted, "She could tell you to go to hell and make you happy to be on your way." Like Fred, she had a quick temper. She spent the summer of 1941 working at the Southern Club to save money for the next year's college tuition. Unexpectedly taken with the "country boy" from Oxmoor, Ruby decided by summer's end not to resume her studies at Tuskegee. After a three-week engagement, they were married on October 20, 1941.[4]

Just before the wedding Fred found a slightly better-paying job at the Alpha Portland Cement Plant, where he earned fifty-four cents an hour working in a quarry, shoveling rock, and performing other miscellaneous chores. At the cement plant, Fred experienced his first real contact with blue-collar whites and racial intimidation in the person of a supervisor named Ewell. Not looking for trouble, Fred kept busy with his duties. On one occasion, when Ewell came to check on the work, Fred's coworkers quickened the pace of their shoveling. Fred, however, continued as before. One of the others needled him, commenting, "Come on, you are mighty slow there." Fred replied, "There's the man. Let *him* say something. He has sense enough to know you ain't doin' this when he's not here." He then added, "I'm gonna do what I do 'cause I think this is the way I ought to do it. Besides, let the man tell me what to do."[5]

With their small increase in income, the couple rented a duplex near the plant. Fred found ways to improve their meager economic existence. The relative deprivation, however, required some adjustment for Ruby, who was accustomed to a more comfortable lifestyle. The Morrises were in a financial position to provide some assistance, but, intent on being the provider, Fred was loath to accept help from his in-laws. Instead, he sought to add to his skills and earnings by enrolling in an auto mechanics course at the Hayes Aircraft Company in Fairfield. He eventually developed enough expertise that later, as a pastor, he worked on his churches' vehicles himself. Never lacking confidence, he later was known to claim that no matter how futile an automotive project might seem, "me and the Lord are gon' get this thing movin'." For her part, Ruby continued to work in doctors' offices until the birth of the Shuttlesworths' first child, Patricia Ann, in early 1943.[6]

The family's new arrival made necessary an even more lucrative source of income. At the suggestion of two friends, Fred decided to seek work in Mobile. From the beginning of World War II, African Americans had seen the war as an opportunity for advancement in the military. In addition, President Franklin D. Roosevelt's creation of the Fair Employment Practices Commission (FEPC), charged with overseeing equality in the defense industry, created a wary economic optimism among many blacks in the South. Hoping for possible advancement, many blacks migrated to the south Alabama port city. Leaving behind his wife and daughter until he could find a job and a place to live, Shuttlesworth joined two friends and ventured to Mobile. Within a day of their arrival in the summer of 1943, they found work at Brookley Air Force Base. Fred was assigned to the uncomplicated duty of driving a truck and earned a wage of $1.80 an hour. Occasionally he drove soldiers around the base all day, but more often than not he spent his time in his parked truck, waiting for his next order. He occupied his idle time by reading the Bible. "I kept a [New] Testament with me all the time," he later commented. Most of his knowledge of the scriptures was gained in this manner. For a short time Fred lived in a boarding house, along with his friends. Also living there as tenants were three single women, one of whom developed a strong amorous interest in Fred. Homesick for his wife and daughter, he rebuffed her flirtations. Another reason was his growing sense of calling to the ministry. Above all he wished to stay on the straight and narrow in the face of these temptations. Besides, the young woman was both light-skinned and making a fool of herself by her forwardness; neither characteristic met Fred's approval. Thus, to salvage both his reputation and his marriage, he quickly found rental property in the housing projects of Maysville, Mobile's "Negro section," and sent for Ruby and the baby.[7]

The young man decided that the family would not stay in the projects for long, however. Interested in advancing his fortunes, and with an eye to obvious opportunity, Fred developed a plan. He had discovered that officials at the base made available concrete blocks and other salvage building materials at little or no cost. He immediately suggested that he and a friend named Sammy Davis buy adjacent lots and help one another build houses with these surplus materials. After making ten-dollar down payments, the two men built two twelve- by twenty-four-foot houses, with Fred's new home facing Ghent Street and his companion's facing Atwood. Later, when Fred and the family left Mobile, they sold the house for $1,200.[8]

While working at Brookley Field, in a clash with a white fellow worker, Shuttlesworth first evidenced the concern for fairness more fully realized in his later civil rights activities. Commenting on the social customs governing blacks in his home state of Mississippi, the man noted that "good nigras" took their hats off on entering white sections of town. When he added that such blacks "knew their place and got along fine," Shuttlesworth retorted matter-of-factly, "You want to know how you got along fine? Because you didn't have no Negroes in your town with guts. I haven't been in your town, and if I ever get there you will see a Negro with his hat *on* walking on your sidewalk. That'll be one time a Negro won't be walking in the street bareheaded." On another, more serious occasion, he protested unfair labor practices. When one of the black workers was threatened with a pay cut, Fred gathered his fellow workers for a complaint to the military superior. In response, the head of operations called for Shuttlesworth to be dismissed as a troublemaker, complaining, "Well, he's a crusader now." Instead of firing him, though, the officer in charge transferred him to office duty for six weeks. Before Fred returned to duty in the field, however, he was told, "This is a government job, and you can't teach men to strike here." Objecting that he had not urged a strike, he responded, "I just went to the head official and told him these men deserve a job and the right pay for doing it."[9]

At that time, the city of Mobile, federal military installations included, was especially sensitive to labor disputes with a racial cast. Scarcely a month before Shuttlesworth's arrival, the Mobile area had been convulsed by difficulties at the Alabama Dry Dock and Shipbuilding Company. The white community of Mobile had begun to stiffen its traditional racial arrangements in reaction to a large wartime influx of blacks into the area. Since 1940 the black population in Mobile had risen 61 percent to nearly two hundred thousand, and white workers became especially concerned over possible desegregation in employment and the inevitable job competition it would create. The FEPC had previously investigated Alabama Dry Dock and ordered the company to upgrade the hiring of blacks, who made up some seven thousand of its thirty thousand workers. After several months of stalling, the company finally transferred twelve African American welders to its Pinto Island operation. The next day, May 25, 1943, white workers brandishing pipes, clubs, and tools rioted and chased the blacks around the island, and eventually violence spilled out into the entire shipyard. Some eighty workers, nearly all of them blacks, were injured before seven companies of state guardsmen and a detail of federal troops from Brookley Field quelled the disturbance. By the time Shuttlesworth came to the city, matters had reached an uneasy equilibrium, but his superiors understandably made every effort to throw cold water on any potential flare-ups or new crusades. At the time, however, any crusades Fred considered had a decidedly religious quality.[10]

After graduating from high school, Fred had begun to think about the ministry as a vocation. His sense of calling had gradually deepened while he was still living in Oxmoor. After serving the St. Matthew AME Church as Sunday school superintendent, he publicly declared his intention to enter the ministry. The church's presiding elder planned to recommend Fred to the AME Annual Conference. If approved, he would receive an exhorter's license, the first step toward ordination. Unfortunately, Fred's arrest for distilling and his resulting probationary period intervened, and later his courtship and marriage occupied his attention. Thus he postponed his plans for entering the ministry. As events unfolded, however, he never initiated the ordination process in the AME Church. Still, his conviction of a call remained. Ruby had minor misgivings about being a minister's wife, but she nonetheless understood that Fred planned a future in the ministry.[11]

Once the family was reunited in Mobile, Fred and Ruby had every intention of settling into an AME Church as soon as possible. The excitable young prospective minister, however, found great difficulty acclimating himself to the spiritual atmosphere at the local AME congregation. Shuttlesworth judged the service to be too formal. He later recalled that the service he and the family attended was "so cold and uninspired. . . . The singing wasn't good, the choir wasn't good, the minister looked like he was straining, and I felt more sorry for him. I left the church disturbed." Fred mentioned his uneasiness to a friend named John Williams, a deacon and trustee of the Corinthian Baptist Church in Maysville. As any respectably faithful church member would do, Williams invited Fred to attend worship services at his church. Not intending to stray from his denominational "raising" but feeling a visit would do no harm, Fred decided to attend the Baptist church the next Sunday. The members of the congregation impressed Fred with their welcome, and on hearing that Fred aspired to the ministry, the pastor encouraged him. "We'd be glad to have you come with us," the Reverend E. A. Palmer assured the prospective member, adding, "'course, if you come into the Baptist church we would have to baptize you [by immersion]." [12]

Obligation to family religious tradition maintained its hold on Fred only temporarily. He decided to give the AME congregation another try. For several Sundays he and Ruby worshipped with the Methodists but were little moved by its liturgy. After the Corinthian Baptist congregation further impressed him with its vitality and warmth, Fred began to waver. One Sunday during Palmer's sermon, a scripture verse spoke directly to Fred: "Here I set my Ebenezer, for hitherto has the Lord helped us" (1 Sam. 7:12). Taking this as a "word from the Lord," Shuttlesworth concluded that God had helped him reach a decision about his church membership. He casually discussed the matter with Ruby, who typically deferred to her husband in such matters. His mind all but made up, the man of the house concluded that they should become Baptists. Explaining this verdict years later, he commented that he "felt that something [was] just leading me to join that church, and all the time all these people were so very warm and very helpful, and I was received in such a way that I felt like I was really somebody." So in June 1944, both Shuttlesworths were baptized by immersion and became proper Baptists. Fred later interpreted this decision as providential, reasoning that had he been an AME minister, his bishop might have curtailed his ministerial freedom and reined in his civil rights agitation. [13]

Within a short time Fred received his license to preach and began filling the pulpit in Palmer's absence. He preached his first sermon on the conversion of Paul and the text "I will show him how great things he must suffer for my name's sake." Shuttlesworth's message focused on two great questions Paul asked of

God: "Who are you?" and "What would you have me to do?" These inquiries, the young preacher exhorted his listeners, are the most important matters human beings must address in their spiritual lives. Like many first sermons, the discourse was preached in less than ten minutes, and looking back on it years later, Fred judged this first homiletical offering as theologically superficial. Fred's preaching early in his ministry generally challenged the converted to conduct their lives in a more committed fashion. Fred was fervently evangelical, but his style never emphasized the salvation of sinners as much as it did the consecration of church members. Before long Palmer, who regularly held services at another pastoral charge, invited Fred to preach at the Corinthian Baptist Church on the second Sunday of each month when he was away. The people of Corinthian received Fred enthusiastically and attended in larger numbers on the Sundays when he preached.[14]

Soon other area ministers discovered in Fred a talented new supply preacher and invited him to preach in their churches. Shuttlesworth would always remember the first time his rhetoric stimulated a listener to "get happy," as the characteristic African American shouting experience is sometimes called. As Fred expounded the text of 1 John ("Greater is he that is in you than he that is in the world"), a worshipper was suddenly caught up in the spirit, walked to the pulpit, grabbed Fred around the legs, and, shouting all the while, literally carried him around in front of the congregation. (Fred never again preached on this scripture passage, apparently leery of its power over a congregation.) As a result of such experiences, his reputation grew rapidly. Moreover, his pulpit activities and the congregants' affirmation confirmed his call to the ministry. As his vocational plans grew more definite, Fred gradually felt the need for more specific theological training or at least the credentials of having attended a seminary or Bible college.[15]

As luck would have it—or as Shuttlesworth always preferred to believe, as Providence would dictate—there was such a school nearby. In Prichard, Alabama, twelve miles to the north, the Mobile Sunlight Baptist Association operated a small school to train its preachers. Organized at the State Street African Methodist Episcopal Zion Church in 1907 for the purpose of educating African American children, Cedar Grove Academy had been reorganized by Palmer for the black Baptists of the area. By the mid-1940s, when Fred began attending classes two or three nights a week, Cedar Grove's faculty was made up of prominent local ministers. Besides Palmer, the school's staff included B. B. Williams, pastor of the St. Louis Street Baptist Church, who taught English, and J. A. Robinson of the Stone Street Baptist Church, who gave instruction in systematic theology.[16]

As a theological student Fred generally performed well and got along well with these ministers. He was especially encouraged in his studies by Palmer and by a white Southern Baptist home missionary, L. S. Maynard, who also taught at Cedar Grove. Nonetheless, the young minister's pugnacious spirit showed itself in a classroom disagreement with a professor of New Testament. One day the prominent Reverend U. J. Robinson, who served as secretary of the National Baptist Convention, U.S.A., and who struck Fred as especially egotistical, commented on the book of Acts and the early Christian practice of common ownership of possessions. The fourth chapter of Acts describes a couple named Ananias and Sapphira, who sold their goods but held back from contributing *all* of the proceeds to the fledgling church. Scripture indicates that as a result of their deception, the Holy Spirit struck the couple dead. Calling such a practice "communism," Robinson criticized its ethical propriety and questioned whether *God* had in fact caused their deaths. Not letting him get away with what he considered a theological error, Fred challenged his teacher's interpretation, asking, "Doctor, did you say that was communism? Are you saying it was wrong since it was generally agreed that everybody sold what they had?" When Robinson replied that he had indeed said just that, a perturbed Shuttlesworth queried, "I thought you said we take the Bible as it is. . . . If [this practice] was wrong, why did the Holy Spirit kill Sapphira? If it was wrong and God did not approve of it, why did the Holy Spirit kill Sapphira?" Robinson grunted, "They just died," to which Fred shot back, "They sure did, and anything else is going to die when the Lord gets ready for him to die." An angry Robinson now aimed a barbed criticism at Shuttlesworth, declaring, "Well, you're not going to make much of a preacher because you're not going to listen." Shuttlesworth rejoined, "When it comes to listening to what man says or listening to God, I'll take what the Lord says, since He's been around all the time." Although never showing the typical fundamentalist fervor to root out heresy, Shuttlesworth remained a strong biblicist, later commenting, "I disagreed with some of what I learned in theology. I must remember that some of it was what man thought and . . . always, when anybody got on theories, it has been my unusual knack to lay them alongside of what I believe is the biblical direction." On this basis, Shuttlesworth confronted an established, well-respected minister with a confidence that bordered on impudence. Until then his "holy arrogance" had had little cause to bubble to the surface. Later, however, it would embolden him to challenge church leaders and to make a mark in the civil rights movement.[17]

With his personal Bible study and the instruction he received at Cedar Grove, Fred slowly prepared himself for the ministry. Cedar Grove notwithstanding, he by and large taught himself the little theology he knew. Except for his elementary and high school teachers, he gave his instructors little credit for influencing his thinking to any great degree. Certainly, teachers such as Maynard and Palmer impressed him insofar as they affirmed and encouraged him to continue, and even to excel, in his preparation. He was especially fond of Palmer and once intervened when some of his church members sought his ouster. Already in his sixties, the unemotional, didactic Palmer served as Fred's "father in the ministry." Among Baptists, older ministers often supervise younger ministerial candidates informally. African American Baptists tend to make this arrangement more official, with the student serving an apprenticeship to a minister of an established congregation. In that context, the young minister would develop preaching and leadership skills in a home church and gradually move on to other congregations. As to the mentor in this instance, Palmer, "a great doctrinal man," impressed the younger preacher by his moral example and by his skill as Bible interpreter. Yet he never became one after whom Shuttlesworth patterned his ministry. For one thing, Palmer shied away from "zooning," or concluding his sermons with the frenzied, chanted delivery that other African Americans call "the whoop." More important, Shuttlesworth related to Palmer not only as a pupil but as a teacher. On one occasion, as Palmer and Shuttlesworth engaged in friendly "shop talk" about the ministry, the older minister confessed that he disliked a certain member of his church. Acknowledging his youth and inexperience and feeling only a trace of impertinence, Shuttlesworth nonetheless advised Palmer, "That's just your cross. You are going to have to bear that. If you can learn not to jump back at him every time he jumps at you, . . . it would be better."[18]

Instances such as this and his dispute with U. J. Robinson marked Fred as a person with a strong self-image. Although psychoanalysts might suspect him of overcompensating for an inner insecurity, he saw himself as a fully competent adult. He owed his teachers respect but was disinclined to fawn over them or defer to their opinions. Moreover, to the extent that he reflected on theological education, he understood it as almost exclusively limited to knowing the Bible. Merely human musings interested him little, and throughout his ministry he continued to affirm, "My basics would have to come from the Bible in the first place. What I believe and what I seek to believe and try to foster is biblical truth."[19] In addition, on the basis of his encounter with Robinson, many a teacher likely would have found his overconfidence annoying and considered him theologically unteachable. Although committed to advancement, he held an instrumental, utilitarian view of education. Determined to achieve the academic training necessary to pastoral ministry, he never became a book-oriented intellectual who saw learning as an end in itself.

Nevertheless, having begun a systematic study of the Bible and Christian theology, Fred soon expanded his denominational horizons. Early on, both external and internal witnesses confirmed his sense of vocation. By their ardent approval of his preaching, ordinary church members corroborated his sense of calling. In addition, Fred developed an intuition or an "inner voice" that produced in him a strong conviction of "God's will." Sustained over lengthy periods of time and affecting him at his deepest levels of consciousness, this intuitive sense continued to provide direction at important forks in the road throughout Fred's life. Within a year or so of his move to Mobile, he began to anticipate a short stay. Acting on his intuition, and perhaps a bit of pure ambition, he became convinced that a successful ministry lay ahead. He told Ruby, "I feel as if my life is designed to touch many lives. . . . I don't know how. I don't know why I feel like this."[20]

With this confidence, he concluded that his ministry might be enhanced by study at a better-known school. The knowledge of such a school, however, did not come to him by any mystical means; he learned of it through the black Baptist network. In 1946 Fred represented Cedar Grove Academy at an oratorical contest at Selma University, the educational pride of the Colored Baptist Convention of Alabama. He competed well enough that Selma University president W. H. Dinkins encouraged him to transfer. Believing that destiny held a significant role for him, Fred decided to avail himself of more and better training. Furthermore, his family's slow financial progress in Mobile necessitated a major change. Noting that in almost four years the family had managed to save less than $100, he complained to Ruby, "I could pick up sticks and save more money than this." Concerned that attending Selma would be fiscally prohibitive, he wrote to Dinkins and indicated his strong interest in transferring if a scholarship could be arranged. The president responded by saying that he would do his best to help Shuttlesworth defray expenses. Although he never came through with a scholarship, Dinkins did invite Fred and Ruby to live on campus in married student housing. Fred prepared to leave his job at Brookley Field and to begin classes in Selma that fall. Ruby's pregnancy, however, postponed the family's move.[21]

Already parents of a one-year-old when they arrived in Mobile, Ruby and Fred had their family increase by three by the time they moved to Selma. After the birth of Patricia (Pat), Fred and Ruby hoped for a boy, selecting the name Fred Jr. When Ruby gave birth to another daughter in January 1945, they resorted to the feminine form and also named her after her mother—Ruby Fredericka. "Ricky" was almost two when in September 1946 a son eventually came along to inherit the name that had awaited him even before his conception. As she and her husband waited to relocate, Ruby cared for the three children, aided occasionally by Fred's sister Cleo, who lived with them for a short time. The proud father exulted over the birth of a son, and just before the family's departure in September 1947, he put his ingenuity to work to ease the strain of moving the larger family. He bought a cow and had it slaughtered, providing enough meat not only to last the entire winter in Selma but also to cause Ruby to swear off beef for years to come. To ensure the family stayed warm, he dug up the pipes of the butane heating system he had built, dismantling it piece by piece, so it could be reinstalled at a new venue. As a late summer hurricane threatened Mobile, the Shuttlesworths headed for the city of Selma with a rented truck piled high with their worldly goods.[22]

The small city of Selma dominated the agricultural region known as the Black Belt. A part of the Gulf Coastal Plain, the Black Belt unofficially bore its nickname because of the strong presence of African Americans. Since the nineteenth century, the population of Selma had consistently been nearly 70 percent black. This percentage held true in the late 1940s when the overall population was fifty-five thousand. In spite of migrations to larger urban areas earlier in the century, many blacks remained in Dallas County, working as small independent farmers. By the time Shuttlesworth began his studies at Selma University, a majority of blacks still worked as tenants in the fields of white landowners. The second largest number of blacks in the first half of the twentieth century worked as domestic servants. White employers excluded most blacks from all jobs other than manual labor until well into the civil rights movement and typically paid them lower salaries for the same work performed by whites. Still, Selma's black population had a larger professional class than other towns in the Black Belt, boasting several doctors and dentists along with a large contingent of teachers. Primarily because of the presence of Selma University, the city also served as a regional center for black education and a focal point for activity among black Baptists. In this connection, Selma provided religious leadership beyond the state line with the Reverend D. V. Jemison, a local Baptist pastor and part-time professor at the university, who served as the longtime president of the NBC. Thus Shuttlesworth found himself in a religious and cultural center that, in attorney J. L. Chestnut's words, set "the trends and standards" for Alabama blacks.[23]

As was generally true among historically black colleges begun in the South during Reconstruction, Selma University became for Alabama blacks a focus of racial identity and pride. Unlike better-known and better-funded colleges such as Fisk in Nashville, Virginia Union in Richmond, and Morehouse and Spelman in Atlanta, all of which were begun either exclusively by or in conjunction with white northern philanthropic organizations, Selma grew from the relatively unaided efforts of black Baptists in Alabama. During this period, African Americans prided themselves on the institutions they built on their own. Black Baptists in Virginia, for example, had two colleges serving their constituency—Virginia Union and Virginia College and Seminary (Lynchburg). Distinguishing between the two schools, some commented that "Union was the white Baptists' gift to negroes. Seminary was *theirs.*" In Alabama, black Baptists, with undivided loyalties, felt the same way about Selma. Education among blacks began sluggishly in Alabama after the Civil War. Since 1832 the state had considered educating blacks to be a crime. Thus, by Reconstruction, black Baptists had only a few learned ministers. To remedy this weakness, the Colored Missionary Baptist Convention of Alabama (CMBCA) at its organizational meeting in 1868 unanimously resolved to encourage ministers to "improve" themselves by reading the Bible, theology, and church history. The next year the convention established a standing committee on education. In 1873, the convention met in Tuscaloosa and voted to begin a "Theological School for young men," going against the advice of the white Baptist convention. In addition, messengers (delegates) to the convention strongly encouraged Baptist individuals, churches, and associations to support the project financially. Within another two years the CMBCA, affirming that "an educated ministry is one of the greatest needs of our people as a race," adopted a constitution for the new school and named a board of trustees.[24]

Over the years the school garnered limited financial support from whites. The American Baptist Home Mission Society of New York, the Women's Baptist Home Mission Society of Chicago, and the Southern Baptist Convention's Home Mission Board all made small financial contributions during Selma University's first decades. Moreover, a white southern Baptist home missionary, the Reverend Harrison Woodsmall, served as the school's first president. The school's founder, W. H. McAlpine, had asked him to become president "because the people seemed to believe in a white person more so than a Negro." Nevertheless, most of the school's faculty, students, and operating budget always came from the black Baptists of Alabama. After three years of fund-raising and debate over the school's location, the board of trustees collected $1,008.44 for its operation and settled on Selma as the place to begin the Alabama Baptist Normal and Theological School. As a "normal school," Selma began primarily as a training ground for teachers, instructing students without high school diplomas in the three "R's," grammar, history, music, and the Bible. In the school's first session on January 1, 1878, meeting at the St. Phillips Street Baptist Church, a faculty made up of Woodsmall, his wife, and the Reverend W. R. Pettiford taught forty students. The next fall the school purchased thirty-six acres of land that had been used for a race track and moved to its own location on the northwest side of town. Although no longer holding classes in the St. Phillips Street Church, the college continued to maintain close ties with that congregation. Institutionally, the church and the college enjoyed a fraternal relationship, growing up together, each lending its influence and reputation to the other. Throughout most of the school's history, the presidents and faculty were either members or pastors of what came to be known as the First (African) Baptist Church.[25]

In 1885 the college was renamed Selma University. Although its academic reputation never equaled that of such other black colleges as Morehouse, the school eventually improved its stature when it expanded its programs to the baccalaureate level. Early on, Selma developed an emphasis on classical education, going beyond the training school educational philosophy of Booker T. Washington and the Tuskegee Institute. Edward Knight Brawley, Selma's third president (1883–1886), stressed *higher* education more clearly than his predecessors. Seeing the school's mission as that of "furnish[ing] the state with men of classical education," he wrote, "I have no patience with a man who says that the low course will do; you have not the mental capacity to grasp the high education. For we have the brain, tact and thrift to acquire the classics. We can not afford to stop with the good English education, but we must go on and attain the highest that can be had." Brawley was like other black intellectuals and religious leaders of his era in committing the college to "uplifting the race" through classical education. Leading these day-to-day efforts were African American women who fostered race advancement by promoting their schools. In Alabama, black

Baptist women forged an especially strong link with Selma University. In time, all the officers of the Baptist Women's State Convention had served as either former teachers or students of Selma University. Eliza Pollard, who led the women's convention at the turn of the century, was married to the Reverend Robert T. Pollard, president of Selma University from 1916 to 1929. The women's convention of Alabama used its newspapers to encourage racial self-help through donations to the university, and at its 1891 annual meeting called Selma University the "child of the Baptists of Alabama." This combination of classical education and the strong identification of black Baptists with Selma University created an institution that inculcated a pride of race and an integrationist philosophy of racial advancement. The college thus became known as the "center of intellectual and spiritual direction and inspiration for more than 300,000 colored people in the State of Alabama."[26]

By the time Shuttlesworth arrived in Selma, the university had developed a long tradition of teaching "true manhood and true womanhood," which involved Christian incentives and moral guidelines. The college demanded that students adhere to middle-class virtues, warning: "This is not an institution for careless, lazy and disobedient pupils. Such when found out, will not be retained." To be admitted, students were required to sign a pledge to obey all rules, "both oral and written." These precepts included strictures against smoking, drinking, profanity, weapons possession, "association between the sexes" (except by permission), and boisterous conduct. In addition, the institution required Sunday church attendance and kept a strict curfew. Through its concern for racial uplift, this strict atmosphere produced an affection among its graduates. "There was something about that school," suggested Shuttlesworth's friend, T. L. Lane, "that it made you not only stand out but to feel proud of yourself." Moreover, this agenda for building pride extended beyond that of individuals to the race. Although never influenced by black nationalism or separatism, the school stressed the African American experience and provided what another alumnus called an education geared toward students' freedom rather than their value in the marketplace. When he began his study at Selma, Fred was attracted less by "black consciousness" than by the school's reputation among black Baptists and its uncompromising moral ethos. A strict disciplinarian, Shuttlesworth naturally gravitated toward a school with high religious and moral expectations, even though matriculating as an adult made his obligations less strict than those of students who were minors.[27]

In September 1947 Selma University still provided instruction from the high school through the junior college level. In addition, the school had a well-attended bachelor of divinity (B.D.) program. The standard ministerial degree, the B.D., had been offered at Selma since the 1890s and the presidency of the Reverend Charles L. Purce (1886–1893). Committed to revising the theological course of study, Purce had pressed students to excel in literary as well as in theological training. "Give the preachers an education," he argued. "Give them a foundation. Let us have an educated ministry. Mere Bible knowledge will not do." Knowledge of the scriptures, however, seemed to suffice for Shuttlesworth, who did not enroll in the theological curriculum. Primarily because he did not hold the baccalaureate degree prerequisite to the B.D., he studied in a non-degree junior college program that anticipated a later transfer to a senior college. Shuttlesworth took general studies courses such as English and literature, mathematics, history, psychology, sociology, and geography. He also studied Greek, Latin, and French, though he never became proficient in any of them. In a three-hour course titled "Negro History," which highlighted exemplary figures from the African American past, the individual self-esteem instilled in him by his mother expanded into pride of race.[28]

As black educational institutions went, however, Selma remained in the integrationist mode. Selma faculty introduced Fred to the thought of W. E. B. DuBois, but if professors and students vigorously rehashed the DuBois–Booker T. Washington debate over accommodation and political activism, it made little impression on Fred. Later, in his mid-sixties, he noted that at Selma "I didn't think too much about DuBois and don't know a whole lot now [about him] to be honest with you." While imparting to students a pride in their race, the school did little to emphasize blackness. As to Marcus Garvey's nationalism (or his "Back to Africa thing," as Fred dismissively called it), Shuttlesworth remarked, "I would never agree with that anyway."[29] Rather oddly for a ministerial student, Fred took only one course in religious studies, a one-hour class in Christian doctrine. Later, he recalled having read only a little of Swiss Protestant theologian Karl Barth and Reformation church history. Thus, although he anticipated eventually going into the full-time ministry, his formal training in theology remained at an elementary level. He earned exemplary grades (a 93.8 average), which were later determined to be the highest in the history of Selma University, and his courses focused on preparing him for a fallback teaching position. Theologically, however, he relied on what he had learned in Sunday school and his personal study of scripture.

Fred's primary contacts at the college were in high places—the president's office and its occupant, William Hovey Dinkins. The president provided Fred with a job firing the furnace in Foster Hall, the girls' dormitory, and working the vegetable garden owned by the college. In addition, as stated earlier, Dinkins made available to Fred and Ruby a small house on the campus. Fred's family became the first to live in the school's married-student housing. Dinkins was the son of Charles S. Dinkins, who had served as Selma's president from 1893 to 1901. The younger Dinkins made a name for himself around Selma both for his straight-laced moralism and for his bookishness. A Brown University–trained historian who knew several languages, Dinkins struck Shuttlesworth as a bit eccentric, probably because of his practice of driving a car and reading the newspaper at the same time. A strong advocate of the middle-class Victorian values of thrift and hard work, Dinkins in daily chapel services often lectured the students on moral concerns. He once talked for forty-five minutes on, in turn, the "chewing gum traffic, the tobacco, and the liquor traffic." On another occasion he insisted that Fred rake leaves only in a certain way and told him, "If you make a penny a day, you are making money." Shuttlesworth later confessed that sometimes "I just thought he was nuts, really."[30]

Fred and the president eventually found themselves at loggerheads. A dyed-in-the-wool Baptist, Dinkins objected to Ruby's taking a nursing position at the Catholic Good Samaritan Hospital. Particularly antagonized by this, Fred answered, "Mr. Dinkins, now you told me when I came up here you would help. I can't feed my wife off these pennies you give me for these windows. And besides," he added, showing a gender-role traditionalism that remained intact over the years, "nobody tells my wife what to do except me." The president then mumbled that he ought to have more pride than to allow his wife to work. "The Bible says pride goes before destruction," answered Fred, only slightly misquoting the scripture text. In spite of this disagreement, Dinkins, the soul of Selma University until his retirement in 1950, affected Fred indirectly through his influence over the college. More important, Dinkins's interest in and patronage of Shuttlesworth became the means by which Fred began his pastoral ministry in Selma. For this young preacher who believed his life "would touch many lives," the experience in Selma and, more particularly, certain religious experiences he had there would prepare him for events of which he could not and dared not dream in the late 1940s.[31]

With a wife, three children under five, a job with the college, and his classroom responsibilities, Fred saw the pace of his life quicken drastically with the move to Selma. While living on campus, he began each morning by milking the cow owned by the college and then made deliveries throughout the day. An old farm hand, Fred often teased Ruby, "the city girl," who did not know how to milk a cow. Ruby, however, had her hands full with the children. Periodically, after financial necessity forced Ruby to take a nursing position, Fred's younger sister Eula Mae lived with them to help with the parental duties. Fred generally left these responsibilities to the women, and they developed a workable division of labor. Although known in the family for her lack of culinary skill, Ruby made breakfast while Eula Mae managed the children and occasionally helped Fred with the cow. On Saturdays both women took care of the washing.[32]

Fred's reputation as a preacher preceded him, and before long pastors in Selma and vicinity were calling on him to fill their pulpits. A country boy, Fred found a home in the rural churches of Dallas County. Within a year of his coming to Selma, churches enticed him to consider becoming their pastor. In July 1948, the Everdale Baptist Church, a congregation of about eighty members ten miles east of Selma, voted to call him as pastor. Fred wanted the position, but a minor snag slowed the process. When the church clerk officially announced that "Everdale Baptist Church calls Reverend Shuttlesworth in the year 1948–1949," Fred discerned that the church issued annual calls. This practice, which was then falling out of fashion in both the white and the black Baptist churches, generally unsettled pastors because it subjected them to a congregational vote of confidence every year. Concerned with job security and with what he considered a breach of biblical propriety, Fred interrupted the proceedings. He asked to hear the statement again. When satisfied that he had heard correctly, he asked pointedly, "And the Holy Spirit told y'all to do that? . . . If the Holy Spirit told y'all to do that, He didn't send me to this church. So y'all don't have a pastor. The Holy Spirit doesn't have to tell you to call a pastor every year." He then told the congregation that if they wished him to be their pastor, they would have to make the call indefinite in length. "But the Holy Spirit," they objected, "told us to call you." Shuttlesworth quickly informed them, "Well, the Holy Spirit is telling me not to accept under these terms. I will not come in here and have you voting on me. Once you vote on me, you don't vote on me again. So if you and the Holy Spirit can get together, we can make some progress."[33]

After a quick caucus, the deacons and other lay leaders acceded to Fred's demand and elected him to an indefinite term. Within a month, Fred returned to the Corinthian Baptist Church in Mobile for his ordination, after which he was installed as pastor at Everdale. His mild ultimatum to the congregation regarding his call suggested an authoritative pastoral style, and within a year he moved further in that direction by turning out a member for failing to support the church financially. As a "half-time church," Everdale held services only twice a month. This made Shuttlesworth available to pastor a second church simultaneously, and within a few weeks, in October of 1948, Fred became pastor of the Mount Zion Baptist Church, which was four miles west of Selma in the rural community of Potter Station. Along with his other responsibilities in Selma, for two years Fred served both churches as pastor, earning from them a combined salary of twelve dollars a week.[34]

After two years at Selma University, as Fred saw his family grow much faster than his financial resources, he resolved to supplement his meager ministerial income and became a substitute teacher. Before long he decided to work toward a teacher's certificate, which would allow him to move into a full-time teaching job. Without apprising anyone in Selma, he suddenly moved the family to Montgomery and began attending Alabama State College in the fall of 1949. Shuttlesworth continued his ministerial responsibilities in the Selma area, driving fifty miles on alternate Sundays to preach at the Everdale and Mount Zion churches. In the meantime, he became acquainted with J. D. Pritchard, a deacon at the First (African) Baptist Church in Selma. As a merchant and owner of the only black print shop in Selma, Pritchard had monopolized the printing business of the black churches in Dallas County to become one of the most successful men in black Selma. By virtue of his prominence in the community, he also came to exercise great influence as a layperson in his church. When his pastor, the Reverend John Frank Grimmett, suddenly resigned in October 1949, Pritchard thought of Shuttlesworth as a temporary replacement. After hearing Shuttlesworth's fiery oratory and warming to his charismatic personality, the deacons invited him to become the congregation's interim pastor. They made clear to him, however, that they would not consider him as a pastor, even hinting that he lacked the social status necessary in a pastor of First Baptist Church. Suggesting he reschedule the time of worship at his rural churches, the deacons commented, "You just preach for us until we get ready to sit down and get a preacher. Just preach until one o'clock, and we will give you ten dollars [a week]."[35]

This interim arrangement was short-lived, however, as several forces combined to nudge Shuttlesworth into the permanent position as pastor of First Baptist. For one, his preaching strongly appealed to many of the rank-and-file members of the congregation. An effective pulpit style has traditionally been a preacher's primary selling point to a congregation. Moreover, among evangelicals in the South, both white and black, an effective style must also be an "affective" style. Intellectual content is often negotiable in sermons, but the ability to move listeners and make them feel the Spirit must be present. In his homespun way Shuttlesworth had this ability, drawing many congregants to him with a powerful charisma. In southern black evangelical churches, particularly those seeking a pastor, this sort of appeal can generate a friendly and quiet clamor from the congregation: "We want *you* to be our pastor." Such a context tempts even the most seasoned minister, who can be seduced by the compliments received from Sunday to Sunday. A young minister, especially one with a large family and a small income, would quite naturally hope to see this interim arrangement become permanent.

In addition, in a congregational polity, Black Baptist boards of deacons or trustees often talk directly with several potential ministers simultaneously in order to discern interest in their vacant pulpits. Such situations create a "beauty contest" ethos. Any minister who had a strong self-image and who was already preaching at the church in an interim capacity might wish to compete for that pulpit. Many would go further and overtly politick for the job, especially if the pulpit in question was particularly prestigious. Few ministers, however, would openly admit angling for a pulpit. The same "spiritualized" terminology that has churches "calling" instead of "hiring" pastors dictates that the "office seek the man, and not the man the office." Given to thinking and speaking in that fashion, Shuttlesworth never admitted lusting after the pastorate of First Baptist—few ministers would—but some members perceived him as doing so. As a teenager J. L. Chestnut, who later became Selma's first black lawyer and a trustee of First Baptist Church, recalled hearing his grandparents talking often about the young minister. "I got the impression," said Chestnut, "that Shuttlesworth was campaigning like he was running for office. . . . The fact that [at] his age that he would be vying for or think that he could pastor First Baptist says a hell of a lot about him right there. Most preachers his age would not even be vying for First Baptist. . . . He wanted to be an effective, important preacher, and he was not necessarily wedded to going about that in the traditional way. Shuttlesworth was prepared to take on the black establishment, if it was going to promote Shuttlesworth." Another member, Louretta Wimberly, acknowledged that some members believed Fred had designs on the pulpit of First Baptist, but they did not see this as unusual or unsavory. Chestnut later observed that "any number" of ministers have conducted themselves similarly and saw Shuttlesworth's ambition as fairly typical.[36]

One other factor made a significant difference in moving Fred toward the pastorate of First Baptist—the active support of W. H. Dinkins, who was a member of First Baptist Church. Some lay leadership in the church wondered whether Fred had the experience and the sophistication necessary for First Baptist. The previous minister had been better educated and more polished than Shuttlesworth, and the congregation had traditionally taken advantage of its longtime relationship with Selma University by seeking pastors among its presidents or faculty. The church had never before considered a student as its pastor. This in itself attested to Shuttlesworth's pulpit appeal, but the support of Dinkins helped. J. L. Chestnut recalled his grandfather, Lewellen Phillips, commenting that "the boy will do alright." As a deacon, Phillips had been privy to discussions in which Dinkins had importuned them on Shuttlesworth's behalf to "give the boy a chance." As Shuttlesworth's sponsor, he possibly argued that the young minister was a morally upright family man, a particularly important quality because the previous pastor had departed under a cloud of scandal. Shuttlesworth had potential; with some seasoning he might make an excellent minister. Eventually, the influential board of deacons, and J. D. Pritchard in particular, acquiesced to the people's attraction to Shuttlesworth and Dinkins's assurances and agreed to call Shuttlesworth as permanent pastor. Fred knew an opportunity when he saw one, and in May 1950 he quickly accepted the congregation's call and their $150-a-month salary. In spite of having relocated to Montgomery only recently, he and his family moved back to Selma and the parsonage at 614 First Avenue.[37]

Without doubt, in becoming the pastor of First Baptist of Selma, Fred Shuttlesworth took a major step up in ministerial prestige. Founded in 1868 when freedpersons in Selma's white First Baptist Church withdrew to form their own congregation, First Church was the third oldest black Baptist church in Alabama. With a membership of only about two hundred during Shuttlesworth's tenure, the members of First Baptist considered themselves the elite church of black Dallas County. Socioeconomic status affects all congregations, and typically the higher their status, the more "dignified" their taste in, for example, worship styles. In the period after Reconstruction, however, many African American churches exaggerated this tendency as a part of the philosophy of racial uplift, which put a premium on Victorian values and "respectability." Historically, the membership of First Baptist took great pride in its large edifice and tall steeple. The story is told of members collecting bricks from the area for use in erecting their first building. Most significant, the membership was largely composed of the professional class, including school principals, teachers, doctors, Selma's only black dentist, eventually its first black lawyer, and several merchants. The church thus came to be known, in the terminology of African American religion, as a "class" or "silk-stocking" church. Thirty-five years after Shuttlesworth served in Selma, the church's pastor observed that his congregation always worshipped in a very organized manner, following a set pattern. The music weighed more heavily on the side of hymns and anthems than on gospel songs. Black Baptists of the area, dating back to Shuttlesworth's time, have said of First Church, "You don't want to go to that church; it's too quiet. You don't want to shout and say 'Amen' and do all the things you want to do."[38]

If other Baptists in the area deemed Shuttlesworth's new congregation too refined for their tastes, First Church responded with a conceit regarding their status as the "mother church" of the other black Baptist churches of Dallas County. Many of the members exuded an almost palpable haughtiness, taking great delight in the title "First Baptist." As Chestnut asserted, they "have always considered themselves to be somehow a cut above most black people." Conscious of class and concerned that his new pastor might identify too closely with the riffraff, Pritchard once advised Shuttlesworth, "You are pastor of First Baptist now; no need to fool around with any of these little niggers." Fred quickly shot back, "J. D., God must have loved little niggers; he made so many of them." After this conversation Shuttlesworth increasingly found his emotional support among those members of modest means rather than from those who "set themselves apart as [having] higher status." The clash of Fred's own socioeconomic background with that of First Baptist, coupled with his often sharp personality and unrefined demeanor, would prove a volatile combination for a young minister in his first full-time pastorate.[39]

Having a full-time congregation, however, does not necessarily constitute being a full-time pastor. Virtually throughout his tenure at First Baptist, Fred continued to attend classes at Alabama State. At first the congregation's lay leadership accepted this arrangement, in part hoping further education would smooth out their pastor's rough edges. The responsibilities of school limited the time Fred could spend on traditional pastoral duties, however, and because congregations ordinarily demand as much time as possible from their pastors, the church's situation boded ill for Shuttlesworth. His predecessor, J. F. Grimmett, had already completed his education by the time he came to the church and had been able to administer a full church program. By the time Grimmett left, the church had come to expect this. Under the press of college obligations, however,

Shuttlesworth could not meet these expectations. Nevertheless, during his tenure, Fred oversaw a modest growth in the membership, the building up of the Baptist Training Union (classes on Sunday evenings designed to train members in the details of church membership), and the development of several missionary support groups called "circles." As time allowed, he visited members and made pastoral calls on others in the community, but he had little time or inclination to adhere to a firm schedule of visitation. As a goal, he sought to reinvigorate the somewhat staid and aging congregation, in part by his energetic preaching and in part by attracting younger members. As a new minister at the most prominent church in the county, he was often invited to preach at revivals and at church anniversaries for neighboring churches. Not yet ready in the early 1950s to "challenge the [racial] conditions of the time," he nevertheless hinted at directions his ministry would take in later pastorates, encouraging voter registration from his pulpit.[40]

Fiery and challenging, Fred's preaching raised eyebrows at First Baptist. Roosevelt's FEPC had kindled a faint hopefulness among blacks, and with Jackie Robinson's integration of major league baseball, civil rights agitation had begun to stir. Still, in the early fifties the note of racial justice rang out infrequently from black middle-class pulpits. From Shuttlesworth, however, perceptive observers detected a hint of militancy, deriving less from his conscious philosophy than from the unconscious exercise of his personality. Louretta Wimberly noted in him an incipient aggressiveness, although she claimed too much by calling this element an early involvement in "the movement." J. L. Chestnut later called this aspect of Shuttlesworth's preaching a "harbinger of what was to come." By the mid-1960s it became clear that some black communities willingly kept intact the racial status quo. In such contexts, some black ministers tacitly agreed to remain silent about instances of overt injustice. Also, such lay leaders as J. D. Pritchard and Lewellen Phillips often curried favor with their connections in white Selma in exchange for crumbs of influence. Shuttlesworth's occasional offhand remarks on racial matters thus jeopardized their arrangements and raised their hackles. At that time, of course, Fred did not nearly approach the vigor he would later demonstrate on civil rights. Although his efforts focused on reviving his congregation's flagging spirituality, he nonetheless manifested a slightly greater sensitivity to racial conditions than his congregation had grown accustomed to.[41]

If the content of his sermons worried the middle-class leaders of the church, so did the style. Perhaps too often to suit the tastes of his more uptown members, Shuttlesworth shifted into the classic style of African American preaching sometimes called the "whoop." A version of what rhetoricians term a peroration, the whoop is a conclusion of a discourse typically delivered with increased zeal and flourish. As a sermonic form, however, the whoop comes in at least three different modes. Usually it is marked by a louder, more rapid, and rhythmic delivery, often using alliteration or rhyming. Phrases are often repeated at regular intervals, such as in the conclusion of Martin Luther King's "I Have a Dream" speech. At a higher emotional pitch, the preacher typically moves into a chant or a singsong delivery. The preacher may even sing outright. In his most intense mode, the preacher may punctuate the repeated phrases with deep, audible gasps for breath. Of this style some African Americans use the onomatopoeic description "hacking." Shuttlesworth periodically used the whoop, though he less often employed alliteration or rhyming.[42]

Beginning slowly, with the deliberate, almost affected, enunciation common among black pulpiteers, Shuttlesworth would lean to the side and gesticulate with an upraised arm. Picking up the pace of his delivery, he gradually boosted his volume and emotional intensity. As a member of his later church in Birmingham observed, "He would give everybody a piece of his sermon." To those who preferred only a sedate discussion of scripture, Fred delivered. Nonetheless, he also satisfied those who preferred a more emotional presentation. Blessed with a fine singing voice, he also often modulated into singing, occasionally concluding his sermon with his favorite song, "My God Is Real," or some other composition. When overtaken by the spirit, he often skipped across the platform on one leg like an oratorical Chuck Berry, shifting to the gasping mode of delivery. One later member of his ministry estimated that in one form or another, Fred whooped almost weekly—or at least so often that if he refrained, some parishioners wondered aloud whether "the preacher must not be feeling good [today]." At First Baptist, though, where the middle class kept an eye out for lapses of "dignity" in the pulpit, some powerful members frowned on whooping of the chanted or gasping variety. "They decided he was a country preacher," Chestnut observed, "and they did not want any country preaching and any country singing in First Baptist." Whether Shuttlesworth perceptively realized that this mode of preaching did not work well in his congregation or whether the Spirit simply led him not to use it where it was not well received depends on one's theology. If he thought about it at all, Fred, with his theology, would have thought about it in both ways. Nevertheless, compared to how often he whooped later in Birmingham, he apparently used it sparingly at First Baptist Selma.[43]

One could speculate that he was too much the country preacher to suit his "class" church in Selma. He later commented, "If they thought it, they didn't say it. . . . It wasn't a matter of open criticism." Probably not. The operative term here is "open." Most members of First Baptist kept this type of criticism out of earshot of their pastor, an act that was typical of many congregations. Shuttlesworth did realize that many of his members "considered themselves to be upper-class," even occasionally needling them from the pulpit that it was "silly for a man to wear his own collar so stiff that it would rub a sore on his own neck." Beyond this, aware of unfavorable comparisons between himself and J. F. Grimmett, Fred himself acknowledged his pastoral predecessor as "highly articulate in his speech, while I was just a country boy." He was self-conscious about his status, but his personality made admitting it difficult, if not impossible.[44]

Even though they tried to camouflage their criticism, some members of First Baptist, especially those among the deacons, disparaged Fred's class orientation. Long-term members later observed that "Shuttlesworth was never really accepted by First Baptist. First Baptist always really considered Shuttlesworth to be beneath that church." Relatively inexperienced in the ministry, Fred lacked the polish, education, and refinement First Baptist believed it deserved. Chestnut reported, "There were vague complaints and rumblings almost from the day he set foot in that church. Privately you would hear, 'Well, he is not our type' or 'He does not speak well enough.' Well, what they didn't like was [that] he was not the president of Selma University. He wasn't a man of great prestige. It was said from time to time, 'He's just a little country preacher. He ought to have a little country church and not First Baptist.' Had Shuttlesworth been the president of Selma University, certain powers at First Baptist would have naturally accrued to him without argument. Because he wasn't, some in that church were determined that he would never have those powers. There were those who considered him temporary there from the first moment he came. He just wasn't their type, and they were not about to give him any powers." Others suggested likewise—that as a pastor and a congregation, Fred and First Baptist were literally "misfit" for each other.[45]

To narrow Shuttlesworth's difficulties at First Baptist Church to a single source, however, would be to oversimplify. Fred's inexperience, his blunt and unpolished manner, his youth relative to the church's lay leaders, and his class differences with important members. All played a part in the developing conflict in the congregation. Another problem may even have been differences in skin tone between Shuttlesworth, whose complexion was very dark and who personally preferred darker hues, and that of some of the leadership. The Reverend L. L. Anderson, a prominent Selma minister for many years, noted a preference in First Baptist Church for light-skinned preachers. "We had some outstanding churches . . . [for example] First Baptist Church," he stated, adding: "They would have real fair preachers because they thought there was something about him that made him . . . , that put him out front."[46] He also noticed that many schoolteachers who attended First Church had light complexions. In a race-conscious nation, non-African features have often allowed some blacks to "pass" for white and use light color as a means of economic advancement. Americans of African descent, most often those of the middle class, have frequently applied white standards of judgment, viewing fair skin as a mark of superiority in intellect and beauty. Given First Baptist's middle-class orientation, this consciousness of skin tone most likely remained an unconscious element in the conflict.

Whether feelings about skin tones entered into the conflict or not, traditional power dynamics in the black church did come into play at First Baptist. Both Fred Shuttlesworth and the deacons who opposed him reflect one of the political roles of the black church, particularly in the period before the civil rights movement. The church historically served many functions for African Americans, who were separated from power in the larger American society. As "the nation within the nation" or "a church with the soul of a nation," the black church gave birth to many of the other institutions of African American life. Excluded from participation in the political system, blacks often created within church life a surrogate political arena, particularly for black males. As J. L. Chestnut aptly noted, "Black men having been denied the opportunity to engage in regular politics and power struggles—and because they didn't have the background or the connections or the money to become industrial giants—all of that more often than not came out inside the black Baptist church. That is where he flexed his muscles. That is the one place he felt that he was a man and in charge." According to this longtime observer, Selma's mother church saw a great deal of male muscle flexing. Deacon leaders J. D. Pritchard, Ben Harris, and Lewellen Phillips functioned as, in Chestnut's words, a group of "tyrants" who "literally ran that church." Phillips's calling Shuttlesworth "that boy" reflected their intention to find a pastor they could lead around by the nose. First Baptist Church thus developed a reputation for conflict with its pastors.[47]

Shuttlesworth agreed. "They were determined," he later recalled, "[that there] wasn't any preacher gon' have any power there anyway." Temperamentally ill suited to leaving such a state of affairs unchallenged, the young pastor soon moved aggressively against the deacons' standard operating procedure. His primary opposition resided in Pritchard, Phillips, a plumber named Ben Harris, and a dentist named Brown—all old enough to be Fred's father and all members of the board of deacons. Harris especially had difficulty adjusting to Shuttlesworth as his new pastor. Earlier, he had been Fred's employer and had grown accustomed to thinking of Fred as an underling. "He would never accept me as his better," Shuttlesworth said, revealing his hierarchical perspective on their mutual roles.[48] In their most significant clash Fred not only contested Harris's status in the church but also cost him some business. When the church decided to install rest room facilities, the deacons assumed that the church would award Harris the contract for the work. The pastor, however, insisted that the church seek estimates from other plumbers in addition to his deacon. The deacons, and especially Harris, accused Fred of pulling rank and challenging their power in the church. Shuttlesworth rather saw himself as trying to get the best price possible for the work through competitive bidding. In his own mind, Shuttlesworth simply intended to guard the financial stewardship of his congregation. As the only black plumber in Selma, however, Harris was understandably disturbed with his pastor for attempting to throw business elsewhere. The deacons could legitimately argue that black institutions such as the church should support black business. Thus, although he single-mindedly tended to the congregation's economic matters, Fred needlessly made the most of an opportunity to confront the deacons.

To Shuttlesworth, these lay leaders failed in their responsibilities chiefly by conducting business without the approval of rank-and-file members, a major shortcoming in the congregational polity of a Baptist church. Once, when Selma student and fellow pastor Nelson H. Smith asked Shuttlesworth to travel with him to Hot Springs, Arkansas, for a Baptist convention, the frugal pastor objected because it would cost money. Smith suggested that they ride together. Perhaps Shuttlesworth had other considerations and wanted to stay close enough to keep tabs on his deacons. Once in his absence, his adversaries decided to sell a vacant lot owned by the congregation. When the pastor returned, he again challenged the deacons. Instructing them in the rules of democratic church polity, he emphasized the responsibility of whole congregations to make decisions and for deacons to *recommend* actions rather than to act unilaterally. Disputes arose so often that the pastor and deacons argued even over whether to hold board meetings. On one occasion, when Pritchard had announced a regularly scheduled meeting, Shuttlesworth exerted his pastoral authority and canceled the meeting. "It is not necessary," he reasoned, "to have conflict and argumentation every month." The deacons responded that the church's constitution required regular meetings. Shuttlesworth prevailed in most of these parliamentary clashes, increasing his stock with some of the less powerful members. One member, Nora Bennett, showing support for Fred, told him the score: "You're the only pastor that has been here for years that lets us know anything about the business of the church, and that's what they are mad at you about."[49]

In another instance, controversy boiled over concerning whether a women's missionary organization in the church, raising money for a trip to Birmingham, should funnel their collections into the general church fund for disbursement or keep it in a separate bank account. Contrary to their own practice in collecting funds, the all-male deacons decided that the women's group should deposit their monies in the general fund. Shuttlesworth shared that view, but again he opted for confrontation. Calling the deacons on their inconsistency, he noted that they kept *their* collections separate from the church's general fund. Thus, he argued, they had no right to insist that the women kick in their funds. The pastor advised the women's missionary leader to hold onto the money until the matter was resolved. When the matter came up for business, tempers flared, and verbal exchanges were sharp. In a meeting of deacons and trustees, Pritchard bluntly asserted: "We ain't gonna have no preacher running this church, and we don't want no women running it. We're gonna run it." In the heat of debate, one pro-Shuttlesworth member cursed the deacons, and Shuttlesworth himself threatened to resign: "If this is your level of religion, the church has to decide whether they want me as a pastor or you." "You're a young man," Pritchard warned. "You better get with us." The pastor countered, "No, you get with me. I'm a young man, but I am still pastor of this church, and that's what you can't accept."[50]

The pastor also initiated controversial policies that grated on the sensibilities of middle-class members. A case in point was Shuttlesworth's all-too-public practice of printing the amounts of members' weekly offerings in the church bulletins every Sunday. Adhering to the dictum "Don't bring our business out on the street," Pritchard and company vigorously objected to Shuttlesworth's actions. Although some congregations still make such figures a matter of public record, few members want their contributions open to general scrutiny. Most churches pressure their administrators to keep financial giving patterns a confidential matter among the parishioner, the church treasurer, and God. For his part, Harris argued that the pastor had no right to publish offerings by name, asking Fred, "Why you got to put that up on the board? You know you ain't got no business." Fred interrupted, "Well, it's their [the congregation's] business what you turn in, isn't it?"[51]

Each incident escalated the tension and soured the relationship. Matters started to come to a head beginning in September of 1951 when, midway through his bachelor's degree work at Alabama State, Shuttlesworth accepted a full-time teaching job. To the deacons' way of thinking, Fred had thus breached his contract with the church. The congregation had accepted his essentially part-time status as pastor because they expected him to finish his degree on schedule and assume full-time duties on graduation. Now, however, it appeared that he had other intentions, and the deacons complained about "part-time pastor, full-time pay." When confronted, Fred asked them pointedly, "Whatcha gon' do about it? Besides, what do you want me to do, baby sit you all? I can't teach you anything." When the deacons delivered an ultimatum, "Stop teaching or else," the pastor asserted, "You just gave me my answer; I'll take the 'else,' whatever it is. I'm gonna to sit right here in the boat and let you rock it. If God has gotten so weak that He would let the boat sink, then God will go down, and I'd go along with Him. God will have made a fool out of Himself if he lets something as little as you sink the boat. If you can sink the boat, then me and God will go down together." With the deacons' mouths doubtless agape with amazement, Fred continued, "You will not have the authority to tell all the other folks what to do. You can recommend to them. Neither will you have authority to tell *me* what to do and what not to do. You can suggest. The only name on that sign up there is mine. If I say it is, it will take a vote of the church to say it ain't, not you. I don't intend to harass you, but I am going to tell you like it is. You all have just gone too far too long."[52]

The pastor-deacon relationship clearly had been deteriorating from the beginning. The deacons' objection to Fred's teaching position became simply the occasion for expressing their long-standing and now festering disapproval of their young pastor. Had this not been so, the deacons also would have pressured Fred's successor, the Reverend Marshall C. Cleveland Jr., to relinquish his second jobs of teaching chemistry and later serving as president of Selma University. His additional employment apparently did not jeopardize his status as minister at First Baptist. He managed to retain his pulpit for forty years. Cleveland, however, had the education, the status, and the polish Shuttlesworth lacked. Thus a whole cluster of perceived deficiencies early on rendered Shuttlesworth's position untenable. In his inexperience, or in his overconfidence, Fred did not realize or admit the weakness of his claim on First Baptist Church. Both the pastor and the lay leaders could be faulted for their arrogance—theological and pastoral in the former, social in the latter. Nevertheless, Shuttlesworth's fiery, "hot-headed" personality, combative style, and inclination to claim God as his almost exclusive partner in disputes further enfeebled his already frail position with the leadership. Now Shuttlesworth's days at First Baptist dwindled to a precious few.[53]

Although Ruby was aware of the problem, she had difficulties of her own that occupied her attention. In 1949 she had given birth to a fourth child, a daughter whom they named Carolyn ("Carol"). Near the same time, Ruby also began adjusting to the church's expectations of a "first lady," as pastor's wives are often called in black Baptist churches. Working as she was able at Selma's hospitals and caring for her children, she remained active enough in church activities to keep the members of First Baptist relatively satisfied. Nevertheless, the women of the church occasionally but good-naturedly joked among themselves that she needed to "stop having these children. Let some of them grow up." Ill health soon made this decision for her. During still another pregnancy, Ruby developed a heart problem that necessitated an abortion. From this point on, Ruby's health difficulties, in part stemming from obesity, became a permanent part of her life.[54]

The couple thus discussed the deacon problem only superficially, less because of Ruby's circumstance than because of Fred's disinclination to reveal "weakness," especially to women. "Ruby always saw me as a strong person," Fred later commented, perhaps protesting too much that he had things under control. Fred did not bring his troubles home, though monthly board meetings made him "nervous and upset" for days before and after. In September 1952, a month after his graduation from Alabama State, Shuttlesworth found himself "grievously vexed," unable to eat or sleep because of the protracted dispute. On a train to Oklahoma City and the annual meeting of the National Baptist Convention, he sleeplessly walked between the cars of the train. About 2:00 A.M. he became aware of a deep darkness. He later narrated the experience: "The train was flying so fast the wind was cutting water out of my eyes, but I did speak to God. I think this is the first time I really actually spoke to God as a person. . . . I think that was the time I really prayed from the situation of actually needing God. . . . It was because I wanted to be sure I was right and that He was with me." So he prayed, asking no special favors from God. Saying he had never asked God to send him to First Baptist, he indicated his willingness to suffer, and for his family to suffer, for God's sake. "I am not asking you to relieve the suffering," he appealed, "but I am asking you to fix me so I don't worry so much." Fred immediately felt his heavy emotional burden lifted. "Look like somebody just reached down and lifted that whole train off me," he testified. Suddenly experiencing what he interpreted as the presence of God affirming him, he went back to his berth and slept peacefully. Later describing this quasi-mystical experience in both physical and emotional terms, Shuttlesworth said, "That experience made me know that God does talk. . . . [It was] a physical and deeply emotional feeling. I was just tired, sagged, sunk down; [afterward] I wasn't tired anymore. I wasn't slumped in my spirit anymore." He considered this experience one of the most significant moments in his life. "The experience most closely related me to the Lord, and I could feel and understand Him actually doing something when I needed it in a way that I could understand it." Nonetheless, this was no "conversion" experience. It did not transform Shuttlesworth into a confrontational personality; the previous two years of interaction with his deacons had already clearly revealed his combative character and pastoral style. The train incident served rather as an "intensification experience" that renewed his faith without changing its structure or content. It moved Shuttlesworth further and faster in the direction in which he was already moving—both in his sometimes overweening confidence and in his conviction that God was allied with him. The train experience reassured him that "God would never forsake me when I was right."[55]

In Shuttlesworth one thus sees a parallel to a classic mode of religious encounter in African American religion, most particularly that of the nineteenth-century abolitionist and social prophet Sojourner Truth. Like her, he underwent a sudden flash of insight that God was "all over" [everywhere] and poised to be his "almighty Friend." Truth described this experience as a release from bondage to freedom; Fred similarly spoke of it as the freedom of a lifted burden. Moreover, both Sojourner and Shuttlesworth "heard" the voice of God, which, both in the encounter itself and after they emerged, enabled them to see their own actions as directly and divinely inspired. For Fred, God's voice was not capable of being heard, and he would later be critical of a ministerial colleague who often claimed to hear God audibly. The experience nevertheless convinced Shuttlesworth that God spoke not only to him but *through* him (although this did not occur in everything he said; it happened only when he had a spiritual impression "in [his] deepest"). Many other ministers believe that somehow God speaks through them. Shuttlesworth was less concerned with the "how"; he was also more certain of it than the average minister. Unfortunately, being allied with God often tempts one to view all opposition as demonically inspired. In this case, Fred yielded. His powerful religious experience fortified him to take on his deacons, or "the devils" as he later called them. His nervousness now vanished, he resolved to bring the contest to a quick end.[56]

Returning home to Selma, Shuttlesworth paid a surprise visit to Pritchard's print shop, deciding to confront the primary instigator of his woes. After exchanging a terse greeting, the pastor got right to the point. "I came by to tell you that I've observed the kind of person you are," he began. "You can shout in the morning and cuss in the evening." Fred continued by saying he had attempted to work with Pritchard and the deacons but that his pastoral calling was not to be the deacons' mouthpiece, but God's. Shuttlesworth further informed Pritchard that he intended to bring a public challenge to the deacons' leadership at the next Sunday morning service. He then concluded, "I stopped by here to tell you to go to hell if you must" and abruptly walked out of the shop.[57]

On Sunday morning Pritchard tried to no avail to convince Fred to drop the matter, warning him, "If you bring that to the church today, this will be the last Sunday you preach at that church." "Then I'm on my way now," he replied, "to preach my last sermon." After the sermon, Shuttlesworth went on the offensive. "I've got something to say to the church," he announced to the congregation and the deacons who were hoping he would let the matter pass. He continued, "Since I have been at this church I have sought to be straight. I have sought to do the best I could. But there must come a time when a man must decide whether he is a man or a mouse. I am not a mouse. If God isn't in this church, I don't want to be here. If the truth can't be told, and if people can't respect the pastor as he tries to lead, then I don't need to be here." Shuttlesworth then informed the congregation of the deacons' ultimatum and delivered one of his own: "Follow me or follow the deacons." He added, "I *cannot* lead this church when the men do whatever they want to do and I'm sitting over here like some kid." At that Shuttlesworth called for a special business conference for the following Sunday.[58]

On October 5, Shuttlesworth wrote up several recommendations designed to put First Baptist under his sway. He requested that the deacon board be dissolved and that the congregation decide church matters by democratic vote of the full body. He recommended that the congregation designate the pastor as the presiding officer at all business sessions. He further requested that the pastor be authorized to countersign all checks issued by the church. He also suggested that the church allow no one to serve on both the deacon and the trustee board simultaneously. (Trustees officially represent the church in *legal* matters; deacons typically help decide spiritual concerns. In actual practice, the roles often overlap.) When in the heat of the moment the congregation passed these recommendations, "all of them devils," as Fred called his opposition, resigned as deacons. The newly empowered pastor soon recruited new ones.

Shuttlesworth thought he had successfully taken power at First Baptist and that the congregation was ready for the changes he had introduced. His victory, however, was short-lived. For the next two months, matters remained unsettled. The older deacons quickly regrouped. Church members gradually became disaffected with the state of affairs and opted to support the men who had long been their leaders rather than the brash young preacher they had known only briefly. By December the former deacons had regained their influence, demanding that Shuttlesworth capitulate to their wishes. When he refused, Shuttlesworth and the lay leadership of First Baptist came to a mutual parting of the ways, one susceptible to divergent interpretations. Members of First Baptist understood the break as a firing or at least a forced resignation; the proud Shuttlesworth claimed he neither resigned nor was fired. As he described his departure, he "just left" at the end of 1952. He may not have given in and formally resigned, but the effect and perception in Selma were the same.[59]

The Shuttlesworths returned to Birmingham to live with family until another pastorate came along. They would not wait long. All in all, First Baptist Church of Selma and Fred Shuttlesworth were indeed "misfit" for each other. From Fred's point of view, the deacons and most of the congregation were too committed to their social status and not enough to their God. From the viewpoint of the lay leadership at least, the pastor had many faults—too young, too inexperienced, too countrified, too unpolished, too abrasive. Still, in Selma he developed his skills as a preacher and displayed a personal charisma capable of garnering a devoted following. More important, the First Baptist Church of Selma became the most significant training ground preparing him for Bull Connor's Birmingham.

Although many Baptist ministers have often magnified contentions with unruly deacons into one of life's great struggles, fighting with deacons hardly compares to challenging segregation and a city bent on defending it. The train experience, in particular, prepared Shuttlesworth emotionally and honed a leadership style ultimately as useful in contesting Jim Crow and Bull Connor as in creating conflict in a Baptist congregation. Expressed in the traditional style of evangelical testimony, Shuttlesworth later said, "From that time on, I never let problems worry me too much, and I think that helped me in Birmingham. . . . God sent me to First Baptist Church Selma to get me ready for Birmingham, Alabama. . . . I was partially prepared before I went to Birmingham for what was coming."[60] Shuttlesworth henceforth relied on such spiritual experiences to confirm his course of action. Selma prepared him in other ways as well. His tenure in Selma confirmed in him certain inclinations of his personality and background. He took to Birmingham a readiness to identify with persons without social status and, if necessary, to contend with middle-class blacks on their behalf. He was ready to contest strong opposition. Most appropriate, perhaps, he was prepared to interpret events as God's intervention on *his* behalf. Good thing, too. Back in Birmingham, he would need it.

Bethel

We could not have been any more reverent than we were
when we saw Shuttlesworth come out of the house.
— Veronica Chappell Flemmon

T he book of Genesis tells of the patriarch Jacob's encounters with the Hebrew God at a village called Luz. At that holy place God eventually changed
the name of the patriarch to Israel, and the patriarch changed the name of the
place to Bethel, the "house of God." Many American Protestant congregations
have named their churches Bethel in hopes of creating a similarly sacred space
where persons might encounter the divine. Shuttlesworth's hometown even had
two black Baptist churches by that name—one in Southside and one in North
Birmingham. Within a few months of Fred Shuttlesworth's unnoticed return to
the "city of churches," he became the minister of the "house of God" on the
north side of town. "Bethel" was an ordinary name for an ordinary church, but
Shuttlesworth and his followers would come to view Bethel Baptist Church as
a wondrous, even sacred, place where the Christian God had been revealed in
personal experience and public miracle. This chapter highlights Shuttlesworth's
early ministry at Bethel, a ministry that began in 1953 and eventually flowed into
the founding of the Alabama Christian Movement for Human Rights. It narrates how, by Christmas night 1956, Shuttlesworth's civil rights involvement
and his extraordinary survival of a segregationist attempt to kill him or at least
scare him off convinced him and his followers that God had endorsed his actions. For Shuttlesworth, returning to Birmingham and going to Bethel eventually changed his role and reputation, if not, like Jacob, his name.

Departing from Selma and First Baptist without a call from another church,
the Shuttlesworths decided to return to Birmingham until a new opportunity
developed. Living alternately with his mother and with Ruby's family, Fred fell
back on his teacher's certificate and began a search for a new pastorate. Within
a few weeks of returning to Birmingham, Fred was invited to fill the pulpit of
a pastorless congregation in Florida. Shuttlesworth accepted the offer, but an
unexpected telephone call from his friend D. L. Motley interrupted his plans.

Motley had recently been elected pastor of Bethel Baptist Church in North Birmingham and was expected to begin his ministry there the next Sunday. Motley, however, had an important program already scheduled at his current church and remained undecided as to whether to accept Bethel's call. While deliberating, he asked Shuttlesworth to fill in for him at Bethel until he could make his decision. Eventually, Fred accepted Motley's invitation to serve as his substitute. On Sunday, February 8, 1953, Fred first filled the pulpit of Bethel Baptist Church, preaching on the second coming of Christ from the New Testament letter of Jude. Impressed with his sermon, the Bethel congregation responded enthusiastically, with some members wishing that they had considered Fred before calling Motley. Not wanting to insinuate himself into a ticklish situation where a church had already committed itself to another minister, Shuttlesworth downplayed Bethel's compliments and dismissed their overtures. The congregation, however, had impressed and encouraged him by their response to his sermon. During the next week, Motley, still dithering over Bethel's offer, once again asked Fred to substitute for him at Bethel. Shuttlesworth objected: "Why would they want me back? I don't play with churches. If you had gone ahead and accepted them, they wouldn't want me back." Apparently inclined to reject Bethel's call and unconcerned that the congregation might come to prefer Shuttlesworth, Motley continued to press Fred to preach there again, adding, "Maybe this is the Lord speaking to you." Agreeing to a return appearance at Bethel, Fred preached to another spirited response. When church officers inquired into his possible interest in their vacant pulpit, Fred answered, "I would be, but I have no business being interested in a church another man has." A week or so later, after Motley finally rejected Bethel's call, the church voted to call Shuttlesworth as pastor. Fred immediately accepted the offer and prepared to begin his new pastorate on Sunday, March 1, 1953.[1]

Situated in the African American section of North Birmingham known as Collegeville, Bethel had enjoyed a strong reputation among the black Baptist churches since its founding in the early twentieth century. Organized on March 27, 1904, by the Reverend P. M. Johnson, the congregation managed to buy a piece of land on Twenty-ninth Avenue North. The church was led by three different ministers during its first six years and called the Reverend A. G. McKinley as pastor in 1910. McKinley was succeeded six years later by the Reverend Milton Sears, who served until 1938 and became the congregation's most influential minister until Shuttlesworth. Under Sears's energetic leadership the congregation built its original edifice, the first in the area to include its sanctuary and educational facilities under the same roof. In 1924 he invited the National Baptist Sunday School Congress to meet in Birmingham and arranged for the congress to meet in the Municipal Auditorium. This was a signal accomplishment for the time inasmuch as a black group had never before gained admission to that facility. Yet Sears, very wise but with little formal education, discerned the limits of leadership in matters of race. Although he pressed for African Americans to be allowed equal use of public facilities, he never openly questioned segregation or encouraged his congregants to do so.

In fact, Sears strongly discouraged any semblance of radicalism among his members. One Saturday night, for example, after discovering Communist Party leaflets distributed around his church, he announced during the next day's services, "If I find any member fooling with this mess, I'm going to turn you out of the church." Sears viewed such radicalism as dangerous and developed a reputation in Collegeville as an anticommunist, making things uncomfortable for the one or two members who held membership in the party. In the spring of 1933, believing Sears had caused one of their comrades to be arrested, a large contingent of local party members interrupted a Baptist Young People's Union meeting at the church and demanded an explanation from the pastor. Forewarned and expecting their arrival, Sears reached down behind his pulpit for a double-barreled shotgun, waved it at the intruders, and yelled to his deacons, "Let them come on. Let them come on. I'll stop them!" Church members and unwanted visitors alike were stampeded out of the sanctuary. In the ensuing panic, police arrived on the scene and arrested twenty-nine persons. When the case went to trial, Sears was fined $250 for drawing his gun on unarmed persons. From then until Sears's death in 1938, party members flooded the minister with nuisance postcards that called on him to "stop working for the police of Birmingham against the Negro people and to leave [the] Collegeville community." Believing his life to be in danger, he appealed to the police for protection. The authorities refused but granted the minister permission to deputize deacons to serve as guards around the parsonage. By force of longevity, Sears's conservatism significantly stamped the personality of the Bethel congregation.[2]

Much like First Baptist in Selma, Bethel had become an aging congregation with a succession of pastors nearing retirement. Shuttlesworth's two immediate predecessors, the Reverends J. S. Gamble (1939–1941) and Chester Laster (1942–1953), had been, in the words of the church's unofficial historian, "older, set-in-their-ways type ministers." Bethel thus seemed an unlikely congregation for a pastor who would eventually challenge the racial status quo. In other ways, however, the congregation was ripe for change. A number of young men had become a part of the congregation after returning from military service during World War II. Few of the church's young leaders had attended college or achieved middle-class status. Having served their country during wartime, however, they were intent on advancement. The desegregation of the armed forces, the establishment of the Fair Employment Practices Commission, and other early rumblings of the civil rights movement had all created a new hopefulness among African Americans in general. Unlike the leaders of Fred's church in Selma, the small cohort of younger adults at Bethel had little to lose and no reason to oppose change in society or in their working-class congregation. Along with some of the older deacons, they warmed to a younger, more vigorous minister. Impressed with Fred's charisma and strength of conviction, the church thus broke with its tradition of calling older ministers, electing him as the youngest pastor in its history. Although they believed Fred Shuttlesworth would attract younger members, they also expected him to motivate the old guard with his new style and new programs. Even they, however, did not expect their new young minister to change their church from a typical "house of God" to one of the centers of civil rights agitation in the South.[3]

Neither did Shuttlesworth, however. He began his ministry at Bethel in a traditional manner. He initially focused on evangelistic canvasses of the community, union meetings, and simultaneous revivals with other churches. He set the typical institutional goals of local congregations—increases in attendance, religious activity, and financial stewardship (tithing). During his tenure at Bethel, he strengthened the church's organizational health, either establishing or increasing participation in the Sunday school, the Baptist Training Union, deacon and deaconess boards, several choirs, mission groups, and two usher boards. During his first few months, he engaged in pastoral and evangelistic visitation to members and nonmembers alike. He combined these two traditional concerns in an unexceptional manner. He later explained his philosophy: "I do evangelism every time I talk to somebody. . . . If I'm talking to a person about a problem, I'm evangelistic in that." Occasionally, members good-naturedly complained to Fred that "all you talk about is the Bible." He characteristically responded, "Well, what am I supposed to talk about? I think Christian folks ought to schedule themselves to, at all times, insofar as possible, be thinking about how good God is to them and therefore witnessing." Primarily because of Shuttlesworth's attractiveness to younger members, Bethel reached its institutional high-water mark of nearly seven hundred members, an increase of more than two hundred, during his first three years as pastor.[4]

Other than through his preaching ability, traditionally a make-or-break element in the success of a black Baptist pastor, Shuttlesworth attracted younger members with the same gregarious personal style that had originally stood him in good stead in Selma. He built a strong relationship with his deacons, particularly those near his own age, who quickly developed a deep loyalty to him. As a result, they put out many potential brush fires that might otherwise have occurred among the members. Fred also developed a personable demeanor with his members, going out of his way to make them feel important. As his involvement in civil rights increased, this personal element of his work at Bethel indicated to his members that despite their pastor's growing fame, they still mattered to him. For most of his tenure at Bethel, this sort of pastoral stroking—typical among ministers—won the vast majority of his members over to his agenda. This approach, which differed little from that which Shuttlesworth had used in Selma, worked more smoothly at Bethel. When he began his ministry in Birmingham, a pastoral colleague offered Fred sage advice, reminding him that "you aren't going to First Baptist when you get to Bethel. So you don't need to go there to fight. Don't go there taking them as though they are fighting. Just take it as if they love you and accept you, and you lead them." More confident of being accepted, and experiencing no differences of class and fewer contests of ego with his lay leadership, Fred managed quite naturally to follow this wise counsel at his new church.[5]

His gregariousness and down-to-earth qualities notwithstanding, Fred continued his hard-line philosophy of ministry. Friendly toward his parishioners, he nonetheless avoided making confidants of his members in order to reserve the right on occasion to challenge them prophetically. Strong pastoral leadership has historically been the norm in black Baptist churches and was the philosophy of ministry taught at Selma University. Both Nelson H. Smith Jr. and T. L. Lane, Shuttlesworth's classmates and later his ministerial colleagues in Birmingham, believed that the Bible prescribes an authoritative role for the office of pastor. Smith, for example, argued that a pastor is given authority by God himself and that a church is a theocracy, not a democracy. Smith also traced this understanding through the history of African American religion, finding Denmark Vesey, Nat Turner, and Richard Allen as strong pastors who took the lead in pastoral matters. Despite often being charged as behaving like a "dictator,"

Shuttlesworth fully agreed that the scriptures prescribe a strong, authoritative pastor. He argued: "God is a benevolent dictator. You don't have to vote on whether or not He's good; He's good without your vote. . . . [Besides] in the Baptist church, although the majority rules, it's not a democracy. . . . The pastor ought to discuss [matters] with his board and leadership. But nobody has a right to get up and outdo a pastor in the church, because the pastor is assigned that church. Not just by the Board of Deacons, which I think some white churches don't understand, but God himself said in Ezekiel [actually Jeremiah] 3:15, 'I will give them pastors after mine own heart.' Being the pastor of a church is a thing that is close to the heart of God, not just somebody who decides to vote for him because he is intellectual."[6]

At Bethel, Pastor Shuttlesworth operated accordingly—and wasted little time in doing so. Within his first few Sundays as pastor, he began to develop a rift with one of his older deacons. Nathan J. Davis, a member of the church for more than fifty years and Sunday school superintendent, took the opportunity near the conclusion of a worship service to compliment Shuttlesworth's sermon, commenting, "Pastor, you preached a g-r-e-a-t sermon today. This is the kind of sermon we been needing to hear." Shuttlesworth appreciated the affirmation but bristled at Davis's setting himself up as public judge of his sermons. Rankled even more when Davis repeated the scene the following week, Shuttlesworth promptly moved to stave off any repeat performances. The next Sunday, just before his sermon, he said, "Let me say one thing before I preach. God hasn't sent anybody out to judge sermons. The test of a sermon is whether it does you any good in life. Sermons are to be lived, not necessarily to be commented on. So after I preach today I don't want anybody commenting on my sermon. This is for everybody equally. If it is good for you, take it and thank God. If it is not good for you, pray for me." If the instruction was indeed "for everybody equally," then only the most obtuse member could miss the sharp point that Davis was first among equals.[7]

Later during Shuttlesworth's ministry at Bethel, the tense relationship between the pastor and his deacon sparked more public disputes. One Sunday after a sermon in which Shuttlesworth had in Davis's mind leveled at him a thinly veiled criticism, the deacon interrupted the service, saying, "Well, you said too much. Seem like you was talkin' to me in your sermon. I been here fifty-some years, and I don't like the way you carried on." Careful to reassert his pastoral authority, Shuttlesworth retorted, "But it isn't up to you to judge what I say." "When something hurts me," Davis countered, "I say it." Fred revealingly answered back, "You characterize women like that, and I don't have no women on my board." He invited Davis to visit him during the next week for consultation on this matter, but when the deacon did not come by, the pastor recommended on the following Sunday that the congregation remove him from his leadership positions. Within a month, the offender issued a public apology and was voted back into office. As justification for the application of public disciplinary measures by a pastor, he claimed, incorrectly, that "the Bible says, 'They that sin openly, rebuke openly.'"[8]

On another occasion, two women leaders, Vivian Durant and Blanche Roberson, disagreed with each other publicly and vigorously about whom to invite as a speaker for the church's annual Women's Day. Their argument degenerated into threats of physical violence, with one of the women threatening the other with a rock and the other reciprocating with an umbrella. Shuttlesworth counseled with them but ultimately forced them to issue public apologies or else surrender their leadership positions in the church. "You can't be ashamed to make these apologies; you weren't ashamed to fight," he told them. "If you can't humble yourself and ask forgiveness of the Lord, then I have to remove you." The two embarrassed women publicly apologized to each other and to the congregation the following Sunday morning just as their pastor required. Shuttlesworth believed their public disagreement had brought reproach to the congregation's good name and that the situation had to be handled publicly. Acting in accordance with his understanding of the pastoral office, Shuttlesworth actively disciplined members whenever he viewed their actions as detrimental to the spiritual life and the public witness of the congregation. Of course, some members might disagree with their pastor's interpretation of a given situation. In such cases, however, exercising the power of both his office and his personality, Shuttlesworth ordinarily won the day.[9]

His understanding of the spiritual life extended beyond private devotion or purely institutional concerns, however. He also sought to raise the consciousness of his members for various sorts of charity work and ministry. Early on, he moved into larger community concerns as a natural outgrowth of his evangelistic canvasses. Seeking to become better acquainted with the community beyond his membership, Shuttlesworth soon took up the physical and social concerns that an African American theology generally views as inseparable from spirituality. Although he had always been "churchy," Fred often worked with persons who were not. For him, the call to be "separate from the world" did not make him hesitant to work with nonreligious persons. On one occasion, for example, Shuttlesworth ministered to a young man who had had his throat cut in a fight at a local honky tonk. As pastor of the nearest church, Shuttlesworth hurried down the street and took charge of the emergency situation. He helped stop the bleeding, counseled the victim and his family, and even worked in an evangelistic witness and an invitation to church. This sort of crisis intervention raised his stock with the citizens of Collegeville.[10]

In addition, he sought to raise the level of civic-mindedness at Bethel and in Collegeville. Although Alabama laws were rife with unfairness, blacks working through the National Association for the Advancement of Colored People (NAACP) and local social organizations and churches nevertheless impressed on their members the importance of registering to vote. In most Alabama counties, eligible black voters exercised the franchise in small numbers. Efforts at intimidation discouraged African Americans from registering. When Fred moved back into Jefferson County and attempted to transfer his voter registration from Mobile County, a registrar told him, "Boy, I don't think I want you to register right now; I want you to come back at a later time." The incident showed Shuttlesworth that "the Negroes' opportunities and chances were all wrapped up in the white man's chance whims. If he said 'No,' no matter how good you were, you couldn't do anything." This experience intensified his interest in encouraging voter registration in his congregation. Shuttlesworth began to encourage, cajole, and even good-naturedly browbeat the members of Bethel to register to vote. He posted rosters of eligible voters on the walls of the church, bringing public embarrassment and a not-so-subtle social pressure to bear on members whose names were not yet on the lists. He added a summons to register to his regular preachments, often calling members by name. He once called on a member named Maude Ellens:

"Maude, it is good to see you and Lonnie in church. Are you prepared to vote?"

"No, Reverend," she timidly replied.

"Okay, I'll be over there tomorrow to take you to register to vote. I'll be by tomorrow at 7:00."

"Don't come at 7:00; I won't be dressed."

"Well, if you don't want me to help you get dressed, be ready," he quipped. The next day Maude became a registered voter.[11]

Shuttlesworth in particular demanded that his lay leaders set an example for the rest of the congregation. The pastor pointedly told some deacons who were prone to long-winded prayers to put feet on their prayers and accompany him to the courthouse to register: "I don't want folks here [kneeling and] wearing the carpet out, saying a lot of lectures to the Lord, when you won't get up and go vote. If you are a deacon, you ought to be a leader. If you are on a mission, where are you going?"[12]

Eventually Shuttlesworth's civic-minded preaching and leadership became his entry point into civil rights activity, but it marked a departure from the sort of ministry he practiced in Selma. Several factors explain this apparent shift of emphasis. In the first place, as a cultural heir of African American religious traditions, Shuttlesworth shared a holistic religious philosophy that did not separate physical, social, or political needs from the spiritual. Whereas white southern evangelical Christianity has historically made such distinctions, black evangelicalism has not, partly because of its African legacy and partly in response to the American experience of slavery and segregation. Although he did not self-consciously think his way toward this "black theology," Shuttlesworth always saw his civic-mindedness, and later his civil rights activism, as part of the prophetic role inherent in the pastoral office. Never expressing his understanding of the Christian gospel in sophisticated theological language, Shuttlesworth nonetheless holistically combined both spiritual and bodily concerns in his spirituality.

Of more significance, Shuttlesworth emphasized, according to the old cliché, a pastor's prophetic responsibility to "afflict the comfortable" rather than to "comfort the afflicted." His particular pastoral context strongly influenced his approach. His first full-time pastorate in Selma naturally served as a training ground for him. The class antagonisms and leadership squabbles he experienced at First Baptist largely submerged the civic activities in which he later engaged in Birmingham. The specific situation at Bethel both necessitated and allowed him to give them more attention. Conversely, the more sedate and satisfied middle-class orientation of First Baptist virtually precluded concerns wider than those of the church's institutional health. In addition, while in Selma, Shuttlesworth attempted to balance his ministerial activities with his academic work, limiting the community ministry he could pursue.

Shuttlesworth's sense of social and racial injustice also grew imperceptibly from his Oxmoor days through his experiences in Mobile and Dallas Counties. He later noted, "There was enough in Dallas County to protest about. Just teaching in the schools showed it to you. You couldn't get to some of the schools when it rained hard. The creeks would rise, and some of the kids couldn't get to school for weeks." These unequal conditions for blacks increasingly offended his highly developed moral sensibilities and created an unease with the status quo, though they did not specifically spawn active protest. He preached a bit about the evils of white supremacy from his Selma pulpit but later confessed that "that was about as far as I went." Over time he concluded that preaching alone could never bring about social change. Unfolding events of the period ultimately sparked a combustion that became the civil rights movement and stoked the fire that already burned in Fred Shuttlesworth.[13]

Probably the best explanation for Shuttlesworth's move toward a more socially conscious ministry lay in his being caught up in a kind of black American Zeitgeist, or spirit of the times. Martin Luther King Jr. later attributed Rosa Parks's refusal to give up her bus seat, thus sparking the Montgomery boycott, to her being "tracked down by the Zeitgeist." Put succinctly, the climate had changed—not merely for Shuttlesworth but also for the entire African American struggle for full citizenship rights. Fred later offered an explanation couched in a homespun philosophy of history: "When the idea and the mood and time and the man and God all conspire—that's when a movement is born. But you go a long time before you get to a movement." Historians might quite rightly list only the human elements at work in a historical movement and reject elements of divine causation; Fred Shuttlesworth never would or could.[14]

Even humanistic historians can agree, however, that events since 1940, an era called "the forgotten years of the Negro revolution," converged to make the time ripe for the civil rights movement. Key developments included Eleanor Roosevelt's high-profile concerns for racial equality, Truman's desegregation of the armed forces, and the formation of the Fair Employment Practices Commission. Perhaps more significant was the growing perception of a duplicitous America—an America that fought the racial ideology of Nazism abroad while leaving racial segregation intact at home. African Americans viewed such events as providential openings to press on toward full citizenship. In that spirit, a national conference of attorneys in 1950 committed the NAACP to a frontal attack on public school segregation. For the next two years, NAACP lawyers filed suits in South Carolina, Virginia, Delaware, the District of Columbia, and Kansas. The latter suit resulted in the U.S. Supreme Court's 1954 *Brown v. Board of Education* decision that declared segregation unconstitutional. Finally, in June 1953, blacks in Baton Rouge, Louisiana, successfully challenged segregated seating in a bus boycott, the first sign that massive direct action might prevail against Jim Crow laws.[15]

Shuttlesworth was part of a younger, less docile group of southern blacks who came of age in this climate of impending change. Lola Hendricks, who later became one of Shuttlesworth's followers, made this sort of generational argument to explain the rise of the movement. Hendricks saw herself and Shuttlesworth as part of a younger adult cohort that, unlike their parents' generation, would accept segregation no longer. She commented: "We just did not want to think about our years [being] spent like our parents' had been spent, and it was time to do something about it." For his part, arriving at Bethel just three months before the Baton Rouge boycott and privy to conversations about it in the network of black Baptist preachers, Shuttlesworth did not immediately launch into full-fledged civil rights agitation. His earliest ministerial activities at Bethel, however, responded to the general context of black America and the particular situation in Birmingham. In the process he made incremental and imperceptible steps in that direction. He later explained that "the conditions were there. You have to have a climate to work in. . . . The climate in Birmingham was such that people were focusing on matters like voting. We strived. There's a song that says, 'Each victory helps you some other victory to win.' So once you get in this, you begin thinking about other things that ought to be."[16]

Not yet in attack mode, Shuttlesworth combatted segregation only indirectly in his first civic victories. Initially he worked with several organizations throughout subsections of Birmingham (Graysville, Hooper City, and Adamsville) known collectively as the Civic Leagues. In particular, Fred worked with the Jefferson County Coordinating Non-Partisan Voters League in his church-based registration drives. Bethel's voter registration more than doubled in Shuttlesworth's first four months as pastor. He also took a leading role in the Interdenominational Ministerial Alliance (IMA) and its efforts to have the city close down certain dives that Shuttlesworth believed bred "loudness, lewdness, and violence."[17] The ministers opposed the licensing of such dens in proximity to black residential areas. Shuttlesworth and others complained that similar establishments were not to be found in white areas near schools, churches, and residential areas and believed that Birmingham police were either operating them or taking bribes to allow their continuance.

Before long, Emory O. Jackson, editor of the city's largest black newspaper, the *Birmingham World*, complimented Shuttlesworth as "active in the community leadership that arouse the churches and citizens of Collegeville to have rowdy places and vice-breeding spots closed." In addition, Shuttlesworth and the others were concerned with raising the quality of life in black areas, giving specific attention to improving the lighting and paving of streets. Civic activities such as these, seeking only a true equality of conditions within the Jim Crow system, became Shuttlesworth's intermediate steps toward the struggle for civil rights in Birmingham. As he later noted, "Everything that I got into whetted my appetite for doing something else to destroy segregation, to embarrass the system and challenge the system from within." Shuttlesworth enjoyed his new success as both pastor and community leader, and his civic activities prepared him, when events would dictate, for a much larger role than even he imagined.[18]

Events dictated that he would not wait long. Like most African Americans, Fred was electrified by the Supreme Court's decision against school segregation. On the afternoon of May 17, 1954, Fred saw the newspaper headlines as he walked near the federal courthouse in Birmingham. He later compared his reaction to "getting religion": "I had felt like a man when I passed the newspaper stand and saw [that] the Supreme Court outlawed segregation. I felt second only to when I was converted. Second greatest feeling in my life. I felt like a man. The Supreme Court decision made me personally feel as if I was a man. I had the same rights, my kids had the same rights as other folks." Like many religious persons who see God's hand in great events, Fred shared the widespread interpretation that "it was in one sense God moving in human history."[19]

Moreover, the high court's ruling provided the legal opportunity for black Americans to push further faster. The judicial branch of the federal government had now moved toward the promise of justice in the nation's founding documents. "We thought that we were almost there," Shuttlesworth exulted. "All we had to do was just rise up and go get it." He later wrote that the decision kept alive smoldering black hopes and intensified their "efforts for freedom and voter registration." Shuttlesworth and other African Americans saw evidence at least temporarily that America's soul was essentially good and could be shamed into delivering on its promises of equality and freedom to all. Later, he came to believe that "you can't shame segregation." As he put it, "Rattlesnakes don't commit suicide; ball teams don't strike themselves out. You gotta put 'em out." Nevertheless, heartened by *Brown*, Shuttlesworth and others in the movement made plans to put Jim Crow laws out as soon as possible.[20]

The same was not true in white Birmingham. Racial tensions, which in the largely blue-collar city always lay just below the surface, had grown even more volatile in the postwar period. Since 1915 Birmingham had enforced zoning laws that restricted black housing to "nigger sections." After the war, however, black families seeking to escape congested black neighborhoods began moving into areas on the fringes of the white sections. As blacks moved into these areas, white reaction brought pressure to bear on them, resulting in some fifty bombings of black homes between 1947 and 1963. During this period the city earned the nickname "Bombingham," and the West End area around Center Street came to be known as "Dynamite Hill." Police rarely investigated these bombings and developed a reputation for brutalizing blacks. Under the direction of Theophilus Eugene "Bull" Connor, who had been commissioner of public safety since 1937, officials typically ruled black fatalities at police hands as "justifiable homicide." In July 1951, the department's notoriety outside Birmingham led the NAACP's annual convention to call for a Justice Department investigation of police brutality in the Magic City. The Connor-controlled department was defiant regarding this criticism and did little to counter a saying popular among African Americans in Birmingham: "If the Klan don't stop you, the Police will; if the Police don't stop you, the courts will."[21]

An opportunity to ease black-white tensions slightly in Birmingham arose in 1953 when, after being caught in a sex scandal, Connor chose not to run for reelection. Connor was succeeded by the comparatively moderate Robert E. Lindbergh, who set out to reform the police department. The reforms sought to raise standards for officers, curb corruption in the department, and, in particular, deal with police brutality toward blacks. These reforms themselves became controversial not only because the power brokers wished to maintain the racial status quo but also because the implementation of these reforms occurred in the same general time period as the *Brown* decision. In light of *Brown*, many white Birminghamians who might otherwise have greeted Lindbergh's reforms more calmly began to view them as local signs of a worldwide conspiracy to subvert the southern way of life.[22]

Reflecting much of the Deep South's paranoia over "the American dilemma," Birmingham gradually joined the region's massive resistance to the high court's order. County solicitors and a group of legislators from all over the state met to devise means of circumventing *Brown*. The press predicted that local school boards would gerrymander school districts in order to retain segregation. Jefferson County's school superintendent, I. F. Simmons, warned that under integration black teachers would not be hired in nearly the numbers in which they were employed in all-black schools. The rise of the most extreme segregationist reactions, however, reflected in increased Klan and citizens' council activity, awaited the stimulus of bona fide black activism in Birmingham.[23]

Amid vitriolic and violent opposition to integration, another incident of corrupt police activity provided a cause celèbre. As a result Fred Shuttlesworth gradually emerged as a leader beyond Bethel. In December 1954, police arrested a black man named Charles Patrick after he argued with a white woman regarding a parking place. When the woman's husband, police officer Jim Siniard, learned of the incident, he and his partner visited Patrick in jail and administered a severe beating. Reformist commissioner Lindbergh fired the errant officers, but his colleagues on the city commission, Mayor Jimmy Morgan and Commissioner Wade Bradley, countermanded the dismissal, merely suspending the officers for thirty days. Reacting to both the beating and the decision of the commission, the local chapter of the NAACP staged a mass meeting at the Sixteenth Street Baptist Church. Congregants at the meeting passed a resolution criticizing Morgan and Bradley and calling for the hiring of black police officers. This latter concern would occupy the attention of blacks in Birmingham for the first half of 1955, eventually bringing Fred Shuttlesworth to center stage and contributing to the return of Bull Connor to power in 1957.[24]

Not all black Birminghamians agreed on the proper strategy regarding racial matters, however. White segregationists often asserted that "good" blacks preferred "their own kind," and at least one member of the African American community publicly corroborated their claim. On January 22, 1955, Collier P. Clay, president of the tiny, obscure, and unaccredited Union Theological Seminary in Birmingham, made a speech in the nearby town of Notasulga before an organization called the Southern Negro Improvement Association. In stark contrast to its namesake organization, Marcus Garvey's Universal Negro Improvement Association, Clay's group eschewed all forms of black nationalism, taking a thoroughgoing accommodationist approach to the race issue. Rumored to have received payments from white segregationists for confirming their views, Clay expressed approval of segregation and criticized "trouble makers." Using a telling analogy, he argued, "You can't hurry God and can't bury the Southern white man. And just like God, you can get anything you need and deserve from the white man, but you have got to ask him in the right manner." The next day a young minister from Montgomery addressed an NAACP rally in Birmingham. Having come to the Dexter Avenue Baptist Church a few days before the *Brown* decision, Martin Luther King Jr. took the opportunity to reject Clay's remarks. Calling for the immediate implementation of the court's ruling, he noted that ending segregation would require that blacks "do more than pray and read the Bible. You must do something about it."[25]

At the same rally, W. C. Patton, the president of the local NAACP chapter, issued a statement disavowing Clay as an "unknown pseudo-leader" whose views "do not truthfully reflect the sentiments of the Negro group with regard to their protracted and valiant struggle for first class citizenship." Other ministerial leaders, including the Reverends J. L. Ware, president of the Birmingham Baptist Ministers Conference, and E. W. Williams, Clay's own pastor, lashed out at Clay's views. Others in the African American religious community were furious over Clay's remarks, and on the following Tuesday, the Baptist Ministers Conference denounced him. They also scheduled a hearing for February 8, at which time they asked him to explain his views, particularly his willingness to equate the "Southern white man" with God. At its next meeting on February 15, the conference expelled Clay from its membership. Clay quickly became persona non grata in the black community of Birmingham; he would emerge later, however, as one of Shuttlesworth's first opponents on the police issue.[26]

For a year or so after the *Brown* decision, Fred tended to his ministerial responsibilities and efforts to clean up vice in the juke joints around Collegeville. In addition, he gradually stepped up his activities with the NAACP, rising to the office of membership chairman. Support for "Negro police" had been increasing in Birmingham for several years, even among whites. Three years earlier, the white Alabama Baptist Convention had passed a resolution favoring the measure in the state's municipalities. In the same year the Interracial Committee of the Jefferson County Coordinating Council noted that eighty-two other southern cities had hired black police and called for Birmingham to follow suit. The *Birmingham World* called on the city commission to adopt this policy, as did the city's two white newspapers. During the first half of 1955, the Patrick incident sparked more frequent and insistent calls for the hiring of African Americans by the police department. This context of support made further public efforts more likely. After the Reverend George Rudolph unilaterally appealed to city hall for black police on June 21 and the *Birmingham World* and the *Birmingham News* again editorialized on the issue, Shuttlesworth was inspired to become involved. Soon after Rudolph's appeal, Fred drafted a petition he hoped a ministerial group would approve and present to the city commission. For several days he privately circulated the petition among his ministerial colleagues and drummed up support for it. In particular, he prevailed on the leaders of three denominational ministerial groups—the Methodist Ministers Alliance, the Central Baptist Ministers Conference, and the United Methodist Alliance—to approve it. After this, he invited a larger group of clergy, the Interdenominational Ministerial Alliance, to meet at Bethel on Saturday, July 9, and Monday, July 11, to discuss the proposal.[27]

Abruptly elevated to the presidency of this organization, Shuttlesworth presented the petition and called on the ministers to endorse it. Fred shrewdly couched the appeal in terms of "crime, delinquency, and lawlessness" rather than the more volatile issue of integration. The petition specifically asked the city commissioners "not to tie the matter of Negro Policemen for Crime prevention" with the issue of integration. "We hold that the two things have nothing in common," Shuttlesworth wrote, adding that "to link them together only clouds and shades the issue at hand." Shuttlesworth expressed alarm over the crime rate, which he traced to "slum housing and uncontrolled crime breeding places." Noting Birmingham's overabundance of brutality and murders, he indicated the ministers' intent not to remain silent witnesses of "the death of our people while the places generating such things roll right along, unmolested and unchecked." Arguing that light punishment constituted "an open and unwritten invitation to murder and crime," he further stated: "In plain words, we believe that a Negro should get the same punishment for the assault or murder of another Negro that he would get for assault or murder of a white man, or vice versa."[28]

Shuttlesworth's pivotal request, however, called for the "immediate hiring of Negro police and detectives in areas populated by Negroes." Shuttlesworth argued for this policy in two ways: first, it was likely to reduce and prevent crime; second, other Alabama cities (Mobile, Montgomery, Dothan, Talladega, and Hobson City) had already used black police with success. In addition to the policy change regarding police officers, the petition requested that officials more rigidly enforce age limits in establishments serving alcohol and that they "especially note amusement places of continued disturbment [sic]—closing down those that remain disorderly." Temporarily accommodating to Jim Crow laws, rather than requesting integrated parks, the statement called for more recreational facilities for African Americans. Finally, Shuttlesworth pledged the ministers' cooperation with the commissioners "in helping to cope with these problems." During the two nights of discussion, some of the ministers appeared hesitant, attempting to table the petition because, they warned, "it's a serious thing." Shuttlesworth impatiently replied, "What's so serious about it—asking for Negro policemen in Negro areas? What's serious about that? What needs to be studied? Besides, I didn't ask you to study it; I asked you to endorse it. Because it's going to the commission with or without your endorsement." Eventually, Shuttlesworth convinced seventy-six of the ministers, who attached their names to the document.[29]

Two weeks later, on Monday, July 25, the large delegation of ministers accompanied Shuttlesworth to city hall to present the petition to Mayor Jimmy Morgan, Commissioner of Public Safety Lindbergh, and Commissioner of Public Improvements Wade Bradley. The commission allowed the ministers to state their concerns but remained noncommittal. After the meeting, in an interview with the *Birmingham World*, Fred expressed his "confidence, faith and belief" that the city commission would favorably consider the appeal. The following day, however, the commission rejected the petition. Although Morgan timidly supported the appeal, Lindbergh and Bradley decided that, in the light of the *Brown* ruling, granting the petition might lead to "serious racial trouble." Lindbergh cited in particular the difficulty of restricting white police to white areas. "Now is not the time; maybe later," he concluded. In the aftermath of this decision, editor Emory Jackson expressed his paper's support for black police. He called Shuttlesworth's petition "a calm, touching, reasoned statement" and complimented the clerical delegation for rendering a "notable public service" by bringing critical problems to public attention. He criticized the city commission: "No real reason has been cited . . . , only excuses and fears."[30]

Believing that broadening the support for the petition might create some movement on the part of the city commission, Shuttlesworth called another meeting of the IMA for August 1. Fred again invited ministers to Bethel to help plan a citywide mass meeting that would reaffirm the need for voter registration and ask laypersons to support the recent civic action program. During the next few weeks the IMA increased the petition's signatories to more than 3,500, a number that included 119 white Birminghamians. Shuttlesworth also lobbied the commission to revoke the license of a certain dive in Collegeville. Shuttlesworth was surprised that Lindbergh had taken his earlier information seriously, and he served as a witness as the commissioner questioned the proprietor concerning violent incidents at his establishment. Shuttlesworth experienced his first taste of success in civic action when Lindbergh followed the ministers' recommendations to revoke the license. This also gave Shuttlesworth some hope that Lindbergh might eventually come around to supporting the petition. In the meantime, Birmingham's Young Men's Business Club (YMBC), an organization that included a number of racial moderates working to change Birmingham's image, voted, by a margin of twenty-eight to two, to endorse the policy of hiring black police. Seeing support for his proposals growing both in black and in white communities, Fred decided to appeal again to the commission.[31]

On September 1, 1955, the ministers appeared before city leaders and presented the earlier petition and a new letter that stated their case. Shuttlesworth argued that there was no doubt as to the "need and validity" of their claims and requests. Articulating his points without great eloquence, and sometimes with solecisms that revealed his lack of polish, Fred nonetheless understood the issues. Rejecting the implication that blacks were "necessarily inclined to do crime," he explained: "Aside from the lack of sufficient Recreational equiptment [sic] and the Slum content, there is a preponderance of Honky-Tonks and Bawdy Houses operating in their areas . . . [and] a definite need of a more positive approach to the problem in Negro Areas. This, we would humbly suggest, to be Negro Policemen." He further noted the commission's authority to help alleviate these conditions and quoted 2 Samuel 23:3–4: "He that ruleth over men must be just, ruling in the fear of God. And he shall be as the light of the morning, when the sun rises, even a morning without clouds." He reminded the commissioners of the YMBC's endorsement and presented the signatures and addresses of the petition's supporters. Finally, he presented copies of letters from white officials in Montgomery and Dothan, Alabama, and Miami, Florida, all of which supported the use of black police. Again, Mayor Morgan accepted the proposal but was outvoted by his colleagues. In spite of their unsuccessful efforts, Shuttlesworth and the other ministers impressed opinion-maker Emory Jackson, who editorialized that they had "made a strong case and presented it with tact and sincerety [sic]." Encouraging the ministers to "stay in there pitching," Jackson wrote: "They deserve the full support of those of goodwill who have the interest of their city at heart."[32]

Heeding Jackson's call to persistence, Shuttlesworth "kept pitching" and renewed his request within the month, receiving the same answer, but this time with a new justification. Just four days before Shuttlesworth's previous appearance before the commission, the body of eleven-year-old Emmett Till had been discovered floating down the Mississippi River after his disappearance from the small Delta town of Money, Mississippi. The national uproar surrounding Till's murder had, in the minds of many southern whites, created another difficult obstacle to racial harmony. When Till's mother provided *Ebony* magazine with a photograph of her son's bloated and beaten body in its casket, African Americans were angered, and whites were put on the defensive. The controversy thus provided a pretext for official Birmingham to continue stonewalling on the

"Negro police" issue. When Shuttlesworth returned to the commission, Lindbergh suggested that emotions stirred up by the Till case had made that particular moment an inopportune time for dealing with the police issue. On this occasion, Lindbergh made use of Collier P. Clay, who had earlier expressed his caution about *Brown* and integration. Lindbergh's convenient mouthpiece, Clay launched into a defense of segregation. His filibuster, however, was interrupted when Shuttlesworth quickly interjected, "I'm sorry, Commissioner, we did not come here to discuss integration. We came to discuss this petition." Lindbergh excused the diversion, meekly explaining, "Well, it's just on our minds." Of course, the Till matter was on the minds of Shuttlesworth and his colleagues as well. Echoing what many African Americans believed, Shuttlesworth said that "only God, only the books in heaven can know how many Negroes [had] come up missing and dead and killed under the system" that resulted in Emmett Till's death. At that strategic moment, however, Shuttlesworth had more pragmatic concerns. "Well, we're going to have to deal with it," Fred admitted, "but right today, we're talking about Negro policemen. Emmett Till's death had nothing to do with Negro police. You are telling us that you won't give them to us; we'll have to fight to get them." Lindbergh stalled once again, took the matter "under advisement," and led Fred to a conclusion about southern politicians he would often repeat to his audiences: "They smile and say 'yes' when they really mean 'hell no.'"[33]

By the end of this round with the city commission, Shuttlesworth's reputation was spreading rapidly throughout the Birmingham black community. It was aided by Emory Jackson, who again complimented him: "The Shuttlesworth leadership has performed a devoted public and civic service in keeping the issue alive. . . . The campaign should be kept on the high level which has characterized it since the Rev. Shuttlesworth and his group moved into action." Within a few weeks Jackson again praised Shuttlesworth for his "enlightened leadership," and the Jefferson County Coordinating Non-Partisan Voters League named him its cochairman. In a letter to Jackson, Shuttlesworth addressed the black community beyond Bethel Baptist, hoping to spur further attempts at civic improvement through the hiring of black police. Noting the white groups that had endorsed the idea, Shuttlesworth claimed optimistically that "our City had grown in good will and mutual relationships." Without mentioning Lindbergh by name, he nonetheless criticized the commissioner's statement that he "has been, still is, and will be so long as he is in Office, against Negro Policemen." He further wrote: "It is good Leaders who make good cities; it is the forward-looking leaders who help people to throw off the unneces-sary things and ideas with which they have been shackled in the past. . . . Times do change and we are changed with them. It is righteousness and just dealings which exhalt [sic] any nation. Wrong in any form is but a temporary and frag-mentary cloud which, though dark and ominous, must finally give way for the brightness of the day. The Almighty will see to it that the day dawns if the righ-teous and courageous will persevere." He called on readers to continue to press for "better thing[s] for all people and the right to share and participate in civic and governmental affairs." He urged obedience to laws, mutual respect, and voter registration and participation in all elections and concluded with the promise: "From our Pulpits and Forums we shall teach Love and persistence with patience; never hate and malice. Against such there is no barrier or law, and from such will come a better Earth, a better City."[34]

Shuttlesworth's references to teaching love and persistence rather than hate and malice evidenced an openness to the "philosophy of nonviolence" he would soon be hearing from Montgomery. He had not read Gandhi at all; instead, his rural southern black evangelicalism provided him a background sufficient for moving into nonviolence. For Shuttlesworth and others like him in southern black churches, Jesus' redemptive suffering at the crucifixion and his message of loving one's enemies served as a more than adequate model for the present moment of struggle. Once he heard Gandhian nonviolence articulated and con-nected with Christian theology by King, he accepted it as precipitously as he made other decisions in his life. Thus in early December 1955, when the news media and the African American grapevine publicized a mass meeting in Montgomery to support a citywide boycott of the buses, Shuttlesworth and some of his IMA associates headed for the capital city to lend their support.

When the Birmingham contingent arrived at the packed sanctuary of the Holt Street Baptist Church, they were recognized and greeted by the leaders of the newly formed Montgomery Improvement Association (MIA). They then heard its new president, Martin Luther King Jr., deliver a speech setting the boy-cott within the theological context of Christian love. Although he would quickly expand his rationale to include the Gandhian philosophy of satyagraha, King began his appeal to the masses on a basis familiar to southern rural evan-gelicals such as Fred Shuttlesworth. For his part, Fred pledged to support the boycott with prayers and financial offerings and made periodic visits to the mass meetings throughout the year-long boycott.[35]

Shuttlesworth had met King in 1954 when ministerial concerns brought King to Birmingham, and Fred saw him again at his NAACP rally address in January 1955. In their first meetings Shuttlesworth had been impressed with King's education and eloquence, but he did not view him as unique among African American ministers of his acquaintance. Similar to many other observers, Shuttlesworth did not immediately discern any particular leadership potential in King. Over the years, the two developed an amicable working relationship. They came to respect one another as public persons, and they were friendly in personal conversation, but they never shared a close, personal friendship. As their involvement increased, particularly after the 1957 formation of the Southern Christian Leadership Conference, they would be in touch more regularly on movement matters. They never became confidants, however. For King that role was played almost exclusively by Ralph Abernathy, whom Fred had known since college days at Alabama State.[36]

Discovering each other during their classes in Montgomery, Fred and Ralph became friends, "talking shop" as young preachers leading congregations while completing their degrees. They discussed religion in general and the trials of the pastorate in particular. They also shared ideas and methods for sermons. Abernathy prepared full manuscripts, whereas Fred depended on the preaching moment itself to add homiletical flesh to his bare outlines. Each of them invited the other to preach in his pulpit, and Fred even advised Abernathy during his courtship with his future wife, Juanita. Believing that Ralph idolized her—"he was going to marry Juanita or die"—Fred cautioned him, "You can make a god out of anything, including your wife or girlfriend." They occasionally discussed matters of racial injustice but without, at least in the early years of their friendship, any intention of challenging the status quo. As their involvement in the protest movement increased, however, these concerns would gradually become the focus of their associations.[37]

During the latter half of 1955 Fred began to expand his leadership beyond Bethel Baptist Church to become the most prominent new civic leader of black Birmingham, as indicated by his name's more frequent appearance on the pages of the *Birmingham World*. His higher visibility earned him an invitation to be the featured speaker for a community-wide program installing a slate of new officers in the local chapter of the NAACP. In two front-page articles, editor Jackson fully introduced him to the community and publicized his forthcoming speech on January 22, 1956. In his first major appearance before an NAACP meeting, Shuttlesworth emphasized the organization's responsibility "to help make the Southland a place of equality and opportunity." Sharply criticizing white groups and officials whose actions showed disrespect for the law, he asserted that "segregation as a way of life is unconstitutional and dead." Calling on the NAACP to reach the masses, he insisted that the organization not "live in tree tops or in a maze of grandiose phrases" and that it should make its goals and principles clear. Borrowing from King's speech on the first night of the Montgomery boycott, he thundered: "Negroes are tired of being the political football in America. Negroes are tired of a backdoor status. Negroes are tired of being murdered with nothing done about it. Negroes are tired of being the last hired and first fired. Negroes are tired of taxation without representation—at City Hall, in Montgomery, and in Washington." Moving into what would become one of his pet themes—weak, docile leadership—he continued, "Negroes are tired and fed up with their own leaders who rise to prominence and then do the Uncle Tom; yes, against those who use their positions for fame and personal aggrandizement. We don't need big shots. Negroes are tired of leaders who will take handouts, sops, and pats on their backs. What we need are men who seek not office, but service; men who will stand for the right." Lapsing into inelegant phrasing, to which he was often prone, he lashed out against "supposed-to-be leaders" throughout the South who were "in open defiance of the constitutional concepts of democracy."[38]

Growing prominence soon taught Fred the price of a leadership willing to rock Birmingham's racial boat. Just days before his NAACP speech on January 17, he received an intimidating phone call in which the caller cursed him for his activities in Birmingham. Two weeks later, his role in Autherine Lucy's attempt to become the first African American to attend the University of Alabama created more serious trouble. On the previous October 10, just after Shuttlesworth's third appearance before the city commission, the U.S. Supreme Court cleared the way for Lucy to enroll by ordering the university to drop its White Only admissions policy. Lucy and Shuttlesworth had been friends at Selma University and had served their graduating class as salutatorian and valedictorian, respectively. After finishing at Selma, the two lost touch but rediscovered each other when they both moved back to Birmingham. When Lucy's suit came to public attention, Shuttlesworth offered her his moral support. In early February Fred accompanied her and her lawyer, Arthur Shores, to the campus to enroll. On this visit, Shuttlesworth became more fully aware of the separateness and the inequality of segregation as he observed the beauty and magnificence of his surroundings at the Tuscaloosa campus—a stark contrast to the impoverished surroundings of the all-black institutions he had attended. On February 18, two weeks after he accompanied Lucy to Tuscaloosa, riders in a passing car threw two bricks through the front window of Shuttlesworth's parsonage. In response, Shuttlesworth called the Birmingham office of the FBI to report the incident. This would be only the beginning of the Shuttlesworth family's experience both with racist backlash and with the FBI.[39]

Meanwhile, his pastoral responsibilities continued. He pastored his congregation with a strong, if not an iron, hand. His preaching typified evangelical Protestantism, though as he became more involved in the civil rights movement, the theme of liberation at the heart of African American Christianity bubbled more frequently to the surface. Still, in these early years at Bethel, his message remained traditional for the black church. His sermons primarily concerned increasing the commitment level of the average church member. "I just think that the Christian religion," he averred, "ought to be lifting, constraining, and compelling in a person's life. And to that extent, most people whose names are on the church rolls are not real [Christians]." He admitted that most had "some residual appreciation of Christ" but generally did not allow Christ to rule over them. Never overly academic, he spent little time studying in his preparation of sermons. Visitors to his messy office found a desk piled high with papers and few books other than a Bible or some devotional or Sunday school material. Although he always took a biblical text for his sermons, he rarely did any extensive exegesis, relying on common sense or literal interpretations. He believed in the literal meaning of Scripture and understood its inspiration in a traditional manner. He believed the Bible was God's book, written "by man into whom God puts his truth." For him the Bible's unified message, despite its diversity of authorship and historical context, constituted the proof of "the truth of the Bible." He understood this process by way of a simple analogy: a mother overseeing her daughter's cooking makes sure she does not add too much salt or other ingredients. "The girl has, in effect, cooked," he observed, "but the mama looks over the cooking." Similarly God would not have "permitted error to the point where it could be critical to His direction of mankind's affairs." In a sermon on the Bible, he argued, "Of all the things known to man, none is more solid or lasting than the Bible—the word of God. It is truly the Old Book for the new age and the newest book for the newer age. . . . Why has it been around so long? It is the word of Him who flung the stars from his fingers. . . . It is the answer to new problems and all problems of man. . . . It leaves no doubt that if you seek, you will find. . . . It speaks freely about life and death."[40]

In addition to warming to his preaching, the members of Bethel viewed their pastor as a good role model for the young people of the congregation and community. He not only was the youngest pastor in the history of the church but also had the most formal education. In spite of his lack of polish and sophistication, he valued education, insisted on it from his own children, and encouraged the youth of Bethel and their parents to aim for college educations. Among the teens who attended Bethel during his ministry, a significantly higher number went to college than under other pastors. Many of them, including all four of Shuttlesworth's children, eventually entered careers in education. He was popular with young people, baptizing many of them into the membership of Bethel. Veronica Chappell, one of twelve whom the pastor baptized on one particular Sunday, later testified, "He was like a father to all of us." He also disciplined his young members as readily as he did his own children, occasionally interrupting his own sermons. Chappell recalled him insisting, "Veronica, turn around and stop talking." Nevertheless, he also impressed the youth with his hunger and with his insistence that they share his hunger for a better station in life. "He wanted education for all. He wanted the young people to do the best they could in all their subjects, to aspire for higher goals and to work for it." He also taught them, "Be sure that Christ is in your life, and he will direct you in the way that he would have you to go. . . . If you believe in a cause, be willing to give your life for it." In time events in the civil rights movement would give their pastor opportunity not only to teach this principle but also to demonstrate it. As adults, many of the young persons who grew up in Bethel testified that they were profoundly influenced by the words, and later the deeds, of their pastor.[41]

In his increasingly high-profile role in the African American community, Shuttlesworth was asked to serve as the membership chairman of the Birmingham NAACP. He immediately began working to increase the size of the organization. Never favorably looked upon in the white South, the NAACP had been committed to the end of segregation since its inception in 1909. In the context of postwar McCarthyism, organizations given to changing the status quo became particularly suspect as potentially subversive. NAACP national executive secretary Roy Wilkins therefore went to great lengths to avoid this impression. In February 1956, he sent a letter to all local chapters to beware of "left-wing groups and individuals" whom he feared might seek to infiltrate local NAACP delegations to the upcoming National Delegate Assembly for Civil Rights in March. He further reminded local workers of the national office's policy "not to cooperate with any Communist-front or left-wing groups." Although Shuttlesworth was fully committed to the capitalist system, he at times poked fun at what he called the "Communist bugaboo." He often said dismissively: "I'm too American black to be Russian red. It doesn't take a communist to tell me how to read the Constitution. . . . It doesn't take communism or Russia or anybody else to tell us what freedom and equality mean." Naturally, he thus worked to raise the membership in the Birmingham branch with little regard for Wilkins's concern. As one of the speakers at a mass rally on Sunday, April 8, he called on his audience to renew their memberships and subscriptions to *Crisis,* the NAACP's national magazine.[42]

Anticommunism alone would have been sufficient to cast suspicion on the NAACP. Litigating the *Brown* case, however, made the NAACP even more of a lightning rod. Within a year of the *Brown* ruling, segregationist organizations such as the citizens' councils hysterically attacked the NAACP, evidenced by their publication of Mississippi judge Thomas P. Brady's polemic, *Black Monday.* Just as implacably opposed to integration were the 101 southern members of Congress who signed and published the "Southern Manifesto" in March 1956. Condemning *Brown* and the NAACP, the document pledged to use "every lawful means" to oppose desegregation. In this context, many Deep South state legislatures began to pass laws monitoring or curtailing NAACP activities within their borders. Alabama attorney general John Patterson fought mightily to uphold the constitutionality of the state's segregation laws, developing a new strategy against the NAACP. He decided to fight through many local cases rather than in a single statewide lawsuit. In light of the Supreme Court rulings, Patterson feared that segregationist forces would never be able to win federal lawsuits brought by the NAACP and instead sought to obstruct their efforts at all costs. He later admitted that "rather than go to court and get decisions that you didn't want, the best thing to do was to avoid decisions altogether. So we went to every extreme to avoid getting involved in litigation with them. And it worked for a long time. It worked for eight years. Simply a delay, though."[43]

Patterson concluded that he could put the NAACP on the defensive with a seemingly endless series of local suits by charging the organization with violating Alabama's corporate domestication statutes. Patterson and Assistant Attorney General MacDonald Gallion discerned a way to prosecute the organization for failure to register as a "foreign corporation." Alabama law considered foreign all corporations chartered outside the state and required them to file certain documents and pay a "non-resident" fee before doing business in the state. Not having met these requirements, the NAACP was thus construed to be operating illegally. On June 1 Patterson petitioned circuit judge Walter B. Jones to enjoin the NAACP from operating in Alabama. This was the first of many such actions that would earn Jones the nickname "Injunctionitis Jones." So designating the judge, Shuttlesworth complained that "officials could ask Jones to issue an injunction against the sunshine [and] I think he would do it." Within an hour of the submission of Patterson's request, Jones agreed with Patterson's interpretations and granted the petitions, effectively outlawing the NAACP and suspending it from all activities for what would become an eight-year period. Moreover, Jones ordered the NAACP to turn over to the state all records and membership lists and levied a fine of $100,000.[44]

Shuttlesworth's activities as membership chairman now potentially placed him in legal jeopardy. Fred was presiding over a small meeting of NAACP workers at the Masonic hall on Fourth Avenue North shortly after Jones issued the injunction. A Jefferson County deputy sheriff soon interrupted the meeting with his intention to serve the papers. Striding confidently into the office armed with a pistol, a shiny gun belt, and a large sheaf of legal papers, the deputy announced, "You're outlawed. I have an injunction against the NAACP." Identifying himself as the membership chairman, Fred asked the officer what the action meant, only to be notified that the order barred them from any activities whatsoever. One of the others asked, "Then what can we do?" "You can't do nothing," the officer replied. Then Fred piped up, "That isn't so. We have to do something. There's never a time when a man can't do anything. You are not going to stop people from trying to be free." Laughing off Fred's comment, the officer remarked, "Well, all I know is that you are enjoined, and I've served it." Determined not to allow this minion of Jim Crow laws the last word, Shuttlesworth shot back, "Well, Sir, it won't stop here. I assure you we *will* do something." "Well, you better be careful," replied the smiling deputy as he exited. Arranging a quick, clandestine meeting with one of his NAACP associates, Lucinda Robey, attorney Arthur D. Shores, and others, Shuttlesworth listened as Shores explained the consequences of the injunction and warned that violators could be jailed for contempt of court. Shuttlesworth replied pensively, "Well, some of us may need to go to jail anyway." As the meeting broke up, the members agreed to be in touch by phone and to think further about their options.[45]

During the next several days calls from all over the city bombarded the Shuttlesworth home. Callers wondered what the NAACP might do to counter the injunction. Stumped for a satisfactory answer, Fred detected a sense of "helplessness and hopelessness." His vexation grew as he cast about for a solution. Talking the matter over with Ruby and his ministerial associates, he became still more troubled when the restraining order went into effect on Friday, June 1. About three o'clock the next morning Fred lay restlessly in bed mulling and praying over the problem when what he took to be God's voice spoke to him saying, "They are trying to kill hope, but you can't kill people's hope." Like the prophet Samuel (1 Sam. 3:9–10), Fred replied, "Speak Lord, for I hear." Shuttlesworth then "heard" the words "Ye shall know the truth and the truth shall set you free" (John 8:32). He concluded that the people had to "know the truth" in spite of the state's efforts to tell them "you cannot be free and you cannot even fight to be free." In a moment of inspiration, he interpreted the experience as divine instruction to let the people decide whether to form a new organization to take the NAACP's place.[46]

Later that morning Shuttlesworth feverishly called Shores, who remained cautious, and Robey, who grew excited, along with several preacher friends who had worked with him on the police petitions the previous year. Before noon the ministers met at Shuttlesworth's home, where he told them of his experience and his decision to call a mass meeting. Oblivious to Fred's warning of the possibility of jail, his colleagues assured him of their support. They began the initial planning for a proposed organization and scheduled a larger planning meeting for Monday afternoon, which was to be followed by the mass meeting on Tuesday night. They then dispersed to finish preparations for their Sunday services, promising to spread the word to other ministers and congregations. Over the weekend, as the news spread, some of the older ministers worried that the younger breed might act hastily. The Reverend Luke Beard, pastor of one of the largest African American congregations in Birmingham, the Sixteenth Street Baptist Church, called Shuttlesworth, raised objections to any action in the face of the court's injunction, and told him, "The Lord told me to tell you to call the meeting off." Shuttlesworth accepted the older minister's counsel politely but had no intention of changing his plans. When Beard called a second time, this time saying, "Seriously, the Lord wants you to call it off," a nettled Fred responded more sharply. "Well, Doctor, now when did the Lord start sending my messages through you? You go back and tell the Lord that I think he told me to call it *on,* and the only way I'll call it off is if he comes down and tells me himself. And tell him to be sure to have the identifying marks of the nails in his hands and spear marks in his side! Otherwise, I ain't gon' call it off."[47]

The next day, following announcements from many of the city's black pulpits, the *Birmingham World* carried a front-page notice of an areawide "Citizens Mass Meeting" set for that Tuesday evening at the Sardis Baptist Church. The paper announced that the emergency meeting would seek "a way to continue the freedom fight in Alabama." While black Birmingham excitedly read the paper and debated whether to attend the mass meeting, Shuttlesworth and his colleagues met at the Smith and Gaston Funeral Home to hammer out plans for the new organization. The session included, in addition to Shuttlesworth, the Reverends Nelson H. Smith Jr., T. L. Lane, Edward Gardner, Herman Stone, C. H. George, and G. E. Pruitt, along with Lucinda B. Robey and several other laypersons. With Shuttlesworth presiding, the committee discussed a set of "Principles and Resolutions" to be presented at the mass meeting. The planners reinforced their own convictions that some new, more activist organization must replace the NAACP and that current groups such as the Jefferson County Betterment Association or the Baptist Ministers Conference were too cautious to push for progress. A consensus had already begun developing among this group that, as Gardner later said, "some action had to be taken and somebody had to go to jail, and they [the older groups] wasn't willing to go that far." He further explained: "The ministers in the Jefferson County Betterment at that time were senior men. Some of them [were] sixty, seventy years old, and they just wasn't willing to venture out. So it took energetic young men who were willing to go to jail. They weren't willing to do that, and they told us they weren't willing to do that. They were gon' call a meeting with the city fathers and try to work out something. But we saw that it was impossible at that time. They [the white officials] wouldn't meet with you." The younger group saw the necessary willingness to "venture out" and "go to jail" embodied in the pastor of Bethel, who by consensus became the leader of the group.[48]

Next the planners addressed the question of a name for the new organization. Shuttlesworth immediately suggested that it be called a movement to distinguish it from the NAACP. The distinction led Shuttlesworth to one of his most oft-repeated and powerful rationales for the new organization: "They can outlaw an organization, but they can't outlaw the movement of a people determined to be free." In addition, Fred insisted that they include the word "Christian" in the name. A natural choice for a group dominated by black Baptist ministers, the term also countered the expected accusations of being a Communist or subversive group. Specifically, Shuttlesworth argued that the organization "should be Christian in all respects, that all our actions, thoughts and deeds would be first, foremost, and always Christian." He finally suggested an emphasis on human rights: "We believe that any 'FIRST RIGHTS' is 'HUMAN RIGHTS.'" Shuttlesworth actually saw little difference between these and civil rights and wasted little time making the distinction, other than to believe his fight was for whites as well as blacks. Then came the suggestion that the name should refer to the entire state of Alabama. Later, some blacks disenchanted with Shuttlesworth would occasionally take this statewide designation as a sign of his delusions of grandeur and overinflated ego. In reality, this idea came from the Reverend R. L. Alford, the pastor of the Sardis Baptist Church, in part because of his expectation that their work would eventually move beyond the local situation in Birmingham, but more directly because the injunction against the NAACP encompassed the entire state. At that point, Alford proposed to call the organization the Alabama Christian Movement for Human Rights (ACMHR), and the motion carried.[49]

Out of their discussions emerged several concerns that eventually became parts of the ACMHR's "Declaration of Principles." They first declared their determination to "press forward for freedom and Democracy and the removal from our society of ANY forms of Second Class Citizenship." Next, as the principal writer of the declaration, Shuttlesworth addressed the question of "outside agitation," noting that the statement represented not "the will or sentiments of outsiders, but our own convictions and will to be free." He further promised to remain "sober, firm, peaceful, and resolute, within the framework of goodwill" and not to "become rabble-rousers." Next, the statement expressed faith in the American court system but noted a significant paradox: Alabama segregationists obeying the ruling of a single state circuit court judge while the unanimous ruling of nine Supreme Court justices was "Openly Flaunted, Disregarded, and Totally Ignored." Acknowledging belief in states' rights but calling for the priority of human rights, Shuttlesworth endorsed federal desegregation rulings and registered the ACMHR's hope for compliance without further litigation. The statement applauded other efforts pressing forward, especially the ongoing bus boycotts in Montgomery and Tallahassee, which had begun the same day as Jones's injunction. Rejecting "vacillation, procrastination, or evasion," Shuttlesworth also denounced "gradualism," declaring, "We want a beginning NOW! WE HAVE ALREADY WAITED 100 YEARS!" Finally, the declaration affirmed: "We Negroes shall never become enemies of the white people. We are all Americans, but Americans born in the struggle for Freedom from Tyranny and Oppression. We shall never bomb any homes or lynch any persons, but we must, because of history and the future, march to complete freedom—with unbowed heads, praying hearts, and an unyielding determination. And we seek guidance from our Heavenly Father and from all men of goodwill and under-standing."[50]

By the end of the meeting the group had approved these principles and de-cided to present them as resolutions at the upcoming mass meeting. The par-ticipants adjourned the meeting and excitedly fanned out into the African American community to drum up strong attendance at the next evening's big event. They did not, however, bear the full responsibility for publicity. Birming-ham radio and television stations announced the meeting, giving the name and address of the leader. About these media announcements, Shuttlesworth sar-donically quipped, "That's the city telling the Klan where to put the bomb."[51]

On Tuesday evening, June 5, by the time the ministerial conveners arrived at the Sardis Baptist Church near the center of Birmingham's black community, a large crowd had gathered, with a palpable air of expectancy. The attractive sanc-tuary seated a capacity of 850 worshippers, and on this night many participants stood in the aisles, in the rear of the auditorium, in the church foyer, and out into the parking area. The pastor estimated an attendance of around one thou-sand participants who spiritedly awaited the leaders. The proceedings com-menced with a fervent "devotional" period borrowed from a typical southern black worship service. For Shuttlesworth the blending of civil rights preaching and church service was consistent with "the religion of Jesus Christ," which, he later wrote, "encompasses . . . freedom, both of body and soul." Thus, a pastor led in chanted prayers and traditional church hymns, building a corporate esprit that had the congregation throbbing with expectancy. A further wave of excite-ment swept through the congregation as the conveners moved in solemn pro-cession to their positions on the dais.[52]

At a moment of high drama, the lean, 160-pound, mustachioed preacher stepped to the pulpit to move the congregation to an emotional zenith with an address part sermon and part stump speech, part prepared text and part im-promptu comment. Shuttlesworth began slowly and somewhat disingenuously, claiming that their new organization had no connection with the recently out-lawed NAACP. Of course, it *was* connected causally, if not legally. "The Citizens' Council won't like this," he jovially affirmed, "but then I don't like a lot of things they do." Warming spiritually to the congregation's responsiveness and physi-cally to the sanctuary's eighty-eight degree temperature, the preacher modu-lated his voice dramatically, wiped his perspiring face with a handkerchief, and called out, "Our citizens are restive under the dismal yoke of segregation. Aren't you?" "Yes, yes," came the rhythmic response. "These are the days when men would like to kill hope," he continued, "when men in Mississippi can be declared 'not guilty' of murder, when men can be shot down on the steps of the courthouse. These are dark days. But hope is not dead. Hope is alive here tonight." After an interruption of prolonged applause, he went on: "We seek nothing which we would deny others. Would you be willing tonight for a white man to sit down beside you?" When the people shouted their assent, he concluded, "Then you believe in integration! The Negro citizens of Birmingham are crying for leadership to better their condition. The only thing we are interested in is uniting our people in seeing that the laws of our land are upheld according to the Constitution of the United States. . . . The action of the Attorney General makes it more necessary that Negroes come together in their own interests and plan together for the furtherance of their cause." He then called on the ministers of the city, both black and white, "to provide the positive leadership" and "start preaching the truth from their pulpits." Moving to a powerful climax, he called on the people to support the new organization despite the efforts of "the enemies of freedom to kill our hopes and keep us from fighting. But they cannot outlaw us all. I think a lot of Negroes are ready to go to jail in order to help get their rights, if such a procedure is necessary. But if anybody gets arrested, it'll be me; if anybody goes to jail, it'll be me; if anybody suffers, it'll be me; if anybody gets killed, it'll be me."[53]

After thunderous applause and a chorus of "Amens," Fred introduced Nelson H. Smith Jr., the pastor of the New Pilgrim Baptist Church in Birmingham. With a deep bass voice and slower-paced delivery, Smith read the new organization's "Declaration of Principles" to the congregation. Cheers and more "Amens" rang out as the congregation pledged to sweep away "any forms of second-class citizenship," and a thunderous ovation broke out with the ringing affirmation, "We want a beginning now. We have already waited 100 years!" When Smith concluded his presentation, Shuttlesworth once more took the podium to moderate the discussions and the vote. Only two dissenting voices were raised. Reverends G. W. McMurray and M. W. Witt argued that there were already enough organizations in Birmingham, warning, "We should think sanely of what we are doing." With the crowd trying to shout them down, Shuttlesworth silenced the audience, allowing the older ministers three minutes to speak their minds. Responding that previous leadership had been too slow and unwilling to push forward faster, Shuttlesworth finally put the matter to a vote. The decision was virtually unanimous. For good measure Shuttlesworth reminded the congregation of the potential dangers of their decision and took two additional votes, each with the same results. The crowd then elected Shuttlesworth as president of the new organization by acclamation, with Alford as first vice president, F. Ellis Bell, a local chiropractor, as second vice president, N. H. Smith as secretary, and William E. Shortridge, a prominent business leader, as treasurer. As the meeting moved toward its conclusion, Shuttlesworth buoyantly assured the congregation that the state may have gotten "the goose that laid the golden egg," as one Alabama legislator had called the NAACP, adding, "but I'm not sure that some of the eggs she laid before [they] got her won't hatch out." He called on the people to be prepared to support the new organization with financial gifts and with continued attendance at weekly mass meetings, warning them once more: "This is not the time for Uncle Toms."[54]

The excitement of the evening was not lost on the home front. Some of the older members of Bethel harbored misgivings about these new activities of their pastor, but a good percentage supported his efforts from the start. One member later estimated that probably 20 percent of the active membership (generally between 200 and 250 people) regularly attended mass meetings of the ACMHR. Shuttlesworth himself more conservatively estimated that he could always expect to see fifteen to twenty of his parishioners at the Monday night meetings. Such a level of support seems high in the context of typical percentages of lay response to any church program. Churches rarely see more than half their members in worship services on any given Sunday, with half of that in Sunday school and half of that in evening services. Monday night mass meetings, held after long days of work and lasting past 9:00 P.M., required high levels of commitment by laypersons even if no one had sensed danger in that particular activity. Thus, for Shuttlesworth to garner between 10 and 20 percent of his church membership in the movement suggested strong support. Indeed, many more supported the ACMHR with financial contributions even when they could not or chose not to attend the mass meetings. Beyond this, in Sunday-to-Sunday conversations they often encouraged him in his efforts. Bethel began with a sense of excitement about their pastor's growing importance in the larger community. The members felt pride in his leadership and accomplishments, believing his activities raised the profile of their church and thus aided its institutional health.[55]

Within the parsonage the Shuttlesworths were still settling into their roles as Bethel's "first family." Ruby enjoyed being back in Birmingham, near her aunt and uncle, who could occasionally care for the children. She participated in community activities as a teacher, but at church she periodically bristled at the "goldfish-bowl" existence of a pastor's family—what she considered the unreasonable expectations and intense scrutiny of the members. Fred, however, accepted traditional roles for men and women and maintained for his family a particularly hard-line approach to what he considered the responsibilities of faith. Believing that a pastor and his family must set an example for the other members of a congregation, Shuttlesworth, like his mother, insisted that his wife and children meet their churchly obligations without fail. For Fred illness alone served as an acceptable excuse for his family not being in their appointed places come church time. On one occasion, after Fred had organized a new choir at Bethel, he expected Ruby to participate in it despite her objections. Concerned that his wife set an example, he told her, "Other folks are supposed to be [in the choir]; you're supposed to be too." His concern that his wife fit the traditional role of pastor's wife coincided with his insistence that she keep up what he viewed as her womanly duties. Ruby's inattention to the housekeeping chores, for example, became a frequent source of irritation to Fred. Because the family lived in a church parsonage, he believed the house needed to be well kept as a matter of pastoral propriety. He did not feel particularly intimidated by the members' expectations of himself or his family, but he largely shared these "principles" and pressed them as vigorously on Ruby and the children as he did on his church folk. That Ruby did not share his solicitude on such matters had begun to create significant clashes between them, particularly when Fred's civil rights activities began to bring more external pressure to bear on their home. Flushed with the activity and excitement of giving birth to a new organization that seemed divinely inspired and destined to bring down Jim Crow laws in Birmingham, however, Fred and Ruby for the time disregarded their own domestic tensions.[56]

Indeed, few disregarded the actions of the ACMHR either inside or outside the black community of Birmingham. Those attending the founding of the ACMHR passed the word, inviting others to a second mass meeting at Sardis on the following Friday night (June 8). That night Shuttlesworth and a steering committee appointed some twenty-nine members to serve on the Education, Recreation, Finance, Hospitality, Transportation, and Youth Committees. The committees were dominated by black Baptist clergy and other males, but they did have nine women, including Ruby Shuttlesworth, Lucinda Robey, and the wife of black millionaire A. G. Gaston. The Reverends J. L. Ware and George MacMurray, who had originally been suspicious of Shuttlesworth and later parted company with him, also served on ACMHR committees. Also paying more attention to the goings-on in Birmingham was FBI headquarters in Washington, D.C., which alerted the bureau's special agent in charge of Birmingham about the new organization. Sending a photostatic copy of a June 7 article from the *Washington Post and Times Herald*, FBI director J. Edgar Hoover told the Birmingham office, "In view of the tense racial situation existing at this time, you are instructed to be alert for any activities of the captioned organization of interest to the Bureau and other Government intelligence agencies. Any pertinent information developed by your office in connection with this matter must be furnished to the Bureau without delay."[57]

Encouraged by the strong community support, Shuttlesworth quickly picked up where the civic leagues and the IMA had left off. In early July he led an ACMHR delegation back to city hall to appeal once more for the hiring of black police officers, only to be rejected with the familiar replies. Unperturbed by this rebuff, he took a cue from Montgomery and began to press for the end of segregated seating on Birmingham buses. On June 4 a federal court panel, following the logic of *Brown* (which had pertained only to education), had ruled bus segregation in Montgomery invalid. Within a month of ACMHR's founding, Shuttlesworth began to apply the federal ruling to Birmingham. On July 7, Shuttlesworth, N. H. Smith, and C. H. George wrote to the president of the Birmingham Transit Company requesting the removal of segregation signs and the establishment of a "first come, first served" seating policy on buses. In addition, they sought the hiring of black drivers for buses and a conference with the company's board of directors within thirty days. Shuttlesworth reasoned that "when Human Relations are in the process of reappraisal and adjustment," true leaders were obligated to find "areas in which these adjustments can be brought about in the spirit of decency, fair play, and Goodwill." Such actions, he pointed out, would "cement the ties of Goodwill, and keep the process of change evolutionary rather than revolutionary." Transit company president D. S. James ignored the request, and three days later Mayor Morgan publicly rejected any arrangements other than the current city ordinances. He acknowledged the ACMHR request to the transit company, but indicated that the matter could not be taken up without a similar request addressed specifically to the city commission. Interpreting Shuttlesworth's thirty-day time frame as a hint of a Montgomery-style boycott, Morgan further warned: "I do not think our colored people here are going to unite in anything of that type which would bring further bad publicity to our city. Our facilities here are good. Everything that could be done has been done. One thing for sure, we are going to enforce the law and no good can come from any attempt to thwart the law." Shuttlesworth hoped a boycott could be avoided, but warned that Birmingham blacks would support such a measure as vigorously as had the black community of Montgomery. He assured officials, "It is not our purpose to bulldoze. We will use a boycott only as a last resort." With optimism, he added, "We feel that in the light of changing conditions the city will do something to show us that they have good will." In addition, he sent to the city commissioners a copy of his earlier letter to the transit company and requested a public notice of their views on the hiring of black bus drivers and the June 4 federal court ruling.[58]

Receiving no reply from the transit company, Shuttlesworth wrote another letter to the city commission on July 16, 1956, requesting again their policies on the matters at hand. In particular, he asked whether a Supreme Court concurrence with the federal ruling of June 4 would cause the commission immediately to apply that decision to Birmingham. After ten more days of silence from both the transit company and the city commission, ACMHR leaders sent still another letter, again asking their views on the crucial issues. Insisting that enough time had passed for a good-faith response, Shuttlesworth accused the commission of "a form of oppression and suppression of equal protection of the laws of the land under the Constitution of the United States." He continued: "It is hard for us to believe that leaders would deliberately ignore or refuse to consider the request of almost half the population which they lead, yet Negroes are expected and indeed called upon to support with their taxes, finance, and their loyalty the economic and moral structure of this city. Not only do we believe that taxation without representation is unfair, but we also firmly believe that continued taxation without consideration is equally unfair and unjust. . . . Know sirs, that we are deeply concerned about receiving a more just and equitable share of this city's economy both in better jobs and better opportunities. This would bring the better relations, and help to keep down the 'bad publicity' of which you spoke." Finally, he wondered how long the commission would take the important matter of black police "under advisement" and registered the hope that the city would "soon act on these matters and help Birmingham to take at long last its rightful place with other enlightened cities on the matter of progressive steps forward in the area of Race Relations." By Friday, August 3, after almost a month of public needling, Shuttlesworth managed to wrest an unproductive meeting with James, but received only continued silence from the city commissioners.[59]

Although he hoped the leaders of Birmingham might relent before the inevitable rulings of the Supreme Court, Fred had grown very skeptical of whites' "will to justice." He believed that segregationists' idea of goodwill typically had in mind "a paternal relationship between whites and Negroes (a father and children fixation) where the Negro is inferior and the white is superior." An authentic goodwill based on equality seemed to him nonexistent in Birmingham, and unfolding events during the next few months would do little to alter his opinion. Invigorated by a movement he believed to be destined for ultimate success, Fred proceeded with abandon. At mass meetings Shuttlesworth and his officers had regularly told their followers, "We're gon' be policemen. We're gon' be everything in the city eventually." In this frame of mind, as opportunity arose, Shuttlesworth exploited any possible area in which to challenge the caste system of Birmingham. A few days after the ACMHR filed for legal incorporation with the Jefferson County Probate Court, Shuttlesworth discovered two possible candidates to challenge the city's racial restrictions in civil service jobs. He warned willing volunteers George Johnson and Clyde Jones of the dangers of pressing for employment as police officers. Their resolve unwavering, on August 20 they applied to the city personnel board to take the requisite examinations for police jobs. Accompanied by Shuttlesworth and the Reverend George Rudolph, the applicants were summarily turned away by the director of personnel, Ray Mullins, on the basis of a Whites Only policy. Entering the fray, Fred told Mullins, "We feel that if our people have the qualifications, then this office should recognize them as applicants for the job." Mullins in turn said that his hands were tied and referred them to the city commission. Undeterred, Johnson and Jones each submitted his application along with the $1.50 fee. When Mullins again refused them, Shuttlesworth assailed the policy as discriminatory and accused Mullins of passing the buck. He added, as his lawyers had informed him, that the Whites Only regulation was not a law but merely an agreement between the city commission and the personnel board. He also advised the men to file suit against the board, advice that was quickly acted on by Clyde Jones.[60]

The next day Jones was fired from his job at the Birmingham plant of the Englander Company, a munitions manufacturer headquartered in Chicago. Reporting for work, he was informed that he had been fired for "extra-curricular activities." Later, Englander general manager R. E. Bishop claimed Jones was released for absenteeism. Shuttlesworth again became involved, arguing that Jones had rather been dismissed for attempting to better his economic condition by applying for a police job. He wrote to Englander offices in Chicago on Jones's behalf, calling on the company to investigate the action for possible discrimination, which he argued would violate "terms of government contracts which call for no discrimination." In addition, he threatened, exaggeratedly, to carry the fight "all the way to the White House, if necessary." Shuttlesworth and ACMHR legal advisors never pursued this strategy, however, focusing instead on challenging the Whites Only policy. By mid-October the two applicants had filed suit in the Jefferson County Chancery Court of Judge William A. Jenkins. Asking for $25,000 in damages for "irreparable injury," they argued that such a policy violated the Fourteenth Amendment and denied them "equal protection of the law, solely because of their race or color." Eventually, in response to the suit, personnel officials secretly removed the White Only restriction from their applications. Jones, however, was never rehired.[61]

Flushed with this first, if relatively private, victory, in early November Shuttlesworth enjoyed more community adulation when the Alpha Phi chapter of Omega Psi Phi fraternity named him "Birmingham's Citizen of the Year." In announcing Fred's award, *Birmingham World* editor Emory Jackson recognized his work as having begun before the founding of the ACMHR and praised Shuttlesworth for inspiring more ministers to stand up and speak out in advancing African Americans toward the "blessings and promises of democracy." Jackson noted that Shuttlesworth had proven false the widely circulated segregationist charges of outside agitation and that the ACMHR had "a wider and more devoted following than . . . any other civil rights organization in the city." Within a fortnight, Martin Luther King would receive the same award for his work in Montgomery, almost simultaneously with the Supreme Court's ruling upholding the June 4 federal court decision striking down segregated bus seating. Rendered by the high court on November 13, the ruling would take effect some five weeks later. This decision ultimately made the Montgomery bus boycott successful and once again catapulted Shuttlesworth and the ACMHR into action in Birmingham.[62]

While waiting for federal marshals to serve the Supreme Court's mandate on city officials, the MIA sponsored a week-long Institute on Nonviolence and Social Change designed to export its methods to the rest of the South. Fred and some of his ACMHR followers attended the December 3–9 conference. Also attending were Joseph Lowery of Mobile, Alabama; C. K. Steele of Tallahassee, Florida; T. J. Jemison of Baton Rouge, Louisiana; and other leaders of national reputation. Held at the Holt Street Church and other Baptist churches in Montgomery, the institute was scheduled as a celebration of the boycott's first anniversary and had as its theme "Gandhi in America." Attending the meeting gave Shuttlesworth the opportunity to learn from and contribute to workshops in subjects such as black voter registration, voting, transportation, and education. In addition, he developed a contact with the Reverend Glenn E. Smiley, field secretary of the Fellowship of Reconciliation (FOR), an organization for social change that had begun as a pacifist response to World War I. Since the third month of the Montgomery protests, Smiley had instructed MIA leaders in the principles of Gandhian nonviolence. He continued that role at the institute, lecturing and leading discussions in five seminar sessions during the course of the week. In addition, he moderated a Tuesday evening (December 4) discussion during which Shuttlesworth joined Steele, Jemison, and Montgomery pastor B. D. Lambert in a forum titled "Nonviolence in Social Change." In his talk Shuttlesworth discussed the difficulties of working for social change in Alabama, "the heart of Dixie," and credited the Montgomery movement with giving "Dixie a heart." He drew a resounding response when he told Montgomery blacks that "because of you, instead of burning crosses, we shall bear our crosses; instead of throwing bombs, we'll throw truth. You have taught us that our greatest contribution must be to bring social change without violence. . . . In the cradle of the Confederacy is the true baby of love that will grow to be a man of the hour." To the crowd of nearly one thousand persons, he stressed the importance of voting, told about ACMHR's suits regarding black civil service jobs, and hinted that Birmingham would likely be the next Alabama city to experience a bus boycott.[63]

In answer to a question the speakers scored white ministers for dragging their feet on the issue of racial justice. Jemison noted that "only two white preachers that I know of have spoken out against segregation," explaining further that "white preachers think of security first and their jobs [their prophetic responsibilities] second." Lambert made a telling comparison: "White preachers' sentiments are made for him by his congregation, while the Negro preacher makes the sentiment for his congregation." Although Shuttlesworth added little to this particular exchange, he shared this assessment of the white clergy and later had many opportunities to express it. On one rare occasion when he had contact with white ministers in Birmingham, one cleric confessed to him that if he preached the truth on matters of race, "I wouldn't have a pulpit to preach in." Shuttlesworth then challenged him, "I'd preach it one time and see if God could give me another one!" Having followed his own counsel in Selma, Fred believed he had credentials for expecting similar courage from fellow ministers. Events in Birmingham would soon give him even greater standing for calling ministers to preach without regard for their security.[64]

On Thursday, December 20, as the writs of injunction were delivered in Montgomery, Shuttlesworth and N. H. Smith awaited word at Birmingham station WAPI-TV. When the expected news came over the wire, Fred grew confident that the Klan would be moving in force to intimidate African Americans off the buses in Montgomery. Thus, in order to take the heat off integration forces in the capital city, Fred decided to press the issue in Birmingham immediately. He sent a telegram to the city commission indicating that the ACMHR now viewed as null and void all laws or policies throughout the state that allowed segregated seating on buses. He also requested that bus seating be desegregated by December 26. Such an action, he averred, would convince African Americans that "Birmingham is in line with the truly democratic process and shall insure that we are truly becoming a brotherhood." Nevertheless, he warned that on the day after Christmas African Americans would ride the buses in an unsegregated manner regardless of the commission's decision. "If there is any interference with the Negroes riding the buses unsegregated," he warned, "we will take whatever action is necessary." He also wrote to the U.S. Civil Rights Commission that "the clear alternative to litigation, then, can only be . . . the relinquishing by officials . . . of the laws and proscriptions which have made and would forever make and keep Negroes in an inferior and subservient status." In a longer letter to transit company president D. S. James, sent the same day, Shuttlesworth and Smith argued that in light of the Supreme Court's Montgomery ruling the continuance of bus segregation would be "in open and flagrant violation" of the Constitution. They urged the company to "remove immediately all discriminating signs on your buses and announce the policy of seating passengers on a first come, first served basis." They added: "There is no better time to do this than now, this Christmas season, in which all hearts are joined in acts and prayer of goodwill, and in giving homage to the Prince of Peace and Fellowship." Offering to meet with James on the issues of desegregated seating and the hiring of black drivers, Shuttlesworth concluded the letter and moved on to await the officials' decisions and prepare his followers for action.[65]

For the next few days emotions ran high as the city commission and the transit company made no comment, pending a "study" of the ACMHR's requests. Segregationist leaders in Birmingham had hoped in vain that the courts would rule in their favor or that the black community would be frightened away from disobeying segregation ordinances by the city's reputation for violence. Wishing to maintain the city's fragile racial "peace," the *Birmingham News* opined: "It would be helpful . . . if action were not pressed at this time to end bus segregation at once here in Birmingham. But apparently action to that end is going to be pressed." The editors encouraged the maintenance of segregated seating for as long as possible. In contrast to the major white newspaper, the *Birmingham World* argued, "No leader . . . who counsels a wait-and-waive philosophy can expect any following in this city" and called for city hall to face the reality of the new order and to exhibit moral courage in support of equality. At this point, Shuttlesworth's attention was temporarily diverted by a household accident. As his daughter Pat tended to her morning responsibility of lighting the family's gas heater, her flannel gown caught fire. In a state of panic, Ruby tried without success to put out the flames by throwing her own gown over the fire. A quick-thinking Fred rolled up Pat in a blanket and patted out the flames, singeing his hands in the process. Ruby and some neighbors then took her to Hillman Hospital, where she remained for several weeks. In the wake of the fire and Pat's severe injury, Shuttlesworth kept a wary eye on the larger events in Birmingham. Along with planning Christmas services at church, he continued attending to movement matters. On Sunday, December 23, gunfire blasted the home of Martin Luther King in Montgomery. That same day, as Shuttlesworth anticipated a rejection of his requests at the city commission's meeting set for the day after Christmas, he reiterated to reporters that blacks would "probably" sit in the "white" sections of buses on Thursday, December 27. The first arrests of blacks for "riding desegregated," he promised, would signal the beginning of the ACMHR's legal battle to have the Jim Crow policies removed.[66]

Christmas Eve 1956 fell on a Monday night—movement night. Never inclined to cancel previously scheduled meetings, Fred went ahead with plans for the Monday night mass meeting. The projected efforts by the ACMHR departed from earlier efforts that sought change by petition or formal request. Now ministers publicly encouraged defiance of Jim Crow ordinances despite the likelihood of arrests. So on Christmas Eve, caught up in the fervor of confrontation, some fifteen hundred persons crowded into the New Hope Baptist Church to hear the latest plans. Shuttlesworth assured them that the strategy remained in force, pending the decision of the city commission. In the meantime, he preached to them again that all actions by the ACMHR would be conducted according to the principles of nonviolence. In the event of any incident, he urged them "to be courteous and not to strike back." The next day, the families of

Bethel attended services at the church, hearing their pastor preach a Christmas sermon sprinkled with unusual references to the upcoming action against Jim Crow laws. In addition, he told the congregation that he expected "a stick of dynamite to go off any day" but that he was prepared to die, if necessary, to achieve integration.[67]

After services, Fred and the family visited Pat at the hospital and later returned to spend a quiet afternoon together at home. That evening one of the Bethel deacons, Charlie Robinson, and his wife, Naomi, paid the pastor and his family a visit. The women and the Shuttlesworth girls, Ricky and Carolyn, watched television in the den while Fred Jr., still dressed in the red football uniform he had received for Christmas, played in the dining room in the center of the parsonage. Pastor Shuttlesworth and his deacon went to the front bedroom for important "man's talk." Dressed in his pajamas and stretched out on his bed with his head leaning against the headboard, Fred conversed with Robinson about the events of the upcoming day. About 9:40 P.M., from the front of the house, Ricky heard a noise that sounded like a newspaper being thrown on the porch. Seconds later, a thunderous explosion strong enough to break windows across the street and down Twenty-ninth Avenue interrupted the quiet conversations in the Bethel parsonage. As the blast knocked out the lights, Fred Jr. immediately smelled and felt dust in his nostrils, with fear descending on him only a few seconds later. He began to stutter as he called out to his family, trying to find them in the dark. Later estimates suggested that between six and sixteen sticks of dynamite had been tossed from a vehicle, landing just under the front northeast corner of the parsonage. The bomb apparently came to rest directly beneath the bedroom where Shuttlesworth lay. The blast caved in the front porch, brought down the roof on the front part of the wooden-frame house, dug a crater in the yard, and blew the supporting pillars fifteen feet into the street. Breaking virtually all the windows in the house, the blast ripped a large hole in the outside wall of the children's bedroom, directly behind the front bedroom.[68]

Inside Fred's bedroom, the blast shot fire out from under his bed before splintering the floor beneath him and demolishing the wall behind his bed. The mattress flew out from under Shuttlesworth and served as a cushion from the mass of flying timber. Physically, he escaped with only a slight bump on the head, but spiritually something irreversible had happened to him. In the milliseconds after the blast, as he instinctively threw his hands in front of his face to protect himself from the falling debris, he instantaneously "knew" the divine meaning of the event. Describing an immediate experience of understanding, sometimes called a "noetic experience," he later testified: "I understood in a moment that I wouldn't get hurt." Without an audible sound, Fred "heard" the words of Scripture, "Underneath [you] are the everlasting arms" (Deut. 33:27). He immediately intuited "that the words were factual" and that God's presence would protect him from harm. Describing the experience later, he said that "you can know something in a second that you never read in a book nor ever will. You can feel something in a second that will be with you the rest of your life." He also instantly connected his survival with his participation in the civil rights struggle: "I knew in a second, [a] split second, that the only reason God saved me was to lead the fight." He told reporters that night that surviving the explosion strengthened his belief that God had called, even destined, him to be a leader in the civil rights movement: "I know it was the hand of God. I know I was preserved for a purpose: to preach the gospel of Jesus Christ and to implement that gospel insofar as possible as it relates to human dignity and human rights."[69]

In evangelical fashion, Shuttlesworth interpreted his survival and his religious experience in the midst of the blast as a divine miracle. Reflecting an indigenous black theology, Shuttlesworth interpreted the event as indicative of God's providential work in history. African American religion understands God's providence as working through the human experience of struggle against the forces of oppression, as James H. Evans notes, "to accomplish something in spite of resistance." Interpreting the bomb experience in this light, Shuttlesworth later described the civil rights fight as "a righteous program between the forces of good and evil, and I am both led and impelled by the Divine Force to take an active part. I feel that I was destined to play this role." Shuttlesworth articulated this theology in a down-to-earth fashion typical of African American religion—through Old Testament stories. In a later conversation with Fred, Martin Luther King offered the opinion that if surviving the bomb "wasn't God making himself plain, there's no way he can." With simple but powerful eloquence, Shuttlesworth harked back to scriptural passages of deliverance long cherished by African American Christians: "Well, God just brought the Bible up to date. You don't have to go back to Daniel in the lion's den or the boys in the fiery furnace."[70]

Police officers arrived simultaneously with Shuttlesworth's neighbors James Revis and Mack Roberson, even before Shuttlesworth and the others had extricated themselves from the wreckage. As a crowd of neighbors rushed toward the house to check on the family's welfare, an officer stopped them, advising them to stay clear of what was left of the house. Seeing electrical wires flashing and smelling the odor of gunpowder, Revis demanded to check the rubble, saying, "Officer, if you're not going in . . . , that's my pastor in there, and if you'll get out of the way, I'm going in." Another bombing in the black community had emotions running high, and many persons arrived at the bomb scene angry and carrying shotguns and pistols. Some of the officers spoke harshly to people as they arrived on the scene, and some feared a pitched battle might break out between black citizens and white officers. One officer then tentatively entered the house to inspect the damage and look for survivors. He encountered Shuttlesworth, who by then had determined that his family and visitors were not seriously hurt. As Shuttlesworth looked for his pants and topcoat, the officer, shaken by the destruction around him, ventured to advise the now homeless minister. "I didn't think they would go this far," he began. "I know these people. Reverend, if I were you, I'd get out of town as fast I could." Drawing him up short, Shuttlesworth quickly replied, "Officer, you are not me. You see God saving me through all this. So you go back and tell your Klan brethren that if God could keep me through all this, then I'm here for the duration."[71]

After the officer led him by flashlight out through the debris, Fred addressed a crowd of an estimated fifteen hundred persons who had gathered in the streets. "The Lord has protected me," he announced to them. "I'm not injured!" Amazed that his minister had survived virtually without a scratch, young James Roberson marveled further as he heard Shuttlesworth, with a demolished home as his backdrop, direct a sermon on nonviolence to the crowd: "Put those guns up. That's not what we are about. We are going to love our enemies. Go home and put the guns away." He then singled out a man carrying a shotgun and commanded those near him, "Take him home. Get him out of here. He's got a gun. We don't need that. We're not going to be violent. We don't want that. This is not going to turn us around." Finally, he assured the bystanders that the bomb had only poured gasoline on the fire of protest in him and that plans to ride the buses had not changed. "We intend to ride the buses. There is no one who can keep us from it, for God will protect us." He told them the ACMHR executive board would meet after the city commission made its decision the next day and that mass meetings were planned for the next night. Unless the commission acted to rescind the segregated seating ordinances, he promised, black Birminghamians would stage the largest "voluntary" integration attempt in history.[72]

The movement would wait for the following day. On that night, however, the people of Bethel Baptist Church hushed into a holy silence akin to that experienced by Jews during the "Days of Awe"—the High Holy Days that follow Rosh Hashanah. Of Bethel's "night of awe," church member Veronica Chappell Flemmon later commented: "If we could have seen Christ walk on water, . . . we could not have been any more reverent than we were when we saw Shuttlesworth come out of the house." The crowd had collectively experienced the "tremendous and fascinating mystery" that scholar Rudolf Otto believed to be the definition of religion. For them it was an experience of the holy that simultaneously attracted and repelled—attracted by the miraculous and repelled by the danger. James Roberson, who followed his father into the rubble of the bombed parsonage, witnessed a rafter that had been blown through what remained of the minister's bed. That Shuttlesworth had been blown out of his bed had actually saved his life. What young Roberson observed that night confirmed his belief that God had protected his pastor and bestowed on him an extraordinary status. He later marveled: "Think about it. The police said eight to eighteen sticks of dynamite went off within three feet of this man's head. He's not deaf, he's not blind, he's not crippled, he's not bleeding. That really made me think he had to be God-sent." When Charlie Robinson himself emerged from the rubble, he told Fred, "Reverend, I'd have been dead, but God saved me because I was with you." When the crowd viewed the parsonage, they saw a symbol of their own lives in Birmingham. Civil rights activist C. T. Vivian later explained that this was the kind of house they lived in every day, a house where everything could be torn loose. But, just as Fred had called this experience God's updating of the Bible, to the people of Bethel and black Birmingham "it was David and Goliath. It was all the Bible stories wrapped up in one." As the people hugged each one who slowly emerged from the house and shed their joyful tears, someone noticed that the night had served up one more ironic "miracle"—the Christmas tree still shining in the center of a parsonage that lay in ruins.[73]

If the bomb led some church members to question the wisdom of having an activist pastor, they were drowned out by the voices of those who saw the divine protection of the pastor as a miracle. Already captivated by Shuttlesworth's charisma and pastoral leadership, they now believed they saw on him God's stamp of approval. As a result, according to Daisy Winston, this event "cemented the church members' attitudes *toward* what Reverend Shuttlesworth was doing." The first Sunday after the bombing, Fred took the pulse of the congregation on the matter of his continuing as their minister. Acknowledging the damage to both the parsonage and the church building itself (which lay only a foot or two from the house), he reiterated his view that "God was there, and I didn't get a scratch. He saved me to lead the movement. That is exactly what I am going to do. Like David, I will run toward the giant; I won't be running from it." Warning them that the church would likely be bombed again and that someone could be killed, he reminded them that it was "the Lord's church that got bombed; not yours, not mine." Finally putting to them the crucial question, he said: "If anybody feels that you want me not to be here at the church, then you can speak now. You have a right as a congregation to say something, 'cause if I stay here, it's gon' get worse. But I am telling you now, I will not take that. I will go further. I will be more challenging, more daring. I am going to preach the social implications of the Gospel, and if you think in the least that I am the wrong person [to be pastor], you say it now." Echoing the sentiments of virtually the entire congregation, one woman shouted out, "G-o-d, don't you leave here! No, don't you leave us now." The others agreed, saying "No, you got to stay here and lead us." The pastor, flushed with excitement over this vote of confidence, replied, "Then you're committing yourselves to going on, full speed ahead, for civil rights."[74]

For the residents of Twenty-ninth Avenue and the people of Bethel, the "night of awe" ended with the practical matters of picking up the pieces and caring for the wounded. Ruby and Ricky had suffered slight cuts, and Fred, Fred Jr., and Charlie Robinson received minor bumps on their heads. Neighbors quickly pulled their cars up to ferry the injured to Hillman Hospital. As six-year-old Carol got into a car, unhurt and unbowed, sucking her thumb and curling into her father's lap, she remarked, "They can't kill us, can they, Daddy?" "No, baby, they can't kill hope," came his reply.[75] For the moment, the people of Bethel believed their pastor. The next few days and the next few years would offer ample opportunity to answer Carol's question.

Agitation

It is people in motion, not people talking, that make
changes, although it takes talk to excite people to motion.
— Fred Shuttlesworth

By sunrise on December 26, 1956, Fred Shuttlesworth's followers had taken
a giant step toward becoming a people in motion—and not just those who
had actually heard the bomb. The African American community throughout
Birmingham began hearing the reverberations on the day after Christmas. The
bomb began a vortex of events that would pull many into it and change Fred
Shuttlesworth, in the eyes of many Birmingham blacks, from an up-and-com-
ing young minister to a virtual folk hero, and, in the view of white Birmingham,
from obscurity to rabble-rouser extraordinaire. This chapter tells of Shuttlesworth's agitation, beginning with the aftermath of the Christmas night bombing through the fall of 1957. In less than a year his actions both put him on the
cover of the *New York Times* and helped put Bull Connor, temporarily ousted
in the wake of a sex scandal, back in office.

Shuttlesworth's response to the bomb agitated many blacks into action. The
bomb convinced many not only that God was present with them in their struggles but also that in this young new leader they might find a courage that would
not desert them. As Shuttlesworth later remarked: "I think that's what gave
people the feeling that I wouldn't run, I didn't run, and that God had to be there.
I think that's what helped build the Birmingham movement." Ministerial
colleague and ACMHR associate Abraham L. Woods Jr. concurred, describing
the galvanizing effect of Fred's sometimes outrageous acts of bravado: "They
served a purpose to pull us together. Not only that, but [they] gave more adher-
ents to the cause. . . . We understood then that here was a man that was not
going to let anyone turn him around. He was a courageous man who was going
to move on even if it meant his life." The day after Christmas thus began a period of persistent actions by Shuttlesworth calculated to agitate the status quo
and stimulate conflict with "the forces of evil."[1]

The first item on his agenda the morning after the bombing was to borrow a suit of clothes from a friend and attend an ACMHR board meeting to discuss the plans for the day. As word of the bombing quickly spread throughout the black community, so did curiosity over whether the bomber's prime target would go through with the integration of the buses. Those closest to Shuttlesworth suspected that the headstrong minister would deliver on his promises, but they nonetheless rushed to the Smith and Gaston Funeral Home to participate in the meeting. Word soon greeted them that the city commission had already met and taken no action on the ACMHR's request, but police commissioner Robert E. Lindbergh had announced that violators would be arrested and that he had called into duty an additional fifty police officers in order to enforce "our law." Expecting the commission to remain stubborn, Shuttlesworth had recruited a coterie of activists who would commit themselves to signing a pledge of nonviolence and ride the buses in spite of the regulations. He also had deliberately left ambiguous the target date of the integrated riding, leading city officials and the press to expect the rides to begin the next day. Hoping to surprise the police, however, he planned the riding to commence that morning. Reporters met Shuttlesworth as he arrived at the funeral home and asked for a statement. He politely requested that they wait outside and promised them a statement after the meeting. As the meeting began, some of Shuttlesworth's board members, frightened by the bombing, recommended caution saying, "We ought to stop and think this thing out." "There's nothing to think out," Fred retorted, waving them off. Believing that allowing the bombing to avert their original plans would be a step backward and leave them cringing in the face of intimidation, Shuttlesworth pressed his case: "We said we're going to ride, and we ride. We do what we say for a change. If you are nervous, I'm not binding you. But I am going to ride."[2]

The president won the argument with little difficulty. He then dismissed the board and headed to the Gaston Motel to meet with the recruits and prepare them for their integration excursion. Caught up in the excitement of what they, like the members of Bethel, deemed a miracle, some two hundred members awaited their leader. Fred's growing reputation and activism had already placed him in position to become the most powerful black leader in Birmingham, but now most of his followers believed God had acted incontrovertibly to solidify Shuttlesworth's status. More definitively, most ACMHR members, 98 percent of whom were Christians (and 88 percent of whom were Baptist), concluded with the Reverend T. L. Lane that Shuttlesworth was "doing the will of God because if he hadn't, he wouldn't have come up out of that. . . . You couldn't find but pieces of the spring and pieces of the mattress or any-thing—and he was *in* the bed. Couldn't nobody do that but God. There ain't no luck that will bring him through that." Others agreed and were thus drawn into the movement. Among the faithful at the board meeting that morning gathered others who had hitherto held themselves aloof from the ACMHR. Among them was an amazed Rosa Walker, who marveled at seeing Shuttlesworth there. She commented, "I knowed how their house was blowed up, and I couldn't figure out how he was there. And I said then, that I'm going into it. And I went into it on that day."[3]

Greeting him almost adoringly as he entered the room, the people came ready to be deployed at his command. "Mr. President, we came to hear you," they said. "We didn't come to hear those scared folks. We want to hear you, whatever you say." Shuttlesworth began by telling them of the events the pre-vious night and by asserting, "If it takes being killed to get integration, I'll do just that thing, for God is with me all the way." Assuring them of his intentions to proceed with the rides according to plan, he admonished them: "We must ride!! History, destiny, America is waiting to see what we do, and we have to do what we said. What we do now will determine whether or not people will be moved to do other things later." He then summarized instructions for non-violent riding—leave spaces for white passengers; no two blacks sit beside each other; respond politely to any incidents; if struck by a police officer, get his badge number. Ready for action, the group dispersed to various city bus stops to board the buses, cheerfully but defiantly ready to sit wherever there was an open seat—even in the white sections.[4]

In the first group to challenge the ordinance, Shuttlesworth, along with companions Henry Lee Anderson, Elizabeth Anders, and Joe C. Lester, boarded a bus on Twentieth Street North. Intending to ride to the hospital to see his daughter, he looked around, said, "This is all right," and took a seat about half-way down the aisle. Realizing what was occurring, two white women asked to get off, and other white passengers moved from the double to the single seats on the bus. As other blacks boarded, they noticed Shuttlesworth and the others seated in the white section and likewise began sitting in the front of the bus. When the bus filled almost to capacity, Shuttlesworth stood to offer his seat to a white woman. Later, noticing a police car cruising in front of the bus and hop-ing to be arrested himself, he asked another African American rider to give him his seat in the white section. After his visit with Pat, Shuttlesworth rode another bus back downtown but again arrest avoided him. Later in the day, however, when he drove up to a bus stop where some black riders were being arrested, the officer ticketed him for driving without a license. By nightfall somewhere between 150 and 200 blacks had ridden the buses in unsegregated fashion without violence or major incident. Some rode as many as five times in an effort to be arrested. In all, police arrested twenty-one riders, four ministers among them, who spent several hours in jail before being released on bond by early evening, just in time to attend mass meetings at two locations throughout the city.[5]

Making the rounds at the simultaneous meetings, Shuttlesworth addressed spirited crowds who had gathered for prayer, celebration, and instructions regarding the future plans. In consultation with ACMHR lawyers, Shuttlesworth had intended to lead only a one-day challenge of Birmingham's bus ordinance. This, they reasoned, would be sufficient to set the stage for suits calling for a federal injunction against the city. At the first meeting of the evening, at St. Paul's Colored Methodist Episcopal Church, after the rousing singing that "we ain't gonna hate nobody," Shuttlesworth addressed the congregation. He informed his audience of his letter to the city commission sent that day that stated that "a declaration today from you rescinding bus segregation laws in accordance with the United States Constitution will strengthen America and set the official pattern for good relations." He further explained the ACMHR's intentions and asked his listeners to resume riding in the Negro sections for the present time. He opined that "we don't need to fill up the jails," pointing out that the twenty-one arrests of that day were sufficient to serve the purpose. Going over the same ground at a second mass meeting at the Metropolitan Baptist Church on Southside, he stated that they had no argument with the police, who were merely doing their jobs in enforcing the law. Their quarrel was with the law itself. He asserted, "There is no further need of mass bus-riding. If they have charged us with violating the segregation laws, that's what we were riding for. Our purpose today was to challenge the law and that's what we did."[6]

Then, as he was recounting his experience and interpretation of the bomb, he was interrupted by the delivery of a telegram from King and the MIA urging the ACMHR to continue riding the buses on a nonsegregated basis. Some four hundred congregants greeted the message with cheers, and when Shuttlesworth put the matter to a vote, they unanimously agreed to continue the unsegregated rides. Buoyed by their decision, Fred acceded to their wishes and exhorted them to maintain "cool heads and warm hearts" in their efforts, warning them that the ACMHR would provide legal assistance only to those who signed pledges of nonviolence. The next day, however, after a two-hour conclave with ACMHR board members and lawyers, Shuttlesworth reverted to the original plan and announced to the press that he was calling off the protests to await the outcome of the court tests. The key point, he noted, was that "we showed we had the courage to do it."[7]

After the high drama and high spirits of the bomb and buses, Shuttlesworth and his family of necessity descended to the more mundane matters of living arrangements. While Fred tended to the details of board meetings, mass meetings, and protest bus riding, Ruby handled salvaging the family's personal possessions from the bomb site and keeping an eye on Pat as she convalesced from her burns. When Ruby returned home to collect her items and surveyed the damage in the light of day, she discovered with delight that a favorite piece of furniture had emerged from the blast unscathed. Not only was her china cabinet left intact, but the crystal inside had also survived. Her spirits quickly fell, however, when the crystal disintegrated as she opened the glass door of the cabinet. In that moment, she might well have wondered what else in her life might disintegrate as her husband and family became increasingly embroiled in the struggle for integration and civil rights. Without doubt, however, their old life of placid pastoral concerns had been blown away by the Christmas bomb, and that dawning new year would usher the Shuttlesworths into a new and unanticipated manner of existence.[8]

As the family picked over what remained of their home and belongings, Fred's and Ruby's families, along with Bethel and ACMHR members, lent helping hands. In the first days after the bombing, city officials condemned the house and wanted to clear the lot immediately. With an eye toward symbolism, however, Fred denied them permission, saying, "It's not hurting anybody. Let the people see what America is." For several days afterward, Shuttlesworth let the house stand while a large parade of curious pilgrims drove by to view the ruins and marvel—not only at what could happen in America but also that anyone could emerge from those ruins with body and soul together. Once Fred gave the go-ahead to begin, the process of rebuilding was aided immeasurably by ACMHR members. The family lived temporarily with both sets of in-laws while friends began the slow process of building a new parsonage.[9]

Treasurer William E. Shortridge spearheaded a fund drive to rebuild the Bethel parsonage. As a funeral home director in Ensley, he cultivated his contacts among black funeral directors across the state and region and sought donations. In addition, as soon as work on the new parsonage was begun, male members of the ACMHR and the Bethel Baptist Church volunteered to serve as guards of the church building and parsonage. Earlier in the century, Bethel pastor Milton Sears, fearing intimidation from union workers, had asked the deacons to watch over his home at night. Now once again deacons would serve as bodyguards for their pastor. Alongside them, several union workers who had been impressed by Shuttlesworth's fiery challenge to segregation volunteered to serve in what became known as the "Civil Rights Guards." One union man, Colonel Stone ("Buck") Johnson, so admired Fred that he disregarded his pastor's view that he was crazy to follow Shuttlesworth. Johnson became one of Shuttlesworth's most loyal followers, often serving as Fred's personal bodyguard in addition to taking periodic night watch duties. The guards did their jobs from a makeshift guard station built beside the house of Bethel deacon James Revis. From the station on Revis's property, diagonally across the street from the church, the guards could simultaneously patrol both the front and rear of the church. Working two shifts, from 6:00 P.M. to midnight and from 12:00 A.M. to 6:00 A.M., they bore their responsibilities every night for the remainder of Fred's tenure at Bethel.[10]

Shuttlesworth's decision, made in consultation with the ACMHR board, to call off the protest rides after one day of arrests demonstrated early on the dual strategy of combining nonviolent confrontation with persistent litigation. As historian Robert G. Corley has suggested, "Shuttlesworth believed in forcing segregationists to defend their institution constantly, whether through the use of police power or legal sophistry." The president of the ACMHR, as the pastor he was, had built the organization as a combination NAACP chapter and Baptist church. Shuttlesworth thus held strong lines of authority in both roles. He answered to the board in his decisions, but the board was filled with loyalists whose admiration for him had been sparked by his willingness to confront the status quo even in the face of threatening circumstance. The more Shuttlesworth's inner fire flamed into outward acts of confrontation, the more loyalty he earned from his board and the more authority they gave him to undertake further such actions. The original eleven-member board was dominated by ministers, including R. L. Alford, N. H. Smith Jr., G. H. George, T. L. Lane, Abraham Woods Jr., and Herman Stone. All but Woods had been participants in the ACMHR from its outset. Lucinda B. Robey was the only woman on the original board. Board meetings usually were held once a month, but they more typically became ad hoc at Shuttlesworth's discretion as events necessitated. Over the eleven years that Shuttlesworth headed the ACMHR, the size and composition of the board expanded to include more women and laypersons, though ministers and Shuttlesworth himself, who was their "chosen leader," always remained the dominant decision makers. Consequently, as sociologist Jacquelyne Clarke noted in her analysis of the ACMHR in 1959, the group was "essentially a one-man organization," which was widely known simply as "Shuttlesworth's organization." His personal charisma and the galvanizing effect of his bravado in large measure made the ACMHR the extension of his fervent persona.[11]

The membership of the ACMHR included anyone who agreed with its purposes and objectives. The dues were one dollar a year. By 1959, according to Clarke's statistics, the organization numbered between nine hundred and twelve hundred members, with a demographic profile less diverse than that of two other Alabama civil rights groups, the MIA and the Tuskegee Civic Association (TCA). Compared to these two organizations, the ACMHR membership was less educated (9.7 mean years of education compared with 11.1 and 15.9 years for the MIA and TCA, respectively) and had a larger percentage of unskilled or semiskilled workers (49.6 percent compared with 44.7 and 7.7 percent, respectively). Similar to the percentage among the general black populace of Birmingham, one third of the ACMHR earned less than $2,000 a year. Sixty percent made less than $4,000, compared with 80 percent for Birmingham blacks in general. Compared with the 20 percent of Birmingham blacks who owned their homes, 55 percent of ACMHR members did so. Such statistics, particularly those regarding income, suggest that the organization was a fairly representative cross-section of the African American community of Birmingham. In spite of these statistics, however, the working-class background of the leader appealed most powerfully to working-class blacks and left some middle-class blacks in Birmingham, such as First Congregationalist minister Harold Long, with the impression that this new group was more representative of the grass roots than Birmingham ministerial groups or even the NAACP.[12]

As 1957 began, the momentum of the ACMHR's first major engagement with segregation reflected the organization's new motto, The Movement Is Moving. Having now begun to attack segregation in earnest, surviving the bomb, and pushing forward with the December 26 bus rides, Shuttlesworth started to receive the attention of the national press and began to establish his credentials as, in Coretta Scott King's words, "a symbol of the southern struggle." The earlier discussions with protest leaders in Montgomery and the recent bus protests in Birmingham and Tallahassee made their respective leaders, Shuttlesworth and C. K. Steele, significant players in the founding of the Southern Christian Leadership Conference. On January 2, Shuttlesworth was among a group of one hundred black ministers from twenty states who met with congressional leaders and

White House officials to press for action toward passage of new civil rights laws that would enforce the Supreme Court's desegregation rulings. Three days later King, Shuttlesworth, and Steele sent out invitations to the other leaders who had joined them in Washington, calling them to attend another conference in Atlanta to consider establishing a southwide organization designed to help co-ordinate and widen the activities of these disparate, local civil rights organiza-tions. About sixty leaders attended the conference on January 10 and 11 at the Ebenezer Baptist Church. On the morning of January 10, King and Abernathy were called back to Montgomery to check on the damage done by several bombs in the city. In their absence, Shuttlesworth and Coretta King led the discussions, which the next day yielded the approval of "A Statement to the South and the Nation." The statement underscored the conference's "God-given duty to help save ourselves and our white brothers from tragic self-destruction in the quag-mire of racial hate." The leaders called on white Christians in the South to con-sider racial justice "a basic spiritual problem" and to join their struggle for jus-tice. They further asked federal officials to call more strenuously for southerners to abide by the Supreme Court rulings and in particular for Attorney General Herbert Brownell to discuss protection for persons who, like Shuttlesworth, stood for justice in dangerous areas and had cause to fear for their lives. In ad-dition to issuing this statement, the conference planned a follow-up meeting in New Orleans on February 14 to institutionalize plans for a permanent organi-zation.[13]

Meanwhile, Emory Jackson praised Shuttlesworth's recent leadership. While criticizing some of the earlier leadership in the African American community as not having "been with the people," he described Shuttlesworth as "a part of a new order of leadership" that was "undisturbed by the scare and stop cam-paign." He further complimented Fred for rejecting "the doctrine of wait and waive, as suggested by those who see the friendly relations between the two groups being upset by any action for integration." Moreover, in a flurry of edi-torials on the bombings, Jackson asserted that Birmingham officials were mor-ally bound to act on the city's unsolved racially motivated bombings, which he argued should be designated federal crimes. He sarcastically complained that the protest bus rides December 26 had driven the Shuttlesworth bombing off the front pages of the white newspapers and asserted that "City Hall must never be allowed to dismiss, write off, or forget the Xmas night racial bombing in Collegeville." He also accused local law enforcement officials of being too weak to handle the situation and challenged them: "If they are in earnest about stopping violence, they will ask the help of state and federal authorities."[14]

If the city delayed its investigation of the bombing, by contrast it acted with dispatch in bringing the twenty-one arrested bus riders to trial. Appearing in recorder's court before Judge Ralph E. Parker on January 3, the riders were convicted and fined $50 each plus court costs. Eight days later, after the ACMHR paid all of the fines, Shuttlesworth and his lawyers sued in federal court, requesting a temporary injunction against the city's segregation ordinance. At roughly the same time, employees of the Birmingham Transit Company went on strike, a decision that management and city officials blamed on the ACMHR protest rides. In response to the accusation, Shuttlesworth wrote a letter to the city commission denying that his organization had called for a boycott or had done anything to harm the company's business. Rather, he argued, he had encouraged blacks to ride the buses even more and to do so on a segregated basis until the courts settled the matter. He did criticize a plan, supported by city officials, that would allow bus drivers to use their private cars as jitneys, expressing concern that drivers would not pick up blacks as well as whites. "Will the City," he asked, "allow Negroes the same rights to operate as drivers in the same fashion?" He suggested further that the high percentage of blacks in the Birmingham population entitled them to "a few places on the Advisory Committee" of the transit company. He concluded by stating, "We must seek equal privileges and opportunities in all public facilities" and called for an immediate answer from the city commission. Whereas in 1955, with Shuttlesworth's work in the Interdenominational Ministerial Alliance, the commission had at least been willing to respond to his requests, the bus protests of December seemed only to harden the commissioners' attitudes. Angered at Shuttlesworth's growing militancy, they ignored his letter. Because the strike reached a quick settlement, Shuttlesworth dropped the matter.[15]

In mid-January, Shuttlesworth requested that officials place sharp controls on the sale of explosives within the city and that they search for the supplies of explosives "as diligently as any drive against the illegal use and sale of alcoholic beverages." At the same time, after police beat a black man named Robert L. Marshall, who had been arrested for drunk driving, Shuttlesworth took up the issue of police brutality. According to police chief Jamie Moore, Marshall had to be subdued by four officers, but having heard such explanations before, Shuttlesworth appealed for "more discretion in the treatment of members of the Negro race who become involved with the law." Once again city officials remained oblivious to Shuttlesworth's appeals. Their unresponsiveness, however, simply reinforced his strategy of attacking segregation on as many fronts as possible. While Shuttlesworth had been busy with the bus protest rides in late December, an incident elsewhere in Birmingham soon provided another front on which to attack. On the previous December 22, Carl and Alexinia Baldwin ran afoul of Birmingham segregation ordinances. As they awaited a train that was to take them on a Christmas visit to Milwaukee, the couple had been arrested for sitting in a white waiting room at the Birmingham Terminal Station. Five police officers confronted them and gave them twenty seconds to move to the "Colored" section. When they refused, the officers charged them with disorderly conduct. These charges were eventually dropped, but the Baldwins, advised by the ACMHR, decided on January 15 to file suit against the station. Soon after the filing of the Baldwin suit, at a mass meeting, an ACMHR member commented to Fred that they could now sit back and watch what happened in court. Not a chance, Shuttlesworth assured him. "Have you ever heard of anybody setting a hen on one egg? One egg is just wasting the hen's time. There won't be just one case; we gon' fill the basket up. We gon' file as many segregation suits as we can."[16]

Militancy of this sort made Shuttlesworth indispensable for the larger civil rights movement. A fiery, hard-boiled demeanor against "the forces of unrighteousness" and a quick-thinking joviality coalesced in Fred Shuttlesworth to make him a persona who challenged more cautious leaders and inspired rank-and-file followers. A toughness of spirit and a certainty of his role in God's work in America, bequeathed to him by both the general Zeitgeist and the particular events of his own life, made him a firebrand among the activists. As such he stoked the fires of the movement to burn hotter than they otherwise would have. Joseph Lowery later said that "Fred brought to SCLC a kind of militancy that maybe was not represented in other preachers . . . a kind of nonviolent militancy that seemed to rest so naturally on Fred Shuttlesworth's shoulders. Fred was a true activist, probably the truest activist in terms of 'shooting first and asking questions later.' Not to waste a whole lot of time in what Martin called 'the paralysis of analysis.' But Fred [was] 'Demonstrate now, and then work out the details later,' where many of us would take a little more cautious approach and make sure we had analyzed and negotiated and then demonstrated and acted. But Fred was impatient with evil."[17]

To King and others in the movement, by pressing forward in spite of the bombing, Shuttlesworth amply demonstrated an impatience with and a resolve unshakable enough to mount a frontal assault on the evil of segregation. In one of their first meetings after the bombing, King, Abernathy, and Lowery marveled not only at Fred's survival of the bomb but also at his resolution to proceed with the protest rides. King commented that in light of the bomb, he himself might have taken time out, as other ministers had, and said, "Let's think this thing out." Still exhilarated by the experience, Fred playfully retorted, "Yeah, and usually, like most folks, when you start thinking it out, you won't do nothing." [18] Stinging comments such as this, while well intentioned and superficially accepted in good spirits, could also make their targets feel ill at ease. Ultimately, this brusqueness limited his influence with King, but in the short run, his bravado made him a rising star. Moreover, although Fred's heedlessness of the consequences occasionally led friends to question his judgment and foes to question his sanity, no one doubted his courage.

Visible examples of such courage were indispensable to widening the movement beyond Montgomery. As leaders converged on New Orleans on Valentine's Day, some seven weeks after the bomb and the bus rides, few besides King had a higher visibility than Fred Shuttlesworth. In early February, Shuttlesworth had received added attention in a chance conversation with former president Harry Truman, who told him he was behind the civil rights movement "one hundred percent." Eight days later, ninety-seven activists, mostly preachers, met at the New Zion Baptist Church to create a permanent organization out of the meeting previously held in Atlanta. The group gave itself the name the Southern Leadership Conference on Transportation and Nonviolent Integration, which was later shortened to the Southern Christian Leadership Conference. The conferees planned to hold their first annual convention in Montgomery in August and elected their officers: King as president, C. K. Steele as first vice president, and A. L. Davis, host pastor in New Orleans, as second vice president. Samuel Williams of Atlanta was elected third vice president, T. J. Jemison as secretary, Medgar Evers of Jackson, Mississippi, as assistant secretary, and Abernathy as treasurer. In a mild snub, Shuttlesworth was not initially elected to an office. The acclaim he had received as a result of his Birmingham agitation might legitimately have earned him the honor of elective office in the new organization. It did not, however, because of his relative lack of involvement in the Baptist preacher network, his loner status, his lack of deep attachment to King, and a blunt personal style that put some people off. Nevertheless, his work in Birmingham gradually increased his stock, and by the SCLC's August convention, Shuttlesworth replaced Jemison as secretary.[19]

The day after the conference in New Orleans, Fred addressed two hundred activists in a meeting sponsored by the Baton Rouge Christian Movement. In his speech, he commended the recent policy of giving aid to anticommunists in Hungary but asserted that "America must not continue to throw bread to Hungarians and bombs at American Negroes." The nation, he argued, must face the problem of equal rights for all its citizens, adding that "the tradition of segregation is legally dead." He scoffed at "silly men of a civilized age [who are] trying to resurrect something that is dead. With anything that is dead, there is nothing to do but bury it. We want to join with our white brethren in arranging for a Christian burial. . . . Segregation laws are keeping good public officials from being good. What we need to do is to move away the legal barriers. The politicians and citizens councils are confusing the good white people. The few do all the bad . . . but it is the good white people who still are responsible [because] they do not speak out." Then turning his attention to the role of blacks in the civil rights effort, he admonished them: "The American Negro is not and cannot ever again be satisfied with less than anyone else. . . . If you are a New Negro, you can't act like the old Negro. We love the man while we hate what he does. We don't hate the man anymore. We have decided not to burn crosses. We're going to bear ours. History will show that social change came by non-violence."[20] His words were carried in newspapers as distant as Chattanooga, though not because of their rhetorical or intellectual power. Rather, in delivering them and the story of the bombing, Shuttlesworth, through his charisma, captivated audiences and fueled a fervor among African Americans that spread as rapidly as his reputation.

Returning to Birmingham, he immediately became involved in a flurry of civil rights activities, with an occasional glance at matters on the home front. Although almost completely ignored by the white press in Birmingham, Fred and his movement became a source of good copy for newspapers and magazines outside the South. To reporter Henry Gitano of the *Militant,* a newspaper in New York, Shuttlesworth ridiculed Birmingham law enforcement's failure to make any arrests for the Christmas night bombing. "Isn't it strange," he asked with tongue in cheek, "that they can't find loose dynamite, that there are no arrests after [these] bombings?" He suggested that officials were winking at the bombings and noted in mock paradox that searches for bootleggers experienced no such difficulty. "When hunting for whiskey," he said, snapping his fingers, "they find it just like that." To the extent that such comments were covered by the local press, they succeeded only in winning for Shuttlesworth the epithet "smart ass nigger" from angry whites.[21]

On February 21, he flew to Chicago to speak to one thousand members of the United Packinghouse Workers Association, the same day federal district court judge H. H. Grooms decided not to dismiss the ACMHR's complaints against the city's segregation ordinance. Grooms did, however, release the Birmingham Transit Company as a defendant because Shuttlesworth's attorneys did not show that the company had conspired to enforce the laws. The day after that, George Johnson and Clyde Jones, who in mid-1956 had applied for and been denied police jobs, brought suit against the Jefferson County Personnel Board. Appearing before Judge W. A. Jenkins, ACMHR lawyers Orzell Billingsley and Oscar W. Adams asked for a permanent injunction forcing the personnel board to allow blacks to take civil service examinations and asked for a $25,000 judgment. In addition, they sought to make the suit a class action, which would allow all Negroes who met other qualifications to take the examinations. Ultimately, this suit was unsuccessful but was later taken up in federal court.[22]

Shuttlesworth also kept his eye on the Baldwin suit, which came before U.S. district court judge Seybourn H. Lynne on Friday, March 1. Although the city had dropped its earlier charges of disorderly conduct against the Baldwins, the couple brought suit against the city, charging that segregated seating in the terminal station waiting room violated their constitutional rights. Lynne dismissed the suit, ruling that the denial of the use of the white waiting room did not constitute compulsion to use a "colored" waiting room. Immediately, the attorneys decided to challenge the court's decision, filing an appeal the next Monday, March 4. Almost as precipitously, Shuttlesworth dismissed Lynne's ruling as mere subterfuge and decided to mount a direct challenge. In his view the judge said that "they couldn't enforce segregation but it was all right for Negroes to segregate themselves. I said, 'We aren't going to segregate ourselves.'" Without discussing the matter with Ruby, who was still slowly putting her household (if not her house) back in order, he announced to her that he planned to buy a train ticket and sit in the white waiting room at the terminal station. "Well, I'm going with you," she insisted, only to be warned by her husband, "You know it's dangerous. You could get killed down there." "Well, I'm going," she assured him, refusing to let him put himself in harm's way alone. Impressed with her determination, Fred agreed that she should come, particularly after realizing that between the two of them, they could simultaneously challenge segregated facilities for both interstate *and* intrastate travel. "Well, if you want to go, why don't you buy a ticket to Atlanta, and I'll buy one for Attalla?"—a small city in eastern Alabama.[23]

On Wednesday morning, March 6, Fred alerted the press of their plans. During the next two hours some seven radio newscasts carried the story, and by 11:15 a large mob had gathered at the station to await Shuttlesworth's arrival. With their children safe at the home of Ruby's aunt, the couple dressed and called on an ACMHR member to drive them to the station. Fred and Ruby got out of the car and immediately noticed the large group of white men in the main entrance of the station. This antagonized assembly consisted primarily of a segregationist group and included Klansman Robert E. Chambliss, often known as "Dynamite Bob." Shuttlesworth, walking slightly ahead of his wife and carrying an empty suitcase to use as a prop or, if necessary, a shield, was met at the door by a scowling young tough. As the wiry, impeccably dressed black minister approached, the young man, whom Shuttlesworth later described as "almost frothing at the mouth," began a verbal exchange:

"You Shuttlesworth?"

"That's right."

"We don't want you in here."

"Well, I don't think it's your place to tell me I can't come in. I have as much right to come inside the station as you do."

"The sign says 'White—intrastate.'"

"I don't have any argument with you. Would you please stand aside and let me go in?"

By this time the crowd inside the station had bunched up toward the doorway and begun pushing outward in an effort to move the Shuttlesworths away. Fred heard someone in the horde shout, "Heave ho!" Just then Shuttlesworth noticed that a squad of police officers, sent by Commissioner Robert E. Lindbergh, had gathered at a side door. He quickly grasped Ruby's arm and followed the officers into the station. The Shuttlesworths went to the window to buy their tickets and then sat down in the white waiting area. Once inside the officers ordered the mob to leave the terminal. Complying with this directive, the group nonetheless refused to leave altogether and loitered for a while outside the building.[24]

Within a few moments of being seated, Fred and Ruby were joined by a white man named Lamar Weaver. A steelworker and unionist who occasionally served as a Presbyterian lay minister, Weaver had declared his candidacy for the city commission as an antisegregationist. In a principled attempt at racial reconciliation, but also in a monumental display of political naiveté, he had spoken at an ACMHR mass meeting two weeks earlier. As one of the first whites to identify with Shuttlesworth and, as a result, certain to forfeit most white votes, Weaver nonetheless committed himself to "the cause of human rights [and] social equality." In addition, he told an ACMHR rally at Macedonia Baptist that he had written to Missouri senator Thomas C. Hennings and offered to appear with Shuttlesworth before the Senate's Judiciary Constitutional Rights Subcommittee in hearings concerning discrimination in the South. His appearance at an ACMHR meeting might somehow be buried in the press, but his coming to Birmingham Terminal Station to lend Fred and Ruby his support could not. Entering the waiting room through the same door as had Fred and Ruby, Weaver greeted them warmly and sat down with them.[25]

As the trio conversed, a burly police officer approached, asking if they had tickets. Fred smilingly replied, "Now, Officer, you know I'd have better sense than to come in here without a ticket. My wife is going to Atlanta, and I'm going to Attalla." Knowing he could not insist that the Shuttlesworths leave, the officer turned and asked Weaver for his ticket. When Weaver said he had none, the officer ordered Weaver to leave the waiting room immediately. The crowd of toughs still waiting outside, now numbering about fifty, had noticed Weaver sitting with the Shuttlesworths. They began yelling, "Yeah, bring him out here!" As Weaver turned away from the mob and headed up Twenty-sixth Avenue North, the intimidators cursed him, called him a "Nigger lover," and began to chase him up the street. Several of the men, identifying themselves to him as members of the Klan, spewed out the threats, "We're going to get you good. We ought to kill you right now." Unfortunately for Weaver, the police officers were still back at the station virtually surrounding the Shuttlesworths, and their absence from the trouble outside gave the antagonists free rein. They punched Weaver several times and smashed him in the face with a suitcase. Surrounding his car, the mob rocked it violently and broke some of the windows. Managing to drive clear of the swarm before they could harm him further, Weaver floored his accelerator and sped away to safety. Other police officers, however, pulled him over and arrested him for reckless driving and running a red light. That day he appeared in recorder's court, where Judge Ralph Parker lectured him on the dangers of agitation and knowingly exposing himself to danger. His participation in Shuttlesworth's "planned maneuver," the judge reasoned, had put

Weaver at least partially at fault. No longer "free of all fault," Weaver had thus forfeited his right to plead self-defense. He was convicted and fined twenty-five dollars. In the aftermath, a wide-eyed Weaver commented in classic understatement: "This is the first time I've ever been in a mob. I never want to be in another one." Now convinced that an ill-prepared South would not accept integration without "serious trouble and bloodshed" and fearing for his life, Weaver withdrew from the commissioner's race and left Birmingham permanently. ACMHR members hid him in the Shortridge Funeral Home and secretly spirited him out of the city in a hearse.[26]

Meanwhile, back in the terminal, with several police officers standing by, Fred and Ruby waited without incident for their departure. An hour and a half after arriving at the station, they boarded a New York–bound train, but both got off in Attalla, where ACMHR members picked them up and returned them to Birmingham. Shuttlesworth had expected to be arrested for sitting in the white waiting room and was surprised to learn that there was actually no city ordinance against integrated seating in the terminal. This error revealed in Shuttlesworth an impetuosity and a penchant for occasionally acting unilaterally and without thinking through all the details. This trait gave some of Birmingham's African American middle class reason to question his judgment and, to some degree, his motives. In a criticism that often came to be leveled by the white community, some blacks suspected him of acting primarily for the publicity.[27]

He indeed acted for publicity, but not *primarily* for that reason. He openly sought to put a spotlight on the discriminations inherent in the system of segregation. Publicizing the travail of blacks toiling for equal rights would rally the power of public opinion and push the federal government to finish what it had begun in *Brown* and other post–World War II strides toward racial justice. Shuttlesworth's agitation was designed both to challenge Birmingham officials and to give its white citizens the opportunity to yield to what Lincoln had called "the better angels of our nature."

In comments to the press after the Birmingham Terminal Station incident, Shuttlesworth suggested that the failure of police to arrest him indicated the death of segregated public transportation in Alabama. Moreover, he complimented police commissioner Lindbergh, who had sent officers to protect him and his wife, as a man of high morals. Apparently, he half-seriously pointed out, because the officers did not arrest him and his wife, arresting future riders would only make authorities look bad, and they should therefore take down the segregation signs. He praised the majority of white southerners as law-abiding citizens but added that "the southern white man is missing a glorious opportunity to show the world that he can meet and master any situation."[28] Finally, he averred that a strong stand by public officials would stop the violence of the Klan and the citizens' councils. His actions, thoroughly planned or not, gave whites in Birmingham the chance to take the stands Shuttlesworth recommended. Perhaps most important, his sometimes precipitous actions continued to inspire his followers and make them proud of one of their number who not only minced no words in saying what most of them felt but enacted those feelings in public view.

White Birmingham did not see things quite that way, however. Reflecting a consensus of white perspectives on Shuttlesworth's latest adventure, a *Birmingham News* editorial analyzed matters in predictable fashion, assuming that racial antagonism could gradually be abated but for ill-conceived efforts to move too rapidly. Making some sport of Fred's challenge of a nonexistent law, the editor identified the minister's sole accomplishment: "Reverend Shuttlesworth's 'test' has resulted in a sharp new arousal of deep-rooted passion." The following week the city commission sounded the same note in a public comment designed to set the stage for the upcoming trial of the twenty-one blacks arrested in the December 26 protest rides. The commission indicated its continued support of segregated seating on buses, which they viewed as "necessary for the avoidance of friction, enmity and violence between the races." At the bus trial on March 18, again before Judge Ralph Parker, the city attorney warned that continued efforts at desegregation would lead to "unpreventable acts of violent resentment." ACMHR lawyer Arthur Shores argued that bus segregation violated the Fourteenth Amendment. Three days later, in a remarkable attempt at revisionist history, Parker declared the Fourteenth Amendment "null and void" and claimed that Congress had "pulled a fast one" by forcing the southern states to approve the amendment without including ex-Confederate whites in the ratification process. Thus, he reasoned, the process had been rendered constitutionally invalid. In an ironic twist, he denounced civil rights activists who "defy the law in regard to segregation and take matters into their own hands," apparently oblivious to his own vulnerability on this very point. In sum, he found the bus riders guilty, fining them fifty dollars each, plus court costs. Immediately, Shuttlesworth and the ACMHR asked the U.S. district court to restrain Birmingham officials from enforcing their segregation ordinances.[29]

After the desegregation attempt at the terminal station, Shuttlesworth maintained his increasingly frenetic pace, trying to balance his pastoral duties with his mushrooming responsibilities as spokesperson for the civil rights movement. The latter role, of course, entailed both a local and a national component. Locally, he kept close tabs on points of weakness in the opposition and stayed up to date on the status of the myriad ACMHR suits. He continued to work with other pastors in the city to schedule the mass meetings on Monday nights, sometimes a difficult task because of many ministers' reluctance to identify too closely with Shuttlesworth and his organization. Fred also scheduled larger events in the movement designed to educate the rank-and-file member in the principles of nonviolence. Two days after returning from the brief excursion to Attalla, Fred led a three-day workshop at the churches of the Reverends Herman Stone, Abraham Woods Jr., and T. L. Lane, all of whom had been participants in the ACMHR. The theme of the workshop was "Social Change through Christian Love," and many of the major players in the organization delivered addresses. Shuttlesworth spoke on the first night's proceedings during a segment called "The Occasion," where he gave an interpretation of the importance of the meetings. Significantly, Shuttlesworth, who did not allow women to make pulpit appearances in standard church services, asked Lola Hendricks, the young secretary at his friend Nelson H. Smith's church, to speak on "The Occasion" in the concluding session on Sunday. He also asked the prominent school principal and loyal ACMHR member Lucinda B. Robey to speak at one of the sessions. Fred also invited Glenn E. Smiley to serve as the workshop leader and to deliver the keynote address on the final day of the conference. Smiley was an expert in Gandhian principles and techniques and had played a similar role during the Montgomery boycott.[30]

With his confrontational activities in what was commonly considered the southern city most antagonistic toward the civil rights movement, Shuttlesworth slowly widened his reputation beyond the local scene. Although he never rivaled King in national attention, his exploits were beginning to capture the attention of such national publications as the *New York Times* and *Newsweek* magazine. Shuttlesworth received a growing number of invitations to speak to northern audiences. For example, the day the ACMHR nonviolence workshop ended, Fred flew to St. Paul, Minnesota, to address the local chapter of the NAACP and a group of African American ministers. At their request, Shuttlesworth responded to claims that the national media were not telling the truth about racial conditions in the South. Impressed by his personal experiences in the movement, the group collected a large offering, a good portion of which

Shuttlesworth took back home as a contribution for the rebuilding of the Bethel parsonage.[31]

Understandably, the excitement of participating in what most African Americans considered a historic as well as a divinely directed movement captured Fred's imagination and his daily calendar. His schedule abruptly became dominated by his civil rights activities. Throughout his tenure at Bethel, by his own guesstimate, the "freedom struggle" occupied 98 percent of his time. Beginning in 1957 he was away from his pulpit roughly half the Sundays of the year. On those Sundays he often telephoned the church to keep a pastoral eye on things, while two assistant ministers filled in for him. The people of Bethel showed extraordinary patience with these absences, an indication of their strong support of Shuttlesworth and his activist agenda. Only very gradually did some members begin to believe that he was investing too much of himself in matters less directly related to his pastoral role. Like other activist ministers in the civil rights movement, Shuttlesworth had developed, to a greater or lesser degree, a self-consciously and characteristically African American theology that made no distinction between the sacred and the secular or between the churchly and the civic. There was a gap, however, between Shuttlesworth's position on this matter and that of the people he proposed to lead. The people generally shared the holistic approach of their minister, who saw civil rights as a central element of pastoral ministry to an oppressed people. The people, like their pastor, also believed that because human beings are both body and soul, Christian salvation was "socio-spiritual." When, however, church members repeatedly needed their pastor's ministrations only to find him unavailable, their patience gradually grew thin. One might strongly support Shuttlesworth's perpetual motion on the civil rights front and view it as a part of the ministry. Nevertheless, if for a period of time Pastor Shuttlesworth missed too many weddings, funerals, hospitalizations, Sunday school promotions, or worship services while out of town on civil rights business, many members could gradually conclude that their minister had forsaken the spiritual health of the religious institution for the moral health of the body politic—or, perhaps more accurately, allowed the prophetic to far outweigh the pastoral.[32]

On the Sundays when their pastor *was* in town, the members of Bethel definitely heard more civil rights and black themes from the pulpit than they had before Christmas night of 1956. Like any preacher whose life experiences inform the themes of his or her preaching, Shuttlesworth naturally addressed issues from the context of civil rights. Because he spent the bulk of his time and energies on these concerns, he could not help but deal with their theological underpinnings in his sermons. As a Bible-centered preacher, he always took a text and explained it with specific applications to the concerns of African Americans in the South. One of his members later recalled that his preaching style became more fervent "after he got more involved in the civil rights movement. . . . Everything he did and said spoke to that." In his sermons at Bethel, he more than occasionally chose biblical texts dealing with war, such as the battle of Jericho. In this instance, he interpreted the Israelites' bringing down Jericho's walls by their trumpets and shouts as an example of nonviolent action. He often expressed a public commitment to nonviolence, which, he often testified, had marked a significant change from his hotheaded and quick-tempered youth. Yet, in his newfound ability to be "passive," he found evidence that "the Lord was using him." Although personal experience typically functions in evangelical preaching, both white and black, to authenticate the words of the preacher, Shuttlesworth's bomb experience led even more directly to his choice of sermon text, as indicated by his frequent quotation of Job 13:15: "Though [God] slay me, yet will I trust him."[33]

Similar themes, along with ideas from the self-help tradition of African American preaching, appeared in a sermon called "The Negro's Hope for the Future." On the basis of the text of Psalm 24:7, which admonishes, "Lift up your heads, O ye Gates, and be lifted up, O ancient doors, that the King of glory may come in," Shuttlesworth used David, the traditional writer of the Psalms, as an example of one who, through faith, was raised to greatness. As a boy, David had learned through such experiences as his defeat of Goliath that "God had done for him what man could not. . . . He had come from the bottom of nowhere to the top of somewhere." Applying this principle to the black experience, Fred charged that

> as Negroes, we are too quick to pin our hopes on things which have not been proved. We sometimes forget to remember that God made us as he did other people. . . . Then, we are somebody after all; the shape and contours of our bodies are the same as others; our customs, actions, desires, yes and our potentialities and capabilities are the same as other people. . . . And everybody that has had a black car, black suit, or anything black knows that black is a color that does not fade so easily. So dark race, lift up your heads. If God had wanted us another

color, he would have made us so. We need to stop trying to be some-body else and be ourselves. Be proud of your color, be yourself.

He castigated those who "want to be white so bad," calling on them to "stop thinking that the white man is God. God is God." He continued:

> Let us lift our heads above Superstition. Then let us stop believing in Hoodooism and conjuration. Too many of us are taking roots and magic bags around for protection. Suppose you lose it? Too many col-ored people waste their money hunting fortune tellers and hand read-ers. But if God be God, then trust him. . . . Lift up our heads above our old habits and standards. The day is out for Uncle Tomism and Aunt Janeism. The day is out for our being tattlers and toters for other people. The day is out for the worst looking head rags downtown, and the cheapest cotton stockings you can find. Get a right view of God and check up on ourselves. Talk to us, David: we are an oppressed people; we have problems inside and out. We worry and can't seem to get what's rightfully ours.

Then his sermon modulated to a second text, "Behold, I have set before you an open door, and no man can shut it" (Rev. 3:8). Shuttlesworth ransacked biblical and secular history, sometimes inaccurately or with an obvious bias, for examples of one of the traditional emphases of African American theology, the "God of the oppressed." He continued: "Yes, my friends, God has a way of stringing along with the underdog. And God has a way of hearing the oppressed, and speaking for them when they can't speak for themselves. Look at the pages of history: Cain oppressed Abel and finally killed him. Nobody had to tell God; the blood cried out from the ground. In the dark days when the Pope at Rome had more authority than the government, Christians were being persecuted and slain. Children thrown down mountainsides, people tortured, and some burned alive. The pope kept the people ignorant; he told [them] what to think, what to believe." Moving to American history, he described early Americans who wanted freedom

> but thought nothing of enslaving black men. Yes, they did it, and thought heaven's door was closed to it. . . . [But] people began to talk—here, yonder there. In Illinois God had a man quoting Scripture,

"A house divided cannot stand." No man has a right to earn his good by wringing it out of the sweat and blood of his fellow man. . . . Meanwhile Congress debated and compromised. But you can't compromise on a wrong principle, so the Missouri Compromise failed, Wilmont [sic] failed, the Kansas-Nebraska Bill failed. But at the same time four million blacks in chains of slavery kept working, kept suffering, kept praying, kept singing. I hear them: "Over my head there's trouble in the air, there must be a God somewhere." "Swing Low Sweet Chariot." Yes, they kept the wash pots sounding and the brush harbors ringing. Then on April 12, 1861, God cracked the door and put his foot in it. Guns started shooting, shells falling, swords rattling, men dying. Yes, the Lord will make a way somehow.

He concluded the sermon by challenging his congregation. He told them that the voice of God still called them to go through the door because "the door is open. No man can shut it."[34]

Still, the cultural and religious needs of an oppressed minority are sometimes at odds with the institutional needs of their congregations. The cultural needs of African Americans under Shuttlesworth's pastoral care demanded the attention he gave to civil rights preaching. Their time and place necessitated it. In isolation from other ministerial responsibilities, however, such preaching and activity do not keep the gears of the local church meshing smoothly. Although Shuttlesworth's emphasis and his charismatic personality attracted many members into Bethel, they also scared off potential members. Moreover, in the long run the constant drumbeat of civil rights fervor in the local church may not have met the wide range of religious needs of Shuttlesworth's parishioners. Although he never wavered in his belief that he acted and spoke at God's behest, and he always believed that the times required his civil rights emphasis, Shuttlesworth later confessed, "I am not sure that you preach pure civil rights sermons and keep a church interested. You have to preach Calvary. Calvary is the important thing that the church is based on. Birth, life, death, resurrection of Jesus Christ. But all of life is related to that."[35]

In April, civil rights leaders put plans in motion for the May 17, 1957, Prayer Pilgrimage to Washington, D.C. A variation of A. Philip Randolph's call in the early 1940s for a demonstration in the nation's capital, the pilgrimage presaged the 1963 March on Washington. It was announced by Martin Luther King Jr. at the founding of the SCLC and was a response to President Eisenhower's continued refusal to speak out in support of desegregation. The pilgrimage had been planned in early April, and by mid-month Shuttlesworth announced his intention to participate. Scheduled for the third anniversary of the *Brown* decision, the pilgrimage intended to show African American unity, give northerners an opportunity to register their support, protest southern legal attacks on the NAACP, protest bombings and other racial violence in the South, and promote the passage of new civil rights legislation. Representatives of every major civil rights organization attended, and King's "Give Us the Ballot" speech electrified the estimated crowd of eighteen thousand. A lengthy series of short "Reports of Southern Freedom Fighters" put Shuttlesworth in the spotlight briefly, as it did such other minister-activists as William Holmes Borders of Atlanta, C. K. Steele of Tallahassee, and A. L. Davis of New Orleans.

In his remarks, Shuttlesworth touched on the issue of bombs that by May 17 had once again disturbed Birmingham. Police officials discovered a box of dynamite outside the Jewish synagogue Temple Beth-El and defused it before it could harm persons or property. In response, Shuttlesworth had released a telegram he sent to U.S. Attorney General Herbert Brownell that called for a federal investigation of unsolved bombings and racial violence in Birmingham. The telegram, signed by representatives of six black organizations, cited twenty-one recent bombings with specific dates listed and complained that bombings were continuing with no apparent progress in apprehending the perpetrators. With these events in mind, Fred told the audience:

> I have been bombed, but I'm alive. . . . It is tragic that, in this day of light, men in a Christian Democracy still find themselves groping in the darkness for these basic freedoms which are by virtue of citizenship. . . . The great job for America in the perilous hour . . . is to see to it that the Constitution *of* the U.S. is the Supreme law *in* the U.S., and that it means the same thing in the South as it does in the North, East, and West. All America's children must be fed from the same loaf; crumbs will suffice no longer. For it is written, "What man is there among you, who, if his son asks for a loaf of bread, would give him a stone." Can America forever give the bread of Charity to Hungarians, Jews, Europeans, and other oppressed people throughout the world and throw bombs at her own Negroes? Is the great American ideal of fair play, equality and justice which even now holds Communism at bay in the four quarters of the earth to fall or fade from view when

challenging the internal enemy of Segregation? . . . Is the ringing Voice of Liberty which is beamed around the world from these shores to become hushed and silent within its own borders?

The Negro Church is taking the lead, and thank God, some in the White Church are at last pleading for justice and reason. We have arisen to walk with destiny, and we shall march till victory is won. Not a victory for Negroes, but a victory for America, for right, for righteousness. . . . This is the real battle for America. . . . Thank God for America, and ladies and gentlemen, I'm glad I'm an American. Wake up, O blessed land! Be not forever guilty of walking in the shadows simply because you refuse to face the light. And though we walk and live in the midst of danger and death, and while threats and cross burnings go on by night and day, while the exploding bomb bursts in the South now match those which exploded in the Revolutionary War, we shall forever shout over the roar and din of battle, "We have set our sails for freedom's shores, and there can be no retreat. Our course is charted as onward up. Give us liberty or give us death."[36]

Clearly Shuttlesworth was no black nationalist, and even when trends in African American thought moved in that direction after the Black Power movement of the late 1960s, he continued to view himself as an American. Later, in the 1980s when many black churches began the practice of teaching and celebrating their African heritage, Shuttlesworth largely ignored the trend, commenting, "I probably ought to have more [events celebrating the African heritage], being a Black church. But I'm not an African. I'm just an American—I am in this American polyglot society which needs every man at his best, white and Black. That's the way I feel about it." His ACMHR followers agreed, as one affirmed, "I am proud of my race and to be an American. . . . By virtue of circumstances, I think of myself first as a Negro; my goal, though, is to begin to think of myself first as an American." Thus, like most of the leaders and followers in the early stages of the civil rights movement, Shuttlesworth accepted traditional notions of American exceptionalism ("Wake up, O blessed land" and "Christian Democracy"). Local elections in 1957, however, would severely test Shuttlesworth's faith in Birmingham's version of "Christian Democracy," signaling as they did the political resurrection of Bull Connor.[37]

As a city that bore among its many nicknames the moniker "The City of Churches," Birmingham would have seemed unlikely to return to power an official who had been involved in public moral scandal. Connor had been caught in an affair with his secretary and pressured out of his post as commissioner of public safety in 1952. His road to political redemption seemed very long. A shortcut was presented to Connor, however, in African American agitation for integration and white Birmingham's reaction against it. Born in Selma in 1897, Connor had moved to Birmingham in 1913 and later worked as a telegraph operator and radio announcer. His popularity among his listeners and his friendship with state senator James Simpson led him to enter politics and won him the commissioner's seat in 1937. A quintessential southern Democrat, Connor led half of the Alabama delegation out of the Democratic National Convention in 1948 as part of the Dixiecrat revolt. A staunch defender of segregation laws, he had the Progressive Party's vice presidential candidate, Senator Glen Taylor, arrested in October 1948 for entering a Birmingham building through the "Colored" entrance. In the early 1950s he coupled the segregation and anticommunist issues, identifying black activists and white integrationists as part of an international conspiracy against American democracy and claiming that Birmingham had been infiltrated by 315 "Reds." In the wake of his scandal in 1952, corruption charges against him were dropped, and he agreed not to run in that year's next election. Voters replaced him with the reform-minded Robert Lindbergh, and Connor bided his time.[38]

By 1957 the times had definitely begun "a-changin'," chiefly in the activism of Birmingham's black community. That agitation, with Shuttlesworth as its unrivaled instigator, had made incumbent commissioner Lindbergh vulnerable. Although Lindbergh had identified himself as a segregationist and believed that law enforcement "without bombast and bluster" was necessary for "these troublous times," his segregationist pronouncements were more vague and less emotive in tone. In the right kind of campaign, he could be painted as soft on integration. Advised by his political mentor, James Simpson, Connor decided to capitalize on white resistance to integration. In the May 7 Democratic primary election, Lindbergh led the field of five candidates, but Connor trailed by only 1,560 votes, forcing a runoff election on June 4. During the runoff campaign, Lindbergh touted his segregationist credentials while distancing himself from Connor's heavy-handed approach, arguing in his advertisements that "it doesn't take AGITATION to maintain SEGREGATION." More important, he exuded a general overconfidence in the race against Connor, who campaigned tirelessly and left no doubt about his stand on integration. On election day Connor surprised even himself by outpolling Lindbergh by 103 votes.[39]

Although the candidates had not specifically intoned the name of Shuttlesworth as the key figure against whom they would defend Birmingham, the "troublemaking" minister's actions provided the backdrop for the race and created an atmosphere that revived Connor's political viability. With his political fortunes now reversed, Connor became the perfect foil for Shuttlesworth's "righteous program between the forces of good and evil." If Shuttlesworth's followers saw him as the embodiment of the force of good, Connor became the devil incarnate. They identified him as the epitome of southern racism and accurately held him responsible for the police department's brutal tactics in handling African Americans. They also suspected him of directly coordinating Klan activity in the city. For his part, Connor was determined to stifle any and all "dangerous" black agitation. His wife later commented that he saw as his primary role "to keep the nigger in his place for his own good as well as the good of the city." This had been the primary plank in his campaign against Lindbergh and became the basis for his antagonism against Shuttlesworth.[40]

In June 1957, while Connor was winning his election campaign, Shuttlesworth acquired a new set of allies in a organization known as the Southern Conference Educational Fund (SCEF). SCEF executive director James A. Dombrowski and SCEF president Aubrey Williams were seeking to recruit reporter-activists Carl and Anne Braden as field secretaries. While in Birmingham to meet with the Bradens, Dombrowski contacted Shuttlesworth to offer his moral support and invite him to breakfast. When Shuttlesworth did not at first show up, Dombrowski speculated that the minister was avoiding them because of SCEF's "subversive" reputation. After a while, Fred called to invite Dombrowski and the Bradens to meet him at the Gaston Motel, where he was staying until his parsonage could be rebuilt. After initial conversations, Fred invited them to ride out to the church to see his parsonage. As they rode to North Birmingham in a cab, Shuttlesworth laughed and told his guests, "You know we're breaking the law," reminding them of Birmingham's ordinances against whites and blacks riding in the same cab. After they had talked for a while, Dombrowski invited Fred to join the SCEF board of directors.[41]

For Fred to align himself with the SCEF was to court additional controversy. Begun in 1938 as the Southern Conference for Human Welfare (SCHW), the interracial organization sought to create a network of white liberals who would speak out on the race issue. Influenced by New Deal thought and the labor movement, its earliest members proposed to support Roosevelt's economic policies, particularly in the South. The SCHW wrote and spoke on a variety of issues, including jobs, labor organization, and farm problems, but gradually focused on the abolition of segregation as the linchpin of its concerns. In 1944 and 1947, the House Committee on Un-American Activities cited the SCHW as a Communist-front organization. After financial problems in 1946 weakened the SCHW, Dombrowski reshaped the organization into the smaller SCEF. From 1948 to 1954 the SCEF sponsored conferences focusing on segregation in higher education and discrimination in hospitals. In addition, SCEF's work consisted of taking polls, circulating petitions, and publishing pamphlets to promote better race relations. On March 20, 1954, after three days of hearings in New Orleans, the Senate Internal Security Subcommittee also concluded that the SCEF was a Communist-front organization. The subcommittee based its allegations on the involvements of Dombrowski and SCEF information director Carl Braden. As a Ph.D. candidate at Columbia University, Dombrowski had written a dissertation titled "The Early Days of Christian Socialism in America," which the Un-American Activities Committee took as illustrative of his "leftist leanings." Dombrowski denied he had ever been a Communist, though he admitted he had once belonged to the Socialist Party and had voted for the Democratic Party since moving to the South. Braden, a former newspaper reporter in Anniston, Alabama, and Louisville, Kentucky, had worked to integrate housing in Louisville and was convicted of contempt of Congress after refusing to answer questions of a House subcommittee, particularly when asked if he was a member of the Communist Party. In the 1954 investigation, Senator James O. Eastland of Mississippi had accused the SCEF of having been "launched by the Communist Party for its own ends."[42]

In spite of the potential anticommunist hysteria if his associations became public, Fred exhibited what Anne Braden called a "moral courage" to go along with his physical courage and became a member of the SCEF board. In turn, the SCEF publicized the racial situation in Birmingham outside the South. In response to the tendency of the Birmingham daily newspapers to black out news of ACMHR's actions, Shuttlesworth often fed information to the Bradens, who in turn passed the item to a newspaper in the North. These northern papers then requested a story from Birmingham through the Associated Press. The SCEF put out releases that were often picked up by the black or student press, eventually coming to the attention of larger city newspapers such as the *New York Times*. In time, Shuttlesworth would credit the SCEF with helping to save his life by getting the word out and drawing public attention to Birmingham. In addition, two years later the SCEF published a major pamphlet on the work of the ACMHR called "They Strike Segregation at Its Core," which for the first time referred to Birmingham as the "Johannesburg of North America."[43]

Buoyed by his newfound colleagues, Fred addressed his followers on the ACMHR's first anniversary, which fell on the day after Connor's runoff victory. At St. Paul AME Church, in his president's address, Fred preached a sermon called "A Faith for Difficult and Critical Times," based on Acts 27:25, a text where St. Paul, in the midst of a stormy sea, reassures his companions, "Wherefore, Sirs, be of good cheer, for I believe God, that it shall be even as it was told me." Picking up on the theme, Shuttlesworth expressed his optimism that his divine impressions boded well for the struggle of Birmingham blacks. He reminded his audience of their year-old efforts to "press forward . . . for the full Rights, opportunities, and privileges of first-class citizenship." Those who tried to "kill our hopes for freedom, and to stamp out by judicial directive the spark of faith that had fired the hearts of the Founding Fathers" and believed that blacks "would never again dare attack the vile god of Segregation" had, he charged, "reckoned without the power of Almighty God or forgot to remember that Faith works its best miracles under difficult circumstances." He continued: "We stood together as one man—pledging each to the other our lives, our fortunes, our sacred honor with massive voice from unafraid hearts, we cried our 'Give us liberty or give us death.' . . . We stood up like men of faith, with love in our hearts, but with determination in our breasts, not only to defy and challenge Segregation practices and customs, but also to say to the 'Uncle Toms' of yesterday, 'Get behind us, Satan, for you are offensive to us.' You have kept us behind long enough."

He noted the white South's criticism of the Supreme Court, its efforts to inhibit black voting, and the failure of the police to make arrests for the Birmingham bombings and identified these rearguard efforts as works of Satan. Shuttlesworth moved them to spiritual ecstasy by saying, as did Paul amid threats of shipwreck, "I believe God. I tell you in plain language that some men are yet trying to hold shut forever in our faces the doors of equal opportunity and privileges. But I read in Revelation that God would set before us an open door which no man could shut. And I believe God." Moreover, he rejected southern whites' professed love for the Negro as mere paternalism:

Nobody fully respects anyone who he can control or maneuver at will. So long as the Negro is docile, quiet, and "in his place"—back doors, back seats, specially marked inferior facilities—his big friend will be sweet and kind; but once in a front seat, or first class facility, this same friend becomes a raging enemy. Segregation is a moral and social cancer which is corrupting the health of the whole Southern body. It is an evil which must be destroyed. It causes otherwise normal men to forget dignity and act like beasts in defense of its laws. It causes men who live together all their lives to fear and be suspicious of each other all their lives. It makes color of skin the criteria for supremacy. . . . The love of segregation has taken precedence over the love of God: thus it becomes relatively easy for some white men to sing "Amazing Grace" on Sunday morning in the choirs, and march at night in robes to burn crosses.

He then concluded with a personal recommitment to the task placed on him a year before:

I speak tonight as a man of faith. I have no magic wand to wave nor any quick solution by which the God of segregation can be made to disappear. I offer myself—my life—to lead as God directs. My family and I—and Bethel Church—have tasted of the bitterest dregs of the vile cup of segregation. But from the pitch black terrors we have learned a faith which cannot be conquered. We have found that there's a Man upstairs who is not asleep; a Man who was there Christmas night, even before the bomb exploded. Truly the angel of the Lord encampeth round about them that fear God.[44]

By July 1957 the Shuttlesworths had settled into their new parsonage. The children had spent the several months since the bombing living with relatives. Now together again, the family hoped to resume their regular routine as Bethel's "first family." In spite of the disruption caused by the bombing, some things returned to normal. The new movement brought new pressures into the new parsonage, however. Almost as soon as the telephone was installed, it began to ring unremittingly. Fred's activities kept him on the telephone with both movement and church matters. Believing he was needed by his followers, he insisted that his family keep the line open even when the home was being bombarded by nuisance and threatening calls. On a light night they would receive twenty-five calls or so and many more when events in the city heated up. The children were forbidden to answer the phone, but once in a while they managed to beat their parents to it nonetheless. On those occasions, they heard loud, piercing whistles, taunts ("Is your daddy in the city or the county jail?"), threats ("We gon' kill your daddy," "Are you ready for the next bomb?"), and the ubiquitous slur, "Nigger!" Of more significance, the danger that Fred's civil rights activities created for his family necessitated an even greater attention to discipline in the home.[45]

Of course, Fred did not need the pressure of civil rights involvements to be a disciplinarian. He inherited a stern insistence on obedience from his mother. Moreover, as a minister Fred prized the self-help tradition of African American thought and preached often on the need for strong parental guidance in the home. In ACMHR mass meetings, for example, in addition to calling his followers to the crusade for freedom, he often spoke on family life in the context of "Negro improvement." On one occasion, he preached a long sermon that called on blacks in Birmingham to be better, stricter parents and to set positive examples for their children. Another time he excoriated parents for having "brought these children into the world without a thought and turned them loose on the streets to steal and fight and curse." He added that "if a Negro ever gets any place they will have to raise their children to be decent," warning that "hell will be full of Negroes for not looking after their children."[46]

Fred was inclined by background and philosophical conviction toward stern discipline, and this predisposition stiffened when things heated up in the movement. Both parents, and especially Ruby, fought to shield their children from as much of the danger as possible. Although the new tensions often made Fred more prickly than usual, the children essentially found their home an oasis of comfort. "At home we felt loved, and we had everything we needed," Pat later said. Nonetheless, just as events caused the phone to ring more often, the circumstances also led Fred and Ruby to clamp down even more tightly on their children's activities. In those times, with bodyguards accompanying their father and watching the parsonage, the children were commanded to go directly to school and return without detour and to stay home until their parents arrived.[47]

For the oldest child, Pat, Fred's words alone sufficed to ensure her obedience, but Ricky often tested her father's limits and led her brother, Fred Jr. ("June") into such transgressions as smoking. Once after Fred had restricted them to the house, Ricky and June ventured away to play with some friends down the street. They kept an eye out for their father's return and raced home when they spotted his blue car heading toward the parsonage. They might have succeeded in getting there first had June not tripped and cut a gash in his head. Later, when he visited his injured but out-of-danger son in the hospital, Fred said, "I'm glad to see you're alright, but as soon as you get out of here, I'm going to kick your butt because you were in the wrong place in the wrong time." In the next instant, though, he asked, "Now are you sure you don't want some ice cream?" Fred believed in corporal punishment and administered it often. Pat recalled that like most children, they preferred to be disciplined by their more lenient mother, whose "licks were light" in contrast to their father, who wielded "his belt like Zorro." [48]

When Fred was busier than usual he occasionally forgot to administer punishment that he thought he owed his children and would "save up spankings." Once when Ruby called on one of the girls to wash the dishes from dinner, Pat and Ricky ignored the directive and argued about whose turn it was. After Ruby reminded the girls several times, Fred impatiently demanded that one of the girls get on with the task at hand. When the girls' dispute proceeded unabated, an angry father tore off his belt to settle the matter. Pat accepted the punishment stoically, but the theatrical Ricky convincingly pretended to swoon as Fred raised the belt. Now worried, the father began to minister to his "fallen" daughter's needs. As her father carried Ricky to her room, Pat noticed her sister giving her a wink and a wry smile. Somehow Pat resisted the urge to blow the whistle on Ricky's ruse and did the dishes. [49]

Just as he followed his mother's example as a strong disciplinarian, Fred likewise insisted on his children's respect for and obedience to all other adults. He delegated to most adults in the neighborhood, and especially in the church, the authority to correct his children. He ordinarily agreed with their expectations of "PKS" ("preacher's kids"), and in disputed stories about the children's misbehavior he almost always believed the adults' version. If they corrected his children outside their home, he repeated the punishment inside. Often the punishment was public. When a member accused Fred Jr. of loud cursing during a sandlot football game, Fred thanked her from the pulpit for bringing the error to his attention, reprimanded his son in front of the congregation, administered a spanking, and grounded him for a week. One Sunday, as Ricky sat behind her father in the choir, he interrupted his sermon, whirled around, and slapped her face for talking in church. Fred took these occasions as opportunities to demonstrate that he practiced what he preached regarding family life and discipline. He made extraordinary efforts to show the members that their pastor's family set the example and lived by rules he advocated for them. His children, by virtue of being offspring of the minister, were to live exemplary lives before the other young people in the community.[50]

Ruby, who bore most of the responsibility for the children, handled discipline much more gently and often argued with Fred regarding his heavy-handed approach. She bristled at her husband's insistence that the children meet the unreasonable expectations of church members and especially resisted his pattern of taking the members' assessments of their children's behavior as gospel. She believed that some of the members' accusations were unfounded and suspected that some of their complaints were displaced criticisms of the pastor or his wife. Thus she often exhorted Fred to be more skeptical of the members' insinuations and to take the children's point of view more seriously. She particularly despised what she viewed as his tendency to sacrifice the needs or feelings of his own children for those of other children in the congregation. On one occasion, as the members boarded a full church bus to attend a church convention in Selma, Fred insisted that Pat relinquish her seat to another child. Angered at this slight, Ruby stormed over to Fred and said, "You don't take *my* child off a bus to give somebody else a seat" and demanded that her husband personally drive Pat to the meeting. On this occasion, Ruby got the better of him, but as a rule the intensity of his unwavering commitments to church and "the struggle" carried the day.[51]

Fred managed to enjoy some lighthearted moments at home. The bombing did not frighten people away from visiting the pastor. His celebrity status and charisma drew people into his circle. His friend T. L. Lane came over periodically to talk religion and to play checkers, and others came to be regaled with stories of his youth and early ministry. His civil rights activities naturally created in his church and in the ACMHR a certain number of fans who wanted to hear him retell his exploits. He often bragged on his children to his visitors, calling them out to recite their lessons from school, sing a song, or give the batting averages of a favorite ballplayer. On these occasions he made the children feel a sense of pride. As Fred Jr. indicated, "Whatever it was, he went off. If it was good, he would go off profusely. Praised you like you just cured cancer."[52]

In the main, however, Fred did relatively little of the parenting. His schedule took him away from home much of the time. When he was at home, his intensity required that he stay busy with church concerns or strategy sessions for the movement. He tended to be involved with his children more often when they needed correcting than in times of play. Typically he spent much of his time at home catching up on his rest, which put additional pressures on the children to behave themselves and play without disturbing their father. His busy activities created in him a good deal of tension and irritability, which exacerbated his insistence that his son and daughters be model children. Often Ruby covered for him, trying with difficulty to explain to them the pressures under which their father worked. Pat believed that her father was "always out of time" and was surprised when Fred managed to attend her high school graduation and treat her to a banana split afterward. Later, Fred Jr. noted wistfully that his father didn't have "time enough to be affectionate with all four of these kids. He didn't have time to play romper room. . . . Me and him didn't go fishing. Uncle Josh took me to the ball games. Ollie [Range] took me to the park. Dad took me to church."[53]

By the end of the first year of ACMHR agitation in Birmingham, Fred was becoming the personification of direct action, even more than King or C. K. Steele. Shuttlesworth had been organizing his movement "without the benefit of a precipitating outrage, such as the arrest of Rosa Parks." Fred, by contrast, pressured Jim Crow laws in Birmingham with radically confrontational acts of courage. In the process he galvanized his followers, jeopardized his family, and antagonized other potential leaders in the city's African American community. Shuttlesworth's intensity led one of his lawyers, Oscar W. Adams Jr.—who later became the first black justice of the Alabama Supreme Court—to call him "a man in a hurry" for whom desegregating at "all deliberate speed" made little sense. A person who demanded immediate actions, Fred continually pestered his lawyers to file suit to desegregate "every nook and cranny" of Birmingham "from kindergarten to high school."[54]

He particularly believed the efforts to integrate the schools were proceeding at a dilatory pace and pressed this point most vigorously. This was partly because the Supreme Court's decision had specifically pertained to school desegregation and also because philosophically Fred saw school integration as most critical in the long run, believing that "when kids go to school together, and play together, they won't be unknown and they won't be enemies."[55] Thus, noting that black teenagers in Collegeville were bused past the all-white and better-appointed Phillips High School to attend the "colored" Parker High, Shuttlesworth took aim at Phillips with intent to desegregate. At the same time that Congress was debating the Civil Rights Bill of 1957 and nine African

American teenagers were being prepared to integrate Little Rock's Central High School, Shuttlesworth began recruiting families willing to send their children into a potentially fiery furnace.

The Pupil Placement Law of 1955 governed school segregation in Alabama. Passed in the wake of the *Brown* decision, the statute gave local school boards wide latitude in determining which schools children in their districts would attend. In effect, the law allowed white superintendents to keep black students out of white schools. It was viewed by Shuttlesworth and other blacks as a subterfuge to delay the Supreme Court's desegregation ruling. Fred apprised several families of the possible repercussions under this law of seeking to desegregate the white high schools. Warning of possible job loss and certain harassment that would ensue, the minister managed to persuade eight sets of parents, largely by assuring them that he would be making the same request on behalf of his daughters and that ACMHR members would guard their homes just as they guarded his.[56]

On August 22, fully expecting their petition to be rejected yet willing to put the law to a court test, Fred submitted a letter to school superintendent L. Frazer Banks requesting that the Birmingham Board of Education admit the children to the schools nearest their homes. Banks advised the parents to keep their children in their current schools until the matter could be studied and a final decision rendered at the September 6 board meeting. The next day both of the daily newspapers editorialized against the move by Shuttlesworth and the others. The *Birmingham News* regretted the petition, warning that such an action "will further enflame a situation already troubled and dangerous." The *Post Herald* argued that "nothing constructive" could come of the effort except "increased tensions and greater misunderstanding" and possibly the abolition of the public school system, which would harm black children more than whites. The number of petitioners suffered from attrition, as two families withdrew their requests almost as soon as the petitions became public. On Friday, August 30, as Senator Strom Thurmond of South Carolina filibustered against the impending civil rights bill for a record twenty-four hours and twenty-seven minutes, a Birmingham meeting of principals and supervisors developed a plan, with the school board's approval, to allow individual school principals to register only those who were "normally and logically members of your school family." Following this meeting, some of the original petitioners backed out.[57]

In preparation for the beginning of the school year two days later, Shuttlesworth wrote another letter to Banks, asking for immediate instruction on whether to present the teenagers for enrollment at Phillips, as indicated in their initial petitions, or to leave them "un-enrolled" pending board action. The superintendent eventually instructed the parents to leave the children in the same school they had been attending until the board decided on their request at their September 6 meeting. Even before Shuttlesworth got his letter in the mail, however, the "already troubled and dangerous" situation, as the *News* had warned, became further inflamed by a horrifying act of racial hatred.[58]

On the evening of September 2, six members of the local Ku Klux Klan discovered an unsuspecting black couple walking along a country road. As part of a ritual ceremony, one of the Klan members sought to prove himself worthy to be promoted to "Captain of the Lair" by getting "nigger blood on his hands." Scaring off Cora Parker, the marauders focused their attack on her thirty-four-year-old companion, Edward Judge Aaron. Known as a docile "white folks's nigger" from Union Springs, Alabama, Aaron was pistol whipped and forced to crawl into his attackers' "lair." In their interrogation of him, they baited him, asking, "You think you're as good as I am? You think any nigger is as good as a white man? You think nigger kids should go to school with my kids?" Before getting down to his vile business, the soon-to-be-captain told him to carry a message to Shuttlesworth: "Stop sending nigger children and white children to school together . . . or we gonna do them like we're gonna do you." Then they dazed him with another blow to the head, took off his pants, and severed his entire scrotum with a razor blade. As he writhed in pain, they poured turpentine on his crotch, inadvertently saving his life by cauterizing the wound. Dressing him, the assailants put him in a car trunk, drove him eight miles, and left him by the roadside. Staggering to his feet, Aaron was spotted by passing motorists who alerted police of the "bloody Negro" along the road. Police who took him to medical care later testified that he looked as if he had been "dipped in blood from the belt down."[59]

Early the next morning Fred Shuttlesworth received information about the Aaron incident and immediately reported it to the Birmingham office of the FBI. As news spread rapidly throughout Birmingham's African American community, the horrific deed had a traumatic effect. The subject of widespread conversation, the assault was particularly vexing because Aaron, as ACMHR member Lola Hendricks said, "was bothering nobody. He wasn't trying to integrate anything. He was not doing anything. He was just walking the street." Shuttlesworth hoped to use this incident to the advantage of the national civil rights movement and was prepared to help take Aaron on the road to speak to issues of racial violence. When, however, Shuttlesworth became aware of the extent of Aaron's injuries, psychological as well as physical, he thought it improper to exploit the matter and subject Aaron to further embarrassment and trauma. Momentarily shaken by the atrocity, Shuttlesworth remained undeterred from integrating Phillips High School. Indeed, he seemed all the more resolved to go forward with his plan. Less than twenty-four hours after the mutilation of Edward Judge Aaron, Shuttlesworth made an official statement to the press that reaffirmed the earlier petitions and reiterated his belief in "the Constitutional right of all children to attend public schools nearest their homes, irrespective of race, creed, or color." He further announced that because Superintendent Banks had promised to deal with the matter at Friday's school board meeting, the parents would withhold their teenagers from enrolling in school until after the board's decision. At the meeting, as expected, the board deliberately avoided mention of the race of the petitioners and authorized Banks to handle the matter as he saw fit. Banks told the news reporters that he would seek other information before rendering a decision, a response Emory O. Jackson of the *Birmingham World* called a "denial by referrals." Concurring with Jackson that Banks and the school board were operating as a "school segregation enforcement agency," Fred resolved to take more precipitous action. Over the weekend, Shuttlesworth caucused with his family and the ACMHR brain trust. In reality, however, he had already made up his mind to take Pat and Ricky on Monday morning to enroll at Phillips.[60]

In discussions with the family, Fred essentially announced to the girls that they were going. With little opposition, Fred convinced Ruby and the girls that they had to be the first to be involved in the attempt to integrate Birmingham's schools. Shuttlesworth insisted that he and the family had to be consistent and set the example for others in Birmingham. He had already committed himself and could not back down without showing weakness. He could not ask others to make sacrifices that he himself was unwilling to make. Above all, however, was the deep conviction of the Shuttlesworths and other African American parents in locales across the Deep South that equality and dignity were ends worth, if necessary, the sacrifice even of their children.

At about the same time of this discussion in the parsonage of Bethel Baptist Church, the Reverend Kelly Miller Smith in Nashville pondered the possibility of surrendering his young daughter on "the altar of black and white together." Quoting the biblical passage about Abraham's sacrifice of his son Isaac, Smith told a white companion, "We're talking about some hard sayings. We're talking about faithfulness to Almighty God. . . . If God says we've got to do it, well, we've got to do it." Fred perhaps put the matter less dramatically, but his reasoning was almost identical. The decision thus made, he gave his daughters rudimentary instruction in the principles of nonviolence, advising them to do or say nothing as they simply followed him into the school. Ruby offered little opposition to her husband's plan, perhaps realizing it was of no use. She insisted, however, on going along to help protect her children. As for the girls, having been taught as the "preacher's kids" to be strong, they played the dutiful soldiers and agreed to the impossible mission with little show of emotion. Still, Pat wondered whether she could resist the urge to strike back against the abuse she anticipated, while Ricky played out various scenarios before blocking out all thoughts from her mind. She just made one wish—that everyone might be blind. She reasoned, "Then nobody would know what color anything was." Both nervous, the girls nonetheless expected their father's presence to calm their worries and trusted his judgment.[61]

At church that Sunday, word spread among the members that the pastor's family intended to follow through with their integration attempt. Sunday school classmates wondered how the girls were bearing up. Their two boyfriends were particularly worried. That afternoon Ricky and James Roberson sat at the organ in the church sanctuary plunking out some tunes and talking. Just as the couple leaned over to give each other a kiss, the imperious pastor Shuttlesworth walked into the room. Jerking herself to attention, Ricky waited for her father to lower the disciplinary boom. Preoccupied with other more pressing concerns, however, and either not noticing their amorous activity or ignoring it, Fred passed through the sanctuary without comment. Relieved to have wiggled at least temporarily off the hook, the couple resumed their conversation while Fred continued mulling over plans for the next day's events. As others in the church learned of the plans, they were told to stay away from Phillips because of potential danger.[62]

Although Ruby and the girls trusted Fred's judgment on integrating Phillips High, not everyone else had such confidence. One of the ACMHR lawyers, Oscar Adams, tried diligently to dissuade Shuttlesworth from going. "Fred, there ain't any point in going down to Phillips. You won't do nothing but get in trouble," Adams maintained. "Fred, you don't have to go down there. We've already got a case in court," he implored, thinking that NAACP Legal Defense Fund cases in other parts of the South would eventually change things in Birmingham. "Yeah, but y'all take too long," Shuttlesworth shot back. "I mo' get it desegregated."

"Naw," the lawyer assured him, "you may get your head beat up going down there. . . . I don't mind being brave, but I don't necessarily think you need to be brave when you don't have to."[63]

The preacher insisted on pressing on. He first wrote an official statement to be released to the newspapers about the time of the party's arrival at the school. Then, gathering some of his closest ACMHR associates, he laid his plans for the next day and assigned the responsibilities. He instructed his ACMHR vice president, Ed Gardner, to deliver the news release to the press around mid-morning. Pointing to another of his colleagues, he said, "Woods, I want you to drive me up to Phillips High School." Abraham Woods, pastor of the Metropolitan Baptist Church, had been an early and enthusiastic follower of Shuttlesworth, but on this occasion he agreed with Adams and had little inclination to follow Shuttlesworth into a lion's den. So, like the biblical Daniel, Woods inwardly prayed. Unlike Daniel, however, he prayed for words to help him avoid this directive while still saving face with his leader. As he paused and fumbled for an answer, the Reverend J. S. Phifer quickly spoke up, offering himself for duty: "I'll drive you up there." Breathing an inward sigh of relief, Woods chimed in, "Yeah, Rev. Phifer will drive you. I'll be the lookout man." With a trace of a smile, Shuttlesworth agreed that Phifer would drive and put Woods in charge of a detail to meet him the next morning at the school.[64]

On Monday morning, September 9, the same day President Eisenhower signed the 1957 Civil Rights Act and other lawyers sought a writ to force Arkansas governor Orval Faubus to permit integration in Little Rock, Shuttlesworth sent a telegram to Commissioner Lindbergh, alerting him of his plans. The telegram read: "Our application for admission having not been specifically approved or denied, and our children needing to be in school, we are presenting them for enrollment at Phillips today, arriving approximately at 10:15. We urgently request protection at the school and upon our complete return home so that no unfortunate incident may happen. As [to] our part, to insure calmness and quiet we have not announced publicly these intentions, nor released this wire." Police officials claimed that the telegram had not been filed until just six minutes before Shuttlesworth's scheduled arrival and did not reach police chief Jamie Moore's office until 11:57 A.M., thus not allowing time for police to provide protection. Shuttlesworth later suggested this time sequence was falsified, noting that he typically gave at least thirty minutes lead time. Moreover, through almost instantaneous radio contact with cruisers, even a six-minute warning would have been enough to put some officers in place. In addition, Shuttlesworth sent advance notice to Birmingham's two television stations in plenty of time for the stations to dispatch cameras to the scene. A little after ten o'clock the Shuttlesworths and Phifer loaded the youths—Pat, Ricky, thirteen-year-old Nathaniel Lee, and twelve-year-old Walter Wilson—into the car and headed for Phillips High School on Seventh Avenue North. When they arrived at the school, the camera crews were in place, but only four officers patrolled opposite corners of the city block.[65]

Pulling to a stop at 10:30, Ruby noticed a mob converging on the car from three directions in groups of eight to ten shirt-sleeved whites. Inside the car, scared silent by the shouts of "Niggers, go home," Ricky wondered, "Are we going in there?" Just then Nathaniel Lee spotted some in the crowd wielding baseball bats, brass knuckles, and chain links. In all this, Shuttlesworth surprised his companions when he got out of the car. Some of the mob gathered around the preacher, while others began beating on the car, denting it and smashing the windows. Police lieutenant E. T. Rouse, observing the melee from the corner, quickly radioed for help and headed toward the fray. Shuttlesworth tried to avoid the mob, running west down Seventh Avenue North for about a hundred yards, but he could not escape. As the swarm reached him, Fred heard a cacophony of howls: "This is the son of a bitch. If we kill him, it'll be all over." Others shouted, "Kill the mother fuckin' nigger" and "Don't let him get away. Kill him, goddammit!" As they began to land blows, Shuttlesworth heard a police officer give the mock order, "Now you ought not to bother him," while he stood his ground without offering to help. Seeing the proceedings, Ruby got out of the car in a vain attempt to lend her aid to Fred. As Ricky began to emerge from the vehicle, someone stopped her by slamming the door on her right ankle. Meanwhile, the mob had repeatedly knocked Fred to the ground with their bats and chains. On reaching the throbbing heap of humanity, Lieutenant Rouse and a few other officers tried to help, but they had difficulty staying with Shuttlesworth and keeping the crowd off him simultaneously. Rouse found one of the men carrying a twelve-inch chain and attempting to pull Ruby out of the car. Ruby had realized the crowd was heading for the car and had rushed back to protect the children. As he tried to help her, Rouse was pushed aside by the crowd, eventually managing to return to her aid. At that point he and three fellow officers each grabbed one of the assailants and took them into custody.[66]

By this time Shuttlesworth had most of the skin scrubbed off his face and ears and had been kicked in the face several times. His vision growing hazy and his consciousness beginning to ebb, he thought, "Well, this is it" as he began to stagger back toward the car. Then, Shuttlesworth later recounted, "something said to me, 'You can't die here. Get up. I got a job for you to do.' And I think that gave me the strength to stagger back to the car." Still dazed and beaten down several times, he got up and gradually located the car. Eventually reaching the car, Fred stumbled into an attacker who was gathering himself for a massive blow. Shuttlesworth fell to the pavement and began to crawl into the car. Phifer pulled him in to safety, while Ruby warded off the last of the aggressors with her purse. The attacker pulled the purse away from her and dropped it on the ground, while the car slowly pulled away from the mob. Even at this point, Shuttlesworth managed to retain a measure of control over the situation, having, as Ricky later recalled, the presence of mind to tell Phifer, "Don't run the stop sign" as they drove off to the hospital.[67]

Shuttlesworth was wheeled into the University of Alabama Hospital on a stretcher. He was conscious and calm, but his breathing was shallow. Ricky was quickly treated for a possible ankle fracture, while Ruby only on arrival at the hospital began to feel a stinging sensation on her backside. Noticing blood stains on the upper part of her buttock, she realized she had been stabbed during the fracas at Phillips High. Still on the hospital gurney and feeling like a skinned pig, Fred asked if the others were safe and was assured that they were. He then noticed that crowds of whites had begun to gather in the halls to steal a peek at the goings-on. Fred smiled at them and, as he waited to see a doctor, bantered with a few of the nurses. One of them told him, "I'll be damned if I'd let somebody beat me up like this. Hell, nothin's worth somebody doin' that to me. What were you trying to prove?" Her colleague replied, "Oh, you wouldn't understand," and Fred spoke up, "That's right, you *wouldn't* understand, but someday you will." At that point, a doctor arrived and extended his apologies to Shuttlesworth that whites had beaten him in that manner. "Well, I'm not angry about it," Fred answered. "I realize that's the price you pay." Then, as the physician examined him for a possible concussion, Fred asked him to hurry things along because he had other things to do. "You're really in this thing, aren't you?" the doctor asked. "With all my heart, Doctor," he replied. The doctor left momentarily while the nurses tended to Shuttlesworth's lacerations and put his arm in a sling. Soon the doctor returned, reporting incredulously that x-rays had detected neither a skull fracture nor a concussion.

"Reverend, even though I know God is looking after you, I thought there would be at least some small crack, as many blows as you took."

"Well, Doctor, the Lord knew I live in a hard town, so he gave me a hard head."

"Still, I'd like to keep you in the hospital overnight for observation," he said shaking his head with a smile.

"Doctor, I'll stay if you order me to, but not unless the police will protect me here." Then realizing that a police department riddled with Klan sympathizers was unlikely to provide him adequate protection, Shuttlesworth said, "I won't die over here in Klan country. If I go home and die, at least I'll die among my friends. Besides, I have a mass meeting to go to tonight."[68]

As the hospital staff finished tending the wounded, city hall responded to the incident. Connor had received word that sometime after the attack at Phillips, Ed Gardner had arrived at the offices of the *Birmingham News* with a news release and Shuttlesworth's prepared statement. Shuttlesworth reminded the city of the black families' good-faith petitions for immediate school admission and charged that Superintendent Banks had responded not with a ruling but with "a sociological treatise on the advantages of segregation for Negroes." He rejected as "a policy of negative evasion" the board's "routine channels" of interviews, studies, tests, and reports to the board, which "in effect mean 'never' without actually saying it." The statement continued:

Now we read (*Birmingham News*, Sept 8) that the applications have been referred to state channels in which they could linger for months. They need time; our children need schooling. We have now no alternative to presenting them for immediate enrollment. From the start, official tone here and elsewhere in the South has been one of defiance of the United States Constitution and judicial process, and of utter contempt for Negroes who would seek rights guaranteed by the United States Constitution and due process of federal laws.

In their failure to recognize the law of the land and to make at least some steps toward eventual compliance, the stage is ripe for tension, confusions, and violence, which they claim to fear. Hence these threats and intimidations of Negroes and these brutally vicious attacks upon innocent Negroes at night by robed white Klansman. The seeds of mayhem are always sown long before the act. . . . But higher official nor blood-thirsty riders can stop our quest for first-class citizenship. This we seek by good will, if at all possible; by law if necessary. We still hope for a reasoning together in love about the great issues of freedom which face us.

In response to both the statement and the events of the day, Commissioner Lindbergh ordered police to prevent anyone without "lawful reason to be at the school" from entering all school grounds in Birmingham, including any African Americans who might attempt to register. "We will use police to keep them out," he warned, disingenuously explaining that although the results would be the same, such an action did not parallel the situation in Little Rock: "The Governor of Arkansas is acting in direct conflict with a federal court order. We are acting under the authority of Alabama law. We are going to maintain law and order." [69]

Before the party was released from the hospital, reporters arrived to seek a statement from Fred. Hearing of Lindbergh's promise to keep blacks out of the white schools, Shuttlesworth announced that the ACMHR would make another attempt to desegregate Phillips *and* Woodlawn High Schools on Tuesday "whether they kill us or not." Asked about the mob's attack on him and his family, he elaborated on the comment he had made to the doctor: "I guess this is the price you pay for freedom. But I am not angry at any of the men who attacked me. I would not accuse the police department of negligence, but except for one policeman, they did nothing to try to stop the mob." Asked whether he thought the police knew about his trip to Phillips in advance, he assured the reporters that he had sent telegrams to both the police and the sheriff's departments. When someone asked what he was working for in Birmingham, he replied, "For the day when the man who beat me and my family with chains at Phillips High School can sit down with us as a friend." At that, he bid the reporters farewell and rejoined his family for the ride home. [70]

Almost as soon as the rowdies at Phillips High had begun to pelt the preacher and shake the pastor's car, the community around Collegeville heard the news. The detail of ACMHR faithful had arrived at the eastern side door of the school just as the commotion began at the front entrance. Running around to the front, Abraham Woods, James Armstrong, and the others arrived only in time to see Shuttlesworth wobble back to the car. They quickly loaded their car and followed Phifer to the hospital. Once there they checked on the injured and placed some calls around town to get the word out. By the time Shuttlesworth and the rest arrived back at their Twenty-ninth Avenue home, a modest crowd of church members, community folk, and a few reporters had gathered. James Roberson and Pat's boyfriend, Calvin Stokes, had cut school that day, waiting on the parsonage porch until the girls and their parents returned. Roberson exploded in anger on learning of the attack, especially when he heard that Mrs. Shuttlesworth had been stabbed. Although he did not act on his first impulse, he wanted to find a gun and kill all of the attackers. He thought to himself, "If I was God, I would just wave my hand and say, 'Away with all the white people who hated black people.'" Likewise, Veronica Chappell, another young member of Bethel Baptist Church, was furious and in a retaliatory mood because her pastor and friends had been beaten.[71]

Fred Jr., arriving from school on what had been until then a normal day, found a crowd milling about his home. He was wide-eyed as he found reporters—the first white people in his house—sniffing out details for their stories. He discovered his father, bruised in body but jovial in spirits, propped up in bed, watching television. Glancing at the screen, June noticed a man being beaten with a chain next to what looked to him like the family car. "Who is this?" he asked. "That's me," Fred responded. Looking quizzically at the sight of his father, bedridden and bandaged, while he was also on the television screen, the boy stood speechless. Pulling June over, patting him on the head, and giving him a kiss, Fred said, "Yeah, it's me. I'm alright. Don't worry about it" as he explained the events being depicted on the screen. Nevertheless, his son remained a bit dumbfounded by his father's lack of concern for his own health and his mirth at having generated some publicity for the movement.[72]

Later that afternoon James T. Montgomery Jr., the Shuttlesworths' family physician, stopped by for a house call. As had the attending physician at the hospital, Montgomery marveled that Shuttlesworth had not been more seriously injured in the attack. He was amazed not merely because Fred had escaped without a skull fracture or concussion but also because, according to hospital records, he had not even registered a rapid pulse or elevated blood pressure. Montgomery later said Fred was "almost made for this thing." As his doctor checked him over, finding bruises, abrasions, and a sprained arm, an excited Shuttlesworth said, "They can hit my head hard, but they can't kill me. We're gon' get this thing changed, Doc." Ruby was sitting gingerly because of the stab wound on her derriere, but complained only that when they all attended the mass meeting that night, modesty would prevent her from showing off her scar.[73]

Fred Shuttlesworth was no more likely to cancel a Monday night mass meeting than he was to cancel a church service on Sunday. Meetings went on as planned regardless of the circumstances and certainly on major events such as this day's. A standing-room-only crowd of more than five hundred awaited the Shuttlesworths' arrival at New Hope Baptist Church. The church's pastor, Herman Stone, barred reporters from the meeting. With his arm in a sling and patches of adhesive tape on his head, Fred sat on the edge of the platform as he addressed a congregation that welcomed him as a hero. Realizing that tempers might be running high, he focused his comments on the need to remain calm and nonviolent. "Now I want everybody to be calm. It happened to me; it didn't happen to you. And if I'm not mad, I don't see why you should get mad. I don't want any violence. We have to control ourselves and keep on fighting." He admonished his followers to avoid "doing anything to any white person for what has happened to me," adding that "God is showing the world that there are some Negroes in Birmingham who are not afraid." After the meeting, Shuttlesworth spoke briefly with reporters, refusing comment on any future plans but vowing that he would "not let up the fight." He once again accused the board of education of evasiveness and denied Commissioner Lindbergh's accusation that Shuttlesworth had acted at Phillips merely for publicity.[74]

That Shuttlesworth operated for publicity's sake was not the only theory circulating. Many doubtless would have agreed with white liberal Charles Morgan's assessment: "I thought he was absolutely off the wall and didn't understand the world he was living in." In reality, he probably understood the Jim Crow world more clearly than most. As did many in the civil rights movement, he perceived that segregation created a world in which those in control would never surrender their power voluntarily. External pressure would have to be brought to bear in order to dismantle the "southern way of life." Publicity became the means of bringing that pressure to bear on segregation. Publicity would indeed fall to Shuttlesworth by virtue of his public acts of confrontation. Just as human events never have single causes, however, human beings never have single motives for their actions. All human motives are mixed. Shuttlesworth wanted publicity, but he unquestionably wanted the end of segregation as well. Clearly the motive of self-interest could be used in the service of the higher motive of ending segregation. Publicity then for Shuttlesworth was a means to a higher end rather than the end itself.[75]

In reality he gained only very limited fame from the Phillips incident. The story and a photograph did make the front page of the *New York Times,* as well as some television news footage, but the story was short-lived. The *Christian Science Monitor* ran a story on Shuttlesworth that covered the Phillips and the terminal station incidents, but although impressed with Shuttlesworth's courage, the writer compared him to other leaders in unfavorable terms: "To reporters accustomed to talking with well-educated Negro leaders, the Reverend Mr. Shuttlesworth appears to be somewhat less polished, and at times incapable of cogent comment about what he is doing." *Time* carried a few lines of the story but only referred to Shuttlesworth as "an ill-advised Negro preacher." The Edward Judge Aaron incident received more attention from *Time* and all the attention of the *New Republic*. *Newsweek* similarly wrote a paragraph about Shuttlesworth and did mention him by name.[76]

In acting publicly Shuttlesworth could hardly control the spin a reporter might give the story. In addition, if Shuttlesworth sought publicity above all, he should have chosen a more opportune time, when the country's attention to the integration issue was not already riveted by the events in Little Rock. Perhaps most important, in a city as violently committed to maintaining segregation as Birmingham, Shuttlesworth had much more to *lose* by acting as he did. His request for police protection indicated that he appreciated the possible dangers not only for himself but also for other members of his family. As Shuttlesworth's SCLC colleague Wyatt T. Walker would later observe, "You don't get yourself half-killed just for publicity."[77] In Birmingham such publicity could easily have gotten the Shuttlesworths much more than *half* killed.

Also, the idea that self-promotion was Shuttlesworth's primarily motivation arose, particularly when it came from whites, out of a widely believed but faulty assumption that African Americans accepted and preferred segregation. It appeared that most white southerners believed, or claimed to believe, that blacks did not want integration, and they convinced themselves that such "integration leaders" as Shuttlesworth could be motivated only by self-interest. As with similar claims that persons in power have traditionally leveled against prophetic types who challenge the status quo, the accusation about Shuttlesworth essentially became an ad hominem argument attempting to discredit the message by discrediting the messenger.

African American concerns about Shuttlesworth's motivations, however, were another matter. Without disparaging the message, some were beginning to be skeptical of the messenger, as was reflected in Emory Jackson's editorial following the Phillips incident: "Whatever judgment one might hold with reference to his methods, motives, and timing, no one has said, or could say, he was violent or forcing his way. He selected one of the ways by which those interested in bringing the local law in line with the highest law might use."[78] Jackson thus defended Shuttlesworth's actions, though he hinted that support for the minister was not monolithic. In essence, Shuttlesworth's single-mindedness had begun to make some other would-be leaders in the black community uncomfortable. Whether he called them Uncle Toms, and sometimes he did, Shuttlesworth, with his uncompromising attack, made them feel like Uncle Toms.

The next morning a bomb threat emptied Phillips High of its 1,850 students for forty-five minutes. That afternoon school superintendent Banks received a second telephone warning, this time indicating a bomb was hidden in the Phillips basement. In another part of town, responding to Shuttlesworth's earlier announcement of an attempt at Woodlawn High School, some fifty students boycotted classes to protest integration. They demonstrated on school grounds, throwing rocks and jeering at buses and cars carrying blacks. Standing near two effigies hanging on the school grounds, others shouted, "We want a boycott!" and "We want Shuttlesworth!" They left disappointed. Not only did their principal threaten to suspend them but also Shuttlesworth canceled plans to integrate Phillips and Woodlawn. He told reporters that he could not take his daughters to school because he was under doctor's orders to stay in bed and that "since I can't be there to lead them," he doubted other blacks would make an attempt. In addition, he postponed his plans because of the school board's promised action on the petitions and also because of Lindbergh's order for unauthorized persons to stay away from the school grounds.[79]

Meanwhile, at city hall, police processed three men whom officers had apprehended at the scene of Shuttlesworth's beating. When I. F. Gauldin, J. E. Breckenridge, and W. H. Cash came to trial in Jefferson County court, Shuttlesworth, his wife, and J. S. Phifer testified against them to little avail. Shuttlesworth positively identified each of the defendants as among his attackers, indicating that Gauldin had struck him with a chain and Cash with brass knuckles and that Breckenridge was on top of him after he was knocked to the ground. Gauldin testified that he had picked up the chain only after the struggle ended. Cash said he had been only passing the school when Shuttlesworth ran into him and knocked him down, and Breckenridge claimed that the mob had caught him up as he watched the disturbance and threw him onto Shuttlesworth. Defense counsel George Rogers rejected a $50 fine for assault and battery. Instead, he opted to allow his clients to be bound over to the grand jury for possible indictment on a felony charge of assault with intent to murder. The reasoning was that a felony charge would be tried before a jury, whereas a misdemeanor would not. Before an October 4 grand jury, the strategy worked, as the defendants' peers refused to indict them even though Shuttlesworth again identified them and their pictures had appeared in the *Birmingham News* on the day after the attack.[80]

Once his bruises healed, Shuttlesworth resumed his perpetual motion at its usual breakneck pace. He traveled to California for a speaking engagement. While he was there, rumors developed that Shuttlesworth had left Birmingham permanently and that if he returned, the Klan would be waiting for him at the airport. Nothing developed, and Shuttlesworth returned without incident. As SCLC secretary he went to Atlanta twice for executive board meetings to participate in discussions of voter registration drives and the need to hire an executive director. In November, after the achievement tests of his daughters and the transfer students had been completed, he threatened to file suit in federal court if the young people were refused admission to the white schools.[81]

Later in the month, he spoke at an annual NAACP banquet in Akron, Ohio, where he delivered an address that revealed much of the theological basis of his agitation for civil rights. Called "Meeting and Matching the Challenge of This Hour," the speech articulated a theological understanding of America's divine purpose long held in African American religion. Although many African American Christians despaired of ever receiving justice in the United States, most believed in an American messianism in which blacks would serve as the chosen of the chosen people, teaching the nation and ultimately the world how to live with its racial pluralism. During the Civil War period, those believers represented by the African Methodist Episcopal Church drew a theological picture of America that excluded the possibility of separated races. Such a nation diverged from the divine decree that America would be "the . . . solving of the great problem of a universal brotherhood."[82]

Hardly deviating an iota from such a theory, Shuttlesworth emphasized the sovereignty of God in human affairs, that the world belonged to God, not to Napoleon, Hitler, Mussolini, or Stalin, nor to the likes of Senators James Eastland (Mississippi) or Herman Talmadge (Georgia). Like the fundamentalist, anticommunist preachers of the McCarthy era, he reminded his audience that God was using Russia's military and technological expertise to get America's attention: "God is saying to the Christian nations: 'Get right or get off; clean up or clean out.' " He continued:

> The great American challenge of the hour is none other than finishing up the unfinished business of the Civil War—of second class citi-

zens in a first class country. Not of conquering the South, but of building a true American brotherhood. Not necessarily of destroying the Southern Way of life, but in seeing to it that any way of life within these borders conform [sic] fully to the American ideals of justice, equality, and fair play. . . . The real crimes of this hour are done in Washington, D.C., where the Eastlands, Talmadges, [Harry] Byrds, and [Richard] Russells can stand with impunity and break the oaths they swore to uphold, and call their misguided fellows back home to defy law, disrespect the courts, and rebel against the constituted authority of the United States. . . .

We shall march with relentless tread to freedom in this day; and shall help America to clean her garments. . . . Integration has become a bad word in the deep South. But the Negro has never confused intermarriage with integration. . . . The Negro only asks for what America means; Democracy means integration. . . . Integration is the right to work and be economically secure; the right to political participation, and the opportunities with all others to participate in and improve upon social activities and standards in the community.

America means integration: else strike from the flag its colors of red, white, and blue. America means integration, else take out of the Declaration of Independence the words, "All men are created equal . . . and are endowed by their creator with certain inalienable rights." . . . America means integration, else take from the pledge, "one nation under God, indivisible, with liberty and justice for all." America means integration, else close down your courthouses, and tear the meaningless signs down from over their doors. America means integration, else send back the Irish to Ireland, the Orientals back to Asia, and the Anglo Saxon back to Europe, the Negro to Africa and call back the Indian from his reservation, give him the keys to the country and make sonnets and epics and build monuments over his heroic war dead, needlessly slaughtered by the American white man. America means integration, else knock down the stature [sic] of Liberty, and chisel off her base the slogan: "Give me your poor." America means integration, else quit singing "Our Fathers God to thee, Author of Liberty." America means integration, else take from the Bible the words, "Of one blood God made all men for to dwell upon the face of the earth." . . . This is

America's challenge of the hour. It must be met and matched in this
hour.

As he spoke with reporters after the speech, he reemphasized his loyalty to
America. "Twice in nine months I was near the icy jaws of death," he noted,
recalling his close calls on Christmas night and at Phillips High School. "In spite
of this I say, 'God Bless America.' It is good to be American. Although we live
in a country that is not fully democratic yet, I still feel the United States is the
best on the face of the earth."[83]

Earlier that fall, Birmingham's version of Americanism had put Eugene
"Bull" Connor back in his familiar seat as commissioner of public safety. To a
significant degree, the agitation of Shuttlesworth and his "people in motion"
had antagonized the most rabid segregationists in the electorate and cracked the
door open for Connor to sneak back into office. Ironically, Shuttlesworth had
helped to resurrect Connor's political fortunes in the Magic City. In October,
rumors spread around town that the commissioners' race would include black
attorney Arthur Shores and the Reverend Fred Shuttlesworth as write-in candidates.[84] The rumor was unfounded, and Connor remained unopposed in the
general election. Nonetheless, an approaching contest between Shuttlesworth
and Connor was no rumor. It was more like a prophecy.

"Bull"fighting

> You generally measure the militancy of an activist's
> character against the intensity of the oppression. . . .
> Fred and Bull Connor were made for each other.
> — Joseph E. Lowery

When Bull Connor swore the oath of office as commissioner of public
safety on November 4, 1957, he might as easily have been pledging his
allegiance to the southern way of life and to resisting Fred Shuttlesworth
"so help me, God." In his inaugural address he argued the constitutionality of
segregation laws and promised to enforce them in Birmingham "to the utmost
of my ability and by all lawful means." Where Robert Lindbergh had waged a
largely defensive war against ACMHR agitation, Connor took the offensive. Connor's return to power was the story of the year in white Birmingham, but in the
black community Shuttlesworth ran unopposed for "Mr. Front Page," the *Birmingham World's* news maker of the year for 1957. Editor Emory Jackson wrote
with prophetic insight, if not *fore*sight, in calling Fred "the target figure of the
bigots, controversial in his approach, outspoken in his convictions."[1]

In reality, anyone with eyes to see could detect a classic battle brewing.
Shuttlesworth and his ACMHR forces noticed the change almost immediately,
and 1958 developed into, in Shuttlesworth's words, "a year of utter harassment."[2]
Direct and often face-to-face encounters between these antagonists yielded a
second bombing of Bethel Baptist Church, another effort at a bus boycott, and
the emotional low point of Shuttlesworth's almost obsessive fight. That year's
continuous parry and thrust between Connor and Shuttlesworth is the focus of
this chapter.

From the ACMHR's inception in 1956, police had regularly issued traffic tickets for improper parking or reckless driving in their attempts to discourage citizens from attending the weekly mass meetings. Soon after Connor came back
into office, plainclothes police detectives began to visit the meetings without
fail. They typically made notes on the proceedings, including summaries of the
speeches and sermons presented, along with who had delivered them. Ordinarily two detectives came to the services, armed with notepads and wired to a tape

recorder in their car. In this manner Connor elevated the intimidation factor and both angered and frightened many in the movement. Some were frightened away.

On one occasion, Shuttlesworth's bodyguard, Colonel Stone Johnson, invited his pastor, R. L. Beverly, to attend a mass meeting. Agreeing, Beverly, who thought Shuttlesworth was crazy and that Johnson was crazy for following him, got only as far as the vestibule of the church when a glance at the detectives stopped him short. He told Johnson, "No, I ain't going no further. I got too much temper. I'll get in there and go to fighting." Johnson, however, remained convinced that a fear of Connor's men drove Beverly away. In addition, Connor, who also ran the Birmingham Fire Department, began to use it as another means of pestering Shuttlesworth and his loyalists. For a protracted period in 1958, Connor pressured fire chief Aaron Rosenfeld to interrupt mass meetings by sending fire trucks to their various locations to search for phantom fire hazards. Bursting into church sanctuaries with blaring sirens and flashing lights, the firefighters primarily fought the inner fire in Shuttlesworth and his friends, failing, in Shuttlesworth's words, "to stampede Negroes or to extinguish the fire that wouldn't go out."[3]

Crank and threatening phone calls to the Shuttlesworth home also increased during this period. When FBI agents occasionally visited Shuttlesworth's home but would never use the telephone, Fred realized the police had tapped it. Occasionally he could detect voices from the police and fire departments on the line; he claimed that the phone actually rang even when it was off the hook. Beyond Connor's direct efforts at intimidating Shuttlesworth's forces were more general impediments placed in their way by white Birmingham. Some ACMHR members were fired from their domestic jobs when they told their white employers they had attended Shuttlesworth's meetings. In addition, the major newspapers in Birmingham tended to bury stories about the ACMHR's activities. More often, the news was suppressed in the local papers, forcing Shuttlesworth to send news releases to SCEF field workers Carl Braden and Anne Braden, who in turn filed stories with the Associated Press wire. As a result, stories often appeared in papers everywhere in the country except Birmingham.[4]

Shuttlesworth responded by redoubling his efforts, in effect seeking to "harass the harassers." In February he kicked off a "Double the Vote" drive, part of an eleven-state voter registration effort coordinated by the SCLC. He issued a strong appeal to church and civic leaders to support the drive and to attend the rally on the February 12 birthday of the Great Emancipator. At the rally itself, which was very well attended, Shuttlesworth arranged for his associates Edward Gardner, N. H. Smith, Abraham Woods Jr., and W. E. Shortridge to be on the program, though he himself had no public role in the event. Also in high-profile roles were insurance executive John J. Drew, wealthy business leader A. G. Gaston, and Dr. John W. Nixon, a dentist and NAACP leader. These members of the black middle class in Birmingham eventually became somewhat critical of Shuttlesworth's style and leadership, but in this instance Shuttlesworth showed an ability to work with them without his needing to be at center stage.[5]

In March ACMHR treasurer Shortridge wrote Emory Jackson to call for increased support for Shuttlesworth. He listed Shuttlesworth's efforts to date to desegregate the police, the terminal station, the buses, and the schools. Contrasting the ACMHR's across-the-board approach with the single-focus methods of civil rights efforts in Montgomery and Tuskegee, Shortridge called Shuttlesworth "the most courageous Negro Leader the County has ever produced." Noting that the cases had to that point cost nearly $25,000 in legal fees, he appealed for stronger support by the black press. In April, with Shuttlesworth's prodding, George Johnson once again unsuccessfully filed suit in federal court against the Jefferson County Personnel Board, charging that he had been deprived of his civil rights after being refused an exam for the police force. In response, he asked the court for $25,000 in damages and for a preliminary injunction allowing him and other African Americans to take the exam. His case before Judge H. H. Grooms was scheduled for July. In the meantime, Shuttlesworth participated in a two-day summit meeting of black leaders in Washington, D.C., and received one of three John B. Russwurm awards from the National Newspaper Publishers Association. Named after one of the editors of the first African American newspaper in America, the award cited individuals and organizations who had advanced the cause of freedom. The year before, the same honor had been awarded to King and white Lutheran minister Robert Graetz of Montgomery.[6]

On May 20, seeking to press issues on Connor's home turf, Shuttlesworth and a small delegation of ACMHR faithful appeared at the office of the Jefferson County Civil Service Board, where they sought and were refused application forms for police jobs. Unwilling to let the matter lie, Shuttlesworth and another delegation of some twenty supporters appeared at a preliminary meeting of the city commission on Monday, June 2. Confronting Shuttlesworth face-to-face for the first time, Connor refused to allow him to make his request on the grounds that Shuttlesworth had not given the commissioners advance notice of his intention to appear before them. The next day, however, at the commission's regular meeting, Shuttlesworth, backed up by an even larger contingent of seventy loyalists, made his presentation. His strategy was to fall back on the issue of black police whenever there was a lull in specific legal attacks. At least on the Negro police issue real progress was possible inasmuch as a majority of even white Birminghamians supported the idea. Armed with the same evidence of such support he had produced in 1955, Shuttlesworth prepared to put the issue before Connor. Even if Connor refused, which was expected, Shuttlesworth reasoned that by generating substantive publicity he would manage both to keep the pressure on Connor and to keep the ACMHR in the eye of Birmingham blacks as the organization that pressed for their needs.[7]

At the June 3 meeting, the three commission officials sat at high desks looking down on their audience. Mayor Jimmy Morgan, seated in the center, called the meeting to order, with J. T. "Jabo" Waggoner, commissioner of public improvements, and Connor on either side. When Morgan called on the delegation of blacks, Shuttlesworth arose to announce he bore a petition for black police officers. At that point, Connor interrupted him, almost shouting, "Are you Shuttlesworth?"

"Yes, sir, I am," he replied politely.

"Are you making this request?"

"I'm making it on behalf of Negro police."

"Well, I think you're more interested in publicity than in police."

"That is not true, sir. I will continue asking for Negro police with or without publicity."

"Well, go ahead and say what you came to say, because I have something to say."

"Well, the letter says what we want to say, and it just asks for Negro police."

At this point, Shuttlesworth began reading his petition. He claimed that "this step would serve not only to grant a social and economic right—well-deserved by Negroes because of their patience, loyalty, and population ratio—but also as a preventive to crime, prevailing now because of the unholy conditions allowed to exist in Negro neighborhoods." He reiterated the results of the polls and other public expressions favoring black police and noted the embarrassment "that a great city of the magnitude and potential of Birmingham should in this day be so far behind all major and even tiny cities" by not having "even a single Negro on either the Police Force or Fire Department." He concluded by stating, "Our people are ready, capable, willing, and anxious to meet responsibilities and fulfill their obligations to society in an orderly and Brotherly manner, using always the Christian approach to problems. There can be no end to our seeking and asking for what is just; for we are divinely urged to 'seek and find, ask and be given, knock until the door be opened.' This door is locked only on the official side. There can be quietness only when elementary conditions for peace and quietness are met."

When Shuttlesworth finished, his adversary snarled, "You know what I think? I think you have done more to set your people back and cause more trouble that any Negro ever in this town."

"Mr. Commissioner," Shuttlesworth replied, "whether I've done more to set them back or you, that's a matter for history to decide. The problem is what will *you* do?"

"I ain't doin' nothin' for you!"

"I haven't asked you to do anything for me. I asked you to do for the Negro community, of whom you are the Commissioner."

Banging his gavel, Morgan called for the antagonists to curtail their arguments. Growing irritated, however, Shuttlesworth shot back, "You're gon' let him say what he wants to say?" Morgan then allowed the preacher his say: "Well, the Commission is on the spot. You are the fathers of the city, and you should do what you're supposed to do, and quit playing ring-around the rosey. Usually when one of you is for it, two are against it." Connor then interjected, "Well, I ain't gon' do nothing for you." As he and his people prepared to exit, Shuttlesworth made one last comment: "Well, I was pretty sure you wouldn't when I came down, but the fact is we asked, and the Bible says ask." At that Shuttlesworth and his delegation were dismissed, bringing the first direct encounter between Shuttlesworth and Connor to an abrupt end.[8]

After the petitioners left, Connor raised the issue of the Bethel church bombing, noting rumors that Shuttlesworth or some of his people had themselves planted the explosives in order to generate publicity. Almost immediately after Shuttlesworth arrived at home, a reporter called with news of Connor's intimations. Turning on the television, Fred watched Connor tell the cameras that state authorities "believe that Shuttlesworth knows more than he is telling about the bombing." Then he invited Shuttlesworth to take a polygraph test. That night Shuttlesworth drafted an official response, releasing it to reporters early the next day. Scoring Connor for his "personal tirades and intemperate remarks," Fred depicted the commissioner "as most unreasonable and discourteous" as he shouted his "contempt and scorn of Negroes." Noting that "official confusion reigns in the city," he further suggested that Connor was a victim of self-deception if he believed he could discredit Shuttlesworth or intimidate his supporters "by his furious rantings." He continued: "Trained men, dedicated to public service, will at least listen to complaints of the people who they govern; but it is utterly childish to close one's eyes against truth, and to get mad when there is no cause for madness. Not to be forgotten is the total negative attitude of the entire Commission as to some of the fundamental rights of Negroes. The struggle must go on. Negroes are not fearful, and need not get angry. It is enough to be right. For righteousness will exhalt [sic] any nation." Then moving to his primary rejoinder, he replied to Connor's appeal to rumors concerning the bombing. "It should seem strange that I would plot to have my own home and church bombed, and then be fool enough to be in bed—directly at the point of blast impact at the time it happened. Mr. Connor should know that tricks of this kind and suicidal ventures belongs [sic] far more to other people than to Negroes." Because Connor sought to discredit Shuttlesworth by appeal to rumor and a lie-detector test, the preacher issued a challenge in kind: "Let us in fairness go all the way and try to clear a lot of rumors and confusion." At that point, Shuttlesworth welcomed the opportunity to take the polygraph test, *provided* the commissioner would follow suit and answer whether he was a Klan member, hated blacks, had been involved in police corruption, or knew about police operating dives in Negro areas.

Appearing before the press on Wednesday, Shuttlesworth followed up his prepared statement by commenting that his conditions for submitting to a polygraph were "directly related to the whole fabric of Klannish violence and law enforcement in our city." He announced that he was ready and anxious to tell what he knew to a lie detector when the commissioner was ready to do likewise, adding, "I believe it is far easier to talk over the airwaves than talk in a lie detector. If there is nothing to hide—and to clear up 'rumors,' let's quit talking and get on with the tests." Connor's initial reaction was to declare curtly, "I am not going to start obliging Shuttlesworth." Later that afternoon, in a more studied reply, Connor answered that some three hundred polygraph tests had been administered without anyone making it a condition that the commissioner of public safety submit to a similar examination. "I don't think I shall begin that practice at the invitation of Shuttlesworth." He further noted that few persons had any doubts about his political beliefs, and he denied that he held membership in the Klan. Then he reiterated that the police department would wait and see whether Shuttlesworth would submit to the test. At that juncture, Connor let the matter drop, at least publicly.[9]

Running the gamut from the Klan to the citizens' councils to the newly formed National States Rights Party, radical segregationists in Birmingham who had put their hopes in Connor soon resented their man's visible standoff with their number one enemy. Having battled to a draw in his public exchanges with Shuttlesworth regarding the lie-detector test, Connor himself intended to be rid of Shuttlesworth at almost any cost. Within a few days, Connor and two of his detectives met with Clarence M. Kelley, FBI special agent in charge of Birmingham operations and later director of the bureau. Connor called the meeting on the pretense of looking into the bombings in Birmingham and arranging a sting operation on potential bombers. Plausible rumors suggested, however, that the Klan or other rabid segregationists had begun to lean on Connor for allowing Shuttlesworth to continue his agitation. Having publicly lost face to his African American adversary and needing to get back into the good graces of his constituents, Connor, with undercover detectives Captain G. L. Pattie and Lieutenant Thomas H. Cook, concocted a plan. The grapevine had indicated that white supremacist lawyer and insurance adjustor J. B. Stoner might be able to arrange another bombing of Bethel. Connor authorized his detectives to contact Stoner and talk with him.

On the afternoon of Saturday, June 21, Pattie and Cook arranged to meet with Stoner and with Klan member and police informant William Hugh Morris in a parking lot behind the Bankhead Hotel in downtown Birmingham. Climbing into Morris's Studebaker, the detectives began their conversation by identifying themselves as steelworkers named G. L. Edwards and Ted Cook. They told Stoner that they intended to stop the integration movement, and then they exchanged greetings and got down to business. After Stoner suggested he had knowledge of the recent unsuccessful bomb attempt on Temple Beth-El, Pattie noted that although he had been opposed to violence, he now thought the previous three years had made the racial situation intolerable and indicated that he indeed had a bomb in mind.

"I've got some boys who are experts in that type of thing, and they could fix a bomb that would go off," Stoner boasted. "In fact, they will guarantee it to go off. If you're really interested, we can talk about it further. The boys will agree if you can furnish the money."

"How much?"

"Say, $2,000? For that amount I can get my people to make a bomb and set it out at a building or wherever you suggest."

They then mentioned several possible targets, finally settling into a discus-

sion of the "Shuttlesworth church." "Yeah, that's one of the places where meetings in the integration movement are planned," Stoner said. "I know where it
is," he added, "[and] know the layout, too. It'll be a little hard to get to, 'cause
it's just niggers that live there." Picking up the cue, Pattie complained about
Shuttlesworth's efforts, in particular his forays at the terminal station and Phillips High School. "We elected Connor hoping he would do something about the
Negro situation," he grumbled, "but we're a little disappointed in him. The only
thing he has done is to engage in a newspaper controversy with Shuttlesworth."
Cook then told Stoner that he and his partner intended to select a responsible
person to arrange for Shuttlesworth's church "to be blown completely off the
map and not leave a brick standing." He added that "some big business people
. . . had promised to come through with some substantial donations to the
cause" if assured that, unlike the attempt on the temple, the mission would be
successful. Stoner said that he could arrange a successful bombing for a price of
$2,000. Pattie then indicated his fond hope that "the total destruction of that
church would persuade Shuttlesworth to leave Birmingham and go up North
where he belongs," adding that if another bombing did not scare the preacher
off, the group "would be willing to go further with another job that would
eliminate Rev. Shuttlesworth completely." Stoner assured the detectives that he
could make either kind of arrangement and that he would not charge them for
an unsuccessful bomb attempt. The detectives then told Stoner and Morris that
if they managed to raise the money and decide on a place, they would notify
them. At that, the twenty-minute meeting ended.[10]

During the next week Bethel Baptist Church received unusual visitors on two
separate occasions. On the night after his meeting with Pattie and Cook, Stoner
himself visited Shuttlesworth's church, apparently to check out the premises.
Having circled the block several times in a cab, Stoner exited his cab and headed
to the front entrance of the church as Sunday evening services were concluding.
As several church people milling near the door greeted him, he said, "I would
like to see Reverend Shuttlesworth. I'm in trouble. I want him to pray for me."
A deacon of the church, suspicious of a white man in the neighborhood,
brushed aside the request, indicating that his pastor was unavailable. At that,
the visitor immediately turned away and walked with a slight limp down
Twenty-ninth Avenue and then got into his cab and departed. The following
Saturday Birmingham police visited the guards stationed outside the church,
charging that they were unlawfully in possession of firearms and confiscated
four rifles from their station on the porch of church member James Revis. Such

an action, in Shuttlesworth's mind, left the church and parsonage once again open to attack.[11]

At about 1:30 the next morning, Revis's daughter, Laverne, returning from her late Saturday night shift at a downtown sandwich shop, spotted billows of smoke rising from beside the church and hurried around to the guard station to alert the men on duty. The two leaders of the guards, Colonel Stone Johnson and Will Hall, sped to the east side of the church and discovered a five-gallon can. A miner with some knowledge of demolitions, Hall realized the sparking fuse would possibly allow enough time to remove the makeshift explosive. Without hesitation, Hall furiously grabbed up the smoking can, running it to the middle of the street. As he carried the potentially deadly pail, the heat singed the hairs of his arms, but Hall managed to set it down at the edge of Thirty-third Street North before it exploded in his face. Just as he and Johnson ran twenty-five feet and dived out of harm's way, the bomb detonated, blasting a crater in the street fifteen inches deep and two feet in diameter.

Across the street from the church, Shuttlesworth instinctively rolled out of bed onto the floor as the blast went off. He hurriedly dressed and ran into the street to investigate, as did other neighbors, who spilled out of their homes in reaction to another nighttime raid. He found Hall and Johnson safe and accompanied them to the point of the explosion. Apprised of what his guards had done to avert more damage, he congratulated them for their bravery and went immediately into the church office to call the police and the FBI. After notifying them, he surveyed the premises to determine the extent of the damage and whether Sunday services could be held as scheduled. On inspection, he discovered that shrapnel had hit the church, shattering all the windows on one side of the building, cracking plaster in some of the walls, tearing a curtain, and marring the pulpit. He and police investigators later learned that the explosion broke windows and tore Sheetrock in the homes of both of Shuttlesworth's neighbors, the Revises and the Robersons. In addition, flying glass injured the six-month-old daughter of Laverne Revis McWilliams, permanently scarring her face and forehead.[12]

Within an hour of the bombing, investigators from both the city fire and police departments arrived at the scene, including fire chief Aaron Rosenfeld and detectives Pattie and Cook. While they investigated the bomb site, police began to confuse matters by the suggestion that Shuttlesworth or others in his organization had planted the bomb. Later testimony by William Hugh Morris indicated strong evidence that Klan-sympathizing police officers regularly arrived at the scene of bombings to destroy evidence. That this may have occurred in this instance seems likely, and the case was not solved until the 1980 conviction of J. B. Stoner.[13]

At the scene, the detectives "suspecting" that Laverne McWilliams had set the bomb requested her to ride with them to the police station to be questioned and to take a polygraph test. She did not object to the test but refused to ride with the officers. Instead, she was driven by her father. In addition, others suggested that Will Hall, who had moved the bomb away from the church, had, as a retired miner, the necessary expertise to have set the bomb himself. In fact, Hall had on occasion talked to Shuttlesworth about retaliating against whites and had mentioned that he knew where explosives might be procured. Shuttlesworth waved aside any such suggestion, given in jest or not, and warned Hall, "If any bomb explodes at any white homes, I'll tell the police that you said you knew where some dynamite was." Eventually, eight persons at the scene of the Bethel bombing, including Hall and McWilliams, gave statements to the police and submitted to lie-detector tests. All of them were ultimately exonerated from any responsibility for the bombing.[14]

Meanwhile, as the initial investigation at the scene proceeded, Juanita Parker, complaint clerk at the police department, received a call at 2:48 A.M., some eighty-eight minutes after the bombing:

"Do you have a pencil and paper before you?" asked a well-spoken voice.

"Yes, I do."

"Write this down: This is General Forrest of the Confederate Underground, and we have just bombed the center of Communist Integration in the South. This is the first of two bombings to take place in . . . " At that point the voice mumbled indistinguishably, resuming after a moment, "We intend to continue this action until the Southern Negro is back in the place where he should be."[15]

The conversation then abruptly ended, but communication with the police officials resumed a few hours later when William Hugh Morris contacted Pattie. Morris had contacted Stoner, who had indeed arranged for the "repair" of Shuttlesworth's church, and he told Morris that "the boys" wanted their money. How soon, he asked, could Morris arrange another meeting with Pattie and Cook? At the next meeting on Saturday, July 12, Pattie got in the rear of Morris's car and sat just behind Stoner in the front passenger seat. "You have really got us on the spot with our people here," Pattie began. "They believe that Cook and I are trying to beat them out of $2,000. The public's general opinion and the opinion of our people is that the negroes themselves set out the bomb at Shuttlesworth's church for publicity for the purpose of raising money. From the newspapers, it seems that the police also believe they did it themselves, or else they would have released the information from the lie-detector tests." He continued with the scenario of Hall having planted the bomb and indicated that the "businessmen" they represented had no intention of being rooked out of $2,000 for a bombing for which Shuttlesworth himself or his people had been responsible.

"The niggers know they didn't do it, and we four know that they didn't do it," Stoner replied matter-of-factly, reiterating that he wanted the money. "Didn't we talk about Shuttlesworth's church as a possible target at our last meeting?"

"Yeah, but we agreed that nothing was to be done until we were satisfied that we were dealing with people who could get the job done," Pattie objected. "Besides, we hadn't even raised all the money or made a payment to y'all. So we didn't expect the church to be bombed. And since it was put in the street, we didn't think you had done it."

"Well, after we talked the last time, I talked with the boys about bombing the church and visited the church myself. I saw the bomb. It was in a five-gallon paint bucket, like the papers said. There was nearly a case of dynamite in it. My boys put it against the wall of the church, and if it had gone off it would have destroyed it. It's just too bad that nigger was there and moved it, but that wouldn't happen again in a thousand years." Again, he asked for the money, indicating he didn't want to report to the boys that he couldn't pay them. "You think you could get half the money from your people. Can you contact them this afternoon?"

"No, they're out of town for the weekend, but maybe we can next week. But why did they go ahead and bomb the church when we told you to wait til we got back to you?"

"You told me you were having trouble proving to your people that you were dealing with people who could do a good job," he replied. "I thought by going ahead, it might arouse the interest of your people and cause them to be more liberal with their money."

Finally, when it became clear that his contacts could not be swayed, Stoner said in irritation, "Well, if they think I've double-crossed 'em, those sonsabitches will probably wire up my car and blow *me* up. They're dangerous folks. People think the niggers did it!" he said derisively. "It's a shame the boys can't sue me in a Confederate court." The detective again told him that they would not be ready for any more bombings until they had raised the money in advance and gotten in touch with him again.[16]

Connor's detectives made no other contacts with J. B. Stoner or "the boys." When brought to trial twenty-two years later, however, Stoner testified that in their second meeting he and the detectives had also discussed the possibility of killing Shuttlesworth for a price of five or ten thousand dollars. Morris corroborated this testimony, although the detectives' reports of the July meeting made no mention of this part of the conversation. Nonetheless, even if they did not discuss killing Shuttlesworth in their second meeting, they had talked about it three weeks earlier. The most significant elements in this unsavory series of incidents remained Connor's role in it and the reality that the bombing of Bethel represented, at least indirectly, the commissioner's effort to rid himself and Birmingham of their troublesome thorn in the flesh. The short amount of time between the Connor-Shuttlesworth face-off over the lie-detector tests, the detectives' meeting with Stoner, Stoner's visit to Bethel, and the confiscation of the guns of the Bethel guards suggest Connor's role in the bombing. He authorized the detectives' meeting with Stoner, and even if he ostensibly did so as a sting operation on a rumored "bomber," he nevertheless buried his department's knowledge of the Bethel bombing and never prosecuted Stoner. What is certain is that even if he did not directly order the bombing, he did not seem to mind that it had taken place. As a result, the stakes in Shuttlesworth's gamble of confronting Connor went up in the process.[17]

In the aftermath of the bombing Shuttlesworth pressed on as usual. Because the explosion had caused no structural damage to the church, Sunday services proceeded according to the typical schedule. Shuttlesworth preached that morning from Philippians 4:11 that, like St. Paul, he was learning to be content in whatever state he found himself. One reason for his contentment was naturally his conviction that God continued to watch over his activities. God's kindly providence had, after all, arranged for Laverne McWilliams to return from work just in time to discover the bomb and avert disaster once again. And although some members likely harbored doubts about the wisdom of keeping a minister who put their church so squarely in "Bull's eye," they remained as elated as he did that God's protective canopy remained over Fred Shuttlesworth and Bethel Baptist Church.[18]

Shuttlesworth saved his public remarks for his president's address at the second anniversary of the ACMHR. Escalating his rhetoric of righteous warfare, he cited Joan of Arc, St. Paul, Daniel in the lion's den, and the three Hebrew youths in the fiery furnace as precursors of those who fought with him and "rose up, as one man, and with one voice to shout their defiance and declared active warfare until this multi-headed cancer to American democracy be removed from our society." More directly, he named as the enemy "Southern America, . . . which only discarded the ropes of yesterday for the explosives of today; and where the cross-symbol of Christ's Sufferings is considered a thing to be burned rather than something to be borne." He continued: "This is a religious crusade, a fight between light and darkness, right and wrong, good and evil, fair play vs. tyranny. We are assured of victory because we are using weapons of spiritual warfare. Against the racist's hate and scorn we are using the love of Christ, against his oppressive and abusive acts we are using the weapon of Prayer on whose mystic wings we sweep into the presence of God to lay out our troubles. Thus we are never tempted to hate white people or to return them evil for evil. . . . Always remember that we are healed by the 'wounds in His side,' not by wounds we inflict upon others. . . . Finally Negroes—be steadfast. Unmovable—except to go forward; be always abounding in good works; for as much as we know our labour is not in vain. . . . Victory waits on those who work for victory. And victory is sure—Thanks be to God which giveth us the victory through our Lord Jesus Christ."[19]

In addition, in a speech in Richmond, California, called "God in Human Affairs," Fred quoted the revolutionary lines of Thomas Paine, "These are times which try men's souls" and criticized "Southern Satanic prophets which now cry out that right is wrong. . . . These are the Southern Seers who are trying to see in 1957 with 1865 glasses on. . . . These Southern voices . . . are condemning and abusing the Court, crying justice while preaching hate and predicting bloodshed, and crying 'Law' while inviting men to be unlawful. . . . Their voices do not tell the whys of the bombs in the South—Why the rebel flags are again flying in the South—Why the K.K.K. is riding again—Why the wcc [White Citizens' Council] is formed. . . . They never explain why Preachers are jailed, and churches and homes are bombed. . . . Where is justice that will give a Negro boy twenty years for attempted rape and turn aloose confessed bombers?"[20]

More public and direct criticism of Connor and Birmingham came from Martin Luther King Jr., who, apprised of the situation by Shuttlesworth, issued a public letter to Mayor Jimmy Morgan that criticized the city's handling of the bombing. Complaining that two weeks had passed since the bombing without any arrests, King rejected officials' public effort to lay blame at the feet of Bethel members. "Could it be," he asked sardonically, "that those responsible for law-enforcement in Birmingham are more intent upon embarrassing and harassing Negroes who stand for interracial justice than in tracking down criminals? . . . The marked failure to ferret out the dynamiters of churches and homes apparently must be attributed to a lack of will and determination to prosecute law breakers if their acts, however violent, serve to bulwark the bastions of racial segregation." In addition, a few local ministers wrote to protest Birmingham's press and clergy, which failed to criticize the bombing of Bethel Baptist Church publicly as they had the April bombing of Temple Beth-El.[21]

Connor then publicly accused Shuttlesworth and the NAACP of attempting to raise money to build a store in Birmingham as a means of setting up a boycott of white merchants. Claiming that Shuttlesworth was planning a new attempt to enroll black children in white schools, Connor said he deplored Shuttlesworth's "harassment" and "agitation": "It is disturbing to see the Reverend Shuttlesworth starting his harassment again. With war with Russia threatening us and American soldiers exposed in foreign lands, this is a poor time for agitation at home by anyone who claims to be a loyal American." Believing that his views of Shuttlesworth and the NAACP were endorsed by the people of Birmingham in his reelection, Connor further attempted to speak for the African American citizens of Birmingham: "I don't believe the Negro people of Birmingham will follow the dangerous leadership of Shuttlesworth." Not willing to let Connor's accusations go unchallenged, Fred scoffed at the commissioner's "total lack of understanding of Negro mentality, aspirations and determination." Harassment and agitation, Shuttlesworth explained, were necessary only "because he [Connor] and others in office cannot find enough good will to voluntarily speed up racial progress." There were, to his knowledge, no NAACP operations in Alabama, he advised. He did suggest that in the near future "Negroes must and will begin teaching their dollars 'to have some sense' and go where they will bring equitable returns and appreciation, the commissioner and the attorney general notwithstanding." Finally, in a sharp rejoinder, he wrote, "The Commissioner might well remind himself that Negroes, following the 'dangerous leadership of Shuttlesworth,' are beginning at long last to apply for civil service jobs, and soon ride buses and sit in seats with human dignity. This 'dangerous leadership' has not led to the bombing of white homes nor the castration of white persons."[22]

Now the ball was again in Connor's court, and he wasted little time in returning the volley. Around four o'clock on Wednesday morning, August 6, a police car crept quietly down Twenty-ninth Avenue beside Bethel church, stopping, according to Shuttlesworth, at the exact spot where the June 29 bomb had been detonated. The officers open their doors and lit cigarettes, creating for Shuttlesworth the impression of another possible bomb attempt. In light of the two bombings and daily threatening calls he and his family received, he imagined persons in the neighborhood or from the guard station approaching the car to investigate. "Bull's boys," Shuttlesworth concluded, were there to intimidate blacks in Collegeville or, worse, to lure them into an altercation or other situation in which they might be charged with "interfering" with the officers in the commission of their duty. Shuttlesworth and the guards sat tight, allowing the police car to depart without incident.[23]

Yet the intimidation paid off in an increased jumpiness among the guards. The next night the guards discovered three men who had been put off a freight train in North Birmingham walking along the tracks near the church. Tense from watching for potential bombers, the guards stopped the transients, asked for identification, and inquired as to their possible knowledge of recent bombings. Discovering nothing amiss, the guards sent the hoboes on their way. A short distance later, however, the men were attacked and beaten by a group of blacks. Within the next three days, without search warrants police investigated the Bethel guards in connection with this incident and made four arrests, confiscating three rifles and a .32-caliber pistol in the process. Explaining the arrests, police chief Jamie Moore commented that the city could not allow vigilantes "to patrol the city's streets, whatever their color"; Shuttlesworth and the guards claimed mistaken identity. Within two weeks the charges against the guards were dropped. In the meantime, Shuttlesworth complained that since Connor took office the previous November, police officers under his command had on three occasions searched the church and homes of some of the guards without warrants. On these raids, as Shuttlesworth called them, police had taken weapons from them in deliberate efforts to hinder their attempts to protect the church and parsonage. On the evening of Saturday, August 9, rather than preparing or polishing his sermon for the next day's worship service, Shuttlesworth wrote several lengthy letters protesting what he considered gross harassment and requesting protection from state and federal officials. Even as he penned his litany of complaints, he noted a 1953 Pontiac with Mississippi license plates repeatedly circling the block. Stopping to report this "deliberate provocation" to the police by phone, he noted that officers never arrived to investigate his concerns.[24]

In his first letter, he addressed the city commission. He noted the police department's refusal to protect the church and parsonage and "other acts which are violative of our rights to be secure in our persons, houses and possessions." Arguing that his guards had been arrested on trumped-up charges, he asked the commission to conduct a "speedy investigation." He complained about the department's "using its vast official powers to molest and intimidate" blacks in "a reign of unholy terror." Young African Americans were, he charged, "being unnecessarily challenged, shaken down, slapped about, and threatened by some of the Officers." He continued: "Why must it be a standard thing almost for the Officers to accost most Negroes they stop about knowing 'that N[igger] Preacher'? . . . Why must people who watch around the Church be intimidated by Police? Why are your officers so prone to strike Negroes? In fairness, these things ought be looked into." Next, he addressed James Folsom, the governor of Alabama, and John Patterson, the attorney general of Alabama, asking both officials to investigate the groundless arrests of the Bethel guards "to see that we as law abiding citizens, we are not only given fair treatment but also Police Protection." Finally, he made an appeal to Connor himself:

> Circumstances dictate that I write you and protest as strenuously as possible the repeated actions of the Police Department under your direction, in continuing to needlessly harass us and interfer [sic] as we try to prevent our Church and Parsonage from being bombed for a third time. . . . Being refused police protection by the Police Department, we have had to voluntarily guard this property ourselves. And since the building of the New Parsonage in July, 1957, the Department knows that we have had to watch all night each night. We believe that it is the duty of the Police Department to offer 24 hours around the clock protection and non-interference with our lawful efforts to keep safe. Since November of 1957 the Police Department has not only offered very little or no protection, but also, through some of its officers, interfered with and molested the men on duty without provocation.

He listed three police visits in which premises were searched, weapons confiscated without warrants, and guards arrested in order "to keep them from voluntarily watching at this place."

Summing up his argument, he wrote: "Sir, personal feelings have no place in this; this is life or death. This involves our constitutional right to be protected in our houses and possessions. . . . These acts and others, Sir, amount to naked intimidation and molestation. . . . The taking of weapons and intimidating of guards are serving to deny us protection and to leave us utterly helpless and at the mercy of bombers. To deliberately or inadvertently allow the property to be bombed again would be a most dastardly act. And the fact that high officials are leading these excursions leads us to believe them the acts of high policy. We ask only that protection due us as American Citizens and law abiding residents of Birmingham, Alabama. . . . Please let us hear from you at once and please return our weapons speedily." Early Monday morning Shuttlesworth sent these letters by registered mail to their respective recipients, along with copies to the Birmingham office of the FBI, asking that the agency "at least look into this problem of improper protection and other problems mentioned in this letter." As he handed the entire package to the postal clerk, he boasted, "Bull Connor finally made the mistake we have been waiting for. We've got him where we want him now." [25]

Shuttlesworth turned out to be overly optimistic about the FBI's willingness to take on Connor, as well as about the possibility of the bureau's weighing into the civil rights debate on the side of African Americans. Director J. Edgar Hoover's antipathy for the movement had not yet become clear, and black leaders at that point still had good reason for hope in the federal government. Shuttlesworth believed a federal investigation could have some salutary effect in curtailing Connor's harassment of his organization. The results were a mixed bag. Even before Shuttlesworth's request in August, on July 24, officials at FBI headquarters, suspecting Connor's possible role in recent bombings, instructed the Birmingham office to keep contacts with the commissioner to a minimum. Yet the bureau refused to become involved in an investigation of the Birmingham bombings or the specific request of Shuttlesworth. Thus the ongoing firefight between the commissioner and the cleric would have to await the next incendiary spark. No one believed either side would wait long. [26]

In mid-October Shuttlesworth and Connor answered a bell rung by the city commission and the Birmingham Transit Company. Anticipating that U.S. district judge H. H. Grooms would strike down the bus ordinance that ACMHR bus riders had violated in December 1956, the commission rescinded the original ordinance in favor of a new one that allowed the transit company to set its own rules on seating. Although the commissioners unanimously approved the new ordinance, they nevertheless called for segregation to be maintained "in the interest of both white and black races." Yet the particular city ordinance requiring segregation, they argued, would "be hurtful to the cause of segregation."[27] On cue the transit company announced its "new" seating policy of having black passengers board from the rear and white passengers board in the front. In reality the only new element in this policy was that it was set by a private company rather than by city ordinance. The new policy, the product of collusion between the commission and the bus company, was a subterfuge, an attempt to undermine the foundation of the ACMHR's federal suit, a ruling on which was scheduled for October 30. In effect, the new policy attempted to hide segregation in a guise of private property rights.

Two nights later an angry Shuttlesworth called a special mass meeting of the ACMHR at Bethel. Blasting the new ordinance as "an unholy conspiracy" between city officials and the transit company, he called on the congregation to adopt a resolution committing the black community of Birmingham to begin violating the policy immediately. Repeating the commitment of blacks to fight for first-class citizenship "in a nonviolent and Christian way" and reminding the transit company of its economic stake in its black customers, he scored the new policy as "an insidious effort to circumvent lawful impending Federal judicial action" and an insult to the blacks' intelligence. The statement rejected the request that African Americans continue seating themselves from the rear of buses and resolved to ride in any available seat. In addition, Shuttlesworth accepted the company's invitation to discuss the policy on October 21. Beyond this, the resolution accused the city commission and the transit company of creating a new condition (breach of peace) under which to arrest blacks who might refuse to ride in segregated fashion.[28]

Shuttlesworth further argued that this maneuver, like the Jefferson County Personnel Board's decision to remove the phrase "White Only" from its applications, sought only to avoid the letter of the law and further court actions. Because there was now no law prescribing segregated seating and because bus drivers were officers of the law, the people would ignore drivers' "requests" and sit wherever seats were available. The final section of the statement gave instructions to black riders who chose to violate the ordinance. Among these were directions that riders remain prayerful, cheerful, courteous, and quiet. They further were asked to avoid boarding when angry or carrying a weapon and not to retaliate if cursed or struck. Ending with a rhetorical flourish, Shuttlesworth opined that "having come this far, through hardship and travail, . . . we are determined not to go backward. Far better would it be, if necessary, to walk in dignity than to continue forever to ride in shame."[29]

The next day, Connor urged city blacks to ignore Shuttlesworth's call to violate the new ordinance. Having investigated circuit court records, Connor discovered Shuttlesworth's arrest for distilling seventeen years earlier and attempted to discredit him as a "liquor law violator." Connor called on "the good Negro citizens of Birmingham" to use their "common sense" to avoid following the advice of the troublesome minister. He further urged that they "follow out the rules and regulations of the Birmingham Transit Company," warning that violations would cause incidents that would "breach the peace." He continued: "I am sure that the agitations that have been fostered by Shuttlesworth have stirred up unnecessary hatreds among both Negroes and whites. This is a time for all citizens to try to work and live together free of the tensions that professional agitators generate for their own personal ends."[30]

At about eleven o'clock in the morning on Monday, October 20, Shuttlesworth called *Birmingham News* reporter Bud Gordon and advised him to go to the Quinn Finance Company on Fourth Avenue and Seventeenth Street North for a story. On arrival at the loan office, Gordon was soon met by television reporter Jeff Smith, who waited with him for Shuttlesworth's arrival. Around 11:30, Shuttlesworth arrived and told them that he and his group would have a short meeting and would be boarding the buses in about five minutes. The preacher gave Gordon copies of his resolution to violate the ordinance and his instructions to the riders. A sizable crowd of some thirty excited Shuttlesworth devotees had crowded into the offices to receive their leader's instructions on how to test the new segregation ordinance. Planning for small groups of riders to board buses on successive days, Shuttlesworth hoped to force the police to make quick arrests or, in effect, allow desegregated riding. If ACMHR riders were arrested on the first day, Shuttlesworth planned to halt further rides in order to conserve funds for legal fees and court costs.[31]

Meeting with the riders, Fred began cheerfully: "Mr. Connor asked us good Negroes to use our common sense and that is just what we are doing." After the short training session, the group split into two groups, one led by Shuttlesworth and the other by J. S. Phifer. Heading for the Ensley and the Pratt-Ensley stops, the two groups boarded their respective buses and without disturbance took seats in the first three rows, which were reserved for whites. The driver of the Pratt-Ensley bus, I. M. Daniel, asked them to move to the rear but was refused. After a call was placed to the police, the stalled bus and passengers were joined by transit supervisor W. H. Webb and, a few minutes later, by police captain W. J. Haley. When the riders refused Haley's order to move to the rear, Haley instructed the driver to proceed to the transit company barn. At the barn, Haley boarded the bus and repeated his order to the riders. Some complied, but thirteen refused and were immediately placed under arrest. Singing loudly as they were transferred to police wagons, they were booked on charges of disorderly conduct. Shuttlesworth, wanting to show Connor that other blacks besides himself were willing to challenge the ordinance, chose not to ride. He was not arrested that day, though he escaped incarceration only briefly.[32]

The next day Connor ordered Shuttlesworth's arrest in connection with the bus demonstrations. When officers arrived at the Shuttlesworth parsonage, they found the minister away. Following his practice of attacking many fronts simultaneously, he had gone to the Western Union office to send a telegram to the city commission that called for the desegregation of Birmingham city parks by November 18, or, he promised, he would seek an answer in federal court. Returning home to the bus matter, he learned that officers had come to arrest him. He called the police to indicate he would be ready at 1:00 P.M. and sat on his porch for three hours awaiting their arrival. When police failed to show up that afternoon, he himself went to city hall to surrender, not wanting to be arrested at night.

Arriving at the police station around four o'clock, Shuttlesworth led police and reporters to believe more riders would challenge the ordinance the next day. "The number will increase daily all this week," he told them. "We are just starting the week off right this Monday morning." Shuttlesworth was charged with inciting to violate the city passenger placement ordinance, inciting to violate the city disorderly conduct ordinance, conspiring to commit a breach of the peace, and conspiring to cause a breach of the peace, and his cumulative bond was set at $1,200. At this, Fred told reporters, "I'm not sure I'll be bonded out. I may prefer to stay in jail rather than to pay bond on a silly charge. . . . Mr. Connor has long expressed his desire that I should be in jail. I don't suppose I could do anything to make Mr. Connor happy except to commit suicide." By the next day, however, Shuttlesworth had posted a $1,200 bond and was released on his own recognizance.[33]

Connor made no public comment, but on his behalf Mayor Jimmy Morgan issued a blistering statement concerning "the ugly serpent of race hatred" that Shuttlesworth had "cast abroad in the midst of the peace-loving peoples of Birmingham." Referring to Shuttlesworth and his followers as "rabble-rousers and agitators" interested only in "unrest, strife, dissension, and discord," he charged them with believing that "the races have been living too peacefully in Birmingham." He continued: "There is one thing of which I am certain; the loyal and decent citizens of the city of Birmingham do not want, will not countenance, and will oppose any and all efforts on the part of rabble-rousers of either race to disturb the peaceful atmosphere of the city." Generations of both races, excepting a "few occasions on the part of hot-heads," had created a "happy existance [sic] in this beautiful valley of ours." But now "unholy forces" sought to "replace peace with unrest, and joy with unhappiness." He then concluded:

> I will never believe that the leaders in this latest move of agitation in their efforts to stir up trouble in the operation of our transit system represent, in any way, the decent colored citizens of Birmingham. . . . The present owners of our transit system are entitled to the complete support of the loyal citizens of both races in their efforts to render this civic service and I am sure the good citizens of both races will again rise up and condemn the efforts of this handful of rabble-rousers in this latest move to substitute chaos for order. Therefore, I call upon all good people to so conduct and express themselves that all may see by their actions that individually and collectively we will not encourage or permit these organized attempts to gain even a toe-hold in our community.[34]

On the evening of Thursday, October 23, Shuttlesworth and the thirteen riders appeared in William C. Conway's recorder's court. None of the defendants offered any witnesses or testified in his or her own behalf. Their counsels, Arthur Shores and Orzell Billingsley, nevertheless were able to show with the uncontradicted testimony of Gordon, Haley, Daniel, Webb, and officer W. W. Gamble that there had been no breach of the peace. None of these witnesses could testify to any loud, disorderly, or profane actions on the part of the thirteen. Gamble testified that the riders had created no disturbance of any kind. He and Haley further indicated that they had arrested the riders only for sitting in white designated areas. In Conway's court, however, this alone constituted breach of the peace. The judge ruled Shuttlesworth and the other defendants guilty and remanded them all, including Shuttlesworth, back to jail without bail, pending sentencing on Monday evening.[35]

Using questionable if not illegal means, Conway in essence acted as the city's instrument for discouraging further efforts by African Americans. The judge's ruling was challenged the next day when ACMHR lawyers filed a habeas corpus petition before circuit judge George Lewis Bailes. Bailes passed the scheduled habeas corpus hearing to Tuesday, October 28, telling Orzell Billingsley that he had failed to meet statutory requirements by personally notifying the attorneys for the opposing party. Failing that, Billingsley then filed two mandamus petitions against Judge Conway, asking that he be required to show cause why the defendants should not be released from jail. Bailes also set hearings for those petitions for Tuesday. In effect, by not airing them until the day after Judge Conway was scheduled to sentence the defendants, Bailes thus insured that the habeas corpus and the mandamus petitions would be rendered moot.

During the weekend, in Shuttlesworth's first significant time in jail, Ruby and other relatives visited him, along with many other church members and ACMHR loyalists. At Bethel Shuttlesworth's assistant ministers got their first of many assignments to fill his pulpit while he did jail time for civil rights activity. During the Monday night sentencing, blacks packed the courtroom while a multitude of at least one thousand congregated on the courthouse lawn in silent prayer and in protest of the arrests. Conway sentenced the riders to a 180-day suspended sentence. Their leaders, Phifer and Shuttlesworth, were sentenced to sixty and ninety days, respectively, and were ordered to pay a fine of one hundred dollars each. Then Conway jailed them once more to await Bailes's habeas corpus and mandamus rulings, sending them away with the admonition to "stay out of trouble." The defendants and their many supporters returned the following morning for Judge Bailes's hearings, which indeed had become moot by the action of Judge Conway the night before. In sum, Conway's sentences remained in effect, and after almost five days in jail, both Phifer and Shuttlesworth were released on $300 appeal bonds.[36]

In addition to the support Shuttlesworth received from his friends in Birmingham, he also accepted expressions of concern from elsewhere in the movement. While Fred was in jail, Martin Luther King Jr. in Montgomery called Ruby to ask whether he or the MIA could be of any help to Fred or to the family. Ruby told King that Fred was faring well, but King nonetheless said he would send a delegation from Montgomery to lend moral support. At this point, the tap that had been placed on the Shuttlesworths' phone came into play. On Tuesday morning, a committee of three Montgomery ministers, Reverends S. S. Seay, H. H. Hubbard, and A. W. Wilson, arrived in Birmingham and called on Ruby and the family at home. No sooner had they arrived and sat down for the midday meal than Captain Pattie and Lieutenant J. R. Davis of the police arrived on the scene. Not finding "proper identification" on the ministers, the officers charged them with vagrancy, took them into custody for five hours, and questioned them. Wilson complained later that the officers had at no time given them any reason for their "entirely unjustified" arrests and suggested the possibility of forthcoming legal action. "There were no abuses," he complained, "but we were treated like any common criminal. We were mugged, fingerprinted, and thrown into a cell with a lot of criminals." He indicated to reporters later the police department's efforts to check "on who was in Birmingham from out of town."[37]

At the time of the arrests, Bull Connor had announced that city officials would likely arrest any "outside agitators coming to our city and dabbling in our affairs." Word of Connor's detention of the Montgomery ministers angered Shuttlesworth and King, and word quickly spread to others in the movement. By the next day NAACP executive secretary Roy Wilkins had induced the Civil Rights Division of the Justice Department to look into the arrests. Two weeks later, U.S. Attorney General William P. Rogers ordered a federal grand jury inquiry into the case on the grounds that the city had violated the civil rights of the ministers. In spite of the federal probe, however, the grand jury was to be composed of members of the local community, leaving Justice Department officials and local blacks pessimistic that an indictment of Connor would be voted. For his part, the commissioner vowed to continue to enforce segregation laws against "crime and disorder." He added sarcastically: "Those three Negroes so dear to Attorney General Rogers' heart came here to aid in an unlawful boycott. . . . I ordered them arrested and will order anyone else arrested who attempts the same thing. If Mr. Rogers thinks he can scare me or the Birmingham Police Department into permitting this city to become the scene of rioting which would follow just to please Negro voters, he is mistaken."[38]

Talk of a limited "protest" boycott in Birmingham began among black ministers soon after Shuttlesworth's release from jail on Tuesday, October 28. Discussions had apparently begun among the ministers during the weekend as a response to Shuttlesworth's and the others' extended incarceration. The Jefferson County Betterment Association (JCBA), an organization of some 110 black ministers, gathered on the same day to discuss a possible boycott. After debating the matter, the ministers expressed their support of a boycott, and on Wednesday, October 29, they wrote to the city commission, threatening action unless the transit company changed the seating policies.[39]

Led by the Reverend J. L. Ware, venerable pastor of the Trinity Baptist Church since 1941, the JCBA seemed uncharacteristically to be thinking along the same lines as Shuttlesworth and the ACMHR. The JCBA served as a sort of secular arm of the Birmingham [Black] Baptist Ministers Conference, incorporating what Shuttlesworth's generation of ministers called "the old guard." Ware, who served as the leader of both organizations, epitomized the old guard's approach to race issues. Shuttlesworth's friend T. L. Lane summarized it thus:

Let the status quo be as it is. Otherwise, don't trouble the waters. Don't try to correct nothin'. Just leave it alone and let the Lord fix it. You see there are some of us who really believe the Lord's not going to do things that you can do for yourself. That is the old school. To me, the new school is to challenge wrong as the prophets did. The Major Prophets did that in the Old Testament as the preachers of the Gospel will do. You have to challenge sin in high places. And that we had done. The new school more focused on the total man. . . . We believe in the total man. See, I can't tell nobody about Jesus when their shoe hurt or they ain't got no shoes to put on his feet. . . . The old school didn't want to shake the water. Leave everything alone and some of them believed the Lord would work it out. . . . I don't think they was mean or bad, but they don't want to mess with the old boss.[40]

More polished and dignified than Shuttlesworth in demeanor, Ware was much less assertive or abrasive than his younger ministerial colleague. Cautious and diplomatic, he was what one younger observer called "a smoothie," who was able to read white folks' minds and get what he wanted without raising their hackles. Long established as a leader of black Birmingham, he had not completely capitulated to white sensibilities, as when he led blacks to forego segregated viewings of the Constitution and the Bill of Rights during a visit of the Freedom Train Exhibit. He advised them not to go to the white first, then black arrangements, commenting, "This is supposed to be the Freedom Train, but we are not free." The repercussions from this incident had weakened his standing among powerful whites and made him more circumspect in later years.[41]

Ecclesiastical protocol created expectations that newcomers such as Shuttlesworth should respectfully defer to Ware and his generation as they climbed the ministerial career ladder one rung at a time. Observers often interpreted Shuttlesworth's brusque interaction with Ware as disrespect and impertinent ambition. To his own way of thinking, Shuttlesworth was following expectations. In his comments to Ware, he sought to maintain a proper decorum and, in his view, never directly challenged the older minister's leadership in the Baptist Ministers Conference. Yet his unsophisticated nature and unpolished manner at times made him unmindful of the way he communicated, through body language and voice inflection, an impatience with Ware's more deliberate style of leadership. According to Glenn E. Smiley, field representative of the Fellowship of Reconciliation, although the two ministers never insulted each other outright, "Fred would intimate, without actually calling anyone an 'Uncle Tom,'" that such thinking was "the old way." Fred was little inclined to go slow even if he had believed it would have worked in Birmingham. In normal times, perhaps, he might have done so. In the extraordinary Zeitgeist of the post-*Brown* era, however, and under what he understood as the leadership of the God who had called him, Shuttlesworth believed he could not afford the luxury of being overly deferential.[42]

Moreover, he increasingly came to believe that his numerous potential sacrifices of life and limb had rightfully earned him the respect of older ministers such as Ware. To James Armstrong and some of Shuttlesworth's followers, however, Ware seemed jealous of Fred and "more concerned about Montgomery" than he was about Birmingham. Indeed, early on Ware had been skeptical of the ACMHR, which he apparently judged an imprudent challenge to whites in Birmingham. At the movement's organizing meeting in 1956, Ware had commented to his more wary colleagues, "Well, brethren, the best thing for us to do is just let it alone. Don't pass any motions, don't say nothing good for it, don't say nothing bad about it. And in two or three weeks, it'll be dead like everything else these little Negroes try to get up around here." An annoyed Shuttlesworth fired back, with a characteristic solecism, "Watch us and see will we die."[43]

Now another minister, the Reverend E. W. Williams, complained that "Shuttlesworth's got these Negroes running around here, but I am not going to BOW down to him." In response, Shuttlesworth told Williams and the others,

> In order to encourage the Betterment society [sic]—to show you that I'm not against you and the Movement is not against you—anything that you agree to do, you have our automatic endorsement. . . . And if we do something, which we are, if you can endorse, we appreciate it. If you can't, just be silent. Of course, if you want to say something against it, we'll just have to struggle anyway. In other words, my brother, if God tells me to jump, it's my place to jump, and it's up to

God to fix a place for me to land. And if God tells me to jump and doesn't fix a place for me to land, I'll still jump on his word. And I appreciate your allowing me this privilege of speaking, and at least I have said to you what's in my heart, and I hope you can understand that you will never have an enemy in Fred Shuttlesworth. I hope you can cooperate with what we do, but if you don't, we're going on without you.[44]

Much of the tension between Shuttlesworth, Ware, Williams, and their respective followings issued from a natural ministerial jealousy. Such professional competition among clergy is more common than piety admits or secularity realizes. The problem, moreover, has historically been exacerbated by the church's role as the singular arena of power for black males. In the civil rights movement, a similar sort of rivalry evolved between Martin Luther King Jr. and National Baptist Convention president Joseph H. Jackson. Older, more established ministers such as Jackson and Ware reacted insecurely to a generation of younger ministers who seemed to them to be unwilling to pay their dues and wait their turn. Shuttlesworth himself saw this as part of his problem with other ministers in Birmingham. Commenting on ministers who were less enthusiastic about civil rights work in the city, he reflected, "Some of the ministers will not work because of their own old priestly philosophy of letting the Lord do it and others do not out of the envy of seeing somebody else move on."[45]

Although the rivalry was real, it should nonetheless be understood within a context of what has been called "conflict in unity." Black religious leaders have often expressed more diversity of opinion than outsiders have noticed. Despite differences of opinion and approach, however, they have shared a larger set of central beliefs and values. In the case of Shuttlesworth and Ware, as with King and Jackson, they shared in different ways the struggle against the common enemies of racism and segregation. Thus an observer of both Shuttlesworth and Ware noted that a rivalry existed between them, "but to the extent and degree that it was truly played out . . . to the point where there was not any agreement amongst and between them, I just don't recall living that experience." In Ware's and Shuttlesworth's mutual threat of a bus boycott during the fall of 1958, one can see quite clearly both the unity and the conflict.[46]

In part because he did not want the JCBA to be perceived as leading the boycott effort, on the Friday night after his release and the arrests of the ministers from Montgomery, Shuttlesworth called another special mass meeting. Nearly one thousand persons crowded into the sanctuary on Halloween night. Before Shuttlesworth addressed the congregation, many persons from all over the city described mistreatment by bus drivers. An ACMHR lieutenant read a new telegram from the Birmingham Transit Company indicating that officials were breaking their agreement to meet with Shuttlesworth for further talks. In a spontaneous action the congregation unanimously agreed to stay off the buses. Caught up in the emotion of the moment, Shuttlesworth announced: "We believe it better to walk in dignity than to pay to ride in chains. Recent action by the Birmingham Transit Company in maintaining segregation on buses, including causing the arrest of Negroes, the mistreatment of Negro patrons by bus drivers, and their refusal to talk about other issues, has caused Birmingham Negroes to launch a protest against the Birmingham bus company." When he learned of Shuttlesworth's new effort, Connor told the press he would jail anyone who attempted to aid a bus boycott in Birmingham.[47]

In effect, the decision to launch a boycott was made by the ACMHR rank and file. Interpreting Connor's earlier arrest of Shuttlesworth as an effort to discourage a boycott, the members rose up to say, in effect, "if 'Bull' thinks arresting us will stop us, he's got another thing coming." Some observers outside of Birmingham believed the boycott was ill conceived and that it fizzled as a result. Glenn Smiley, who had taught the principles of nonviolence to the MIA and spent several days in Birmingham working with Shuttlesworth and the black community later confessed that "we tried . . . to take Montgomery to Birmingham and fell flat on our faces because Montgomery was not exportable." Chief among the reasons for the perception of failure, Smiley said, was weaker intellectual leadership, which made the appeal of nonviolence more difficult in Birmingham. He believed the blue-collar, "redneck" nature of Birmingham made it tougher to sell those principles. Such an assessment would have been more accurate if the intention had truly been a Montgomery-style boycott. Shuttlesworth, however, doubted the likelihood of duplicating Montgomery. During the first weekend of the boycott, when many blacks continued to use the buses, he registered some reservations about its prospects of "Montgomery-style" success: "I am looking for it to grow, but to what extent it will grow I can't say."[48]

In their discussions Shuttlesworth and his board enumerated the reasons not to attempt a thoroughgoing boycott patterned after Montgomery. First, the intensity of police intimidation made carpooling untenable. Police cruisers followed most buses, and some parents who transported their own children to school were stopped by police and threatened with arrest. Second, Shuttlesworth did not believe ACMHR coffers were deep enough to furnish vehicles to substitute for the buses, particularly after Connor's officers began impounding such cars that had been used. Third, large numbers of the black clergy did not support the boycott. Their distancing themselves largely had to do with fear and their uneasiness with the sometimes prickly leader of the ACMHR. Competition between Shuttlesworth's and Ware's groups, particularly regarding which organization was leading the boycott, exacerbated this problem. Fourth, the sheer size of Birmingham and distances of travel required made a full-fledged boycott much less feasible than had been true in the smaller city of Montgomery. Finally, Shuttlesworth believed that Montgomery had been the right place and the right time for such an action but that by 1958 boycotts were old hat. Thus he did not anticipate that a boycott in Birmingham could garner enough outside sympathy and financial support to sustain a major effort.

Nevertheless, Shuttlesworth and the board allowed the effort to go forward primarily as a response to the will of the members and to test how much support actually could be marshaled. Fred later noted that he never believed Montgomery could be repeated, and five months after the "boycott," he wrote: "No attempt was made to organize a bus boycott in Birmingham. This was, in contrast to Montgomery, a voluntary protest wherein a few—maybe a thousand—people declared their intention not to ride." Yet he continued to issue public calls for a boycott in order to let the fervor of the moment buoy the spirits of ACMHR members and keep the heat on Connor.[49]

Shuttlesworth intended to keep the heat on by various means. The day before the boycott was announced, U.S. district judge H. H. Grooms denied the ACMHR permission to amend its federal court suit against bus segregation in Birmingham. Now that the ordinance that was challenged by the ACMHR in 1956 had been replaced, attorney Arthur Shores intended to substitute a challenge to the new law that in effect maintained the policy of segregated seating. Grooms ruled that the new ordinance on its face was constitutional, though the key issue was whether it would be constitutional in its application. He took under advisement the city's argument that the original suit had been rendered moot by the repeal of the specific ordinance it challenged.[50]

Within two weeks Shuttlesworth mounted a new challenge to the 1958 ordinance, asking for $100,000 in damages and an injunction restraining the city commission and the transit company from acting in accordance with the ordinance until the case was tried. In addition to the proliferation of legal challenges, the ACMHR stepped up its efforts in the boycott. On occasion black-on-black violence occurred against some who continued to ride the buses. Typically, Shuttlesworth preached against it, but he could not always control everyone on the margins of the movement. In fact, in board and mass meetings he occasionally passed on a joke he heard from King about a black who, during the Montgomery boycott, had asked where she might catch the bus. "You catches it right over there," she was told, "but you gets your ass beat right around there." Moreover, when ACMHR treasurer Bill Shortridge joked about heading a "physical persuasion committee," Shuttlesworth responded in kind by saying in mass meetings that "Bill Shortridge is not quite nonviolent." Thus, Shuttlesworth's occasional joviality at times gave the impression that his call for nonviolence was being delivered with a wink. In the meantime, Ruby Shuttlesworth traveled to Chicago to speak at a rally held by the African American Heritage Association. There she told her audience that although the white press was silent about it, the boycott was gaining momentum. In these protests, she noted, southern blacks were fighting, one hundred years after the Civil War, for "rights that were already won in that war."[51]

Naturally, Connor also saw matters in military terms and launched a counterattack. Within a week of Ruby's appearance in Chicago, Samuel Hoskins, a reporter from the *Baltimore Afro-American,* visited an ACMHR meeting. After talking with detectives reporting the proceedings, Hoskins was granted an interview with their boss, Bull Connor. "Just bring him on in," Connor bellowed to his secretary as Hoskins arrived.

"I know what you fellows print up North," he commented.

"Baltimore? Is that North, sir?"

"Well, anyway, you and the rest of the papers, I know what you print. But I'll talk to you anyway."

Hoskins then began to talk about the ACMHR mass meetings, eventually asking him why he sent detectives to report on them. Connor replied, "Yes, we assign them because we have to know what goes on down there. Otherwise we would wake up one morning and be in a hell of a fix." When Hoskins wondered aloud whether such surveillance was lawful, Connor gleefully remarked, "Damn the law. We don't give a damn about the law. Down here we make our own law." Concerning his arrests of the three Montgomery ministers, the commissioner boasted that he had indeed ordered their arrests on a charge of vagrancy "until we could find out what they were doing here. We're not going to have outsiders coming here stirring up trouble. If they come here and do the wrong kind of talking, they'll see the inside of our jail." Continuing his war of words, he specifically took aim at Fred. "Excepting Shuttlesworth, the colored people of Birmingham are satisfied with present conditions. As for Shuttlesworth, his interest is in what he can get out of it. He stirs up trouble and you people up North send him a lot of money which he pockets and uses to his own advantage."[52]

Words, however, turned out to be only part of Connor's arsenal. During the bus protests, a period in which Shuttlesworth and the ACMHR hoped to spark more fervent interest from the grass roots, Connor's detectives became particularly unwelcome at mass meetings. Shuttlesworth complained that their presence intimidated potential followers and kept them away from the meetings and the movement. In response, ACMHR members passed a resolution that complained about the detectives and requested that the commissioner stop sending them. Connor ignored the resolution, and the detectives returned the next Monday night. On that occasion, the Reverend Charles Billups, leader of the ushers, stood outside the door of the First Baptist Church of Ensley admitting members who flashed their ACMHR membership cards. As two detectives approached the door, Billups held his hands up to stop them and asked them to state their business.

"We've come to attend the meeting," one of the men replied.

"We voted last week not to let y'all in anymore. If you want to arrest anybody, and you have a warrant, you are welcome to do your duty."

"What is your name?"

"I'm Reverend Charles Billups."

"I'd like to see one of the higher-ups."

"I *am* one of the higher-ups. What do you want?"

"What about Reverend Shuttlesworth?"

"He is not in at present."

"Is Reverend Gardner or Phifer in?"

Billups then found Gardner and Phifer, who took over the discussion with the officers. Standing to one side, Billups listened in until he overheard the detectives ask the others if Billups drank. He then rejoined the conversation in order to assure the detectives that he did not drink. Just then Shuttlesworth arrived, reiterating that the congregation had voted not to admit the officers. At that, the detectives replied, "Well, they told us not to force our way in." "Well, you can't come in," Shuttlesworth repeated as the detectives turned to leave, adding, "You tell them I said so." Angered by the rebuff, Connor sent the officers on a retaliatory mission. The following evening the officers appeared at Billups's home with a warrant for his arrest. Taking care of his children at the time,

Billups asked to be allowed to call his wife, who had gone out to a meeting. The detectives at first refused his request, but they eventually relented and allowed Billups to summon his wife home. When she arrived, the officers grabbed Billups under the arm, taking him into custody without indicating the charge under which he was arrested. After processing, Billups was told he had touched the lapel of one of the officers when he stopped them from entering the church the night before. Actually he had merely held up his hand, and the officer inadvertently walked into his hand. This constituted interfering with an officer in the commission of his duty. Ultimately, Billups was convicted and sentenced to sixty days and a one hundred dollar fine. Later, on appeal in circuit court, Billups pled guilty in order to have the sentence dropped.[53]

In a more serious way, the commissioner began to act on his threat to arrest persons who aided a bus boycott. Apparently judging that arresting Shuttlesworth himself would only make more news and create more interest in the boycott, Connor set his sights on intimidating one of Shuttlesworth's underlings. Purchasing the services of an informant in the East End Baptist Church, Connor discovered that the Reverend Calvin Woods had preached the boycott. Urging his members to stay off the buses, Woods instructed them that so long as they paid their money, they were entitled to sit wherever they pleased. They should further refuse to relinquish their places to anyone. Two days later, police arrested him as he worked his second job as a janitor in a downtown office building. As he was carried to the Southside jail in a patrol wagon, he shouted his name to bystanders in hopes that word of his arrest would get out. During interrogation he was told that he had been arrested for urging a boycott of a legal business. By late evening Shuttlesworth had learned of his detention, raised enough money to post bond, and delivered Woods back to his home.[54]

Angered by Connor's blatant effort to bully them into silence, several ministers discussed a response. In this instance differences over personalities and strategies paled into insignificance, and ACMHR-affiliated ministers worked in tandem with some who had kept Shuttlesworth and his group at arm's length. Three days after Woods's arrest, the Reverends N. H. Smith Jr. and J. L. Ware called a press conference to register their disapproval of Connor's tactics. Two weeks later, the weekend before Woods went on trial in the court of misdemeanors, the ministers held another press conference in support of their colleague. In a prepared statement to reporters, twenty African American ministers, including Shuttlesworth, called Woods's arrest "an unwarranted and illegal invasion of the inviolability of the Christian pulpit." Ware seemed less concerned with the matter of the buses, arguing that "the big thing we're interested in is that we do not have to clear our sermons with officials." Objecting on the grounds of church-state separation, the ministers argued:

> No earthly authority has any right to interfere with the minister in the discharge of his duty. Once a breach is allowed here the whole concept of the separation of church and state on which our democratic society rests has been destroyed. . . . We declare our Christian solidarity with him in this action and on Sunday, December 14th, each of us is resolved to make this known to his own people from the pulpit and to counsel them along similar lines with regard to the concrete issues of discrimination and segregation confronting our community. We note, finally, that in thus discharging our Christian responsibility . . . we are also rendering a patriotic service to our country and to the cause of democracy. Freedom of thought, of speech, of conscience, of religion, enshrined in the Constitution of the United States is what distinguishes a free from a totalitarian society. This distinction we are resolved to do all in our power to defend and maintain in this age when democracy is gravely threatened in many parts of the world.[55]

In his remarks at the press conference, Shuttlesworth virtually worked himself into a lather, vowing that he would preach the crusade against segregated riding until the "sin of segregation" was ended. "You sin when you yield to the bus company's sins of segregation," he preached. "I call upon you to use passive resistance to defeat this evil." Answering Connor's efforts to silence the black pulpit, Shuttlesworth averred, "Only God can tell me what to say in the pulpit. And I'm going to tell my people to stay off those buses if I have to go to Kilby prison." Connor dismissed the ministers' support for Woods, commenting only that, had he wished, he could have arrested them then and there.[56]

As the boycott effort began to dwindle, Shuttlesworth continued to skirmish in a variety of theaters. Connor's effort to cower Birmingham blacks into forsaking the movement verged on the violation of civil liberties. Emory Jackson editorialized with the arrests of Billups and Woods in mind. "The clear purpose of such arrests," he wrote, "seems to be to crush protest, intimidate civic leaders, and thwart the cry for seating freedom on buses." In a renewed response to Connor's detectives, Shuttlesworth wrote to the city commission and lodged a "strenuous protest" of their continued presence at ACMHR meetings.

He compared the commissioner's policy of sending his minions to meetings, ticketing parked cars, and arresting Woods with actions of the Gestapo. He also scornfully criticized a police department that could "deploy several cars and many officers around our Mass Meetings" but could not manage to protect a church that had been bombed twice. He further pointed out: "We have never met for hate purposes: thus no Negro has ever left a Movement Mass Meeting and bombed a home, nor castrated a white person. . . . On the other hand, subversive groups have met with the knowledge of the police and such groups have not only conspired against the rights of others, but actually have plotted and done violence—including castration." He suggested that if detectives intended to continue taking notes of ACMHR meetings, then they should also make notes of meetings of the Klan or citizens' councils.[57]

His central request, however, was that the commissioner stop assigning detectives to attend meetings unless police protection was needed. On the same day that Fred sent his letter to Connor and his brethren on the commission, Shuttlesworth and Phifer went on trial on an appeal of their convictions for violating the new bus ordinance. Hearing the same evidence presented earlier in recorder's court, Jefferson County circuit judge George Lewis Bailes upheld the convictions and the respective sentences.[58]

The relationship between black leaders in Birmingham continued to be problematic. In the long run, the rivalry between Shuttlesworth and the ACMHR and Ware's JCBA was hardly a significant contest. Shuttlesworth's bold—many called them "foolhardy"—confrontations with segregationists, launched in staccato fashion since 1956, had won a larger, much more fervent following among working-class African Americans. Eventually the JCBA would be overshadowed by the ACMHR, and its support would be reduced to quiescence. During the weak boycott efforts, however, the competition between the two organizations took on a larger importance. Glenn E. Smiley, who came to Birmingham as a consultant during these weeks, believed the rift weakened the boycott effort, though he doubted its chances of success in any event. He observed that "feeling sometimes runs rather high" between the two groups and their leaders. The boycott, he believed, had been called with too little preparation or publicity and was "itself part of the competitive picture between the two groups."[59] Thus Smiley spent his time in Birmingham trying to coordinate the efforts of the ACMHR and the JCBA.

At a November 10 meeting, Smiley, Shuttlesworth, Smith, Ware, and the Reverend Luke Beard, pastor of the Sixteenth Street Baptist Church, had a "long, frank talk" on common purposes and actions and made a beginning of what Smiley called "cooperation at a minimal level." After the meeting Smiley wrote a lengthy letter to FOR colleague Bob Gussner that related his regret that the boycott suffered from "little organizing" and "no effort to form a car pool." He thus judged the boycott as "of small but growing importance," operating at between 5 and 15 percent effectiveness.[60]

Smiley, however, had also convinced Shuttlesworth, Smith, and Ware to accompany him to a December workshop in organizational procedures and the principles of nonviolence at FOR headquarters in Nyack, New York. The trip to Nyack made a significant impression on Fred, convincing him more firmly than ever of the soundness of nonviolence as a tool for social change. In addition, the conference enabled him to widen his connections with a network of persons and organizations who were working for civil rights and civil liberties around the nation. Furthermore, the attendance by both Shuttlesworth and Ware solidified their cooperation, at least for the short term. On their return home, the *Birmingham World* ran a brief front-page article on their trip, presenting to the black community a picture of a united front between its primary leaders. Yet the aftermath of the trip would result in an incident that would shake Shuttlesworth and bring him to an emotional low point in his battle with Connor.[61]

Back from Nyack with the Birmingham delegation, Glenn Smiley returned to tie up some loose ends before closing up shop on the boycotts and, his wife hoped, getting home by Christmas. Two days after arriving back in Birmingham, on Sunday, December 14, Smiley attended church services, only to be met by Connor's top henchmen, Detectives G. L. Pattie and Thomas H. Cook. The men questioned Smiley and asked to search his hotel room. Thinking of nothing that could be incriminating, he let them look. The detectives gravitated toward a briefcase and discovered a copy of Smiley's letter to Gussner. The detectives confiscated the letter and took Smiley down to headquarters for several hours of questioning. Later, as he released him, Pattie offered to buy Smiley a cup of coffee. Not wishing to be observed, Pattie found a table in a darkened area in the rear of a local bar. Over their coffee, Pattie told him, "I am dying of guilt. I feel terrible about what I did to you and what Mr. Connor is forcing me to do." He paused and then said, "And what I did to Shuttlesworth," thinking of his role in the bomb attempt at Bethel. Asking the minister to pray for him, he confessed, "And I'm not sure that I can maintain my sanity." As Smiley finished consoling the distraught detective, he left Birmingham more concerned about Pattie than with what Connor had discovered in his briefcase.[62]

The following Sunday a front-page article in the *Birmingham News* stunned Shuttlesworth. In a public statement the preceding night, Connor had accused "local Negro integration groups" of working with "a Communist-front organization"—his epithet for the FOR. On the basis of information his detectives had extracted from Smiley, the commissioner described the black leaders' trip to Nyack, barely containing his amusement as he pronounced the report "interesting." Connor ostensibly used the information to convince the citizens of Birmingham that its police department was "in a lawful, orderly, peaceable, but we hope effective manner, doing its utmost to protect our community from being plunged into bus boycotts such as struck Montgomery, rioting and disorders, bloodshed and possible closing of our public schools." His overriding intent, however, was to embarrass and undermine Shuttlesworth by revealing the contents of Smiley's seized letter to Gussner. In the letter, Smiley acknowledged that the boycott was "led by Shuttlesworth almost entirely at the moment" and catalogued Fred's weaknesses: "Shuttlesworth is a courageous leader, but devoid of organizational knowledge, headstrong and wild for publicity, almost to the point of neurosis, undemocratic and willing to do almost anything to keep the spotlight on himself."[63]

Angry and deeply aggrieved by what he viewed as a betrayal, Fred privately railed that Smiley, who had eaten in his home and been taken into his inner circle, could so strongly criticize him in a letter. He fumed that Smiley had had ample opportunity to raise questions in discussions with the ACMHR board without ever having done so. Indeed, the entire family was shaken by Smiley's letter. The older children had difficulty believing the words were Smiley's, and Ruby felt the pain of a loneliness borne of misunderstanding and questioned motives. Outside the family, some of Shuttlesworth's close friends suggested that Connor had merely twisted Smiley's words to his own purpose, while others denounced Smiley as "a treacherous white man, a Judas." Shuttlesworth protested to himself and his supporters that Smiley did not fully appreciate the needs of Birmingham. In his view, the needs of the moment called not for "a model organization on paper" but rather someone with the conviction that God was directing and the courage to act (not just talk) to bring Birmingham blacks out of Bull Connor's nightmare. Moreover, he was incensed that Smiley did not see that.[64]

Soon after the story broke, Smiley received a call. "All hell's broken loose," Martin Luther King told him. "Fred's mad as hell at you." King explained Connor's ploy and told Smiley that Bayard Rustin, one of King's most respected advisers in the SCLC, had somewhat pacified Shuttlesworth. In a telephone call, Rustin said, "Fred, don't overreact. All of us have our neuroses. Granted, this is a very embarrassing thing. But the only way you can defend yourself is to defend Smiley. Because you know good and well that all they want in Birmingham is to drive a wedge between you and Smiley." As Smiley worried about the harm his words had caused, King tried to console him by joking, "I've said a lot of worse things about Fred than that." Still conscience stricken by the news, the remorseful Smiley immediately sent a telegram that confessed his sins and begged Shuttlesworth's forgiveness. The message read: "In a confidential memo to a colleague taken from me illegally by the Birmingham police, and about which you already know, I was indiscreet, unkind and unjust. That memo has now been publicized by the police in an attempt to divide us and weaken our common purpose. I send you my deepest regrets for the pain I have caused you and my prayer is that your generous nature which I have come to know so much better in the last few weeks can encompass forgiveness. We must not let this trickery undermine our faith in one another or divert us from our joint struggle towards the goal of Christian brotherhood."[65]

In response, Fred penned a lengthy letter that revealed a pained leader who felt the burden of holding his movement together, as Wyatt Tee Walker later commented, "with spit and scotch tape." Smiley's letter had brought to Fred's mind an earlier comment by Smiley concerning Fred's interest in publicity. Fred had now learned, however, that beneath Smiley's offhand remark lay more telling concerns. Fred took Smiley's letter as reflecting a "contempt and disdain" for his and ACMHR's efforts in Birmingham. "It is amazing," he wrote, "how close people can come to you—even to the point of uninhibited fellowship in one's home and business—and yet not really be true." Describing his family's disbelief at Smiley's comments, Shuttlesworth inferred that "in their hearts they know that Bull wouldn't have quoted it if you hadn't written it." Furthermore, he speculated, "Surely nothing could have suited Mr. Connor's purposes" more than Smiley's "profoundly critical estimation of me. . . . Your statement gives him sharpshooting ammo, and shoot it he will." He also wondered whether his ministerial colleagues who because of fear, indifference, or envy had remained aloof from the ACMHR might now discover "some long awaited excuse" for their "inaction and noncooperation." "A completely vitriolic enemy of mine," he complained, "could not have made a more thoroughly adverse criticism of me." Smiley's characterization of him as virtually neurotic and "willing to do almost anything" for the spotlight cut him most deeply. "What better terminology," he wrote, "could be used to disqualify any person of leadership, or of any sound ability at all? I would to God that you had told me before I read it. I have always felt that we were close enough to discuss things frankly—even things about our persons."[66]

Next, he poignantly rehearsed to Smiley his adversities in the "dangerous Birmingham field." His listed the "apathetic tendencies" that he believed prevailed among his fellow clergy before 1956. Lapsing into his occasionally awkward phraseology, he criticized them as lacking civic-mindedness, fearful to the point of opposing the ACMHR: "You would be shocked at . . . how certain of our biggest Preachers (I'll call no names) pleaded with me to call off the Mass Meeting; how many tried to take a stand against the Movement, and would have publicly except for public sentiment. . . . You cannot imagine how tedious and painstaking it has been to forge together this organization in Birmingham; nor how difficult to keep in line moving forward. . . . Surely you would be shocked to learn how many times, but for me standing alone, certain officials would have flunked the movement." Returning to his providential worldview, he reminded Smiley of "the unpopularity of certain key decisions and acts which now are seen to have clearly been guided by His hand." Finally, turning from his recitation of the past and Smiley's recent letter, Shuttlesworth concluded:

> Knowing from whence we came, and how that only by His grace we have come thus far, I can clearly forgive you for what you have done. Having in my deepest conscience that the thoughts and acts of mine have been inspired by the Savior, I can do this without hypocrisy. Let me say that we be Brethren, and . . . you are and will be as welcome as before to sleep, eat, talk, pray, and work with us. . . . So far as I am concerned, the things that would divide us will never be as great as the things that bind us. Wishing the best for you and yours this season and much happiness and success in the new year, I am
> Always yours, Fred[67]

In context, Smiley's evaluation of Shuttlesworth's organizational skills sought to answer Gussner's specific question, "Does he know anything about organizing for nonviolence?" On that particular score, Smiley was accurate. He nonetheless recognized the ACMHR as "a powerful organization" that testified to Shuttlesworth's general organizational abilities. As to his craving for publicity, Smiley later commented that Shuttlesworth "was not enamored of television in order to get his picture thrown around the country." He understood the instrumental value of publicity and had long since established his willingness, even eagerness, to put himself in harm's way in order to get it. That fact alone led many observers to question Shuttlesworth's mental health, even if merely in jest. Nevertheless, in time Smiley concluded that to whatever lengths Shuttlesworth would go for publicity, he did not seek it as an end in itself. Moreover, whatever his own reservations and Ware's defensiveness about Shuttlesworth, Smiley affirmed that he had to be helped, inasmuch as "his group is the only one that is moving."[68]

This, of course, was also Shuttlesworth's evaluation of the Birmingham situation. He and his followers viewed themselves as the only force actively pushing hard against the forces of Bull Connor. More important, Shuttlesworth's movement seemed to be substantiated by the God who had intervened more than once to save their leader. Only Shuttlesworth was moving; only Shuttlesworth was being protected by God.

Hence his leadership seemed undeniable, and his support among the working class did not waver in response to Connor's use of the Smiley letter. A few days after the incident, a faithful ACMHR member told Emory Jackson, "We aren't paying what he [Connor] said no attention." Jackson indicated that the member's comment reflected "what so many others of her racial group are saying" and completely ignored Smiley's critical remarks about Shuttlesworth. Connor's ploy could not shake the loyalty of rank-and-file ACMHR members to Shuttlesworth. His defiance of Connor had won their uninterrupted devotion, and God's apparent favor on Shuttlesworth had cemented it. Will Hall, who had already risked his life in the second bomb attempt, embodied their fealty to Shuttlesworth as their leader. One particular Monday night, Shuttlesworth deviated from his usual practice of being driven to the mass meeting by an ACMHR member and drove himself. When the meeting ended and Fred got into his car, Hall hurried over and pulled him out of the car. Fearing another bomb attempt, Hall started the leader's car for him and told Fred, "If I die, it won't make no difference, but if you die, the movement won't be led."[69]

Nevertheless, Connor's attack on Shuttlesworth struck a vulnerable spot in Shuttlesworth's emotional armor. He expected little better from Connor, but he felt a keen sense of betrayal at the hands of a colleague. Although he offered Smiley his forgiveness, the two never worked together again—a parting of the ways attributable as much to Smiley's embarrassment as to Shuttlesworth's pained response to the letter. The incident intensified Shuttlesworth's perception of being the lone force for change in Birmingham. Fissures in black leadership only barely perceptible at the outset of the ACMHR began to widen. Criticism of Shuttlesworth from the upper echelon of the black community began to grow louder. Fred's typically unflappable demeanor was buffeted by an occasional sense of isolation. A fellow minister and ACMHR devotee, Abraham Woods, later told of at least one instance when Shuttlesworth inadvertently let his guard down and revealed a flash of vulnerability. One morning as Woods and his family were enjoying a mid-morning breakfast, Fred and Ruby unexpectedly appeared at their door. Woods invited them to join his family for breakfast. While Mrs. Woods engaged the Shuttlesworths in conversation, her husband ducked out the back door to the nearest market for a pound of sausage. Woods later reflected, "I had a perception that sometimes he felt a little lonely. . . . They sat there and ate for the longest. Seemed like they just wanted to get away from home."[70] For a moment Connor had the upper hand. The parry and thrust, however, would continue.

Alberta Robinson Shuttlesworth, mother of Fred Shuttlesworth, at her home in the Oxmoor community outside of Birmingham, ca. 1930. Her right eye was accidentally put out in an altercation with her husband, Will. (Courtesy of Fred Shuttlesworth)

High schooler Fred Shuttlesworth *(front)*, with brother Eugene and sister Cleola, ca. 1940. (Courtesy of Fred Shuttlesworth)

Ruby Keeler Shuttlesworth,
pictured here later in life, and
Fred Shuttlesworth were married
on October 20, 1941. (Courtesy
of Fred Shuttlesworth)

Fred as a graduate of Alabama
State College, August 8, 1952.
(Courtesy of Fred
Shuttlesworth)

"A Fire You Can't Put Out": Shuttlesworth the preacher, late 1950s. (Courtesy of Fred Shuttlesworth)

A church service at Bethel Baptist Church with Pastor Shuttlesworth at the pulpit. (Courtesy of Fred Shuttlesworth)

The Reverends Fred Shuttlesworth
and Ed Gardner, president and
vice president, respectively, of the
Alabama Christian Movement for
Human Rights, founded June 5,
1956. (Courtesy of Fred
Shuttlesworth)

A bomb leaves shattered the Bethel Baptist Church parsonage on Christmas
night, 1956. The collapsed left side of the house is the bedroom from which
an uninjured Shuttlesworth emerged. (Courtesy of Fred Shuttlesworth)

An interior view of the bomb's damage. (Courtesy of Fred Shuttlesworth)

Shuttlesworth is beaten by a mob as he attempts to enroll his daughters in the all-white Phillips High School, September 9, 1957. (AP/Wide World Photos)

Shuttlesworth meets with the press on his release from the hospital after the incident at Phillips High School. (Courtesy Birmingham Public Library Archives, Cat. #829.1.1.62)

Shuttlesworth under arrest in 1960. (Copyright by *The Birmingham News*, 1998. All rights reserved. Reprinted with permission.)

Jefferson County sheriffs confiscate the Shuttlesworths' car after Shuttlesworth and three other ministers are found guilty of libel in *Sullivan v. New York Times*, February 3, 1961. (Courtesy Birmingham Public Library Archives, Cat. #827.1.1.1.1)

ACMHR Monday night mass meeting. Shuttlesworth is to the right of the pulpit. Martin Luther King Jr. is behind and left of the pulpit. (Courtesy of Fred Shuttlesworth)

Bethel Baptist Church after its third bombing, December 1962. (Courtesy Birmingham Public Library Archives, Cat. #827.1.1.8.29)

Marchers sing "We Shall Overcome" in the Gaston Motel courtyard, April 3, 1963, at the beginning of Project C. (Robert Adams, *Birmingham News*. Copyright by *The Birmingham News*, 1998. All rights reserved. Reprinted with permission.)

Fred Shuttlesworth assembles marchers in the Gaston Motel courtyard. (Copyright by *The Birmingham News*, 1998. All rights reserved. Reprinted with permission.)

The Good Friday march led by Shuttlesworth, Abernathy, and King, April 12, 1963. (Courtesy Birmingham Public Library Archives, Cat. #1125.11.20)

King, Shuttlesworth, and Abernathy announce the May 10, 1963, truce agreement with Birmingham business leaders, ending five weeks of demonstrations. (Copyright by *The Birmingham News,* 1998. All rights reserved. Reprinted with permission.)

Desegregating Graymont Elementary School, September 5, 1963. *(Foreground, right to left)* Shuttlesworth, Floyd Armstrong (age 10), Dwight Armstrong (age 11), James Armstrong Jr. (father), attorney Oscar Adams Jr. (Copyright by *The Birmingham News,* 1998. All rights reserved. Reprinted with permission.)

Fred Shuttlesworth at age 35.
(Courtesy of Fred Shuttlesworth)

Revelation Baptist Church's
pastor and "first lady," Fred
and Ruby Shuttlesworth.
(Courtesy of Fred
Shuttlesworth)

Shuttlesworth statue, Birmingham Civil Rights Institute and Museum. The inscription reads: "Rev. Fred L. Shuttlesworth, Birmingham's Civil Rights Freedom Fighter: With singular courage he fired the imagination and raised the hopes of an oppressed people." (Courtesy of Andrew M. Manis)

The aging warrior: Fred Shuttlesworth in 1997 at Samford University, where he preached in the A. H. Reid Chapel. (Samford University photograph/Caroline Baird Estes)

Stalemate

Maybe the Reverend Shuttlesworth is a glut[ton] for publicity.
Maybe his methods are wrong. Maybe he has too much nerve.
If he had sought no publicity, had the right methods, and was
timid enough, would his critics accept him any more than now?
Or would they find something else wrong with him?
—— Emory O. Jackson

lthough brought low by Connor's public airing of the Smiley letter, Fred
Shuttlesworth refused to stay down long. His moments of emotional
weakness usually and quickly gave way to a religious hopefulness and a predisposition to project an image of strength. A *real* man should be strong—and his
fixation on strength fought fiercely to root out every vestige of "weakness" he
found in himself. "If somebody's real sick and you want to cry," he was wont to
say, "crying won't help. Somebody's got to be well enough to give the medicine.
. . . If *you're* weak and *I* get weak, and we both major on weaknesses, nobody'll
be strong." Moreover, an African American and evangelical faith in providence
fortified this feature of Shuttlesworth's personality. This popular tenet of African American religion remained unwaveringly at the center of Shuttlesworth's
spirituality. He maintained, "I always had a sense after I got into this thing, that
God was leading me step by step, and that everything was gon' come out alright
in the end, regardless of what the traumatic situations were. . . . I just don't believe I have to cringe before a thing when God's already promised. And the question comes down to . . . 'Do you believe in God or not.'" The God in whom
Shuttlesworth believed apparently kept Fred's combative and combustible spirituality alive through events that threatened to douse it completely. By force of
will Shuttlesworth typically fanned the flicker back to a fiery blaze.[1]

Consequently, his sometimes lonely battles not only continued but soon expanded to some additional fronts—and, not surprisingly, among friends as well
as foes. During 1959 and 1960 Shuttlesworth continued his feverish pace, tan-
gling with attorneys, black business professionals, and other black ministers in
what came to be called Birmingham's "leadership stalemate." While telling this
story, this chapter also highlights another stalemate as Shuttlesworth tried with
only partial success to press King to increase the sclc's activities in Birmingham. Finally, this chapter recounts Shuttlesworth's continuing public standoffs

with Connor, epitomized by his 1960 suit against the commissioner and police chief Jamie Moore.

By early 1959 Shuttlesworth's efforts to desegregate city parks, along with renewed attempts to integrate the Birmingham public schools, kindled a new controversy—this one, however, with some of the ACMHR's erstwhile allies.[2] Shuttlesworth had retained a new attorney, Ernest D. Jackson Sr. of Jacksonville, Florida, to handle the ACMHR's new park and school desegregation efforts. In consultation with the ACMHR executive board, Shuttlesworth judged as excessive the fees levied by Arthur Shores, Oscar Adams, Demetrius Newton, and Orzell Billingsley. Since the inception of the organization, the legal costs had amounted to some $24,000. Shuttlesworth also objected to the agreed-upon pay schedule of half down and half after the initial arguments. Jackson had agreed to take cases for $4,500 rather than the $6,000 the others had required. In response, the Birmingham lawyers asked federal judge Seybourn Lynne for a court order requiring out-of-town attorneys to associate with a local firm. During the next few years the attorneys' action annoyed Shuttlesworth, who believed his own single-minded attention to the struggle for civil rights should be shared by all black professionals in Birmingham. On occasion he even called the lawyers his "Calhouns," comparing them to the ethically questionable lawyer of the *Amos and Andy* show. In addition, these disagreements had the effect of slowing down the ACMHR's direct challenges to segregation and restricting them to litigation already in the courts or that which resulted from further arrests.[3]

By May Shuttlesworth commented on the dispute. Of significance, he made his remarks in the context of larger complaints about the failure of black Birmingham to fall in line completely behind him and the work of the ACMHR. He distinguished between himself and the ACMHR ministers, whom he classified as part of "the prophetical line . . . who set out to turn the world upside down for Christ," and those of more priestly or "status quo" concerns. He further noted his disappointment in the level of support of local physicians, dentists, and attorneys, the latter of whom "had been willing to take some cases for us (for a fee), but cooperation even here has broken down. They feel they may be attacked for stirring up litigation." Citing total expenses of $40,419.79 incurred by the ACMHR, most of which came from legal expenses, he commented: "This lawyer situation is a regretful one, particularly in view of the fact that this struggle is so sacred and so encompassing. I think the lawyers, up to this point, haven't had anything but small fees and somehow see this as a chance to make big money, although, in some cases, they may actually end up losing money. In their effort to get big money (although we have no objection to paying reasonable fees), they forget that they have a part also in this program to realize first-class citizenship for all Negroes."[4]

His feeling that the lawyers were using the movement to their own financial advantage galled him, particularly in light of his own practice of contributing all his honoraria from outside speaking engagements to ACMHR coffers. This practice was causing strain within his own marriage because Ruby believed the family's sacrifices for the movement deserved remuneration. Unmoved by that argument, Shuttlesworth tenaciously insisted that all contributions from around the country belonged to the movement. Thus, self-righteously holding others to his own standard of commitment, he chafed at what he took to be the lawyers' opportunism.

The problem with the black professionals in Birmingham occupied his mind as he embarked on an extensive speaking tour to the midwest and the eastern seaboard. His most widely reported stop on the tour occurred in Louisville on May 22. Speaking at an SCEF rally, he stressed the linkage between what he titled "Civil Rights and Civil Liberties." His address, given at the West Chestnut Baptist Church, protested congressional proposals to revive state sedition laws. Shuttlesworth told his audience, "If the state can dictate to Negro preachers what to say and what not to say, when to do and when not to do, how to act and when to act, then Americanism has become far less than that which the Founding Fathers established, and what we have for so long proclaimed." He warned: "Negroes should not be fooled at the tactics of the segregationists. This is one big fight. We must contend as one man, white and colored together, for the total liberties guaranteed by the Constitution and the Bill of Rights. McCarthy, known as the modern prophet of hysteria, is dead; but the segregationists have taken up his line. . . . If the House Un-American Committee is really interested in uncovering un-American activities, why does it not investigate the bombings, the lynchings, the mob violence against Negroes in the South?"[5]

After his speech, in an interview with *Louisville Defender* editor Frank Stanley, Shuttlesworth criticized the Birmingham lawyers and ministers. The interview "created a flurry of inquiries" concerning the growing controversy, and several national publications ran stories on what came to be called the "leadership stalemate" in black Birmingham. On the basis of information provided by Shuttlesworth, Stanley editorialized that "the Negro lawyers of Alabama are hindering the work" of the ACMHR by setting high fees and colluding with the courts to keep "outside lawyers from participating in the movement."[6]

On his return from his speaking tour, Shuttlesworth prepared for the ACMHR's third anniversary. Much of the black community anticipated his responding to the "stalemate" in his president's address. He opened his remarks with a rehearsal of the organization's aims and objectives, and he noted the membership's steadfastness in the face of obstacles, saying, "We only pray that *our* methods will always be Christian, that no hate will ever be found nor practiced in our hearts and actions, and that out of the intensity of this struggle, we Negroes will become more religious, more consecrated, better Americans."

Then, reviewing the ACMHR's financial status, he marked a thinly veiled contrast that "no personal gain has been secured for anyone from Movement funds. This is an organization where we sacrifice for Freedom, not grab for personal gain." Most of his comments centered on the ACMHR's legal situations; he reviewed the current status of five bus-related cases, the school case, the police and personnel cases, and the terminal station case. He also summarized the dispute with the lawyers, indicating that pressures from fellow attorneys and Judge Lynne induced Demetrius Newton to reject associating with attorney Ernest Jackson. He explained that he had met with the lawyers to discuss matters and to head off the unfavorable publicity that had developed but that such efforts had not led to any resolution. He concluded by affirming: "The Cause of Freedom is greater than any of us. Let us in these critical days be friendly and truthful in our relations, restrained and courteous in our conversation, and always considerate of others. Finally, we need all of our resources—lawyers, doctors, preachers, housewives, ditch diggers, Christians, sinners—everybody to win this struggle to make our country to become the Land of the Free, and the Home of the Brave."[7]

Shuttlesworth treated the dispute in a surprisingly restrained, even conciliatory, manner. The verbal pyrotechnics were provided by Ella Baker, then serving as interim executive director of the SCLC. After being introduced by Ruby Shuttlesworth, Baker addressed the leadership question sharply. "Beware of the accommodating type of Negro leader," she warned, "who says what he thinks local Southern officials want to hear. The leader, self-styled or otherwise designated, who is quick to limit the Negro's drive for civil rights to some one phase, such as voter-registration, and who pointedly avoids mention of desegregation of schools, buses, housing, public facilities, etc., is as dangerous as those white persons who lump together the NAACP and the White Citizens' Councils as the 'two extremes.' Both are misrepresenting the facts and befuddling the issues." She advised her audience instead to "choose and follow leaders who, like Reverend Fred Shuttlesworth, have proved by their actions, their courage and dedication, that they are determined to secure the full loaf of freedom and not just the crumbs."[8]

Also supportive of Shuttlesworth was Emory O. Jackson, who commented on the ACMHR anniversary by noting, "No other organization has had to withstand as much opposition, pressure, discouragement, and suffering as the leaders of the Alabama Christian Movement for Human Rights. Bombings, jailings, betrayals, and harassments have not chilled their ardor, upset their dedication, or checked their drive." Taking the side of Shuttlesworth in the controversy with the attorneys, he gently criticized

> a section of our local leadership failing to be of as much service as freedom and the whetted desire for first-class citizenship would seem to require. In this freedom struggle there should be no room for the obstinate selfish. Our leadership should be broad-minded enough, sensitive enough, and interested enough not to stand in the way of the determined and honorable efforts of our group to move against the obstacle to meaningful citizenship. Let us appeal to all sections of our leadership not to try to make harder this heroic struggle. . . . Selfish leaders in the long haul are usually found on the losing side. History is likely to deal roughly with those who try to hold back the children of God's freedom.[9]

On June 20, Judge Lynne made the dispute all the more onerous by refusing Ernest Jackson's request to file the park integration suit without associating with a local attorney. In response to the judge's decision, the *Birmingham World* issued an editorial titled "The Leadership Stalemate." Jackson saw the ruling as dramatizing the need for a committee of black leaders to end the impasse. "The little folk who foot the bill, who pay off our professionals, who feed our businesses are beginning to talk," he warned, implying that the dispute revolved around a disagreement over the scope of civil rights activism in the city. Jackson did not endorse Shuttlesworth's multipronged attack outright, but he did quote Baker's speech and observed, in language that could have been written by Shuttlesworth, "The blame-swappers are using this stalemate to even justify individual do-nothingism." Reminding his readers that segregationists took comfort in a divided black community, he averred that certain power brokers in the black community "could break the leadership stalemate if they were truly interested in trying to advance the group forward."[10]

In a second editorial, Jackson touched on the wounded feelings of the local attorneys who felt the public airing of the stalemate "was a calculated effort to embarrass and hurt them." They believed that, having made a national name for themselves in the civil rights cases to date, they were entitled to call the legal signals. He defended the lawyers against claims of some ACMHR members that they were deliberately seeking to slow down the movement by playing along with segregationist judges, and for a second time he called for a committee to help find a solution.[11]

No solution was forthcoming, and the dispute once again appeared in the black press outside of Birmingham. In October, *Pittsburgh Courier* reporter Trezzvant Anderson wrote an article titled "Birmingham's Big Need." Calling for a unified black leadership, Anderson cited Shuttlesworth as "the only really outstanding Negro leader with a large following," who, "by his dramatic and daring moves ha[d] kept the interest of the masses aroused." Yet, he added, Shuttlesworth's controversial nature had led "other influential Negro leaders" to hesitate to fall in line under his banner. "There are a goodly number [of leaders]," he wrote, "who do not approve of some of the tactics of the Rev. Mr. Shuttlesworth. They would do it differently, if it were up to them, some will tell you. So let them choose one man around whom they can rally and let that man carry the banner. There is glory enough to go all around."[12]

For ACMHR members there was *not* enough glory to go around. In their estimation, Shuttlesworth had earned the glory with his scars. As for Shuttlesworth himself, though he insisted that recognition was never his main goal, he freely believed that his bravado and his acts of confrontation, along with what he considered God's confirmation of them, had merited the status of leader and the respect of others who had never shared his risks. His followers, dubbed "Shuttle-lites" by some of Fred's critics, agreed with an Emory Jackson editorial written early in the year, just as the lawyer dispute was beginning:

> The Reverend F. L. Shuttlesworth, the colorful, courageous, controversial, uncompromising president of the Alabama Christian Movement for Human Rights, was a center-of-fire leader on the local desegregation front. *Time* magazine, *Jet* magazine, and other publications recognized him as Birmingham's No. 1 crusader for civil rights. He is the sparkplug, if not the symbol, of the unpopular local integration

struggle. . . . History pours itself through men. Men are the pipelines of history. The Rev. Shuttlesworth has gone to court, sweated it out in jail, and lifted his voice on the platform seeking to remove racial discrimination from state-supported services. He has his critics; he has opposition, yet he commands substantial support from those cut the deepest by damaging discrimination.

As long as Shuttlesworth maintained this "substantial support," the stalemate continued. It indeed did continue throughout his work in Birmingham, and Shuttlesworth gradually impressed Jackson with his willingness to learn. A year and a half later, when feelings regarding this dispute were less frayed, Jackson editorialized again: "Today the Rev. Shuttlesworth is a more seasoned leader. His presidential speech at the fourth annual anniversary of the ACMHR reflected no less. He seems to better understand teamwork leadership and is beginning to adjust his approach to some of the realities of struggle. . . . Birmingham has civil rights leadership depth. It has teamwork leadership. . . . Yet the 'wanted man' sign, figuratively speaking, seems to hang over the head of the Rev. Shuttlesworth." [13]

Problems with other ministers also surfaced occasionally. Fred periodically fought off theological challenges of brethren who believed activist ministers had overstepped the bounds of their ministerial calling. On June 15, the *Birmingham News* ran a letter from the Southern Negro Improvement Association, the prosegregation group that in 1955 had challenged the *Brown* decision. The group condemned such black ministers as Shuttlesworth, whom they believed had abandoned traditional biblical interpretations for "integration and other social doctrines as a basis for their sermons." Shuttlesworth viewed such remarks as "Uncle Tom" organizations making their statements primarily for white consumption. If he even noticed the letter, he ignored it in his public statements. He nonetheless continued to articulate his African American brand of "social gospel" to his church members and movement followers. [14]

His understanding owed little to his formal education or to his reading of any of the classic exponents of the social gospel, such as Walter Rauschenbusch, whose writings had influenced King. Shuttlesworth never read Rauschenbusch or other such thinkers. He certainly heard some of those ideas recycled in sermons and in conversations with King and other more educated black ministers in the movement. For Shuttlesworth, however, these "authorities" carried weight only insofar as they corroborated his reading of scripture. In particular, he often referred to the social implications of Jesus' teachings and ministry. Thus, he later argued, the church has a right and a duty to work for social change. "I interpreted Jesus' life," he explained regarding the sources of his views and added, "I didn't have to ask somebody over yonder, because any great man, however great he was, was not the perfect man Jesus Christ, who is the example for our generation and all generations."[15]

Much of his understanding derived from a "prophetical" view of the church. In his criticism of nonsupportive ministers, whom he categorized as "priestly," he also judged Jesus himself as a prophet. Thus, for Shuttlesworth the church's role extended beyond itself as an institution to challenge society itself. He later explained:

> [Religion] ought to have the same thrust that John the Baptist had when he went to tell Herod he was wrong . . . and when Elijah went to Jezebel . . . or Elijah when he challenged the 450 prophets [of Baal]. It's "both/and." It has to do with your prayer life and your living life and it also has to do with how you live, whether you live under oppression. Whether or not somebody's challenging the oppression. Because it was never God's will, in my estimation, though he permitted it, for oppression to be the order of the day anywhere. . . . I always remember what Dr. [William Holmes] Borders said: "The Book of Acts is an action book. The gospel will get you in trouble; but God will get you out." That's a true statement. And if you aren't . . . running over somebody's feeling, making and overcoming enemies, then it's not the gospel. . . . I think civil rights is a part of what God always intended for the gospel. "Let my people go" is the basis of all of it. That tells me God has always been on our side, and God has allowed it that men have had to fight in all generations.[16]

Armed in part with this progressive theology, Shuttlesworth fared somewhat better than a stalemate with his allies in the SCLC. He seemed to translate the loneliness he felt after the Smiley incident into a portrait of his group as the spearhead of a "worldwide revolution which is a divine struggle for the exaltation of the human race." The ACMHR, in conjunction with the SCEF, published a pamphlet whose title depicted the organization as the vanguard of the civil rights movement: *They Strike Segregation at Its Core!* The pamphlet reviewed Shuttlesworth's exploits since 1956 and solicited outside financial support. The entreaty was based on Shuttlesworth's view, increasingly shared by the SCLC, that as went the struggle in Birmingham, so would go its success throughout the South. "Wherever you live," the tract explained, "if you believe in human dignity and brotherhood, Birmingham Negroes are fighting your battle. Birmingham is the strongest bastion of segregation in America. When equality and right win there, the key line of segregationist defense will be breached. From then on, victory for human rights will be easier everywhere. Birmingham in a sense is the test for America's future."[17]

In this period, Shuttlesworth, as SCLC secretary, first began to press King to step up his activities and give particular attention to the situation in Birmingham. During the years between the Montgomery bus boycott and the 1963 campaign in Birmingham, according to historian Adam Fairclough, most of the movement's dynamism came from such local leaders as Shuttlesworth, C. K. Steele in Tallahassee, and James Lawson in Nashville. Part of King's difficulty had to do with his adjusting to his growing role as central leader of the movement while balancing his role as a local pastor in Montgomery. As a result, by the end of the year, he decided to resign his pastorate and move back to Atlanta in order to give full-time attention to SCLC activities. For his part, Shuttlesworth, through his activities, had earned the respect of the more militant spirits in the SCLC, and his influence increased in this period despite significant differences of style with King.[18]

King's education and theological sophistication contrasted starkly with Shuttlesworth's biblicist approach to doctrinal matters. On one occasion, he sharply differed with King and Abernathy regarding the nature of Christ's resurrection, which they spoke of as an image or apparition. Although King and Abernathy may have been merely speculating about views they had studied, Shuttlesworth took their comments as doubt concerning the historicity of the event. Shuttlesworth further took the incident as Martin's good-natured effort to provoke a response from him. Theological doubt was for Fred another kind of weakness in which he would never allow himself to indulge. On this occasion he challenged King's indulging in it, asking, "Well, Martin, what did the disciples see?" King hypothesized that they experienced something like an apparition, "something that's not exactly real, but yet real." Fred answered, "If God lied about that, he lied about everything else. If God lied about anything, then God was not God. It's impossible for God to lie. . . . That would be the biggest lie, the biggest fostering of something on people than ever."[19]

Shuttlesworth reacted so intensely to this suggestion, he later acknowledged, that Martin seemed uncomfortable discussing theological matters with him. They never did so again. Fred later convinced himself that Martin did not really believe the views he had expressed. Had Shuttlesworth believed this about King, he later said, he would have prayed for him to change his view, given his belief that no true Christian can doubt this doctrine. Nevertheless, his courage and persistence had won King's admiration. As "one of the most cussed and discussed men in the integration movement in America," as the SCEF's newspaper, *Southern Patriot,* called Shuttlesworth, he had earned the right to be taken seriously in the inner counsels of the SCLC.[20]

With his influence rising within the SCLC, Fred began prodding King to stronger efforts. In early April the SCLC Administrative Committee met in Montgomery to discuss various difficulties. One problem was the weak leadership of Executive Director John Tilley, and his resignation was requested. Tilley's job was taken over temporarily by Shuttlesworth ally Ella Baker. In early 1960 the SCLC chose Wyatt Tee Walker, a Petersburg, Virginia, pastor, as the permanent replacement. With his outspoken nature and sometimes prickly personality, Walker was akin to Shuttlesworth in spirit, though better educated and capable of smoother diplomacy. By placing Baker and then Walker in the position of executive director, the SCLC had moved into the more militant position that Shuttlesworth had exemplified and on occasion advocated. Three weeks after the meeting in Montgomery, Shuttlesworth, insisting on more action by the SCLC, wrote King to complain that segregation in Alabama was not being attacked vigorously enough. He saw civil rights leadership in Alabama as "much less dynamic and imaginative than it ought to be."[21]

More frustrating were setbacks recently experienced by the ACMHR. One of these was the Klan beating of ACMHR colleague Charles Billups. In two other situations that posed more strategic problems, the Alabama legislature had introduced several segregation bills, and the Alabama Court of Appeals had declined to review Shuttlesworth's and his colleagues' convictions for disorderly conduct, charges stemming from the bus-riding attempts the previous October. The appeals court dismissed the case because lawyers had filed the transcript of trial testimony three days after the deadline. As Shuttlesworth wrote his letter to King, he was under pressure to file another appeal or begin serving his jail term within fifteen days. Perturbed that nothing had been done in response, he called for organized protests uniting local groups and hit on his pet theme—action must follow words. "When the flowery speeches have been made," he wrote, "we still have the hard job of getting down and helping people. . . . We [the SCLC] must move now, or else [be] hard put in the not too distant future, to justify our existence." Looking forward to a forthcoming SCLC board meeting, he hoped that "we can really lay some positive plans for action. . . . Now is the time for serious thinking and practical resulting actions."[22]

In June, Shuttlesworth wrote another impatient letter to King that reiterated his call for action. "I had certainly expected to hear from you further on this matter before this time. . . . It is my feeling that the times are far too critical for us to get good solid ideas on what should be done in certain situations, and then take too long a time to put these ideas into action." Particularly galled by recent statements critical of civil rights agitation by wealthy black business leader A. G. Gaston, Shuttlesworth warned that such "backward statements" could negate their own leadership. "Any local Negro appointed to high position," he wrote, "should not be allowed to make Uncle Tom statements so far as the rights of Negroes are concerned and get away with it. Surely, with his wide business interests among Negroes, Mr. Gaston's statement will have a lot of effect. I hope you take action at once."[23]

In October, Fred attended the SCLC's major fall meeting in Columbia, South Carolina. The Executive Committee discussed the weaknesses of the SCLC frankly, concluding, much as Shuttlesworth had observed, that little had been done to improve voter registration or to put together any concerted effort among local affiliates. The SCLC had not developed, in their words, "a positive, dynamic and dramatic program." Recognizing the prohibitive size of the Administrative Committee, they appointed a subcommittee to assist Ella Baker in planning the program for 1960. Soon the Future Program Committee, to which Fred was appointed as a member, called on King to consider giving his full attention to the work of the SCLC. By the end of November, King submitted his resignation as pastor of Dexter Avenue Baptist Church, effective January 31, 1960. In addition, the November issue of the SCLC's newsletter, the *Crusader,* carried an article that described Birmingham as the "South's Toughest City." Referring to Birmingham as the "Johannesburg of North America," the article reviewed recent developments in Shuttlesworth's efforts, including Judge Grooms's November 23 dismissal of the 1958 bus suit and Judge Lynne's dismissal of the three-year old Baldwin suit. Shuttlesworth was quoted as calling the rulings "worse than the Dred Scott Decision."[24]

In a significant indication of Shuttlesworth's influence in the SCLC, the board met in Birmingham in early December to finalize plans for 1960. Resolutions adopted by the board commented on the symbolic importance of meeting in

Birmingham and commended the efforts of the ACMHR and Shuttlesworth. Moreover, King pressed to move beyond mere voter registration to a full-scale assault on segregation, expressed in classic Shuttlesworth style as "stepped-up action on all fronts." Having drawn up the plans in a morning meeting, leaders presented them at a joint mass meeting of the ACMHR and the SCLC that night at St. James Baptist Church. This period thus saw the strengthening of Shuttlesworth's hand in the SCLC, but not yet to the point of convincing King to commit the organization fully to combining forces with the ACMHR in a direct action challenge to Bull Connor. The time had not yet arrived.[25]

Tensions also began to invade the Shuttlesworth home. Fred's single-minded attention to his civil rights responsibilities and his extended travel schedule put added pressure on the family. He and Ruby found themselves arguing over Fred's expectations of her and the children. An intelligent and somewhat independent woman, Ruby increasingly chafed at the responsibilities of keeping house and family intact while her husband trotted around the globe on the speaking circuit. Shuttlesworth expected his wife to be active in the movement. Ruby shared his excitement for the struggle and participated in a goodly number of ACMHR and SCLC events. In May Fred and Ruby flew to New York for an event sponsored by the SCEF's New York Committee. In a posh reception in the Crystal Room of the Hotel Delmonico, Fred was feted as one of the guests of honor. Both he and Ruby were congratulated by the committee's honorary chairperson, Eleanor Roosevelt. The next day the Philadelphia Friends of the SCEF held a reception to honor Ruby. At the event, Ruby recounted her family's experiences in the segregation fight and plugged for financial support of the movement. Occasionally she participated in various workshops sponsored by the ACMHR or the SCLC, such as a conference jointly held by the SCLC, FOR, and the Congress of Racial Equality (CORE) at Atlanta's Spelman College.[26]

New pressures brought on by Fred's movement activities exacerbated long-standing difficulties between Fred and Ruby. Tensions regarding his expectations of the members of the household as a minister's family, discipline of the children, and what Fred considered Ruby's weaknesses as a cook and housekeeper persisted. Fred's extensive time away from home and his insistence on giving all outside financial contributions to the ACMHR rankled Ruby. She believed that her husband's sacrifices had earned him the right to a portion of the proceeds, a view that Fred never shared. The miserly Reverend Shuttlesworth found what he considered his wife's spendthrift ways a major annoyance, and Ruby thought the same about Fred's tightfisted approach to family finance. As a result of her dissatisfaction regarding their financial situation, Ruby decided in 1959 to return to college, transferring her original work at Tuskegee to Alabama State. Ruby spent the weekdays in Montgomery taking classes and left the care of the children to her aunt, Adell Morris. She returned to Birmingham on weekends, but her time away from home bothered Fred, and the couple argued often enough to cause Fred to doubt the survivability of the marriage.[27]

Even with his difficulties with friends and foes alike, Shuttlesworth kept up his tenacious assault against Jim Crow laws in Birmingham on as many fronts as possible. Legal challenges already in motion continued to be dismissed by the courts, only to be appealed. In addition, he and the ACMHR developed new attempts in the schools, in the city's recreational facilities, on buses, and, beginning in 1960, at the lunch counters of downtown department stores. All efforts overlapped with one another and at times gave white Birmingham the sense of being under siege. Progress was so gradual and cumulative in effect that Shuttlesworth became convinced that no real breakthrough would come apart from massive direct action with the help of King and the SCLC. Only rarely, however, did Shuttlesworth find himself downcast; he was full of conviction that eventually the walls would indeed come "a-tumblin' down."

As the school year in Alabama began in 1959, Governor John Patterson commented that blacks in the state would be wise to ignore the leadership of Martin Luther King Jr. and his ilk, warning that King's policies could result in the closing of the state's public schools. This, he pointed out, "would be to the detriment of Negroes." In response, Shuttlesworth sent a letter to the governor, with a copy to the press, which stated that the governor's attack on King gave "the impression of a desperate man." King had won his following as "a shining symbol of the hope of a people tired of oppression, disfranchisement, abuse and economic exploitation." He further criticized Patterson's vow that integration would come to the state only "over my [dead] body." Such language, Shuttlesworth argued, constituted an "indirect call—coming as it did from the state's highest office—to certain groups, for the harassment and intimidation of Negroes."[28]

On Monday, October 26, Shuttlesworth, acting on behalf of some eighty black families, sent a special-delivery letter to the city's new superintendent of education, Dr. Theo R. Wright. As "tax-paying Citizens of Birmingham, Alabama, and parents of school-age children," Shuttlesworth's group petitioned the board of education to desegregate and open all schools to "all children without regard to race, creed, or color" as ordered by the Supreme Court decisions of May 1954 and June 1955. He further wrote: "It has been five and four years respectively since these rulings have been rendered, and your Honors, as a Board and Superintendent, have made no effort to comply. The Supreme Court announced that the local School Boards had the primary responsibility, and ordered 'a prompt and reasonable start' toward compliance." Noting that several similar petitions had been submitted to the board only to be either denied or ignored, Shuttlesworth offered to meet with the board "to discuss any positive plan designed to desegregate the public schools." Warning of possible litigation, the petition asked the board to declare a nondiscriminatory policy in the public schools and to direct all employees of the school system to abide by the new policy. The petition also called on officials to announce a plan of desegregation by December 1. Eight days later Shuttlesworth resubmitted the same petition, which had originally been submitted without signatures. This time the form had 135 signers. In response, Superintendent Wright announced that the petitions would be discussed at the next meeting of the board, which was scheduled for November 20. He added, however, that the Alabama Pupil Placement Law provided only for individual school assignment, without provision for class actions. Thus, few in Shuttlesworth's camp were surprised when three days after the board meeting, the signers were informed that their request was not "appropriate" inasmuch as the placement law provided for only the individual assignment of students. Undeterred, Shuttlesworth proceeded to other pressure points.[29]

At about the same time as Shuttlesworth's petitions to the board of education, the park suit, which early in 1959 had been slowed by the dispute with the attorneys, was once again filed. In response, Connor appealed through the press to the "decent, thoughtful, and good Negroes" of Birmingham to render a "great service" by ignoring Shuttlesworth's agitating ways. If they did not, he warned, they would face the closing of the parks. He attributed Shuttlesworth's activities to a desire for "personal exploitation" and communist leanings. As evidence of the minister's subversive activities, he cited Fred's trip to Europe during the previous summer to an international conference of the Fellowship of Reconciliation, attended by, according to Connor, "left-wingers and out-and-out communists."[30]

Shuttlesworth answered with a letter to Connor, taunting him as "a once-mighty lion" who now appeared "impotent with a thorn in the foot." He further pointed out that white citizens would be more inconvenienced than blacks by the closing of the parks and called for the formation of a biracial committee.

"The days of frank discussion around the conference table are upon us," he wrote. "Negroes want to talk and be brothers." He continued: "Good Negroes wonder why it is that of all the 'decent, thoughtful, and good Negroes' in Birmingham with education and qualifications of all kinds, there has not been, nor is there yet, one Negro policeman, or one Negro fireman, or one Negro clerk or one Negro secretary, working for the city of Birmingham. Good Negroes noted the difference in your action when Bethel Baptist Church was bombed the second time with no special efforts on your part to apprehend the guilty, and in the attempted bombing of Beth-El Temple when the Commissioner made great display of official concern." He accused Connor of insulting the intelligence of blacks with his comments about how little taxes were paid by black citizens, who had paid considerable taxes and viewed the results as taxation without representation. "What the Commissioner and the Commission think of Shuttlesworth personally," he argued, "is not nearly so important as what they do for Negro people. . . . It is a tragic day when . . . some officials only diagnose the word integration as being Communism; and can only label those persons, white or black, as Communists who ask for what the U.S. Constitution promises by lawful petition, earnest prayers, and legal action when necessary. Shuttlesworth seeks not publicity but progress." He then challenged Connor to a public debate on the issues as soon as possible. No debate was forthcoming, and U.S. district judge Grooms dismissed the ACMHR suit on November 1, stating that the suit failed to state any relief that might be granted and that it showed no "justifiable controversy." Along with another suit seeking to integrate the public schools, Shuttlesworth and the ACMHR filed another parks suit against the city in mid-1960, both without success.[31]

Along with Shuttlesworth's efforts to desegregate the schools and parks, court dockets once again brought up older efforts related to the city buses. Shuttlesworth decided immediately to challenge the city's new bus seating ordinance, which left seating policies up to the Birmingham Transit Company. Filing an action in U.S. district court in mid-November 1958, Shuttlesworth and the ACMHR achieved a partial victory in Judge Grooms's November 23, 1959, ruling. From Shuttlesworth's perspective, Grooms ruled negatively by holding that the October 1958 arrests did violate the plaintiffs' civil rights but that the ordinance did not set a policy. The judge disingenuously ruled that "evidence from one case was insufficient" to conclude that the transit company had conspired with the city to deny blacks their rights. As a private business firm, the company retained the right to set its own policy, and thus blacks were "not entitled to injunctive or declaratory relief." Seating arrangements, the judge opined, "were a matter between the Negroes and the Birmingham Transit Company." Grooms further ruled, however, that a "willful refusal to obey a request to move from the front to the rear of a bus when unaccompanied by other acts tending to disorder, does not constitute a breach of the peace." Police could no longer arrest blacks simply for refusing to ride in designated Jim Crow sections. Grooms also ruled that "all forms of governmental racial discrimination, whether cleverly fashioned or free of disguise, are illegal. . . . There is a very strong presumption that public officers will in good faith discharge their duties and observe the law."[32]

Puzzled by the ruling, Shuttlesworth nonetheless assured reporters that "Negroes in Birmingham will not be satisfied with anything less than desegregation." Ultimately he and his lawyers settled on appealing this ruling as well, doing so on December 23. In the meantime, however, Shuttlesworth took advantage of the situation, interpreting Grooms's more positive ruling to mean that blacks could no longer be arrested for sitting in "white" sections of the buses. On Monday, December 7, he dispatched an ACMHR committee, composed of Ed Gardner, Abraham Woods, and W. E. Shortridge, to meet with transit company officials. Requesting that the segregation signs on buses be immediately removed, they were told that the highest officials of the company were out of the city. The next day, Shuttlesworth sent a strong letter to the company recapping the outcome of the previous day's meeting and citing favorable sections of Judge Grooms's ruling. He further reiterated the ACMHR's request for the removal of segregation signs within six days.[33]

That evening, in a joint mass meeting between the ACMHR and the SCLC, whose board had been meeting in Birmingham, Shuttlesworth pressed his people to ride the buses in an unsegregated manner. In a meeting at St. James Baptist Church, Shuttlesworth tangled with fire chief Aaron Rosenfeld, who under Connor's orders interrupted the proceedings by looking for fire hazards. The angry minister at first refused to move the meeting, informing Rosenfeld that "the fire we have in here you can't put out with hoses and axes." Finally relenting, Shuttlesworth moved the meeting to another nearby church and told his followers, "This is a helluva city." Criticizing Grooms's ruling, he commented: "It is a terrible thing when the federal judiciary diligently seeks ways to deny people their rights." Informing the crowd of his efforts with bus officials, he roared his advice: "Damn the torpedoes, full speed ahead! We gonna ride these buses again if jail be our destinies."[34]

By the time of their mass meeting a week later, the ACMHR request had gone without a response from the bus company. That night Shuttlesworth led the activists to adopt a resolution that announced their intentions to begin riding buses in any available seats. Reiterating the ACMHR's publicized desires for the end of segregated seating, their repeated arrests and jailings, their unsuccessful lawsuits, and the failure of the transit company to respond to their requests, the resolution rejected any suggestions that blacks voluntarily accept such seating. The statement further resolved that "we are free NOW to ride in ANY SEAT available on ANY BUS. We shall ignore Segregation Signs, and shall ride henceforth FIRST CLASS ON FIRST CLASS FARE. We urge our people in riding buses and waiting in waiting rooms, to do so in quietness, with calm dignity, and in a prayerful and understanding spirit."[35] Shuttlesworth also gave his audience handbills for distribution throughout the downtown area and the African American community. The circulars announced: "Negroes Can Now Sit Anywhere on Buses. There is no law to make Negroes go to the back, and no policemen or driver can make Negroes move. Start now—ride desegregated on buses."

Soon Connor spoke up against what he called the "dangerous" circulars. He charged that the handbills propagated false information "seeking to deceive the Negroes into false beliefs." Attempting to counter the ACMHR message, the commissioner argued that company drivers could lawfully require passengers to follow their seating instructions, which according to current company policy called on whites to be seated from the front of the bus and blacks from the rear. "Bus drivers," he continued, "have lawful authority to remove any person, colored or white, who refuses to comply with company rules." He accused those distributing the circulars of being "agitators seeking to cause more race trouble in Birmingham." Finally, he warned, "If violence and disorder occurs [sic] by reason of reckless deception being propagated by these circulars, it can and will be quelled by the police department. My advice to our many Negro citizens is to ignore the circulars by taking them for what they are—a sure-fire way to stir up trouble."[36]

Shuttlesworth's immediate rejoinder denounced the comments as "another pathetic attempt to deceive Negroes." He said that his followers viewed both his statement and the 1958 ordinance as "old bull wrapped up in a new plan." Negroes would ignore the segregation signs on buses on the basis of Judge Grooms's ruling "that a refusal to obey a request to move from the front to the rear of a bus is not a breach of the peace." He spoke of African Americans' determination to emerge from second-class status as "a major fact of the twentieth century . . . and that includes Birmingham." He taunted the failure to threaten Negro arrests because Connor knew that he and the bus company were power-less to stop them. "In fact," he concluded, "they are as powerless as a hound dog with his teeth extracted. Neither should the Commissioner think he can fool Negroes by his use of the words dangerous, violence, and stirring up trouble. We have not come so far just to stop here. In olden days, the contest for jus-tice and righteousness was between God and Baal; today it is between God and Eugene Connor."[37]

After three years of struggle with the city commission and the transit com-pany, Shuttlesworth and the ACMHR had what the *Southern Patriot* called a "bus victory in Alabama." A more personal taste of success occurred as the Shuttles-worth children boarded a city bus. Just as the driver was about to order them to the rear, a white passenger quickly warned him, "Some of those are the Shut-tlesworth children." "Well, I'd better not bother them," he replied as he left them to sit wherever they wished. Still, in a sense the victory was only partial. In the midst of Shuttlesworth's controversy with Connor over the circulars, the Alabama appellate court rejected the appeals of the fourteen ACMHR members convicted for integrated riding in October 1958. Judge Robert B. Harwood ruled them out of order because trial transcripts had been filed three days after the March 6, 1959, deadline. Thus, though the 1958 bus ordinance had been partially struck down by Judge Grooms, Shuttlesworth and the others remained liable for having challenged it, and jail time loomed as an eventual likelihood.[38]

Flushed, however, with the modest victory, a reenergized Shuttlesworth moved on to fight Connor on a new venue. On February 1, 1960, four students from the North Carolina Agricultural and Technical College in Greensboro launched the sit-in movement at southern lunch counters. Ten days later, while preaching revival services in High Point, North Carolina, Shuttlesworth learned of plans for thirty high school students to conduct sit-ins at the downtown Woolworth's department store lunch counter. Along with local ministers J. Elton Cox of High Point and Douglas Moore of Durham, Fred observed the sit-in and called the new tactic "a strike for democracy" that would spread throughout the South. In an interview with the local press, Shuttlesworth criticized North Carolina governor Luther Hodges and countered Hodges's recent statements that blacks were satisfied with the progress toward integration to date. "That's not true," he assured them. "Our people here will not be satisfied until every vestige of discrimination is gone." He also quickly called the SCLC office in At-lanta to report on the sit-ins. Shuttlesworth was the first of the SCLC inner circle to observe these activities, and his commendation carried significant weight. He enthusiastically advised Ella Baker, "This is the thing. You must tell Martin that we have to get with this right away. This can really shake up the world." On returning home, Shuttlesworth met with students from Miles College to discuss similar efforts in Birmingham.[39]

Two weeks after the sit-ins in High Point, thirty-five Alabama State students asked for food service in the cafeteria of the Alabama state capitol. When Governor John Patterson threatened to cut off appropriations for the college unless President H. Councill Trenholm expelled the "law violators and race agitators," larger student protests ensued. King, Abernathy, and Shuttlesworth headed for Montgomery in the students' support. The next day the *Birmingham News* carried a front-page announcement by Connor that warned against similar demonstrations in Birmingham. It also stated that the city would not tolerate any actions by any groups that threatened to breach the peace.[40]

During the weekend, Montgomery students and SCLC leaders planned further protests for Monday, February 29, while Miles College and Daniel Payne College students engaged in sympathy demonstrations in Birmingham's Kelly Ingram Park. Shuttlesworth had advised the students to launch their own sit-ins, but they instead opted for a "Prayer Vigil for Freedom." Connor's officers picked up twelve students and fingerprinted, photographed, and otherwise intimidated them before advising them to behave themselves. Learning of the students' arrests while still in Montgomery, Shuttlesworth wired the city commissioners, expressing his concern regarding the arrests of students "who violated no law by standing in the cold on public property to protest injustice."[41]

During the next week the Montgomery students' protests petered out as a result of police arrests and weak support from the adults of the MIA. Abernathy had recently taken over the MIA presidency as a result of King's move to Atlanta, and he and Shuttlesworth quarreled over what Fred considered Abernathy's weak leadership. When the MIA board refused to support the students by public statement or mass meeting, Fred blamed Abernathy, believing his old friend had failed to rule his MIA board with a strong enough hand. "If it were Birmingham," he noted, "I wouldn't have to be frustrated." "But Fred," Abernathy objected, "I'm not a dictator." Shuttlesworth shot back, "You're not a dictator, but once the board had finally agreed to do what you wanted to do, you said, 'Well, I'm not too sure y'all want to do this.' You got your promise, why not move on it?" Abernathy quieted Shuttlesworth, however, by reminding him of his own ineffectiveness in drumming up adult support for sit-ins in Birmingham. Still,

Shuttlesworth continued to believe the intensity of his situation made Abernathy's more democratic approach dangerous in Birmingham. He told Abernathy, "We don't do this in Birmingham. We don't spend our breath arguing among ourselves. We hit the road in Birmingham." Too much discussion among ACMHR board members, he argued, "wouldn't have done anything but get a lot of us killed. Birmingham was far different from anywhere else."[42]

On the basis of the notoriety he had developed in the movement during the previous four years, Shuttlesworth enjoyed many opportunities outside the South to encourage these efforts. For a time, the *Pittsburgh Courier* asked him to write a weekly column called "A Southerner Speaks." Interviewed in the *National Guardian,* Shuttlesworth criticized the Birmingham city government as "venal and reactionary" and vowed, "I may die in this city, but I shall always fight for the principles in which I believe. They will never drive me out." He also spoke at Progressive political rallies in Chicago and Mobile.[43]

Back home, he and Edward Gardner accompanied a young woman to FBI offices to report her beating by two city police officers. Meanwhile, he savored a challenge of Connor's assurances that no sit-ins would be forthcoming. Viewing Connor's boast as an affront both to blacks' intelligence and courage, he thus continued planning sit-ins for downtown lunch counters. On Wednesday, March 30, Shuttlesworth sent his colleague Charles Billups to bring students James Gober and James Albert Davis to his home, where he recruited them to participate in sit-ins and promised bail money and legal representation. Ten students ultimately volunteered to sit in at five department stores. They were given enough money to buy a pair of socks and instructed on how to converge unobtrusively at the lunch counters at a given moment.[44]

The next morning at 10:30 five pairs of African American students simultaneously attempted to take seats at lunch counters at the Loveman, Pizitz, Kress, Newberry, and Woolworth department stores. Only the students at Kress's managed to be seated before being arrested and charged with trespassing after a warning. As the officers took the students into custody, Connor, standing nearby, commented, "That was quick, wasn't it?" Later, he told reporters, "That's the way it's going to be from now on. We're not going to put up with this sort of thing in Birmingham. It looks like I've been police commissioner long enough for the Negroes to have learned I'm not going to put up with this kind of carrying on." At four o'clock that afternoon, police detectives C. L. Stevens, C. L. Pierce, and Thomas Cook arrived at the Shuttlesworth home with an arrest warrant. They surprised Shuttlesworth, however, by charging him not in connection with the sit-ins but rather with giving false information to the police more than a month earlier.[45]

Shuttlesworth and the ACMHR had received a report about another possible emasculation of a black man on February 24. Their sources mistakenly indicated that police had perpetrated this crime, and Shuttlesworth immediately wired FBI offices in Washington and Birmingham, the local sheriff's office and police department, and the state attorney general and asked for a full investigation. Connor later concluded that the attack had been committed by the victim's wife, but he decided to hold the results until such time as it might be used against his nemesis. Commenting on his arrest, Shuttlesworth quipped that "my arrest apparently is their answer to a two-month request for an investigation." When interviewed by the warden at the city jail, Shuttlesworth noticed that the warden scrawled "vag. warrant" on a report, leading him to object that as a full-time pastor he should not be charged with vagrancy. Such a charge, by Birmingham statute, had the effect of denying him the right to make bail until the disposal of the vagrancy charge. Another of Connor's efforts at intimidation, this ploy constituted a way to keep Shuttlesworth in jail overnight.[46]

While Fred was in police custody, Ruby called the Birmingham office of the FBI to report her husband's arrest. Realizing that Fred's earlier report to the bureau on the alleged sexual mutilation might now be of value, she inquired whether a record of that report had been filed in the Birmingham office. She learned that the report had been furnished to Washington the day it was submitted. In addition, Ruby handled calls from reporters, informing them that Shuttlesworth's incarceration would not interfere with a mass meeting at Bethel that night.[47]

The next morning, which ironically was April Fool's Day, Shuttlesworth was allowed to post a $300 bond on the false information charge. Shuttlesworth, however, was not fooled into believing he had seen the last of Connor's jail. He fully anticipated returning soon in connection with the sit-ins. As expected, under questioning that day the students indicated that Shuttlesworth had advised them concerning their actions at the lunch counters. Still, he drove to Montgomery for some personal business and stayed overnight. The next day, he was alerted that Birmingham police had been to his home with a warrant for his part in the sit-ins. Returning to Birmingham, he consulted with his attorneys and surrendered himself into custody that afternoon. With Charles Billups, he found himself charged with aiding and abetting in violation of a city ordinance and, again, with vagrancy. Interviewed around midnight concerning his knowledge of the sit-ins, he declined comment. He was released on $300 bond the next afternoon, having missed his regular Sunday morning pulpit obligations. He faced trial in recorder's court on Monday.[48]

Returning to his home, Fred took care of a few pastoral concerns and contacted William Rogers, the U.S. attorney general, to request an investigation of his arrests. Noting "serious violations of constitutional rights" by the Birmingham Police Department, Shuttlesworth related his experience of Connor's use of vagrancy charges to hold citizens in jail without bond. He also indicated that police had handled another minister, the Reverend C. Herbert Oliver, in the same manner. In a letter later that month, he told Rogers, "We believe the actions herein related are clear-cut violations of due process of law, and merit speedy action by your department. It is apparent that the vagrant charge is being applied unconstitutionally." He asked the attorney general to review matters in Birmingham and to authorize the Civil Rights Division to "seek injunctive relief" for the ACMHR. During the day on Monday, Shuttlesworth met with Arthur Shores in preparation for his court appearance that evening. As he arrived at city hall, he was greeted by a message from King in Atlanta that pledged the SCLC's absolute support. King continued: "We are always deeply inspired by your courageous witness, and your willingness to suffer in this righteous cause. You have transformed the jail from a dungeon of shame into a haven of freedom and a badge of honor. I know that you will face this situation with the same courage that has always guided your epic making career."[49]

Buoyed by this and many other telegrams of support, including one from Eleanor Roosevelt, Shuttlesworth proceeded to his place in Judge William Conway's now familiar recorder's court. He was tried simultaneously for the false information and sit-in charges and was summarily found guilty on both counts. Each conviction earned for him, respectively, fines of $100 and 180 days in jail. The conviction for giving false information stood even though the victim of the alleged castration, James Mallory, admitted that he had given three different versions of his story. During the next three years, Shuttlesworth was denied appeals of the sit-in charge in the Alabama Court of Appeals (twice) and the Alabama Supreme Court (twice) before the charges were reversed by the U.S. Supreme Court on May 20, 1963.[50]

On still another front, Shuttlesworth soon found himself in a new case that, like his sit-in conviction, would eventually wend its way to the Supreme Court. On April 19, 1960, he was named as a codefendant in a libel suit by the city of Montgomery against the *New York Times*. Ironically, Shuttlesworth was already embroiled in a controversy involving the newspaper. Five days earlier the *Times* had carried a front-page article by reporter Harrison Salisbury that portrayed Birmingham as gripped by "fear and hatred." Salisbury had described Shuttlesworth's arrests and a city "fragmented by the emotional dynamite of racism, reinforced by the whip, the razor, the gun, the bomb, the torch, the club, the mob, the knife, and many branches of the state's apparatus." In lurid detail Salisbury painted the Birmingham known by its black citizens. He related a particularly horrific incident in which one of the students involved in the February 29 prayer vigil was attacked. A few days after that silent protest, seven hooded men beat the student, his mother, and his sister with pipes, clubs, and blackjacks. The mother, hospitalized the next day for a smashed head and crushed hands, became terrified when she was visited by two of her attackers. When the *Birmingham News* accused its New York counterpart of slandering the city and the city commission voted to bring a libel suit against Salisbury, Shuttlesworth could not resist entering the fray.[51]

In a letter to the editor, Shuttlesworth responded that however whites might deny the Birmingham described by Salisbury, the city's African Americans easily recognized the reporter's alarming portrait. He ridiculed white Birmingham's "frantic efforts" to denounce the *Times* and the *Washington Post* as "slanderers of the South." Defending the article as factual, he tweaked the editor for "sparing no pains in trying . . . to cover up the nasty things written in the articles." Salisbury, he speculated, must have been sickened by "a great city and state being strangled and cut in its jugular vein by men in public office who are so obsessed with the failure of 1865 that their words and acts serve as a deterrent to racial progress in 1960." One could see, he observed, from Connor's and Governor Patterson's vituperations why so many "raw acts of terror can happen and why so many of them have gone unsolved." Finishing with a flourish, he taunted the paper's misrepresentation of the ACMHR:

That ours is a "continued high-pressure program" cannot be disputed. . . . But ours is not a pressure which arouses men to act like beasts. Thus, in four years no Negro from our organization has bombed a home, or mobbed a white man, or castrated a white man, or broken into a home for violence. In fact, no white today is in danger from a Negro and our churches will not close their doors to a white person. Our pressure helps men to know the meaning of brotherhood and commits them against the evils of segregation which forbids them to act and live like brothers. Our high-pressure is praying, singing, teaching Christ, and suffering long for freedom. Would to God that others would be so pressurized.[52]

While feelings were still frayed over the Salisbury article, city officials in Montgomery launched a more direct attack on the *Times* and Shuttlesworth. When the state of Alabama brought Martin Luther King up on tax evasion charges, the SCLC used recent events in Montgomery in an effort to raise funds for King's defense. On March 29, the *Times* ran a full-page advertisement called "Heed Their Rising Voices" sponsored by SCLC advisor Bayard Rustin and singer Harry Belafonte. Reviewing the efforts of the Montgomery police to squelch the February protests, the advertisement described the students' expulsion after "truckloads of police armed with shotguns ringed the Alabama State College campus." Rustin and Belafonte unwittingly involved Shuttlesworth in the matter by listing him, along with Abernathy, Lowery, and Montgomery minister Solomon S. Seay, among a large number of signatories.[53]

In reaction, the Montgomery police commissioner, L. B. Sullivan, and the mayor, Earl D. James, brought libel suits against the newspaper and the four ministers. They charged that though the advertisement had not specifically named them, it had subjected them, as the city officials responsible for police activities, to ridicule and embarrassment. This claim was more than a little disingenuous because in reality their efforts to stifle segregation protests enhanced rather than harmed their reputations with their voting constituency. Their inclusion of Shuttlesworth and the other ministers as codefendants, however, would make the suit a significant strike at the protest movement in Alabama.

By naming the ministers in the suit, lawyers for Sullivan and James denied the *Times* the option of removing the case to a federal court, which could review a case only if the parties resided in different states. Because the plaintiffs and the codefendants were all Alabama residents, the case was restricted to state courts, which were particularly unfriendly to "race agitators" and their journalistic advocates in the North. By the end of May, Governor Patterson filed a similar suit, asking for one million dollars in damages for the "false, malicious . . . defamation of the citizens of Alabama and particularly public officials." Sullivan and James sought damages of $500,000. The case came before circuit court judge Walter B. Jones in Montgomery on November 2. In a pretrial hearing, attorney T. Eric Embry sought to challenge the Alabama circuit court's power to bring the *Times* before it, arguing that the sale of 394 copies out of a circulation of 650,000 did not amount to enough business in the state to come within the jurisdiction of its courts. On August 5, Judge Jones ruled that the *Times* did enough business in Alabama to bring it within the jurisdiction of its courts and set trial for November.[54]

As the trial began, Embry objected to the use of the word "nigger" in the opening statement, but Jones denied the motion on the basis of customary pronunciation. The bad omen was not lost on the minister-defendants, who entered the courtroom expecting another "lynching." Nonetheless, Shuttlesworth managed to retain a good humor. He flashed a broad smile, partly owing to his policy of trying to look happy whenever in the presence of whites. Not smiling, he later explained, "made white folks think you were worried." As he and the others took their seats at the defendants' table, Fred ribbed Lowery, who, though nattily attired in a new suit, had crossed his legs, inadvertently revealing to Shuttlesworth a hole in the sole of his shoe. Fred chuckled, nudged Lowery, and suggested that he uncross his legs lest the all-white jury convict them merely because of the contrast between his suit and his shoes.[55]

As arguments proceeded, the plaintiffs' attorney brought forth a series of witnesses, including the editor of the *Montgomery Advertiser,* who testified that the students' arrests had reflected badly on police commissioner Sullivan. On cross-examination Embry attempted to wring from the witnesses admissions that the advertisement, rather than embarrassing Sullivan, had raised his political stock in Alabama. One witness said he did not believe the ad had damaged the commissioner. Another admitted he had not seen the ad until shown it by the plaintiffs' lawyers three weeks before the trial. Other testimony, uncontroverted by the defense, revealed that the advertisement had contained several erroneous statements, most of which were imprecise or slightly exaggerated claims.[56]

On the second day of testimony, November 3, Shuttlesworth and the others testified that they had been ignorant of the advertisement and its use of their names. They learned of it only when they received Sullivan's letter notifying them of his suit, some ten days after the ad appeared in the *Times.* Bayard Rustin testified that without consulting them he had included their names on the basis of their involvement in the SCLC. Attorney Fred Gray, specifically representing Shuttlesworth and the others, moved to have his clients dropped from the case because no testimony had tied them to the publication of the advertisement. Jones overruled. In closing arguments, suggesting that the ministers "had no business in the case," Gray asked, "How could these individual defen-

dants retract something—if you'll pardon the expression—they didn't 'tract?'"
After two hours and twenty minutes of deliberation, however, the jury found
the defendants guilty and returned a judgment against each defendant of the
requested damages of $500,000, the largest such award in Alabama history.[57]

The day after the verdict, Embry announced plans for an appeal to the Ala-
bama Supreme Court, thus beginning the case's eventual route to the Supreme
Court in 1964. Early in 1961, Judge Jones denied a motion for a retrial of the
Sullivan case and prepared to try four sister suits to be brought by Mayor Earl
James, Governor Patterson, and two other Montgomery officials. The James case
came to trial on January 30, 1961. As proceedings opened, James and several
other city officials entered the courtroom sporting beards to commemorate
Montgomery's Civil War Centennial. Not surprisingly, the jury's February 1 verdict matched that of *Sullivan*. Two days later the cars of Abernathy and Lowery
were seized by Montgomery County and Mobile County deputies. In addition,
officials also confiscated parcels of land owned by Abernathy and Seay.[58]

On Saturday, February 4, the Jefferson County sheriff's office ordered Fred
to begin his settlement within five days or be subject to levy on his property
without further notice. Other than his automobile, Shuttlesworth had few possessions, he told reporters, and attorneys planned to ask Judge Jones to excuse
the ministers from posting a $1 million joint bond. This would have postponed
final settlement while the cases were appealed to higher courts, but again Jones
denied the motion. Meanwhile, just two days after the ultimatum to Shuttlesworth, deputies J. M. Jones and O. E. Kinney arrived at the Bethel Baptist parsonage to take possession of the pastor's late-model Plymouth. The state sold
Shuttlesworth's car, along with the property expropriated from his ministerial
colleagues, at public auction. Responding to his loss, Shuttlesworth said, "We
expect these intimidations, but we know we are right, and we are prepared to
lose all that we might gain for freedom for our people." Abernathy and Lowery
made similar comments. Without his car, Shuttlesworth found a friendly taxi
service provided by his friend and fellow minister T. L. Lane and by various deacons and ACMHR members. Within a few weeks contributions from ACMHR and
Bethel members provided enough resources for Fred to buy a new car.[59]

Further losses for Shuttlesworth and the others were negligible because they
appealed for relief in forma pauperis, and the state did not file motions necessary to attach their most personal possessions. Nonetheless, four years of legal
wrangling and the filing of numerous appeals left them liable for additional
damages and kept them busy raising money for their defense. State courts de-

nied all remedies; the Alabama Supreme Court upheld Judge Jones's ruling on August 30, 1962.[60]

Matters began to take a positive turn for Shuttlesworth and his colleagues the summer before when federal district judge Frank M. Johnson Jr. ordered that the remaining libel cases be moved to federal court. Johnson ruled that the ministers had been "fraudulently" named as codefendants because they had had no knowledge that their names were being used. "From the facts available to this court," opined the judge, "no liability on the part of the four resident defendants existed under any recognized theory of law."[61] He also rejected the contention that the ministers had endorsed the ad simply by virtue of their involvement in the sclc. Johnson's ruling affected only the pending cases, not the *Sullivan* and *James* cases that had been decided and were on appeal. Thus, further liability remained a possibility for Shuttlesworth until the U.S. Supreme Court agreed to review the case during its 1963 session.

Seeing in *Sullivan* an important First Amendment case, the high court heard oral arguments on January 6, 1964. On March 9 the justices voted nine to zero to reverse the lower court ruling. The opinion authored by Justice William J. Brennan held that the rule of law applied by Judge Jones violated the First Amendment's free speech protections. In sum, Brennan ruled that requiring a critic of a public official to "guarantee the truth of all his factual assertions" would deter public criticism and limit public debate. Public officials, therefore, may not recover damages for defamatory falsehood unless they can prove "actual malice." In other words, a public official suing for libel can be awarded damages only by proving that his or her critic published statements knowing they were untrue or with "reckless disregard" for whether or not they were true. The ruling ultimately vindicated both the *Times,* which in economic terms emerged from the case relatively unscathed, and the ministers, who did not. Yet eventually the state of Alabama returned to the ministers the money it had received from the auction of their automobiles, and Shuttlesworth found himself inadvertently involved in one of the most important free speech rulings in the history of the Supreme Court.[62]

That victory seemed improbable and far away in 1960, when Shuttlesworth had several other fights on his hands, none of which offered much promise of success. A true agitator, the minister continued to fire rounds at Connor and other Alabama officials largely for the purpose of keeping integration before the public, even when there was little chance of making any headway. One such instance involved Governor Patterson's firing of Professor Lawrence D. Reddick, head of the history department at Alabama State College, for his progressive writings and statements as well as for his involvement in the MIA and the SCLC. Shuttlesworth participated in a joint statement of protest with King, Abernathy, and Lowery, but also sent an individual telegram to the governor on August 16. Shuttlesworth charged that the governor's attempts to discredit and dismiss Reddick "prove that the basic freedoms of thought, speech, and association can be denied in Alabama under any pretext." He observed that Patterson's efforts to fire Alabama State president Councill Trenholm, even after he expelled students on the governor's order, gave evidence that acquiescing to or cooperating with segregation offered no real reward and would assure further attempts to desegregate other colleges in the state. "I suggest a cancellation of the communist charges against Dr. Reddick, a withdrawal of the dismissal order, and a public apology to him. This would be the only right thing to do," he suggested. Patterson predictably ignored the protests.[63]

A few hours after finishing his telegram to the governor, Shuttlesworth found himself embroiled in a new controversy. At 9:30 that evening, Fred was interrupted by a phone call from his daughter Pat, who, with her sister and brother, were in jail in the northeast Alabama city of Gadsden. Pat, Ricky, and Fred Jr. had spent the previous six weeks in a youth project at the Highlander Folk School in Monteagle, Tennessee. Since the 1930s, Highlander had functioned as an experimental and interracial "school" sponsoring interracial programs and workshops. As one of the few places in the South where blacks and whites mixed together freely, Highlander and its founder, Myles Horton, had been targets of intimidation. Near that same time segregationists placarded a photograph of King at Highlander with the caption, "Martin Luther King at Communist Training School." The program attended by Pat, Ricky, and Fred Jr. afforded them their first extended opportunity to interact with whites because it brought together forty-five white, black, Hispanic, and Native American youngsters. Years later Fred Jr. talked about the experience at Highlander: "Your whole purpose was to get to know each other . . . to sing songs that make you come out of yourself. Go out and play ball and be yourself. . . . What impressed me was that they [whites] was all just like me." Moreover, Fred sent the youngsters to Highlander to introduce them to the principles of nonviolence, and the next year he began a program to train the children of ACMHR members in direct action techniques. This extension of the civil rights movement to children would come to fruition in the later demonstrations of 1963.[64]

On their Greyhound bus trip home, Ricky and Fred had given their seats in the rear of the bus to an elderly couple and stood. Later, when passengers got off at a local stop, all three young people took seats near the front. In Gadsden, the driver, a resident of Birmingham, announced a fifteen-minute stopover and returned with several police officers, who ordered the young people to move to the rear of the bus. Pat, a recent high school graduate, knew that segregated riding, particularly on interstate buses, had been outlawed by the Supreme Court and asked why they should move. Asked another time to move, Pat replied, "We aren't going to move anywhere." At that the ranking officer announced to them, "You are all under arrest." Later, the arresting officer testified that he had heard persons outside the bus calling, "Get those damned niggers off the bus, or we'll throw them off!" Although he could not identify anyone making such threats in court, he testified that he arrested the youngsters for their own protection. The charges of disturbing the peace suggested, however, another version of the story. The officers forcibly removed them from the bus and took them to the city jail.[65]

Officers first questioned Pat, who acknowledged that they were the children of "that Birmingham Shuttlesworth." Ricky gave her name in a loud voice that annoyed the desk sergeant, who scowled and objected that he was not hard of hearing. Ricky informed him that with her ears stopped up from a cold, she *was* hard of hearing. Angered by what he took as impudence, he bolted from around the desk and grabbed her by the arm. She pulled away, and he grabbed her again, finally slapping her twice across the face and bruising her eye. At this, Fred Jr. leaped to his sister's rescue. The officer whirled, grasped the thirteen-year-old in a choke hold, bent back his index finger, and shouted, "You had enough?" Subdued, the threesome were allowed their phone call and then were placed in jail cells for the night. The two girls shared a cell with a prostitute, while Fred Jr. occupied a cell one floor beneath the girls. Pat and Ricky took turns sleeping, concerned over jail guards who oiled their guns and talked aloud about what they would do to "that cotton-pickin' nigger" when he got to town. "We had to stay awake," one of the girls said later, "so that we could warn Daddy how many men there were, how many guns they had, and what they were fixing to do to him." From his cell, Fred Jr. tried to cheer up his sisters by singing loudly the songs they had learned at Highlander. Ricky later said, "I could hear my brother in his cell singing 'Because all men are brothers.' Just hearing his voice gave my sister and me courage not to be afraid."[66]

Meanwhile, Shuttlesworth quickly recruited several of his followers to go with him to Gadsden to retrieve the children. He made arrangements for bail bonds from a local bonding company and alerted the Etowah County Sheriff's Office, the Alabama Highway Patrol, and the Birmingham office of the FBI regarding his intended journey. Seeing about these matters, he said to his travel partners: "I know y'all may think I'm crazy, but if you got any weapons, I don't want you to go 'cause you ain't gon' do nothin' but get put in jail. But just to see all of us coming, we won't have no trouble, and ain't nobody gon' bother us. I got confidence that the Lord will take care of us." Shuttlesworth's loyal bodyguard, Colonel Johnson, laid down his .38-caliber revolver, and after some others did likewise, the contingent drove off to Gadsden. On the way, Shuttlesworth was stopped by the highway patrol for speeding and as a result had his driver's license suspended. As the convoy reached the Gadsden city limits, Johnson, lagging behind the others, stopped at a stoplight to ask a police officer for directions to city hall. The officer asked Johnson, "Y'all come up here to take our town, didn't you?"

"Oh naw," he answered. "We just accompanying Rev. Shuttlesworth. His children are in trouble, and he is our leader."

"What kind of weapons y'all got?"

"We don't have any," Johnson answered.

The officer then demanded that Johnson open his trunk. His search turned up a saw, a crowbar, and a hammer, which Johnson used in part-time carpentry. "Oh yeah, you come up here to fight," the policeman ventured. "You got a hammer." Johnson replied, "No sir, we nonviolent." Just then, noticing Shuttlesworth and another officer approaching, Johnson called out, "Hey, Reverend Shuttlesworth, come here. I want you to hear what this guy is saying." "What's the matter?" asked Shuttlesworth. "This guy says we come up here to fight. He's tellin' me my carpentry tools are fightin' tools." As the officer proceeded to give Johnson a ticket for running a traffic light, Shuttlesworth objected, "How are you going to give a man a ticket for running a red light at one o'clock in the morning when the traffic lights are cut off?"[67]

Moving on to the police station, Fred addressed the officer on duty: "Captain, I'm Reverend Shuttlesworth. You have my children here. I came to get the children." After visiting with his children in their cells, reassuring them, and on close inspection determining that they were not seriously hurt, the concerned father returned to the officer on duty to begin the process of bonding the youths out of jail. As he produced the documents he had brought with him, the captain informed him, "These bonds are no good; they're Birmingham bonds." He added, "You came up here with a gang, didn't you?" Shuttlesworth replied, "I do not have a gang; I like company, and people like to accompany me. So long as you have my children here in Gadsden, I will be here. I know I have that constitutional right." Smiling, as if switching to the offensive, he asked, "Now you seem to be angry, Officer?" Ignoring the question, the policeman instructed Shuttlesworth that he would be required to find Gadsden citizens to secure his bonds. Someone in his party knew of a black physician named Stewart and was familiar with another Gadsden resident and made a few phone calls. Arrangements were made, even though it was now well after midnight, and Shuttlesworth quickly headed for the men's homes, trailed by two Gadsden police cruisers. Returning to the station, Shuttlesworth was then told the property bonds had to be checked against the city tax rolls, even though the police officers who had followed them could verify that they were indeed signed by Gadsden residents of financial means. "We'll see you in the morning if these bonds are any good," the captain said dryly.

The vexation continued, however, as the captain next announced that he was going to arrest one of Shuttlesworth's followers as a vagrant because he had been unable to produce identification. "Now listen, Officer," Fred rejoined, "you have better sense than that. You can't put this man in jail when you know he's with us." The officer backed away from that threat but proceeded to issue a ticket to Colonel Johnson for running the red light. Johnson objected, but Shuttlesworth advised him, "Johnson, take the ticket. What difference does it make? We didn't come up here to argue with these policemen. We don't want to give them any occasion for stumbling, and they are having as difficult a time of it as we are. Let's be Christians and take the ticket whether you deserve the ticket or not." Johnson agreed, but the officers were not done yet. As Shuttlesworth's party exited the station, the captain told them, "You won't loiter in the street here; we have loitering laws, and we'll use them."[68]

Smiling, the minister turned to his men and, except for his friend James Armstrong, sent them back to Birmingham. As the men got into their cars, Johnson advised them with tongue in cheek, "Drive slow 'cause they'll give you a ticket for standing still if they want to." With one last effort to provoke a confrontation, the captain taunted Shuttlesworth, "You act like you're scared." "You read about me before you saw me, and you know I'm not scared of anything," Shuttlesworth retorted. "But that isn't the point. You have my children locked up. As long as these children are here in jail, I'll be here getting them out." Excusing himself, he and Armstrong found a hotel room. By noon that day the youngsters were free and heading for home.[69]

In the aftermath, both the NAACP and the SCLC asked the Justice Department to investigate the arrests. In Washington, NAACP representative Clarence Mitchell requested an inquiry on the grounds that officials arrested the Shuttlesworth children for resisting segregation on interstate bus travel, barred by the Supreme Court in 1945. Responding quickly, Harold R. Tyler, assistant attorney general in the Civil Rights Division, discussed the matter with the U.S. attorney in Birmingham, William L. Longshore, before concluding that the facts of the case warranted a preliminary investigation. Soon thereafter he contacted FBI director J. Edgar Hoover and requested that he have the matter investigated "as expeditiously as possible." Hoover in turn ordered his special agent in charge of Birmingham to initiate the investigation, with interviews of victims, arresting officers, and pertinent witnesses to be completed by August 23. Agents carried out the orders and conducted the probe "expeditiously" but without any results satisfying to the victims or to their father.[70]

The inquiry did reveal that the arrests of the youths garnered a good deal of attention in the North, a reality that portended the outpouring of reaction to the "children's crusade" three years later in Birmingham's major demonstrations. Gadsden city officials were flooded with protests concerning their arrests of Pat, Ricky, and Fred Jr., which may have ultimately influenced the final outcome of the case. One writer from Florida commented that "irrespective of certain intransigent sentiments prevalent to our Southern communities, few of our states have sunk so low as to visit them on children." A telegram from New York journalist Nat Hentoff and his wife called for officials to drop the charges against the Shuttlesworth children, who "have done no wrong except to exercise their American rights." Someone else wrote, "The jailing of the Shuttlesworth children is a disgrace to all America. Their immediate release should be made in the name of human decency."[71]

A similar inquiry was requested by the SCLC. When Shuttlesworth and the others returned to Birmingham, the first person (after Ruby) to look the children over was the new executive director of the SCLC, the Reverend Wyatt Tee Walker. He quickly passed the facts of the case to King in Atlanta, who immediately wired the attorney general, the Interstate Commerce Commission, and the national office of Greyhound Bus Lines to call for full investigations. Walker also forwarded a letter to the national offices of the NAACP and to the Congress of Racial Equality and threatened to call a national boycott of Greyhound. The angry father told the *Birmingham World*: "There is no shadow of doubt that there has been a flagrant abuse of the civil liberties of these children and we intend to push it all the way." He did complain of their treatment in the press and in letters to the Gadsden mayor and police chief.[72]

The incident also resulted in a series of letters from white youth wanting to be a part of the movement. One fifteen-year-old white girl wrote that she had never spoken to an African American on an equal basis, adding: "Since you and your group have begun this noble work, I feel there is hope that I may yet have the chance to associate with and really get to know people of different races, creeds, nationalities, etc. . . . I feel much more that it isn't so useless to be for equal rights down here. . . . Maybe if all of us can have the courage you and others have, we will get somewhere soon." Another letter writer identified himself as a white who believed in equality. "Therefore," he noted, "it pains me deeply to see my own family so prejudiced on this subject." Thus encouraged about the future, Shuttlesworth told the *Southern Patriot:* "These contacts from the white youth of Birmingham prove again that there is no solid white South—even in Birmingham."[73]

At her hearing, Pat faced Etowah County judge W. W. Rayburn; the cases of Ricky and Fred Jr. were assigned to juvenile court. In a three-hour proceeding Pat was charged with conduct calculated to cause a breach of the peace. Rayburn heard testimony that the girl had obstructed other passengers by putting her feet in the aisle and caused other disturbances on the bus between Chattanooga and Gadsden. Judge Rayburn, however, decided to transfer the case to the county juvenile court, over which he also presided, to be considered along with those of her sister and brother.

On September 16, all three young people appeared before Judge Rayburn. The Shuttlesworths' attorney, Len Holt, called twenty-five adults from Birmingham as character witnesses but did not put Pat, Ricky, or Fred Jr. on the stand. The prosecution called only three witnesses, including the bus driver and the two police officers who had taken them into custody. Rayburn adjudged the youths to be delinquent and placed them on indefinite probation. Holt told reporters that he would appeal the decision to the circuit court, but ultimately nothing came of the effort. Not content with the slow and uncertain appeals process, a few weeks later Shuttlesworth filed suit against Southeastern Greyhound on behalf of his daughter in federal court in Atlanta, where Pat had begun attending Spelman College.[74]

By the first of the year, the defendants succeeded in having the suit moved to U.S. district court in Birmingham because the incident occurred in Alabama and because all principals in the case resided in the state. The suit sought $9 million in damages and claimed that Pat had been "arrested and falsely imprisoned" and that the conduct of the driver had provoked hostility toward the girl on the part of the passengers and police in Gadsden. In November 1961, Judge Seybourn Lynne dismissed the suit for lack of prosecution.[75]

The first two years of Connor's regime in Birmingham had seen sustained attack and counterattack between the commissioner and the ACMHR leader. Shuttlesworth had quickly become the litigation king of the civil rights movement, and his defiance of Connor had won him the admiration of black Birmingham. Even the attorneys and black professionals who often bristled over his demanding style had to reckon with his popularity among the working class. Nevertheless, other than on the bus issue, by 1960 he still found himself in a standoff with Connor. As fervent as was Shuttlesworth's faith that God had chosen him to lead the fight against Jim Crow was Connor's resolve to defend segregation and to put Shuttlesworth on the defensive. His harassment of his local, "inside" agitator continued without respite.

Indeed, his devotion grew more volatile and eventually more violent as each successive event upped the ante. During the uproar in Birmingham over the Harrison Salisbury article, Connor stoked up the rhetoric in a speech to the Selma Citizens' Council. He told his avid audience that the NAACP and communist-front organizations sought black supremacy rather than equality. "I'll tell you right now, unless the South makes up its mind to stop this plague—and it is a plague—we are going to find Negroes who can't read or write . . . enforcing our laws." Noting his own efforts in Birmingham to stem the tide, he boasted about his surveillance of black mass meetings. Summing up with a peroration filled with the football imagery so beloved in Alabama, he roared: "Yes, we are on the one-yard line. Our backs are to the wall. Do we let them go over for a touchdown, or do we raise the Confederate flag as did our forefathers and tell them . . . 'You shall not pass!'" A personality such as Fred Shuttlesworth could not resist taking up such a gauntlet. He responded to Connor's speech obliquely in his Birmingham News letter concerning the Salisbury flap. He had another tactic in mind, however, one that would, in his words, "harass the harassers." If he could not back Connor into his own end zone, perhaps he could embarrass him by the effort.[76]

Shuttlesworth and Charles Billups had decided to bring a lawsuit against Connor and police chief Jamie Moore in an effort to keep them from sending detectives to report on their mass meetings. Such regular visits by the police hardly stopped the revivalistic proceedings, but they did somewhat dampen attendance. The police department's notorious record of intimidation made many African Americans loath to place themselves in a position to be hectored by angry officers. ACMHR leaders and members alike knew that the presence of the detectives frightened away many potential participants. The revivalistic spirit of the mass meetings, particularly the call and response between charismatic leader and the congregation, had a powerful effect. Caught up in the communal nature of African American religion, regular attendees at mass meetings found a community of support for their aspirations of freedom from Jim Crow and were more likely to give financially or to volunteer for protest actions. Thus the detectives' note taking in some measure suppressed involvement in the ACMHR. If successful, the suit would very likely increase the active membership of the organization and presumably speed the Birmingham movement along.

Shuttlesworth had no illusions of winning a suit against Connor, particularly not in U.S. district court, where Judge Seybourn H. Lynne would decide the case. The National States' Rights Party newspaper, the *Thunderbolt*, had recently referred to Lynne as "our judge," and Shuttlesworth kept a realistic view of the matter. He knew, however, the morale-boosting potential of a public confrontation with Connor. Even his members at Bethel, who in larger numbers had begun to complain about how his prophetic activism was swallowing up his pastoral duties, nonetheless warmed to his public battles with Bull. Years later Bethel member Daisy Winston, who believed that her pastor's single-minded focus on civil rights led him to neglect some of his traditional pastoral duties, still indicated that she enjoyed seeing someone stand up to the commissioner.[77]

The minister thus decided to file this suit and to win if possible, but at any rate to lift both his own spirits and those of his followers. Moreover, he hit on another idea calculated to raise the stakes even more. He relished the idea of challenging Connor verbally, in person, and in a court of law. Besides the sheer fun of putting Bull on the witness stand and goading him for himself, Shuttlesworth knew the theatrics of such a face-to-face confrontation would multiply its impact with potential activists in black Birmingham. So Shuttlesworth decided, mostly for dramatic effect, to try the case himself. Acting on his own and Billups's behalf, he filed the suit in early September 1960.[78]

The suit sought $97,000 in damages and a permanent injunction to restrain the city defendants and their agents "from continuing the odoriferous practice of intimidating and seeking to intimidate Negroes who desire immediate and full integration of the races in Birmingham." Shuttlesworth claimed that Connor's actions in effect denied them freedom of assembly and violated the Fourteenth Amendment. They further stated that the class represented by the plaintiffs was intimidated for "seeking to hurriedly bring an end" to racial segregation. By attending their meetings, they argued, detectives had "thwarted, intimidated and discouraged Negroes from attending." After a request for a temporary injunction, which was denied, the new "law student" recruited attorney Len Holt to coach him in the fine points of litigation. Shuttlesworth, after all, wanted to give his client the best possible advocacy. Other black lawyers with whom he had dealt were less than amused. Oscar W. Adams did not think much of Fred's plan, but he nevertheless marveled at how capable he was of keeping up with all the cases in which he was involved. Adams later commented, "I don't mean to say he was a good lawyer, but it was amazing how much that he would know. Sometimes he would bring something to my attention that I didn't know." When the matter came to trial on November 22, Shuttlesworth was ready and eager to make his case.[79]

"Attorney" Shuttlesworth first called a series of six witnesses, all officers of the ACMHR, to testify regarding the attendance policies of the organization, the role of officers, and the presence and activities of police detectives at the meetings. In particular, they testified that persons of their acquaintance had stayed away from the meetings because of the presence of the detectives. As a result ACMHR ushers had on occasion asked the detectives to leave. On at least two occasions, they testified, the entire ACMHR had passed resolutions asking them to desist from attending the meetings. Charles Billups recounted his arrest for interfering with police officers in the conduct of their duty and related that the detectives' presence had occasionally caused persons to leave the meetings.

On cross-examination, defense attorney J. M. Breckenridge established that Billups had ultimately pled guilty to his charges, only to have Shuttlesworth show that Billups had done so as part of a plea bargain. Breckenridge also elicited testimony that Shuttlesworth had once stated publicly, "I wish all of the policemen would put their guns down and come on in here and be with us." Shuttlesworth also led ACMHR member and Bethel guard Charlie Brooks to testify that in addition to police going into the meetings, others waited outside in squad cars or on occasion cruised the neighborhood in patrol wagons, thus adding to the intimidation effect. Attempting to establish that police attended meetings in order to protect the meetings, Breckenridge wrung from Brooks admissions that meetings had not been interrupted by outsiders and that he had served as a guard at Shuttlesworth's church because he felt "protection was necessary for that church." At that point, Shuttlesworth called a new witness, missing an opportunity to show that police had repeatedly declined Shuttlesworth's requests for protection for Bethel while regularly monitoring the flow of information at ACMHR meetings.

The entertainment value of Shuttlesworth's questioning of witnesses took a decided upturn when he called police chief Jamie Moore to the stand. After establishing Moore's responsibility for police activities, Fred asked, "Do you consider it unlawful for persons to gather together to plan methods to peaceably end segregation?" The defense quickly objected and was sustained by Judge Lynne. Moving on, Shuttlesworth, in his sometimes unpolished verbal style, asked, "What other meetings in the City of Birmingham do you regularly incur the assignment of policemen?" Pointing out the awkward phrasing, Breckenridge asked, "What was the verb?" "Assign," Shuttlesworth answered. Proceeding, Shuttlesworth drew out Moore's admission that he himself had never assigned officers to the meetings but that he nonetheless received reports from them. Testimony failed to reveal detail of these reports, even though witnesses had readily observed the detectives' note taking. Years later the Connor papers were found to contain large files of reports from the meetings. The reports, however, began not in 1956, when the ACMHR was founded, or in 1958, when Connor regained the commissioner's seat, but in 1961, when Shuttlesworth's harassment suit had been completed. Connor apparently destroyed the reports from 1958 through 1960. Shuttlesworth's questioning did, however, lead Moore to testify inconsistently that he had known of the ACMHR's activities for only two years, while at the same time acknowledging that his assistant had visited Bethel in connection with the 1956 bombing. The chief confessed, however, to a fuzzy memory of those early reports. Concluding his examination of the witness, Shuttlesworth mischievously responded, "You said you didn't get reports regularly back there. In that respect the Police Department is a little more efficient now. You get reports regularly."

"We object to that," replied defense co-counsel Henry A. Simpson.

"Sustain the objection to the question."

"I think that is all," Shuttlesworth announced.

"That is all," Breckenridge agreed.

"Next witness."

"The Commissioner, please," answered Shuttlesworth, with a trace of a smile.

Connor took the stand, ready to answer matter-of-factly and without elaboration. When Shuttlesworth quickly asked, "Mr. Connor, do you feel one of the important duties of your office is the maintenance of racial segregation in the City of Birmingham?" the defense's sustained objection absolved him of responsibility to answer. The fireworks had begun, however. Shuttlesworth got Connor to admit to knowing of detectives' attendance and to receiving reports of the meetings. Shuttlesworth continued:

"Is it your position that all of the meetings held by this organization are supposed to be supervised or have police assigned to them?"

"I wouldn't say they were supposed to be supervised. I think there should be officers there," he replied.

"So you feel that their being there is right?"

"I really do."

"Are you aware, sir, of the purposes of the Alabama Christian Movement for Human Rights?"

"I have no idea what it is."

"You have no idea of what it is. You just think police officers ought to be there?"

"That is right. I do."

"You are saying, sir, to the Court you think every meeting held in any church ought to have officers assigned to it?"

Shifting to whether police held membership in the ACMHR, Shuttlesworth commented, "In fact, you are not concerned whether they are members or not?" The objection was sustained. Connor next admitted that in spite of requests that the detectives not attend, they were expected to continue to attend the meetings. Taking another tack, Shuttlesworth introduced Connor's interview with the *Baltimore Afro-American* and asked Connor if he recalled stating, "Damn the law, we don't give a damn about the law down here. We make our own law." Judge Lynne sustained the objection, but Shuttlesworth mildly challenged the ruling: "Wouldn't this show the attitude of the Commissioner?" "I sustain the objection," came the judge's reply. Reading from a copy of the newspaper and its interview with Connor, Fred asked whether the commissioner had said, "The police have to keep up with what is going on. If they didn't we would wake up one morning and find ourselves in a hell of a fix." This time the judge overruled Breckenridge's objection. Connor asked what paper had written the comment and then categorically denied making it. Finally, before finishing with his obviously hostile witness, Shuttlesworth established that Connor saw the detectives' attendance as essential to "keeping up with what people are doing" and that he intended to continue assigning them to the meetings.

Just as he had in his cross-examination of Chief Moore, in questioning Connor Shuttlesworth intended to demonstrate that police department policy was to monitor both integrationist and segregationist meetings. Connor testified that he intended to treat all such organizations, from the citizens' councils to the NAACP, alike and to "know what is going on." At this point, Shuttlesworth missed another opportunity by not showing, as he had in his redirect examination of Moore, that the police department did not regularly send officers to *all* meetings of segregationist groups. As the defense prepared to introduce a request from the segregationist States' Rights Party, Shuttlesworth interrupted,

"We object, your Honor. It has not been stated they requested parades or caused disturbances. The letter would have nothing to do with this."

"We submit," Breckenridge replied, "that it shows the absence of any discrimination between this organization and the others which are apparently contrary to it."

"Might I say we are not at this time saying whether it is discrimination or not. We are contending against this as a violation, what the Police Department is doing as a violation of our rights of freedom of assembly and speech." Judge Lynne reserved his ruling and moved the proceedings to Shuttlesworth's redirect examination.

After Connor admitted that he had never received reports of any disorder at the meetings, Shuttlesworth asked his reason for assigning detectives to the meetings. "For protection for you, if you want me to tell you the truth. If I pulled the policemen away from there, there is no telling what will happen." The preacher reminded him that no disorder had occurred at the meetings prior to his assigning the detectives. Annoyed, Connor retorted, "Before I came in office your church was dynamited, and since I have been in office they have attempted to do it again. I am trying to see that you don't get dynamited, if you want to know why the policeman is there." The judge interjected that matters were straying from the issues of the case. "I believe that is all," Shuttlesworth replied, and he called *Baltimore Afro-American* reporter Samuel Hoskins as his next witness.

Hoskins testified to visiting Birmingham in November of 1958, when he attended two ACMHR meetings. There he spoke with the detectives and later interviewed Connor. He identified himself as the author of the article from which Shuttlesworth had read. Hoskins further stated that Connor had indeed made the "damn the law" statement and the comment on his need to "keep up with what is going on." Breckenridge repeatedly objected to this line of questioning, only to be repeatedly overruled. On cross-examination, Breckenridge, hoping to pit Hoskins's word against Connor's, established that neither Connor's assistant nor his secretary had been privy to the interview.

By this time, testimony had recessed and resumed, continuing through an afternoon session. Shuttlesworth once again called Nelson H. Smith Jr. to the stand, essentially to testify that Birmingham police had on a few occasions followed the ACMHR to mass meetings held outside the city limits. Defense attorneys merely sought to obfuscate this matter by casting doubt on how many occasions Smith had noticed Birmingham detectives in Bessemer and Midfield.

As a final effort, Shuttlesworth gained permission to read into the record a report of Connor's Selma Citizens' Council speech, quoting the commissioner's statement that "the Negro is my brother, but not my equal." With that, the preacher rested his case. Breckenridge immediately moved to "exclude the evidence," but Lynne stopped him, announcing, "Now Mr. Breckenridge, I don't want to interrupt you. There is no such thing in this Court as a motion to exclude the evidence." He did, however, promptly rule that he had seen no evidence that any defendant or any subordinate had ever restrained anyone from attending an ACMHR meeting. No constitutional guarantees had been violated, and Judge Lynne accordingly denied the injunction. As expected, "Lawyer Shuttlesworth," as legal documents typically referred to a black attorney, had lost his first case.[80]

He had, however, managed to confront Connor personally and publicly, and to some extent he raised his profile even higher as a leader willing to tangle with Bull. The suit, of course, was open to interpretation. Those who admired Shuttlesworth saw it as a useful way of getting under Connor's skin. More pragmatic, professional types saw it as showboating or as frivolous litigation unlikely to have any real effect. After the suit, the state of affairs between the combatants Shuttlesworth and Connor remained in rough equilibrium. The stalemate continued until 1961, when reinforcements from CORE and truly "outside agitators" and the Freedom Rides once again put Connor and the state of Alabama again in national headlines. As an "inside agitator," Shuttlesworth gained some mileage from the suit, reinforcing his reputation as a fighter. The long, historical view, however, understands this effort as part of a "culture of resistance" shared by African Americans since the time of slavery. Just as in 1860 blacks deliberately deceived whites in order to "put on ol' massa," Shuttlesworth similarly carved out a niche of dissent in the ethos of Jim Crow by attempting, as the preacher often put it, to "de-horn Ol' Bull."

Jailbirds

Ordinarily, I do not carry on correspondence with jailbirds.
— Mayor Art Hanes

The inauguration of a new young president created among many Americans an almost euphoric feeling of possibility. As far back as during the New Deal, black America had begun shifting its political allegiance away from the party of Lincoln, and the 1960 presidential campaign of candidate John F. Kennedy significantly moved the transition along. In large measure, he won southern black hearts—and votes, such as they were—with his concerned phone call to Coretta King asking about her jailed husband's welfare. The new president's campaign rhetoric impressed King and the civil rights community, who believed Kennedy's heart was in the right place. Kennedy, however, still needed to win them over with legislative action. Although political realities and public opinion gradually moved Kennedy to action, civil rights activists occasionally complained that "it's a difficult thing to teach a president."[1] By the tragic end of the Kennedy administration, events in Birmingham and Alabama had taught him a great deal. Throughout those events, Fred Shuttlesworth would never be far from the center of the action.

This chapter covers the fifteen-month period beginning in January 1961, when Shuttlesworth's actions would deepen the difficulties in his marriage and result in his accepting a new pastorate in Cincinnati, Ohio. In spite of his new residence, however, his continued activism would give him a central role in the 1961 Freedom Rides, which would once again put Alabama in the national spotlight. His actions in civil rights would also entangle him in a web of legal wranglings, one of which landed him in Bull Connor's jail for thirty-six days, the longest incarceration of his civil rights career.

Early on, the president had done little more than talk in terms agreeable to such activists as Shuttlesworth. Birmingham's inveterate man of action, however, warmed quickly to the new chief executive. The president's movement toward civil rights reform might be considerably slower than Shuttlesworth's, but in the preacher's view, it was a great improvement over that of Kennedy's predecessor. Critical of Eisenhower as "almost a dumbbell," who "saw nothing, felt nothing, heard nothing, and he did nothing until he had to," Shuttlesworth took the pulpit at the first ACMHR mass meeting after the inauguration to complain that blacks had "no friend in Ike. . . . No Negro ever played golf with Ike." Regarding Kennedy, he exulted, "What a wonderful President we have now!" Less than a year later, he would tell another mass meeting crowd that he was "thinking more and more of becoming a Democrat" because of Kennedy's record of appointing African Americans to the federal bench. Kennedy, he said, "is . . . the man for the Negro race."[2]

Prospects for the Shuttlesworths in 1961 were mixed, however, despite Fred's hopefulness over the new president. The excitement of participating in the civil rights crusade always captured Fred's imagination and fired his soul with enthusiasm. Thus, absorbed in his fervor, he was often oblivious to developing problems close to home. Indeed, if he noticed them at all, they seemed to him to pale in importance beside the call to, in the words of the SCLC motto, "redeem the soul of America." On the one hand, his profile in the SCLC remained high, and both he and Ruby traveled widely to stump for the movement. In February, for example, Fred was the featured speaker at a benefit for the Highlander Folk School at New York's Carnegie Hall. Over the next ten-day period, Ruby went to Chicago twice for speeches to a union audience and traveled to a return engagement at the Afro-American Heritage Association.[3]

In his role as an SCLC officer, in early March Shuttlesworth attended an Administrative Committee meeting in Atlanta to help develop consensus on the organization's directions. Shuttlesworth pressed for King, Abernathy, and himself to tour various cites to mobilize the African American clergy and raise money. He argued that "the three symbols of the movement" would be able to raise great amounts of money and commitment from the churches. Ministers should get to know the leaders of the movement, and their exploits should be kept before the people in the churches. The SCLC had already staged events such as this on a small scale. One was "The SCLC Hour" by Wyatt Walker, and Shuttlesworth had noticed that "even old, shut-in women" who rarely left their homes enthusiastically attended. Shuttlesworth called for expanding that practice. King, however, leaned toward a focus on voter registration. Fred held that his proposal could easily be tied in with voter registration, but the brain trust was swayed by King's inclinations and took Shuttlesworth's idea under advisement. The tour never materialized, primarily because other events and speaking obligations would distract King.[4]

Shuttlesworth also began a process of getting much wider attention when television reporter Howard K. Smith decided to produce a program for CBS *Reports* called "Who Speaks For Birmingham?" On March 13 a film crew visited a mass meeting, allowing Shuttlesworth and others to tell their story to a national audience. In the piece, Smith and producer David Lowe put a national spotlight on Birmingham once again, as had been the case with Harrison Salisbury's *New York Times* articles. Smith called Shuttlesworth "the man most feared by Southern racists and the voice of the new militancy among Birmingham Negroes." Also interviewed was Episcopal bishop C. C. J. Carpenter, who angered Shuttlesworth by suggesting that the *Brown* decision "came too quickly." "There are many of us," Carpenter added, "who were working along pretty satisfactorily, we thought, before the Supreme Court decision. We felt we were making progress in the relationship between the races. I think we were. We've been set back."[5]

Shuttlesworth believed that anyone who thought things had progressed "satisfactorily" had not consulted him or his people, who were no longer willing to wait for whites to move toward equality. On camera, Shuttlesworth described the Christmas night bombing and his beating at Phillips High School. He criticized Connor as wanting "the white people to believe that just by his being in office, he can prevent the inevitable, so he has to talk loud . . . because when the sound and fury is all gone, then there'll be nothing." Issuing his war cry, he promised, "We mean to kill segregation or be killed by it." After the filming, Smith, a native southerner who grew up in Ferriday, Louisiana, had tears in his eyes as he listened to Shuttlesworth's stories. When Fred asked how he might acquire a copy of the film, Smith replied, "Aw hell, Fred, anybody who can live in Bull Connor's town like you do and keep fighting and keep the spirit and be as cheerful as you are now, I'll send you the film." Within a week of its broadcast—ironically in the middle of a week of violent response to the Freedom Rides—Shuttlesworth received his copy.[6]

Life in the Shuttlesworth family increasingly showed the strain of Shuttlesworth's notoriety and his frenetic activities. Pat was now away at college, but the other children remained in the tense Birmingham setting, worrying about further bomb attempts and fending off criticism of their father. Along with frequent threatening phone calls, they dealt with prank calls of persons calling their father a jailbird or asking whether he was in the city or the county jail. Fred and Ruby's relationship was strained by his many absences and his hard-line approach to Christian duty when he was at home. Ruby continued to resent Fred's insensitivity to her struggles against church members' expectations. His inattention to her and his refusal to shield her from the members' petty criticisms increasingly raised Ruby's hackles. She vigorously disagreed with Fred's view that her role as "first lady" required her to tolerate whatever carping the members dished out.

More significant, however, the couple bore a heavy financial strain, and their conflicting philosophies of fiscal management fueled many heated arguments. One trait Fred mercifully had not inherited from his mother was the propensity for physical violence toward his spouse. Although loud enough to be overheard by the children and sometimes profane, their arguments did not deteriorate into violence. Financial problems had recently become more acute as the family now had one daughter in college and another a year away from attending. The loss of their car in the *Sullivan* settlement exacerbated the situation. In the face of this, Shuttlesworth continued to give all honoraria for his speaking to the ACMHR or the church, and Ruby continued to fume over both his decision and the unilateral way he made it. Looking back on this issue years later, daughter Pat sided with her mother, candidly commenting that, at least in this particular instance, "as a marriage partner, I don't think he was fair." Ruby insisted that his sacrifices for the movement, especially those involving the physical and emotional health of his family, deserved some remuneration. "You have put your kids through a lot," Ricky overheard her mother say to Fred. "You have given all since '56 to the movement. It's time to give to your children." Soon after state authorities confiscated the car, the prayers of a worried Ruby were apparently answered when another church began inquiring into Fred's interest in moving to a more prestigious and slightly more lucrative pulpit.[7]

In late 1960 Shuttlesworth had preached at a service celebrating the anniversary of the Reverend L. Venchael Booth as pastor of the Zion Baptist Church in Cincinnati. Knowing of Shuttlesworth's difficult times in Birmingham, Booth mentioned to Fred that another church in the Avondale section of Cincinnati was looking for a new pastor. The Revelation Baptist Church, a vigorous middle-class congregation of some eight hundred members, was seeking an established pastor whose prestige equaled that of the church. Shuttlesworth seemed uninterested in leaving Birmingham, particularly in light of his promises to stay in the Magic City until its slogan, "It's Nice to Have You in Birmingham," became a reality even for African Americans. He also knew a move to a new church would look like a show of weakness, which his high regard for "being a man" was loath to allow. Booth told Fred that he had done a good job in Birmingham but that he did not have to be there to stay in touch with the movement. Unconvinced, Fred returned to Birmingham with little intention of pursuing the Cincinnati pulpit.[8]

Booth did not leave matter solely in the Lord's hands, however, as he took the initiative to recommend Shuttlesworth to Revelation's pulpit committee. Delighted with the possibility of securing a high-profile minister, a spokesperson for the committee contacted Fred and invited him to preach at the church. Early in 1961, Shuttlesworth agreed to fill the pulpit at Revelation, though at first not in view of a call as pastor. Nevertheless, the congregation responded so fervently to Shuttlesworth that after the first few Sunday services together they elected him as their pastor without his approval. Furthermore, although he declined their invitation to lead their church, the pulpit committee and the people at Revelation refused to take his "no" for a final answer and continued to court him.

In the meantime, Ruby ardently advocated shaking Birmingham's dust off their feet. Although she had been a loyal supporter of the movement, Ruby had a raft of reasons for wanting to move. She typically saw more clearly than Fred the repercussions of the crusade on the family. She had in mind not just the emotional scars of past events but also the movement's effects on her children's future. At Revelation, Fred's higher salary would more easily enable the children to go to college. In addition, she thought the University of Cincinnati or other schools in the area would academically outrank schools available in Alabama. Another factor was the North's more hospitable atmosphere, which would allow greater employment opportunities for the children—certainly more than were likely in a state where black skin and the name "Shuttlesworth" could be a deadly combination. Ruby also hoped a move to Cincinnati would more effectively shield their youngest child, Carol, from the pressures of life in Birmingham. As for personal concerns, she also hoped a new start in a new place would reinvigorate her marriage by diminishing the couple's need to argue over money. Perhaps she even believed that if she were going to live as a pastor's wife, at least a larger "goldfish bowl" would allow her a bit more room in which to swim.[9]

Fred, though increasingly interested in Revelation, remained unconvinced and awaited some convergence of factors that would make the decision clearer.

One such consideration was the very human tendency for a pastor to be intrigued by overtures from other congregations. New attentions ordinarily have a powerful lure on a prospective pastor, typically the kind of person who is vulnerable to being wanted and needed by a new congregation. The attraction is even stronger when, as was true in this case, the new church is larger and more prestigious than a minister's current charge. That situation can be intensified when, like Shuttlesworth, a pastor has been in one pulpit for several years and is naturally susceptible to new challenges.

For Shuttlesworth, however, the old challenge of fighting segregation in Birmingham still occupied his attention and obstructed his view of a growing disaffection. He still commanded great loyalty and fondness from the members at Bethel. His recent courtroom tangles with Connor had lifted their spirits, and they had vigorously congratulated him (and themselves) for his besting Connor in their earlier skirmish over taking a polygraph test. The members, especially the younger adults, continued to be inspired by his activities both as pastor and as civil rights leader. A significant number, however, had begun to tire of their pastor's frequent, even regular, absences. The pastor occasionally tried to make light of the problem, even joking with the congregation from time to time, "Be glad when you see me and pray for me when I'm gone." The members were glad and did pray. Nonetheless, many complained when, according to member James Roberson, an all-too-frequent Sunday morning refrain became "Reverend is in Detroit" or "Reverend is in Chicago."[10]

The members strongly supported their pastor's civil rights crusade, and for the most part, they believed that he balanced his responsibilities as pastor and civil rights leader admirably. Some struggled, however, to come to terms with what they saw as a new role for their pastor and church. As member Daisy Winston later indicated, "I don't think it was negativism toward what he was doing. It was more or less finding it hard to accept that this was going to be one of the roles of our church." Quietly and without rancor toward Shuttlesworth, Winston thought the movement was causing some of the pastor's traditional duties to be neglected. "His pastoral duties were neglected in a sense," she surmised, "because he saw it [his dual role as pastor and civil rights leader] all as one." Another member, Reuben Davis, had no doubt that civil rights had overshadowed Shuttlesworth's pastoral activities, putting the issue bluntly: "I could feel that he was more involved in the political and civil rights struggle than he was at Bethel. . . . All of us were aware of the fact that he was more than just pastor of Bethel Baptist Church." Another member, Vivian Durant, reported that "there came a time . . . when the church felt it was being neglected." James Roberson believed that the discord "became profound," and he saw this as the primary reason Shuttlesworth realized the time was ripe for a change and left Bethel before matters deteriorated further.[11]

Shuttlesworth remained oblivious to this small and slowly growing sentiment in his congregation. Had he known of it, or allowed himself to believe it existed, he would have been more inclined to stay and fight it out. Years later, he held that conditions at Bethel continued to be favorable toward him and did not figure significantly into his considering the pastorate at Revelation. The members' testimony, however, suggests the presence of the problem even if the pastor remained unattuned to it. In fact, quiet criticism of Shuttlesworth's civil rights involvements slowly began to develop among a minority of members after the second bombing of the church. His status as pastor and his following as civil rights leader made voicing those opinions unpopular within the membership. For Fred Shuttlesworth the noise of battle on the civil rights front rendered such criticism inaudible. Yet evidence of the congregation's dissatisfaction—not with Shuttlesworth in particular but with having a pastor so involved in the civil rights movement—may be suggested by Bethel's choice of the Reverend V. C. Provitt as Fred's pastoral successor. Although honoring what Shuttlesworth had done as their pastor, they found in Provitt a more traditional minister who never participated in civil rights concerns. This choice also suggests that rank-and-file church members in the African American church did not always share the unified view of ministry and civil rights activism held by such ministers as Shuttlesworth and King. Member Laverne Revis Martin commented on Bethel's failure to call a civil rights preacher as Shuttlesworth's successor: "The church and the movement is separate. When we got ready for a pastor, we were looking for a minister, a preacher. Somebody that could preach to the congregation, and a leader. We wasn't lookin' for a movement . . . you know, because the movement and the church is different. We were looking for a pastor of the church." Perhaps more significant, Bethel never hosted any other ACMHR mass meetings after Shuttlesworth left Birmingham.[12]

Troubles at Bethel may have played a minimal role in driving Shuttlesworth away; his major obstacle in contemplating a move remained balancing the needs of his family with his commitment to continue the fight in Birmingham. As he weighed his options, he showed to only a few confidants his growing concern for his family. On a trip through Louisville, he discussed the matter with friends Carl and Anne Braden. In a rare admission of discouragement, he told them,

"If I could see any possibility of anything ever changing in Birmingham, I'd stay, but I don't. I just don't know how much longer I should put my family through this." Yet despite difficulties in Birmingham, pressure from Cincinnati, and Ruby's appeals, Fred resolved to stay put unless he convinced himself that he could somehow attend to both concerns.[13]

Impetus toward a resolution came from an unlikely source. Early in 1961 Fred's sometime rival J. L. Ware, along with most of the black Baptist community, heard rumors that the Cincinnati church had been courting a reluctant Shuttlesworth. After Shuttlesworth had preached a rousing sermon at the Sunday School District Congress, Ware congratulated him on the sermon and offered his advice. "Fred, you are tied to Birmingham, you are tied to civil rights. You can't see nothing else but that. But now, open your eyes. Maybe God wants you to move."

"Well, he's trying to get me out of Birmingham," came Shuttlesworth's suspicious first thought. But before he could form his words, Ware continued, "Your wife will never get a job in Birmingham or in Alabama. Your children are growing up."

Surprised to hear Ruby's arguments coming from Ware, Shuttlesworth overcame his natural urge to dismiss the older minister's advice and listened further. Now Ware's homily moved to its second point. "God may want you to do something else. Just think about it. . . . I know you will never leave the movement. But don't close your mind to bettering the condition of your family."[14]

Shocked by Ware's perceptive reading of his situation, Shuttlesworth thanked him for his kind words and began to reconsider the offer from Revelation. Soon after this conversation and more discussions with Ruby, Fred decided to reopen negotiations with Revelation. Contacting the pulpit committee, Shuttlesworth reminded them of his ongoing commitment in Birmingham. He refused even to consider the church's call except on condition of free rein to return to Birmingham for ACMHR activities whenever he deemed necessary. For most churches, this request would have been a deal breaker. Revelation, however, so fervently coveted the prestige of having a major civil rights leader as its pastor that the committee accepted Shuttlesworth's proviso. That door now open, Fred and the committee moved on to the more conventional discussion of the prospective pastor's "program."

Baptist churches often seek to know a prospective leader's agenda or plan of action he (rarely *she*) intends to implement once installed as pastor. Ordinarily, the request amounts to a statement of the candidate's philosophy of ministry.

In certain instances, however, churches seek or ministers unilaterally provide a more specific program. African American Baptist churches generally treat the enunciation of the program with a mixture of both formality and informality. If a congregation has been smitten by the preaching skills of a candidate, a vote can be taken while the people are still in the throes of an emotionally rousing service of worship. Moving quickly, the congregation may say to the preacher, "Tell us what you want and when you can come to take over." They seek a somewhat formal, sometimes written, statement—a kind of ecclesiastical prenuptial agreement—that serves as the basis for their relationship as pastor and congregation. Up until Ware's comments and further discussions with Ruby, Fred and the lay leaders at Revelation had not proceeded to this point. By mid-April, however, Shuttlesworth had submitted a list of fifteen recommendations that served as conditions for his further consideration of their offer.[15]

Most of Shuttlesworth's recommendations focused on general matters typical of churches of Revelation's size and status. He expected to build a church with ample educational and recreational facilities, a church bus, active denominational involvements, a Baptist Training Union, a youth program, and financial pledges and building funds. More characteristic of his commanding pastoral demeanor, yet not unusual for a black Baptist pastor, Shuttlesworth proposed certain policies designed to keep his prospective members in line. He insisted on an annual call of trustees and deacons, with no church officers to serve without the approval of the pastor and the larger congregation. All groups and persons working in the church were to be subject to the direction of the pastor, and members were expected to contribute financially to the church's ministry. Shuttlesworth would continue his policy of publishing quarterly reports of congregational giving, with noncontributing members disqualified from voting in church business matters. The policy also included dropping slackers from the membership rolls if their financial neglect of the church persisted beyond six months. Shuttlesworth further stipulated that the church would make no expenditures without his consent and would grant to the pastor the right to countersign all checks.

Although this last stipulation was slightly unusual, it was not an unheard-of expectation among African American Baptist ministers of the period. At any rate, the committee and membership of Revelation registered no objections and reaffirmed their call of Shuttlesworth as their pastor. Now they simply would have to await his final answer. It did not come for two months, partly because of his indecision, but primarily because of his involvement in what would turn out to be some of the most important episodes in the entire civil rights movement—the Freedom Rides.

In early February, the Congress of Racial Equality, led by national director James Farmer, decided to dramatize restrictions in public accommodations by sending a group of "freedom riders" through the Deep South. Despite Supreme Court rulings since the late forties that ordered the desegregation of interstate buses, most Deep South localities maintained segregated seating on buses and in waiting rooms, arresting African Americans who challenged those arrangements. At this early stage of his new administration, President Kennedy had decided on a go-slow approach to civil rights, concentrating on winning African Americans the vote in the South rather than introducing legislation into an unsympathetic Congress or using executive orders. The planners of the Freedom Rides thus hoped to cast a national spotlight on the difference between national law and regional custom and put pressure on the new Kennedy administration to step up its efforts on the civil rights front.

Farmer and his associates recruited a dozen or so persons to go on the rides and brought them to Washington during a week in April 1961 for training in nonviolence. Leaders formulated an itinerary for a trip that was to begin in the nation's capital on May 4, proceed through Virginia, the Carolinas, and the Deep South states, and arrive in New Orleans on May 17, the seventh anniversary of the *Brown* decision. More than a month before departure, Farmer wrote President Kennedy, the attorney general, FBI director J. Edgar Hoover, the chair of the Interstate Commerce Commission, the presidents of Greyhound and Trailways bus companies, and local officials along the travel route and notified them of the plan and the itinerary.[16]

CORE drew its participation chiefly from northern activists with few ties to and little interest in the black church, and its efforts depended in large measure on the church-based movement affiliated with the SCLC. The rides would have been an unmitigated disaster without the early financial backing of SCLC supporters in the African American churches along the route of the Freedom Rides. Executive Director Wyatt T. Walker bluntly observed, "The truth of it is, the Freedom Rides would never have been continued without SCLC. . . . In the South particularly, if you don't go to a Negro church you can forget it. They never did really have any outposts in the South because of the attitude that they wanted to be non-religious."[17]

From his SCLC office in Atlanta, Walker lined up Shuttlesworth to serve as the primary contact for the riders as they made their way through Alabama. At a Monday night mass meeting on May 8, Shuttlesworth told his audience that with Connor having recently been reelected he intended to "do more integrated riding and playing golf" than ever. At the same time, he mentioned that "our Freedom Riders" were scheduled to arrive in Birmingham the following Sunday, making a specific point of reminding Connor's detectives to pass the information along to city hall. As they made their way along their route, the riders encountered relatively minor obstacles. One was arrested in Charlotte, North Carolina, for entering a white barber shop, and another was slugged in Rock Hill, South Carolina, after entering a segregated rest room. Their reception in Alabama, however, was destined to raise the stakes considerably.[18]

On Sunday morning, May 14, Shuttlesworth awoke prepared for a Mother's Day sermon at church and certain of action in Birmingham against the arriving Freedom Riders. Before services Fred received a call from one of the riders, Jim Peck, apprising him of the arrival times of the buses in Birmingham early that afternoon. Shuttlesworth warned Peck to expect trouble when they arrived. Rumors had circulated for several days that a mob would greet them at the bus terminal when they arrived. In fact, CBS producer David Lowe and news reporter Howard K. Smith, in Birmingham to finish up work on the "Who Speaks for Birmingham?" program, caught wind of the report and called black minister C. Herbert Oliver, who in turn notified Shuttlesworth. Fred gave Peck his address and told him he would be looking for him and the others. Hanging up, he immediately dialed Western Union, wiring Connor and Jamie Moore about the riders' expected arrival and requesting protection at the Greyhound and Trailways bus stations.[19]

Later, during worship services, Pastor Shuttlesworth expressed his concern for the riders and led the congregation in prayer for their safe arrival. Soon after dismissing the service, he learned that a mob had answered his prayers by visiting violence on the interlopers. One badly beaten rider had staggered to a cab, asking the driver to take him to Shuttlesworth's home. When the rider arrived at Bethel, church ushers ministered to him and summoned Shuttlesworth to the rear entrance. Fred spoke quietly with the victim and learned that the attack at the Trailways station had been the second round of violence of the day.

As the buses pulled into Anniston, an angry mob met the Greyhound bus, bashed its sides with clubs, broke the windows, and slashed the tires. A few minutes later, after failing to dislodge the riders, the mob firebombed the bus and severely beat the travelers as they emerged, choking and coughing, from the vehicle. The next day a photograph of the bus in flames graced the front page of newspapers around the world. Meanwhile, several white toughs had boarded the other bus. The driver announced, "I ain't movin' this bus another foot until the niggers get in the back of the bus where they belong." When none of black riders obeyed the command, the whites began beating those parked in the front seats. When two white riders, Peck and Walter Bergman, tried to intervene, they were beaten unconscious. Turning their attention back to the African American riders in the front, the attackers moved them bodily into the rear as the bloody bus slowly began moving west toward its next destination. The young thugs remained on the bus, standing guard over the riders for the entire two-hour drive to Birmingham.[20]

Shuttlesworth immediately called several of his ACMHR faithful, who had already heard of the attack in Birmingham. He recruited several carloads to caravan to Anniston on a rescue mission to retrieve the stranded riders. When Shuttlesworth appeared intent on going along, Colonel Johnson and some of the others protested that he should remain available for the riders who had taken their lumps in Birmingham. Seeing the wisdom of the suggestion, Shuttlesworth acceded to their request, but not before instructing them once more: "Gentlemen, this is dangerous, but I know you mustn't carry any weapons. You must trust God and have faith." Shuttlesworth's men apparently disobeyed the directive; Hank Thomas, one of the CORE volunteers, later remembered that each of the cars had a shotgun in the floorboard in case of trouble. The convoy, however, gathered up the Anniston wounded and speedily returned to Bethel without further incident.[21]

As Shuttlesworth talked with the first rider, another wounded arrival pulled up to the front of the church, followed by a battered and wobbly Jim Peck. Alarmed by vast amounts of blood and a gash in Peck's forehead wide enough for Shuttlesworth to view his skull, the preacher told Peck, "Man, you need to get to a hospital." He quickly called an ambulance and rounded up some of his church members to carry him into his house. Ruby instructed them to lay Peck on the bed in the guest room even though so doing ruined her beautiful white bedspread. Repeatedly shooed away from the frenetic activity, Ricky, mesmerized by more blood than she had ever seen before, kept peeking around the corner into the room. Finally mustering the courage to tiptoe toward the victim, she asked, "How do you feel?" Peck uttered a deep sigh and replied in a whisper, "I'm okay."[22]

Peck and fellow rider Charles Person had encountered a mob of some twenty-five whites who had gathered at the Trailways station when they learned the Greyhound bus had been destroyed in Anniston. Peck later said he could have sworn he noticed the gang licking their lips as he and Person took deep breaths and heard them say to each other, "Here we go again." Several of the attackers forced Peck and Person into an alley, where they beat them with bare fists and iron pipes. One of them shouted, "Get him, get him. Jesus, get him good." In the midst of the attackers, FBI informant Gary Thomas Rowe heard Peck call out, "Before you get my brothers, you will have to kill me," just before he lost consciousness. Waking sometime later, Peck wiped his blood with a handkerchief and found Walter Bergman, who helped him toward a taxi. Refused by two drivers, Peck and Bergman managed to get a third cabbie to agree to take them to Shuttlesworth's home.[23]

Nine of the Freedom Riders were injured in the attack, as were *Birmingham Post-Herald* photographer Tommy Langston and radio newscaster Clancy Lake. Accidentally caught in the brawl, Langston was beaten and had his camera smashed. The mob attacked Lake as he broadcasted an account of the melee from his car. As the mob smashed his windows, Lake shouted for help, and his radio transmission went off the air. All of the carnage occurred within a few blocks of police headquarters. Officers, however, did not arrive on the scene for some ten minutes after the riders' arrival. By the time police approached, the mob had disappeared as if on signal.

The signal had come directly from Connor. To later inquiries into the absence of officers from the scene, Connor replied that because it was Mother's Day, he had let a number of them off duty in order to visit their mothers. He apparently had given Chief Moore and a police sergeant the day off and was in his office and personally in command of the police department that day. Both from Rowe's reports through the FBI and from Shuttlesworth's telegram, he knew in advance of the riders' arrival time and place. Connor passed the information to the Klan through detective Thomas H. Cook, along with a promise to keep police officers away from the scene and with the admonition, "By God, if you are going to do this thing, do it right!" Rejecting appeals even from his Methodist minister, the Reverend John Rutland, that he protect the riders, Connor deliberately kept police away from the Trailways station and personally encouraged Klan violence against the Freedom Riders. Years later an FBI teletype message from the Birmingham office to Director Hoover quoted Connor as saying he wanted the Freedom Riders beaten until "it looked like a bulldog got a hold of them." The message also indicated that the police department promised the Klan fifteen unimpeded minutes during which to get the job done.[24]

In contrast to their performance at the bus station, Connor's police found no difficulty arriving at Shuttlesworth's home in short order. Noting that white and black riders were piling together into the Bethel parsonage, the officers threatened to arrest them for breaking residential segregation laws. Shuttlesworth challenged them, "You can't arrest these men. They are sick! They are going to the hospital, or they can stay at my house." Later that afternoon, Connor himself called Shuttlesworth and threatened the minister with jail, but Fred shot back, "They are out here, and this is my house. What are you going to do about it? If you provide them a hotel downtown, I will be glad to release them; otherwise, they stay here. I am going to give them hospitality." Apparently satisfied merely to harass Shuttlesworth and the riders further, Connor made no arrests at the parsonage. After the police departed, Shuttlesworth turned his attention back to getting the injured riders, especially Peck, to the hospital. Before the ambulance drove Peck away, Fred gave him a dime and told him to call as soon as he had received medical care. Then warning him that the Klan would be on the prowl, he instructed Peck to stay inside the hospital until he came to pick him up.[25]

After offering care to the riders with more superficial wounds, Shuttlesworth rounded up his temporary boarders, Bethel and ACMHR members, and a few reporters for a small mass meeting at Bethel that night. A relatively small crowd heard victims describe their experiences in Anniston and downtown Birmingham. With chairs set up across the front of the sanctuary, the riders became physical exhibits of the mob's violence. Bergman, a retired professor from Michigan State University, first explained CORE and their goals for the rides. He then told of the attacks against him that afternoon, showing off his swollen left eye and several cuts on his face. Other Freedom Riders told their stories and called on the local blacks to pick up the fight for integration.[26]

One young Bethel member, Veronica Chappell, marveled at the integrationists' willingness to continue the fight in the face of their injuries. She was particularly impressed by the middle-class whites among the riders, whom she realized had little to gain and much to lose personally from their participation in the rides. "We want you to know," they told their audience, "that we're doing this because we're dissatisfied with the way things are. We need you to take up from this." By the time Shuttlesworth addressed them, the group had been electrified with religious fervor, shouting "Amen" and "Yeah" as he told them, "This is the greatest thing that has ever happened in Alabama, and it has been good for the nation. It was a wonderful thing to see these young students—Negro and white—come, even after the mobs and the bus burning. When white and black men are willing to be beaten up together, it is a sure sign they will soon walk together as brothers." Caught up in the spirit, Shuttlesworth exclaimed, "No matter how many times they beat us up, segregation has still got to go. Others may be beaten up, but freedom is worth anything."[27]

After concluding the mass meeting with lusty hymns and impassioned prayers, Shuttlesworth led "his people," as he had begun to call the riders, back over to the parsonage for a meal and to talk over plans for continuing the Freedom Rides the next day. About 2:00 A.M., with Freedom Riders and Shuttlesworth teenagers sleeping on the floors, Shuttlesworth received a call from Peck, now with fifty-three stitches in his head, saying he was being released from the hospital. The minister once more reminded Peck to sit tight until he came for him, assuring him he would pick him up shortly. Summoning a driver, Fred immediately headed downtown.

The men drove up to the door of the hospital and waved to Peck, who had been waiting just inside the glass door. Just as the car pulled away from the hospital, a police cruiser began to follow, finally stopping them after a few blocks. The officer went through the routine questions but then accused the driver of having stolen the car. At that point, Shuttlesworth called out, "Officer, this is not a stolen car, and you know it." "And who the hell are you?" the officer asked. "I'm Reverend Fred Shuttlesworth, and I'm sure you're familiar with the name," he shot back, adding, "We don't want any interference from the police tonight." The officer then mumbled to his partner that Shuttlesworth was with the driver. Shortly thereafter Shuttlesworth heard the dispatcher over the police radio say, "Oh hell, let 'em go." As the officers drove off with a loud uproar, a smiling Shuttlesworth told Peck, "They don't want to get in another tangle with me." After they reached the Shuttlesworth home, Peck, still woozy, was escorted into the living room and fell asleep on the family couch. Fred was still keyed up from an eventful day and found little room or opportunity for sleep.[28]

On Monday the voices of white Birmingham criticized Connor and the police department. In a front-page editorial the *News* pointedly asked in the headline, "Where Were the Police?" Recalling Harrison Salisbury's indictment of their city, the paper admitted, "Fear and hatred did stalk Birmingham's streets yesterday" and acknowledged that "Mr. Connor did not do what could have been done Sunday." At the same time, the Young Men's Business Club rebuked the commissioner for "letting the people of Birmingham down" by not deploying enough security to stave off violence at the bus station. For his part, Connor defended himself by commenting, "I have said for the last twenty years that these out-of-town meddlers were going to cause bloodshed if they kept meddling in the South's business." Throughout the day large crowds of Klan members and sympathizers gathered at the bus terminal awaiting another opportunity to shed more Freedom Rider blood.[29]

Meanwhile, Shuttlesworth, the ACMHR, and Bethel Baptists provided food and encouragement as their guests decided to resume the Freedom Rides. In addition, Shuttlesworth discussed matters several times with Robert Kennedy, who kept close tabs on the situation in an effort to avoid further incidents. "Mr. Shuttlesworth, what do you think I should do?" the attorney general asked the minister. "Give us some protection down here," he quickly answered. Promising to arrange security, Kennedy then called Connor and with some vigor argued him into an escort for the bus to the city limits. When Kennedy called back to report on his plan, Shuttlesworth was dissatisfied. "Mr. Kennedy, they were escorted to the city line in Anniston," Fred reminded him, "and that's where the bus burned. So we are not going to leave the station until they can be escorted to the Alabama state line." Kennedy then turned to the matter of negotiations with Governor John Patterson. In the meantime the attorney general promised Shuttlesworth and the riders that he would induce Connor to provide them an escort to the bus station. Before hanging up, Kennedy offered reassurance, saying, "Mr. Shuttlesworth, we are concerned about your problem. Do you have my phone number?" Pleased to have such access to the corridors of power, Shuttlesworth ended the conversation, and the party went to the bus terminal.[30]

Shuttlesworth and his church members ferried the riders from North Birmingham to the downtown Greyhound terminal, arriving at 2:45 P.M. Entering the terminal, James Peck told reporters, ""It's been rough, but I'm getting on that bus to Montgomery." As they bought their tickets, a police officer approached Shuttlesworth.

"What are you doing down here?" the officer asked.

"You know why I'm down here. I have business down here. These people are down here."

"You got a ticket?"

"No, but I'm going to get one."

"You better, or you can't stay in here with these folks."

Purchasing a ticket to Montgomery, Shuttlesworth sat in the waiting area with the riders, but he soon learned that Greyhound drivers had decided not to drive any bus carrying the riders. The riders quickly huddled with Shuttlesworth, who told them, "There are two ways to handle a strike—we can either abide by it or break it."

"What do you mean 'break it?'" someone asked.

"Well, now that the station is integrated, we can stay here and wait them out. They are bound to put a bus through sooner or later. But, of course, the decision as to what to do is up to y'all."

Putting off the decision until events developed further, Shuttlesworth and the group made themselves comfortable in the waiting area until government officials made final arrangements for their departure. As the group waited, reporters observed that the party seemed undisturbed by the situation, passing the time by reading magazines and raiding the vending machines. At one point, an angry drunk approached them, blustering that he wanted to take them all on. Noticing Shuttlesworth's familiar face among the group, the man came after him, shouting, "There is the one I want." A police officer immediately grabbed the would-be attacker by the arm and diverted him out of the terminal. Watching the proceedings, Fred grinned at both the drunk and the novel experience of being protected by the Birmingham Police Department.[31]

Discussions resumed as Attorney General Kennedy alternated calls between Shuttlesworth, Governor Patterson, and the bus company. Shuttlesworth spoke again with Kennedy, apprising him of the latest development. Kennedy then called the manager of Greyhound's Birmingham terminal, George E. Cruit, insisting that he "get in touch with Mr. Greyhound" if necessary to find a driver and get the bus on its way. When Cruit reiterated that his hands were tied, Kennedy threatened to send down an air force plane if some progress could not be made on finding a driver.[32]

Conversations with Patterson turned out to be less fruitful because the governor reneged on an earlier promise to have Alabama State Safety Director Floyd Mann accompany the bus from Birmingham to Montgomery. Patterson now said that having the riders remain in the state could be dangerous and refused to guarantee safe passage. "The citizens of the state are so enraged that I cannot guarantee protection for this bunch of rabble-rousers." Offering to have a patrol accompany them directly to the nearest state line rather than to their preferred destination, Patterson declared, "We will not escort them to any other cities in Alabama to continue their rabble-rousing."[33]

At that point, the riders concluded that their purpose had been accomplished by the national publicity regarding the previous day's events and that further delays would foil plans to rally in New Orleans by Wednesday, May 17. On that basis they booked a 6:50 P.M. flight to New Orleans. Shuttlesworth once again contacted some of his loyalists to come and collect the riders and deliver them to the Birmingham airport. After bomb scares forced the cancellation of two flights, the riders managed to board a plane and escape Birmingham at 10:30 that night.[34]

After depositing the riders at the airport, Shuttlesworth had his eventful day continue as he hurried to the Kingston Baptist Church for the regular Monday night mass meeting. News of the events of the previous two days had raised attendance and stimulated the zeal of some 350 congregants anxious for a firsthand report from their leader. The vice president, Ed Gardner began the rollicking meeting by poking fun at the detectives, noting with irony that "our Commissioner sends them here each Monday night, but we can't find them when we need them." As the meeting proceeded, Shuttlesworth moved back and forth between the sanctuary and the pastor's office, keeping posted on unfolding developments at the airport. At 9:15 P.M., Fred took the pulpit to fire up the troops. Knowing he had wired Connor on Sunday morning with word of the riders' arrival, he complained bitterly of the absence of the police: "This is the worst city in the world, where Mr. Connor or any other Commissioner of the Police Department will say, 'We didn't know violence would happen.' They are a damn liar." He then held them spellbound, recounting the events of Mother's Day.[35]

The audience shook their heads in dismay at his description of Peck's injuries and exulted with Shuttlesworth on his commentary regarding the police avoiding "another tangle" with him. After he left once again and returned from another phone call with Robert Kennedy, the crowd cheered their leader who was on a first-name basis with the brother of the president of the United States. They especially reveled in Shuttlesworth's boast that the attorney general had told him, "If you can't get me at my office, just call me at the White House." The triumphant meeting concluded with a congregation caught up in the shouting experience of African American religion and with Ed Gardner leading the cheers for Shuttlesworth: "Don't we have a great president who has courage and conviction!"[36]

On Tuesday, May 16, as the Birmingham papers again criticized local police and the governor for not protecting the Freedom Riders, Shuttlesworth tried to catch up on his rest, having been awake since Sunday morning. That evening, however, Shuttlesworth's respite was interrupted by a call from Diane Nash, a leader of the Nashville Christian Leadership Conference. She advised him that student protesters from Fisk University and the American Baptist Seminary in Nashville had decided to come to Birmingham to resume the Freedom Rides. Jolted awake by this news, Shuttlesworth blurted out, "Young lady, do you realize what's happened here already?"

"Yes," she answered, "but we can't let violence interfere with our constitutional rights."

"I agree with you, but you must realize that here you might get killed. These people almost got killed coming down."

Unperturbed, Nash replied, "That's exactly why the rides must not be stopped. If they stop us with violence, the movement is dead. Anyway, the students have decided. They'll be leaving in the morning. We just want to know if you can meet us."[37]

Agreeing to meet them at the bus station, Shuttlesworth advised them to call back when travel plans were set and, because his phone line was tapped, to use a code. Nash was relieved that Shuttlesworth would support continuing the rides. Some of the ministers in Nashville opposed the students' decision, and she believed that Shuttlesworth's dependable support would convince the student movement to follow through with their plan. Early the next morning Nash called back and indicated, as Fred had suggested, that ten new chickens (Freedom Riders) would soon be shipped, including both hens and roosters (males and females), some Rhode Island Reds and some speckled (an integrated group), and were scheduled to arrive in Birmingham Wednesday morning sometime after eleven o'clock.[38]

Shuttlesworth immediately fired off a telegram to Connor and the press to alert them of the arrival of a new wave of Freedom Riders and to request that the commissioner use the powers of his office "to see that these citizens reach all points of their destinations and are afforded full protection while at stations within your jurisdiction." He and Ed Gardner then went to the bus station and bought tickets to Montgomery in order to be allowed to remain in the waiting room. As they waited, a crowd of several hundred gathered outside the terminal. The bus pulled into the station a little after noon, and the police held the eight black and two white Riders on board for almost an hour until the officers, avoiding the problems of bloody Mother's Day, separated the bus from the crowd. Above the noise, someone yelled, "Y'all take the police away, and we'll move the other people out!" Finally, the riders were allowed off the bus, with the police requesting that they not mingle interracially in the waiting room. They answered that they intended to wait in accordance with the Supreme Court's rulings desegregating interstate travel and that they planned to board a five o'clock bus. Playing the gracious host, Shuttlesworth welcomed them into the station and led them to the window to buy their tickets to Montgomery.[39]

As the departure time approached, a worried driver told the riders, "If you get on, I will not drive the bus." Returning to the waiting room, Shuttlesworth and the riders were met by police chief Moore, who said, "It is dangerous for you and for others for you to stay here" and put them under "protective arrest." Shuttlesworth immediately protested, "These students came here to ride out on a regularly scheduled bus. That is our irrevocable position. The challenge has to be made. This is a continuation of the Freedom Ride which was stopped temporarily here in Birmingham. When it is proven [that] people can ride through Birmingham without molestation, it will all be over here." Heedless of the preacher's sermonette, Moore reiterated his intention to arrest the riders, to which Shuttlesworth insisted, "If you are going to carry them to jail, I am going too." Moore asked him to move, and when Shuttlesworth refused, the police chief personally placed him under arrest for refusing to obey and for interfering with an officer. As Moore placed Shuttlesworth into a squad car, the crowd still gathered at the rear of the station broke into a loud cheer. Shuttlesworth and the Nashville group were processed into the Southside jail, where five hours later the minister was released on bond.[40]

Because the riders were still in custody, Shuttlesworth held a meeting at his home early the next day to map out future plans with Wyatt Walker, Joseph Lowery, the Nashville movement's Reverend J. Metz Rollins, and Len Holt, an attorney from Norfolk, Virginia. Public statements in the press denounced Shuttlesworth for his role in the local upheavals. Connor charged that Shuttlesworth had conspired with the Nashville Freedom Riders to disturb the peace and that Shuttlesworth had known of their arrival. "As early as 9 A.M.," Connor fumed, "he began precipitating trouble by making statements to newspapers and radio stations and sending telegrams and otherwise warning people." He further said that he would consult the legal department in an effort to have Shuttlesworth charged for inciting a breach of the peace. The *News*'s editors commended Connor for this course of action. They likened Shuttlesworth's activities to shouting "Fire" in a crowded theater, an action beyond the Constitution's free speech provisions. In a front-page editorial announcing, "Shuttlesworth Shouts 'Fire,'" the paper called on the city to prosecute him: "Shuttlesworth cannot be allowed to threaten this city with turmoil."[41]

During the day, Chief Moore offered to release the riders a few at a time if they would leave the city in private transportation. The riders themselves began a hunger strike, and at an 8:00 P.M. press conference Shuttlesworth and the others announced that they continued to support the riders, who would leave the city only on a regularly scheduled bus. Around midnight, Connor himself walked into the cells of the riders, introduced himself, and transferred them to black limousines. Along the highway toward Nashville, the commissioner and the students engaged in unexpectedly friendly repartee. After the group had traveled for a period of time, Connor ordered the driver to stop. He told the riders, "This is the Tennessee line. Cross it and save this state and yourself a lot of trouble." His young opponents promised to see him again in Birmingham around noon. Laughing, Connor got back in his car and returned to Birmingham.[42]

Now stranded, the students found a phone and called Diane Nash, who in turn sent cars to retrieve them. Then she called Shuttlesworth to alert him that the riders had been released and would be returning to Birmingham that afternoon. On Friday Shuttlesworth welcomed old and new riders who trickled into the Bethel parsonage during the afternoon. After providing a quick meal and final instructions, Shuttlesworth accompanied a group of Freedom Riders back to the Greyhound depot for the third time in a week. Once there, Shuttlesworth was arrested for the second time in a week, this time on charges of conspiring a breach of the peace, as Connor and the *News* had advocated the day before. The riders, once again detained by another set of refusals by bus operators to drive, spent the night at the terminal. Shuttlesworth rejoined them as soon as he bonded himself out of jail.[43]

During their overnight wait Shuttlesworth again kept Robert Kennedy and Burke Marshall, assistant attorney general for civil rights, abreast of the latest developments. When Shuttlesworth informed Kennedy that the riders intended to go through Mississippi via Montgomery, the attorney general begged Shuttlesworth to persuade them to fly directly to New Orleans, adding, "Oh my God, Reverend Shuttlesworth, the Lord hasn't even been to Mississippi in a long time."

"But we think the Lord *should* go to Mississippi, and we want to get him there," Shuttlesworth quipped, refusing to persuade them otherwise.

At that, Kennedy asked him, "Are you going to ride the bus?"

"Mr. Kennedy, would I ask anybody else to do what I wouldn't do?" Shuttlesworth answered. "I'm a battlefield general. I lead troops into battle. Yes, sir, I'm gon' ride the bus. I've got my ticket."

"Well, I respect that, but you don't have to ride, do you?"

"Well, why would I ask anybody else to ride?" he shot back. "Yes, if the buses roll, I'm going to ride."

After another round of discussions with both Greyhound officials and with Governor Patterson, the attorney general finally negotiated both a driver and a security detail for the bus. A high-spirited Shuttlesworth presided over the final preparations for boarding, joking with state troopers about their next assault on Mississippi. He laughed aloud, exclaiming, "Man, what this state's coming to! An armed escort to take a bunch of niggers to a bus station so they can break these silly old laws." He led the riders in singing, "He's Got Governor Patterson in His Hands" and promised once again to make a "steer out of ol' Bull." At 8:30 on Saturday morning, just as he prepared to board the bus for the ride to Montgomery, Shuttlesworth felt a hand take him by the back of the collar and heard a voice behind him call out, "Freddie Lee . . . where are you going?" Recognizing the voice of police chief Jamie Moore, he turned and said, "I'm getting on the bus."

"No, I'm giving you an order not to get on the bus."

"What you mean, I can't get on the bus? I have my ticket. You can't stop me from riding."

"Well, no, but I can get you for refusing to obey the lawful order of a policeman," he explained. "And I'm telling you to go home."

"I ain't going home," came an annoyed reply.

"Then I'm arresting you for refusing to obey a lawful order."

"But you can't arrest me when I've got a ticket to ride," he insisted.

"Well, that's just what I'm arresting you for."[44]

Taken into custody again, he watched from a squad car as the Freedom Riders once and for all pulled out of the bus terminal with state protection. Released a few hours later, Shuttlesworth learned through the news media that apparently the state escort dropped off at the Montgomery city limits and that the riders were victimized by another mob beating at the Greyhound station in the capital city. News reports told of many injuries. At that point Shuttlesworth, perhaps overestimating his own importance to the civil rights movement, became convinced that Robert Kennedy, Jamie Moore, and divine providence had worked together to keep him from riding the bus and possibly being killed in Montgomery. Kennedy's insistent efforts to dissuade him to ride the bus that day led Shuttlesworth to believe—though he readily admitted, without hard evidence—that Kennedy had privately asked Moore to arrest him in order to keep him out of possible danger in Montgomery. That scenario perhaps would have required an unusual level of cooperation between Moore and Kennedy and an unexpected prescience of what lay in store for the Freedom Riders in Montgomery and thus seems unlikely. It took little clairvoyance, however, for Kennedy to anticipate violence in Alabama in 1961, and interestingly enough, Birmingham police records or news accounts listed no arrest of Shuttlesworth on May 20. Collusion between Kennedy and Moore for a sham arrest was thus an unlikely possibility, though one that Shuttlesworth was inclined to believe.[45]

Returning home after his release, Shuttlesworth received a call from Katherine Burke, one of the Nashville students, who confirmed the reports of another bus station attack on the Freedom Riders. As the bus reached the outskirts of Montgomery the police escort and the helicopter overhead disappeared, leaving the bus unprotected as it approached the downtown area. Pulling into the terminal, Freedom Rider John Lewis noticed an eerie lack of activity as they prepared to get off the bus. Suddenly whites began pouring in from all over, beating the riders with clubs and fists. Robert Kennedy's personal representative, John Seigenthaler, in town to mediate between his boss and Governor Patterson, was beaten unconscious as he physically stepped in to protect two female Freedom Riders from attack. Reports estimated the mob as numbering near one hundred, who were cheered on by bystanders shrieking, "Get those niggers! Hit 'em again!!" Sitting in a car near the station, police commissioner L. D. Sullivan, asked by a reporter if he had anticipated trouble, replied, "We respond to calls here just like anyplace else. But we have no intention of standing guard for a bunch of troublemakers coming into our city."[46]

That afternoon, after several unsuccessful attempts to coax Patterson to call out the Alabama National Guard to protect the Freedom Riders and restore order, Kennedy induced federal judge Frank M. Johnson Jr. to issue an injunction against interference with travelers on interstate buses. In addition, to enforce the injunction the attorney general mobilized four hundred federal marshals, who were assembled on Saturday night and Sunday morning at Maxwell Air Force Base. For his part, Patterson objected to what he saw as federal intrusion, commenting, "While we will do our utmost to keep the public highways cleared and to guard against all disorder, we cannot escort bus loads of rabble rousers about our state from city to city for the avowed purpose of disobeying our laws, flaunting our customs and traditions, and creating racial incidents. . . . If the federal government really wants to help in this unfortunate situation, they will encourage these outside agitators to go home."[47]

Still bothered that his arrest had interfered with his becoming a Freedom Rider and on fire to be part of the action, Shuttlesworth called some of his ACMHR followers to go with him to Montgomery as soon as possible. In too big of a hurry to get there, he accidentally shaved off half of his moustache and decided to shave it off completely—the only time in his adult life he appeared without it. He quickly called on an associate minister to handle Sunday services at Bethel and made arrangements to stay with Ralph Abernathy in Montgomery. He headed for the capital with little thought of the threatening conditions there. After surviving the Christmas night bombing, he had taken literally the saying of Jesus that "he that loses his life for my sake shall find it, and he that finds his life shall lose it." Thus, in later interviews, Shuttlesworth occasionally asserted, "I really tried to get killed in Birmingham. I exposed myself deliberately, and I felt [that] if I did give my life that the country would have to do something about it." His actions in Birmingham since 1956 had long since demonstrated the intensity of this prophetic "fire in his bones." So intense was the fire and so reckless were his actions that some observers—some in jest, some in seriousness—questioned his sanity. This would be one of those occasions, as he apparently "tried to get killed" in Montgomery as well.[48]

On Sunday CORE and SCLC leaders laid plans for a special service to honor the Freedom Riders that evening at First Baptist Church, where Ralph Abernathy served as pastor. Word of the service emerged in the media, and as dusk approached mobs began to gather around the church. Martin Luther King Jr., the main speaker for the evening, arrived at the airport in the late afternoon and was escorted by federal marshals to the church on Ripley Street. James Farmer, who had conceived of the Freedom Rides but had not participated in them because of the funeral of his father, was also scheduled to arrive that afternoon. He was met by Fred Shuttlesworth, who had volunteered to pick him up at the airport. As they drove toward the church, the wiry preacher updated Farmer on the worsening situation. By that time the mob around the church exceeded one thousand in number and had begun beating up blacks, closing in on and before long besieging the church.

"Can you get me into that church, Fred?" Farmer asked uneasily.

"Wrong question, Jim. The only question to ask is: how will I get you in?"

As they came within a few blocks of the church, a crowd of whites waving Confederate flags and shouting rebel yells blocked the car and began to rock it back and forth. Shuttlesworth slammed the car into reverse, screeched to a stop once out of the mob's grasp, made a U-turn, and tried another approach.

Blocked again, Fred turned and headed for a black taxi stand. "I have Jim Farmer," he told a cabbie. "How can I get him into that church?" The cab driver suggested they try a third route, park the car, walk through a nearby cemetery, and approach the church from the rear. Shuttlesworth obliged, but once they crossed the cemetery, they realized the mob had blocked that way as well.

"Jim, we have no choice. We'll have to go right through them!"

"We're going to have to do *what?*" replied a wide-eyed Farmer.

"We're gon' have to walk through that mob!" he repeated.

Before Farmer could answer, however, Fred began to march into the teeth of the horde and elbowed his way toward the church, shouting, "Out of the way. Let me through. Step aside." Farmer, a much larger man than his trailblazer for the day, scuttled up to follow in Shuttlesworth's train, while the ocean of angry white hoodlums obeyed his word. In an occurrence Fred saw as tantamount to the parting of the Red Sea, a path opened up through an ocean of angry whites, allowing Shuttlesworth and Farmer to make an exodus into the "safety" of First Baptist Church. Less inclined toward seeing the miraculous, Farmer chalked the incident up to what was called "the crazy nigger syndrome"—"Don't mess with that nigger, he's crazy."[49]

Once inside, Shuttlesworth and Farmer discovered that the uprising had finally forced Patterson to declare a qualified martial law and to give troops under Adjutant General Henry V. Graham authority to do whatever was necessary to restore order. Later, Patterson told an interviewer, presumably with a straight face, "There was never any breakdown of law and order in Alabama. We never were in a position where we couldn't enforce the law." Yet by eight o'clock, when Abernathy strode to the pulpit to present the Freedom Riders to a capacity crowd of between twelve hundred and fifteen hundred worried worshippers, the mob had grown to an estimated twenty-five hundred. Outside the sanctuary, a phalanx of U.S. marshals faced off against the angry crowd gathered in a park across Ripley Street. Some shouted, "Let old King come out. Let the niggers come out. We'll take care of them." Some set a car on fire, while others threw bricks and bottles at the church. When marshals began trying to disperse the crowd with tear gas, the mob temporarily retreated more deeply into the park, but within minutes they surged forward, once more driving the marshals back to the church. Soon members of the swarm learned to act quickly and hurl the tear gas canisters back into the marshals, causing the gas to waft into the church through broken windows.[50]

Inside the church, the congregants choked on smoke and rubbed their eyes from tear gas, singing and praying for protection from the mob. At times the shouting and sirens outside rivaled the sound of singing inside the church. The Reverend Solomon Seay called on the congregation to remain calm and keep singing. "I want to hear everybody sing," he exhorted, "and mean every word of it." As an officer called out on a bullhorn, "This is the police. Everybody clear the area," the congregation sang, "There'll Be Freedom in That Land Where I'm Bound." The ministers took turns stepping to the pulpit, preaching homilies to the crowd to bolster their courage. In calming tones King lamented Patterson's actions: "His consistent preaching of defiance of the law, his vitriolic public pronouncements, and his irresponsible actions created the atmosphere in which violence could thrive. Alabama has sunk to a level of barbarity comparable to the tragic days of Hitler's Germany." Shuttlesworth echoed that sentiment, commenting, "It is a sin and a shame before God that, in a day like this, that these people who govern us would let things come to such a sad estate. But God is not dead. The most guilty man in this state tonight is Governor John Patterson."[51]

Back in the pastor's office, a harried confab of King, Abernathy, Walker, Shuttlesworth, and Farmer much less calmly wondered why federal officials were so slow in breaking up the mob and protecting the people in the church. Contemplating a worst-case scenario in which the mob actually broke into the church, King suggested that in order to save the people in the sanctuary, the leaders might give themselves up to the mob. As Walker wondered to himself whether King had lost his mind, Shuttlesworth said, "Yeah, well, if that's what we have to do, let's do it." After ten o'clock, after chief federal marshal James F. McShane asked the leaders to keep the congregation in the church overnight, King placed a call to Robert Kennedy to lodge his complaints. When Kennedy suggested that the Freedom Rides enter a cooling-off period, Farmer replied to King, "We've been cooling off for three hundred years. If we cool off any more we'll be in the deep freeze!"[52]

Shuttlesworth, inclined toward speech even less diplomatic, wanted to tell him, "Shit, goddammit, do something." He did not speak to Kennedy until 1:30 A.M., by which time his frayed nerves were somewhat more under control. By that time the combination of federal marshals, Alabama National Guard, and Montgomery police had restored a semblance of order. Still, the crowd in the church sang quietly or slept in Sunday school rooms until dawn when law enforcement officials escorted them in small groups to their homes. Shuttlesworth again noted the irony of the state of Alabama being forced to protect them even while trying to defend segregation, telling his ACMHR mass meeting on Monday night, "When I left the church this morning, Pat's marshals carried me home."[53]

All but addicted to the excitement of the movement, Shuttlesworth returned to Montgomery on Tuesday to have his say in discussions of whether to continue the Freedom Rides. The young firebrands of the Student Nonviolent Coordinating Committee (SNCC) pressured King and Farmer, older and more conservative leaders, to press on through Mississippi to New Orleans. Farmer agreed to join the ride, but a reluctant King told the students he had to choose "the when and where of his own Golgotha." Some of the students derided King's messianic language and began calling him "de Lawd," disillusioned at what they regarded as timid leadership.[54]

Although Shuttlesworth never actually became a Freedom Rider, he nonetheless earned the students' admiration for his eagerness to agitate against segregation. Occasionally rolling their eyes at his incessant "God language," the students savored his poking fun at the icons of Jim Crow and honored his willingness to suffer for the cause. The same impulsiveness and bluntness that led some black professionals to look askance at Shuttlesworth made him a hero to the younger activists of the movement. Over the course of her movement activities, Diane Nash judged that King, in order to raise money, was occasionally forced to make decisions she considered damaging to the "people as a whole." Shuttlesworth, however, because of his persona of fearlessness, always made Nash feel secure that he had the interests of the people at heart. "Fred was practically a legend," she later recalled. "I think it was important—for me, definitely, and for a city of people who were carrying on a movement—for there to be somebody that really represented strength, and that's certainly what Fred did. He would not back down, and you could count on it. He would not sell out, [and] you could count on that."[55]

Thus, despite not participating directly in the Freedom Rides, Shuttlesworth played a significant role and did more than anyone to involve the SCLC with them. The riders spent more time on Shuttlesworth's turf than any other place along their route, and his role of encouraging, housing, providing medical care for, and ferrying the riders to the bus station was indispensable. On Thursday, May 25, after the students decided to continue their foray from Montgomery through Mississippi, a group of SCLC leaders, including Abernathy, Shuttlesworth, and Walker, accompanied another group of Freedom Riders to the Trailways terminal for the Montgomery-to-Jackson leg of the journey. Montgomery police arrested the integrated group as they asked for service at the coffee shop.

This amounted to Shuttlesworth's third jailing in eight days, making him the incarceration king among SCLC leaders. Released on bond two days later, he told reporters at the Montgomery airport that "our fight has gained a new dimension" and headed back to Birmingham to take care of business.[56]

An almost incessant part of Shuttlesworth's business in Birmingham remained legal in nature, and his role in the Freedom Rides generated another round of litigation. Just three days after Shuttlesworth emerged from jail in Montgomery, the Alabama Court of Appeals decided one leftover piece of business by upholding Shuttlesworth and Billups's sit-in conviction from 1960. The next day, he faced two breach-of-peace charges stemming from his role in the Freedom Rides.[57]

Before Jefferson County judge Francis Thompson, Fred somewhat disingenuously denied knowing of the riders before their arrival or of having arranged for their coming to Birmingham, claiming that he sought police protection for them only after learning that they were on their way. He further denied he was a member of CORE and held that he had been notified concerning the Freedom Rides because of his notoriety in the movement. He also stated that he had not had any part in the return of the Nashville group after Connor delivered them to the state line. For his part, Connor testified that the preacher had been the person most responsible for the events of May 14 and 17, judging that mobs had gathered at the bus stations only because Shuttlesworth "advertised it all over the country." In a later mass meeting, Shuttlesworth made great sport of Connor on this point. His delighted audience roared when their leader said, "I sho' must be somebody. Ole Bull says the riders only came here because of me, and they been coming from New York and all over. Well, all I know is I am catching Hell for being somebody." In the end, the hell he caught from the judge was a conviction on both counts, fines of $500 for each, and two sentences of ninety days in jail.[58]

Next came another appearance in William Conway's recorder's court, where Shuttlesworth and Phifer had been convicted for violating bus segregation ordinances in 1958. This time the troublemaking minister appeared before Conway for interfering with and refusing to obey the police chief's order at the May 17 arrest of the Nashville Freedom Riders. Moore and two other officers testified that Shuttlesworth had interfered not physically, but by talking and lending moral support to the group as officers attempted to take them into protective custody. Fireworks then began as Conway ordered the defendant to take the stand. Shuttlesworth's attorneys raised strenuous objections to Conway's forcing their client to testify. Overruling them, the judge said to Shuttlesworth, "We know what your conduct has been in the past. Now we want to know what it is going to be in the future. Do you plan to continue to break these ordinances as you have been doing?" Again counsel lodged objections, this time invoking the Fifth Amendment. Overruled once more, attorney Orzell Billingsley, whom Shuttlesworth believed to have been at that moment under the influence of alcohol, fairly shouted, "It is the legal right of my client not to testify. Your honor, you can force him, but I am directing my client not to testify." "Well, I am ordering him to take the stand," answered the judge. Billingsley continued to argue despite Conway's threats of a contempt citation until Shuttlesworth told him, "Man, just be quiet! I'll handle it. Hell, you stay out of jail so you can get *me* out!"

Turning to the judge and feigning ignorance, Shuttlesworth asked, "Your Honor, must I take the stand?"

"Yes, you must take the stand. Take it now." As Shuttlesworth took his seat, the judge offhandedly tipped Fred off that his ruling would likely be the same, whatever his testimony.

"What do you want me to say, Your Honor?" Fred asked in needling fashion. Flushing with anger, Conway barked, "You know what I mean!"

"What do you mean? I don't understand."

"You know what I mean! Are you going to violate any more of our segregation laws?"

Controlling his first inclination to reply, "Hell, yes!" Shuttlesworth answered, "Your Honor, it's hard for me to answer that. I truly don't know."

"You know how to answer. Just answer the question. Are going to violate any more laws?"

"Your Honor, I can't answer that question."

"Lock him up!" Conway angrily ordered the bailiff as he declared Shuttlesworth guilty of the charges and cited him for contempt. The convictions won him a $200 fine and sixty days in jail; the contempt citation carried a $10 fine and twenty-four hours in jail. In addition, Conway placed him under a $5,000 peace bond for his manner of testifying. As was typical of Shuttlesworth's legal strategies, all convictions were appealed and upheld in all state courts. The appeals process continued to the Supreme Court, but in the meantime, Shuttlesworth turned back to more ecclesiastical concerns.[59]

After several months of weighing church, family, and movement needs, Fred finally agreed to accept the new pastorate in Cincinnati. Announcing the decision on Friday, June 2, 1961, the same day Judge Conway cited him for contempt, Shuttlesworth made Revelation Baptist Church one of the few congregations ever to call a new pastor while that individual was in jail. In his announcement he acknowledged that he intended to retain his residence in Birmingham temporarily and that his commitments in civil rights would continue. His tenure at Revelation would begin August 1, and in the meantime he would preach in Cincinnati whenever possible.[60]

The Cincinnati press greeted the news of Shuttlesworth's coming with speculation on the new minister's importance to the civil rights movement: "Perhaps no other Negro in recent times has been jailed more, become involved in more litigation, and absorbed as much abuse. . . . Shuttlesworth is one of the nation's important symbols of the non-violent militancy of the new Negro." The *Cincinnati Herald* ran an article headlined, "Rev. Shuttlesworth Involved in More Legal Battles Than Any Other Freedom Fighter in U.S." His legal involvements were figured as amounting to nine criminal and twelve civil cases and as entailing total sentences of 810 days in jail and $2,400 in fines. Shuttlesworth commented: "Sometimes I have a hard time keeping up with all of them myself. You know, I didn't really mean to get involved in so much. I just want to be free." Another article quoted Martin Luther King's comment that "the departure of the Birmingham leader is a sad thing for Alabama and Birmingham in particular, and the state will take a long time to find someone to fill the shoes of the young leader." Shuttlesworth, however, had no intention of letting anyone fill those shoes.[61]

That seemed to hold true for Bethel as well as for the ACMHR. By the time the Shuttlesworth family bid farewell to the congregation, some members had begun to grumble that he was attempting to pastor both churches simultaneously. Because of their pastor's frequent trips out of town, particularly to Cincinnati, some of the Bethel congregation thought he had accepted Revelation's call even earlier than June. Others complained that his period of notice to Bethel was too lengthy or objected that he accepted full salaries from both churches between June and August. In reality procedures for pastoral transition in Baptist churches, white or black, vary greatly and depend on the particular congregation and pastor involved. Shuttlesworth had been in pulpits other than Bethel so often for so long that he hardly noticed any difference when he began alternating Sundays between Bethel and Revelation. In the church's eagerness to procure such a prestigious pastor as Shuttlesworth, Revelation willingly put him on salary during the period between his announcement and his assumption of pastoral duties, and he was within his rights to accept both salaries. Nevertheless, the matter created a small firestorm of protest, particularly from a member named Reuben Davis.[62]

The disagreement put only a slight temporary damper on his departure from Bethel. On his final Sunday, at the "Concluding Services and Friendship Hour," Fred spoke from Pauline texts about his forgetting the past and pressing toward the mark of God's high calling (Phil. 3:13–14) and about his having "fought the good fight, finished the race, and kept the faith" (2 Tim. 4:6–7). Church members James Revis and Veronica Chappell, representing the trustees and young people, respectively, gave tributes to Shuttlesworth for his work at Bethel. Fellow pastors J. L. Ware, T. L. Lane, and J. S. Phifer celebrated his accomplishments both in the congregation and in the city. In a column for the *Pittsburgh Courier*, Shuttlesworth reflected on his tenure at Bethel. He recounted the harassment, crank calls, and phone taps by which the police attempted to drive a wedge between him and his congregation. Yet they "carried on with a faith that we had a date with destiny, a job to do, and a determination to do it. The mere threat of a bombing—much less harassment—would have been enough to depose a minister from most any church in Birmingham. The extra sacrifices of additional light bills, gas bills, and things needed for the comfort of the guards, have never proved a sore point at Bethel. She is a great church, and only history can accord her full glory." He thus bid them farewell, saying with some satisfaction, "I leave them further along than I found them on the road to freedom."[63]

His following in the ACMHR responded to his pastoral move by affirming their loyalty to him without regard to his place of residence. Just after making his move public, Shuttlesworth addressed them at their fifth anniversary celebration. In his president's address Shuttlesworth told them, with no indication that his move to Cincinnati would affect his activities in Birmingham in the least, that "we must go forth, not knowing what the future holds for us; but trusting in him who holds the future. We must keep our faith that freedom is worth suffering for and, if necessary, worth dying for." In his characteristic manner, common to many preachers and easily interpreted by skeptics as false humility, he said: "As your leader, I do not seek the applause or praise of men, for these are changeable and unlasting. Rather, I seek the favor of Him who chose me, who called me, who leads me, and who has brought me so far. My native state would like to disown me. I am wounded here in my own city and state, but I am healed by the wounds in His side. . . . Jesus is my director and my Captain; and woe unto me if I preach not the gospel—the social gospel of freedom, of peace, justice and humanitarianism." The natural ease with which Shuttlesworth wrapped a boastful confidence in the packaging of pious humility often grated on the religious sensibilities of some of Birmingham's African American middle class. His loyal ACMHR members, however, long since won over by his actions more than his words, lapped it up. They unanimously adopted a resolution to reassert their support of Shuttlesworth's leadership despite his impending move to Cincinnati. Extolling his "personal courage, personal sacrifice in the face of perils, complete honesty, integrity," and commitment to nonviolence, the members pledged continued support for him as leader and urged others to do likewise. In addition, they "declared that he has full authority, as in the past, to do all things at all times necessary to insure the continued progress of this Movement."[64]

Shuttlesworth had earned a powerful and at times breathtaking loyalty from his followers in the Birmingham movement. In 1959, when sociologist Jacquelyne Clarke conducted her survey of the membership, some 80 percent disagreed with a statement that "leaders have too much to say about organizational affairs." Of those, almost 62 percent strongly disagreed with the view that leaders—and that primarily meant Shuttlesworth—wielded too much authority. Thus, at one of the final mass meetings before Shuttlesworth's departure, one speaker called on ACMHR members to go by train with their leader to Cincinnati as a "farewell gesture." Even Commissioner Connor's detectives observed and testified to the ACMHR's fervent love for Shuttlesworth when, at a mass meeting, they noted treasurer Bill Shortridge's salute to Fred's financial integrity, telling the crowd that Shuttlesworth "did not receive one penny from the organization." Shortridge added: "God gave him to us, and he is our leader. We will follow him." The audience rose for an extended standing ovation and then, in the detectives' words, would "jump up and go down to shake hands with Shuttlesworth."[65]

Later in the year, the detectives heard Ed Gardner complain that like Christ before Pilate, Shuttlesworth's legal pilgrimage proceeded from one "crooked court" to another. On still another occasion, a minister, with Shuttlesworth in mind, reminded the mass meeting audience that "the Lord sent a Jew to free the Jews, and now, he has sent a black man to free the black people." Such devotion remained unshakable among a vast majority of members. With adulation of this magnitude, it is no wonder that Shuttlesworth once told a mass meeting audience, "If I was sick you would make me well with all the enthusiasm you have for me," promising, "I will never leave Birmingham permanently . . . until the fight is over." He left for the new parsonage at Revelation convinced that further battles remained, particularly over the effort to integrate Birmingham's parks and downtown department stores.[66]

Through the summer and fall of 1961, Shuttlesworth began the process of acclimating to a new city and a new pastorate. His notoriety after the Freedom Rides and the attention generated by the CBS broadcast of "Who Speaks For Birmingham?" won for him a new opportunity to write an opinion piece for the *Pittsburgh Courier*. His prominence in the movement also led a contingent within CORE to call for Shuttlesworth to replace James Farmer as national director. At CORE's convention in September, Gladys Harrington, a member of CORE's New York branch, sought Farmer's ouster, in part because Farmer had married a white woman. Campaigning among a number of the CORE chapters, Harrington needed a prominent name in the movement with which to counter the popularity of Farmer. She contacted Shuttlesworth, who remained noncommittal. Nonetheless, rumor spread among the delegates that Shuttlesworth had agreed to accept the position if it actually became available. Farmer in turn phoned Fred, who confirmed that he had spoken with Harrington but had indicated no interest in replacing Farmer. Eventually Farmer's supporters squelched the attempted coup in the corridors and gave him a strong vote of confidence. The incident, however, gave evidence of Shuttlesworth's prominence in the movement.[67]

Earlier that month Shuttlesworth and more than thirty other African American ministers rushed to Martin Luther King's defense in an ecclesiastical-political controversy of the first order. King and National Baptist Convention president Joseph H. Jackson had developed a powerful national rivalry, much like the rift between Shuttlesworth and Ware in Birmingham. Jackson had been president of the convention since 1953 and a friend of the King family since Martin was a boy. The younger King, now the most prominent African American in the nation, had designs on Jackson's fiefdom. Although little interested in the presidency for himself, King had hoped to establish the NBC as a national base for the civil rights movement. Jackson, politically conservative in addition to being jealous of King's meteoric rise, opposed the movement's growing advocacy of direct action and civil disobedience. On one occasion Jackson criticized the civil rights movement, complaining, "Some Negroes talk too much about racial integration, and not enough about racial elevation." Shuttlesworth scoffed at what he called "a sickening statement." He asserted to the contrary: "I think every time a preacher preaches to a black congregation, he's talking about elevation. . . . And I think it just shows how far back he was either talking or thinking, because you can't talk about America without talking about integration."[68]

Aiming for a showdown, King's forces had spent great energy recruiting Brooklyn minister Gardner C. Taylor to run against Jackson and a large contingent of ministers committed to supporting the "Taylor Team" at the 1961 convention in Kansas City. At the meeting emotions ran dangerously high. In a crowded hall tempers flared, and a shoving match between two columns of conventioneers accidentally caused an elderly minister to fall backward off the stage. The minister, the Reverend A. G. Wright of Detroit, died of a crushed skull two days later. After his election victory, Jackson blamed King for "master-mind[ing] the invasion of the convention floor . . . which resulted in the death of a delegate." Less concerned with denominational matters and less convinced of the NBC's usefulness to the civil rights movement, Shuttlesworth nonetheless attended the convention and enthusiastically supported Taylor. He also signed a joint telegram calling for Jackson to retract his character assassination of King, which would only "serve the purposes of the segregationist forces in America."[69]

Shuttlesworth did not follow King's lead uncritically, however, and was occasionally put off by King's careful, deliberative style. In September, Shuttlesworth quickly decided in favor of petitioning President Kennedy to grant clemency to activist Carl Braden, whereas King delayed a decision on the matter. A field secretary of the Southern Conference Education Fund, Braden had been convicted of contempt of Congress after refusing to answer whether he was a communist before a House subcommittee. He had also been convicted of sedition in a Kentucky state court. After Braden began a prison term in May 1961, his wife, Anne, sought the support of King, Shuttlesworth, and other civil rights leaders for a clemency petition.[70]

Shuttlesworth had signed onto the idea immediately, but King, worried about possible accusations of communist associations, hesitated. Asked to sign the petition, King responded with a nervous laugh and said, "Don't you know they call me a communist, too?" "Yeah, but nobody believes it," she replied unfazed, explaining why his support was crucial to the effort. She left King to think over her request and waited two weeks without word. Finally, a somewhat exasperated Shuttlesworth told Braden, "Now, Anne, we just got to go ahead with this thing. We can't wait any longer on Martin. I'll tell you about Martin. It just takes so long for Martin to get up that mountain of decision on anything. Carl will be out of prison before we get this going. Just forget about Martin." When a group of ministers and other activists went to the White House in late September to deliver the petitions, Shuttlesworth, Abernathy, and Wyatt Walker represented the SCLC among them; King did not attend.[71]

Still, the most important element of Shuttlesworth's activity remained his return to Birmingham every other week for mass meetings and strategy sessions. Shuttlesworth's strategy was partly determined by the steady stream of legal decisions affecting him. In late September the Alabama Supreme Court refused to review Shuttlesworth's convictions in both the Freedom Rides and the 1960 sit-in case.[72] A month later, on October 23, Fred returned to Birmingham in anticipation of a ruling on the desegregation of the city's recreational facilities. Having pursued this goal since 1958, Shuttlesworth had followed with a suit a year later in U.S. district court. As Shuttlesworth returned for a mass meeting on the night before Judge H. H. Grooms would hear arguments, the minister expected what would become one of his most important victories.

Ed Gardner, the vice president of the ACMHR, explaining his own role as a "vice" that merely held things together "until the real thing comes along," introduced Shuttlesworth to an audience of some 350 persons at Bethel AME Church. Calling on the congregation to give Shuttlesworth a standing ovation, Gardner made the congregation repeat the ritual when the level of their fervor did not meet his satisfaction. Taking the pulpit to the cheers of his followers, Shuttlesworth told them:

> Every time I am in the city of Birmingham, I am looking some judge in the face. I have never been before any judge for doing anything that hurt anyone. All the times I have been before a judge was for trying to get rights for my people. . . . Tomorrow, when I go before Judge Grooms, I will be depending on God. If I have to go to court, God will go with me. I have been in jail and court before. I am ready to go. I have stood before judges all over the state, and I feel sorry for these judges. I am right and they are wrong. God is not with these judges. God has been talking to me and he tells me what to do. . . . God will take over the courts and run them. God is with us in the Federal courts.

. . . We lose all our cases in the lower courts, but when we get to the bigger courts we will win. We know we will win because God is with us.

The immediacy and the certainty with which Shuttlesworth "heard" the voice of God vexed the more rationalistic spirits of some in Birmingham's black professional class, but they spoke powerfully to the less sophisticated members of the ACMHR. Buoyed by their leader's confidence, several women were caught up in a frenzy of religious ecstasy, repeatedly shouting, "God is with us; we will win!"[73]

The celebrations, at least in the African American community, began in earnest the next day when Grooms fulfilled the ACMHR's expectations. In August the judge had ruled unconstitutional a city ordinance that made it "unlawful for Negroes and white persons to play together." With the same logic Grooms now voided all ordinances segregating all of Birmingham's recreational facilities. He ruled that the city was not required to operate or maintain the parks but that any such facilities run under city auspices "must be [operated] upon a precisely equal basis by citizens of all races and colors, entirely without discrimination of any kind or nature based upon race or color." Grooms further issued a permanent injunction restraining the city from enforcing segregation in any recreational facilities after January 15, 1962. The expansive ruling desegregated Birmingham's art museum, Municipal Auditorium, six swimming pools, four golf courses, thirty-eight playgrounds, and sixty-seven parks. It also included Legion Field, where every year crowds of fifty thousand watched the University of Alabama football team square off against their hated rivals at Auburn University.[74]

The day after the decision, Connor announced a forthcoming appeal and simultaneously asked Grooms to delay integrating the parks until the Supreme Court had ruled on the appeal. In the event that the judge rejected the request, Connor vowed that the city commission would close all facilities affected by Grooms's decision. He concluded with the opinion that the "great majority of the people in Birmingham do not want integration. We have given Negroes public parks . . . and I don't believe the great majority of Negroes are behind this Negro lawyer from Jacksonville, Florida [Ernest Jackson] and the so-called Rev. Shuttlesworth, who now lives in Cincinnati. These two are pushing this thing for financial benefits."[75]

At his next mass meeting Shuttlesworth rejoiced with his followers, reminding them of all the activities suddenly open to them. "Last year the white people and the Negro people swam together in Louisville, and for the life of me," he chuckled, "I could not see where any black had faded off in the water. Get you a bathing suit and go swimming with the white people and dare any Policeman to bother you." Saving his more acerbic words for Connor and the city commission, he threatened that there would be no peace in the city until officials were willing to confer with the Alabama Christian Movement for Human Rights on the closing of the parks. "The Negro people do not want the parks closed—the white people do not want the parks closed. Three men in our city have the power to do what they want to with these parks. If 300,000 people are fools enough to let three men close their parks, then let them close them. But after January 15, if a white man goes into these parks, let there be Negroes with him."[76]

The city commission had no intention of integrating the parks. Both Connor and Commissioner of Public Improvements J. T. "Jabo" Waggoner had recently been reelected, running on strong segregationist platforms, as had the new mayor, Arthur J. Hanes. Judge Grooms had set his January 15 desegregation date just two days after their inauguration, and the commissioners argued that to integrate the parks would be a step closer to integrated schools, a prospect that was anathema to them. In early December Hanes ordered the dismissal of every park's employees, effective on January 1, 1962, and the closing of all recreational facilities on the same date. In quick succession public statements opposing this course of action were issued by such white groups as the Birmingham Jaycees, the Young Men's Business Club, and the Baptist Pastors Conference, which pledged to work with officials "to arrive at a Christian solution to these problems." Other private citizens wrote Connor to register their support. One woman particularly took issue with the ministers who, she argued, "would do more good to attend to their church work and quit dabbling in politics—let their members who have the largest number of children have their say, not the ministers." Bolstered by their perceptions of the people's views, Connor and the commission proceeded with plans to close the parks. In addition, Connor once again attacked Shuttlesworth as an irresponsible leader with communist sympathies, while the mayor, ignoring the requests of many of his own supporters, publicly refused to meet with African American leaders on the parks issue.[77]

On New Year's Day, 1962, city officials closed the parks and put up No Trespassing signs at their entrances. The commission rejected a petition bearing the names of more than twelve hundred whites calling for the parks to be reopened and garnered still more criticism in the process. The Birmingham Chamber of

Commerce and the two major newspapers supported open parks, which in turn strained relations between the business community and the commission. Decisions such as these, coupled with national embarrassment over Birmingham's responses to the Freedom Rides, gave business leaders reason to fear for the city's economic development if the city's political leadership remained as it was. By the summer of 1962 young lawyers David Vann and Charles Morgan launched a petition drive to change Birmingham from a commission to a mayor-council form of local government.[78]

Meanwhile, in the African American community, ministers J. L. Ware and C. Herbert Oliver, leaders of the Inter-Citizens Committee (ICC), issued a statement supporting open parks. Indicating their unreserved approval of Judge Grooms's ruling, Ware and Oliver also congratulated Shuttlesworth and the ACMHR "for the courageous fight they have been waging against the evils of segregation. They have exercised great fortitude and patience, and have shown great faith in American democracy." The statement further criticized those who sought to "thwart the effect of the court ruling." Such attitudes, argued the ICC, would not strengthen "the moral fiber of our nation" and "could weaken and destroy our national structure."[79]

Some two weeks earlier, an ad hoc group of leaders known as the Committee of 14, which was led by millionaire business leader A. G. Gaston, met on December 14 and 21 with a group of white leaders to discuss the situation. It is significant that the group neither included nor mentioned Shuttlesworth and remained silent on the decision regarding the parks. Gaston and his associates, erstwhile attorney Arthur Shores and wealthy insurance executive John Drew, called for a mass meeting for Friday, January 5, to report the results of their meetings with white leaders and to plan further action. These meetings revealed efforts by members of the black middle class to circumvent Shuttlesworth's leadership and negotiate with their white counterparts without his input. They excluded Shuttlesworth in part because white business leaders who differed with Connor over the parks issue nonetheless shared with Connor a desire not to legitimize Shuttlesworth's claims to leadership. The black professionals also used Shuttlesworth's new residence outside of Birmingham as a cover for their major reason for excluding him—namely, their uneasiness with his style. Such efforts to minimize him as a leader eventually antagonized Shuttlesworth and created among his followers a resentment toward "leaders" they saw as Johnny-come-latelies who, unlike Shuttlesworth, had been unwilling to risk anything for the movement. For the moment, however, the economic power structure of

Birmingham was beginning to take seriously the calls to confer with the city's black citizens. This was a step forward, even if the commercial elite remained fearful of being seen meeting with Fred Shuttlesworth.

In any event, Shuttlesworth had more pressing matters on which to focus. Eight days into the new year, ACMHR faithful were hoping for a Supreme Court reversal of Shuttlesworth's and Phifer's 1958 disorderly conduct convictions in connection with nonsegregated bus riding. Instead, in a brief order, the high court announced its refusal to review the case on the basis of a technicality—ACMHR lawyers had failed to file papers in the Alabama Court of Appeals within sixty days of the original conviction. Receiving the news while in Birmingham for his regular mass meeting, an irritated Shuttlesworth lashed out at his attorneys. "From now on I will tell them how to fight my cases," he pledged, his mind on forthcoming appeals of the Freedom Rides convictions. "I will get another sentence tomorrow when I go back to court, but this time I am going to see that my Calhouns don't mess things up for me again." At the same meeting, Diane Nash, who had worked with Shuttlesworth in coordinating the Nashville Freedom Rides, encouraged the crowd to march to city hall and demand to be jailed with Shuttlesworth and Phifer. "If Shuttlesworth and Phifer are guilty, we all are," she argued.[80]

Acting quickly to come to Shuttlesworth's aid, SCLC executive director Wyatt T. Walker penned an emergency letter requesting that all SCLC board members wire their concerns to Attorney General Robert Kennedy. Walker advised that board members request an audience with Kennedy before February 1, the tentative date of Fred's surrender to Birmingham authorities. Within a week King sent a joint telegram to Robert Kennedy on behalf of several civil rights organizations, including the SCLC, SCEF, SNCC, ACMHR, MIA, and others. Apprising the attorney general of Shuttlesworth's situation, the wire asked him to intervene and help prevent "the execution of these sentences."[81]

The statement pointed out that both the district court (Judge Grooms) and the circuit court of appeals had ruled that the ordinance had been unconstitutionally applied. Shuttlesworth and Phifer were thus arrested, convicted, and subject to serve sentences for violating an ordinance that had been declared unconstitutional in two federal courts. Acknowledging the lawyers' mistake in filing the appeal, the statement argued that "no technicality should be allowed to make two American citizens serve jail sentences on charges that our federal courts have declared were illegal in the first place—especially on an issue such as bus segregation which our courts and the public opinion of the nation have so clearly denounced as wrong." Reminding Kennedy of the tense racial situation, especially in light of recent controversy over the parks, supporters noted the particular danger of subjecting Shuttlesworth to incarceration in Birmingham: "The man who has led the drive for this great victory for human rights, as well as so many other civil rights battles in Birmingham in recent years, is Mr. Shuttlesworth. To the Birmingham segregationists, he is a symbol of this struggle; he is hated by many people, just as he is honored by all right-thinking people both South and North. But because of the emotion involved, we frankly fear for his physical safety if he has to serve this sentence." The Justice Department offered a great deal of sympathy but little concrete assistance. Assistant Attorney General for Civil Rights Burke Marshall held to a strict constructionist theory that limited federal intervention in matters of law enforcement and could not "discern any basis upon which this Department might possibly intervene."[82]

By January 16, bombs—legal, political, and otherwise—had fallen in Alabama, or at least in Birmingham. That night three African American churches fell victim to bombers who had not done their research—they targeted churches that had not participated in ACMHR meetings or activities, including the New Bethel Baptist, which they mistakenly thought to be Shuttlesworth's church. Later, Connor told reporters, "We know that Negroes did it." Of more significance, earlier that day Judge Grooms sentenced five assailants of the Freedom Riders to a year's probation and gave the sixth a concurrent term with a prior burglary conviction. The irony, as Taylor Branch later noted, was that whereas none of the assailants served any jail time for attacking the Greyhound bus, Shuttlesworth would serve ninety days for sitting at the front of a city bus. In perhaps the biggest blockbuster of all, Connor announced the night before that he was running for governor of Alabama and promised to buy one hundred new police dogs for use in the event of more Freedom Rides. He also ordered the arrests of Shuttlesworth and Phifer.[83]

On January 24 *Birmingham World* editor Emory O. Jackson made light of white reaction to the Supreme Court's nondecision on the Shuttlesworth case. Mocking white southern newspapers that treated the decision as if it had reversed previous rulings outlawing bus segregation, Jackson viewed the matter, based as it was on a legal technicality, as a minor setback. "The Reverend Mr. Shuttlesworth, an old hand in the fight to civilize Birmingham, long ago must have reached the conclusion that freedom is not worth much to anyone unless he is willing to go to jail or risk his life for it." The next day Shuttlesworth willingly surrendered to Birmingham police officials in the lobby of the A. G. Gaston Building. Although Ruby and the children worried about his spending time in Bull Connor's jail, Fred, once his pique with his lawyers had passed, cheerfully shared a cell with his friend Phifer. They sang and prayed together and preached to many of their fellow inmates, some of whom were converted by their impromptu sermons. The preachers' spirits were lifted as well by the celebrity status they enjoyed while in jail. Fellow prisoners treated them as special, offering them sugar for their coffee and presenting other tokens of respect. The preachers regaled a constant stream of visitors with stories of their imprisonment and pious homilies of how God was keeping them safe in the "Bull's den" or would soon deliver them altogether. ACMHR colleagues Georgia Price, Lola Hendricks, and Fred's cousin Julia Rainge helped Shuttlesworth take care of movement and churchly business by placing long distance calls. They also kept Ruby and the family posted on his condition and the latest happenings in Birmingham.[84]

Outside Fred's cell, activities became more frenetic as King and his SCLC staff stepped in to help speed his release. Wyatt Walker called on New York attorney William Kunstler to fly to Birmingham to assist Shuttlesworth's attorneys Arthur Shores and Orzell Billingsley, who applied for a federal writ of habeas corpus. A hearing before Judge Grooms, who would determine whether Shuttlesworth had been lawfully detained, was scheduled for Wednesday, February 2, eight days after he had been jailed. King again appealed to Robert Kennedy on Shuttlesworth's behalf, writing, "The Reverend Mr. Shuttlesworth does not shrink from jail-going, but I have grave fears for his safety in the light of the recent rash of bombings and general bitterness directed toward this courageous non-violent leader. It is clear that hundreds of segregationists, in and out of jail, would like nothing better than to do bodily harm to the Rev. Mr. Shuttlesworth. We respectfully request immediate surveillance by your office of this situation as a precautionary measure to insure his safety." King also wrote letters to most of his clergy friends, asking them to take up offerings in the church services to help defray legal expenses.[85]

In still another effort of support for Shuttlesworth, King and the SCLC joined with the ACMHR and the Cincinnati Ministers Conference to supply preachers for Shuttlesworth's and Phifer's pulpits while they were in jail. Thus Revelation Baptist Church enjoyed a stellar lineup of pulpiteers, including Wyatt T. Walker, C. K. Steele of Tallahassee, Kelly Miller Smith of Nashville, Ralph Abernathy of Montgomery, and King himself. If the incarceration continued, Fred's Birmingham colleagues Edward Gardner, Nelson H. Smith Jr., and J. C. Parker would fill in, followed by Cincinnati ministers L. V. Booth, Otis Moss, and T. L. Lane. In addition, the Sunday school superintendent at Revelation spearheaded a campaign that collected six hundred lettergrams and night letters to be forwarded to the U.S. attorney general asking for intervention into the matter.[86]

The night after Shuttlesworth and Phifer were jailed, a mass meeting was held at the Metropolitan African Methodist Episcopal Zion Church under the auspices of A. G. Gaston's ad hoc organization. Many ACMHR followers attended the meeting, in part to gauge the resolve of the middle class to support their leader. Although skeptical, the ACMHR faithful left relatively pleased when the body passed a resolution "giving unanimous endorsement to the efforts and sacrifices and spirit of the Rev. Fred Shuttlesworth and the Rev. James Phifer, and we pledge to Rev. Shuttlesworth our prayers, our support, and our services."[87]

The following Monday night, at their regularly scheduled meeting, ACMHR members heard leaders read twenty telegrams of support for Shuttlesworth, including one from former Alabama governor James A. "Big Jim" Folsom, a liberal on race issues who was then running for another term. Another telegram, receiving a much less enthusiastic response, came from Burke Marshall. It expressed the attorney general's sympathy in the matter but said that any action on Shuttlesworth's behalf would have to come from local courts. As the meeting concluded, treasurer Bill Shortridge admonished the congregation to send letters of encouragement and support to Shuttlesworth and Phifer in care of the city jail. Soon, however, Shuttlesworth and Phifer complained through Shortridge to the FBI special agent in charge of Birmingham that their mail was being withheld unless the ministers allowed it to be censored by police authorities. This was another ploy, judged Shortridge, to harass Shuttlesworth and to discourage other "freedom-loving citizens" from rallying to his support.[88]

Few persons seemed inhibited from supporting Shuttlesworth and Phifer. Meeting on Abraham Lincoln's birthday at the Sixteenth Street Baptist Church, the largest African American church in Birmingham, a capacity crowd gathered, with several hundred lingering outside without seats, to hear King pay tribute to the Birmingham movement and its leader. Sixteenth Street Baptist Church, formerly pastored by Shuttlesworth opponent Luke Beard, had not been a regular site for ACMHR meetings. The church's new minister, the Reverend John Cross, who had come to Birmingham in part to participate in civil rights activities, reversed his predecessor's policy and opened the sanctuary to the

ACMHR. Still, the congregation's ideas of middle-class decorum held the more emotionally vigorous style of Shuttlesworth and his organization at arm's length. Even Connor's detectives noticed a change in the worshipers' demeanor at this meeting: "The service was conducted differently from the usual meetings. . . . Rev. [C. Herbert] Oliver was then called on for prayer. His prayer was an extended one, but delivered more dignified than any I have heard since attending these meetings." With A. G. Gaston, Miles College president Lucius H. Pitts, and the Reverend J. L. Ware in attendance, the black professionals were out in force—primarily in order to hear King. After two standing ovations, before moving into a boilerplate civil rights address, King complimented the ACMHR and its president. He said that Shuttlesworth would be remembered in history "for what he has done for Birmingham and all the nation. He is in jail, but he has transformed it from a place of shame to a place of dignity."[89]

In a similar meeting in Cleveland, Ruby Shuttlesworth drummed up moral and financial support for Fred. Quite willing in her own right to play the public martyr, Ruby told the audience:

We have been beaten, jailed, bombed and suffered many indignities before. We have learned to live with fear and understand the price that must be paid for the struggle for our civil rights and first-class citizenship. . . . I am part of this struggle. I have been ever since it started. We all feel that no sacrifice is too great to make. I have no feeling other than to cooperate in the work of obtaining first class citizenship with him. I am happy that our sacrifices are beginning to bear fruit. . . . I have been shouldering the burden along with my husband and will be with him no matter what the cost. This latest episode, however, could just be the one that could tax my physical stamina to the very limit.

The crowd responded warmly to Ruby's recounting of the family's struggles, and her appearance was covered by the local black newspaper, the *Cleveland Courier,* which heralded Fred's role as "a national hero to nearly 20 million Negroes."[90]

Meanwhile, if Shuttlesworth and Phifer had played the roles of apostles Paul and Silas, engaging in jailhouse singing and preaching (Acts 16), Shuttlesworth also followed Paul's epistolary example. He managed to smuggle letters and news releases out of jail by hiding them in the garbage. Once Shuttlesworth stuffed a message in a biscuit. Another time he hid one under the shirt of an ACMHR member. In one instance that gained attention in Birmingham, Shuttlesworth managed to write a petition, later signed by seventy-four ACMHR members, to Mayor Hanes and the city and county commissions. Amused with his own efforts at getting under his adversaries' skins, Shuttlesworth asked them to desegregate the courthouse facilities in Jefferson County, including water fountains, rest rooms, courtroom seating, and city jobs. Noting the inscription over the courthouse door and quoting Hebrew scripture, he wrote: "It is inconceivable that denial of rights and due process would continue at the courthouse, where the public inscription reads: 'Equal and exact justice to all men of whatever state or persuasion.' And in the administration of justice and affairs of people, we believe that those in authority should be the first to 'do justly, love mercy and walk humbly with thy God' (Mic. 6:8). We have confidence in your honor and your capabilities to quickly eradicate wrongs and exalt equality and human dignity." Connor became almost apoplectic over the lapse of security. Out in a hallway he complained loudly enough to be overheard by a gleeful Shuttlesworth: "How in the hell can they be making news releases in the damn jail?" The mayor's reply captured the commissioner of public safety's sentiment, but expressed it in a somewhat more civil tone: "Ordinarily, I do not carry on correspondence with jailbirds, however, inasmuch as you insist on being extraordinary people, I shall treat you as extraordinary jailbirds. This letter is to acknowledge receipt of your ridiculous so-called petition and to let you know that action is being taken immediately—that is, to throw it in the waste basket. My advice to you is to do the best you can on K. P. [Kitchen Police] duty while confined in the city jail, and I will do my best in running the Mayor's office."[91]

Shuttlesworth could not resist a needling response of his own. He commented on the "honor" of receiving a letter from the city's highest-ranking official during "our unjust and unnecessary confinement." In mock amazement that Hanes had become so exercised over a petition that reflected the traditional and lawful manner of seeking redress of grievances, Shuttlesworth continued:

> Your immediate response of throwing it into the waste basket may indeed have served you a momentary relief of the burdens of office. But it no more relieves you of your responsibility of sane and righteous action on it than did Pilate's cowardly washing of his hands relieve him of the duty to set Jesus Christ free. . . . Waste baskets cannot be substituted for the courage to honestly face racial problems and the will to keep step with time. Rather, the proper place, and correct way, is

around the table of conference, men to men, people to people. . . . The fact that you gloat over our serving jail terms for actions declared by federal courts to be Constitutional is, in itself, an indictment of the City of Birmingham—and especially its leadership. Your calling us . . . jailbirds . . . can only be interpreted as official acknowledgment of our determination to win freedom, even if we must suffer the indignities of working 12 hours [a day], 7 days a week in jail, washing thousands of dishes, and lifting heavy garbage cans and cartons of food. Finally Sir, we surrender voluntarily to Birmingham officials because we fully believe in that which we seek: Freedom and Justice for all. If serving this or other terms will hasten that day when men will cease to act as enemies, then we are at your service.[92]

Amused by Hanes's and Connor's responses to his communiqués, Shuttlesworth bided his time and entertained his visitors as his counsel prepared legal maneuvers to secure his release. On February 1, Arthur D. Shores, Orzell Billingsley, and William Kunstler arrived at a packed courtroom for Shuttlesworth's habeas corpus hearing before Judge Grooms. They found, however, a main courtroom undergoing repairs and the smaller courtroom crowding hundreds of Shuttlesworth's followers out of witnessing the proceedings. When Shuttlesworth and Phifer were brought into the room, Kunstler, who had never met his new client, introduced himself and said, "I hope that we'll be able to do something for you, Rev. Shuttlesworth." "Hope is all I live on," the preacher replied. "Just do the best you can."[93]

As proceedings began, Shuttlesworth's lawyers would have to show Grooms that no recourse was left to them in Alabama state courts. The Alabama and U.S. Supreme Courts had ruled that by filing a transcript of the original trial with the Jefferson County Circuit Court three days after the sixty-day time limit, Shuttlesworth's lawyers had deliberately avoided available state procedures. In response, lawyers brought forth testimony showing that a court reporter had miscalculated the time in which to transcribe his shorthand notes. The defendant, they argued, was therefore not at fault. Judge Grooms nonetheless dismissed the petition and ruled that state remedies had not yet been exhausted. As the bailiff led Shuttlesworth out of the courtroom, Fred stopped at the attorneys' table and said with a broad smile, "Don't worry. You'll find a way."[94]

The next step, an appeal to the U.S. Fifth Circuit Court of Appeals in New

Orleans, led to another dead end because on February 12 Judge Richard T. Rives upheld Grooms's ruling. When this approach failed, Kunstler and the other attorneys, now unable to test Grooms's ruling and believing that the case contained important constitutional issues, filed another writ of habeas corpus directly with the U.S. Supreme Court. They argued that Birmingham officials had not specified the defendant's misconduct, but rather had arrested him because he had been seen in the company of some African Americans immediately prior to their taking "white" seats on a city bus.[95]

On February 26 the Supreme Court acted on Shuttlesworth's petition in a brief unsigned but unanimous opinion ordering Grooms to release Shuttlesworth on bail within five days if the Alabama courts failed to do so. This meant that his lawyers were forced once more into Alabama state courts, this time to contend that Shuttlesworth had been convicted unjustly. The next day Orzell Billingsley requested and was denied a habeas corpus writ and a petition for bail by Alabama Circuit Court judge George Lewis Bailes. On the following day Billingsley filed a request for bail in the Alabama Court of Appeals and after being denied there made a similar request in the Alabama Supreme Court. Finally, on March 1, when the Alabama Supreme Court also denied the request for bail, Shuttlesworth's attorneys had exhausted all state remedies and were free to take their requests back into the friendlier federal court of Judge Grooms. Reaching the judge's Birmingham office late that afternoon, Shuttlesworth lawyers Shores and Billingsley presented the requisite papers to Grooms, who immediately ordered their client's release on $300 bail.[96]

Legal wrangling over *Shuttlesworth v. Moore* continued until Grooms eventually decided the case as it came to the end of what he termed its "devious course." In a nine-page opinion the judge ruled that there had been "no evidence whatever in the record to support the conviction" on the basis of his having declared unconstitutional the very ordinance on which the conviction was based. The ACMHR and its leader would have to wait until December 1963 for this final outcome. For now, however, the ACMHR celebrated the release of their hero. At their next mass meeting, they cheered as Wyatt Walker with euphoric exaggeration hailed Shuttlesworth as the "greatest man in the nation." Bull Connor had found out, Walker preached, that Shuttlesworth "could not be scared, or bluffed, and that he was one man that would not back down." Whites could have John Glenn as their hero, he told them, but African Americans had Fred Shuttlesworth.[97]

The elated ministers shook thirty-six days worth of the dust from Bull Connor's jail off their feet. Jubilant in victory, Fred issued a not-so-veiled threat to the city before departing for Cincinnati: "Whites can't stop us now. Negroes are beginning to realize Birmingham is not so powerful after all—not in the face of a federal edict. . . . There was no peace for 'Bull' when I was in Jail and certainly will be no peace for him now that we are out."[98]

Shuttlesworth had even bigger plans for Birmingham. Midway through his hitch in the Birmingham jail, he had indicated his intentions in a letter to Walker. He wrote primarily to thank the SCLC staff and the preachers who had helped fill his pulpit. He indicated his delight in being a part of an experience in which "brotherhood is being demonstrated for the world to see." He also registered his pleasure that his wife, family, and congregation were being comforted by the presence of civil rights leaders. "It is good for the Church," he wrote, "to be affiliated in the 20th century suffering for freedom."[99]

Unintimidated by his incarceration, however, he pressed the SCLC to stir up further action in Birmingham, suggesting they challenge segregated fountains and toilets in the city's new airport. Also, he speculated, the SCLC could send a mixed delegation to stay in segregated hotels during the upcoming SCEF meeting scheduled for Birmingham in April. Always pressing for immediate action, Shuttlesworth wrote, "This should be done at once, or something similar."[100] Compared with the challenges Shuttlesworth had already launched, "something similar" indeed lay in store. But with it would come stunning confrontations, with whites *and* blacks, such as Birmingham had never seen before.

Confrontations

It's Nice to Have You in Birmingham
—Birmingham Chamber of Commerce

S huttlesworth's combative persona naturally created opportunities for conflict, and between March 1961 and the eve of the major demonstrations in 1963, Shuttlesworth clashed with individuals on several fronts. As he pressed for the SCLC to aid his cause in Birmingham, he ran afoul of the black middle class and the white business leaders, both of whom hoped to stave off any appearance of King and the SCLC in Birmingham. This chapter narrates these confrontations, along with those between segregationist and more liberal forces in the political climate of local Birmingham and statewide races. Over this two-year period Shuttlesworth's smaller confrontations had set the stage for a major cataclysm in April 1963.

The Birmingham leader's confrontations with some of the black middle class necessitated postponing a decisive confrontation with Birmingham's white power structure. By the time Shuttlesworth was released in early March, relations between the often prickly minister and some of the black business leaders had become more frayed. Businessman A. G. Gaston and insurance executive John Drew, leaders in the black community by virtue of their wealth, often bristled at Shuttlesworth's fiery, unpolished style. As Birmingham's wealthiest African American, Gaston had prospered by working within the system as it stood, and his pace toward change was much slower than that of Shuttlesworth, whom he occasionally considered a hothead. John Drew, longtime friend of the King family, preferred Martin's more deliberate approach to civil rights leadership. As a classmate of "Daddy" King at Atlanta's Morehouse College, Drew shared with the Kings the aura of being "Morehouse men." Other southern blacks often perceived this school pride as conceit. The best-known black college in the South, Morehouse was known as the educator of the black middle class. Middle-class sentiments of polished classical learning prevailed there, and in Drew's estimation Shuttlesworth suffered by comparison.

Because he lacked skill in the social graces, Shuttlesworth sometimes struck middle-class black professionals as gauche. Shuttlesworth's sometime attorney (and later the first black justice of the Alabama Supreme Court) Oscar W. Adams Jr. noted this element in the middle class's reaction to Shuttlesworth: "They objected to his style. They thought he was crude." One of Shuttlesworth's ACMHR colleagues, Abraham L. Woods Jr., agreed, acknowledging, "He was not as polished. His demeanor was not as dignified as some would like for him to have been." Drew remembered Shuttlesworth visiting his home and continually calling out to the Drews' maid, "Give me some lemonade." The annoyed servant later complained to her sympathetic employer, "What kind of man is this?" To Drew, he was "unsmooth" and ill educated. Other instances led Drew and others to believe that Shuttlesworth had enormous ego needs. Drew later observed: "The only thing that used to sort of annoy me a little bit was his quest for the limelight. I mean I remember when his church was bombed. I think Dr. King was here, and we called trying to find out how he was. He said, 'Doctor, talk to me. Did you see me on television?' He wanted to be in the limelight. He didn't want to be left out, and I sort of thought that wasn't too important."[1] Drew and others of the black middle class disliked Shuttlesworth's uncultured and maladroit mien, even as they disagreed with his methods and suspected his motives. Later in life, Fred tried to minimize his rift with the middle class, claiming he never encountered their hostility. The claim is believable. Shuttlesworth's single-minded focus on his own actions often made him oblivious to the negative ways his actions and words were received by observers. In sum, his social naiveté caused him not to notice the way his rough edges sometimes grated on middle-class sensibilities.

Various middle-class persons also questioned Shuttlesworth's judgment and disliked his unilateral decision making. Many saw him as overly reckless, thereby making matters more difficult in the black community than they needed to be. Some of the ministers considered him a martinet or a dictator and called his followers "Shuttle-lites." Abraham L. Woods Jr. recalled Shuttlesworth's critics saying occasionally, "You all are fools. You all ain't got no sense following crazy Rev. Fred Shuttlesworth. All y'all ain't nothing but fools." Others, he noted, simply thought the followers were "just ignorant, stupid." Woods resented such criticism, though he admitted that there were times when he himself privately questioned Shuttlesworth's decisions. Nevertheless, he continued to follow Shuttlesworth and defer to his judgment. Shuttlesworth's toughness and tenacity, his seeming invincibility and divine protection, overpowered

Woods's occasional doubts and those of other ACMHR faithful. Woods later averred: "Here is a man who seemed to be specially anointed by God—the dynamite can't kill him, you know. . . . So we followed his leadership even at times when, [if] we had to make the decisions ourselves, we probably would have done something else. . . . At times in our minds we differed with him, but he was the anointed one."[2]

Another matter struck more at the heart of the middle-class aversion to Shuttlesworth—his activity was a reproach to more timid African American clergy and professionals. Wyatt Walker, executive director of the SCLC, believed Fred's confrontational activism simply intimidated the vast majority of clergy in Birmingham who had been cowed by segregation: "[Fred] made a lot of black people uncomfortable. . . . He had angered a lot of people in the black community because he was very blunt in his language—you know, talking about Uncle Toms. I don't blame him, because that is what they were. . . . The presence of Fred Shuttlesworth in the early sixties made black people ashamed of themselves. See, it was the uncomfortableness that the presence of a Fred Shuttlesworth created. You have to understand how segregation is like a stain and it's on everybody and Fred represented the person who had the task of going around trying to wash the stain off." On the reluctance of other ministers to challenge segregation in Birmingham, Shuttlesworth was typically blunt: "The cat needed to be belled, but when it came down to who's gon' bell the cat, all the rats got silent."[3]

The few ACMHR faithful with professional status agreed that Shuttlesworth's courage and sacrifice of personal safety stood in stark and embarrassing contrast to the caution of the middle class. Principal Lucinda Robey, an active ACMHR participant from the beginning, often defended Shuttlesworth against the criticism of other black professionals. These professionals, argued Lola Hendricks, "feared for their jobs and did not want us to be involved in this movement. They wanted us to let everything stay as it is." Chiefly, they feared that participation in Shuttlesworth's movement would cost them "our jobs and our homes and our status." James T. Montgomery, the only black physician in Birmingham active in the ACMHR, agreed with Oscar Adams in criticizing other black professionals who believed public support of Shuttlesworth would jeopardize their jobs or get their homes bombed. Beyond this, however, Montgomery pointed to their tendency to see Shuttlesworth as a usurper of their "leader" status in the black community. Shuttlesworth's barber and ACMHR activist

James Armstrong assessed matters even more bluntly: "They were waiting for somebody else to shake the tree and they get the grapes."[4]

Despite middle-class misgivings, Shuttlesworth's six years of bravado had so galvanized large numbers of the African American community that the "black bourgeoisie" were reluctant to disparage Shuttlesworth in public. His popularity among the common people far outstripped theirs and forced them to take him seriously. Hoping to present a united front in their struggle with whites, these economic leaders kept their difficulties with Shuttlesworth a "family matter" within the African American community. At times, events demanded that they defer to his charismatic hold on his followers. Shuttlesworth's imprisonment in early 1962 turned out to be one of those times. Because they had kept their distance from Shuttlesworth's movement since 1956, they had rarely witnessed firsthand the tenacious loyalty of the ACMHR rank and file toward Shuttlesworth. In addition, though they truly admired his courage and persistence, they often speculated that Fred, enamored of his own press clippings, sought to use the civil rights struggle to win a larger, more prestigious pulpit for himself. That having been accomplished with his move to Cincinnati, these black professionals underestimated Shuttlesworth and his following, expecting him gradually to disappear from the action in Birmingham. Shuttlesworth's thirty-six-day incarceration proved that Birmingham still had much to hear from its not-quite-favorite son.

White Birmingham's gradual realization of the wisdom of negotiating with the black community also became an element in Shuttlesworth's confrontations with the black middle class. In December 1961, the desegregation of the city parks convinced some white business leaders of severe economic repercussions if the city commission carried out its threats to close the parks. During the Freedom Rides, a group of white business leaders attending an International Rotary Club convention in Tokyo was embarrassed by worldwide news accounts of the debacle in their city. Now convinced that the city's hard-line approach had to be moderated, Sidney Smyer, president of the Birmingham Realty Company and incoming president of the chamber of commerce, vowed to help limit Connor's role and avoid similar embarrassments in the future. Soon after returning home, he formed the Committee of 100, a resource group composed of the chief executive officers of virtually every business, law firm, and professional group in Birmingham. Along with the Birmingham Downtown Improvement Association, Smyer's supercommittee resolved to form a biracial subgroup to study racial problems. Racial polarization, however, made any compromise seem like a sellout of principle. Smyer and his committee feared that negotiating with a hard-liner such as Shuttlesworth would stimulate a similarly hard-line response from Connor's following, thus jeopardizing efforts to build wider support for their initiatives. In addition, to the degree that white business leaders had any African American contacts at all, they were primarily with their counterparts in the black business community. Consequently, when black and white groups secretly began to consult on ways to avoid the closure of the parks, they both failed to invite Shuttlesworth to the table. The whites did not want to invite him; the blacks did not insist that they do so. Shuttlesworth's stay in the Birmingham jail, however, made his absence from the table impossible to ignore.[5]

As long as he remained in jail, Shuttlesworth, because of the high-profile support of ACMHR and SCLC colleagues, forced the Gaston group, known as the Committee of 14, to maintain its public support of him. Beneath the surface, however, they believed him too antagonistic to be able to win any concessions from cautious whites. When Shuttlesworth left the custody of the Birmingham police, the ACMHR, Reverend J. L. Ware's Inter-Citizens Committee, and Gaston's group were locked in a not-completely-private power struggle. Southern Regional Council field workers Paul Rilling and Reggie Robinson noted the divisiveness. Rilling described meetings of the Committee of 100 with Ware, Gaston, William Shortridge, black dentist Frederick Taggart, Arthur Shores, John Drew, and new Miles College president Lucius H. Pitts. Rilling noted that Gaston was "quite critical of Shuttlesworth's leadership" and that he preferred "conservative leadership." In addition, Rilling reported general agreement that "Shuttlesworth does not command the loyalty of as many as fifty percent of the Negro citizens." These meetings resulted in the removal of segregation signs from the drinking fountains of several downtown stores and from the elevators of one office building. Still, Robinson reported that Shuttlesworth's approach had driven away from the local movement "people who can think for themselves." Nevertheless, Fred's loyal followers continued to believe that "without Shuttlesworth the Negroes of Birmingham will remain—now and forever—in the dark. He is the one and only."[6]

The middle-class uneasiness with Shuttlesworth also related to the warm relationship he had developed with a group of activist students at Miles College. Led by Korean War veteran Frank Dukes, who had been elected president of the Miles student body, this group of students had been impressed with Shuttlesworth's brash efforts to desegregate Birmingham. Dukes and Shuttlesworth quickly formed an informal coalition and collaborated on the 1960 sit-ins. Dukes willingly allowed his student movement to be considered a part of the Alabama Christian Movement for Human Rights, and Shuttlesworth supported and offered counsel to the student group. Shuttlesworth offered his advice without attempting to co-opt or take credit for what the students were doing, and in late 1961 he publicly supported the students' publication of a statement called "This We Believe." In their manifesto, the students warned, "We do not intend to wait complacently. . . . We cannot tolerate in a nation professing democracy and among people professing Christianity the discriminatory conditions under which the Negro is living today in Birmingham, Alabama."[7]

Within a few weeks the students grew still more militant and formed a new organization called the Anti-Injustice Committee (AIC). Their first order of business was to discuss an economic boycott of downtown department stores. At this point Miles president Lucius H. Pitts intervened, prevailing on the students to postpone the boycott and to negotiate with the white merchants. Pitts had recently come to Miles from Albany, Georgia, where he had been involved in civil rights activities with the Negro Teachers' Association. He believed that as the president of a black college, his fund-raising responsibilities required a deft touch around potential white benefactors. He supported efforts to pressure whites, but his financial attachments to whites necessitated a behind-the-scenes support to the movement. Thus he avoided public statements of support while privately encouraging and advising the students in their negotiations with whites. He nonetheless allowed students and faculty to participate in the movement, even occasionally excusing faculty member Abraham Woods from classroom responsibilities in order to attend to movement matters. While offering advice to both the ACMHR and the AIC, he managed to reassure his contacts in the white community that his moderating influence could keep the movement from getting out of hand. Pitts impressed white minister Norman Jimerson, who worked to establish interracial dialogue in Birmingham through the Alabama Council on Human Relations. Jimerson strongly supported the ACMHR, though he at times differed with Shuttlesworth on tactics.[8]

On January 22, 1962, just days before Shuttlesworth surrendered to police officials for his thirty-six-day incarceration, Pitts spoke at an ACMHR mass meeting. Addressing the topic "How Christian Is the Christian Movement?" Pitts called on the ACMHR to deemphasize such confrontational approaches as the boycott and to concentrate on increasing black voter registration and supporting black businesses. With oblique criticisms of Shuttlesworth, he advised the group to conserve its financial resources "instead of spending it on fines and doctor bills and court costs." He further emphasized the need to trust whites and negotiate. Afterward, Shuttlesworth made a few short remarks but seemed to police detectives to be displeased with Pitts's remarks. Shuttlesworth, however, did not debate with Pitts or contradict his speech in any way. In conversation afterward, Pitts reiterated his suggestion that they trust whites' good faith and begin negotiations. "Fred, I tell you the truth," he said. "I get so darned tired of talking to these people. They're always talking to me, trying to get us divided, but I'm with you basically. But I can't come out [publicly] and be with you. But I tell you what, if you try this [compromise effort], and if they go back on this, I'll get out and march myself." Shuttlesworth understood Pitts's need to remain in the good graces of both the white and the black elite for the sake of his college, and he was satisfied for the president not to make any public statements against his movement. He also was willing for a biracial committee to begin discussing the Birmingham situation, even without his initial participation. Although he had little faith that whites would do much more than talk, he believed that sooner or later both the Smyer committee and the Gaston group would be forced to bring the ACMHR and its leader to the table. After the mass meeting, some ACMHR members whose feathers were ruffled by Pitts's remarks urged Shuttlesworth to ignore the college president's advice. "That's just the white folks trying to quiet us down," they said. Nonetheless, Shuttlesworth assured his followers, "Nothing wrong with trust. But the tree is known by the fruit it bears. So that if there be negotiations, we'll be waiting to see the fruit." The key, Shuttlesworth believed, was to keep the pressure on with a constant threat of a boycott by working with Dukes and the Anti-Injustice Committee.[9]

Shuttlesworth took the position that anything any other group did to fight segregation, either on its own or in conjunction with the ACMHR, would have the unquestioned support of the ACMHR. Dukes and Shuttlesworth helped each other expand their base of support and together requested that white merchants remove segregation signs and hire African Americans as sales clerks. The merchants refused to meet with Shuttlesworth, ostensibly because he no longer lived in Birmingham, but they also viewed him as too militant. Even had they been inclined to meet with him, his stay in the Southside jail made this impossible. They could not be seen as parleying with a jailbird. They agreed, however, to meet with the students. The students, along with Pitts and Gaston, met with the merchants several times during the month of February. Dukes kept

Shuttlesworth abreast of his meetings with white leaders and bounced ideas off Shuttlesworth and the ACMHR leadership. Meeting with the students had a militarizing effect on Gaston, who assured the whites that blacks were unanimous in wanting their full citizenship rights. By the time Shuttlesworth was released from jail in March, negotiations had stalled, and the AIC moved closer to a "selective buying campaign"—a euphemism designed to help them circumvent Birmingham's ordinance against boycotts.[10]

Dukes wrote letters to white merchants asking for concessions in their stores, but he received no response. After several more meetings with Sidney Smyer, Emil Hess (president of the Parisian Department Store), and Episcopal bishop C. C. J. Carpenter, Dukes's Anti-Injustice Committee learned the limits of the merchants' willingness to change. "There's nothing we can do," they objected. "Bull's got this town in the palm of his hand. We're really afraid of him. If we ask him to let us integrate, we'd lose our business." In mid-march, Dukes's group began showering the downtown area with leaflets that bore such messages as "Wear Your Old Clothes for Freedom" and "Use a Dime's Worth of Common Sense." Several students appeared downtown in sandwich boards that read "Don't Buy Where You Can't Be a Salesman." On March 29, Pitts told an Anti-Defamation League representative that the boycott enjoyed the complete support of the black leadership "from Shuttlesworth on the left to A. G. Gaston on the right." They were unified behind Dukes because all parties involved could support the boycott without jeopardizing their own status as leaders.[11]

In only two weeks, the selective buying campaign, sponsored by the AIC but endorsed by Shuttlesworth, had reduced black trade in downtown stores by 15 percent. There were reports of unauthorized efforts to intimidate African Americans who did business as usual with the downtown stores. Groups of other blacks met shoppers and insisted that they return their purchases. One group destroyed a fifteen-dollar hat purchased by one woman. One store owner anonymously told reporters that although they were hurting his business, he sympathized with the boycotters and complained that compromise could be worked out if not for the "adamant position of City Hall."[12]

The merchants soon saw even more of the commission's recalcitrance. When they pleaded with Mayor Hanes for assistance in their crisis, the business leaders were unceremoniously rebuffed. When they asked if any actions on their part to desegregate their stores might result in arrests or fines, Hanes warned them that prosecuting any violations of city ordinances would be within the purview of Connor's duties rather than his own. Connor learned from detectives that the ACMHR did "a lot of bragging about the boycott of our downtown stores." Shuttlesworth had spoken at length on the successes of the boycott, boasting that within six months "any store in Birmingham would be glad to hire Negroes." Galled at Shuttlesworth's temerity, Connor suggested that in retaliation for the boycott he and his fellow commissioners immediately cut off the city's regular appropriations to Jefferson County's surplus food program. Reminding the commissioners that some 95 percent of the ten thousand families receiving aid were black, Connor swaggered, "I don't intend to sit here and take it with a smile." The commission then voted unanimously to support Connor's punitive approach, thus denying the program 45 percent of its regular contributions. Joining with Connor, Hanes warned that "if the Negroes are going to heed the irresponsible and militant advice of the NAACP and CORE, then I say let these leaders feed them, because in excess of 90% of the recipients of the free food handouts are Negroes." Shuttlesworth called the commission's action a shame, complaining, "This is going to hurt the wrong people. It is going to hurt the poor Negro rather than those who are a buying force in the city."[13]

The next day Shuttlesworth and Phifer ventured downtown to observe the latest effects of the boycott. When they arrived at the Newberry Department Store, they were met by several boycotters on the front sidewalk some twelve feet in front of the door. The group, partially blocking the path to the crosswalk on Second Avenue North, were approached by three police officers and asked to disperse. Most did so, but Shuttlesworth and Phifer held their ground. After being given another warning, Shuttlesworth complained, "You mean to tell me we can't stand on the sidewalks?"

"You're blocking the sidewalk," answered the officer.

"If you say I'm blocking the sidewalk, I'll go in the store," Shuttlesworth replied. Before he could enter the doorway, however, the officer arrested him and Phifer for obstructing a sidewalk and refusing to obey an officer. The next day in recorder's court, Judge Charles H. Brown found the two ministers guilty and sentenced them to 180 days of hard labor and levied a $100 fine, plus costs. An appeal to the Alabama Circuit Court resulted only in the addition of sixty-one more days in jail. Ultimately the ruling was quashed by the U.S. Supreme Court in November 1965.[14]

At the next ACMHR mass meeting, movement leaders commented on Shuttlesworth's and Phifer's most recent arrest and the surplus food situation. Gardner offered the empty boast that if the city did not feed the African Americans on the food program, the ACMHR would step in to do so. When the boycott's fire began to flicker by the late spring, ACMHR meetings continued to try to stoke the flame. At times the rhetoric grew sharp, with Gardner hurling accusations of treason after spotting some African Americans carrying packages from downtown stores. He reminded them of Shuttlesworth's five-week sojourn in jail and his most recent arrest, calling on them not to let the leaders of the movement down by shopping in the downtown stores or continuing to ride in the back of city buses.[15]

Gradually it became clear that neither the ACMHR nor the AIC would be able to sustain the boycott indefinitely. Yet the effort made a significant cut into the sales figures for the major downtown stores, especially during the Easter season when the African American community spent large sums on clothing. The boycott reduced Easter sales by 12 percent compared with the previous year and claimed 90 percent of black trade with the downtown stores. The efforts also drew national attention, and eventually even the local white press weighed in against the city commission's retaliatory strikes, calling for open communications between blacks and whites. The boycott proved to both white and black leaders in Birmingham that economic pressure could be brought to bear on the racial status quo. Perhaps even more significant, it developed a cadre of previously uninvolved students who became potential activists for a major direct action campaign the next year. More than two-thirds of the college students involved in the selective buying campaign participated in the 1963 demonstrations. Shuttlesworth and other local blacks began to believe that the factions in the black community could indeed unite against Bull Connor and the business elite of Birmingham.[16]

Shuttlesworth, as usual, was ready to press on. Although his direct role in the boycott was essentially limited to cheerleading, among the students and regular ACMHR members he retained his status as hero and living "martyr" of the movement. His losses as a result of the *Sullivan* case and his jail time had made him appear once more to be the person most willing to sacrifice his own well-being for the cause. Enduring long absences from his family, he nonetheless continued a frenetic pace of travel among Cincinnati, Birmingham, and other locales on behalf of the movement. The weekend after his release in Birmingham he received a hero's welcome at an SCLC Administrative Committee meeting in Atlanta. Discussions centered on the legal aspects of the *Sullivan* case. In other matters, the committee agreed to push a church-oriented voter registration drive, and Shuttlesworth also reminded the committee of an earlier decision to conduct a caravan of southern leaders of the movement to stimulate more activity in local areas.[17]

That same weekend Shuttlesworth and several of the SCLC leaders drove back to Birmingham from Atlanta to attend a large rally celebrating Shuttlesworth and Phifer's release from jail. King spoke at a banquet in their honor at L. R. Hall Auditorium. Afterward, Roy Wilkins, the executive secretary of the NAACP, paid tribute to them at a mass meeting at the Metropolitan AME Zion Church. Making his first appearance in Birmingham since 1956 other than as a witness in court, Wilkins praised Shuttlesworth and Phifer as soldiers who "fought the system that has kept their people in bondage and in humiliation. They fought in spite of threats and beatings and bombs. They have persisted in the face of derision and insult from elements in the white community who should and do know better. The courage and the persistence of these men and of their people reveal the shame of this city." Wilkins also called on the state to heed Shuttlesworth's call to put a quick end to "the whole segregated pattern of life—public schools, public recreation, public transportation, housing, and employment."[18]

The adulation continued at another ACMHR mass meeting when Shuttlesworth returned to Birmingham to preach the newest phase of the civil rights crusade, the students' selective buying campaign. As he choreographed the offering, calling on the congregation to come forward with their contributions, Ed Gardner announced, "The house is loaded, so let's all unload our pockets for the collection. Our President has come to town, so let's knock him down with the money." After Gardner led the congregation in singing "Happy Birthday" to Shuttlesworth, who had turned forty the day before, Phifer took the pulpit to introduce Shuttlesworth, claiming, "We can follow a man that will stand up for us." A bit carried away in the eulogistic spirit, Phifer even told the congregation, "Shuttlesworth is God Himself."[19]

In his remarks Shuttlesworth told the crowd, "When the white people see you mean business, they will step aside. . . . I am a glutton for punishment and I will not stop now." Calling on them to drag out their old clothes for Easter, he charged them not to buy anything "from anyone that is not for us." He poked fun at Connor, who recently had been involved in a minor car accident, saying, "I am glad it didn't kill him. I want to pester him some more. I am glad it did not put out his eye, for I want him to see me some more when I ride the buses with Negro drivers later on." He bragged that "all the big boys know me.

I now go to see the top boys when I want something done." Still later, caught up in the spirit, he moved into a whoop. Overcome with emotion, he was eventually helped into a chair by two ACMHR faithful. So overwhelming was the ecstasy of the service that the police detectives, showing traditional prejudices about black religious expression, observed: "The crowd went wild, like a bunch of cannibals, hollering, dancing, and making all kinds of noise that a human would not make."[20]

Back in Cincinnati and invigorated with a renewed sense of divine protection, Shuttlesworth later boasted at a testimonial dinner in his honor that "Bull Connor almost had my neck, but God wouldn't let him pull the string." In a jovial mood, he wrote another letter to the Birmingham City Commission. "I do hope that you will read this letter prior to throwing it in the waste paper basket as you did the last one I wrote you," he needled them. "During Rev. Phifer's and my recent confinement in your fine jail, the members of the Alabama Christian Movement for Human Rights, who are of course strongly in favor of public education for all of our children, regardless of race, have raised $100 for the rebuilding of Jones Valley High School. They have authorized me to send to you the enclosed check to assist the wonderful people of Birmingham in their efforts to rebuild a high school here."[21]

Shuttlesworth's levity won a much more serious response, though one that caused the ACMHR to marvel that divine protection extended beyond their leader to one of his subordinates. After Shuttlesworth moved to Cincinnati, treasurer Bill Shortridge became one of the more prominent of the local ACMHR leaders. Deeply committed to the movement, outspoken in calling on the black community of Birmingham, and especially its middle-class professionals, to support the ACMHR financially, he found himself receiving an abundance of threatening phone calls. In response he obtained a gun permit, which was soon rescinded by city officials. Two days later, on March 28, 1962, as he emerged from his car to enter the front door of his home, four shots rang out from an old-model Cadillac passing in front of the house. Shortridge quickly dropped to the floor of his porch. Inside the house, his wife, Pinky, was holding her baby as she talked on the phone. One of the bullets knocked the receiver out of her hand and ricocheted into a wall. She instinctively fell to the floor with her child as she waited for the reassuring silence. Seconds later Shortridge entered through the door unhurt.[22]

After realizing that, beyond a minor bruise or two from hitting the floor, no one had been hit, Shortridge told his wife he had caught a glimpse of his would-be assassin, a black man from Ensley who was rumored to have worked occasionally for the police as a pimp. Sometime later, a man claiming to be the gunman called Shortridge and said that Connor had arranged for a $2,000 contract, believing Shortridge to be "the brains of the ACMHR, and that if they got rid of him, things would improve in Birmingham." To assure Shortridge that he was not joking, he accurately described the contents of the glove compartment and trunk of Shortridge's car. In Birmingham's atmosphere of intimidation, Shortridge and Shuttlesworth found the scenario plausible, but believed they could do little to prove the claim or bring the conspirators to justice. The ACMHR guard detail was transferred to the Shortridge home because after Fred's move to Cincinnati the Bethel Baptist parsonage no longer needed protection. Shuttlesworth, for his part, determined to press on in the face of persecution of the movement.[23]

Stories of such intimidation became Shuttlesworth's contribution to discussions the next week when he accompanied King, Abernathy, Walker, and several others to Washington for three days of talks with government leaders. The delegation hoped to induce President Kennedy to end segregation "with a stroke of a pen" by issuing a second Emancipation Proclamation the next year during the centennial of Lincoln's 1863 decree. King asked Shuttlesworth to attend the meetings as a symbol of Jim Crow's persistent persecution of blacks who challenged the status quo. In their April 9 meeting with Robert Kennedy and his assistant, Burke Marshall, King criticized the president's civil rights record. He pressed the administration to denounce segregation more forcefully and reiterated their hope for another proclamation. To buttress the case for federal protection of black voting rights and civil rights activists, King asked Shuttlesworth to tell of his travails in Birmingham. Tickled to be walking in the corridors of power, Fred recounted his and the ACMHR's exploits from 1956 through the recent attempt on Shortridge's life. He was particularly delighted finally to meet the president's brother, with whom he had often spoken by phone but had never met in the flesh. He left impressed with the combination of Kennedy's boyish appearance and forceful personality and used the meeting to rhetorical advantage at a later mass meeting. He told a congregation at St. John's AME Church, "We see a lot of signs on Highways and at Airports saying, 'It is nice to be in Birmingham.' What is nice about a city that closes our parks? Me and Bob Kennedy are going to do something about it. If the white people can go to the parks, colored people can do so also."[24]

One concrete measure Shuttlesworth had in mind for Connor was to bring reinforcements into Birmingham. Ultimately, he wanted to bring the SCLC into town for a direct action campaign such as had been attempted in Albany, Georgia, during the latter months of 1961. Such major plans would be postponed as King's organization geared up for another assault on Albany during the summer of 1962. Shuttlesworth, however, remained undeterred, agitating strongly for the SCLC to put more pressure on Birmingham. For starters, Shuttlesworth hoped to get Birmingham's attention by bringing a coalition of civil rights organizations together for a workshop in the Magic City. Given Connor's frequent boast that he would never allow such a meeting within his jurisdiction, the tension of the parks crisis, and Shuttlesworth's jailing, many more cautious heads concluded that this was the wrong time to try to hold a major integrated meeting in Birmingham. As usual Shuttlesworth had other ideas.

Early in 1962 Fred attended a meeting of the Southern Conference Educational Fund, the civil rights–civil liberties education organization that had disseminated information about Fred's activities in Birmingham through its newspaper, the *Southern Patriot*. Since 1957 he had served on the SCEF board of directors, and when the board cast about for a place for SCEF's semiannual meeting, Fred challenged the group to come to his domain. His proposal elicited a lengthy period of dead silence, followed by a cleared throat and a suggestion of Atlanta or New Orleans. Shuttlesworth slowly looked around the room with a grin and piped up, "I think y'all are *scared* to come to Birmingham." He argued that confronting the serpent of segregation meant attacking it at its head, declaring, "The time has come to hold an integrated meeting in Birmingham, and we're going to do it." A skeptical Herman H. Long, director of the Race Relations Institute at Nashville's Fisk University and SCEF vice president, asked, "Fred, how are you going to deal with this in Birmingham? Where we gonna sleep? Where we gonna eat?" Waving off these and other objections, Shuttlesworth replied, "Don't worry about that. Y'all come to Birmingham," adding with a chuckle, "unless you're scared to come to Birmingham."[25]

Anne Braden later admitted, "He was right, but nobody wanted to be called a coward." The SCEF board sheepishly picked up Fred's challenge and committed itself to holding a joint conference with the SCLC, SNCC, and the ACMHR in Birmingham on April 13–14. Opposition to the meeting persisted, however, particularly among some of Birmingham's white liberals. One of their number declined an invitation to speak and complained about the timing of the conference. Holding the conference during the Alabama gubernatorial race, he warned, would result only in the election of a less-desirable candidate. Shuttlesworth scoffed at this argument, saying, "The conference is on. What do we care who is elected governor? One of them is as bad as the other." He added, "We have to take a position. It's time to have an interracial meeting in Birmingham. When it's time to do something, it's time to do it—regardless of the consequences. Those who aren't ready can stay home. Those who *are* ready can go ahead."[26]

The first major civil rights event in the city since Shuttlesworth's release, the workshop on "Ways and Means to Integrate the South" was dubbed "Shuttlesworth's Answer to Birmingham." The conference brought together black and white activists from ten states to consider special difficulties in civil rights progress and to study how techniques successful elsewhere might be adapted to the Deep South. As conferees began to assemble at the Gaston Motel for lunch just before the conference kickoff, many of them still harbored a palpable nervousness about being an interracial group in Connor territory. In high spirits, Shuttlesworth walked into the restaurant with a wink and a wisecrack, crowing, "Well, I'm glad to see everybody. I'm glad you're here and glad you're not scared to come to Birmingham." Braden mustered a laugh and replied, "Fred, we're scared to death, but we're here."[27]

That Friday night, the conference began with a mass meeting at the St. Paul Methodist Church, the largest integrated gathering in Birmingham in twenty-five years. The next day Shuttlesworth presided at a series of workshops held at the Gaston Building. The workshops were led by such prominent civil rights workers as W. P. Mitchell, secretary of the Tuskegee Civic Association; SNCC's James Forman; Ella Baker, by then working with the Southern Regional YWCA; Carl Braden, field secretary of the SCEF; the Reverend G. Murray Cox, chairman of the Mississippi Advisory Committee to the U.S. Civil Rights Commission; Kelly Miller Smith, leader of the Nashville Christian Leadership Conference; and C. T. Vivian of the Chattanooga Council for Cooperative Action. Howard Schomer, president of Chicago Theological Seminary, spoke to the conference on the subject "Religion in the Struggle for Civil Rights and Civil Liberties." Unable to attend because of a schedule conflict in South Carolina, Martin Luther King Jr. sent his greetings to the mass meeting.

At the end of the conference, Herman Long read a tribute to Fred written by SCEF's outgoing president, Aubrey Williams, and the SCEF board established a $1,000 educational scholarship fund for the Shuttlesworth children. Presenting the gift "in recognition of the contribution he and his family have made to the cause of democracy," Long said that Shuttlesworth had "in the incredibly short span of seven years become a force for social justice in all parts of this country and a symbol of courageous leadership in many lands." Afterward, Anne Braden paid tribute to Ruby and the four children, noting that they had not only supported Fred's activities but also "marched into the struggle with him." She predicted that someday Alabama would find its greatest pride in the fact that "this was the state which produced and gave to America not only the Rev. Fred L. Shuttlesworth, but the Shuttlesworth family."[28]

Shuttlesworth swelled with pride over the successful conference, especially because Connor had made no effort to interrupt the proceedings with arrests, proving Fred's point that interracial meetings could take place in Birmingham. The only interference the workshops encountered was a larger than normal number of police, taking pictures of persons entering the mass meeting. Still, one veteran civil rights leader quipped, "When the segregationists are reduced to shooting people with cameras in Birmingham, Alabama, it's a sure sign that the world is progressing." Buoyed by the relative success of the selective buying campaign and the successful conference in April, Shuttlesworth, who had been nudging King on the matter since at least 1959, began pressing him urgently to launch a direct action campaign in Birmingham. Like most activists in the movement, King shared what Anne Braden called the "general feeling that there are certain places that have symbolic meanings." Birmingham was such a place, and a major confrontation with integrationist forces was close at hand. The attention of King and the SCLC, however, remained in Albany. An attack on Birmingham, with all its symbolic potential, would have to wait.[29]

As Albany and Birmingham played tug-of-war with King and the SCLC, white segregationist candidates confronted each other for election to Alabama's highest office. Judge George C. Wallace led the pack in the May 8 Democratic primary election for governor. Promising to disobey "any illegal Federal court order," Wallace vowed to stand in the schoolhouse door in person if necessary to resist the integration of Alabama's public schools. He told voters, "This state is not going to be big enough for me as the elected sovereign of this state and a bunch of Supreme Court yes-men appointed for life trying to run Alabama's school system; one of us is going to have to go." In the May vote, Wallace led all his opponents, but he failed to win a majority and faced a May 29 runoff election against Ryan deGraffenreid, a popular state legislator from Tuscaloosa. Bull Connor, who had campaigned for the office promising to increase the Birmingham police department's K-9 Corps by one hundred police dogs for use against Freedom Riders, managed to finish a weak fifth place with only twenty thousand votes.[30]

At the first ACMHR mass meeting after the primary election, Shuttlesworth poked fun at the tepid response to Connor's run for governor, wisecracking that he himself could garner more than twenty thousand votes in Jefferson County alone. Shuttlesworth had supported former Alabama governor James E. "Big Jim" Folsom, the only racial liberal in the contest. In 1958 Folsom had been defeated by John Patterson's harder line against integration and by his well-known alcohol problem. Shuttlesworth (who could no longer vote in Birmingham) and most of the African American community supported Folsom, though he had little chance of winning. Fred often voiced his support of "Big Jim" at mass meetings. Detectives reported such comments to Connor, who in turn released Shuttlesworth's statements to the press in order to discredit Folsom among white voters. Although he supported Folsom, Shuttlesworth nonetheless remained clearheaded about the ex-governor's weak chances of being elected again and believed that on racial concerns "there wasn't a dime's worth of difference" between the candidates—as Wallace would later say about his 1968 presidential opponents Nixon and Humphrey. Wallace defeated deGraffenreid in the runoff, and his rise to power was thus virtually assured in the November general election because of the weak state of the Republican Party in Alabama. To that point in Alabama's 1962 election year, there were few surprises. Political developments in Birmingham, however, soon took a decidedly different turn.[31]

During an August 28 special election to choose ten new state legislators, attorney David Vann, head of the Jefferson County Democratic Campaign Committee, placed a petition booth outside every voting precinct to drum up support for changing Birmingham's government from a commission form to a mayor-council system. With the support of business leaders, Vann and his colleagues worked assiduously to keep information about the booths from public consumption. They feared that segregationists, hoping to keep Connor, Hanes, and Waggoner in power, would stir up opposition to the change. When the figures were tallied, almost twelve thousand Birminghamians had registered their support of the mayor-council form of government. The next day Mayor Hanes, under pressure from Connor, announced that the group calling for the change in government were Communists. On the basis of this "new information" he refused to call a special election on the issue. On October 2, however, Judge J. Paul Meeks ordered a special election for November 6. The pro-change forces successfully defused the racial element by arguing that Connor supporters could simply elect him mayor, thus giving him full power in Birmingham rather than dividing his power with two other commissioners. On election day, the mayor-council option prevailed by a nine-hundred-vote margin. Vann and other white liberals hailed the results as a progressive step forward, and mayoral elections were set for March 5, 1963. In the same election, George Corley Wallace was elevated to the governor's mansion.[32]

Meanwhile, in mid-May, as the governor's race moved into high gear, Shuttlesworth attended an SCLC board meeting in Chattanooga, where he continued to lobby King to bring his forces and the national media to Birmingham. Although of significantly different background and temperament than Shuttlesworth, King admired Fred's toughness and considered him "a most energetic and indomitable man." Shuttlesworth had been an active member of the SCLC from its inception, and most of that time he was an officer. As the SCLC cast its net widely throughout the South, Birmingham's Alabama Christian Movement for Human Rights became its strongest affiliate organization. Partly to placate Shuttlesworth's dogged insistence on bringing the SCLC to his city and partly to spotlight the selective buying campaign, King announced in his opening remarks that the SCLC's annual convention would be held in Birmingham on September 25–28. King and the board continued to discuss a direct action campaign but remained noncommittal, though they promised Shuttlesworth they would investigate the matter further.[33]

In early June, Fred returned to Birmingham for the sixth anniversary of the ACMHR. In his "State of Freedom" address, he rallied his troops in what he called a "most dangerous, desperate, and critical hour. Birmingham and Alabama persecute us because we fight segregation," he asserted. He continued: "Men who occupy seats of power appear to use passion and madness rather than calmness and reason. They continue to misread history and misjudge the future." He further criticized the absence of prophethood in the white church: "Perhaps the worst part of this madness is that the white church is for the most part an incubator of classism and racism." Shuttlesworth especially despised the timidity of the white clergy. "The white pulpit is captive," he chided, "afraid to stand and speak to men's hearts on the issues of freedom, justice, equality, and brotherhood." Turning his ire toward similarly spineless counterparts in the African American church, Fred thundered, "It is a shame for any Negro preacher to be afraid to speak about freedom in this day."[34]

After six years at the helm of the movement, Shuttlesworth remained set on seeing real change in public accommodations in Birmingham regardless of the claims that his family and new congregation placed on him. The distance between Cincinnati and Birmingham made little difference to Shuttlesworth and most of the ACMHR faithful, a few of whom only gradually began to realize that Fred's nonresidence in Birmingham was becoming a hindrance to the movement in the city. The distance in reality created more travel and more absence for Fred, and more pressure and tension when he was home, than had been the case at Bethel. The Revelation congregation, larger and more demanding on a pastor's schedule, at first basked in their pastor's fame, just as they had when calling him. His absences and dictatorial leadership style would eventually begin to wear on many members' patience, but they caused no major problem at this point in his Cincinnati ministry. One could see what lay in store for Revelation when he told a Birmingham mass meeting audience about "taking the bull by the horns." This time, however, he did not have Commissioner Connor in mind. He described his "running the church and firing one particular woman" who had been a member and teacher at Revelation for thirty years.[35]

Besides Fred's frenzied travel schedule, other elements remained as they had been in Birmingham, among them the nuisance and threatening telephone calls. Early in his tenure in Cincinnati, Shuttlesworth had reported such calls to the local office of the FBI, just as he had in Birmingham. The special agent in charge of the Cincinnati office, E. D. Mason, interviewed Shuttlesworth on a wide range of issues, including whether he was a communist or would allow communists into his organization. Although he had at times been critical of what he considered Martin Luther King's overconcern with "the Communist bugaboo," Fred assured Mason that he would not knowingly admit communists to the ACMHR. Shuttlesworth quickly struck up a friendly relationship with agents in the Cincinnati office, which soon afforded him some important information. On Monday, July 16, Shuttlesworth had been in federal court on a case regarding an attempt to integrate the Dobbs House Restaurant at the Birmingham airport. His court appearance left observers with the impression that Fred planned to lead a visit to the restaurant to press for service within the week. At the mass meeting that night, however, he made only brief mention of the airport case and introduced his lawyer, Eric Bell. He then hurried back to Cincinnati.[36]

That weekend FBI agents in Cincinnati called the Shuttlesworth home to warn Fred of impending danger. Ruby informed them that her husband was away from home preaching revival services in a church in Cleveland. Contacting him there, the Cleveland office told Shuttlesworth that informants in Birmingham had stumbled onto a conspiracy to kill him when he sought to integrate the Birmingham airport restaurant on July 21 or 23. They indicated that they had notified the Birmingham police and that Chief Jamie Moore had promised to place a detail at the airport as a protective measure. Fred told the agents that he had no plans to be in Birmingham on those dates but that he anticipated returning to the city on July 30. He further promised he would handle the information in strictest confidence and thanked them for their tip. As a result of the FBI's information, Shuttlesworth proved he was not invariably disposed to courting danger because he changed his plans and stayed away from Birmingham on July 30. The integration test of the Dobbs House, however, came on the Saturday before, July 28, led by one of Shuttlesworth's ACMHR underlings, the Reverend Calvin W. Woods. The contingent of thirteen African Americans was refused admittance at the door of the Dobbs House. Taking seats on the floor twenty feet from the main door, the contingent observed white patrons being served in the restaurant. After four and one-half hours of waiting, the ACMHR group was served without incident. Shortly afterward Shuttlesworth met again with FBI agents in Cincinnati. He expressed high regard for the bureau and volunteered to keep FBI officials posted of his forthcoming activities. As a result, the Cincinnati office, having "no question whatsoever concerning [his] patriotism, . . . health, reliability, stability, or integrity," recommended that the bureau "exploit and establish" Shuttlesworth as a confidential informant. There is no indication, however, that Shuttlesworth ever functioned in that capacity for the FBI.[37]

Back home, however, the threatening calls and the alleged attempt on Fred's life added to Ruby's worries. Although like her husband she projected a tough public persona, Ruby was gradually falling victim to the stress. Already suffering from heart disease, which was worsened by her weight, Ruby had begun to have blackouts that she and her husband attributed to the pressure of Fred's civil rights struggles. Her ill health became common knowledge to the principals of the movement. King had mentioned her in his February appeal for funds to get Fred and Phifer out of jail, and ACMHR mass meeting congregations were frequently reminded of Ruby's illnesses in regular catalogues of the sacrifices of the Shuttlesworth family. Fred, however, remained oblivious to the toll his life was taking on the health of his wife or his marriage. No one in the civil rights movement interpreted it as a religious crusade as literally or as consistently as Fred Shuttlesworth, and he fully expected the crusade to require some sacrifices. Even in the face of his wife's failing health, he refused to curtail his involvement. In fact, his pace would quicken in the next fifteen months, as matters moved to a climax in Birmingham.[38]

By the end of 1962, SCLC efforts in Albany, Georgia, had fizzled, largely because of discord between the NAACP, SNCC, and the SCLC and because of the "nonviolent" response of Albany police chief Laurie Pritchett. King had not enjoyed a national civil rights victory since the Montgomery boycott, and the SCLC had not been central to the action in the Freedom Rides. Now, in the first attempt at massive direct action against segregation in Albany, King and the SCLC were perceived as having faltered. The *New York Herald Tribune,* for example, had called Albany "the most stunning defeat of King's career." Expectations for a reversal of SCLC's fortunes rose dramatically after Albany, and many supporters clamored for an immediate and visible success.[39]

After Albany, Shuttlesworth noted in a later interview, "SCLC needed a movement. It needed something to revive itself and there was just nothing else"—at least nothing else that promised victory and avoided the problems of Albany. Birmingham did that. Shuttlesworth reasoned that, despite the occasional opposition of the black middle class, civil rights activism in Birmingham, unlike Albany, was essentially unified under his leadership. He was convinced that the loyalty of the ACMHR could deliver a core of five hundred to one thousand volunteers who would in fact be able to "fill the jails"—as King had vainly hoped to be able to accomplish in Albany. "I could guarantee," Fred later recalled, "that they would be received and wouldn't be run out, and wouldn't have . . . a lot of problems." Division and internecine warfare between black organizations, which had so hampered the Albany campaign, remained a potential problem in Birmingham. Shuttlesworth was convinced, however, that the SCLC could counter potential disunity with the strength of the ACMHR's loyalty to its leader. King already considered the ACMHR to be the SCLC's strongest affiliate and Shuttlesworth to be "the most courageous civil rights fighter in the South." In addition, King's relationship with some of Shuttlesworth's critics—Drew and Gaston—led him to believe that lingering rivalries in the Birmingham black community were surmountable. As to the other salient problem of Albany—the absence of extreme reaction to demonstrations—few even entertained the possibility of Birmingham following Albany's example. The presence of Bull Connor and a hard-core, violent racism made it unlikely that the temperate responses of Laurie Pritchett would be duplicated in Birmingham. Birmingham thus was strong where Albany had been weakest, and conditions augured well for a decisive confrontation.[40]

On the other hand, Shuttlesworth and the ACMHR needed some tangible success as much as the SCLC did. Seven years of occasional legal triumphs struck Shuttlesworth as "Pyrrhic victories." Most of Birmingham remained segregated, even after the ACMHR's six-year effort. Recent attempts to desegregate the parks and downtown department stores had yielded only mixed results. Although often ridiculed as hankering for the spotlight, Shuttlesworth had indeed been appealing to King for several years to come to Birmingham. He actually countered his own reputation as a loner by realizing that Birmingham "needed something more than what we [the ACMHR] were doing" and by inviting King and the SCLC to conduct their campaign in "his" city. One item the ACMHR needed was the national glare of television lights, which would accompany King and the SCLC. In addition, King's organization was larger and better trained in the tactics of nonviolence than the ACMHR and more capable of teaching these principles to large numbers of volunteers. In Shuttlesworth's estimation, therefore, the "SCLC needed something and we needed something," and in board meetings he continued to lobby King for joint action: "Birmingham is where it's at, gentlemen. I assure you, if you come to Birmingham, we will not only gain prestige but really shake the country. If you win in Birmingham, as Birmingham goes, so goes the nation."[41]

For a while, it seemed inevitable that Birmingham would see massive demonstrations led by both organizations during the SCLC's annual convention in September. In May, Shuttlesworth had promised his ACMHR members that King, Abernathy, and SCLC reinforcements would be in Birmingham in September. "We want to integrate everything we can then," he told them. Observing the police detectives making their notes, Shuttlesworth challenged them: "Tell Bull to get ready because F. L. is ready. Write everything I said down because I won't retract one word of this statement." Although the white media almost never reported announcements like this from the African American mass meetings, word spread through the grapevine that major demonstrations would accompany the SCLC convention.[42]

Learning of the plans, Birmingham Chamber of Commerce president Sidney W. Smyer and his colleagues hoped to avoid both eventualities if possible, but demonstrations at all costs. At the end of August, Smyer formed a new biracial committee called the Senior Citizens Committee, which was made up of leading merchants and included a contingent of black leaders. Among those asked to serve were John Drew, A. G. Gaston, and L. H. Pitts. Early on in their negotiations, Smyer's committee tried to ignore Shuttlesworth and sent an emissary to SCLC headquarters in Atlanta to attempt to stave off demonstrations in Birmingham. King and Walker sent back word that the ultimate decision rested with "Birmingham civil rights leaders" and recommended that they deal with

Shuttlesworth. At this point, Gaston and Pitts reiterated their advice that any meaningful agreement regarding demonstrations had to negotiate with the persons most likely to do the demonstrating, namely Shuttlesworth and the ACMHR.[43]

On Sunday morning, September 16, Smyer met privately with L. H. Pitts and Norman Jimerson, the northern white minister and director of the Alabama Council on Human Relations who acted as liaison between black and white groups. Pitts again emphasized to Smyer that only Shuttlesworth had the power to postpone demonstrations. In exchange, Smyer had to make visible concessions, such as the removal of segregation signs in the downtown department stores. Smyer was confident that he could have the signs removed within forty-eight hours, but he was not in a position to make a firm commitment that would be binding on the other business leaders. Shuttlesworth remained on the periphery of the negotiations.[44]

On September 20, four days after Smyer's meeting with Pitts and Jimerson and five days before the start of the SCLC convention, a contingent of black leaders traveled to Washington to meet with Attorney General Robert Kennedy and Burke Marshall. Shuttlesworth, Shortridge, and Gardner represented the ACMHR, and they were accompanied by black bourgeois leaders Pitts, Gaston, and Drew. Also attending were several prominent but "nonaligned" leaders. Among them were Shuttlesworth's doctor, James T. Montgomery, and his sometime attorneys Arthur Shores and Oscar W. Adams. Together the group hoped to apprise Kennedy of the latest developments in Birmingham and to induce him to weigh into the situation and pry a concession from the white business leaders. Although the meeting yielded no obvious results, the next day Martin Luther King announced that his trip into Alabama for the SCLC convention would include a tour throughout the state to "recruit a nonviolent army for a new front of the attack of the system of segregation in the whole state."[45] On the eve of the SCLC convention, Smyer's Senior Citizens Committee finally invited Shuttlesworth to the table.

Years later, Shuttlesworth minimized his differences with the black leaders, speculating that at the beginning of their talks with Smyer's group, the middle-class leaders tactically chose to criticize Shuttlesworth as a means of gaining concessions. In other words, he believed they played up their differences with Shuttlesworth for white consumption as a means of establishing common ground for discussion. This ploy represented a modern instance of African

Americans' "strategic deception" of whites with power—"Got one mind for massa to see / Got another for what I know is me." By convincing Smyer's group that they too had reservations about Shuttlesworth, the black elite established themselves, unlike Shuttlesworth, as, in a common phrase of the day, "reasonable Negroes of good will" and won the white leaders' trust. At that point, they could say that although they too were suspicious of Shuttlesworth, they believed his relationship with the SCLC and his powerful hold on the people's loyalty made negotiations impossible without him. In a moment of personal triumph, Shuttlesworth relished every moment as he accompanied Gaston, Pitts, Ware, and several others to join Smyer and other white business leaders.[46]

Six years of ACMHR activity seemed to flash before Shuttlesworth's eyes—the Christmas night bombing, his beating at Phillips High, the attempted bus boycotts, the arrest of his children, the confiscation of his car, the tensions of his home life, the fulminations of Bull Connor, and the silence of the respectable white community. Feeling a twinge of anger at white Birmingham as its commercial "representatives" belatedly greeted him, he could not resist adopting an imperious air as he took his seat at the table. He would make Smyer and the others squirm for not having taken him and his movement more seriously in the past. Gaston broke the ice, commenting, "Mr. Smyer, like I told you, I got a million dollars, but I can't stop the people from demonstrating if they want to. You've been talking to us, but we got no power to keep Dr. King from coming to Birmingham. The only man who can keep him from coming to Birmingham is Shuttlesworth, and you have to deal with him." Shuttlesworth suppressed a smile as Gaston continued: "Like I told you, we're just businessmen, and we don't have no say. You got to talk to Fred. He's the one with the marbles. He's the man with the folks. He tells them to march, they march; he tells them to stop, they stop."

Smyer stuck out his hand—shaking slightly with nervousness—to Shuttlesworth and said, "Well, Dr. Shuttlesworth, I'm glad to meet you." Ignoring the pretentious sign of respect, Fred matter-of-factly replied, "Well, I'm no 'Doctor,' but I am glad to meet you . . . although it's very late. We should have met a long time ago. This is the first time we have met, and I've been here fighting for seven years. So I don't think that you have any particular regard for me, and my church has been bombed twice, and I haven't heard anything from a white minister or white church. I've been in jail any number of times for nothing, and you all know it. You businessmen haven't done anything about it. You've been meeting with Dr. Pitts and others, but I'm interested in what you can do. I'm not interested in just sitting around and talking. 'Cause that's all we've been doing and will be doing. So I'm concerned about what you can offer."

Shifting uncomfortably during the minister's quiet tirade, Smyer changed the subject: "Well, we just wanna know what we can do to help keep Dr. King out of here."

"Let's get one thing clear," Shuttlesworth began. "You have signs up here that say, 'It's So Nice to Have You in Birmingham.' We think Dr. King is a nice person and that those signs mean Dr. King as well as anybody else. Now let's talk about the issue of confrontation. You're concerned about your business, and my concern is, are you willing to do for us now so we won't have the demonstrations? Because we are going to have it."

At that, someone objected that they could not make decisions for all the downtown merchants. Fred shot back, "Well, we talkin' to the wrong folks then. You all are wasting my time. Gentlemen, I'm not noted for wasting time. I don't want to waste y'all's time; I know y'all are busy making money, and I'm trying to be busy making justice. I'm not your darling, and I don't have time to be here wasting time when I'm out trying to get freedom. If y'all can't do nothing, call me when you can. So as far as I am concerned, the meeting is adjourned." The merchants objected, "But we can't make—" "Alright then," interrupted Fred. "When you can all get together, gentlemen, I'll be glad to meet with you. See what you can do."[47]

Called back to resume discussion the next day, Shuttlesworth tangled with Isadore Pizitz, owner of Birmingham's largest downtown department store, who rejected the notion of desegregating his store's rest room facilities. Before Shuttlesworth could reply, Gaston spoke up: "Mr. Pizitz, you and I started around here at the same time. You used to carry your clothes around here on your back, selling them to Negroes. Both of us got our fortunes off poor folk and black folk." Impressed with a statement like this coming from Gaston, Fred added, "The problem is, we got to have some give. We're tired of our ladies coming into your stores—can't use the rest rooms, can't change clothes, can't try on dresses and things." Pizitz, however, reaffirmed his objections to desegregating rest room facilities, offering to desegregate the water fountains instead. "Oh no, gentlemen. Let's don't play with each other. We done passed water a long time ago," Fred said without noticing his own double entendre. "We got to have toilets. We can't agree that we'll be in the stores and buy if we can't relieve ourselves when necessary." Ready to suspend the discussions again, he insisted, "That's elementary, and there's no use in our talking any longer. We must not only have the water; we must have toilets. Besides, some Negroes want to see what's in those toilets that makes you white folks act so crazy."[48]

Shuttlesworth's attempt at humor was lost in the moment, and Pizitz remained adamantly opposed to any concessions on toilets. After a few more minutes of throat clearing and meaningless offers, Fred drew matters to a conclusion. "Well, Mr. Pizitz, I see why we can't make no progress in this town. This is what I meant when I said the white people, when they smile, they really don't mean anything. But I've just made a decision: I've decided that when the demonstrations start, Martin and Ralph and I will be arrested from *your* store. Last time [during the 1960 sit-ins], it was unknown students who were arrested, but next time it'll be Martin Luther King and Fred Shuttlesworth. We're going to sit on your stools, and we ain't gon' walk out. They're going to have to carry us out of the great Pizitz store. The camera will get all that. And then when we go to jail, we won't eat. We'll fast. Won't shave. Folks will see how bad we're treated, and I'm sure there won't be nobody shopping with you. Now that's just the way it is, and if this is all you've got to say, we'll bid you good day."[49]

At that, Roper Dial of Sears, Roebuck stopped Shuttlesworth to suggest he might be able, after all, to have his janitor paint over the White Only signs in his store. After excusing himself to make a phone call, Dial returned to announce, "My janitor accidentally painted over a sign." With a smile, Shuttlesworth said, "Now you're a white man with some sense. Maybe all of y'all could accidentally paint them over?" As the merchants fell in line with Dial, agreeing to remove the signs from water fountains and rest rooms, Shuttlesworth promised not to make a public announcement about agreement. "All we want is progress," he told Smyer. "We're not interested in publicity, if that's what y'all are worried about." A relieved Smyer said, "Doctor, I offer you my hand. We'll work this thing out." Extending his own hand, Shuttlesworth offered one last warning, "Okay, Mr. Smyer. I don't have illusions about white people doing things that they don't really want to do. Remember Cincinnati is only one hour's flight from Birmingham, and Atlanta is less than an hour. We can start anytime, because the war is on. If the signs go back up, the fight goes on."[50]

After the two negotiating parties bade each other farewell, some of the black professionals—Drew, Pitts, and others—complimented Shuttlesworth on his coolness in the negotiations and expressed surprise that he willingly accepted the merchants' promise without publicity. "We were surprised that you would agree to something like this," they said. Accepting their congratulations, Fred nonetheless replied warily, "Yeah, and all you thought I wanted was publicity, but I want progress. Progress is my thing, not necessarily publicity. Publicity is what I have to fight [for] to get progress." As the contingent celebrated their victory, a skeptical Shuttlesworth warned them not to expect too much from the merchants. Later, in conversations with SCLC staffers, he predicted that the Jim Crow signs would reappear as soon as the SCLC left Birmingham without major demonstrations.[51]

On Tuesday, September 25, Shuttlesworth welcomed the SCLC to his turf as the convention gathered to consider a theme that could easily have been borrowed from Fred's approach—"Diversified Attack on Segregation." Shuttlesworth and other leaders of the ACMHR played relatively minor roles in the proceedings of the convention, primarily serving as designated "pray-ers," leading invocations and benedictions or giving the introductions of other speakers. No ACMHR personnel delivered any of the major addresses or led in any of the convention, all of which duties were handled by SCLC staff or invitees. The ACMHR choir, directed by Carlton Reese, did, however, lead the music throughout most of the convention. Shuttlesworth presided at the Wednesday evening session, allowing Ed Gardner to greet the delegates on behalf of the ACMHR.[52]

The convention itself resulted only in announcements by both King and Shuttlesworth that SCLC activities would be expanded in the near future in Alabama, which King described as "still a hard core state." King and other speakers lauded the efforts of James Meredith to enroll at the University of Mississippi and called for similar attempts to integrate Alabama's comparable institutions, the University of Alabama and Auburn University. In response, gubernatorial candidate and front-runner George Wallace pointedly commented, "I am going to have more to do with that than any rabble rouser since I am going to be governor of Alabama, and there will be no integration while I am Governor of Alabama." Undeterred by Wallace's threats, the SCLC further announced that its "diversified attack" on segregation in Alabama would include a four-pronged strategy of direct action, lawsuits, boycotts, and voter registration. King and Shuttlesworth also met with fifty-five black leaders from Mobile, Tuscaloosa, Talladega, Huntsville, Marion, Tuskegee, Montgomery, and Dothan to discuss ways of uniting for a full-scale assault on segregation in the state.[53]

King announced a Christmas boycott "somewhere in Alabama," though the Drew-Gaston group raised questions in his mind about attacking Birmingham now that negotiations were finally beginning to have some effect. Shuttlesworth, in characteristic fashion, pressed King to tighten the screws on the merchants, explaining, "They took those signs down because you were coming to town, and they'll put 'em up again just as soon as you leave." Publicly, Fred told reporters that no demonstrations were planned "as of now," though he held out the threat: "There is a possibility that demonstrations will take place, but this will be determined by the actions of the power structure of the city." He identified the power structure as "the merchants, those who control the money," issuing a direct challenge to the city's public servants: "It's time for other white leaders also to act to prevent what could happen." The convention's most sensational result turned out to be an unintended one. While King addressed the group on Friday morning, a young Nazi Party member from Arlington, Virginia, approached the stage of the L. R. Hall Auditorium and punched King in the face. The crowd stood in stunned silence as King received several blows without retaliation. As onlookers pulled the assailant away, King told the congregation to remain calm and respond nonviolently. Police quickly took the attacker into custody. Within four hours the assailant had been sentenced to thirty days and fined twenty-five dollars.[54]

After the SCLC convention, Shuttlesworth's prediction that Jim Crow signs would soon reappear was fulfilled in short order. In early October, Connor sent building inspectors to the department stores, threatening to close several of them for building and fire code infractions if they did not replace the signs. He forced one merchant to make $9,000 worth of repairs on an elevator system. In addition, when word got out that the proprietors had integrated their stores, a dangerously large number of customers canceled their charge accounts. As a result, the progress that King and the black elite were banking on proved short-lived. By that time, the action on the national civil rights front had temporarily shifted to James Meredith's enrollment as a student at the University of Mississippi. Nonetheless, even while the eyes of the nation and the president were focused on events in Oxford, a contingent of leaders returned to Washington to discuss the fragile situation in the Magic City.[55]

On this occasion, however, Shuttlesworth and the others were able to see the president as well as the attorney general. At one point in their chat, President Kennedy asked the group what they would advise him to do in response to Governor Ross Barnett's challenge of Meredith's attempt to matriculate at Ole Miss. Before anyone could answer, ACMHR treasurer William Shortridge thrust his thumb in the air and exclaimed, "J-a-i-l him!!" Amused, the president asked, "How'd you say that, Mr. Shortridge?" "J-a-i-l him!!"—same gesture, same voice inflection, came the immediate reply, followed by a good-natured laugh by the group. Kennedy just smiled and said, "That's just what he wants me to do. That'll make a martyr out of him in front of his people." Shuttlesworth left the meeting still chuckling at Shortridge's outburst and preening that he had actually sat in the attorney general's chair. The Kennedys had been too preoccupied with Mississippi matters to settle decisions on Birmingham. On the way to Birmingham, Shuttlesworth stopped in Atlanta for a strategy meeting with Wyatt Walker and other SCLC staff members. That night he told his ACMHR mass meeting audience that major demonstrations were in the offing. "Demonstrations," he warned, "remain an imminent possibility. I must confess that some face to face talks [with white business leaders] have taken place but these talks must be followed by good faith action. Some signs have come down—and gone back up. We are serving notice on Birmingham that SCLC and Martin Luther King have assured me they are still on call if Birmingham needs them." Reached by reporters, Walker disclosed that SCLC plans "revolved around the decisions of Fred Shuttlesworth and the Alabama Christian Movement for Human Rights."[56]

Throughout the fall, Shuttlesworth relished his newfound access to political power, boasting to the ACMHR faithful, "I can go to the White House any time I want to, and Bull can't even get there. I can sit down and talk to the Kennedy boys because I have something to say." As the November gubernatorial election neared, Shuttlesworth advised the African American community to support Folsom and poked fun at "that little knucklehead George Wallace." Meanwhile, he continued to press King for joint demonstrations between the ACMHR and the SCLC to commence for the Christmas buying season. On Sunday afternoon, December 9, King came to the city to participate in the installation service of his former associate, John T. Porter, as pastor of the prestigious Sixth Avenue Baptist Church. Afterward, King and Shuttlesworth once again discussed a massive direct action campaign. Still, King's travel and fund-raising schedule hindered him from making a firm and immediate commitment, though his attention increasingly focused on Birmingham. As the new year approached, major demonstrations, for which Shuttlesworth had cajoled the SCLC for years, seemed imminent.[57]

Five days after Shuttlesworth's meeting with King in Birmingham, bombers, apparently unaware that Fred had moved to Cincinnati, struck Bethel Baptist Church for the third time since 1956. At about 9:25 P.M., detective E. K. Alley and fire chief Aaron Rosenfeld later speculated, six to eight sticks of dynamite were placed in a cast-iron pipe, which in turn was placed in a paint bucket. Like the 1958 bombing of the church, the explosion rained shrapnel in all directions.

All the church's windows were shattered, and the brick porch supports and roofs of the parsonage and the neighboring home of James Revis were severely damaged. At the time of the blast, several children were in the basement of the church rehearsing a Christmas play. Two of the children received minor facial cuts when the basement was showered with broken glass and were hospitalized. ACMHR and Bethel people telephoned Shuttlesworth with the news of the bombing. The next afternoon he appeared on a Cincinnati radio news program to appeal for financial contributions for repairs of the church and private homes and then left after church services at Revelation on Sunday evening to fly to Birmingham to see the damage for himself. While he was in town, police officials publicly speculated that the bomb had been designed not to destroy the church building as much as to attempt to intimidate Shuttlesworth. He characterized the bombing as "an act of vengeance and retaliation . . . because of the gains being made by Negroes in Birmingham. We have been having many victories, and Negroes are going places where they never went before." Reading the bombing as a personal attack on himself, he commented, "I have always been a symbol of the Negro freedom movement here, and that is why the church where I used to be pastor has been bombed again. This is Birmingham's shame and America's tragedy."[58]

On Monday afternoon the *Birmingham News* finally broke its self-imposed silence on the bombing of black churches, offering a reward of one thousand dollars to any person providing information on the Bethel bombing. The *Post-Herald* offered a similar figure, and within two days total rewards had risen to $4,000. In addition, the Reverend Edwin Kimbrough, president of the Ministerial Association of Birmingham, started a fund drive to raise money for the repair of the church. Fred attended the regular Monday night mass meeting, where the bombing was the primary topic of conversation. Before addressing the crowd Shuttlesworth nodded his head in agreement as he heard Ed Gardner mock Birmingham's motto, "It's Nice to Have You in Birmingham," which could no longer be inscribed on license plates "because it is now known as 'Bomb Land.'"[59]

Shuttlesworth came to the podium in a subdued mood, telling the crowd of his fatigue and his plans to visit the steam baths of Hot Springs, Arkansas. He felt humbled as some of his followers brought him Christmas gifts of new clothes and an overcoat and as a child presented him a stick of candy. He then told them that illness had struck his entire family and that he had spent more money on medication over the last year than he had in the previous twenty-one years combined. Working the congregation's sympathy, he described how his daughter Pat had worried aloud to the people of Revelation that when her father went south she never knew whether he would come back to Cincinnati alive. In spite of these travails, he assured them he was all right and that he was ready to give his health, his life, his all for the movement. His voice rising in intensity, he said God had appointed him to lead the ACMHR because of his hardheadedness. Thus he intended "to go forward and never quit" and promised, "I'll give my life for you." In a rambling disquisition, he noted with satisfaction that the white ministers of the city had begun to act and called on all white churches to take up offerings for bombing victims. Finally, he congratulated his successor at Bethel, the Reverend V. C. Provitt, who had banned ACMHR meetings from the church, for being at the meeting that night. "That is the only place for this pastor to be," he asserted, "to go forward with this movement."[60]

His slightly drooping spirit now restored by the charismatic energy of the mass meeting, Fred ended a long day at the Gaston Motel. At the same time in Cincinnati, Ruby's sleep was interrupted by a number of crank phone calls related to the bombing. At about 1:20 A.M. she answered the phone, only to hear the repeated shouts of "Communist! Communist!" followed by the click of a phone being disconnected. Immediately the phone rang again. The voice was the same, but the message was more specific this time: "Fred Shuttlesworth is a Communist, Communist, Communist. You'd better get back down south. You'd better get back down south." This time Ruby hung up. Four hours later came a call from a different, but more inquisitive, caller: "Do you remember December 1956? Do you think you're too far? Do you think you're safe?" Ruby shot back with feistiness, "Do you know a call like this can be considered a threat?" This caller quickly clicked the conversation to an abrupt end. Then at 8:30 A.M. came a message from a third caller: "Bombs fly in Hiroshima. Bombs fly in Alabama. Bombs fly in Ohio. Communist, Communist, Communist."[61]

Early in the new year, on January 8, an ebullient Shuttlesworth preached to his mass meeting audience a sermon titled "Free in '63," explaining the difference between the Klan and the ACMHR. "The Ku Klux Klan," he pointed out, "is always mad, but our organization is always glad." Part of the reason for Shuttlesworth's effervescence lay in being on the verge of talking King into committing the SCLC to major demonstrations in Birmingham. Two days later, Fred attended a meeting of King's brain trust at the Dorchester Conference Center near Savannah, Georgia, to plan the demonstrations. King, Abernathy, Shuttlesworth, and Joseph Lowery—who had constituted those preacher-activist meetings in Montgomery in the early days of the boycott—were accompanied by SCLC staff persons such as the executive director, Wyatt Tee Walker, and staff members Andrew Young, Jack O'Dell, Stanley Levison, Dorothy Cotton, Clarence Jones, and James Lawson. During their two-day conversation, the group gradually came to consensus that Fred's long-standing persistence had to be taken seriously. Also, the mark he had made in Birmingham, challenging Bull Connor without fear but with limited success, inclined King to commit to Birmingham. Shuttlesworth's friendship played a role in the decision, but more important, it was a case of King's national civil rights movement owing Shuttlesworth's indigenous movement its aid, a matter of King honoring Fred's courage with the SCLC's support.[62]

The discussions at first rehashed the lessons of the SCLC's difficulties in the Albany campaign. Shuttlesworth quickly reiterated his argument that victory was there for the taking in Birmingham if the SCLC joined forces with his ACMHR shock troops. His organization—his movement, as he often called it—had proved itself large enough to "fill the jails" and induce the federal government to take action on civil rights legislation. Furthermore, in King's estimation Shuttlesworth "had proved to his people that he would not ask anyone to go where he was not willing to lead" and had thereby created a following loyal enough to avert the organizational and leadership disunity that had hampered efforts in Albany.[63] In addition to the ACMHR, three new ministers inclined toward participation in the larger civil rights movement—if not always Shuttlesworth's movement—had recently become pastors of the largest African American churches in the city. John Cross at the Sixteenth Street Baptist, John Porter at the Sixth Avenue Baptist, and Martin Luther King's brother, A. D., at the First Baptist of Ensley became leaders of congregations that could supplement Shuttlesworth's ACMHR core with a significant number of volunteers.

Bull Connor had proved himself as well. As Shuttlesworth and other Birmingham watchers virtually guaranteed, the primal, visceral racism represented by Connor would, in Wyatt Walker's words, "inevitably do something to help [the] cause." From bitter experience, Shuttlesworth saw Connor as the "symbol of police brutality in the South." Expecting Connor to be defeated by former lieutenant governor Albert Boutwell in his upcoming run for the mayor's office and preferring to attack while his longtime nemesis was still at the helm, Shuttlesworth told King, "I think it's time to give Bull hell before he's finished." He added satirically, "We don't want to be unfair to the new man; he didn't start it. It will be better for Boutwell when it's over." Andrew Young later explained that at Dorchester, Shuttlesworth, not King, emphasized the necessity of confronting Bull Connor and Birmingham as the means of "shaking up the country." King "went to Birmingham," Young testified, "because Fred Shuttlesworth pleaded with him to do it." Shuttlesworth told King, "Look, we've got to move in Birmingham. We've been hammering away for seven years with no impact. If segregation is going to fall, we've got to crack Birmingham. In fact, if you can break the back of segregation in Birmingham, Alabama, then you can break the back of segregation all over the nation."[64]

The SCLC not only relied on Shuttlesworth's organization to provide the personnel for protests in the Magic City but also built on the strategy already put in place by the ACMHR and the Miles College Anti-Injustice Committee. At Dorchester, King and the others settled on using African American economic clout in the downtown stores as the instrument for applying pressure on Birmingham's business elite. King had already assigned Wyatt Walker to draw up a strategy for the demonstrations. As Walker, Shuttlesworth's kindred spirit, finished briefing the others on his plan, in which he called the demonstrations "Project C"—for "Confrontation"—Fred smiled with excitement, ready to approve any strategy that attacked segregation on every front. Still, Walker and Young worried aloud about the scope of support for major demonstrations among the black clergy, noting that John Cross had recently pestered them for reimbursement of his church for electric bills incurred during the past September's SCLC convention. In addition, the large churches included many of the black business elite who were still skeptical about Shuttlesworth and still harbored hope that the change of city government and a possible defeat of Connor for mayor would make demonstrations unnecessary. Shuttlesworth downplayed this potential problem. Ever confident, and in this case *over*confident, he waved off such concerns, assuring King, "Don't worry, Martin. I can handle the preachers." "You better be right," King replied warily. Then King began a dramatic warning, in life-or-death tones reminiscent of Shuttlesworth's homilies on giving his life for the movement, of the serious danger of this projected campaign. After Stanley Levison reminded the group of Connor's efforts in putting down Birmingham's budding labor movement in the 1940s, King spoke up: "I want to make a point that I think everyone here should consider very carefully and decide if he wants to be with this campaign. . . . I have to tell that in my judgment, some of the people sitting here today will not come back alive from this campaign. And I want you to think about it." Shuttlesworth, having long since thought about and clamored for the campaign, smiled, nodded his approval, and, in call-and-response style, said, "That's right!"[65]

Although Dorchester settled the issue of whether the joint forces of the SCLC and the ACMHR would launch major demonstrations in Birmingham, it did not iron out the details of when and how. In the days following the Dorchester meeting, Walker consulted with Shuttlesworth and other ACMHR participants to help determine the lay of the land. Scouting the five main department stores where sit-ins had occurred in 1960, Shuttlesworth and the others enabled Walker to plan demonstrations to the last detail. Within a week, the SCLC staff set March 14 as their tentative date. Scheduling the campaign for a date after Birmingham's March 5 mayoral election represented a concession to the black business elite and white liberals who hoped to avoid protests until after the electorate had the opportunity to replace Connor with more moderate leadership. Both groups feared that demonstrations before the election would stir up the radical segregationist vote and enhance Connor's election chances. With good reason, however, Shuttlesworth believed Boutwell would be no real improvement over Connor. In their heart of hearts few white liberals expected Boutwell to challenge Birmingham's racial status quo. When Boutwell underwent surgery, liberals joked that "it wasn't an appendectomy or an operation to take anything out. It was an operation to put guts in." A committed segregationist, Boutwell had written Alabama's Pupil Placement Act, which Shuttlesworth had challenged in the 1957 Phillips High School incident. For that reason, Fred considered Boutwell little more than "a dignified Eugene Bull Connor—a crying or trembling Bull instead of a bellowing Bull." Yet Shuttlesworth knew that postponing the demonstrations would push them back into the Easter buying season and thus allow more economic pressure to be applied to the downtown stores. Largely on that basis, he yielded to King's and the SCLC staff's decision to hold off until after the elections.[66]

In the meantime other considerations demanded attention. On January 16, George Wallace took office as governor of Alabama with the words, "I draw a line in the dust and toss the gauntlet before the feet of tyranny. And I say, 'Segregation now! Segregation tomorrow! Segregation forever!'" That same day King began a speaking tour to raise money for Project C, though without naming the specific venue of the protests. At the end of January, he told an audience in Chicago that his organization was preparing for "the most difficult campaign I have yet undertaken." Shuttlesworth spent most of this time in Birmingham, to the extent that his colleague Abraham Woods hardly noticed he had moved to Cincinnati. He attended a mass meeting in which ACMHR treasurer W. E. Shortridge hinted to the crowd, "In March we hope to show you something that has never been shown before in Birmingham, something you will all be proud of." Picking up the cue, Shuttlesworth energized the audience, admonishing them: "We must endure pain and heartbreak. Some more of us may yet be fired from jobs. Some may yet be beat with chains. We are going on with God. We don't care who goes in or out at City Hall."[67]

While King did the lion's share of fund-raising for the protests, Wyatt Tee Walker spent some sixty days in Birmingham planning the logistical details of the demonstrations. In mid-February, when Walker kissed his wife and children goodbye in Atlanta, he wondered whether he would ever see them again. He would later comment, "I didn't see how King, Shuttlesworth, Abernathy, myself, and maybe one or two others could ever get out of Birmingham alive."[68]

Not very familiar with the city, Walker depended on the firsthand knowledge of Shuttlesworth and other ACMHR people to help him plot the tactics of their protests. Fred told Carter Gaston, a young ACMHR member who later became pastor of Bethel Baptist, "I want you to get with Wyatt Walker and show him all of the eating facilities that are off limits." Some fifty different followers of Fred Shuttlesworth, including Lola Hendricks, Georgia Price, James Armstrong, Carlton Reese, and Abraham L. Woods Jr., impressed Walker with their availability and usefulness in his planning. "You got fifty people available to do whatever you ask them to do," he later commented. "That's a formidable operation." Hendricks, for example, had contacts with A. G. Gaston and helped talk him into renting the vacant Smith and Gaston Building and the A. L. Smith Auditorium to the movement in spite of his reservations about the protest effort. Woods often drove around the downtown area while Walker made notes. Walker divided his assistants into five committees: the Local Organization Committee became the recruiters for the demonstrations, dividing the city's African American residential areas into eleven pockets. Committee members listed persons who were willing to participate in Project C. By the beginning of the demonstrations, Walker had amassed a list of three hundred potential activists. Other committees included Telephone, Transportation, Food, and Jail Visitation.[69]

As the demonstrations approached, King and Shuttlesworth hammered out an agreement between themselves and their organizations for conducting the forthcoming demonstrations. Their arrangement stemmed largely from what the two leaders needed from one another. King needed a victory for his organization, in particular a victory with national ramifications. Shuttlesworth, of course, had a vested interest in success at the local level. He needed King and the SCLC to tip the balance in Birmingham and remove the remaining vestiges of segregation. With these varying goals of the national and the local civil rights movement, one view is that Shuttlesworth had concluded that complete victory in Birmingham was impossible without additional pressure from the SCLC. Shuttlesworth and King, therefore, had different goals for the demonstrations and, as a result, different ideas of what would constitute success. Accordingly, to King the complete integration of Birmingham mattered less than appearing successful enough to a national audience to induce the federal government to intervene.[70]

This perspective probably makes too great a distinction between national and local goals. The difference was primarily a matter of emphasis, and local success was intertwined with national progress in civil rights. Moreover, Shuttlesworth did not call in reinforcements because of the ACMHR's failures; it was rather on the basis of his *victories* that he called in King and the SCLC. By nature Shuttlesworth had great difficulty acknowledging his own or his organization's limitations. He believed that his going it alone would eventually prevail but that progress would be quicker and larger in scope if the ACMHR and the SCLC combined forces. As he later explained, "Look at how far we had come with only a few people, and . . . without massive demonstrations, without SCLC, we have done [all] this; now *with* SCLC enlarging the influence, with national celebrities and figures coming in, and with all of us together, we ought to be able to turn things upside down."[71]

In inviting the SCLC, Shuttlesworth had hopes of "enlarging upon what we were doing to the maximum." Shuttlesworth believed the SCLC could help complete and nationalize his earlier, limited victories at the local level. That is why Shuttlesworth later argued that had King entertained notions of anything less than genuine change in the local situation, he would never have invited King to join forces. "We would not have gone through it . . . had I felt in the least bit that Martin was using Birmingham to just stage something in his own interest, rather than progress in Birmingham *as well as* a victory [for the SCLC]. See, we all needed a victory, so that to that extent, our goals were the same. . . . Insofar as I was led to believe or could see or could discern, Martin was as concerned about a total victory, which included not only victory over segregation—a clear-cut victory, a filling of the jails—but also some progress in the local Birmingham situation. I wouldn't have agreed any other way. . . . Martin never gave me any indication that he was any less concerned about total and complete victory in Birmingham, Alabama, itself. Because victory in Birmingham, Alabama, itself meant victory to the nation."[72]

Similarly, Wyatt Walker minimized any distinctions between national and local goals, arguing that "one hand washes the other. . . . You can't better a specific situation until you better the whole situation. Montgomery . . . isn't going to be any better on voter registration until they get a fiat from the federal government." This element of unity between the two organizations, as contrasted with what happened in Albany, necessitated a series of agreed-upon policies between Shuttlesworth and King. First, decisions during the demonstration were to be made in consultation with Shuttlesworth and the ACMHR. Second, all communications with the media were to be made jointly by the two organizations. Third, because he had sworn never to give up until tangible progress was reached and had developed the trust of his people, Fred insisted that King and the SCLC "could not stop in Birmingham unless we got some definite commitment" from the city's economic elite. King recognized Shuttlesworth's claim on the movement in Birmingham, and on the eve of the March 5 mayoral election, King and his organization entered the city in agreement with Shuttlesworth's terms of engagement.[73]

Events in early March portended important political change for Birmingham. On March 1 the Alabama Supreme Court upheld the efforts of the Progressive leadership petition to change Birmingham's government to a mayor-council form. This decision thwarted the commissioners' suit to retain the old system and fully legitimized the mayoral elections set for March 5. Election day brought news regarding another judicial decision that impinged even more directly on Shuttlesworth and similarly augured well for the civil rights movement: the Alabama Court of Appeals had reversed Fred's two breaches of the peace in connection with the Freedom Rides. The court found that the state provided insufficient evidence that Shuttlesworth's notifying of the press and the police of the approaching Freedom Rides had "conspired to cause mobs to form" at the bus station. On learning the news of his court victory, Shuttlesworth quipped, "This may be a sign that some of the people in the Alabama court system are getting some religion." Most of Birmingham's white progressives thought additional good news arrived in the day's election returns, as Boutwell led the way with 17,434 votes to Connor's 13,780, followed by 11,659 votes for liberal candidate Tom King. The results set up an April 2 runoff election between Boutwell and Connor. Because King had been considered the most liberal of the candidates, local politicos expected most of his support to fall to Boutwell, making likely a defeat of Connor.[74]

The infinitesimal difference between Boutwell and Connor on segregation suggested to Shuttlesworth that the "promised land" still lay some distance away.

For him a Boutwell victory hardly heralded the arrival of the millennium. He told audiences at mass meetings that "whoever is elected is going to catch hell." Demonstrations would be necessary in either event. Nonetheless, his bitter experience with the commissioner made him hope for Connor's eventual ouster, and he believed Boutwell to be marginally better for Birmingham in the long run. Fred therefore viewed Connor as a definite contender in the runoff and counseled that Project C again be postponed until after the elections. This advice coincided with that of others, such as Miles College president Lucius Pitts, who worried that demonstrations would have deleterious effects, especially if held before the election. In a March 9 meeting with Alabama Council on Human Relations director Norman Jimerson, Pitts noted that he and others in the black business elite were "convinced that demonstrations mean blood on the streets." He further indicated that Connor hoped to create an incident by hiring a former Miles student to sit next to him at a political event and "start a ruckus." Pitts had learned of the ploy and convinced the student not to be Connor's pawn and to return the money. Two weeks before election day, Connor, hoping to galvanize his far right-wing support, made a radio comment that "Negroes are already planning something to come off during the election." Stopping over in Atlanta on his way back to Cincinnati, Shuttlesworth heard Connor's comment on the wire services and immediately called Lola Hendricks back to Birmingham. He complained, "If Bull can win on his own merits, that's one thing, but to use cheap tactics to fool the white and Negro communities makes him unfit as a public servant. If anything happens, the general public will know it has been staged by unscrupulous politicians." He then dictated a statement of rebuttal to Hendricks, denying responsibility for any racial incidents that might occur before election day. "We have received information from several reliable sources," Shuttlesworth announced, "that an incident with racial overtone is to be staged in Birmingham by persons supporting one of the Candidates for Mayor. This faked action is to be blamed on the Alabama Christian Movement for Human Rights." He then sought to assure the public that his organization "has planned *no* action or incidents during the election, which would aid or abet the election of any Candidate, and will not participate in any." He concluded by urging "all citizens Negro and white" to avoid any incidents that might "create an atmosphere of hysteria in the midst of such a critical election."[75]

Shuttlesworth's announcement temporarily assuaged the black business elite and many of the African American clergy. In truth, however, with its more gradualist approach to civil rights, this middle-class element opposed major demonstrations regardless of their timing. In the weeks before the runoff election, A. G. Gaston argued against the demonstrations, and the Reverend J. L. Ware, president of the Baptist Ministers Conference, unsuccessfully tried to pass a resolution asking King to stay out of Birmingham. Many of the business and ministerial elite still bristled at Shuttlesworth's claim of being the city's exclusive black leader. Having expected Shuttlesworth's role in Birmingham to diminish after his move to Cincinnati, a number of them considered him an "absentee autocrat." John T. Porter, pastor of the sizable Sixth Avenue Baptist Church and former associate to King at Dexter, grew increasingly hesitant concerning Project C and developed a dislike of Shuttlesworth, whom he viewed as an "unstable dictator." A sophisticated "Morehouse man," Porter was closer to Shuttlesworth in age, but, like Ware, he had an intellectual and polished manner. He bristled at Fred's leadership style and considered Shuttlesworth an insecure loner who, unlike King, "was not the kind [of leader] who could allow input." "Fred just didn't have that sense of security," Porter later told an interviewer, "[and] really could not deal with groups." He later speculated that Shuttlesworth's insecurities lay in his academic limitations, and after moving to Birmingham he clashed with Fred regarding Birmingham's Episcopal bishop Charles C. J. Carpenter. Porter saw the bishop as a sincere white clergyperson with whom blacks could work. Carpenter, however, had earlier angered Shuttlesworth with public statements that race relations had been making progress until the rise of civil rights agitation. Carpenter also disgusted Shuttlesworth with his prognosis that fifty years would be a reasonable length of time for racial equality gradually to develop in the South. Fred never got over his disdain for Carpenter and concluded that if Porter trusted Carpenter, he was not ACMHR material. As a result, Shuttlesworth refused to name Porter to his board.[76]

Porter saw Shuttlesworth as an authoritarian and later recalled an instance when an angry Shuttlesworth made it clear that he viewed himself as black Birmingham's sole leader. As the two disagreed on some particular, Shuttlesworth told him, "Porter, this is my movement! You get in line or you get out." Porter increasingly came to believe that Shuttlesworth was emotionally addicted to the limelight. Porter later recalled another occasion, during Project C, when Shuttlesworth arrived at King's motel room to find a news conference already in progress, with national television cameras whirring as King explained the situation for that day. Noticing Porter sitting on a sofa next to King, Shuttlesworth became infuriated and insisted that Porter get up so he could sit next to King. Porter interpreted the incident as an example of Shuttlesworth's need to be the center of attention. Still, Porter could not deny and did admire Shuttlesworth's raw courage, acknowledging his importance to the civil rights movement as the instigator of "public acts that lit the fire" in Birmingham.[77]

In contrast to Birmingham's black middle class, ACMHR members and supporters were less antagonized by Shuttlesworth's sometimes heavy-handed leadership style. For one thing, as predominantly working-class persons they were less concerned than the middle-class elite about sharing power with their leader. Of more importance, they believed what observer Vincent Harding later wrote concerning the loyalties of the African American masses in Birmingham: "Negro leadership is now largely determined by the willingness of a man to suffer for the people." Shuttlesworth's proven record in that regard made him, as Harding further observed, "the key figure among the Negroes of Birmingham." James T. Montgomery, Shuttlesworth's physician and one of the few truly middle-class ACMHR members, expressed more sympathy with Fred's dictatorial ways and believed he had earned the right to call the shots. He bluntly asserted, "You see, if you've been out there, and been cut and hit and bombed, it's not hard for you to say 'This is my thing.' And it *was* his thing." Other "Shuttle-lites" resented what they considered efforts of prominent "Johnny-come-latelies" to assume leadership without paying the price of suffering. Shuttlesworth's follower and bodyguard, Colonel Johnson, believed that Porter, for example, sought to parlay his ministerial prestige too quickly into civil rights leadership, hoping to "come in as a vice president." True or not, most of Shuttlesworth's loyalists unquestionably viewed John Porter in that light.[78]

Still others took offense at other ministers' tendency, as the civil rights movement grew more popular with their parishioners, to claim greater involvement in the movement than the facts merited. This tendency to exaggerate one's involvement, significant during the civil rights struggle itself, became even more pronounced in retrospect. Thirty years after his involvement in the Danville, Virginia, movement, Thurman Echols commented that "some people claim to have been in the movement who were not, but I've got the pictures to prove I was there." James Orange, a young Birminghamian who recruited for the demonstrations and later was an SCLC staff member, vehemently denied, on the one hand, that anyone active in the Birmingham struggle thought ill of Fred Shuttlesworth. On the other hand, however, Orange admitted that negative comments did occasionally surface, but that these criticisms always occurred among those who were least involved with the movement. In essence, both perspectives are true: Shuttlesworth's authoritarian style did grate on the sensibilities of many prominent African Americans in Birmingham. It is also true that to some extent he had earned that right. Furthermore, it is undeniable that in hindsight many persons marginally involved with the movement claimed more involvement and importance to the struggle—sometimes including Shuttlesworth—than was deserved. This is to be expected as an oppressed minority looks back on a historically momentous movement such as this one. As the struggle revved up in 1963, however, the movement certainly enjoyed less popularity within the black middle class than would be the case a generation later.[79]

Thus in mid-March King and Shuttlesworth responded to the black professional elite in both public and private ways. King became a sounding board for complaints about Shuttlesworth, convincing them that he had Fred under control. Using his considerable personal and diplomatic skills, King gradually brought the middle-class advisors under the tent and secured their support for the demonstrations. He was aided, however, by the vortex of events, and the reluctant supporters did not fall in line until the demonstrations were well under way. Publicly, to white critics as well as black, King and Shuttlesworth answered objections that the impending demonstrations were "untimely." First, they argued that some segregationists would never see any protest efforts as "timely." Second, influenced by Fred's understanding of the situation in Birmingham, they countered that they saw no evidence that Boutwell would move fast enough to suit their needs. Third, again shaped by Shuttlesworth's expectations and experience from the previous fall's negotiations, they reminded their critics that segregation signs had returned to Birmingham stores after the SCLC convention—without demonstrations those negotiations had failed to bring lasting progress. Finally, they pointed out that protests during the Easter season would both economically affect an important buying season and, by emphasizing their willingness to suffer for a righteous cause, carry an important religious symbolism.[80]

Shuttlesworth thus agreed only to letting the middle-class leaders act as an advisory board to the collective efforts of the ACMHR and the SCLC. He had no intention, however, of being governed by the timidity of his critics. "'Advisory Board' means advisory—advice," he later explained. "We are free to take it or not." So the business elite's caution regarding the demonstrations and their willingness to allow Boutwell a chance to prove himself made little impression on Shuttlesworth. Boutwell, he surmised, would prove only that he "was gon' talk nice and do nothing." Although the advisory board alerted the public that they "stood ready and willing to negotiate with the new mayor," Fred intended for the ACMHR-SCLC coalition alone to determine the future course of events: "We didn't ask the Advisory Board to vote as to whether or not we were gon' demonstrate, or the type of demonstrations we would have. That was not in their hands, and I made that plain to start off with." Meeting with them, Fred told them in typically certain terms, "You didn't invite him [King] in; you can't put him out. And if you try to put him out, you'll be in trouble. You'll be against what the movement is about, and we can't have these poor folk thinking you are selling them out to the white folks." Shuttlesworth was prepared to make at least one concession to the advisory board. Concurring with the consensus in black Birmingham that demonstrations might aid the Connor campaign for mayor, Fred supported postponing the start of demonstrations until after the runoff election.[81]

In the fortnight leading up to the demonstrations, Fred participated in innumerable planning sessions. In mid-March he wrote to Wyatt Walker and King because he was unhappy that targets for the demonstrations were limited to desegregating the lunch counters of the primary downtown department stores. On Shuttlesworth's recommendations, Walker had settled on sit-ins at Loveman's, Pizitz's, Newberry's, Britt's, and Woolworth's. Nonetheless, Shuttlesworth registered his preference that the demonstrations attack segregation more broadly than just the lunch counters. "My feeling," he wrote, "is that we should cover the waterfront—including Parks implementation (golf, 'Kiddie-Land'); Roving squads to ride Taxis, Buses, etc.; Picketing, if necessary, Marches, and even a Prayer meeting at City Hall." Initially, Walker and King stuck to their narrower focus on the lunch counters, but as Project C got under way the course of events gradually expanded the attack to include most of what Shuttlesworth had advocated. In other matters, his letter communicated his concern "that we have not clearly defined areas of action, points of emphasis, the degree of commitment, and the time and methods by which other Groups will be allowed to participate." He reminded King and Walker that the SCEF and SNCC had made commitments to join the demonstrations but held firm that it would be better to begin "with local people and SCLC," with other outside organizations welcome to join after action had begun. Of significance, he added that activities of the SCEF and SNCC would remain "subject, of course, to direction by ACMHR-SCLC." Of even more significance, he listed his own organization first, indicative of his concept of the chain of command.[82]

Fred thus felt no limitations to involving himself in all phases of the planning for Project C. Bearing the scars from the previous seven years of battle with segregation and Bull Connor, Shuttlesworth was particularly useful to King's money-raising efforts. On their most lucrative foray, Shuttlesworth and King went to a function at the apartment of entertainer Harry Belafonte in New York City. King and Belafonte introduced Shuttlesworth to the gathering, which included actors Ossie Davis, Ruby Dee, Frederic March, and Anthony Quinn, along with editors James Wechsler of the *New York Post* and Jimmy Hicks of the *Amsterdam News.* King told the many SCLC supporters of the impending demonstrations, letting them in on the plans that remained closely guarded in Birmingham. He reminded them of Birmingham's status as the most segregated city in the South and mentioned that protests were scheduled to begin on April 3, the day after the mayoral election. King indicated, however, that the project would proceed as planned even if the more moderate candidate, Albert Boutwell, won the election. He concluded by emphasizing the necessity of hitting Birmingham during the Easter season for reasons of religious symbolism. By the time King finished, his urbane and politically astute audience was prepared for Shuttlesworth's more emotional appeal.

Reviewing some of his own travail against Connor, Shuttlesworth told them that "the time is ripe to end segregation in Birmingham forever." His ACMHR troops were fully mobilized and ready to march as soon as the word was given. "Birmingham Negroes have endured too much for too long," he importuned. "If freedom doesn't come now, it may be too late for it ever to come. We hope that you will join us in the good fight. If you don't, we are prepared to go it alone." Picking up King's earlier Easter theme of death and resurrection, Fred concluded, "You have to be prepared to die before you can begin to live." As Shuttlesworth finished, King jerked his head slightly in a nervous tic, while the rest of the group hushed into a shocked silence. King was impressed with Fred's comments, later suggesting that his status as a walking-talking symbol of the dangers of confronting Jim Crow in Birmingham served the fund-raising effort to great effect. He wrote that Shuttlesworth "brought a sense of the danger as well as the earnestness of our crusade into that peaceful New York living room." In response, the attendees dug into their deep pockets and contributed $475,000 to underwrite Project C. All that now remained was to await the dawning day after the election.[83]

Cataclysm

We hope to show you something that has never been seen
before in Birmingham, something you will all be proud of.
— ACMHR treasurer William S. Shortridge

A lmost two months before the cataclysmic demonstrations in 1963, Birmingham police officer W. E. Chilcoat noticed speakers at mass meetings
tipping off ACMHR members of something momentous in the offing. At an
early February mass meeting, Bill Shortridge hinted that the big event would
occur in March, and Ed Gardner spoke of the need to "mix politics with religion." Connecting their civil rights activism to the traditional evangelistic language of the "Great Commission" (Matt. 28:19–20), Gardner intoned, "We have
got to observe all things. We have got to teach others. Teach Bull Connor things.
Teach George Wallace things. The church must take the lead." For his part,
Shuttlesworth, operating this night on a somewhat less lofty plane, seemed concerned that he was not getting his due from the congregation: "You are not like
some audiences," he complained. "They go wild when they see me. But to see
this large crowd does me good." He reminded them of a recently televised program on religion and race, noting, "I'm in the picture. King's in the picture. I
made the closing statements in that picture."[1]

Fred's occasional boastful comparisons to King reflected a concern not to be
outshone now that King and the SCLC were coming to his turf. On such occasions Shuttlesworth could appear to nonpartisans as petty in his concern for
personal glory. Some of that was no doubt there, but Shuttlesworth was not con-
sumed by feelings of competition with King. Rather, after seven years of difficult work, he wanted to be sure that ACMHR members—and, of course, their
leader—got the credit they deserved now that the national press was finally
poised to follow King into Birmingham. As cameras began to roll, Shuttlesworth insisted that he and the ACMHR faithful remain in the picture not just
for the sake of self-aggrandizement but also to be sure that King and the SCLC
ultimately held Birmingham's feet to the fire. On the day after the election,
"a fire you can't put out" was set to overwhelm Birmingham. This chapter

describes the events that captured national and international attention during the five weeks from April 3 to May 10, 1963, when the ACMHR and the SCLC carried out Project Confrontation.

With the election returns now official, the *Birmingham News* on April 3 heralded "New Day Dawns for Birmingham" with a front-page color cartoon of a bright sun over the city. Mayor-elect Albert Boutwell triumphantly announced, "Birmingham at last is ready to move—forward and upward to its rightful place as a real leader among Southern cities." Connor had been defeated, but he and the other city commissioners refused to give up their offices, charging that the earlier election on government change had been fraudulent and arguing that the commission remained the rightful government in the city. The matter would eventually be decided in court, but in the meantime both governments sought to administer the affairs of Birmingham. Two mayors, Art Hanes and now Albert Boutwell, occupied the mayor's suite at city hall, and as attorney David Vann later noted, when visitors asked to see the mayor, the receptionist had to ask, "Which one?" This divided government aided the developing demonstrations by inhibiting rapid, clear responses to ACMHR-SCLC actions. Still, just as Boutwell's election left Shuttlesworth and King undeterred from proceeding with their protests, so did the wrangling over who held Birmingham's reins of power. Asked whether the fuss in city hall affected their plans, Fred simply commented, "It's unfortunate, but I don't see anything to do but to go ahead with our program."[2]

So on Wednesday morning, April 3, the majority in the Magic City read the election results they hoped would make both Connor and Shuttlesworth disappear. While they perused the newspaper that morning, around ten o'clock Fred dispatched Lola Hendricks and the Reverend Ambus Hill, pastor of the Lily Grove Baptist Church, to city hall to request a parade permit. They were greeted by Connor, who grumbled, "No, you will not get a permit in Birmingham, Alabama, to picket. I will picket you over to the City Jail if you don't get the hell out of here." Over in the vicinity of the Sixteenth Street Baptist Church, Shuttlesworth himself was helping to distribute copies of the "Birmingham Manifesto," a statement announcing to the press the onset of protest demonstrations. Written by Wyatt Walker and going out under Shuttlesworth's name, the manifesto reminded the city of its broken promises of the previous fall and professed African Americans' faith in "our Hebraic-Christian tradition, the law of morality and the Constitution of our nation." The statement appealed to black and to white citizens to join the protests, concluding: "This is Birmingham's moment of truth in which every citizen can play his part in her larger destiny." The following day, the ACMHR-SCLC released a second statement to the press that outlined the aims of the protests. First, they sought the desegregation of all downtown store facilities. Second, they called for the adoption of fair hiring practices by those stores. Third, they called for all charges from previous protests to be dismissed. Fourth, they demanded equal employment opportunities for blacks within the city government. Fifth, they called on officials to reopen on a desegregated basis all of the city's closed recreational facilities. Finally, Shuttlesworth and King called for the establishment of a biracial committee to pursue further desegregation.[3]

Later on Wednesday afternoon Shuttlesworth spoke to reporters who, like Birmingham's white liberals and more than a few black leaders, wondered why black protests were being launched so soon after the election of a more moderate mayor and asked why they would not give Boutwell a chance. Ignoring suggestions that Boutwell's victory made any real difference, Shuttlesworth reminded them that demonstrations had been postponed three times in the previous year in the hope that merchants would agree to desegregate. He also noted that they had been put off in order to avoid becoming part of the political rhetoric of the mayoral race. Now, however, he noted, "Birmingham's rigid and inflexible history in race relations leaves us no alternative but to make this moral witness. We can no longer defer Birmingham's confrontation with that which is right and just."[4]

Timed to coincide with Shuttlesworth's press conference, some two dozen volunteers began the initial protests of Project C by converging on the lunch counters of four downtown department stores. Recruited at a mass meeting the night before, the protesters brought a religious fervor to their commitment to risk a visit to Bull Connor's jail. Young Carter Gaston had mulled over the decision, finally convinced by an irrepressible feeling that if he "had not gone to jail that next day I just would have died." Once arrested and placed in a paddy wagon, Gaston and his twenty cohorts rocked the wagon with rousing strains of the hymn "Shall We Gather at the River." Other ACMHR faithful were among those arrested, including the Reverends Abraham Woods and Calvin Woods and Carlton Reese, director of the ACMHR choir. After the protesters were booked into the city jail, other inmates warmed up to them once they realized they were "King and Shuttlesworth men" and soon began to sing along.[5]

The religious ardor and the enthusiastic singing continued that evening at the first of the nightly mass meetings held for the duration of the demonstrations. Some five hundred congregants crowded into St. James Baptist Church to cheer the demonstrators and to rally behind the leaders. Ed Gardner warmed up the crowd by poking fun at Connor: "Old Bull has hollered so loud for so long, [but] he is now out in the pasture." Following Gardner, Shuttlesworth told the crowd to enthusiastic cheers that "some people think Negroes are going to put on a big bluff, that it will soon go over, but we are just getting started." He then described his conversation earlier in the evening with a white liberal who asked him whether blacks "wanted progress or attention." "I told him, 'Go over to the City Jail and ask twenty-one Negroes in jail what they want.'" With members of the congregation shouting, "That's right!" Shuttlesworth continued:

> Birmingham must wake up and join the rest of the world. We have been in this fight for seven long years, and we don't intend to quit now. Twenty-five people came to me this morning and said, "Here's my body." I told them unless you are ready to go to jail and give your body and your soul to our movement, then go home. What did they do? They went to jail. Last September the merchants of downtown met with us and promised certain things, and they have not lived up to them. "Old Art" . . . and Boutwell said it was silly of us to make this movement at this time, but I will tell you now we don't think it's silly, for the time for action is now. We are tired and we mean business. As I came into Birmingham I walked underneath a sign that said, "It's Nice to have You in Birmingham." I thought to myself, "For what? So we can be arrested and put in jail."

Winding up his stump speech, Shuttlesworth modulated into a spirited introduction of King, calling him a symbol of the movement and enjoining the crowd to "follow him to jail. In the end he will lead us to freedom." King then used some of his diplomacy on the crowd by noting how closely he had worked with Fred over the years. "We in Atlanta have come to the aid of Fred Shuttlesworth. He called on us, and we were glad to come because of the injustice in Birmingham." Then after reminding his listeners that, in spite of criticisms of the timing of the protests, "the time is always right to do right," he outlined the principles of direct action and nonviolence on which the demonstrations were to be based. Finally, Abernathy addressed the crowd, now throbbing with the spirit, and extended an altar call for volunteers to participate in the demonstrations. Some seventy-five or eighty persons flocked down the aisle as if being converted at a revival meeting, and as in an evangelistic service, they were escorted into a back room for preliminary instructions for the next day's protests. Shuttlesworth took the dais once more to issue a few announcements, and then the movement, encouraged by modest success, called it a day.[6]

Establishing a routine of activities did not take Shuttlesworth long. As did the Atlanta contingent, he lodged at the Gaston Motel for the duration of the demonstrations. During "off" hours, of which there were few, he visited his mother and sisters in Oxmoor or some of his friends and former parishioners in North Birmingham. The bulk of his time was spent overseeing the protests in the downtown area. He always considered himself a hands-on general in the civil rights wars, a Patton as compared with King's Eisenhower. Consequently, around ten o'clock each morning he headed for the Sixteenth Street Baptist Church to check out activities at the nonviolence workshops. At these workshops SCLC subordinates Andrew Young, James Bevel, and Dorothy Cotton taught the young volunteers the principles of nonviolence prior to their participation in the demonstrations.[7]

King and Abernathy frequently visited the workshops, but Shuttlesworth, with his do-it-yourself style, tended to be present a good deal more than the others. One of the young volunteers, James Orange, noted Shuttlesworth's particular ability to fire up the troops, especially the youth. At mass meetings both he and Abernathy excelled at what evangelists might have called "drawing the net," dramatically extending the invitation for volunteers to go forward to the "mourner's bench" and join the movement. Whereas Abernathy tended to do this through humor, Fred's status as a symbol of fearless activism inspired younger persons to follow his example. What Fred did at mass meetings he did on a smaller scale during his visits to the morning workshops. In addition, he served as an advisor to Bevel, Young, and Wyatt Walker, reminding them on occasion, "This is my town, and I know this town; I know them rednecks." Pressing to have something done according to his wishes, Shuttlesworth "almost always" saw planners defer to his suggestions.[8]

On the second day of protests, a mass demonstration planned for the noon hour failed to materialize, as did sit-ins at the same lunch counters where protesters had sought service on the previous day. Four of the five department stores closed their lunch counters, and the fifth posted a heavy-set young tough at a narrow entrance who carried a sign that read, "We reserve the right to refuse service to anyone." Thus, where twenty-one protesters had been taken into custody on the first day, on this day police made only four arrests. Still, Connor fumed that although he did not know how much longer he would remain in office, the citizens of Birmingham could "rest assured that I will fill the jail if they violate the laws as long as I am at City Hall." Despite the disappointing showing in the day's protests, King and Shuttlesworth thought it was too early to worry about eventual success and went into the evening's mass meeting in an upbeat mood.[9]

At the meeting King expounded on the need for an all-out boycott of purchases at all downtown stores, including merchandise obtained by telephone and credit card. Imploring the people to be prepared to go to jail, King then turned the pulpit over to Abernathy, who convinced some fifty volunteers to commit themselves. Shuttlesworth used a young man named Robert as an object lesson. Telling the congregation of the young protester's having been jailed but subsequently released because of illness, Fred had the young man tell the crowd he intended to go back to jail the next day. Shuttlesworth proudly pointed at Robert and assured the congregation, "This is why we will win," and then urged them to pray for those who remained in jail.[10]

On Friday King and the other leaders responded to further criticism from whites over the timing of the demonstrations. Mayor-elect Boutwell had chided the civil rights leaders as "outside elements and agitators" in spite of the leadership of the ACMHR. Choosing to ignore Shuttlesworth and the ACMHR's work as the homegrown core of the current SCLC demonstrations, Boutwell predicted: "When these outsiders learn they are not going to get any more publicity out of this thing, they will move on to more profitable fields." To prove they had little intention of moving to other venues, leaders decided to launch protest marches on Saturday morning. Also, the department stores' ploy of closing their lunch counters had resulted in too few arrests on the first three days of demonstrations. This necessitated some action designed to generate larger protests. The brain trust decided that larger marches in the direction of city hall would infuriate Connor and goad him into more visible and possibly violent measures to put them down. More important, such reactions by Connor's police would likely spur larger numbers of volunteers for later marches. Thus, protest marches would begin on Saturday morning; furthermore, both to involve one of the key leaders and to counter Boutwell's "outside agitator" criticism, Shuttlesworth insisted that he would lead the first one. This would make him the first of the primary leaders to go to jail during Project C.[11]

More nettling than Boutwell's criticism, however, had been a speech by Father Albert S. Foley, a Jesuit priest and professor of sociology at Mobile's Spring

Hill College. Foley, chairman of the Alabama Advisory Committee to the U.S. Civil Rights Commission, addressed a banquet in Birmingham on the first day of the demonstrations. He delivered a broadside, accusing King of inhibiting racial progress in the city. Calling the demonstrations "poorly timed and misdirected," Foley told his white audience that "Negro leaders have told me they are suspicious of the motives of Shuttlesworth and King coming into the city to stir people up, hold mass meetings, raise money, then move elsewhere." Foley angered the leaders of Project C by criticizing King as a leader for "one failure after another," citing his difficulties in the Albany campaign. King and Shuttlesworth were most irritated by the cleric's implications that the protests were being launched for the leaders' personal gain. Consequently, Foley became the target for the preachers' rhetoric at Friday night's mass meeting. King fired a salvo of criticism at Foley. Speaking more bluntly, Abernathy called Foley a hypocrite and complained, "We're sick and tired of white folks picking our leaders for us." He called for Shuttlesworth to send a telegram to President Kennedy and John G. Hannah, chairman of the Civil Rights Commission, to inform them that Foley was unfit to serve on the Alabama Advisory Committee. Shuttlesworth quickly assured Abernathy and the congregation that this would be done. Before the service had ended, Wyatt Walker had released a statement to the press that the four hundred persons in attendance voted unanimously to "condemn the statements of Father Foley." The statement also called on the president to remove Foley from his post. Shuttlesworth announced that protests would be stepped up the next day—he himself would lead a march on city hall. Feeling at once jovial and defiant, he joked that he wanted "to drink some of that *white* water in the City Hall and see if it tastes any better than the colored water." [12]

About eleven o'clock the next morning Shuttlesworth met with Walker at the Sixteenth Street church to go over last-minute instructions with the participants for the march. Fred believed that his arrest would give the demonstrations a needed spark when the news reached the African American churches the next morning. What really made the difference, however, was the decision to dispense with sit-ins as the primary tactic. Too easily foiled by the act of lunch counters being closed down ahead of time, sit-ins quickly had to be replaced by larger, more public marches, which, led by Shuttlesworth and other prominent ministers, would generate more arrests. After reminding his forty-two fellow marchers of their tactics, Shuttlesworth, along with Charles Billups, led them from the church across Kelly Ingram Park to Fifth Avenue North. [13]

After walking double file for three blocks toward city hall, with police chief Jamie Moore and Connor looking on, the marchers were stopped by police in front of the federal building. Calling to them through a bullhorn, Moore warned them that they were violating the city ordinance that prohibited parading without a permit and ordered them to disperse. Another police officer, Captain George Wall, repeated the order twice. On the third order, Shuttlesworth turned and called on his charges to kneel with him in prayer. At that point they were arrested. Shuttlesworth and the marchers were loaded into three paddy wagons. One of the wagons was so crowded that closing the door required four officers. As they were herded into the wagons, Shuttlesworth led the group in the singing of "We Shall Overcome."[14]

After being booked at city hall, Shuttlesworth and the others were taken to Southside jail, where he sent word of his arrest to Ruby in Cincinnati. Assuring her that he was safe, Fred instructed her to ask his associate minister, Aaron Bland, to preach at Revelation the next morning in the pastor's absence. In the meantime, he learned that King had convinced reluctant Birmingham ministers John Porter and N. H. Smith to risk arrest by leading marches that day. At the Saturday night mass meeting, while Shuttlesworth remained in jail, Smith admitted to the congregation that his seven-year activity in the ACMHR had not resulted in his being arrested but that the Easter season was a symbolically appropriate time, and he was now ready to go to jail for the cause. The next afternoon, on Palm Sunday, Smith, along with Porter and A. D. King, led another march on city hall.[15]

During the march, problems developed when African American bystanders, who had not participated in the SCLC's nonviolence training but who to most white police and reporters were indistinguishable from bona fide marchers, became angered by a new police tactic, the use of dogs. One such bystander named Leroy Allen reportedly slashed at one of the dogs with a clay pipe. The dog immediately attacked, tearing the sleeve of Allen's coat and pinning him to the ground. Other African American onlookers rushed toward him, which in turn drew more police officers with two more dogs to the scene. Twenty-six marchers and onlookers were taken into custody, bringing the total arrests to 102 since the beginning of the demonstrations. Learning of these developments in jail, Shuttlesworth simply commented that he had expected such a reception from Connor's police department. Back at the Gaston Motel, the movement's headquarters, Walker and Dorothy Cotton "celebrated" the use of the dogs, saying,

"We've got a movement. We had some police brutality. They brought out the dogs."[16]

Although not quite as exuberant as Walker and Cotton, Fred, when his work detail at the Birmingham prison farm gave him time to think about it, knew that the demonstrations had reached a transforming moment. Connor's use of police dogs and the incident involving Leroy Allen created the kind of drama that the ACMHR-SCLC forces desperately needed. King and the others understood that these developments, though tragic in the short run, would generate more local support of the movement than anything else. Events on Monday bore this out.

That Monday afternoon, while Shuttlesworth remained in jail, King and Abernathy attended a meeting of the Baptist Ministers Conference, hoping to drum up clerical support now that demonstrations had begun. Most of the pastors displayed a marked reluctance to support the protests. J. L. Ware agreed with the city's white liberals that Boutwell deserved a chance to prove himself. King's appearance before the conference without Shuttlesworth turned out to be a fortunate happenstance. Shuttlesworth's rash actions and blunt criticisms of ministers who avoided the civil rights movement had long since rubbed many of the brethren the wrong way. His absence from the meeting helped take the focus off his often polarizing persona.

Much more important, however, was King's national reputation and diplomatic approach, which enabled him to overcome the ministers' timid resistance in ways that Shuttlesworth never could. In effect, increasing numbers of the black elite found saying "no" to King much more difficult than saying "no" to Shuttlesworth. The black community at large had begun to frown on those who failed to support King, and other ministers could ill afford for their congregations to know they did not back African Americans' national leader. In the words of one observer, Ware "was distinctly opposed to the demonstrations" and still wielded great influence with the ministers; nonetheless, the situation in Birmingham had reached critical mass. In addition to King's eloquence, the newspaper photos of five police dogs hovering over a lone African American turned the tide. Thus, largely against the wishes of a still-reluctant J. L. Ware, King and the situation at hand convinced some 125 black Baptist ministers to endorse the protests or at least not to oppose them publicly.[17]

That night Fred was released on bond and conducted a brief press conference, telling reporters that protest leaders had turned down a request from

Robert Kennedy's office for a moratorium on their protests. He assured the press that the marches would continue until the downtown merchants met each of the ACMHR-SCLC demands. There seemed no reason to put on the brakes because the violence of the previous day's march had generated a head of steam for the protests. Then he returned to the Gaston Motel to catch up with developments in the demonstrations. The numbers of demonstrators had increased to a level high enough to lead even Connor to marvel, "The mystery of the whole situation is how can these simple home folks be talked into going to jail by a bunch of rabble rousers." Shuttlesworth was pleased that the action in the streets had intensified and that the ministers had finally come on board. He also learned that King had met that day with a contingent of black professionals seeking their more vigorous support for the demonstrations now that police violence had broken out.[18]

Although millionaire business leader A. G. Gaston had been initially hesitant about the protests, after the meeting he announced his full support and called for whites and blacks to work together to end injustice. In a statement to the press, Gaston said he regretted "the inability of the white merchants and white power structure" to communicate with the city's black citizens. Attempting to inform the white community about the "aspirations of the Negro citizens in this community," he said, "We want freedom and justice, and we want to be able to live and work with dignity in all endeavors where we are qualified. . . . We also want the privilege of access to those facilities that will make an individual qualified." Later, when Mayor Art Hanes phoned Gaston and tried to elicit the businessman's aid to pressure King to stop the demonstrations, Gaston replied: "We will never accept the status quo, never." At that night's mass meeting, Shuttlesworth informed the crowd of the ministers' and business and professional leaders' support, boasting, "We not only have the poor Negroes in Birmingham, we have the rich Negroes in this movement now." Abernathy pledged their intention to wear overalls until the city merchants treated African Americans fairly, while King announced that he would lead marches and personally submit to arrest within the week.[19]

Gloating that events were at long last dragging the African American elite into the movement, Shuttlesworth now prepared for another important meeting—with Sid Smyer, spokesperson for Birmingham's white business leaders. The escalating violence and increased black support for the demonstrations had finally induced Smyer to arrange a secret meeting with the minister and to consider the terms set by the ACMHR and the SCLC. A key business leader and president of the Birmingham Chamber of Commerce, Smyer had sought to avoid meeting with protest leaders, in part because the merchants were not empowered to speak for the city government and partly to avoid the perception of being pressured to the bargaining table. To buffer himself further from public opinion, Smyer asked Norman C. Jimerson, director of the Alabama Council on Human Relations, to call the meeting. On Tuesday evening, prior to his appearance at the mass meeting, Shuttlesworth and two associates met with Smyer; Emil Hess, owner of the Parisian Department Store; Boutwell's representative, W. C. "Billy" Hamilton; and Birmingham lawyer Charles Morgan.[20]

The meeting got off to an inauspicious beginning when Smyer bluntly asked Shuttlesworth, "What is it you niggers want?" "Probably not to be called niggers, for one thing," came a mumbled reply from Morgan, a liberal sympathetic to the concerns of black Birminghamians. Unperturbed, Shuttlesworth smilingly answered that whites would have to grant the movement's requests, plus commit themselves to prompt school desegregation. Absent these concessions, he warned, the city could expect further massive demonstrations. At that Hamilton reminded the group that the mayor-elect could as yet make no promises. Shuttlesworth replied, "We understand that," probing further into what Boutwell *would* do. He received no clear answer other than a rather nebulous discussion of appointing a biracial committee. The meeting ended without any firm decisions, but the negotiation process had nonetheless begun. Another meeting was scheduled for a week hence, with intentions to broaden the number of participants.[21]

Although Tuesday had gone well for the demonstrations, events on Wednesday constituted something of a downturn. In the *Birmingham World* Emory Jackson published an editorial critical of direct action and called for a more indigenous program for the city based on "dependable hometown leadership." The editor took a similar tone the following week when he commended local leaders, such as Ware, who did not "play to the grandstand or exploit the spotlight." With Shuttlesworth likely in mind, Jackson also criticized "the non-responsible, the non-attached, and the non-program 'leader'" whose role was "to cluster around a glossy personality and share in the reflections of his limelight without the obligation of . . . being held accountable." Shuttlesworth was somewhat surprised by the comments, which seemed to be a public breaking of ranks with the protests. Jackson had typically been supportive of the minister's efforts in Birmingham, attending ACMHR mass meetings monthly and occasionally speaking at them. Shuttlesworth passed the editorials off as having been written, or at least influenced by, *Birmingham World* owner and publisher C. A. Scott, who also owned the *Atlanta World*. Scott, more conservative in his approach to civil rights, often criticized the work of King. Jackson, by contrast, had occasionally complained to Shuttlesworth about Scott's restrictions on him, commenting on what he could get away with and what he could not. Shuttlesworth believed Jackson to be more supportive personally than he was allowed to be in the pages of the *World*. In the heat of battle, of course, Shuttlesworth was little inclined to muse over criticism—there was nothing new in it, and white Birmingham, not given to reading black newspapers, was oblivious to it. Consequently, the editorials were largely ignored.[22]

The movement could not afford, however, to ignore the day's other development. Attorneys for the city had appealed to circuit court judge William A. Jenkins for a temporary injunction against the protest leaders for encouraging demonstrations calculated to provoke breaches of the peace. From the beginning of Project C, movement leaders had planned for a possible injunction against the demonstrations. Shuttlesworth fully expected such an action, but King argued that "not every judge will issue an injunction; we can't assume that." Countering what he viewed as King's naiveté, Shuttlesworth answered, "Where are those converted judges? Where did niggers ever move and law was not used to beat our heads, with the judges helping?" King put the discussion to a temporary end with a dismissive reply: "Well, we can't take that for granted." Now, however, Shuttlesworth seemed to have the better of the argument because an injunction was imminent. Hearing rumors that Jenkins's order was forthcoming, Shuttlesworth called Constance Baker Motley, assistant director of the NAACP Legal Defense Fund, asking for someone to be sent from New York to coordinate the local legal efforts. Motley quickly dispatched Norman Amaker to handle matters in Birmingham.[23]

Judge Jenkins signed the order about nine o'clock that night, and the papers were served a little after one o'clock in the morning. Deputy sheriff Raymond E. Belcher found King, Abernathy, and Shuttlesworth sitting at a table in the restaurant of the Gaston Motel. After receiving the papers, King read portions aloud for television cameras and reporters. Shuttlesworth called the injunction a flagrant denial of their constitutional rights and assured the reporters that the movement would not be deterred by such an injunction. He later added that although he had respect for federal injunctions, he had learned that state courts typically favored the wishes of local governments and that "if the police could not handle the situation, then the mobs could." Characteristically more cautious than Shuttlesworth, King indicated that nothing would be done until SCLC law-yers had examined the order. Still, the Baptist preacher in King emerged as he commented that the movement's main concern was to obey its "injunction from heaven." The gathering soon broke up, with King and Shuttlesworth announc-ing a more formal press conference for that day at noon.[24]

After a few hours' sleep, Shuttlesworth was up again, tending to legal and other matters. At nine o'clock in the morning he met with Amaker, giving him a copy of the injunction and informing him of the upcoming press conference. Meeting with reporters, Shuttlesworth deferred to King, who took the lead in articulating the movement's position on the injunction. Indicating a willingness to obey a *federal* injunction because the federal judiciary had established inte-gration as the law of the land, King observed that courts in the Deep South had proved their willingness to perpetuate segregation. He noted, in language that would soon be incorporated into his "Letter from Birmingham Jail," that just as the protest leaders could not in good conscience obey unjust laws, they could not yield to the unjust use of the courts. Out of love for the Constitution and a hope to purify Alabama's judicial system, he explained, the protests would go forward in spite of the consequences.[25]

Applause and cheers from a crowd of African American spectators greeted King's remarks. Shuttlesworth then followed with comments that echoed King's. He denounced what he called Alabama's unwritten rule that "if the mobs don't stop Negroes, the police can; and if the police can't, then the courts will" and promised that demonstrations would continue regardless of the in-junction. He viewed the injunction as another torpedo "thrown in our way" and announced the movement's only appropriate response: "Damn the torpedoes! Full speed ahead."[26] After the thirty-minute press conference, Shuttlesworth headed for the Sixteenth Street Baptist Church to oversee the day's marches. Along the way the minister had a chance meeting with his old nemesis, Bull Connor. Despite his usual antipathy toward Shuttlesworth, Connor greeted him in an unexpectedly jovial manner.

"Hi, Shuttlesworth."

"Hi, Bull."

Noting Shuttlesworth's informal attire, the commissioner said, "Shuttles-worth, if you wear those overalls to jail, they are going to work you real hard over there."

"I'm wearing them so I might save the city a few pennies worth of work clothes," came the lighthearted retort.[27]

In spite of concerns over the proper response to the injunction and the movement's dwindling financial resources for posting bail, the frivolity continued that evening at the mass meeting. Ed Gardner poked fun at the detectives' transmitter, which he called a "doohickey." Shuttlesworth reveled in his enthusiastic audience, telling them triumphantly of his encounter with Connor that afternoon. "Today is the first time that Bull has ever smiled at me." Abernathy announced to the crowd that the movement planned to break the injunction. "You hear that, little doohickey? . . . And biting dogs and ain't nothing else going to stop me. . . . We ain't afraid of white folks anymore. We are going to march tomorrow. We are going to a higher judge than Judge Jenkins. Fred Shuttlesworth and I are marching on Good Friday!!" King appealed for more volunteers, and Wyatt Walker closed with an anecdote emphasizing the call for African Americans to boycott the downtown stores during the Easter season. One woman went into Loveman's with the intention of buying shoes for her baby. The appalled clerk upbraided her potential customer for spending money in the store while "your people [are] out there on the street getting put in jail." She refused to sell the woman any merchandise and sent her elsewhere to make her purchase.[28]

After the mass meeting the leaders retired to King's motel room to discuss the pros and cons of disobeying the injunction. Some worried that fundraising efforts would languish if King were jailed. Others argued that as leader King was now committed to marching and symbolically had to make the sacrifice. Early Friday morning, King himself yielded to the latter argument and cut the discussions off with an announcement that as an act of faith he would march that day and submit to arrest. Now, he said, echoing Shuttlesworth's long-standing argument, talk and philosophy must give way to action. In the process, he believed, God would use the publicity of the arrest as a means of refilling the movement's coffers.[29]

After a short night's sleep, King, Shuttlesworth, and Abernathy arrived at the Sixteenth Street Baptist Church just after noon on Good Friday, April 12. Expecting to be in jail by mid-afternoon, the leaders reviewed details of the campaign that would be continued by SCLC lieutenants Wyatt Walker, Andy Young, and James Bevel. At about 2:30 P.M. the blue jean–clad leaders led some fifty volunteers out of the church. The preachers' sermonic use of Good Friday symbolism took effect; some worshipers in the church said of King, "There he goes, just like Jesus." Some five hundred to one thousand onlookers fell in behind the marchers as they moved up Sixth Avenue North. Met by a large contingent of police officers, the protesters unexpectedly turned south, away from city hall and toward the downtown business section. The marchers turned east again on Fifth Avenue North, where redeployed police met them halfway down the block. Connor shouted, "Stop them there!" As King and Abernathy knelt in prayer, two motorcycle officers and two detectives seized them, twisting their arms behind them and piling them into paddy wagons along with the other marchers. As the wagon pulled away, headed for Southside jail, someone asked Connor if King had been among those arrested. He laughed and replied, "That's what he came here for, to get arrested. Now he's got it." Shouts of anger came from bystanders witnessing the arrests. Others began singing and clapping hands. All of the demonstrators were arrested.[30]

Shuttlesworth, however, was not arrested until later that day. He had intended to avoid arrest in order to continue the movement's fund-raising efforts. Peeling off from the march, he returned to church and then to the motel. Sometime later that afternoon, police officers appeared at his door to place him under arrest. Shuttlesworth protested that the officers had not attempted to arrest him during the march. "Yes, but we got pictures showing you in it," replied the officer. Shuttlesworth then submitted to arrest for parading without a permit, but he was bonded out of jail that same day. While the movement awaited financial reinforcements from Belafonte in New York, Shuttlesworth continued to wring contributions from Birmingham blacks. On Saturday, he put on his pastor's hat and flew back to Cincinnati for Easter Sunday services.[31]

Back at Revelation, he performed a wedding ceremony in his office and preached his Easter sermon wearing the same dungarees he had worn in the Good Friday march. The congregation passed a resolution of support for their pastor and the Birmingham demonstrations. The statement commented that the campaign "led by Reverends Shuttlesworth, King, and Abernathy is necessary for the fulfillment of the American dream of Democracy." They accepted Shuttlesworth's civil rights activities as "necessary leaves of absence," noting that "Gospel Ministry is to 'All the World,' and the Gospel Message deals with man's body as well as his soul." Buoyed by his members' full support, Shuttlesworth boarded the first available plane back to Birmingham, determined to return as soon as possible.[32]

Quite a bit had happened in his absence. After the arrests of the "Big Three" on Good Friday, the congregation at that night's mass meeting heard Bevel and Walker call for grade school students to volunteer to enter the protests. Walker argued that the students could "get a better education in five days in this jail than five months in school." In addition, the preachers called for volunteers to test the segregated white churches on Easter Sunday. On Saturday, six blacks were jailed after sit-ins at Atlantic Mills, a North Birmingham discount shopping center. Also that morning, the *Post-Herald* carried an article by several Birmingham ministers calling the ACMHR-SCLC protests "unwise and untimely." Learning of the article, King began penning a response that would become the most famous writing of the civil rights movement, his "Letter from Birmingham Jail." On his return to Birmingham, Shuttlesworth learned of the ministers' criticisms and of King's forthcoming response. The next week, when the letter became public, Shuttlesworth became mildly annoyed because it had not gone out as a joint statement of King and himself or at least as an ACMHR-SCLC statement. The response had violated King's agreement to issue joint statements, but Shuttlesworth kept his own counsel even though inwardly he felt that his more famous associate was overstepping his bounds. On the other side of the response to the letter, Episcopal bishop C. C. J. Carpenter, one of the ministers whose statement spawned King's missive, sighed to his coadjutor, George Murray, "This is what you get when you try to do something. You get it from both sides. George, you just have to live with that."[33]

Meanwhile, in Southside jail King and Abernathy were held incommunicado, and Wyatt Walker encouraged King's wife, Coretta, to request assistance from the White House. By Easter Sunday afternoon word had reached the vacationing president, who had Robert Kennedy return her calls and inquire into the Birmingham situation. In a much more public manner, the movement made two other statements to white Birmingham on Easter Sunday. Encouraged and led by Andy Young, groups of African American worshipers attempted to attend services at several white churches. Young himself and two women were seated at First Baptist Church. The pastor and several members greeted them, but one member refused to shake hands with Young or accept an offering from him. At the Sixth Avenue Presbyterian Church, the Reverend Bernard Lee and two others were turned away at the door. Pointing toward another place of worship, an usher told them, "Go to the colored church. This church was built by white people, and white people worship here."[34]

After church services that afternoon, protesters launched a sympathy march for their jailed leaders. Some five hundred teenagers gathered around the Thirgood African Methodist Episcopal Church, and A. D. King, Martin's brother and pastor of the First Baptist Church of Ensley, led a group of marchers from the church toward downtown. Along the way the march was blocked by police, who arrested thirty of the protesters, including King and John Porter. The delayed arrival of a paddy wagon allowed a crowd of angry spectators to gather at the scene. As the paddy wagons departed, spectators threw rocks, smashing the windshield of a police motorcycle. Police moved toward the rock throwers, and several blacks were clubbed as the officers tried to contain a crowd that had grown to some two thousand people. Most of these individuals were spectators who streamed in beside and behind the marchers, singing and clapping as they went. Consequently, bystanders swept up in the excitement and often prone to violence came to be confused with actual marchers who had received nonviolence training. This circumstance turned out to be a two-edged sword when handled by the press: although it inflated the size of the protest marches and thus made the demonstrations seem larger than they were, it also led reporters to pin accusations of violence on the ACMHR-SCLC troops. As a further result, the situation gave occasion for whites to refer to the demonstrations as *riots*.[35]

On Monday morning, April 15, ACMHR-SCLC attorneys Arthur Shores and Norman Amaker filed an application to dissolve Judge Jenkins's injunction. Appearing before Judge Jenkins, they argued that the injunction was invalid on eleven grounds. Most important of these was that the injunction violated the ministers' right to due process because it was issued without notice or opportunity for them to be heard prior to its issuance. Also, they argued that the order was so broad that it was impossible to know what specific actions were prohibited. On constitutional grounds, they argued that the injunction constituted an unlawful "prior restraint" on the ministers' rights of free speech and that it was designed to enforce unconstitutional segregation policies. At the same time Birmingham's lawyers, J. M. Breckenridge and Earl McBee, filed contempt charges that stated that the Good Friday march amounted to criminal contempt and that the statements at the April 11 press conference constituted both criminal and civil contempt.[36]

In this case, criminal contempt constituted the less-serious violation, carrying a penalty of only five days in jail. The civil contempt charge, on the other hand, threatened the demonstrations more severely. It carried an indefinite jail sentence by lasting until the defendants "purged" themselves by recanting their public comments and promising not to disobey an injunction again. In response, Jenkins signed the order requested by Breckenridge and McBee for the defendants to "show cause" why they should not be found in civil contempt. Jenkins set two hearings—one on whether to dissolve the injunction, the other on the city's contempt charges—to occur simultaneously on the following Monday. He told reporters, however, that the hearing on the city's contempt charges would take precedence over the motion to dissolve the injunction. During the next week, lawyers for the movement, including New York attorney William Kunstler, who had recently joined the group, petitioned for relief from the federal district court in Birmingham, but none of the three district judges could consider the cases for two weeks.[37]

Shuttlesworth attended the hearing on Monday morning, speaking briefly to King and Abernathy in the courtroom. They informed Shuttlesworth that unlike other prisoners, they were being denied mattresses on which to sleep. When they complained that their cells were cold at night, Shuttlesworth promised to take their topcoats over to them later that afternoon. He also assured them that he would pass along their message to the mass meeting congregation to "keep the movement moving." While at city hall he decided to test the public facilities to see what "white water" tasted like. He found the rest rooms locked and the water fountains turned off. As he leaned over to drink from the "white" water fountain, Connor came out of his office and said, "Well, I caught you." Shuttlesworth bantered with his long-time opponent, laughing about having to use the rest room across the street at the bus station. Entering the bus station, the preacher found several police officers taking advantage of the facilities. He asked jovially, "What y'all doing in here?"

"Hell, Reverend, segregation is hard on us, too," an officer replied. "Bull has got us in the same position that you Negroes are in. We have to come over here to use the rest room. We are locked out."[38]

"Well, then that means y'all ought to get with us, and we'll get it over with then."

That evening, the mass meeting crowd roared its approval as Shuttlesworth regaled them with his retelling of his encounters with Connor and the police officers. "Today we all got equal treatment, and that's what the law means. Equal and exact. Nobody could use the water, 'cause the water fountain went dry. The judge couldn't drink nothin'. I couldn't drink anything. The sheriff, with all that power, couldn't drink anything." Switching his attention to another matter, he said, "Now tomorrow—we have always wondered what made these white folks act so crazy over these toilets. Whatever it is, we'll find out tomorrow. Tomorrow, we will use white toilets. I don't want a black man in a black toilet tomorrow. Let them use ours a while, and we'll use theirs."[39]

He and other speakers commented on the swearing in of Albert Boutwell. In thinly veiled but indirect comments, the new mayor had such outsiders as King and Shuttlesworth in mind when he said, "Whatever our shortcomings may be, they are our own local problems, and we shall resolve them by local efforts and local unity. We shall not submit to the intimidations of pressure or to the dictates of interference." Speakers took such words as a challenge, renewing their intentions to press on, and they made great sport of Connor and the city commission's refusal to give up their offices without a court fight. They also poked fun at the prospect of two city governments competing for the same office space and conducting the same business until the courts settled the matter. (Later, this state of affairs led one wag to observe that Birmingham had "two mayors, one King, and a parade everyday.") Shuttlesworth and other leaders told the mass meeting congregation that they rejected Justice Department requests to postpone direct action until Boutwell and the new city council were in full control. Instead, they celebrated that fifty-five public figures, including Harry Belafonte, Marlon Brando, Steve Allen, and Mrs. Ralph Bunche, had sent telegrams to the president and attorney general that urged federal action in Birmingham. At the same time, however, Burke Marshall, the assistant attorney general for civil rights, said that "the federal government has no authority to take legal action to intervene in Birmingham as the situation now stands." He further made clear in a telephone conversation with the *Birmingham News* that there would be no such federal intervention unless some federal law was violated.[40]

At Monday night's mass meeting, Wyatt Walker took these indications from Burke Marshall as his cue to shift the focus of the demonstrations from a floundering selective buying campaign to a voter registration drive, which would be of more interest to the Justice Department. Thus, most of Shuttlesworth's time on Tuesday was devoted to helping Walker and Young plan a voter registration clinic for the next day and getting updates on the various legal situations pertaining to the demonstrations. ACMHR-SCLC attorneys planned to file suit in federal court to restrain the city from denying African Americans the right to protest in Birmingham. That evening he met with whites in a second but largely futile negotiating session. The most notable development at the meeting had to do with some verbal sparring between Shuttlesworth and Rabbi Milton Grafman and some other ministers. When Grafman mentioned overhearing members of his synagogue complaining about the demonstrations, Shuttlesworth's fiery temperament and prophetic zeal flashed a quick response: "What do you let your people hear you say, Rabbi? I think it's important that they hear from you. . . . I think the pulpit is supposed to advise the pew."

When another minister protested that he did not speak for God or for his people, Shuttlesworth asked, "Then who *do* you speak for?"

"I'm just speaking for myself."

'Well, your self is a very little particle in the wide problem we face," came Shuttlesworth's annoyed rejoinder. "And if you aren't speaking for God and you're not speaking for your people, who in the Hell are you speaking for? I think that's a problem."[41]

Such exchanges added to Shuttlesworth's sense of moral superiority and confirmed his "hothead" status in the eyes of most white ministers, but they did little to advance the negotiations other than to convince the whites of the movement's resolve (or, from the white point of view, its stubbornness). Discussion shut down, and white leaders backed away from continued meetings until a court decision was rendered in the city commission's attempts to retain control of city government. Unlike Shuttlesworth and the others, the white leaders believed Boutwell differed enough from Connor to merit calling off the demonstrations.[42]

During the next few days, the preacher participated in the voter registration marches by sending police chief Jamie Moore and Mayor Art Hanes telegrams that asked for police protection for a group marching to the Jefferson County Courthouse. Instead of granting protection, Moore interrupted a registration workshop at the Sixteenth Street Baptist Church, warning that they would be arrested if they left the church as a group. Undeterred, the march went on as planned and yielded some fifteen more arrests. At the same time, thirty other protesters were arrested in department store sit-ins, bringing the total arrests to more than three hundred.[43]

The same day, King and the movement took some additional ministerial criticism, this time from evangelist Billy Graham, who asked King to "put the brakes on a little bit." He criticized the timing of the demonstrations, which he said had complicated the progress that been made in Birmingham, and indicated that friends had told him that the local African American community did not truly support the efforts. Shuttlesworth contemptuously sniffed at the comments, which he viewed as "a typical churchman's view—putting the brakes on when you ought to be taking the brakes off, going as fast as you can because you hadn't gotten anywhere before." Some days later he would use Graham's words in a mass meeting sermon, asserting: "We have had the brakes on too long, and we have taken them off the car, and we are going a hundred miles an hour."[44]

He was hardly inclined to spend too much time or worry over another white minister's timid gradualism; he had more pressing concerns at hand. Because King and Abernathy still languished in the Birmingham jail, someone was needed to go on the stump for financial support. Walker and Young were busy with the day-to-day logistics of the demonstrations, and Shuttlesworth was the one member of the Big Three free to substitute for King. On Thursday night, April 18, Shuttlesworth replaced King as the speaker in the "One Hundred Years of Freedom" series sponsored by the Capital Press Club in Washington, D.C. In his speech he narrated his personal struggles over the years, with dramatic and emotive attention to his travails in the Birmingham movement. Despite the hundred years of freedom, he lamented, African Americans still were not free, and the time was ripe for a second Emancipation Proclamation. Of course, he also updated the audience on the state of the current demonstrations in Birmingham.[45]

Still, on this trip Shuttlesworth had even bigger fish to fry. Before leaving Birmingham, Walker had arranged for Fred and SCLC representative Walter Fauntroy to meet with Burke Marshall at the Justice Department on Friday morning. Walker thought it was important for Marshall to meet with and learn about the Birmingham struggle from Shuttlesworth. Fauntroy later indicated to Walker that Shuttlesworth had very effectively apprised Marshall of the situation in Birmingham, particularly laying to rest some questions concerning the timing of the demonstrations and the new city government. Marshall told the two emissaries that the federal government would do all it could but that it could not order these businesses how to run their affairs. To that point, he added, he saw no reason for the government to intervene. After the meeting, Marshall said that "it was good to have the opportunity to discuss [the demonstrations] directly with Reverend Shuttlesworth" and reported to Robert Kennedy that the atmosphere in Birmingham remained dangerous.[46]

Always excited to be walking in the corridors of power, Shuttlesworth rushed back to Birmingham eager to share the news of his conversations with Marshall at the mass meeting. Such narratives always served to invigorate the audience and give the preacher a renewed sense of importance, particularly when he thought, as he did occasionally during the five weeks in Birmingham, that the demonstrations were slipping from his control. Shuttlesworth took to the pulpit to tell the crowd that he had just returned from Washington, where everyone had welcomed him with open arms, and assured them that the reporters at the Capital Press Club sent the message that "the whole world is concerned with what is happening here." He complained, "Why can't the *Birmingham News* put some of this stuff on the front page when it is front-page news all over the country?" He evoked loud laughter when he read a *News* article about the demonstrations that claimed that "many local Negro and white leaders oppose this outside interference." Moving toward his crescendo, he cried out that the local paper was lying and that African Americans who did not "want to go forward should get in the back and shut up." With this he gave an altar call, and thirty more volunteers walked the aisle to join the movement.[47]

The next day, April 20, King and Abernathy were bailed out, and their wives drove over from Atlanta to greet them on their release. Shuttlesworth spoke with Mrs. King and Mrs. Abernathy for about forty-five minutes, briefing them on the state of the demonstrations before accompanying them to the jail to meet their husbands. After an impromptu press conference at the Gaston Motel, the three leaders quickly left Birmingham for the weekend, returning to their respective pulpits on Sunday. Back at Revelation, Shuttlesworth had his parishioners pat him on his back for his television appearances and praise the courage of the demonstrators. At home with his family, he updated his wife and children on the inner workings of the movement. All over the church sanctuary and parsonage there were feelings of pride and excitement over the pastor's public role and national importance. Again, however, Shuttlesworth's time back home was limited because he wanted to be back in Birmingham the next day when the contempt trial began.[48]

Between 150 and 200 persons, mostly white reporters or black supporters of the movement, filled Judge Jenkins's courtroom on Monday morning, April 22. Shuttlesworth entered the courtroom fully expecting a sentence of five days for criminal contempt and anticipating that Jenkins would prefer not to give the movement additional publicity through an indefinite sentence for civil contempt. As he took his seat in the courtroom he joked aloud, "Well, let's get on with the hanging." Jenkins began the proceedings with consideration of the contempt citation. Shores objected, arguing that the motion to dissolve had been filed prior to the contempt petition and that the court did not have jurisdiction to issue an invalid or unconstitutional order. Following generally accepted practice, however, Jenkins ruled that in this case the only matters to be determined would be whether the court had had jurisdiction to issue injunctions and whether the parties named had been properly notified of it.[49]

Attorney Earl McBee called several witnesses to establish that the integration forces had been duly notified and had deliberately violated the injunction. One witness testified to observing the injunction being served at the Gaston Motel. Another described Walker's comments that the movement had support in Birmingham "sufficient to create a revolution." Still another witness, police detective Maurice House, recalled Shuttlesworth's public criticisms of southern courts and the statement that "if the police couldn't handle it, the mob would." In reality, of course, the argument that King, Shuttlesworth, Abernathy, and the others had violated the injunction was easy to sustain. Nevertheless, testimony continued through Wednesday. The court then adjourned until Friday morning when Jenkins rendered his decision. Jenkins found the defendants guilty of criminal contempt, ruling that the defendants' actions constituted "deliberate and blatant" denials of the court's authority and, as Shuttlesworth expected, sentenced them to five days in jail. King and the others were released pending appeal. In other courtroom developments that week, circuit judge Edgar Bowron ruled that Boutwell and the newly elected city council constituted the legitimate government of Birmingham. In response, Connor, Hanes, and Waggoner appealed the decision to the Alabama Supreme Court, which eventually sustained Bowron's ruling. The same day, Judge Clarence W. Allgood of the U.S. district court rejected petitions by movement lawyers to transfer 286 cases from the city recorder's court to federal court.[50]

At Wednesday evening's mass meeting, Shuttlesworth was in rare form before a congregation at the First Baptist Church of Ensley. Ed Gardner began the meeting by telling the people who had no money to contribute to the movement to relinquish their seats to those who did. That day a group of integrationists, including Marti Turnipseed, the daughter of a white Methodist minister, were arrested during a sit-in at Woolworth's. The protests, according to later reminiscences of attorney William Kunstler, seemed to be losing the interest of both the media and the protest volunteers. Shuttlesworth, Bevel, Walker, and Young had begun discussing the possibility of mobilizing youngsters from the high schools and junior high schools as demonstrators. The activities of college-age persons, especially such whites as Turnipseed, encouraged Shuttlesworth, who warmed to Bevel's insistence that younger protesters be used. At the mass meeting, Shuttlesworth introduced Turnipseed and two other white students from Birmingham-Southern College. Standing between the two young women, Shuttlesworth put his arms around them, to the enthusiastic approval of the congregation and the apparent disgust of the white detectives. The preacher exulted: "White people used to be afraid to come to the meetings, but they are not afraid to come anymore. They are not afraid of Bull Connor or the police. Bull came into the court this morning and was looking bad and mean. The past six years that the movement has been on has just about pulled all of Bull's horns out, and what they hadn't got, Judge Bowron got this morning. . . . Seven years ago we started a dangerous and difficult task. Tonight we have come close to realizing our goal." King then took the podium and indicated his delight that the three white students had joined the movement. Noting that two of them were children of Methodist ministers, he congratulated them for "doing what they learned in Sunday School." Then Abernathy called for volunteers, saying, "I was born under an injunction, and have lived under an injunction all my life. When my mother gave birth to me, and the doctor discovered my skin was black, I was under an injunction." His altar call yielded another forty-four volunteers, including Marti Turnipseed.[51]

During this time, James Bevel began conducting daily workshops for nonviolence training for high school and elementary school youth. He more than anyone advocated the use of children. He believed, first of all, that young persons would add great numbers and enthusiasm to the demonstrations. Second, Bevel argued that the youth would increase the publicity of the demonstrations. Last, because they were too young to hold jobs, the children were less susceptible to economic reprisals. King deliberated intensely over whether to approve using the youngsters in the protests. He feared for their safety and worried that encouraging them to march against the wishes of their parents would undermine the already tenuous support for the demonstrations. As they began hearing rumors that the movement was planning to use young persons, such middle-class ministers as John T. Porter registered their grave concerns. King held out as long as he could before approving the tactic. He was finally pressed into doing so by Project C's weakening momentum. Shuttlesworth, who had used his own children in the movement long before now, immediately sided with Bevel, telling the recruits in the workshops, "You are soldiers, and you live in America, and nobody can tell you not to march." Arguing with Abernathy, who focused on the concerns of parents, Shuttlesworth observed, "No parent sees his child every day, every hour of the day, and sometimes you have to raise them so they'll be people on their own." Agreeing with Walker, he believed that "the best education was being educated to destroy the system which kept them enslaved."[52]

On Thursday, April 25, Robert Kennedy and Burke Marshall met with Alabama governor George Wallace in Montgomery. In the seventy-five-minute discussion, mainly about the desegregation of the University of Alabama, the subject briefly turned to matters in Birmingham. Wallace lectured Kennedy about the administration's easy treatment of King, complaining about Kennedy's telephone call to Mrs. King. Most significant, the governor vowed that he would not retreat from his pledge to defy any federal desegregation orders. The meeting left the attorney general shaken. He wondered: "It's like a foreign country. There's no communication. What do you do?" That night at the mass meeting, Shuttlesworth knew what to do: use the meeting to rhetorical (and comical) advantage. "I don't believe George wants to go to jail. I'm glad Bobby came down, and I wish he would come to Birmingham. But he can hear the noise we are making one hundred miles away."[53]

By Friday, April 26, the decision to use young people had all but been made. All that remained was for King, ever slow about making momentous decisions, to sign off on the tactic. Other leaders, including Shuttlesworth, sensed that King would eventually be won over. Anticipating large demonstrations for the next week, Shuttlesworth petitioned both city governments for a parade permit for May 2, a date Walker dubbed "D-Day," the first day that youth would be sent into the fray. Mayor Boutwell recommended that the city council deny the request on the basis of Shuttlesworth's recent contempt conviction and his fear that such a parade would provoke further disorder. In a public statement, Boutwell added, "I will not expose the people of Birmingham, white or colored, to danger, and I will not saddle our police department with an extra burden just to satisfy Rev. Shuttlesworth." The mass meeting crowd that night at the Sixteenth Street Baptist Church heard Abernathy announce that a youth rally was scheduled for Saturday morning. He informed the crowd that there would be no marches on Saturday but that a massive one would be scheduled for sometime the next week. With this march, he promised, "We will close Ullman and Parker and the rest of the high schools." King, Shuttlesworth, and Abernathy all left Birmingham for their ministerial responsibilities at their churches, leaving Walker, Bevel, and Young in charge of workshops and mass meetings over the weekend.[54]

Events during the next few days bore out Bevel's prediction that using the young persons would elevate both the numbers and the enthusiasm of the demonstrations. On Saturday, nearly 150 persons volunteered for sit-ins at some forty white churches the next day. Younger SCLC staff persons, such as Bevel, Young, and Dorothy Cotton, recruited young persons such as James Orange, William "Meatball" Dothard, and Andrew Morrisett from among Birmingham high schoolers first nurtured by Shuttlesworth. These workers virtually idolized Shuttlesworth as their hands-on leader and became ACMHR-SCLC's connection to the black high schools in Birmingham. They would be the key to tapping this human resource. At the first of the week, police detective M. H. House learned from an FBI agent that movement volunteers had put out hundreds of leaflets at the black high schools. The leaflets called on students to leave school, with or without the permission of parents or school officials, at noon on Thursday, May 2, for a massive march. Alexander Brown, also a Shuttlesworth-influenced recruiter, remembered school officials' locking the doors of the schools in an attempt to dissuade their students from volunteering. Such efforts met with dismal failure as many students climbed out of windows to volunteer for the demonstrations. Disc jockey "Tall Paul" White used codes to tell students where to go to volunteer. Abraham Woods remembered: "You could see the students coming from every direction from high schools and some elementary schools to go to take part in the demonstrations."[55]

As King feared, the use of young students as demonstrators proved controversial in the African American community as well as among whites. Who might get hurt? What might Connor do next? When would the next bomb go off? All these questions surfaced in common conversations, which also occasionally included criticism of King and Shuttlesworth. African Americans carried, as the Reverend C. Herbert Oliver later recalled, a sense of foreboding that "something tragic would happen, with a touch of hope for something positive." During the height of the demonstrations, business leader A. G. Gaston publicly condemned the tactic of using the youth, commenting, "As a responsible citizen of Birmingham, I deplore the invasion of our schools to enlist students for demonstrations during school hours." Harold Long, minister of the First Congregational Church, complained to Andrew Young regarding admonitions to students to defy their parents if necessary to participate. Long remembered Young replying, "In this kind of a struggle, you just have to do certain things."[56]

On Monday, after the Big Three returned to Birmingham from their weekend preaching engagements, King brought together his brain trust to discuss further a possible "children's crusade." After almost four weeks of protests, police were making fewer arrests, and the press was ignoring the demonstrations. A bold stroke was needed to generate momentum once again. King remained reluctant to use the young people but understood clearly the movement's desperate need for a shot in the arm. He tentatively okayed the massive young people's march for Thursday, May 2, for which Shuttlesworth had sought a permit the Friday before. Shuttlesworth grew restive over King's soul-searching and enthusiastically opted with Bevel to utilize the resources of youth. He felt twinges of concern that his input was not being adequately considered. Still, on Tuesday he traveled to Memphis for an SCLC board meeting and planned to return, though not on the same plane, with King, Abernathy, and Walker late Wednesday afternoon.[57]

Both Shuttlesworth and King returned in time for Wednesday night's mass meeting. William "Meatball" Dothard exuberantly announced that the movement was set to "give the employees of the Negro schools a holiday tomorrow because the students are going to march." Another speaker informed the audience that the students would meet for a training session with Bevel at the Sixteenth Street church, after which they would move en masse into the city. Shuttlesworth quite surprisingly told the congregation that the decision to march on Thursday was not yet final but would be determined after a summit meeting of movement leaders. Shuttlesworth's cryptic remark reflected King's continuing indecision over using the young students.[58]

The next morning—"D-Day"—as Walker and Bevel prepared hundreds of truant African American students for the noon march, King wrestled with his conscience and wrangled with a contingent of black professionals criticizing him for even considering using the youngsters. Much more committed to pressing forward with the "children's march," Shuttlesworth maintained his hands-on approach, not content to remain at the Gaston Motel for the tortured decision making. Instead, he rose early to go to the Sixteenth Street Baptist Church to preach rousing sermonettes to the swarms of hooky-playing students. By eight o'clock the church was crowded with students who were clapping hands and singing the old spiritual "Woke up This Morning with My Mind Stayed on Freedom!" Shuttlesworth darted back and forth to different parts of the church, watching the training sessions led by Walker, Bevel, Young, and Cotton and giving his own input whenever the spirit moved him. And the spirit indeed moved him that morning. On what he later called "one of the most exciting days of my life," he gave the young recruits short inspirational talks. He called them "freedom fighters, as much so as those in the army. But without weapons." He added: "Still, you are expected to be as disciplined as soldiers." He was particularly moved because he knew that demonstrations of this size had the potential to burst the city jails at the seams.[59]

As lunch time approached, WENN radio personality "Tall Paul" White aired coded instructions: "Kids, there's gonna be a party at the park. . . . Bring your toothbrushes because lunches will be served." Just after noon Walker and Bevel committed the forces to the streets. As hordes of young marchers invaded Kelly Ingram Park, Connor's cool was finally broken. The presence of schoolchildren and the size of the demonstrations unnerved and perplexed him as to an effective response. Squad cars arriving to take the marchers to jail were quickly overwhelmed by the numbers, as were the later arriving paddy wagons. Finally, Connor called for school buses to transport the arrestees. Watching wave after wave of the students submit to arrest, Shuttlesworth later asserted, "I really knew that God had involved Himself in our struggle." As Shuttlesworth wandered from the church to the downtown area, a police officer called out, "Hey, Fred, how many more have you got?" "At least a thousand," he called back. "God A'mighty!" exclaimed the shell-shocked officer. As a second wave of demonstrators headed for downtown, fire trucks arrived on the scene, poised to put their powerful high-pressure hoses to work. Connor barked orders: "Let those people come to the corner, Sergeant. I want 'em to see the dogs at work. Look at those niggers run." By nightfall more than one thousand young protesters were in custody, with females in the detention home and males divided among the Southside, Bessemer, and Jefferson County jails. The next day Birmingham was again in the headlines.[60]

Almost everyone in Birmingham and many throughout the nation were horrified by the use of young people as demonstrators. Mayor Boutwell excoriated outsiders "who will not have to live with the fearful consequences" and who used "innocent children as their tools." Robert Kennedy worried, "School children participating in street demonstrations is a dangerous business. An injured, maimed or dead child is a price that none of us can afford to pay." Malcolm X huffed that "real men don't put their children on the firing line." Birmingham's frustrated juvenile court judge Talbot Ellis set bond at $500 for first-time offenders and $750 for return offenders. Seeing an eight-year-old under arrest, he complained, "That's what makes my blood boil," adding that those who recruited the students "ought to be put *under* the jail." Of course, public opinion differed greatly that night at the Sixth Avenue Baptist Church, where the ACMHR-SCLC forces met despite pastor John Porter's earlier opposition to the use of the students.[61]

Between eighteen hundred and two thousand fervent participants heard King declare that he had never seen anything like what had happened in Birmingham that day. Events having made his decision for him, he indicated that the young peoples' demonstrations would continue until the movement's demands were met. Shuttlesworth interrupted the proceeding several times with announcements and pep talks. He asked the students not to go to school and implored the parents to keep their children at home if they didn't want them involved with the protests. He praised "our little folks" for marching to city hall to pray and rejoiced that "Bull had to call the sheriff for help today." He gleefully celebrated that "they locked the gate at Parker [High School], but the school children climbed the fence" and concluded that "the whole world is watching Birmingham tonight." James Bevel moved the crowd to ecstasy, three hundred of whom waved their arms, sang, shouted, and marched around the sanctuary when he boasted, "There ain't going to be no meeting Monday night because every Negro is going to be in jail by Sunday."[62]

On Friday Connor prepared his forces, both police and fire departments, for another blitz. At the outskirts of Kelly Ingram Park, barricades were erected and fire hoses stood at the ready. At the Sixteenth Street church, Shuttlesworth and the younger leaders repeated the scene from the previous day, stoking the fervent fire of another thousand young protesters. Once again the black high schools were virtually emptied of students. One report had only 887 of the city's 7,386 black high school students actually attending classes. At approximately one o'clock in the afternoon, several groups of demonstrators began their orderly procession into the downtown streets in different directions. This day would be different, though. Fire hoses only displayed the day before were now activated. As a group of about sixty teenagers reached the corner of Seventeenth Street and Fifth Avenue North, Captain Glenn V. Evans called out, "Halt and disperse, or you're going to get wet." For two hours firefighters obeyed Connor's orders to train their hoses, powerful enough to take the bark off a tree, on the teenage protesters.[63]

Onlookers enraged at the actions of the firefighters and police began to throw bricks and broken bottles in the officers' direction. Two firefighters and a news photographer were injured. The demonstrators, for their part, were battered by the water. One girl's face was cut as she skidded across the pavement; an older woman's nose was bloodied by a blast from a hose. In the face of the violent stream some of the youth cowered, others sat down, and still others sprawled out awash in the spray. One woman tugging a four-year-old boy led a new wave of protesters toward a police line. She cried out, "This baby is mine, and he's in it, too!" Then, as another group of demonstrators marched from the church and met police at the fringes of the park, Connor brought out the canine corps, largely to quell the violent outburst of bystanders angered by the fire hoses. Photographers captured the gruesome scene of fifteen-year-old-bystander Walter Gadsden being attacked by a snarling German shepherd.[64]

Scenes such as these turned the tide for Project C. In light of the violence against the youth, virtually all opposition to the ACMHR-SCLC efforts in the African American community evaporated. A. G. Gaston was speaking to David Vann by telephone at the very time of the Friday marches. As Gaston was expressing his resentment that King had begun the demonstrations just as a new city government was in place, the business leader interrupted himself—"But lawyer Vann, they've turned fire hoses on those black girls. They're rolling that little girl right down the middle of the street. I can't talk anymore." Vann later commented: "There, in a twinkling of an eye, the whole black community was instantaneously consolidated behind King." Whereas adults had previously remained aloof from the demonstrations, Birmingham's African American community now rallied to its abused children. As one writer noted, the violence had "extended the emotional involvement into countless homes." Perhaps more significant, the young people's resolve against segregation's violent resistance enlightened even some of Birmingham's whites out of their traditional misconceptions. Another white attorney commented: "You just can't say that the Negroes are contented when they are willing to let their children go to jail."[65]

By Friday night Fred Shuttlesworth was among a team of movement leaders slated to meet with white business leaders. The massive demonstrations on Thursday and Friday had induced Sid Smyer to reopen negotiations. In addition, Burke Marshall, after conversations with King and Robert Kennedy, planned to come to Birmingham on Saturday to help bring the disorder to a peaceful conclusion. In the meantime, on Friday night Shuttlesworth and Gardner represented the ACMHR at a meeting held at Smyer's Birmingham Realty Company, accompanied by Gaston, Arthur Shores, John Drew, Miles College president Lucius H. Pitts, Harold Long, and Andrew Young. The white contingent included young attorneys David Vann and Abraham Berkowitz; business leader Roper Dial of Sears, Roebuck; Vincent Townsend, publisher of the *Birmingham News;* Boutwell's representative, W. C. "Billy" Hamilton; and Smyer.[66]

Over the course of the negotiations, Shuttlesworth's influence gradually weakened as white representatives tried to ignore him. For several years, since the formation of the ACMHR, his name had been, according to David Vann, "a real curse word in the white community."[67] The whites really did not want him at the meetings, partly because of his history in Birmingham and partly because he now lived in Cincinnati. Also, the business leaders hoped to avoid negotiating with King and thus, by extension, with Shuttlesworth, linked as he was with King, probably the only African American more hated in Birmingham than

Fred. Consequently, in their sessions white negotiators found it easier simply to bypass Shuttlesworth and deal with the others.

One other matter caused Shuttlesworth to grow dissatisfied with the negotiating process. Early on the whites established that because they represented only private businesses, they could not make promises or commitments for the city government(s). Also, Connor's challenge to the new mayor-council government was still pending in the Alabama Supreme Court, where segregationist justices could still rule in his favor. The white leaders therefore argued that their concessions had to remain within the private sector and could carry no governmental guarantees. This meant that three of the original demands of the protests (the dropping of charges from previous protests, equal employment opportunities for blacks within city government, and the reopening of the city's closed recreational facilities on a desegregated basis) were likely to be gradually surrendered. Because these were the most significant and long-lasting concessions sought by the ACMHR, Shuttlesworth's disgruntlement grew as the negotiations proceeded. When other black negotiators accepted the whites' limitations and King's public statements began to reflect this shift in focus, Shuttlesworth grew increasingly unhappy with the developments.[68]

Saturday morning found Martin Luther King hanged in effigy in the courtyard of a Catholic church and protesters and police anticipating another day of massive protests. To that point in Project C, no public protests had occurred in the downtown area during the weekends. Now, however, the zeal of the young demonstrators overcame earlier policy. As marchers left from the Sixteenth Street Baptist Church and the Greater Apostolic Overcoming Holy Church simultaneously, Connor once again utilized the fire hoses. Onlookers again threw rocks and other missiles. Connor's forces eventually sealed off the two churches, trapping the trained marchers inside and leaving only bystanders outside threatening further violence. In the excitement James Bevel borrowed a police bullhorn and called out, "Okay, get off the streets now. We're not going to have violence. If you're not going to respect policemen, you're not going to be in the movement." He then called off demonstrations for the day and for Sunday as well. In the day's activities, another 211 protesters were arrested, some 111 of them under age eighteen.[69]

On Sunday afternoon a large prayer service spilled out of the New Pilgrim Baptist Church into the downtown area as a spontaneous march to the Southside jail, where the marchers intended to hold a prayer vigil. When they reached a police cordon two blocks away, Connor ordered the nearly one thousand sing-ing demonstrators to halt. "You have no parade permit," the commissioner yelled. "Reverse your direction and return to the church and leave in your cus-tomary manner. If you do not, then we will have no alternative but to dis-perse you in whatever way we can." Their leader, the Reverend Charles Billups, defying Connor, turned to the marchers and shouted, "Let them use their dogs. Let them use their water. Let them do what they want to. We are not leaving!" The crowd then began chanting in support, some kneeling in prayer and asking forgiveness for Connor. Fire hoses were aimed at the crowd, and police dogs and billy clubs were at the ready, but Connor never ordered his men into action. The officers held their ground as if paralyzed. Slowly the marchers arose and moved past the officers, who quietly stepped aside and allowed them to move to a park near the jail, where they prayed and sang for another twenty minutes.[70]

The weekend's behind-the-scenes story was the federal government's in-volvement with the negotiations in the person of Burke Marshall. The assistant attorney general arrived by noon on Saturday accompanied by Joseph F. Dolan, the assistant deputy attorney general. Immediately they began setting up meet-ings with the negotiating parties—separate meetings, though with a view to-ward facilitating biracial talks. As much as any of Birmingham's white negotia-tors, Marshall hoped to limit discussions to private sector concerns—public accommodations and jobs—rather than take on such public matters as deseg-regating schools or voting rights. Marshall took the approach of an arbitrator in a labor dispute, shuttling back and forth between white and black negotiating teams, trying separately to nudge them closer together. The racial element and the reluctance of whites to be perceived as giving in to King and Shuttlesworth's demands also made such an approach necessary. Marshall later noted that "there were many whites that wouldn't talk to any blacks, and there were many more whites that wouldn't talk to certain blacks, and there were no whites, I think, except for David Vann, who would talk to Martin King"—or, he might have added, Fred Shuttlesworth.[71]

Shuttlesworth should have understood the white team's limitations, but his impatience with white Birmingham and his experience of being ignored by the city's leaders made him wary of Marshall's approach. Although he was happy to see the Kennedy administration finally involved, he complained to King about the separate meetings Marshall had set up. "I think he ought to get all of us together, and not be talking to one side and then the other, [and then] we can all know what everybody said." King's pleasure at having the federal government weighing into the negotiations, however, seemed to Shuttlesworth to override all other considerations, and King more or less mollified Shuttlesworth and avoided dealing directly with his concerns—at least until he and Marshall thought the time was ripe. With misgivings, Shuttlesworth withheld his criticisms out of respect for King and allowed negotiations to proceed. On Saturday evening representatives of the downtown merchants met with Marshall to discuss the worsening situation. They heard reports that the ACMHR-SCLC forces were prepared to reduce their demands and that their control of the demonstrations was threatening to dissipate. Because African American bystanders were angered by Connor's dogs and fire hose resistance, the likelihood of serious violence became palpable. As a result, the merchants decided to meet again on Sunday with a larger, more representative group.[72]

Returning from his Cincinnati pulpit, Shuttlesworth was disappointed at missing the "parting of the Red Sea" that afternoon at the Southside jail. Arriving in time for the negotiating session, he joined Shores, Gaston, and Pitts, along with the white contingent, at the home of African American business leader John Drew. Each side accused the other of negotiating in bad faith, and one merchant commented that he had been indirectly warned by Governor Wallace against any settlement. The blacks presented their four "Points for Progress." These included (1) the immediate desegregation of all store facilities, including lunch counters, rest rooms, and fitting rooms; (2) the immediate upgrading of store employees and nondiscriminatory hiring; (3) merchant pressure on the city government to drop charges against the jailed protesters; and (4) merchant pressure on city government to establish a biracial committee to deal with such future problems as the hiring of black police officers, the removal of obstacles to voter registration, the desegregation of schools, the reopening of all municipal facilities, and the desegregation of all theaters and hotels. White negotiators rejected points three and four, reiterating their lack of authority in governmental matters. In response, Shuttlesworth interrupted the discussions, which had been led by Shores and Gaston, to warn the merchants that if they did not help the government come to some just decision on segregation, their businesses would continue to suffer as they had during the demonstrations. "We can keep it like this for a while," he warned. Chiding Smyer and the other white business leaders for their fear of Connor, Shuttlesworth admonished them to remember that "this is your city. Bull Connor is not the whole city." In spite of his misgivings Shuttlesworth nevertheless believed the whites were negotiating in good faith and recommended that the ACMHR-SCLC team keep talking.[73]

By nine o'clock Monday morning some four thousand young people had gathered both in and outside the Sixteenth Street Baptist Church. They had been recruited with fliers that read, "Fight for freedom first, then go to school. . . . It's up to you to free our teachers, or parents, yourself, and our country." As the students prepared for their march, Shuttlesworth and Bevel worked out a deal with police chief Jamie Moore: during the afternoon demonstrations, police would agree to arrest protesters without the use of dogs and fire hoses if marchers agreed to remain orderly. By 2:30 that afternoon police arrested one thousand more demonstrators, some 90 percent of whom were juveniles. Hearing the strains of the protesters' freedom songs, Connor fumed to reporters, "They don't even know what freedom means. If you ask half of them what freedom means, they couldn't tell you. You ask them, and they'll tell you, 'My preacher told me to march.' Boy, if that's religion, I don't want any." Arrest totals for the day exceeded any of the other protests, bringing the five-week total to 2,425. Negotiations for the day proved futile. In the morning session city leaders refused to meet any of the "Points for Progress." Matters moved forward only barely that night, as the African American committee agreed to accept promotions as good faith attempts to improve employment in the downtown stores. The white negotiators, by contrast, immediately rejected the blacks' repeated requests that the merchants pressure the city government to drop the charges against and prevent the expulsion of the protesting schoolchildren.[74]

Tuesday, May 7, would turn out to be Project C's moment of truth. Birmingham's jails were now bulging, and ACMHR-SCLC forces were determined to keep the pressure on in what were the largest and most chaotic marches of the entire protest effort. Around ten o'clock that morning, before the beginning of the day's demonstrations, Shuttlesworth and King held a news conference at the Gaston Motel. Noting that for the first time in the history of the civil rights movement integration forces had succeeded in filling the jails, the leaders called recent developments "the fulfillment of a dream."[75] Once again, they warned that demonstrations would continue until the city made concessions. After answering a few more questions for the press, King returned to his room, and Shuttlesworth headed for the action at the Sixteenth Street church.

On his arrival he found Dorothy Cotton and James Forman, the leader of SNCC, in charge of a tactic called "Operation Confusion." This stratagem divided demonstrators into fifteen or so groups and dispatched them into the downtown area via different routes. Fred began his usual routine of stoking the fires of the young demonstrators, calling on them to prepare themselves to go back downtown en masse. A first wave of demonstrators began their march before noon, surprising police and firefighters, who had grown accustomed to demonstrations starting around one o'clock in the afternoon. Some of the protesters taunted the firefighters, daring them to use their hoses on them. Some of them, along with many more of the bystanders, began to throw rocks at the police while Bevel and Shuttlesworth began herding them back to the church. Police and firefighters moved hundreds of protesters and bystanders off the streets with hoses and an armored car. Violence broke out after an estimated twenty-five hundred to three thousand protesters moved through the business district.

When the police finally got to the area, they blocked the line of students, confiscated and destroyed their picket signs, and told the youngsters to go home. In the confusion Shuttlesworth meandered through the area, barking instructions to the youthful protesters. He noticed a motorcycle officer whirling his vehicle around too hastily in an effort to chase down one of the crisscrossing squads of marchers. The cycle got away from him and turned over on top of him. In what the policeman probably took as mock concern, the minister said, "Don't hurt yourself, Officer."[76]

Fred Shuttlesworth was never more enthusiastic as he marveled at the powerlessness of the police and fire departments. Seeing in the motorcycle mishap the symbol of that impotence and the sign that victory was at hand, Shuttlesworth rushed back to the Gaston Motel to get King and Abernathy. He burst into King's room and shouted, "Martin, this is it! You need to come out and see this." He commandeered a car and hurried the slow-moving tandem into it. He drove them three or four blocks and circled the area, narrating everything he had seen on his earlier foray. All the while, he kept insisting that the city's will was now at the breaking point. "All we got to do," he boasted, "is hold it like this a few more days." After giving King and Abernathy the tour of *his* town, he took them back to the motel and then returned to the Sixteenth Street Baptist Church. Receiving a hero's introduction from Wyatt Walker and a boisterous ovation from the young crowd, Shuttlesworth revved up the troops once more: "We're making history in that we've literally filled the Birmingham jails. Bull Connor thought the jails were like hell to us, but you all have made a heaven out of the jail. Or you have at least made the jails heavenly by singing and praying in the jails. You are as good a soldier as any that go across the water. Because you are fighting for what your country is and what it will be."[77]

An afternoon march began as a police officer entered the church to announce that the jails were full and to ask the students to go home. Instead, some two thousand of them proceeded to march downtown. They soon encountered some three hundred police officers, aided by the canine corps and a battery of fire hoses. Just before three o'clock in the afternoon a riot was sparked when blacks crowding the sidewalks on the south side of Kelly Ingram Park began throwing rocks at police and firefighters. Still caught up in the excitement, Shuttlesworth and Bevel crisscrossed the park several times in an effort to restrain young demonstrators from throwing bricks or rocks at the officers. After separating from Bevel, Shuttlesworth continued sauntering up Sixteenth Street, pointing youngsters back toward the church as he went. The way between himself and the church looked clear as he crossed Sixth Avenue North. Just as he approached the stairs descending to the church basement, a firefighter who had been training his hose on a group of demonstrators led by James Orange noticed the preacher heading toward sanctuary. Uncorking seven years of white Birmingham's bottled-up irritation with the pesky, *inside* agitator, the firefighter said, "Hey, let's put some water on the Reverend!" He turned, trained his nozzle on the minister, and violently baptized him with Bull Connor's fire hose. Having moved about freely among the police and firefighters all day without incident, Shuttlesworth was surprised by the firefighter's words. Looking in the direction of the firefighter, he caught a glimpse of a large column of water just beginning its downward arc toward him from a range of less than fifty feet. He had time enough to cover and turn his face away, but he was not able to evade the force of the water completely. Hitting him in the back of the shoulder and ribs, the powerful stream broke a rib and rolled him several feet toward the church, slamming him against the brick wall and continuously pounding him until he lost his breath and almost his consciousness.[78]

When the water abated, he lay in a hump, temporarily paralyzed, but again certain that God had protected him in the midst of the ordeal. Bracing himself for the impact of the water, a prayer flashed through his consciousness: "Lord, I've been coming this way a long time. This is it. I'm ready when you are." Just as instantaneously he experienced a presence saying, "Not here; not yet." The first to reach the prostrate leader was James Orange, who found him dazed and visibly in pain. Still, battered and awash in Birmingham's spray, Shuttlesworth's "fire you can't put out" remained unextinguished. Regaining his typical bravado, he told Orange and the others, "Let's go! I'm ready to march." Orange, ACMHR faithful "Buck" Johnson, and the Reverend T. L. Fisher ignored his protestations and convinced him it was time to see a doctor.[79]

Just then someone opened the basement door of the church and discovered the wet and bruised minister at his feet. Turning to colleagues inside the church, he called out, "Hey y'all, it's Reverend Shuttlesworth!!" They quickly carried him into the church basement and called an ambulance. Staggering but still conscious, Shuttlesworth was carried to an ambulance. Amid the confusion word filtered back to police officers in the downtown area that Shuttlesworth had been hit by a hose. In mock disappointment, Connor replied, "I waited a week to see Shuttlesworth get hit with a hose. Damn, I'm sorry I wasn't around to see it! It must have been funny as hell." Told that his longtime nemesis had been taken from the scene in an ambulance, he snorted, "I wish they'd carried him away in a hearse."[80]

At Holy Family Hospital, Dr. James T. Montgomery treated Shuttlesworth's ribs and chest and tried to calm him down with a sedative. ACMHR friends Ed Gardner and C. Herbert Oliver, staying with him at the hospital until Ruby could arrive from Cincinnati, watched him rest fitfully for several hours until Montgomery returned to check on his patient.

"You should be asleep," complained the physician.

"Well, Doctor, this is no sleeping time. I should be back at the mass meeting."

"But you need your rest. You've been in a serious situation here!"

"Well, I'm not dead, and as long as I have life, I want to use it," asserted Shuttlesworth. "How soon can I get out?"

"Well, you will have to sleep some," Montgomery insisted and administered a second sedative.[81]

The downtown demonstrations had long since reached cataclysmic proportions, with televised pictures going around the world that would bring international opprobrium to the "Magic City." In a morning negotiation session the participants discussed the possibility of martial law. Burke Marshall advised against such an action, calling on the Senior Citizens Committee to achieve a lasting local solution. Sidney Smyer, hoping to avoid another humiliation for Birmingham, called the entire group into emergency session. Meeting that afternoon as demonstrators continued to swarm around the downtown area, seventy-five of Birmingham's business leaders heard Jefferson County sheriff Mel Bailey explain that 904 juveniles were in custody and being held not only at the city jail but also at the county jail, the Bessemer jail, and in dormitories at the fairgrounds. Other juveniles were being detained at the overcrowded juvenile court.[82]

Somberly, he repeated that the jails were full and that "if we arrest any more demonstrators we will have to set up a barbed wire fence at Legion Field." He added in warning, "Pictures of that won't look very nice." He advised the leaders to find a way to reach a settlement or face the alternative of martial law. David Vann later noted that Bailey's report made a powerful impression on the group, which immediately voted unanimously to appoint a subcommittee to develop an agreement with "responsible Negro leadership." That night a group led by Smyer and Vann met with Arthur Shores, Lucius Pitts, Andrew Young, Burke Marshall, and Boutwell's representative, Billy Hamilton.[83]

Marshall's pressure on King to accede to white overtures in turn resulted in pressure on black negotiators to water down the original demands of the protests. A general settlement was proposed by Andrew Young. It called for "immediate 'token' employment of Negroes" in downtown stores, with gradual increases during the next year to 10 percent of the total number of employees at each store. This represented a compromise in the original demand, which had sought the "immediate upgrading" of employment. Second, the desegregation of store facilities and the dropping of charges against demonstrators would await the full empowerment of the new city council. White negotiators agreed to the eventual desegregation of store facilities and to the establishment of a biracial committee to deal with long-term problems. The sticking point remained the question of dropping charges against those arrested. When the team of black negotiators, which by this time no longer included any active ACMHR members, accepted a promise of eventual rather than immediate progress on three of the four points, a truce agreement was in sight. Early on Wednesday morning the ACMHR-SCLC Central Committee, led by Lucius Pitts, convinced King to accept these terms, even though the original non-negotiable demands had been surrendered for some immediate actions and a number of future discussions. In exchange, King promised to declare a moratorium on demonstrations.[84]

At the hospital on Wednesday morning, Ruby found her husband restless and unhappy. Herbert Oliver had watched him toss and turn all night, moving in and out of a mild delirium, unconsciously muttering his refusal to be shunted aside by the movement's decision makers. He later claimed that he never thought King and the SCLC had taken over *his* movement but that he had become perturbed by what he considered King's "habit of making statements without clearing them with anybody." He was irked that as the demonstrations unfolded King had increasingly failed to consult him on important decisions. They *had* agreed to make joint statements to the press, and King *had* occasionally failed to keep that agreement.[85]

More telling was Shuttlesworth's self-image as more of an "action man" than King or Abernathy. As stated earlier, he saw himself as the movement's General Patton, marching and fighting with the troops, to be compared favorably to King as an Eisenhower-like leader who philosophized from a high-command post. Not a drop of water from the fire hoses had touched King or Abernathy. By contrast, the fire hoses had put Birmingham's indigenous leader in the hospital with a bruised rib. Thus Shuttlesworth understandably complained that neither King nor Abernathy had come to the hospital or called to check on his condition. When Ruby arrived that morning with Ed Gardner, she found her husband too keyed up to get any rest. She called Dr. Montgomery to voice her concerns. He advised her to take him back to the Gaston Motel, where he thought being close to the action might enable Shuttlesworth to relax a bit more. Back at the motel, Shuttlesworth had just gotten into bed when Andy Young knocked on the door to summon him to the home of John Drew for an emergency meeting. Still wobbly from the medication, Shuttlesworth managed with Ruby's help to dress and head to "Dynamite Hill" to talk to King and the others.[86]

On the way Shuttlesworth seethed over King's sending for him to meet him at Drew's home rather than King and Abernathy coming to consult with him. He was rather vexed that Drew and the black professional elite appeared to have more input into decisions than he did. Most important of all, he had concerns that King had yielded to Burke Marshall's pressure to call off the demonstrations before wringing full concessions from the merchants. When he arrived, his worst fears were realized. Shuttlesworth entered the Drew home escorted by Gardner on one side and Ruby on the other and sat down heavily in an armchair in the living room. "Martin," he began, "why did I have to get up out of my sickbed to come out to John Drew's house. What's so important?" King stood silent, looking out over the Drew's backyard with his hands in his back pockets, a pose he often struck when he was worried. King seemed to be avoiding turning to look at him, and when his silence continued, Shuttlesworth enquired once more, adding, "You and Ralph didn't even come to see me, whether I was dying or living." Finally turning to address Shuttlesworth, King said, "Fred, we got to call off the demonstrations."

"Say that again, Martin?" Shuttlesworth replied.

"The merchants say they can't negotiate while we are demonstrating."

"Well the merchants have *been* negotiating with Burke Marshall," said Shuttlesworth, who had early on objected to Marshall serving as a mediator between black and white negotiating teams.

At this point John Drew's wife, Deanie, chimed in, "I want to know why we can't call them off." By this time beginning to breathe fire, Shuttlesworth gave a withering response: "You can't call them off because you ain't called nothing on and ain't got nothing to call off. Besides, I didn't come out here to talk with you." Turning back to King, he continued, "I tell you what, Martin, since you're going to go against all that we've promised, if you got to call it off, you go ahead. But my position is that we ain't gon' call nothin' off. Not a damn thing! We ain't calling nothing off! People have said this of you before—that you come in and get people started, and then you go off and leave them to their trouble. But I've been here. People have been hurt, and I've been here to help heal. That's why I'm respected in Birmingham. They know I'm not going to change. We came in with the idea to say to Birmingham and the world, and we agreed before we got here that we wasn't gon' call it off no matter what, even if we had to go to jail. So if you want to go against that, go ahead and do it. But I will *not* call it off, and I don't think you can call it off without me. But you go ahead and do what you want to do."

He rose to leave, but still dizzy from his medication, he fell back into the chair. Then Abernathy ambled over to mediate the dispute, even getting on his knees to implore Shuttlesworth to reconsider his decision.

"Now, Fred, we're friends, ain't we? We went to school together, and I can talk to you, can't I, Fred?"

"Ralph," Shuttlesworth shot back, cutting him off, "get off your damn knees. You can get on your knees or get on your damn belly, it won't make no difference. We're not gon' call it off."

Then Marshall interrupted, "But I made promises to these people."

"Burke, any promise you made that I didn't agree with is not a promise. You go back and tell them that. Besides, I never agreed with you going to talk to the white folks and then talking to us." Someone then mentioned the upcoming press conference. "Oh, you called a press conference, huh?" Shuttlesworth demanded from King. "I thought we were going to make joint statements. You go ahead and have your press conference. Go ahead, Mr. Big, and call it off. I'm going back home and get in the bed. I'm gon' wait until I see on TV that you've called it off, and then with what little strength I have left, I'm gon' get up and lead those three or four thousand kids back in the streets, and you'll be dead."

Just then he overheard Joe Dolan talking to Washington from a phone in an adjoining room, saying, "We've hit a snag. . . . The frail one is hanging things up." Shuttlesworth now aimed his fire at Dolan. "I guess you're talking to the president or his brother. Well, tell them they don't live down here, and I'm frail but not that frail, and we're not gon' call it off."

A worried King now turned to Marshall, saying, "Burke, we got to have unity. We just got to have unity." Shuttlesworth shot King a fierce look and promised, "I'll be damned if you'll have it like this. You may be Mr. Big now, but if you call it off, you'll be 'Mister Shit.' You're way up here, but you'll fall way down low, and you'll be Mr. Nothing. I'm sorry, but I will not compromise my principles and the principles we established." With that the bitterly angry minister rose to leave. Before he could make his exit, however, Marshall tried once more to mollify him. "Don't worry, Fred, they're going to agree to your demands."[87]

The next few hours did little to calm Shuttlesworth down. Back at the Gaston Motel, he tried to get some rest, but still fumed about King's decision. Word of his confronting King soon filtered out of the Drew's living room and out to the African American community. Some of Shuttlesworth's ACMHR friends came by his motel room to congratulate him and to find out exactly what had happened. The fiery leader continued to denounce King as a double-crosser who was squandering this perfect opportunity to put Connor away. "Ain't no use scalding the hog on one side!" he told them. "While the water is hot, scald him on both sides and get him clean. If the water gets cold, you ain't never gon' clean off that hog."[88]

Shuttlesworth's bitter outburst came from a combination of concerns. He was in considerable pain from his injury and very close to nervous exhaustion. Like many of the movement leaders, he had functioned on very little sleep for the latter weeks of the protests. His feelings were genuinely hurt by King's and Abernathy's failure to visit him in the hospital. He was even more annoyed by King's failure to consult with him over the course of the demonstrations, which violated his initial agreement with King. Thus when he learned of King's decision to halt the protests now that they had gained the international exposure that King had so coveted, he feared that Burke Marshall and the Kennedy administration had pressured King to end the demonstrations without extracting any real concessions from the city. This was his primary concern—that the local movement for which he had sacrificed for seven years might achieve some real gains and not merely obtain national exposure that would force federal intervention and pass civil rights legislation.

Shuttlesworth was one of the first leaders around King to discern that the local struggle in Birmingham would certainly have national ramifications. Indeed, he used precisely that argument to convince King and the SCLC to come to Birmingham in the first place. Thus he was eager for the local situation in Birmingham to push the nation's civil rights agenda forward, but not apart from real improvements in the city where he had labored for seven years. By the end of the demonstrations Shuttlesworth believed that King was willing to sacrifice local progress in Birmingham in exchange for federal intervention. Thus Shuttlesworth interpreted King's calling off the demonstrations as King's reneging on their mutual promise to Birmingham blacks to continue the protests until *all* of the original goals had been met. Now, Shuttlesworth accurately surmised, King was giving up the fight without a full-fledged victory—at least not a complete victory for the *Birmingham* movement. Having seen city officials go back on promises before, Shuttlesworth was convinced that Birmingham's power structure was trying to maneuver ACMHR-SCLC forces into a position where they could say, "You called it off because you couldn't win. We didn't promise you a damn thing." Shuttlesworth was convinced that from such a position the movement would lose any chance of forcing any concessions from the city.[89]

As in many important historical events, certain accidental factors also help explain the incident. Of course his injury and resulting absence from the negotiations could not be helped, nor could King's failure to seek Shuttlesworth's approval for ending the protests. Unfolding events caused Shuttlesworth's absence, and under pressure King simply forgot to confer with him. In addition, King made an unfortunate and unintended choice of words at the Drews' home when he told Shuttlesworth of his decision. Instead of indicating that he had agreed to a one-day moratorium, King told him, "Fred, we got to *call off* the demonstrations." Shuttlesworth understood this to mean the protests were being ended for good, not a temporary suspension. In interviews, he later indicated:

Martin used the word "call off." If Martin had said "moratorium"—a moratorium is different from "calling off." . . . He didn't say "moratorium," and he didn't say "we got to call 'em off for a day" or "the merchants have asked us to call them off for a day or two." He just said to me, "We got to call the demonstrations off." The word "call off" might have been the most tragically misused word in that statement because I'm sure if Martin had said . . . "Fred, the merchants have asked us to do a moratorium of one or two days." . . . If there was an error, it was on Martin's part, and maybe he was under so much pressure he just misstated or misphrased. . . . If, for instance, there had been some communication with me that evening . . . [but] this was given to me cold turkey and was said to me, "We got to call the demonstrations off." No time period. No [time] frame. No word "moratorium." And no saying—even then—"And the merchants will sign this thing [on] X day." . . . So to that I had to say, "No, No, Hell no, a thousand times no."

Even years later, reflecting on the incident, Shuttlesworth remained convinced that King had intended a complete cessation of the protests: "I don't think he meant suspension. I don't think he meant moratorium. I think he meant "call it off." [90]

During the next two days Shuttlesworth continued to complain about King's decision and was able to rally a good deal of support among the Birmingham youth, many of whom enthusiastically wanted to continue the demonstrations. More militant activists, such as James Forman, believed that King had sold out the masses of young persons who had been the backbone of the Birmingham protests. He fumed that the people had become too militant for the Kennedys' (and Burke Marshall's) tastes or King's image. King announced the moratorium on protests with his hope that a settlement might be reached by the next day. That afternoon, however, King, Abernathy, and twenty-five other activists were called into Judge Charles H. Brown's recorder's court for a trial on the Good Friday charge of parading without a permit. Brown found the defendants guilty and sentenced them to $300 in fines and 180 days in jail. He also broke precedent in setting an appeal bond of $2,500, whereas earlier appeal bonds had been set at $300. King and Abernathy refused to pay the exorbitant figure and chose to go to jail. Walker and A. D. King threatened to "pull out all the stops tomorrow." [91]

Less patient with such developments, Shuttlesworth declared the moratorium over, donned his "marching shoes," and prepared to leave the Gaston Motel to return to the streets. Others, such as Andrew Young and Wyatt Walker, tried to slow him down. As Shuttlesworth moved toward the door, Young physically restrained him while Joe Dolan frantically got Robert Kennedy on the phone. Just as Young prepared himself to tackle Shuttlesworth to the floor, Dolan grabbed his arm and said, "The attorney general would like to speak with you, Reverend Shuttlesworth." After a few minutes of conversation with Kennedy, Shuttlesworth was mollified. By that evening, Shuttlesworth joined King and Abernathy, who had been bailed out of jail by A. G. Gaston, for another press conference. Shuttlesworth convinced them to threaten to resume demonstrations on Thursday if an agreement had not been reached by 11:00 A.M. Addressing reporters himself, Shuttlesworth indicated that the jailing of King did "not destroy our faith in the people we are dealing with. If there are demonstrations, they will be limited. We do believe that honest efforts to negotiate in good faith are under way." That night Shuttlesworth, recovering from both his physical and his emotional wounds, skipped the mass meeting at New Pilgrim Baptist Church.[92]

On Thursday Shuttlesworth continued his convalescence and was tempted to mutter, "I told you so," when King postponed his press conference three times without reiterating his earlier threat to resume demonstrations. This convinced Shuttlesworth that King was caving in to pressure and ending the demonstrations without a clear-cut victory. The original 11:00 A.M. deadline had long since passed when King and Abernathy, without Shuttlesworth, finally announced the imminent end of the campaign. Journalists had sniffed out reports that Shuttlesworth "was not happy over the peace terms being considered," but King publicly attributed his absence to his injuries. King's announcement signified further compromise on the movement's original demands. Some unspecified future desegregation of Birmingham's public facilities would now be acceptable, he indicated, along with the gradual upgrading of black employees. The demand that charges against the arrested demonstrators be dropped was itself dropped, replaced only by King's hope that the merchants would recommend this action "in a very strong manner." King no longer demanded specific timetables for integrating school, parks, and theaters and removing obstacles to voter registration, accepting merely that whites would follow through in appointing their representatives to a standing biracial committee.[93]

Even the *New York Times* perceived the dimensions of King's compromise, indicating that agreement was reached "after Negroes had scaled down their demands." King had accepted mere promises "in lieu of immediate action," the report noted, and observers speculated that as in Albany, King had settled for less than half a loaf. This, however, was far from the note sounded at the mass meeting later that evening at the St. James and Thirgood Baptist Churches. Substituting for King and Shuttlesworth, Abernathy told his audience of twelve hundred that negotiations with the white leadership were continuing and that "we are not going to back up one bit, so I want all of you to be at the Sixteenth Street Baptist Church in the morning in case we have to march."[94]

By that time, there was little chance that ACMHR-SCLC forces would reenter the fray. Overnight and throughout the morning, negotiators Charles Morgan, Vincent Harding, Andy Young, and Arthur Shores worked on the exact wording of the truce agreement to be read by King and Shuttlesworth at Friday's press conference. Getting wind of the imminent agreement, white leaders in Alabama and Birmingham denounced the merchants for negotiating with King. Birmingham mayor Art Hanes called the white negotiators "a bunch of quisling, gutless traitors." In Montgomery, Governor Wallace commended Bull Connor's handling of the protests and pledged that he would not "be a party to any such meeting of compromise on the issues of segregation." At the Southern Baptist Convention meeting in Kansas City at that time, messengers (delegates) considered a resolution criticizing Birmingham officials and expressing solidarity with "2,400 of our brethren in Christ" jailed in the city. Prominent Birmingham minister Lamar Jackson, pastor of the Southside Baptist Church, immediately opposed the statement, asking his fellow Southern Baptists "to hold in abeyance [their] judgment of our good city."[95]

Such sentiment remained standard fare in Birmingham's white community, whose leading downtown merchants insisted on racially separate announcements of the final agreement. King's forces, who had originally claimed to be fighting for the *end* of segregation in Birmingham, ironically accepted the idea of segregated press conferences. At 2:30 in the afternoon on May 10, 1963, Shuttlesworth joined King and Abernathy at a patio table in the courtyard of the Gaston Motel for the black announcement. Appearing gaunt and frail to at least one of the reporters, the Birmingham leader had temporarily lost his fire and bravado. Instead, he sat dazed, swaying with exhaustion as he began reading the prepared statement. His two gold teeth flashed as he opened his mouth to announce: "The city of Birmingham has reached an accord with its conscience. The acceptance of responsibility by local white and Negro leadership offers an example of a free people uniting to meet and solve their problems. Birmingham may well offer for twentieth-century America an example of progressive race relations, and for all mankind a dawn of a new day, a promise for all men, a day of opportunity, and a new sense of freedom for all America. Thusly Birmingham may again become a Magic City."[96]

Events larger than his ego had forced Shuttlesworth to join King and Abernathy before the cameras. Still skeptical of the agreement, but bowing to the inevitable, he continued reading the statement that had in fact compromised all four Points for Progress. First, instead of the immediate desegregation of all store facilities, such would occur within ninety days. Second, instead of the immediate upgrading of store employees and nondiscriminatory hiring, such would take place within sixty days. Third, instead of having the charges against jailed protesters dropped, the movement was able to arrange for their release only "on bond or their personal recognizance." Finally, instead of the immediate establishment of a biracial committee, the ACMHR-SCLC accepted the promise of one within two weeks.[97]

When he finished reading the statement, Shuttlesworth, along with King, began answering reporters' questions. Shuttlesworth fielded a query as to whether he believed whites were sincere and would implement the agreement. He meekly assured journalists that he was satisfied "that they [the whites] are dealing in good faith. I wouldn't double-cross my people; they know that. We must now move from protest to reconciliation." During the next question his physical endurance began to ebb. He shakily arose from his seat and said, "Gentlemen, I hope you will excuse me. I have to go back to the hospital." With applause ringing in his ears, he moved toward a waiting ambulance and was whisked away to the segregated Holy Family Hospital. After examination the now less-than-fiery minister was judged by his doctor to be suffering from "complete physical and mental exhaustion." Meanwhile, King finished the press conference, vowing that civil rights leaders would continue to evaluate the situation in Birmingham for the next ninety days. In the white press conference held later in the day, Sid Smyer emphasized the emergency situation that necessitated the merchants' negotiations with protesters in an effort to stave off further violence. He concluded by asking all Birminghamians to do nothing that would destroy the peace so recently forged.[98]

At the hospital Ruby Shuttlesworth kept a watchful eye on her husband's condition as he rested in his room. She fended off a visit by the Reverend Paul Stagg, a denominational bureaucrat from the white American (Northern) Baptist Convention who wanted to make a financial donation to Shuttlesworth, telling him to take it to that evening's mass meeting and place it in the offering plate. Four ACMHR members sent by Ed Gardner arrived at the hospital to volunteer to sit with Shuttlesworth, but they were turned away. Not making the same mistake he and King had made the last time Shuttlesworth had been hospitalized, Abernathy came by late that afternoon to check on his condition. He also was refused entrance into Fred's room. Later that night at the mass meeting, Abernathy played to the crowd by telling them of his thwarted attempt to see their leader and that he "threw a fit with the nurses." He vowed, "If I was dying I would want Fred on one hand and Martin Luther King on the other, and my wife holding my head and wiping my brow."[99]

Despite his public adulation of Shuttlesworth, calculated to appeal to his fervent and loyal followers, Abernathy nonetheless harbored some displeasure toward Fred for becoming an obstacle to the final negotiations. Years later he revealed some of his hidden thoughts on the matter, along with an amazing amnesia regarding Shuttlesworth's civil rights career in Birmingham. He criticized Shuttlesworth's bitter anger and his view that the SCLC had taken the movement away from him, adding that "in reality, without us there would have been no movement in Birmingham at all."[100]

To the extent that such a comment reflected Abernathy's feelings at the end of the demonstrations, it boded ill for Shuttlesworth's future relationship with the SCLC. Even to consider such a thought was for Abernathy to overlook some significant realities. Leaving aside the seven years he had stirred Birmingham's waters, Shuttlesworth, because of his work with the ACMHR and with the black students from Miles College, had provided the core of volunteers for the cataclysmic waves of protest known to movement activists as Project C. Arrests numbered more than twenty-four hundred, though many of those arrested were juveniles who were detained but not charged and thus were not counted on the warden's docket. From April 3 through April 27, a total of 339 protesters were arrested and charged with parading without a permit or trespassing after a warning. Another 274 younger demonstrators were arrested in the children's crusade. In his comments Abernathy forgot that Shuttlesworth's followers provided the bodies and the fiery spirits that forced Birmingham to take the civil rights movement seriously.[101]

Shuttlesworth soon returned to Cincinnati to resume his pastoral work and to continue to keep a wary eye on Birmingham. The demonstrations concluded with their indigenous leader less than totally satisfied with the outcome for his local movement. Nonetheless, he still believed that he had won an important victory. Birmingham *had* made concessions it had never made before. As the ripples from Birmingham extended outward to the nation, Shuttlesworth would come to see that victory more in national than in local terms. The demonstrations did not wring from Birmingham's power structure everything the African American community had wanted. Shuttlesworth understood that, but he nonetheless viewed Project C as a victory—a victory that eventually would have more impact on America than on Birmingham, a victory that would have been impossible without him. If that was not clear to Abernathy or to certain others in the SCLC, it was nonetheless clear to Shuttlesworth and his followers.

More cataclysms lay ahead in the civil rights life of Fred Shuttlesworth. How many of them he would encounter in the good graces of the SCLC remained to be seen. Although Shuttlesworth retained his office within King's organization, his role in the civil rights movement unquestionably changed after May 1963 as the movement's focus gradually moved away from Birmingham. He would never again be as close to the national spotlight. The flash fires of his life would become more local and spread to venues ecclesiastical and familial. Persisting through them all, however, would be his combustible and combative demeanor and his "actionist" ways, even as he adjusted to life in the shadow of Martin Luther King Jr. and gradually became a living icon of the civil rights movement.

"Actionist"

City Minister Has No Plan to End Fight
— *Cincinnati Enquirer* headline, June 17, 1979

F red Shuttlesworth's involvement in civil rights after 1963, and certainly after Martin Luther King's death in 1968, attracted less national attention than had been the case up to that time. Still, he retained his status as, in his words, an "actionist." His actions ordinarily provoked strong reactions, whether they occurred in civil rights or, more and more likely, in his church or family. His civil rights adventures became less noticeable as King moved to venues away from Birmingham, always followed by the national media. As long as King continued to work primarily in Alabama and the South, Shuttlesworth remained a part of SCLC activities. Birmingham, however, eventually became old news, and as the events of 1963 receded into the background of public memory, Shuttlesworth became less useful to King's purposes. The central reality was that King and the SCLC were reluctant to resume major efforts in Birmingham—to return in force was tantamount to a public admission that the 1963 demonstrations had not been the victory the SCLC had claimed them to be. If Birmingham were no longer in the national spotlight, there were fewer reasons for Shuttlesworth to be a central participant.

Beyond this, a few hard feelings lingered over Shuttlesworth's criticisms of King at the end of the 1963 demonstrations. At the end of July 1963 Wyatt T. Walker, always Shuttlesworth's temperamental soul mate, stepped down as SCLC's executive director and was succeeded by Andrew Young. Shuttlesworth often saw Young as too conciliatory in spirit, too anxious for compromise. Years later Shuttlesworth complained that Young "talks shitty," trying to argue both sides of an issue. At the end of Project C, Young had tangled with Fred over his initial objections to the Birmingham truce agreement. As one of the chief negotiators of the agreement, Young had been the target of much of Shuttlesworth's ire. In interviews years later, Shuttlesworth still had an edge in his voice when he recalled Young's tactics in hammering out the final agreement. Like most of the participants, Young was exhausted during the closing days of the demonstrations and lost patience when he feared Shuttlesworth's objections would undo all that the negotiators had accomplished. In spite of his admiration for Shuttlesworth's courage, he was prepared to resort to physical force if necessary to restrain Shuttlesworth from renewing protests in those last days before the May 10 settlement. When Young was promoted within the SCLC hierarchy, Shuttlesworth was used less. Young's increasing authority in the SCLC may have contributed indirectly to Shuttlesworth's star falling, but it was not the main reason.[1]

King remained the key to Shuttlesworth's involvement in the SCLC. Although on the surface King and Shuttlesworth made their peace, their relationship, never truly close, remained somewhat strained after their disagreement. Nevertheless, King's magnanimous spirit dictated that he never seriously considered dropping Shuttlesworth altogether from his role in the SCLC. He involved Shuttlesworth in SCLC direct action whenever he believed Fred's talents could be put to good use, at times having him substitute for him at speaking engagements and making sure Fred kept his office as SCLC secretary. To whatever degree he was privately peeved at Shuttlesworth, King always respected and often lauded him in public for his courage and contributions to the movement. At the same time, though occasionally disagreeing openly with King, Shuttlesworth nevertheless maintained a healthy respect for him as the leader of the movement and consistently deferred to him in public settings.

Even more important to Shuttlesworth's apparent disappearance from the national scene were the demands and stresses of his local situation. He continued as best he could to merge his civil rights life with his church and home life. He maintained a hectic schedule as a pastor while also keeping busy as a prophet of social justice—but all this increasingly took place in and around his home base of Cincinnati. Difficulties in his church and in his family gradually limited his "actionist" impulses. As his fiery, combative nature continued to flare up in his relationships within the civil rights movement, it also reasserted itself in his congregation and with family. The combination of civil rights, church, and family concerns took its toll on him personally and cut into his opportunity to continue his involvements at his typical fever pitch. Concerns in Cincinnati allowed fewer and fewer excursions to Birmingham and other hot spots. This chapter narrates the course of Shuttlesworth's life and ministry after 1963. It highlights his continuing confrontational activities, which occurred intermittently in various civil rights arenas (Birmingham; Danville, Virginia; St. Augustine, Florida;

and Selma) but increasingly in his church and in his home during the 1970s and 1980s.

Cataclysms continued to rock Birmingham and the nation for the remainder of 1963. While Shuttlesworth recuperated from the injuries he sustained in Project C, the aftershocks spawned by those protests began to occur. While most of the city's African Americans took a wait-and-see attitude toward the settlement, white leaders publicly fumed about it and denied that any agreement with agitators was binding on them. Connor called the agreement "the lyingest face-saving" statement ever issued, while Hanes called it hogwash and vowed to have violators of the city's segregation codes arrested. The next evening the Klan met in the Birmingham suburb of Bessemer. By the light of two burning crosses, the knights prayed for the demise of King and the Kennedys while their leader, Robert Shelton, admonished them to action: "Tonight we are facing the greatest darkness that this nation has ever faced. Tonight we as God-fearing men and women can turn Alabama upside down for God."[2]

Early on Sunday morning, May 12, the Ensley home of A. D. King and the Gaston Motel were bombed. Seven hundred Alabama state troopers dispatched by Governor Wallace to Birmingham on May 8 had been patrolling the area but were mysteriously withdrawn at the time of the blast. Suspecting a setup, an estimated twenty-five hundred enraged blacks in the business and residential areas stormed into the streets, throwing bricks and rocks. As state troopers quickly returned to the scene, the violence escalated and was not calmed until 4:30 Sunday morning. Some fifty troopers marched into the driveway of the Gaston Motel with carbines at the ready. A number of blacks were clubbed with night sticks or gun butts, among them the wife of Wyatt Walker, who had come from Atlanta to visit her husband. By Sunday evening the White House announced that army units including approximately seven thousand infantry, paratroopers, and military police had been moved from Fort Benning, Georgia, to Fort McClellan, some eighty miles east of Birmingham. These forces remained ready for action in Birmingham if necessary.[3]

On Sunday and Monday, the president and Governor Wallace exchanged telegrams regarding the presence of troops and the possibility of martial law, while King and Abernathy hurried back to Birmingham to try to dissuade angry blacks from further rioting. Their pilgrimage to preach nonviolence in the city's pool halls was effective, and matters calmed to an uneasy peace. Leaving the hospital, Shuttlesworth went back to the Gaston Motel and telegraphed Kennedy to inform him of harassment of African Americans by brutal state troopers. He told the president that African Americans expected his "immediate action" would be to send federal troops into the city to protect black citizens. He complained, "We want the city police, who we respect, to take charge." Accusing Wallace of trying to ignite a violent incident to sabotage the May 10 agreement, the preacher called on the governor to remove the troopers from Birmingham.[4]

In other public statements, he guaranteed there would be no more violence from African Americans if the troopers left the scene. He also expressed a certain wary confidence in the downtown business leaders who agreed to the truce, saying, "We believe the businessmen can grant Negroes freedom without more demonstrations or martial law or troops. If they don't, there will be more demonstrations, and I will lead them personally."[5]

During the next week, King, Abernathy, and Shuttlesworth sparred with business leaders, who sought to meet the provisions of the truce agreement by hiring only one African American clerk. Dissatisfied with this minimalist reading of the agreement, movement leaders countered that they had meant one clerk in each store. Shuttlesworth added, "The very word 'clerks' and 'salesmen' precludes the idea of one clerk to be hired and fired at will." Still, the leaders had little inclination to resume demonstrations, stating in a private letter to David Vann, Sidney Smyer, and Burke Marshall that the misunderstanding required clarification but would not be viewed as a violation of the agreement.[6]

On Friday, May 17, Fred and Ruby finally returned home to Cincinnati for a week of rest before the minister resumed a full schedule of activities. Met at the airport by a crowd of church members, well wishers, and reporters, Shuttlesworth told them that recent developments in Birmingham signaled "the beginning of the end of segregation in the South." He appeared magnanimous when asked to react to Connor's wish that Shuttlesworth had been carried away from the Birmingham demonstrations in a hearse, chalking it up to Connor's lack of religion and his fatigue: "He didn't use his religion, if he has any. He was tired, and when people get tired, they often say things they wouldn't say otherwise."[7]

Still bothered by his injuries and fatigued by the intense pressure of the demonstrations, Shuttlesworth tentatively resumed his pastoral duties at Revelation and his civil rights concerns. During the summer he continued to travel to Birmingham every other week and often accompanied King to important fundraising engagements for the SCLC and the movement. On Tuesday, May 28, he attended a rally at the Washington Tabernacle Baptist Church in St. Louis. Shuttlesworth regaled the congregation with stories of his treatment at the hands of the Birmingham police and echoed King's call for President Kennedy to issue a second Emancipation Proclamation. He publicly answered a Cincinnati television editorial critical of the Birmingham movement. He also defended the SCLC when ACMHR treasurer William Shortridge complained that King's organization had not paid its share of the bills accrued during Project C. He wrote Shortridge to reprimand him for sharp statements he and Ed Gardner had made in a recent strategy meeting with the SCLC. He affirmed that the "SCLC does not owe us one cent," adding, "I think it would be silly at this point to go back to the old pattern in Birmingham of Negro Organizations squabbling over money. ACMHR is a local organization, and irrespective of anybody's feelings is not supposed to match the statue [sic] or do the work of SCLC."[8]

Back in Birmingham for the seventh anniversary of the ACMHR, Shuttlesworth celebrated the Birmingham victory in his annual president's address. Speaking on the subject "Birmingham—A Little Closer to Freedom," Shuttlesworth boasted that because of the recent demonstrations segregation would soon end in America:

> How glorious it is to realize that Negroes in Birmingham, Alabama, have not only helped to bring about a change in local government, but also a change in the attitude of the National Government about the racial situation. . . . The New Frontier is trying to catch up with the Negro frontier. Unless the President moves with dispatch, vigor, and with a degree of dedication as that which was shown by Abraham Lincoln, Negroes will be demonstrating in every nook and cranny of the nation. . . . The hour has arrived when Kennedy must end segregation and discrimination with his stroke of a pen.[9]

Clearly Kennedy was closer than ever to proposing wide-ranging civil rights legislation to Congress, pushed in that direction by events in Birmingham. The bombings of May 12 and the ensuing riot, connected as they were to the April-May demonstrations, moved him toward martial law, though that was eventually avoided. Now Governor Wallace's defiance pushed him inexorably toward some federal response such as what King and Shuttlesworth were advocating. On May 18 Wallace had conferred with Kennedy in Muscle Shoals, Alabama, after the president gave a speech at Vanderbilt University. Sharing a limousine ride to Kennedy's next speech in Huntsville, Wallace complained about developments in Birmingham and notified the president that he had filed suit in the U.S. Supreme Court to contest the use of federal troops. The governor blamed

Birmingham's troubles on King and Shuttlesworth, whom he considered charlatans. On June 11 the Wallace-Kennedy confrontation escalated still higher when the governor stood "in the schoolhouse door" to block the desegregation of the University of Alabama. This action forced Kennedy to federalize the Alabama National Guard, which in turn compelled Wallace to give up his quixotic effort.[10]

That night the president addressed the nation to announce his intention to introduce a bill that later became the Civil Rights Act of 1964. He called integration a moral issue that "is as old as the Scriptures and is as clear as the American Constitution." He recounted international concern regarding recent events in Alabama and asked, "Are we to say to the world . . . that this is the land of the free, except for the Negroes?" Answering his own question, the president said the time had come for America to fulfill its promise. He then connected his forthcoming actions to the Birmingham demonstrations: "The events in Birmingham and elsewhere have so increased the cries for equality that no city or state or legislative body can prudently choose to ignore them." Discord over racial justice threatened violence and human lives, he warned. Moving toward his conclusion, he announced: "Next week I shall ask the Congress of the United States to act, to make a commitment it has not made in this century to the proposition that race has no place in American life or law."[11] King, Shuttlesworth, and other civil rights activists hailed the president's words and took credit for setting the stage for executive action.

A few days later Shuttlesworth and some two hundred other leaders visited the White House to hear the president make another speech on civil rights. Shuttlesworth and Abernathy publicly praised Kennedy, but called for a firmer stand, with the Birmingham leader insisting that the president make a "good will tour of the South" to refute the statements of segregationists. Less than a week later, after the civil rights bill had been introduced into the House of Representatives, King, Shuttlesworth, Abernathy, and others were back at the White House to celebrate the victory and to inform the president about a massive march on Washington being planned for later that summer. Kennedy quipped that Bull Connor ought not to be judged too harshly. "After all, he has done more for civil rights than almost anybody else." According to Shuttlesworth, the president also added, "But for Birmingham, we would not be here today." Whether Shuttlesworth actually recalled the president's exact words or was drawing an inference, the historical judgment of the statement was valid. A private comment such as this one was consonant with the president's public statement on June 11. Clearly, the Birmingham demonstrations convinced the president to propose new, far-reaching legislation on civil rights. Fred Shuttlesworth and King were among the many leaders who agreed on the significance of Birmingham as the turning point of the civil rights movement.[12]

Shuttlesworth could hardly savor the moment, however, because he was embroiled at the time in a new controversy over his relationship to the Southern Conference Educational Fund. He had been on the SCEF's board of directors since 1958 and had been elected president of the organization in June 1963. Since 1948 the SCEF (originally a part of the Southern Conference for Human Welfare) had narrowed its early attention to a variety of liberal causes to focus on aiding the civil rights movement. In 1963 the organization saw the Birmingham demonstrations as signaling the beginning of segregation's end and sought to widen its concerns once again to issues of economic and racial justice. The SCEF board believed that Shuttlesworth's prominence, particularly after the events of the spring, would assist in organizing whites and blacks for its varied projects. Since the McCarthy era, however, the SCEF had often been criticized as a "Communist-front" organization, and within days of his election as president, Shuttlesworth read the sensational headline "Cincinnati Pastor Named as Head of 'Red Front.'" *Cincinnati Enquirer* writer Jack Lotto had turned up old reports from Mississippi senator James O. Eastland's internal security subcommittee and the House Committee on Un-American Activities that described the SCEF as an organization set up to "promote Communism throughout the South." In an accompanying article, the paper carried Shuttlesworth's defense of his associations with the SCEF. Shuttlesworth dismissed such charges as verbal gymnastics. "I have seen nothing on the part of any persons with whom I have been associated, to give any substantiation to these charges." He added in sharp tones that southern members of Congress "will label any organization subversive or communistic that seeks to further the American aims of integration, justice, and fair-play. To a segregationist, integration means Communism. I can think of nothing more un-American than the House Committee on Un-American Activities."[13]

Shuttlesworth's associations with the SCEF could have had a negative effect on his relationships with other civil rights organizations that were wary of being stuck with the Communist label. Since 1956 NAACP president Roy Wilkins had warned branches not to cooperate with Communist-front or left-wing groups, and he was nervous about the NAACP Legal Defense Fund's handling of some of Shuttlesworth's pending court cases. In a phone conversation Shuttlesworth told Wilkins of his intention to continue working with the SCEF and offered to give up NAACP legal representation if he thought it prudent. Hearing that the *Jackson (Mississippi) Daily News* had also criticized Shuttlesworth's involvement with the SCEF, Wilkins laughed off the minister's offer. "Oh hell, Fred," he affirmed. "If you say its right—in fact, if the *Jackson Daily News* says its wrong, that makes me know you're right."[14]

When Shuttlesworth similarly informed King and Abernathy of his new role in the SCEF, Abernathy huffed and advised him, "Yeah, you need to get out of there as quick as you can." Fred immediately shot back, "No, I didn't take it to get out. In fact, I came to this meeting to offer my resignation." Turning to King, Shuttlesworth said, "Martin, if you feel hard pressed because of this Communist issue, we've been talking about it, and it's going to come up. But I've decided that this is what I am supposed to do, and I am prepared to resign, both as secretary and board member of SCLC." Like Wilkins, King assured Shuttlesworth of his continued support and urged him to follow his conscience on the matter.[15]

Closer to home, however, his SCEF involvements created additional tension, especially for Ruby Shuttlesworth. On June 10, while Fred was out of town, Ruby received a phone call from an unknown male identifying himself as "Mr. Hoffman." On learning that Fred was away, the caller asked Ruby her opinion of the recent newspaper article about her husband. Lacing his comments with profanity, he then warned Ruby that she should expect her home to be bombed and that he hoped "to blow off Fred Shuttlesworth's head." Ruby immediately reported the call to the local FBI office, who arranged with the Cincinnati Police Department to make periodic spot checks for any suspicious activity around the Shuttlesworths' Dana Avenue home. A week or so later Ruby received another threatening call in which the caller asked for "Comrade Shuttlesworth" and said, "You give him a message for me. Ask him if he wants it in the belly or back. Wherever he is we will find him."[16]

Nothing came of such threats, and even when George Wallace associated Shuttlesworth with the SCEF and called him a Communist during a Senate subcommittee hearing, the preacher continued his support of the organization. More controversy developed in October when Louisiana state troopers and city police raided SCEF offices in New Orleans. Under the authority of the Louisiana Subversive Activities Communist Control Law, the raid was conducted at the request of the Louisiana Joint Legislative Committee on Un-American Activities. Officers confiscated a truckload of records and office supplies and arrested SCEF officers James A. Dombrowski and Benjamin Smith and member Bruce Waltzer on charges of criminal conspiracy, participating in a subversive organization, and distributing Communist propaganda in the state. The next day Shuttlesworth denounced the raid, saying that "anybody who says the organization is guilty of communist activity is telling a dirty lie." Rather, he argued, the incident was part of a conspiracy among the states of Alabama, Mississippi, and Louisiana to "prop up the crumbling walls of segregation." He added: "So far as these people are concerned, anybody, white or black, irrespective of his color, who believes in integration, will be called a subversive and a Communist. To these gentlemen, anti-segregation means Communist." Eventually two Louisiana state judges ruled that the seizure of SCEF records had been illegal. Shuttlesworth continued as president of the SCEF until 1972.[17]

Other actions during the summer of 1963 took him to Danville, Virginia, where local civil rights forces had called on King and the SCLC to lend a hand in breaking down segregation there. On Wednesday, July 3, Shuttlesworth arrived in the sleepy southern Virginia city in King's place. On the previous day a federal judge had issued an injunction barring "violent or unruly demonstrations." Speaking to a crowd at the Langston High School football field, Shuttlesworth denounced the injunction, arguing that it did not ban peaceful demonstrations. Reading from the court order, which specifically prohibited "upsetting noises," he thundered, "If singing 'We Shall Overcome' is upsetting, then let's upset the hell out of Danville. It needs to be upset when it keeps people down." He concluded with what turned out to be an idle threat that King would arrive the next week with a large force of lawyers, clergy, and civil rights fighters. The next week King did follow up Shuttlesworth's visit, though without a large contingent, speaking to a much more sizable crowd and promising that the SCLC was considering making Danville "the next Birmingham."[18]

Shuttlesworth concluded that Danville was too small a city and its local civil rights organization too disorganized to provide a social framework for massive demonstrations on the order of Birmingham's. During the summer and fall the SCLC considered an all-out campaign in Danville, but events in Birmingham divided the movement's attention. As autumn moved toward winter, it looked as if a major Danville campaign might have gotten off the ground, with Wyatt Walker, Shuttlesworth, and other SCLC officers going there on November 18. After President Kennedy's assassination on November 22, however, plans for direct action in Danville fizzled.[19]

Matters in Birmingham continued to occupy much of Shuttlesworth's attention as he pressed the SCLC to keep tabs on developments since the close of the demonstrations. Still, the success of Birmingham was spinning off local movements in other parts of the nation, and nudging the Kennedys in the direction of the struggle had given national developments a greater impetus. Plans for a great March on Washington had evolved from ideas put forth by A. Philip Randolph in the early 1940s. The fledgling civil rights movement had staged a smaller version with its Prayer Pilgrimage for Freedom in 1957. Shuttlesworth had been one of the speakers at the pilgrimage, and in the wake of the Birmingham demonstrations he expected to fill that role again. As a result of their success in Birmingham and the administration's pending legislation, civil rights leaders began to plan a march that would bring to Washington a quarter of a million persons to celebrate the victory in Birmingham and to call the nation's attention to its unfinished business. In practical terms, march coordinators hoped it would put added pressure on the president and Congress to strengthen the civil rights bill to include provisions for creating new jobs to deal with acute black unemployment.[20]

The march was officially directed by Randolph, who put Bayard Rustin in charge of the day-to-day organization of the event. Plans to "lobby Congress en masse" were eventually dropped in an effort to placate the president, who worried that a heavy-handed approach toward Congress would turn swing votes against the civil rights bill. More militant members of the movement complained that the march was being run by the White House. Shuttlesworth was attuned to the problem but thought Kennedy's worries about antagonizing Congress were a legitimate concern. In a June 26 meeting in Birmingham, King, Abernathy, and Shuttlesworth discussed the matter, with Shuttlesworth suggesting that dropping plans to lobby Congress "might relieve the apprehension of the President."[21]

When Shuttlesworth returned from a month-long vacation to Europe in mid-August, Rustin's plans for the march were complete. Those plans included, of course, a list of speakers, and to the chagrin of his ACMHR followers, Shuttlesworth's name was not on it. His ego was bruised once again, though this time he could not blame King for the slight, and he attended the march in spite of his hurt feelings. Nevertheless, King and Rustin knew of his displeasure. Events soon gave them the opportunity to make amends. While leaders tried to convince SNCC leader John Lewis to soften his speech criticizing the Kennedy administration, Rustin called on Shuttlesworth to give a short speech to kill some time. Just after the singing of the national anthem, the leader of the Birmingham campaign began the freedom rally by telling the estimated crowd of between 200,000 and 300,000: "We came here because we love our country, because our country needs us and because we need our country. . . . Everybody in America ought to be free. If the politicians want peace, if the judges want to unclog their court calendars, then turn the Negro loose in America. Then we will all be free!"[22]

Shuttlesworth lacked the native ability and the time to prepare, and thus his words that day could not match the soaring rhetoric of King. His "I Have a Dream" peroration turned out to be an extemporaneous deviation from his prepared text. Twenty-five years later Shuttlesworth commented on the speech's significance: "There are good words said every day. But every once in a while, God intervenes in such a way that you know only God could do it. That was God preaching the gospel to America through King. It helped change the mindset of America." The speech and the march as a whole inspired the movement to return to the South to continue the push for "jobs and freedom." Shuttlesworth now prepared to go back to Birmingham to help desegregate the city's public schools. He would return also to another cataclysm, indeed the greatest of them all.[23]

As the rest of the nation reflected on King's words, Birminghamians focused on the matter at hand. The day after the march on Washington, Birmingham police chief Jamie Moore and Jefferson County sheriff Mel Bailey called on the city's ministers to use their pulpits to call for order and peace during the next week's first efforts to integrate Birmingham's schools. Many white ministers did so, most of them calling for Christian obedience to law and order. The next night, however, the Reverend Ferrell Griswold, pastor of the Minor Heights Baptist Church, addressed a meeting of some one thousand Klan supporters. Criticizing King and the Kennedys, the minister attributed the troubles between the races to "the Communist scheme for world domination." On the eve of the first desegregation attempts, which included five African American students attending three previously all-white schools, the National States' Rights Party held an anti-integration rally in the Birmingham suburb of Midfield. J. B. Stoner, the Georgia lawyer who had earlier arranged for the bombing of Shuttlesworth's church, fired up the crowd, telling them they "should use any and every method to stop" the integration of their schools.[24]

Along with students who integrated Ramsay and West End High Schools on Wednesday, September 4, 1963, Floyd and Dwight Armstrong were set to attend Graymont Elementary School. Their father, James Armstrong, a faithful ACMHR member since its beginning, asked Shuttlesworth to accompany him and his sons to the school that morning. White rage erupted at all three schools, and once more Shuttlesworth was called on to face a hostile crowd. The preacher contacted the FBI on the group's behalf, asking them to provide protection for the students, but his request was denied because it was against bureau policy. Undeterred, Shuttlesworth's contingent proceeded to the school. They were met by a group of some two hundred Confederate flag–waving whites who chanted, "Two-four-six-eight, we don't want to integrate! Eight-six-four-two, Albert Boutwell is a Jew!" Others waved placards that read "Close Mixed Schools" and "Keep Alabama White." A number of women pleaded with white parents to take their children home. One shouted, "If you don't, one day there may be a Negro child in your house." About half the parents heeded the warning and refused to register their children in the integrated school. Shuttlesworth and the others passed among the demonstrators without incident, however, as the preacher defused the situation with good-natured banter with some of the crowd.[25]

That night at 9:40, as Shuttlesworth rested at the Gaston Motel, the home of black attorney Arthur Shores was bombed. African Americans from other homes in the area and the housing project at the foot of "Dynamite Hill" angrily poured out into the streets. Within minutes Birmingham police were on the scene with another riot on their hands. Quickly driven to the scene by one of his ACMHR loyalists, Shuttlesworth arrived and with civilian defense captain James Edward Lay tried to calm the mob. As he walked through the crowd, Shuttlesworth was approached by a wing of police officers formed in a wedge and moving toward Shores's house. The officers kicked and clubbed rioters as they proceeded. Shuttlesworth hit the ground to protect himself and was kicked in the side as the wedge of police passed over him. Angry rioters then launched a volley of rocks, bricks, and bottles while state troopers and city police tried to disperse them by firing over their heads with pistols and automatic rifles. Standing some ten feet from the minister was twenty-one-year-old army veteran John Coley. In the melee Coley was shot in the back of the neck and later died. Witnesses later told reporters that a section of armed whites mistook Coley for Shuttlesworth, calling out, "Kill that nigger Shuttlesworth! That's the nigger Shuttlesworth there! Kill that nigger."[26]

The next day Shuttlesworth denounced the shooting and the bombing as "part of a plot to enmesh the city in trouble" and to give Wallace a chance to stop the integration of the schools. The governor did not disappoint Shuttlesworth, choosing to close the schools in Birmingham, Tuskegee, Huntsville, and Mobile that very day. Shuttlesworth further criticized the Kennedy administration, which he believed was "making a mistake in playing cat and mouse with George Wallace and regarding this as a purely local matter." He also issued "A Call for Calmness and Restraint during the Racial Crisis" to his ACMHR faithful and the larger African American community. He admonished all Birmingham citizens to use restraint and "be not carried away by momentary passions." Reminding his readers of biblical passages that called on Christians to overcome evil with good, he asserted, "This is a good time to believe the Bible we read, practice the religion we profess, and honor the fathers who founded this Nation." To contribute to the calming of the city, he gave specific admonitions to African Americans: "(1) Stay away from the schools except on business; (2) Respect the police; (3) Avoid crowds; (4) Be friendly; (5) Be prayerful; (6) Remember that true brotherhood means being concerned about life, living, peace, happiness for others, as well as for ourselves."[27]

The next week the schools reopened, and the rowdy white demonstrations against integration resumed. On Wednesday, September 11, almost five thousand persons attended a Midfield Parents for Private Schools rally, led again by segregationist minister Ferrell Griswold, who ignored board of education pleas for full school attendance and asked parents to "keep your children away from these integrated schools." Almost two thousand students were truant from the integrated schools. Motorcades of students and adults raced through the city from one school to another, blowing horns, shouting segregationist slogans, and waving Confederate flags. On Saturday students gathered across from city hall and heard another segregationist sermon. In response, they stormed the mayor's office, waving Confederate flags, dropping lighted cigarettes on the carpet, and standing on the mayor's desk. By then Shuttlesworth had returned to Cincinnati to prepare for services at Revelation, but he spent the next week in Birmingham keeping tabs on the situation and accusing the police of failing to provide adequate police protection for the black students at Ramsay, West End, and Graymont. Little did he realize the extent to which African American schoolchildren in Birmingham also needed protection in their churches.[28]

The next day, September 15, he found the phone ringing just as he returned home from church. A church member gave him staggering news from his hometown: Birmingham's twenty-ninth bombing since 1951 had taken place at 10:25 that morning at the Sixteenth Street Baptist Church. Four young girls had been killed just after leaving a Sunday school class where they had studied a lesson on "The Love That Forgives." After ascertaining as much as he could from news broadcasts, Shuttlesworth immediately called ACMHR member Georgia Price for further details. For one of the few times in his life, he wept as he grieved over the senseless loss. Waves of disgust swept over him as he struggled to keep his emotions under control. Gradually composing himself, he told his wife and children the news and made his arrangements to return to Birmingham as soon as possible.[29]

Along with King, who had flown in from Atlanta, Shuttlesworth arrived in a city poised to go up in flames. The bomb had injured fourteen others in addition to the four young victims and set off another riot in the black community. As the victims' bodies were carried out of the rubble, an elderly man cried, "My grandbaby was killed. I feel like blowing the whole town up." Another wondered aloud, "I don't know how much more the Negro people of this city can take." The explosion brought hundreds of angry African Americans out into the streets, some of whom attacked police with stones. Police dispersed them by firing shotguns over their heads. Responding to requests from Birmingham officials, the governor sent five hundred men from the National Guard and three hundred state troopers to help restore order in the city where sporadic gunfire sounded in black neighborhoods and small bands of residents roamed the streets. Another 500 city police and 150 deputy sheriffs, armed with riot guns, carbines, and shotguns, cruised the neighborhoods in an effort to stifle the latest paroxysm of rage.[30]

By that night the Kennedy administration had sent twenty-five FBI agents, including bomb experts, to Birmingham in a contingent led by Burke Marshall and Joseph Dolan. Although he had arranged a meeting with black leaders at the home of John Drew, Marshall was reluctant to venture into the black residential section for fear of violence. Finally convinced to come to the meeting, Marshall traveled across town with a helmet on, hiding in the back seat of the car. In spite of his own fears, however, he argued against federal military intervention. At that moment, King did not want to press the president and was on the verge of being won over to Marshall's view when the others, led by Shuttlesworth, raised strong objections. Attorney Oscar W. Adams Jr., later a justice on the Alabama Supreme Court, thought the scene was laughable: "When he came at first he was shivering. You could tell he was visibly upset. Even though he had been afraid to come, he said he didn't think it was serious enough to merit use of federal troops to restore order." Along with the others, Shuttlesworth helped convince King to disregard Marshall and to call the president to insist that he do something about the situation.[31]

Thus on Monday morning King and Shuttlesworth appeared on the *Today Show* as they prepared for an early press conference at the Gaston Motel. In both appearances they urged the president to occupy the city of Birmingham with army regulars to halt racial terrorism. King called the situation a "state of civil disorder" that demanded that the president intervene with "the full weight of the federal government, even to the presence of federal troops." He further denounced Governor Wallace, whose defiant public statements had "created an atmosphere for violence and turmoil all over this state" and whose hands he believed were stained with the victims' blood. Shuttlesworth echoed these sentiments and at that night's mass meeting won the fervent approval of his audience of five hundred by proposing that further violent incidents would spark a mass march to the state capital in Montgomery to deliver a black wreath to Governor Wallace. Also that evening Birmingham black leaders, including A. G. Gaston, J. L. Ware, and Lucius Pitts, wired Washington and requested an immediate conference with the attorney general.[32]

On Tuesday, because of the administration's refusal to occupy the city with army regulars, Shuttlesworth threatened the possibility of renewed demonstrations similar to those of the previous spring. He told reporters that the Sunday bombing had exhausted the patience of the black community and that the May agreement with business leaders had turned out to be a fraud. He predicted that the mass march to Wallace's doorstep would soon be mobilized. He also spoke on King's behalf at the funeral of one of the bomb victims, Carole Robertson. To the fifteen hundred persons in attendance, Pastor John Cross of the Sixteenth Street Baptist Church spoke of the girls' redemptive suffering, while Shuttlesworth hailed Carole as an innocent victim, though in truth she had been a soldier killed in a great battle for justice.[33]

Attending the funeral was Diane Nash Bevel of SNCC, who had arrived in Birmingham with a proposal for getting "some concrete gain . . . out of the tragedy." After the funeral Bevel conferred with Shuttlesworth, suggesting that movement leaders launch the mass march on Montgomery with the added notion of attempting to sever communications between the state capitol building and the surrounding city. Shuttlesworth heard her out but did not think such a plan was in order at the moment. He agreed with Bevel that some strategy meeting should take place, assuring her that one would be arranged after King returned. He asked her to type up a copy of the proposal but not to release it to the press until it had been discussed.[34]

Bevel continued to pitch the idea to others and reiterated to Shuttlesworth the need to put the proposal forward at the collective funeral of Cynthia Wesley, Denise McNair, and Addie Mae Collins, which was set for Wednesday. She told Shuttlesworth that the people wanted to implement her proposal to express their anger and grief. Growing impatient, Shuttlesworth counseled her, "Well, I know that, but right now, Diane, we gon' express grief by mourning. And if you get out here and do other things that would take away from the sacredness and sanctity of the funeral, then I will have to call a press conference and say that I asked you not to do this for the sake of the family, for the sake of the occasion. If you want to do it later, you can organize and do it, and to what extent I can support you I will, but right now I won't. But a funeral is not the time to do what you're talking about." Silenced by Shuttlesworth's rebuke, Bevel waited to discuss the proposal again with King and the other leaders after the funeral. She viewed that meeting as unfruitful, though discussions of the plan continued during the next week. Ultimately King and other leaders decided not to implement the plan but to give the federal government a chance to address the problems of Birmingham.[35]

Meanwhile, thinking along somewhat the same lines as Bevel, King *had* convinced the families of the remaining victims to allow a collective funeral as a statement to the nation. The families were led into the sanctuary of the Sixth Avenue Baptist Church by a minister intoning the words, "I am the resurrection and the life." Seeing the entourage, many in the congregation burst into tears, several sobbing into their hands. As King delivered an eloquent eulogy on the meaning of redemptive suffering, strains of "We Shall Overcome" were audible from the crowd outside the church. Among that throng were some three hundred persons organized by SNCC leaders to launch into a protest march. They were dissuaded from that action by the Reverend Charles Billups.[36]

White Birmingham stayed away from both of the funerals. Only one member of the city council and an assistant to Mayor Albert Boutwell had attended the service for Carole Robertson on the previous day; on this day only the Reverend Joseph Ellwanger, minister of St. Paul's Lutheran Church, who participated in the service, was in attendance. One white moderate later admitted that for white leaders to attend the funerals would have been a nice gesture, but most could not afford to be viewed as supporting King and Shuttlesworth and chose to stay away. Speaking on the day of the funeral to a citizens' council meeting in Mobile, Bull Connor expressed his hope that the bombers would be caught, but raised the possibility that "King's crowd" had perpetrated the crime.[37]

Not all white responses in Birmingham were cut from this cloth, however. In one school in a lower-middle-class neighborhood a fourth grade teacher had her students compose their views of the bombing. One of her students wrote, "I think the person that bombed the church should get a tral and [be] sinunst for life. And I think if the people wood stop waving the Confederate flags bombers woodn't do all this."[38]

By the next afternoon a contingent of African American ministers led by King and Shuttlesworth were at the White House for a conference with the president. Sitting on either side of the president, King and Shuttlesworth began the conversation by informing Kennedy that Birmingham's black community was "on the verge of despair as a result of this reign of terror." Shuttlesworth told Kennedy that the bombing had blown away the remaining patience of Birmingham blacks and that demonstrations would resume if federal protection were not provided. As the ministers and the president discussed possible federal responses, Shuttlesworth shook his head in disbelief at the recent turn of events. "Mr. President," he interjected, "if you think of these four little innocent girls, not in war, but just studying a Sunday school lesson, and they're blown away. People look to us, and we are on the spot. It's up to us to say something." Kennedy answered, "Yes, I know, Reverend Shuttlesworth. I know exactly how you feel. But you have to tell your people that in every situation there are some innocent people who get killed. In a war, more bystanders get killed than those on the battlefield. And somehow you have to communicate to your people that this happens." At this point, Shuttlesworth reiterated his suggestion that the president make a goodwill tour of the South, arguing that his presence would send an important signal that the executive branch was poised to enforce the law. Pressing his desire for "the White House to be closer to our house," he suggested that the president's personal visit would communicate his concern for the victims of racial violence, tantamount to the human contact of a head of state at the scene of a disaster.[39]

The president remained noncommittal regarding a tour of the South, but he gave the group firm assurances, as King later told the press, that the administration "would not stand idly by and allow the lives and property and rights of Negro citizens to be trampled." Kennedy announced that at Mayor Boutwell's request, he would confer with white civic leaders on the city's steps to reestablish confidence that law and order would be maintained. He further indicated he would send two retired military officers, General Kenneth Royall and Colonel Earl "Red" Blaik, to Birmingham as his personal representatives to help Birmingham work together to overcome its current suspicions. After the session, which lasted more than one hour, the ministers backed off their earlier calls for army regulars in Birmingham because, as King told the press, they thought mediation should be given a chance. Echoing that sentiment, Shuttlesworth said, "We felt assured by his statement that he would take appropriate steps to protect the lives of all citizens." Reflecting on the appointments of Royall and Blaik, King added, "We welcome this action by the President and state our unanimous desire to cooperate with the President's representatives."[40]

Royall and Blaik arrived in Birmingham five days later, on Tuesday, September 24, the same day that the SCLC held its annual convention in Richmond, Virginia. Shuttlesworth attended the convention, and then he returned to Birmingham to attend a meeting set up by the president's representatives. Their task was to develop a cross section of views from the nearly five hundred residents they interviewed during their ten days in Birmingham. Shuttlesworth's return to the convention, however, overshadowed his meeting in Birmingham because the SCLC honored him as the recipient of the Rosa Parks Freedom Award. With King and Abernathy looking on, attorney William Kunstler noted Shuttlesworth's leadership in the spring demonstrations in Birmingham, telling the audience that "no man better characterizes the enormous power of mass direct action, relentlessly and continuously applied." Birmingham remained one of the central topics of conversation at the convention, and many attendees complained about the lack of progress there since May. One unidentified activist criticized Kennedy's choosing Royall and Blaik as his emissaries, citing Royall's earlier opposition to integrating the army and the absence of African Americans on Blaik's football teams at West Point. Some, including Wyatt T. Walker, recommended the Bevel plan as the SCLC's response, but Shuttlesworth objected to it as counter to the policy of nonviolence. King was also reluctant, though he believed some action might soon be necessary. In his presidential address on the final evening of the convention, King scored the failure of Birmingham law enforcement to find the Sixteenth Street church bombers, telling the audience that if something were not done soon in Birmingham, he would "recommend to Rev. Fred Shuttlesworth and others that demonstrations be resumed there."[41]

Indeed, little would be done in Birmingham, at least until Royall and Blaik departed on October 4. Their visit left little changed, and their report to the president merely reiterated what the black leaders had told him, that all of Birmingham, but especially the black community, lived in terror because of the bombings. They noted that almost everyone with whom they conferred approved of the city's hiring of black police, though they noted whites' "unsound" fear that hiring blacks would cause dissension and resignations from the current police force. As a result of pressure from Royall and Blaik, representative groups did request that the mayor and city council consider establishing a black police precinct. The city council, however, dragged its feet and postponed any decision indefinitely, blaming the "time-conditioned threats of non-Birmingham Negroes."[42]

On this point, the president's representatives seemed to agree, arguing that the continual threats of renewed demonstrations had come "at psychological times" and exacerbated the ill will between the races. On the other hand, they also criticized the white leaders for managing to put together a biracial Group Relations Committee only by October 1, well after their promise of May 10. In addition, they noted the disagreement over the number of black clerks to be hired in the downtown stores. They largely upheld the merchants' claim that one clerk in each store was not unambiguously in the agreement. Some individual merchants had nonetheless hired black clerks, but most of them were later fired for what the merchants considered "good cause."[43]

Even before the president's emissaries left Birmingham, Shuttlesworth dismissed the Group Relations Committee as a sham. He and King asked for direct talks with Boutwell and the city council, who in turn refused to negotiate with "professional agitators." Shuttlesworth denounced Gaston and Shores for backing Royall and Blaik and for opposing further demonstrations. At the end of September, Shuttlesworth induced an ACMHR mass meeting congregation to adopt a statement reasserting its claim that Shuttlesworth was its president and local leader. "Mr. Shuttlesworth" the statement insisted, "is a voting resident of this city, maintaining a residence and a telephone, and has on his body the grim scars of leading the fight for seven and a half years." Shuttlesworth wrote to Royall and Blaik to criticize the merchants' default on their May agreement and called on the president's representatives to nudge city officials toward face-to-face talks with him and King. Little did he realize at that time that Royall and Blaik themselves, like Boutwell and the council, had Shuttlesworth and King in mind when they spoke of "non-Birmingham Negroes." In order to make such a meeting more politically palatable for the new mayor, the minister offered to hold the meeting in private, noting wryly that "despite words to the contrary, we are more interested in progress than publicity." His offer and his request were ignored by the president's men as well as by Boutwell.[44]

Also in early October, three suspects in the church bombing were arrested for possession of dynamite. Two of the men posted their own bail of $300. That day Shuttlesworth had been found guilty in circuit court for parading without a permit during Project C and released under a $2,500 bond. Comparing the amount of bond levied against him with that placed on the bombing suspects, an angry Shuttlesworth denounced the bombing investigation as "a sham on the part of law agencies, in an effort to sooth the national conscience and placate Negroes." He added: "Where are the FBI and the federal experts brought in? And what part did they play in this? Is this the best the nation can expect of the combined efficient forces of the federal, state, and local law agencies?"[45]

In mid-October Shuttlesworth continued to juggle his pastoral duties in Cincinnati with his civil rights concerns in Birmingham. He and King put out ultimatums that unless Birmingham hired twenty-five African American police officers by October 22, new massive demonstrations would be launched. For at least one weekend, however, Shuttlesworth would be forced to give attention to matters at home. His oldest daughter, Pat, was scheduled to be married on October 12. Many friends and colleagues had come from the South to the Shuttlesworth home for the wedding, and the family was naturally busier than usual. The day before the wedding, the *Cincinnati Post and Times-Star* received a phone call indicating that Shuttlesworth's home would be bombed that evening. An hour or so later, Ruby Shuttlesworth received the same call. The evening passed without incident, but Shuttlesworth's son, Fred Jr., took another such call on his sister's wedding day. Again the family and their friends took the warning seriously and vacated the home for a few hours. The traditional wedding went on as planned, though Pat's concerns that day were something more than those of a typical bride.[46]

Another potential crisis averted, Shuttlesworth turned his attention once more to Birmingham, returning with King for a mass meeting on October 14. King challenged the audience to mount another boycott, and Shuttlesworth complained that the middle-class leaders of black Birmingham—Gaston, Shores, Drew, and the like—were undermining progress by talking to Boutwell behind their backs. Together they continued their ultimatums, but on October 24 the city council postponed once again the matter of black police. King was torn between resuming protests in Birmingham and launching a new set of demonstrations in Danville, Virginia. After meeting with several of the black middle class, he concluded that resuming protests in Birmingham had too little support. Shuttlesworth continued to press King to keep the pressure on Birmingham to honor the May agreement. In November Shuttlesworth wrote King, stating that he was "concerned that we not lose the initiative in our struggle over the fall and winter months." He called for "people to people meetings throughout Alabama in December or January, in preparation for massive demonstrations in the spring. If this was not done, he warned, "we will have failed the Movement." He continued: "I hope that you will consider that, as the Symbol of the Movement, you must lead in planning and stirring up people in the South and that writing and some speaking in the North may be less crucial at the moment. . . . We must move now to intensify and solidify the desire of the Masses to move now, or else forever be frustrated." He further called on King to consider new forms of civil disobedience, arguing that the masses were mobilized to resume massive protests. The weeks since the Sixteenth Street church bombing had convinced him that massive protests were again in order, and he reconsidered a version of the Bevel plan to march from Birmingham to Montgomery with some thirty-five thousand to forty thousand demonstrators. He concluded: "The masses are with us, but we can lose them by inaction and indecisiveness. . . . I have come to understand that we must either keep leadership or give it over to more active elements. I hope I am not frightening you, but some immediate thought, action, and planning are necessary; for many people in many parts of the country think that we are in a period of vacuum. . . . May I hear from you at once?"[47]

Although Shuttlesworth's views were shared by King's close adviser Bayard Rustin, King nevertheless remained reluctant. Shuttlesworth would continue to argue for renewed massive direct action for some time, but the assassination of President Kennedy temporarily took the air out of all protest plans for 1963. If the church bombing was not able to rally Birmingham's activist troops for massive direct action once again, little could. For the next five years Fred Shuttlesworth would continue to try to fire up the troops for another major battle. The civil rights movement, however, had moved on, leaving Birmingham to fend for itself. Shuttlesworth could do little to change that reality. Nevertheless, the fire in his belly kept burning, and he kept trying—at least until matters at home forced him to relocate the fight to Cincinnati.[48]

Shuttlesworth's prominence in the high-profile efforts in Birmingham had long since placed him on a short list of speakers for civil rights teach-ins and public addresses at colleges and churches across the United States. A dynamic and lively speaker, able to both amuse and inspire an audience, Shuttlesworth often was asked to tell his story, and after 1963 he increasingly played this role. In early 1964 he participated in a session at prestigious Haverford College, located outside Philadelphia. He was the main speaker at a rally at Shiloh Baptist Church in Canton, Ohio, where he criticized President Johnson's reported willingness to compromise on the public accommodations section of the civil rights bill: "We don't want Johnson to mess up what Kennedy started. I respect LBJ. I'm going to do all I can for him by putting pressure on him."[49]

In March Shuttlesworth won a personal victory when the Supreme Court reversed convictions he had earlier suffered at the hands of Alabama courts. In the 1961 Freedom Riders case, he had been convicted of interfering with the police. The Alabama Supreme Court dismissed a petition for review because the plea had been filed on the wrong-sized paper. The U.S. Supreme Court set aside the lower court ruling in a blunt, unsigned, three-line opinion, indicating that the conviction rested on particularly thin grounds. At the same time, the high court also reversed the $500,000 libel judgment against the *New York Times* awarded to Montgomery police commissioner L. B. Sullivan. In the precedent-setting ruling, the Court held that the Constitution bars a public official from recovering damages for a defamatory falsehood unless the official could prove "actual malice." The Court also set aside libel verdicts as applied to Shuttlesworth and the other ministers named in Sullivan's original suit regarding the March 29, 1960, *Times* advertisement titled "Heed Their Rising Voices."[50]

Unfortunately, Shuttlesworth's efforts to move matters along in Birmingham were not faring nearly as well. Lobbying for the hiring of African Americans on the police force or in clerical and other civil service jobs, he continued to request meetings with Mayor Boutwell, who continued to ignore his requests. Still threatening to resume pickets and more demonstrations, he requested a meeting with the mayor and downtown merchants. When this request was ignored, Shuttlesworth sent another telegram, notifying Boutwell that the ACMHR would begin their picketing of city hall that day and requesting police protection for the demonstrators. On March 19 he tried to stoke the protest flames among the Birmingham faithful with an extensive news release called "Why We Must Demonstrate." In that statement he accused the merchants of neglecting the hiring of blacks, which Shuttlesworth considered the "most meaningful point in the May 1963 Agreement." Royall and Blaik reported in an interim report to Robert Kennedy that city officials were stonewalling against Shuttlesworth and other "outsiders" who sought to force them to act. Even John Drew complained, "First they said, 'Give us until the first of the year,' then, 'Give us until Easter.' I don't know what it will be next. . . . The new administration is a complete disappointment to us. It had such a great challenge, but it is a do-nothing administration."[51]

Through it all, Shuttlesworth kept up public claims that the summer of protests in Alabama would be very hot, with "more massive efforts than last summer." Privately, however, he believed that King was dragging his feet by refusing to bring massive direct action back to Birmingham despite continually dangling the possibility before Shuttlesworth and the city. In June, as the SCLC was beginning its actions in St. Augustine, Florida, Shuttlesworth complained to Gardner: "I have tried my best to get Martin to understand that Birmingham could be the center of the Alabama Integration program, but what has he done? First, he gets stuff stirred up in Montgomery, then he pulls out and goes over to Atlanta without desegregating Montgomery. He stays in Atlanta working until it is partially on the right road and then pulls out for Nashville. Nashville is still segregated, and he pulled out from there, and now they tell me he is in St. Augustine, and I bet he pulls out of there. If he would listen to me. . . . " Shuttlesworth had argued for combining the work of all civil rights organizations to push matters in Alabama and staying in a specifically chosen city until it was fully desegregated. "In that way," he continued, "we can all work together and do a complete job." He fumed that "this police thing here in Birmingham has fizzled and . . . we have lost the summer as far as demonstrations because the kids are not organized here, and I couldn't commit myself not knowing what M. L. was going to do."[52]

King, however, could not be convinced to return in force to Birmingham because his trust in Birmingham's black elite and their hesitancy hindered him from renewing major demonstrations in Birmingham despite Fred Shuttlesworth's insistence. Even more important, though they may not have realized it at the time, King and the SCLC could never return to Birmingham for major demonstrations. To do so would be to admit that Project C had not been the success it was claimed to be. King's failure to return to Birmingham hurt Shuttlesworth's chances of preaching up a new crusade. At the same time, Shuttlesworth's inability to charge up the faithful made it even less likely that King and the SCLC would return.

To some extent, Fred's problem in Birmingham was compounded when his erstwhile ACMHR lieutenant N. H. Smith became the head of an SCLC chapter in Birmingham. At first, the ACMHR and the Birmingham SCLC tried to work together, but over time jealousies between leaders weakened both local organizations. A related problem concerned Shuttlesworth's residence in Cincinnati, which in some ways made the epithet of "outside agitator" more applicable to him. Some of the black middle class, who had long been skeptical of Shuttlesworth's style and leadership, now used this argument to help stave off new demonstrations. Amid Shuttlesworth's threats of new demonstrations if the city did not hire black police, A. G. Gaston wrote Boutwell a friendly letter, arguing that hiring black police would be "a great shot in the arm for those of us in the Negro community who want to avoid outsiders coming . . . and taking the leadership of our people for more direct action."[53]

Clearly Gaston could now consider Shuttlesworth an outsider because he no longer lived in Birmingham, and the argument was not lost on some of the members of the ACMHR. Abraham L. Woods later indicated that friction gradually developed between the ACMHR and the local branch of the SCLC and that eventually, even within the ACMHR, many believed that Shuttlesworth's hold on the organization's presidency was "selfish and unreasonable." Try as Shuttlesworth might to be in the city regularly and often, being away from Birmingham made it increasingly difficult for him to give hands-on leadership to the ACMHR. Some in the organization believed that as a nonresident of Birmingham, Shuttlesworth was away too much and should give up his role in the ACMHR. By 1967 Woods himself had adopted that view. Once at a board meeting, Vice President Ed Gardner told Shuttlesworth that "he believed that the Spirit told him to tell me to go on to Cincinnati and let them do it."[54]

Unimpressed, Shuttlesworth clung to the ACMHR reins as firmly as ever. He prepared to celebrate the eighth anniversary of his organization on June 5, 1964. In his president's address he quoted President Kennedy's comment, or at least his version of it, that "but for Birmingham, we would not be here today." He stated, "How little did we know or even dream in 1956 that we would carry on and discipline ourselves as a movement that destiny would use . . . as a vehicle to make America come to grips with its conscience! . . . But for Birmingham, the Civil Rights bill would not be before Congress today!" Within days of the anniversary, Shuttlesworth heeded King's call to help in the SCLC's attack on segregated facilities in St. Augustine.[55]

The SCLC had been in St. Augustine for the previous four weeks demanding the desegregation of public accommodations, the formation of a biracial committee, and the hiring of more blacks by the city. King had requested help from across the United States when the local movement in the Florida city had made a tepid response to SCLC efforts. He asked the Birmingham activists to join them as a "spearhead force" to reinforce the SCLC's "nonviolent army." On June 18 Shuttlesworth and SCLC staffer C. T. Vivian led a contingent of some seventy demonstrators, including seventeen rabbis who had arrived from across the country, to the restaurant of the Monson Motor Lodge. When the marchers refused his request for them to disperse, manager James Brock began pushing Shuttlesworth and the other leaders. At that moment, five African Americans in swimsuits emerged from a nearby car and dived into the motel's pool. Brock then grabbed containers of muriatic acid, a cleaning agent, and poured them into the pool. The swimmers were uninjured by the chemical and remained in the pool until an off-duty police officer physically removed them. Local police arrested Shuttlesworth and forty others, including the rabbis, who joined black Baptist ministers Shuttlesworth and Vivian in a cell for something of a jailhouse theology colloquium.[56]

A week or so later Shuttlesworth and Vivian led another protest, a "wade-in" at one of the city's beaches. Court authorities had given them the legal authority to swim at the beach, but Klan forces, which were very strong in the area, were determined not to allow blacks to swim in "their" ocean. As the protest group marched toward the beach, a contingent of Klansmen stationed at the edge of the tide taunted the would-be swimmers in an effort to lure them into water deep enough to "baptize" them. Nearing the water, Shuttlesworth asked Vivian out of the corner of his mouth, "Can you swim?"

"Yes, but not good enough for oceans," he replied.

"I can't swim," Shuttlesworth informed him, "and I'm not going out in that water and get drowned, and I'm not going to be responsible for these kids getting drowned."

Vivian countered, "But we got to go, Fred."

"We're going," he said, "but we ain't going as far as they think we're going."

Just then the Klansmen called out, "Y'all come on in, you goddamn niggers! The judge said you could swim. Come on in and swim!" Shuttlesworth, trying to maneuver his would-be attackers further back into the water, shot back, "Don't worry, buddy, we're coming. Get on back. You're in our way. Move back, white folk, we're coming. We can't swim on the bank. That ain't deep enough. We want to swim in deep water. Get on back!" The Klansmen moved back until they were shoulder deep in the ocean. Then Shuttlesworth told Vivian to pass the word back to the thirty other marchers to follow him. At that, Shuttlesworth marched his column into the surf at an angle, calling out, "Alright, white folk, we're coming in." Just when swimmers were hip-deep, he called out, "Left face," and his column began to back away from the water. Before the waders retreated very far, however, the Klansmen pounced on them and wrestled them into the water. Eventually the police intervened and separated the combatants. When the episode ended, Vivian marveled that Shuttlesworth would wade into such a situation without knowing how to swim and in the face of Klansmen more than willing to "baptize" the minister permanently. Shuttlesworth left St. Augustine with its inconclusive result, having spent two days in jail for trespassing and breach of the peace. He then headed back to Cincinnati to preach the word the next day and planned to return to Birmingham the next week to test the Civil Rights Act of 1964, a new law he had helped make happen.[57]

On Thursday, July 2, 1964, in the East Room of the White House, President Johnson signed the bill into law, cheered on by an audience of more than one hundred guests, including Martin Luther King Jr., Roy Wilkins, and A. Phillip Randolph. Not among those invited, Shuttlesworth had arrived in Birmingham early enough in the week to lead his regular Monday mass meeting at the New Pilgrim Baptist Church, where he offered instruction on how the new law would be tested and gave thanks to God for its passage. Then on Thursday evening, just after the signing ceremony had been completed, Shuttlesworth assembled a small group of his followers in downtown Birmingham to test the law. He warned his contingent to be prepared for massive resistance and reminded them of their pledge of nonviolence. He and his entourage entered the Parliament House, one of the city's posh hotels, completely without incident and were immediately seated in the dining area. Reports from all over the city—from movie houses and Britling's Cafeteria—bore the same message: no one had been refused service. Dumbfounded that there were no incidents, the minister was also surprised to find John Drew entering the restaurant at the same time. Drew greeted him and invited him to join him and his group for dinner. Ed Gardner, like many ACMHR faithful, was still wary of Birmingham's black elite and of Drew in particular. Concerned that his leader might forsake the little people in his moment of triumph, Gardner asked Shuttlesworth privately, "Well, Doctor, you gon' eat with us who walked with you, ain't you?" "You bet I am," came his reply.[58]

Having won access to public accommodations with the Civil Rights Act of 1964, civil rights forces next focused on voting rights, which had been largely denied to African Americans by the redeemers of the turn-of-the-century

South. King was now poised to mount an attack in Selma, Alabama, where voter registration practices had discriminated against the black majority of Dallas County. Flushed with victories in Birmingham and the enactment of the new civil rights law, King was in a position to make greater strides toward freedom than ever before because of still another development—his winning of the 1964 Nobel Peace Prize. The award brought King additional international prestige, which in turn brought him more influence for his work in America. Such influence could now be brought to bear on Alabama once again.

A large entourage of family and friends accompanied King to Oslo, Norway, to receive the prize. Viewing the award as an international endorsement of the entire civil rights movement, King early on intended to devote the financial award of $54,000 to the struggle and to allow some of his co-laborers to share the experience. Thus in addition to his family he invited along Ralph and Juanita Abernathy; advisors Bayard Rustin, Harry Wachtel, and Wyatt Walker; and SCLC associates Bernard Lee, Andrew Young, and Dorothy Cotton, among others. Fred Shuttlesworth, however, was not on that list, and he was hurt by the omission. He was proud of King's accomplishment, which he believed was deserved. Nonetheless, he also believed that he had earned the courtesy of being personally informed about the award by King, even if he was not invited to make the trip with him. Fred called Martin to register his hurt feelings, telling him that his ACMHR had put King on the road to fame and that if there had not been a Birmingham (and, by extension, if there had not been a Fred Shuttlesworth *in* Birmingham), there would have been no Nobel Prize. Unhappy with what he considered too little favorable publicity from King, Fred threatened to resign as secretary of the SCLC. Thinking of this snub years later, he grumbled, "If it had been me, I couldn't have gone [to accept the award] without carrying the person who . . . concretized my greatest success in the world." King apologized to Fred, saying he simply had neglected to think the matter through. Several weeks later, however, when he was honored at a dinner in Atlanta to celebrate the Nobel Prize, King once again failed to invite Shuttlesworth and reopened the wounds. These hurt feelings would complicate Shuttlesworth's involvement in the protests in Selma.[59]

As efforts there began during the first few weeks of 1965, Shuttlesworth was already involved on two fronts: in Birmingham he sought to convince voting registrars to increase the number of hours they enrolled new black voters, while in Cincinnati he joined a campaign with twenty-eight local black ministers to see William N. Lovelace appointed as the city's first African American municipal court judge. Selma, however, gave Shuttlesworth the chance to address his concerns about the lack of black voting in his former hometown. When he pastored Selma's First Baptist Church, he knew of only seventy or so black voters in Dallas County, and returning in 1965 he found the number had dropped. The SCLC and SNCC were also concerned about the matter, and during January and February both organizations aided a local group led by Frederick D. Reese in protesting discriminatory registration regulations.[60]

In early February Shuttlesworth visited a rally in Selma, speaking to a group of three hundred, which was composed primarily of high school students. Preceding him at the podium was Malcolm X, who in this instance was participating in one of his few active involvements in the mainstream civil rights movement. Malcolm arrived with an entourage of reporters, warning that if Dallas County officials did not heed King's requests, he would come in with *his* army. Shuttlesworth privately dismissed Malcolm's claim and knew Malcolm was playing on white fears of the Black Muslims. When he introduced Malcolm to the crowd at Brown's Chapel AME Church, he advised the press to note in particular the contrast between Malcolm's methods and those of the SCLC.[61]

In his remarks Malcolm registered his support of black voting rights but admonished the group to use any means necessary to get them. Shuttlesworth countered Malcolm's calm, scholarly disquisition with a spirited and demonstrative sermon on nonviolence. "In our struggle to be free," he preached, "we hold and affirm that not one hair of one white man will be harmed." Urging them to take the same pledge, he told the audience that his many trials in the movement had convinced him all the more of King's idea of the redemptive power of unearned suffering.[62]

By the next week, the fifth week of protests in Selma, more than three thousand demonstrators had been jailed. Dallas County sheriff Jim Clark had used extensive violence on the protesters and had arrested leader James Bevel. Bevel's five-day jail sentence had temporarily deprived the protesters of their leader, and in his absence Shuttlesworth flew into town to appeal for more volunteers. At the same time, he continued to try to instigate a similar march for voter registration in Birmingham, scheduled for Monday, February 15, largely so as to steal some of the publicity away from the SCLC's activities in Selma. An anonymous police report, probably provided by Ed Gardner, revealed, "It is believed that this is his big push for national publicity as he failed to get any at all from King in Selma. They have answered all newspaper men that this is definitely a march by the Alabama Christian Movement for Human Rights and not King's movement." The mercurial leader, however, canceled those plans to be part of a group led by King to press for black voting rights in Camden, Alabama.[63]

Despite denials in later years Shuttlesworth held a residual anger toward King after Birmingham and had an emotional need to compete with him for publicity. In addition, he quarreled with King's not keeping the heat turned up in Birmingham, to some extent disagreeing with King's decisions to mount protests in St. Augustine and Selma. He nevertheless continued to support and participate in these protests as a way of reclaiming his place in the movement. He also remained committed to the civil rights movement wherever it landed and always wanted to be in on the action.

In late February the stakes of the protests were raised when an Alabama state trooper shot and killed civil rights worker Jimmie Lee Jackson in Selma. Responding to the tragedy, the SCLC proposed a fifty-four mile march from Selma to the state capitol in Montgomery. On "Bloody Sunday," March 7, six hundred peaceful marchers were halted at the Edmund Pettus Bridge by state troopers and local police using tear gas and billy clubs. Dramatic photographs and film footage immediately sparked a national furor. King called for a second march across the bridge for Tuesday and called up civil rights sympathizers from across the nation to join the effort. In a press conference on Monday morning Shuttlesworth told reporters, "Alabama is in open rebellion against the United States and its laws. Negroes are being prevented from exercising the American right of peaceful protest. The soul of America should be ashamed today." He added: "The tear gassing and beating of Negroes in Selma, Alabama, yesterday by state troopers and county officers upon orders of Governor Wallace clearly dramitizes [sic] the sordid facts that Negroes are not respected . . . and are treated worse than cattle. No act of the Ku Klux Klan thus far is worse than the dastardly deeds done by Alabama law officers upon defenseless Negroes. . . . The federal government under the Constitution has the duty to insure peaceful assembly and guarantee domestic tranquility."[64]

He sent telegrams to President Johnson and the Justice Department to insist that the administration protect the marchers with federal marshals and troops. He also called on the president to appoint federal registrars throughout Alabama and demanded that the government prosecute Wallace for malfeasance in office. Shuttlesworth immediately headed for Selma and called for a mass sympathy march in Cincinnati on the following Saturday. "I'll be back here Saturday," he said in his departing words, "unless I'm in the hospital in Selma."[65]

On his arrival Shuttlesworth found the SCLC, SNCC, and federal officials engaged in discussions on whether to proceed with the march. That day U.S. district judge Frank M. Johnson Jr. issued an injunction against the march, calling on activists to postpone it until he held formal hearings on March 11. King had always obeyed federal courts and feared marching as scheduled would mean marching without federal protection against Wallace's forces. Joining in the late-night discussion, Shuttlesworth agreed with SNCC workers that the march should go forward. He believed that, as in Birmingham, there was no alternative to going back across the bridge; to do otherwise was tantamount to letting violence have the last word. Eventually, through federal mediation, King secretly struck a deal to halt the march and return to Selma just after reaching the far end of the Pettus Bridge. Shuttlesworth was among the fifteen hundred marchers who, making a symbolic statement but falling short of disobeying Judge Johnson's injunction, knelt in prayer with King just across the bridge. After the "partial" march, some of the marchers criticized King's decision. Shuttlesworth defended it, however, believing it to have made the point without unnecessarily endangering the lives of the marchers.[66]

That night Shuttlesworth walked with the Reverend James Reeb from Brown Chapel, where mass meetings had just ended, toward a restaurant on Broad Street. As they rehashed the day's events, they encountered a group of young toughs, one of whom called out, "Are y'all sure y'all are gonna win?" Shuttlesworth flashed his trademark smile and replied, "We intend to!" Moments later he parted company with Reeb to go to Birmingham with some of his ACMHR followers. The next morning he learned that Reeb, a young Episcopal priest, had later had his skull fractured in several places by a blow from behind. Two nights later, a few hours before Reeb died, Shuttlesworth led 450 marchers on the streets of Birmingham with signs reading "God bless and save our brother, Reverend Reeb." The next week he organized a march in Cincinnati as an expression of sympathy for oppressed blacks in Alabama and as a memorial for Reeb. In his speech Shuttlesworth paid tribute to Reeb, whose death, "like that of the four Birmingham girls and the three civil rights workers killed in Mississippi, and Medgar Evers, and John F. Kennedy, and all those who died for Freedom—from Crispus Attucks on the Boston Commons to this day—is another installment paid in blood for justice, human dignity, and brotherhood." Noting President Johnson's recent campaign slogan, Shuttlesworth suggested to the five thousand Cincinnatians who had marched from his church to gather at the Hamilton County Courthouse: "Let all America now demand that LBJ go 'all the way' to end racism in this country." Federal intervention, he argued, could have prevented the deaths of Jimmie Lee Jackson and James Reeb. That day the president, in an address to a joint session of Congress, proposed voting rights legislation. Shuttlesworth repeated his performance the next day in Birmingham at a large rally celebrating Johnson's action as well as remembering Selma and its fatalities. Taking advantage of the national momentum, he once again called for Birmingham to hire African Americans as police officers and firefighters. His remarks were adopted by the crowd as its official statement and sent to Mayor Boutwell.[67]

The next day Judge Johnson approved the Selma-to-Montgomery march, and President Johnson's voting rights bill reached the floor of the Senate. Soon after that the president federalized the Alabama National Guard and sent troops, marshals, and the FBI to protect the marchers. Shuttlesworth joined the thirty-two hundred marchers who left Selma for the state capital on Sunday, March 21. He marched several miles but, like many of the other leaders, returned to Selma and did not sleep on the highway as did some of the marchers. On March 25 he rejoined the throng that had grown to more than twenty-five thousand by the time they reached Montgomery. Speaking briefly at the capitol before King spoke, Shuttlesworth told the crowd that "our goal is not out here, but in there where Jeff Davis stood."[68]

Meanwhile, having devoted so much of his time and attention to the civil rights movement, Shuttlesworth began to hear some of the same complaints at Revelation in Cincinnati that had occasionally surfaced at Bethel Baptist Church in Birmingham. Since becoming pastor of Revelation in 1961 many of the key events of the civil rights movement had taken Shuttlesworth away from his parishioners, albeit not as often as from his pulpit. He was never one to spend a great deal of time in pastoral care and counseling members in their everyday problems, and he certainly could not provide such ministry from afar. Complaints of "full-time pay, part-time pastor" began to roil the congregation. During the Selma campaign the church seemed to be on good terms with the pastor, hosting an appreciation dinner to honor him for his leadership in the local church and to recognize his importance to the civil rights movement. The year before, on Shuttlesworth's third anniversary as pastor, the church celebrated his accomplishments: three hundred new members had joined; the church had bought and paid off a parsonage; the church had paid $24,000 for new office furnishings; and the church's budget had more than doubled and had reached a new high of $68,000. In appreciation the congregation gave the Shuttlesworths a love offering of $1,700 plus a new color television set. The 1965 appreciation dinner featured members who gave testimonials about their minister and climaxed with the reading of a proclamation from Ohio governor James A. Rhodes that honored Shuttlesworth. The lovefest was not to last, however.[69]

In late June, Shuttlesworth wrote a letter that rebuked the trustees of the church for showing disregard for the church's program. He had always insisted that deacons and other church officers were more responsible for supporting the church's ministry tasks than ordinary members, and they had absented themselves from the Deacons, Deaconess, and Trustees' Annual Day and several other meetings. The pastor insisted that the officers meet with him the next Sunday and bring an offering of at least five dollars to the church as a sign of their support. Any trustee who had to work or be out of town was to contact the pastor and send his offering by other means because, Shuttlesworth wrote, "I expect each man to be represented."[70]

After coming on board as pastor, Shuttlesworth periodically butted heads with church trustee chairman Jack Grigsby and Sunday school superintendent Autieve Smith, both of whom had considerable influence within the congregation before Fred's arrival. The new pastor's policy of personally approving all church leaders antagonized them and threatened their influence. When Shuttlesworth publicly suspended the membership of several church leaders for causing discord in the church, Grigsby accused Shuttlesworth of claiming too much authority. Shuttlesworth returned fire, asking, "Where do you think I get it from?"

"From the people," Grigsby replied.

"I'm sure that's a mistaken notion," Shuttlesworth countered. "When you voted for me to become pastor, you acceded to the fact that God had appointed me as pastor."[71]

Later, when Shuttlesworth led the church to buy a piece of property in the Mt. Auburn section of town, Grigsby withheld his signature from the deal, raising the possibility of a breach-of-contract suit against the church. As a result Shuttlesworth orchestrated Grigsby's dismissal as trustee chairman. Autieve Smith also differed with Shuttlesworth over the land purchase, arguing that the lot he wanted to buy was too small to allow the church to expand. She also challenged him on his policy of dropping children from the church's membership rolls unless they made at least one financial contribution a year. During the first years of Shuttlesworth's pastorate Smith had had several similar conflicts with him, at one time leading Shuttlesworth to suspend her from her church position.[72]

Matters simmered for three weeks until dissident members interrupted a Sunday morning service with their complaints. As Shuttlesworth stood in the pulpit, deacon I. E. Hayes, who had butted heads with the pastor some months before, approached Shuttlesworth to ask him to call a meeting to discuss certain grievances. Using his microphone, Shuttlesworth drowned out their voices and berated some members for their sins. Then another deacon, Robert Pierce, arose, took a microphone in the choir loft, and announced that the trustees had called a meeting scheduled for September 3 to discuss the church's financial affairs. When the pastor ruled Pierce out of order, some two hundred of the members began chanting, "We want a meeting!" The commotion continued for an hour while police stood by to make sure matters did not get further out of hand.[73]

The dissident members had hired attorney Smith Tyler Jr. to draw up a petition complaining of the pastor's dictatorial manner of dealing with deacons and trustees. The petition also raised questions about Shuttlesworth's use of church finances. The angry members charged that besides spending $75,000 on the new church property without the congregation's full approval, Shuttlesworth had run up large accounts at a local department store and had incurred heavy telephone and travel expenses. Shuttlesworth called a press conference Sunday afternoon to explain what had happened that morning. The disturbance, he said, was rooted in satanic desires "to offset the will and purposes of God" and was being pursued by persons with "little knowledge of Baptist discipline or rules of procedure." He noted that trouble had been brewing for some time because he was a "strict disciplinarian" and because he had dismissed Smith from her church office. Accused of being a dictator, he commented, "If I'm a dictator, I'm a benevolent one. I sleep with my parishioners on my mind, thinking of their misdeeds and the evil in their hearts." He added, "I certainly don't mean to be a dictator, but I will run this Church according to the way God directs me." Given his experience in Birmingham and his rejection of the "outside agitator" label for himself, he ironically claimed that the disturbance had been "brought on by outside influences."[74]

In the next few days the anti-Shuttlesworth group filed suit against their pastor, charging him with misappropriation of church funds. In addition, they convinced common pleas court judge Frank Gusweiler to issue a temporary restraining order that prohibited Shuttlesworth from interfering with the activities of the trustee board. The judge ordered an audit of all church funds spent since Shuttlesworth had become pastor and prohibited the church's savings and loan companies and its banks from distributing any church monies until "further order of the court." In addition one of the dissidents sent a telegram to Martin Luther King to seek his help in getting Shuttlesworth to treat church officers and members "as free intelligent human beings and not as illiterate slaves." The telegram was sent on behalf of the "Freedom Committee of the Revelation Baptist Church." Releasing the telegram to the press, Lovie Lowe commented, "We just want our pastor to practice what he preaches—freedom for all." She also indicated that some one hundred members hoped that Shuttlesworth would resign as pastor of the church.[75]

Learning of the communiqué to King, Shuttlesworth laughed it off, expecting King to urge members to be loyal members of their church. Shuttlesworth's reaction to the suit, however, was more serious. He filed a cross-petition against seven of his members, prohibiting them from disrupting any services, threatening the pastor or other church officials, or calling special church meetings without the pastor's approval. Late the next night a fire destroyed part of a shed behind the Shuttlesworth home, and fire department officials suspected arson. On Sunday morning another disturbance interrupted the church service. The next day King responded to the dissidents' telegram, coming to the defense of his colleague. He wrote: "The freedom struggle has produced few leaders of the stature and determination of your pastor, Fred Shuttlesworth. Often the very determination which makes it possible for a man to confront segregation's bastion in Birmingham is interpreted by others as a threat to their freedom and dignity. Surely this misunderstanding can be resolved, for you are a great church and Fred Shuttlesworth is a great man."[76]

Fortified by his support from King, as well as by a statement of support from the SCEF board, Shuttlesworth told reporters that through this church dispute the "right wing" was seeking to discredit him and create division in the civil rights movement. He noted that the dissidents' legal counsel, Smith Tyler, had led the Goldwater for President forces in Cincinnati in the 1964 election. He accused Tyler of personally putting up the $1,000 bond to cover possible damages against petitioners in the court action and of orchestrating the recent disturbances at Revelation. In addition, he filed a motion for a contempt-of-court citation against the ten members who caused the second interruption of church services. He also sought to restrain Tyler from disrupting services of meetings with church officers. "I didn't come from fighting lions and tigers in the deep South," he boasted, "to bow before cats and used-to-be tigers here." Tyler labeled Shuttlesworth's accusation of a conspiracy to discredit him "a smoke screen." The following week common pleas court judge Otis R. Hess met with attorneys for both sides of the dispute, and the parties agreed to name an auditor for the church's financial records and an independent moderator for church meetings. The court's decision calmed matters briefly, but only until the results of the audit were released at the end of September.[77]

Finding nothing amiss, auditors exonerated Shuttlesworth of the misappropriation-of-funds charges. The dissident group, however, refused to be satisfied. They ignored the audit's findings and renewed their complaints against the pastor. Weighing into the dispute in the hope of coming to Shuttlesworth's aid, the board members of the ACMHR in Birmingham issued a letter of support. Ed Gardner and Georgia Price asserted that "there was absolutely never any question about the integrity of Mr. Shuttlesworth in matters of money. Complete financial records from the nine years of the existence of the Alabama Christian Movement for Human Rights bear this out. Furthermore, it is common knowledge here in Birmingham that Mr. Shuttlesworth not only directed the spending of money wisely; he sacrificed his own welfare to put money into our treasury."[78]

Such statements notwithstanding, the angry members continued to make their charges and disrupt services, calling for the church to fire Shuttlesworth as pastor. Shuttlesworth refused and once again blamed right-wing attorneys for the difficulties, citing the large number of hate letters he received from strangers as far away as California. Many of these letters referred specifically to charges leveled by his church people even before those charges had received national publicity. As the controversy continued to swirl, many of the youth of the church issued a statement of support for Shuttlesworth.[79]

By this time, however, the controversy was taking its toll on the congregation. Some families were divided over the issues, with enough criticism of Shuttlesworth on the deacon board to bring the issue of his continued tenure as pastor to a vote. Analyzing the dispute for the city's black community, a writer for the Cincinnati Herald criticized the church's deacons for not fully supporting their pastor and thus helping avoid a showdown. The deacons supported him by a fifteen to four vote, but on November 4 the congregation took the deciding vote. There Shuttlesworth's margin of victory was much narrower, 284 to 276, though many members refused to take part in the proceedings. Still refusing to give up, lawyers for the anti-Shuttlesworth faction filed a motion with the court to declare the vote illegal, charging that proper procedure had been violated. In characteristic fashion, Shuttlesworth claimed that the narrow margin of victory would not limit his capacity to function as pastor. In reality, however, it would. A few days later, the Baptist Ministers Conference of Cincinnati and Vicinity issued a statement of support for Shuttlesworth and called on the dissidents to allow the majority vote of the church to stand without further legal challenge. "Any action to the contrary," the ministers warned, "will be looked upon by us as both malicious and immoral."[80]

The following Sunday the dissidents interrupted another church service and found themselves criticized in the pages of the city's African American newspaper, the *Cincinnati Herald*. The editor wrote: "In spite of defeats on every hand, the small group of insurgents seem determined to continue their divisive tactics. In the beginning their plight garnered them much public sympathy . . . but now they seem bent on a personal vendetta against Rev. Shuttlesworth. . . . The loser[s] should stand tall, admit their defeat, and go about the business of mending the rifts that they have caused in what has been one of the Great Churches in our community."[81]

In December Judge Otis Hess issued a twenty-seven page opinion overruling the dissidents' motion and upholding the November 4 vote to retain Shuttlesworth as pastor. As much prophet as judge, Hess noted that "a house divided cannot long endure." The next day, however, an article in the *Cincinnati Post* noted that the pastor was experiencing similar travail as leader of the ACMHR in Birmingham, where some critics were calling him "a tyrant firmly holding on to power." At this point, his victory seemed meaningless and his clinging to his office futile. The Reverend L. V. Booth, who had been instrumental in Shuttlesworth's coming to Cincinnati in the first place, convinced him to consider the possibility that it was time to resign.[82]

Before Shuttlesworth had time to make that decision, however, a group of 150 supporters within Revelation Baptist Church, tired of the "disgraceful conduct of the dissident members" began the process of organizing a new church. "Without any encouragement at all from Reverend Shuttlesworth," as they indicated in their public statement, these former members of Revelation "felt it necessary to leave that body." They met on January 16, 1966, in an old YMCA building for public worship service with more than three hundred persons attending, and their first order of business was to vote to call Shuttlesworth as their pastor. Next, they welcomed twenty-four new members. Meanwhile, back at Revelation, Shuttlesworth had decided to resign the pulpit, indicating on the first Sunday of 1966 that his resignation would be effective in May on his fifth anniversary. Developments with new Greater New Light group, however, induced him to move up the effective date, and on the same day that the new church conducted its first services Shuttlesworth made his earlier resignation effective immediately. He told the Revelation congregation that the dissidents had shown that "they would go to any lengths to prevent unity and reconciliation." He concluded: "Enough bitterness and strife has taken place. Enough shame has been brought to the Church, and enough injury done to the Cause of Christ. . . . I leave as I came: unfettered, unashamed, unbowing except to Christ, and undaunted in my spirit, devotion, and zeal for the work of the Kingdom."[83]

That night Shuttlesworth delivered his inaugural sermon at Greater New Light. He told an applauding, cheering congregation, "If your motive is to serve God, I would have no objection to accepting this church and spending a lifetime." He reiterated that his civil rights activities would continue, though he would begin to focus more on situations in Cincinnati. As he had often told his people at Revelation, "You should be glad when you see me and pray for me when I'm gone. The whole world is my pulpit, and I will go wherever the cause of civil rights leads me." The next week Shuttlesworth led the congregation to purchase property on North Crescent Avenue in the Avondale section of Cincinnati, and a new congregation—the Greater New Light Baptist Church—was born. By mid-year the church had grown to nearly four hundred members and formally dedicated a new church building exactly one year after founding the new congregation.[84]

As the summer of 1966 approached, Fred still made his biweekly trips to keep tabs on developments in Birmingham. Voter registration efforts flagged, and Shuttlesworth continued to lead small demonstrations and to threaten larger ones if city and county officials did not make registration convenient for African Americans by opening the registrar's offices six days a week with evening hours. City officials largely ignored him and picked up the pace only as federal registrars exerted pressure. The demonstrations in Birmingham never returned to the size or fervor of 1963. The African American community had grown weary, and a number of its elite members were telling them that the city was making progress, imperceptible though it might sometimes seem. There was still some talk in Birmingham that Shuttlesworth should give up the leadership of the ACMHR. Now there was a brand new church to build in Cincinnati, and Fred began to consider laying the Birmingham burden down.[85]

In June 1966 the organization would celebrate its tenth anniversary; it seemed a good time for a change. In his president's address, Shuttlesworth recounted the travail of ten years and assured his followers, "We shook up the Country and made America conscious of its morality and its commitment to the ideas of justice and humanitarianism." He once again credited the Birmingham movement with helping America achieve the Civil Rights Act of 1964 and interpreted Selma and the Voting Rights Act of 1965 as an extension of what they had begun in Birmingham. He noted that as many whites were beginning to listen to their consciences, "Negroes must never follow the illusory impulses to create a 'black society' to replace white supremacy. . . . Negroes . . . must always seek to be what they ask others to be." As he concluded his address, he announced his resignation as president of the ACMHR to be effective in early fall.[86]

Georgia Price and Lola Hendricks, longtime ACMHR members, immediately got busy planning a banquet to commemorate Shuttlesworth's departure. They put together a week-long program to begin October 17 to honor him. Part of the celebration of Fred Shuttlesworth Appreciation Week was a "This Is Your Life" theme, in which they gave him a giant scrapbook that reflected his accomplishments as ACMHR leader. Two thousand persons attended the festivities held in the now-integrated Municipal Auditorium, where his followers rejected his resignation and convinced him to continue as president. Moved by their devotion and prevailed on by their request, he pointed to work left undone: "Birmingham, Alabama must integrate its school; City Hall must cut tokenism and hire more Negro Policemen and Clerical Workers. Police brutality must cease in this town; and the stores must afford more job opportunity for our people. . . . You are asking that I stay, and I believe it is God's will that I stay with you."[87]

It was apparently not God's will that Shuttlesworth accomplish much more in Birmingham in his three additional years at the ACMHR helm. During that time rivalries continued to develop regarding who spoke for Birmingham blacks. The SCLC had installed a Birmingham branch, which by 1967 was being led by Joseph Lowery, who now pastored a Methodist church in the city. Shuttlesworth and Lowery clashed regularly during this period in which demonstrations dwindled. At times Shuttlesworth made rather pathetic claims and indirect criticisms of Lowery, whom he considered to be the black elite's leader of choice. In late February 1967 he told an ACMHR gathering: "I don't care how much the power structure likes anybody. If they don't have the soldiers they can't stop the marching. . . . I'm tired of the so-called upper crust Negro. Every time you turn around they run down to City Hall and come back with nothing. . . . You got to deal in a marble game with the boy with the marbles. . . . In the army you have to deal with the man with the troops. If I can shake the city, I ought to do part of the talking."[88]

In reality, however, Shuttlesworth could no longer shake the city. No one could. Nevertheless, he kept trying to fire up the troops for demonstrations regarding voter registration, police hirings, and police brutality. In February and March of 1967 he protested the killing of ten blacks by police during the previous fourteen months. Little changed in Birmingham, though the assassinations of King and Robert Kennedy made the Magic City look better by comparison. Local concerns in Cincinnati more and more claimed his attention, and by 1969 Shuttlesworth decided again to resign from the presidency of the ACMHR. He reasoned that the danger of local officials destroying the organization was past, and thus it no longer needed, in his words, a "national symbol of the movement as leader." He also had stayed on partly because he and other Birmingham blacks remained tied up in various courts, from local ones to the U.S. Supreme Court, in cases from the early 1960s. He had always insisted that if anyone would be jailed, he would be the first. Thus, when in March 1969 the Supreme Court wiped his slate clean, he thought he could give up activities in Birmingham without leaving any of his followers in the lurch. In the late summer of 1969 he relinquished the ACMHR presidency to Ed Gardner.[89]

Shuttlesworth's status as an "actionist" for civil rights and what later came to be called "justice issues" persisted beyond his office as president of the ACMHR. As the *Cincinnati Enquirer* wrote, the "minister had no plans to end the fight." The civil rights movement found new venues as it moved to northern cities, places where Fred Shuttlesworth had little experience or expertise. Primarily a southern black folk preacher, his social critique of American life was often simplistic. Blatant southern segregation, based so centrally on evangelical Protestant cultural understandings, was susceptible, though certainly resistant, to the prophetic preaching of a *Southern Christian* Leadership Conference. In spite of his ministry outside his native region, Shuttlesworth remained an African American Baptist preacher from the South. Nevertheless, he remained engaged in justice issues as he encountered them in Cincinnati. Shuttlesworth always argued that as a conservative Republican city, Cincinnati was much like his hometown of Birmingham. Thus, though increasingly focused on local concerns, his "actionist" status remained intact.

Among his first causes in Cincinnati was his work with a group of ministers (which suggests, contrary to the view of many in Birmingham, that he could work with others without being "in charge") to protest the firing of eight black employees at the city's Drake Memorial Hospital. In early 1966 the hospital, which had a record of discrimination against blacks, dismissed the workers for "incompetence." In June Shuttlesworth and two other African American ministers, the Reverends Bennie W. Smith and Floyd Davis, became involved when arbitration had produced promises that the dismissed workers would be rehired. Meeting with the Hamilton County commissioners, the hospital administrator, and the chairman of the Ohio Civil Rights Commission, the ministers argued that the firings were unjustified. "Some of the Negroes," Shuttlesworth posited, "were fired after sixteen years for incompetency. Does it take sixteen years to learn that a man cannot do his job?" Smith noted that black workers with seniority had trained the man who later became their supervisor. Davis warned that the ministers would take direct action against the hospital in the near future. Along with the three ministers, fifteen community leaders signed a resolution committing themselves and their organizations to a confrontation with the hospital unless the fired employees were reinstated with retroactive pay and fringe benefits, along with the upgrading and hiring of blacks in all departments.[90]

On Saturday, June 25, after the administration made no move toward the workers, the ministers' group began picketing the hospital. Hospital administrator Maurice Packwood rejected the ministers' complaints as false allegations. In a public statement to the protesters, he asserted, "We will not be intimidated in this matter nor have reemployment dates dictated by this group." He then demanded that the pickets be removed. Through the month of July Shuttlesworth continued to participate in, but not lead, demonstrations at the hospital, garnering an arrest and a trespassing charge in the process. During the protests Shuttlesworth deflected an erroneous report that the protesters were considering the use of violence. Disavowing violence, he told reporters he had met with fifty African American leaders who believed it would take drastic action to move the city along but that they had in mind civil disobedience and nonviolent sit-ins rather than violence. "Every big northern city, including Cincinnati," he warned, "is a potential powder keg. . . . I think America is driving its Negro minority to give a meaning to 'Black Power' that was never intended. We are headed on a collision course." Eventually, however, in Cincinnati the violent collision was avoided when the hospital board of trustees rehired all eight employees and hired Tony Yates, an African American basketball star at the University of Cincinnati, as head of the hospital personnel department.[91]

A year later violent riots broke out over arrests stemming from nonviolent demonstrations in the Avondale section of Cincinnati. General impatience with the slow pace of improvement simmered in northern black communities in the mid-1960s as King's nonviolent approach began to give way to the Black Power movement. In most places conditions were ripe for any local injustice to touch off a major firestorm. In Cincinnati, after a young black male named Posteal Laskey was convicted of murder and sentenced to die in the electric chair, small protests called for the conviction to be reversed. During the demonstrations another African American was arrested and charged with interfering with traffic, which sparked another round of larger demonstrations. Some of these protesters grew unruly as they gathered at a Cincinnati high school and heard an official make a speech endorsing the city's no-loitering ordinance. When police entered the area, the demonstrators' anger escalated, and for nearly two hours black youth battled the police, with the protesters throwing rocks and bottles and smashing windows in at least two dozen stores.[92]

The next night violence erupted again, spreading into the integrated residential sections of Evanston and Walnut Hills. That day the city council met in special session with African American clergy to seek to head off further violence. The leaders asked for the immediate repeal of the no-loitering ordinance, requested that charges be dropped against those arrested, and called for black youth to be employed in all sections of Cincinnati. At nine o'clock that evening police chief Jacob Schott requested and received the support of the Ohio National Guard. Forty-seven persons were arrested, and some thirteen were injured, as teenagers and young adults hurled Molotov cocktails, smashed windows, looted, and set fires. More than eight hundred guardsmen joined with nine hundred police officers to quell the riots.[93]

Along with a number of the city's clergy, Shuttlesworth met with city officials and with groups of the rioters. After the second night of violence the clergy group met again with the city council and with Mayor Walton S. Bachrach. As Shuttlesworth addressed the officials, a number of blacks waiting outside the chambers for a chance to be heard were dispersed by police, and Clyde Vinegar, a former leader of CORE, burst into the room to report the incident. Blacks had come to the meeting at the request of city officials, Vinegar said, only to be insulted by police and guardsmen. "We will never accept another invitation to come down here again!" he shouted. At that all but a handful of the blacks walked out, leaving Shuttlesworth at the microphone trying to be heard over the uproar. He told officials that riots would likely continue throughout the country "until whites learn to give a hearing to Negroes who outline their grievances in nonviolent demonstrations."[94]

When Shuttlesworth and the Reverend Otis Moss, pastor of the Mt. Zion Baptist Church, met with the young protesters, they found less respect for their positions or perspectives than Fred had been accustomed to in Birmingham. As they spoke one young female asked derisively, "What's this preacher saying? Get these preachers out of here." When the pastors counseled them to avoid violence against the police and guardsmen, another young militant commented, "Well, I know I'll get me one." Shuttlesworth quickly replied, "If you get *one*, you haven't got your quota. There's twelve of them to every one of you. If you gon' talk about killing, there are twelve white folks to every one of you. So you must understand that the race loses if you're just going to kill off one to one. You got to kill *twelve*." Then he added, "I think long before you kill twelve folks you will come to understand that killing isn't what you need to do."[95]

In dozens of conversations with young blacks, Shuttlesworth came to believe that the northern urban blacks were caught up in a trend toward violence that had to run its course. Young militants often replied to his preachments by saying, "You go along home and pray, Reverend, and let us take care of it now." Analyzing the riots for reporters, Shuttlesworth offered the view that nonviolence did not meet the same success in the North as in the South because, as in Cincinnati, the white power structures could not differentiate between violence and nonviolence. Noting his sentence of twelve months' probation for trespassing in the Drake Hospital protests the year before, he said, "That's more than many of the rioters receive." Many Negroes, Shuttlesworth said, had become convinced that violence could accomplish things that nonviolence could not. He added, "They will not abandon this belief until they come to realize that violence engenders the very hate and bitterness that we are trying to destroy. They've got to come to see that when you say 'Whitey' then everyone who is white feels in danger." He added, however, that "a lot of people who aren't out there rioting with them think that maybe the rioting will do some good and get them better housing and more jobs." With an approach such as this, and against the more threatening backdrop of the Black Power movement, it is no surprise that less than two months after these riots, the FBI removed Shuttlesworth from its "Rabble Rouser Index."[96]

As times changed, the fiery minister found he missed the excitement of the old days. Asked by an interviewer if he had enjoyed the danger of his days in Birmingham, he replied, "Tell you the truth about it, I did. . . . It was thrilling, in that you were challenging the system, and you knew that something had to move. . . . I wish to God people would get a-moving again." Still, throughout the 1970s and 1980s, as in Birmingham, he always remained with his marching shoes at the ready. In June 1979, at age fifty-seven, he led two bus loads of people to the Ohio statehouse to protest unfair utility practices. He also planned a massive voter registration campaign and pushed to change the system of electing Cincinnati city council members. Quoted in an article titled "City Minister Has No Plan to End Fight," Shuttlesworth said, "We are fighting the same fight we fought 23 years ago, and it upsets me to know that people think we are so far ahead when we are not. We are not fighting the Ku Klux Klan, but we are fighting people with a Klan mentality."[97]

That summer, as chair of the Direct Action for the Coalition Concerned for Justice and Equality, he marched on Cincinnati's city hall as the first of several speakers opposing a decision to grant police .357 Magnum handguns and hollow-point–controlled expansion bullets. Shuttlesworth spoke out against police brutality and increased police firepower. Some days later he and other ministers warned the city council that the preachers would organize voter registration and that the council could count on little African American support in their November elections. Always harking back to his Birmingham experience, he told the council: "Only a fine line of difference separates the backwardness of pre-1963 Birmingham and present conditions in Cincinnati today. We are prepared to struggle for our freedom." During the next month, Shuttlesworth called for a boycott of Cincinnati's downtown businesses, an action that won the support of the city's most influential African American group, the Committee of Fifty. Lasting less than two months, the boycott ended with negligible effect on the businesses because the city council voted to increase black representation on the police force by suspending state civil service regulations. Shuttlesworth promised continued vigilance in pushing the city toward affirmative action and said the controversy produced between five and six thousand new voter registrations and increased awareness in the African American community.[98]

During the Reagan era, Shuttlesworth fervently preached against the administration's massive budget cuts in social programs and the president's frequent use of racial code words, such as his attacks on welfare and affirmative action. In addition, early in Reagan's first term the preacher left a White House tour group with seven other African Americans to conduct a sit-in on the grounds, where they prayed for "strength and resistance for black people" in the face of the Reagan budget cuts. When asked by police to move, the eight continued to pray and were arrested. Only Shuttlesworth, however, remained in jail overnight because as a visitor to the District of Columbia, he was ineligible for a special bail bond program. Pleading guilty to unlawful entry, he received a sixty-day sentence and one year's probation. On his release, he commented, "We can't go back in time. We can't lose the civil rights gains that were won in the '50s and '60s. We must protest the militarizing of this country and the world and the budget cuts that will surely hurt the poor."[99]

Shuttlesworth's protest was a part of a larger effort organized by the Community for Creative Nonviolence in which such activists as Benjamin Spock and Father Phillip Berrigan were also arrested. Returning home to Cincinnati, Shuttlesworth joked, "The jailbird is back home." Two years later Shuttlesworth was arrested again in Washington, this time at the Capitol rotunda with 162 persons protesting Reaganomics. Later, in an address at New Orleans's Xavier University, he exulted, "The last two times I went to jail was in Washington, D.C. because I couldn't let Ronald Reagan come to Washington and get out comfortably without my saying something to him."[100]

During the 1980s and 1990s, Shuttlesworth became involved with the Southern Organizing Committee for Economic and Social Justice (soc), headquartered in Birmingham. Along with his longtime friend and fellow activist Anne Braden, Shuttlesworth served as a cochair of the soc's executive committee. The soc is a multi-racial and multi-issue network seeking to coordinate community activists from across the South. The organization does its work through networking, coalition building, providing information and education, and training activists. Grassroots organizing by the soc brings together various people's movements, including tenant groups, labor unions, peace groups, and environmental and antiracism organizations.[101]

Concerned about the increasing number of the homeless in these years, he began to use some of his growing financial resources as a means of lending a hand. In 1989 he established the Shuttlesworth Housing Foundation to help provide low-cost housing for low-income families. Since the early 1970s the preacher had acquired a million dollars' worth of real estate in the Cincinnati area, buying two small one-bedroom buildings as a tax shelter. By trading up he gradually acquired four apartment buildings with a total of eighty-four units. The purchase price of the buildings ranged from $35,000 to $285,000, but rents at these apartment complexes remained within the range of lower-middle-class tenants—$160 for a one-bedroom apartment and $240 for a two-bedroom apartment. Although they provided Shuttlesworth with a reasonable income, they by no means made him wealthy. He continued to live in the comfortable but not grandly appointed parsonage of the Greater New Light Baptist Church. He owned but one car, a late-model used Ford.

His toughness in his preaching, insisting that his flock toe the line, translated into making him a no-nonsense landlord. From 1980 through 1982 he filed more than sixty eviction notices, prompting some to call him a slumlord. Most of his tenants disagreed with that charge. Evelyn Nettles, against whom Shuttlesworth had earlier filed an eviction notice, told reporters, "I don't have no complaints. If he evicts you, you best believe you've been warned. He's a lot more understanding than a lot of them." He saw no conflict between preaching against the Reagan cutbacks and his string of evictions. "Just because I'm a minister and fighting for human rights," he explained, "[it] doesn't mean I have to be furnishing people free rent. . . . Even the Bible tells us a man that don't work, don't eat." [102]

In 1988 he decided to use his acquisitions to help the poor. He sold two of the buildings for $300,000, put up a third of that toward establishing his foundation, and sought additional donations from the religious, civic, and corporate communities to add to the start-up fund. The plan was that the foundation would provide grants of up to $5,000 as down payments on homes for persons at or below the poverty line. By the next year the foundation had provided a working mother, Carol Anderson, with $1,300 toward a $2,500 down payment on a five-room, $33,000 home. Shuttlesworth provided financial counseling for applicants and encouraged them to confer with bank officials on their ability to keep up payments. In its first five years the foundation became affiliated with the Better Housing League and the Greater Cincinnati Foundation and assisted 105 low- and moderate-income families in buying homes. Grants to applicants averaged $1,183 each, and, all told, recipients eventually owned more than $6 million in housing. [103]

Although Shuttlesworth's fire for action was never completely extinguished, there were times when it was reduced to a flicker. Certain personal travails dampened his spirit for periods of time and made it more difficult for him to work in civil rights. Differences with King that lingered since 1963, the movement's turn to the North, the broadening perspectives of the movement to preach to issues of militarism and economics, the shift to Black Power, and Shuttlesworth's new calling to help build a brand new church in Cincinnati—all of these factors to some extent lessened his action in the national civil rights movement. Just as significant were his troubles at home. In the late 1960s the difficulties in Fred and Ruby's marriage became insuperable.

An imperfect union from the start, the couple was never deeply in love, and years after the marriage ended, Shuttlesworth said wistfully, "We grew up and grew apart." The stress of Fred's almost manic activity, in both the churchly and the civic arenas, exacerbated the particular pressure points that weakened their marriage. Part of the problem stemmed from their widely divergent backgrounds and personalities. Ruby's relatively privileged upbringing had accustomed her to having most of her material needs met. This differed greatly from Fred's poorer, rural background, which created in him a pronounced conservatism in financial matters. Such differences significantly weakened the marital ties. "Fred was taught to squeeze the penny," explained his brother Eugene, "and she probably threw the penny away." One time Fred accidentally discovered some $5,000 in bills for items his wife had charged at various stores in Cincinnati. Horrified, Fred insisted on taking over her financial affairs, paying her bills, and putting her on a $100-a-month allowance.[104]

The couple often fought over the use of monies Fred received from speaking engagements on the civil rights or ecclesiastical circuits. Shuttlesworth insisted on giving the offerings to the movement or to the church, whereas Ruby argued that he was sacrificing his family's needs to those of his causes. Like many crusaders, Shuttlesworth had a fire to preach righteousness in the pews and in the streets that burned too hot for even his family to survive. He could never see Ruby's point—until it was too late.

To a great extent the authoritarianism that antagonized many in his churches and in the civil rights movement also took its toll on his marriage. A rather traditional male chauvinist (for example, he always rejected the idea of women pastors), Shuttlesworth believed in the husband as the head of the family. As the monarch of the family, his rule was law. From the vantage point of his oldest daughter, Pat, Shuttlesworth engaged in little meaningful consultation with his wife concerning the needs of the family. "As a marriage partner," asserted his daughter, "I don't think he was fair. I wouldn't stand for it in one that I had." His second daughter, Ricky, agreed that her father "was not always cognizant of those who were supportive of him." Both daughters recall lying awake many nights hearing their parents argue, mostly about money and his impossibly high expectations of Ruby and the children.[105]

Such arguments arose from their differing views of duty and discipline. A legalist who fanatically insisted on doing one's Christian duty, Fred had little patience with Ruby's leniency. She cared little whether she and their children set a high example of morality and piety for the rest of the congregation. She strongly believed such expectations on a pastor's family were unfair and refused to bow to Fred's unyielding demands that they meet them. Fred saw these matters as more than merely the whims of church people who expected more of a pastor's family than they did of themselves; for him they were the will of God. For him, being extraordinarily faithful to church matters *was* what God expected of ministers and their families. The pastor's wife was obligated to keep a perfect home and a spotless house; Ruby, though, tended to slack off such mundane duties, especially when her husband was away. Traditional domesticity was never one of her gifts. When he returned to preach on Sundays, he often found the parsonage in disarray. Consequently, the family's weekends were often filled with discord as he frequently and bitterly reproached her for what he viewed as neglect of her duties. Never finding resolution for such matters gradually escalated anger in both husband and wife.[106]

Eventually the anger seemed to wear Ruby down. Tired of her husband's absences and neglect, Ruby began to stay away from home for extended periods of time. She once confided to a friend that she was merely playing a role at home, and in her anger she sought refuge in her friends, refusing to go home until late at night. She absented herself as well from church obligations, becoming increasingly hostile to her husband and threatening to "tear up the church." In 1969, when her husband spent four days in the hospital for stomach problems, Ruby did not even visit him and left it to Fred's secretary to check him out of the hospital. Rarely a man to share his family problems with outsiders, Shuttlesworth nevertheless revealed their situation to his physician, Dr. George C. Hale. "Looks like we're having real problems. Nothing seems to be working. I hate to go through a public thing with a divorce, because I know anything that happens to me is news." Hale acknowledged that he had suspected difficulties and had advised Ruby to get help. He told Shuttlesworth, "Your wife is fighting your image. It's almost as if she exists to tear it down."[107]

Shortly after her husband returned from the hospital Ruby apparently reached the breaking point. Knowing that Fred did not believe in divorce, she seemed determine to change his mind. After several days of conflict the anger of both spouses boiled over with less than reverent verbal exchanges in the parsonage of the Greater New Light. When a pushing match finally led Fred to the threshold of physical violence, Ruby smiled and taunted him, "Go ahead, hit me. I know that's what you want to do, and that's what I want you to do. I'm gon' make you destroy yourself." Reining in his inclinations, Fred collected himself and replied, "I know that's what you want me to do, but it won't work." He turned away, went into the kitchen for a drink of water, and determined that the marriage was over. A short time later Ruby moved out of the parsonage. At the end of the church service the next Sunday, the minister candidly told his congregation: "I want you to know something. I try to be fair with the church. You're going to hear about it, and I'd rather you hear it from me than in the street. I know you're going to talk about it, and it's alright to talk about it if in your talking you will talk to God about it. That will help me and you. My wife and I have decided to separate. That's final. You can't do nothing about it, and we won't do nothing about it. We just ask for your prayers."[108]

In later years Fred admitted his failures at home. "I didn't pay attention to Ruby," he confessed. He recognized his own limitations too late to salvage the relationship, acknowledging that his physical and emotional absences were largely responsible for the destruction of their marriage. Occasionally counseling his son-in-law Harold Bester to avoid the mistakes he had made, Shuttlesworth told him, "Men always want to be the dominant figure. It's not always about that. . . . If I hadn't been so abrasive, our marriage would have been different. It's the thing of giving and taking. It's not that you are always the authority." It was the fire—always the fire to "redeem the soul of America," always the fire burning inextinguishably in his soul, but eventually burning away the marriage and the last vestiges of love in Ruby's heart. Later, overlooking the personal ruins that the fire had left behind, Fred Shuttlesworth was forced to concede, "I think I helped save the country and lost the family."[109]

After twenty-nine years, the Shuttlesworth marriage legally ended on April 20, 1970. The personal difficulties, however, did not end then. When their parents finally decided to divorce, three of their now-grown children sided with their mother. Even Ricky, who had always doted on her father, was awash in grief, disappointment, and recrimination. Her sister Pat was particularly angered by the divorce and blamed her father. For a good while after the divorce, her relations with Shuttlesworth were so strained that the minister even suspended the church membership of his own daughter for using profanity during a church meeting. In an effort at ecclesiastical discipline, Pastor Shuttlesworth sent a group of deacons to Pat's home to counsel her on how to be reinstated into the church's fellowship. Livid and refusing to hear anything of it, Pat barked at them: "Y'all can't tell me anything. I doubt that you have anything to say that I need to hear. You're not doing anything but bringing me his philosophy, and until he understands my point, we don't have anything to say. So get the hell out of my house." At that point, Ruby intervened, advising her daughter to make allowances for her father and do what was necessary to get back in the congregation's good graces. Nevertheless, Pat's fury lingered. Some ten months after the divorce, Ruby suddenly succumbed to her longtime heart disease and was found dead in her home on February 1, 1971. Once again devastated and grief stricken, Pat handled the funeral arrangements and refused to allow her father any role in the funeral, bitterly charging, "You treated her like dirt in life, and you will not be near her in death." Fred acquiesced to his fiery daughter's wishes, commenting to church people who were seeking his counsel over what to do, "Whatever Pat says, you do it."[110]

In good time, however, broken hearts were mended, and the children were reunited with their father. Pat, Ricky, and Fred Jr. remained in Cincinnati and continued their membership in the Greater New Light Baptist Church. They followed teaching careers in the Cincinnati public schools, and their younger sister, Carol, earned a Ph.D. and taught at Howard University in Washington, D.C. All of them regularly brought their children to visit their grandfather, who never remarried, for Sunday dinners. Chastened by former sins of neglect, the aging preacher became more attentive to kinfolk, typically saying grace over family meals or admonishing a granddaughter, "Remember to give your tithe to the Lord."[111]

Epilogue

I believe those sidewalks on Sixth Avenue running from Sixteenth
Street Baptist Church toward City Hall are as sacred . . . as the
ground at Valley Forge or Yorktown.

— David J. Vann

Martin Luther King was a messianic figure to his people. After his martyrdom, those who had worked closely with him unwittingly found themselves part of a process of becoming his apostles—at least such was the popular perception. Since his assassination, King has become a mythic figure, joining the elite pantheon of titans who shaped or reshaped American democracy. Remembering him on a holiday in his honor takes Americans back to a "sacred time" when America's civil religion finally expanded to include the sons and daughters of Africa. Over the years such persons as Fred Shuttlesworth were left behind to retell the "sacred story." As those events receded into the past, particularly after the deaths of King and Abernathy, Shuttlesworth's recollections could always transport listeners back to "movement days." More important, as one of the key instigators of the action in the "sacred time," his memory conferred on him a partly unwanted status.[1]

The theology of Eastern Orthodox Christianity teaches that icons are pictures that open a window into the sacred world. In his latter years Shuttlesworth activated his memory, retold the story, and like an icon became the means by which younger generations entered the sacred time. His frequent retelling of the civil rights story in church sermons and speeches at schools, colleges, and seminaries served as a window into the "sacred" past. In such settings his role as a central participant, his courage as a fighter, and his charisma as a speaker enabled him to achieve the unofficial status of unsung hero and icon of the civil rights movement.

Fred Shuttlesworth always believed that King had been chosen by God as the central leader of the movement. He told reporters in 1978 that in King "the hour, the idea, and the man met up. Every movement has to be personified by somebody. I recognized there is but one leader at one time—one Moses, one Joshua. I recognized he had the leading prophetic role." Still, he took pains to remind celebrants of King's holiday that though Martin was the leader, he never was the single hero of the movement. Back in movement days, Shuttlesworth often muttered to King's SCLC colleagues, "Martin can't do this by himself." Fifteen years afterward, his ego and bravado intact, to those same reporters he added, "But Martin didn't make Birmingham; *I* made Birmingham." The momentum of the King holiday made it easy to roll past such comments as if they were merely egotistical efforts to claim more for oneself than was deserved. The effect of the King holiday, though conceived as a civic ritual to remind the nation of the civil rights movement, ironically made it more difficult to see that historical period as it actually was—a movement of many important actors whose names are rarely recited on the third Monday in January. That holiday, which Shuttlesworth supported and honored, turned him into a living icon bearing witness to King's work but always trying to carve out for himself and for the local movement in Birmingham a share of the sacredness.[2]

Within minutes of King's death, Shuttlesworth was busy bearing witness. When violent riots quickly broke out as news of the assassination spread, Shuttlesworth reminded listeners in Cincinnati of King's frequent statement that "'not one hair on the head of one white man shall be harmed by us.' . . . I certainly think that he would want no violence to come as a result of his death. We know that violence, from whatever source, is self-defeating." Three days later Shuttlesworth delivered the sermon at a memorial service for King at Cincinnati's St. Peter's Cathedral. "Today," he told the congregation, "that eloquent and appealing voice, which should have been eagerly welcomed and vigorously supported, has been stilled. . . . God gave him to this generation for this hour; but this generation either understood him not or mistook the words he spoke." From that week on, Shuttlesworth was continually called on to bear such witness and to provide a memory for a younger generation.[3]

The context of these oracles was most often seen in the speeches he gave while accepting the avalanche of awards he received to commemorate his role in the civil rights movement. Local in nature, these awards rarely brought him back into the national spotlight, as he had been in the early 1960s. Leading the way in these awards were those from civil rights organizations: the 1975 Martin Luther King Civil Rights Award from the Progressive National Baptist Convention; the 1977 SCLC Founder's Award; the first F. L. Shuttlesworth Award of the Birmingham Chapter, SCLC, in 1980; and the 1987 Founders and Their Families Award, presented to the Shuttlesworth family by SCLC women. Universities and colleges, both predominantly white and historically black—among them

Birmingham Baptist College, Selma University, Boston University, and Colgate-Rochester Divinity School—gave him honorary degrees and awards of merit. Governors—James Rhodes of Ohio, Otis Bowen of Indiana, and even a repentant George Wallace of Alabama—gave him certificates of appreciation or commendation. He received keys to the cities of Selma and Gadsden, Alabama; Lansing and Detroit, Michigan; Cincinnati, Silverton, and Cleveland, Ohio; Richmond, Indiana; and Savannah, Georgia. He was honored with Fred Shuttlesworth Days in Lincoln Heights, Cleveland, and Cincinnati, Ohio.[4]

In September 1978, fifteen years after the events that sent images of Birmingham around the world, Shuttlesworth joked about being a criminal returning to the scene of the crime. Civil rights veterans from around the South gathered at the Sixteenth Street Baptist Church to celebrate the most satisfying Fred Shuttlesworth Day of all. Martin Luther King III called Shuttlesworth "a burning torch of courage," and the Birmingham City Council belatedly proved that a prophet could have honor in his own country. In a resolution, the council expressed their "esteem for this truly remarkable man" and commended him "for his most courageous efforts in leading a peaceful demonstration which eventually led to the 1964 Civil Rights Act and the 1965 Voting Rights Act guaranteeing all citizens the right to vote." Less than two months later he returned once again, this time to speak at a civil rights conference at the University of Alabama at Birmingham, the first time a predominantly white institution invited him back to Birmingham. At that conference Birmingham mayor David J. Vann, who as a young lawyer had helped negotiate the concluding agreement of the 1963 demonstrations, told his audience: "I believe those sidewalks on Sixth Avenue running from Sixteenth Street Baptist Church toward City Hall are as sacred . . . as the ground at Valley Forge or Yorktown."[5]

On such occasions, Shuttlesworth was always called on to reminisce about his role in the movement and was typically forced by questioners to connect his role with that of King. His role thus changed from actionist to icon, his task to interpret the movement, explain his role and King's, and help usher his ever-younger listeners back to the sacred "movement days." Typically his fiery charisma won over legions of young ideologues for whom King and "his lieutenants" were inspirational heroes. In 1978 Shuttlesworth visited the Southern Baptist Theological Seminary in Louisville, Kentucky, where King had made a controversial visit in 1961. Students who studied King's book *Why We Can't Wait* in ethics classes were delighted when Shuttlesworth gave guest lectures and preached in the seminary chapel. Using the exodus motif, Shuttlesworth in his narrative sermon had Moses telling the pharaoh that Israel's God, I Am, says, "Let my people go." "Who in the hell is I Am?" asked Shuttlesworth's pharaoh, and the chapel full of apprentice white preachers laughingly roared their approval. A palpable excitement greeted him when he told them that preaching is to "comfort the afflicted and afflict the comfortable." These sermonic pointers were hardly fresh advice, but hearing them anew from an icon made the experience an emotional high point for the seminarians.[6]

Ten years later, after the bill authorizing the King holiday had been passed by Congress, Shuttlesworth addressed the Martin Luther King Jr. Week of Peace at Xavier University of Louisiana. Young students cheered his clichés and roared with laughter at his humor. Older professors, ordinarily not given to approving simplistic preachments, were nonetheless heard to comment, "This was one of the greatest events we've ever had on this campus." They said it not because of the eloquence or profundity of Shuttlesworth's words but rather because of the events of his life and his status as an icon. His courage during the sacred time and his closeness to the mythic hero vested his words with power to transfer his audience back to the days of the movement. In the latter years of his life, two days a year were certain to bring reporters to his office at Greater New Light: the King holiday and April 4, the anniversary of King's death. Occasionally the resulting newspaper articles bore the headline as well as the subtext: "In the Shadow of King." The articles always contained his respectful paeans to King; they often communicated as well his own importance to the movement. In speeches to local public schools, colleges and universities, and religious groups, Shuttlesworth was a favorite King Day speaker.[7]

In 1986 Birmingham mayor Richard Arrington proposed that the city build a civil rights museum. After a bond issue was defeated on May 10, 1988, Arrington called on Shuttlesworth and local ministers to lend a hand and petition the city council for support of the project. In August Shuttlesworth joined with a dozen African Americans (still no whites) in calling on the Birmingham City Council to move forward on the plan. Shuttlesworth presented the council a petition with the names of more than two hundred ministers asking for action on the museum. Insisting on the importance of Birmingham for the history of the civil rights movement, Shuttlesworth said, "There is no place more than Birmingham that should have the monuments, the symbols, or the legacy of a civil rights museum."[8]

Over the next four years the mayor's task force, with the aid of Shuttlesworth and other ministers, raised private and public funds for the completion of the

Birmingham Civil Rights Institute and Museum. Shuttlesworth served as a member of the board of directors, a group created by Arrington to oversee the development of the institute. From the beginning, museum director Odessa Woolfolk and others on the board viewed Shuttlesworth as the most prominent activist involved in Birmingham who was unattached to the Martin Luther King Center for Nonviolent Social Change in Atlanta. His position as a former local minister and founder of the local civil rights group, the Alabama Christian Movement for Human Rights, accorded him the status as the key figure who, in the absence of King, could inform the decisions of the board. Indeed, board member Marvin Whiting argued that Shuttlesworth would have been the key figure even in the *presence* of King.[9]

In November 1992 the Birmingham Civil Rights Institute opened to the public, hallowing the ground David Vann had declared sacred fourteen years before. Across from the Sixteenth Street Baptist Church lay Kelly Ingram Park, the venue of the 1963 demonstrations. On the corner of Sixteenth Street and Sixth Avenue North stood a statue of King. Diagonally across the park was unveiled a depiction of three ministers kneeling in prayer. In between the sculptures of King and the three ministers, in the bowels of the park, visitors found three dramatic statuary scenes from Project C: police dogs attacking a demonstrator; fire hoses trained on a group of protesters; and a depiction of children behind bars.

Controversy surrounded the depiction of the three ministers. This monument was originally conceived to portray the actual three ministers who were arrested in the Easter Sunday demonstrations in 1963: A. D. Williams King, N. H. Smith, and John T. Porter. Rumors swirled that some in Birmingham's civil rights community, a pro-Shuttlesworth faction and probably Shuttlesworth himself, objected to Porter's being glorified in this manner. Porter had long since drawn the ire of Shuttlesworth's loyal ACMHR followers for his criticisms of their leader and in their view for claiming more of a role in the movement than he had actually played. Eventually plans were changed, and the monument was sculpted to depict three generic, unidentifiable ministers. Sometime later an easily identifiable sculpted head was delivered to its subject, John T. Porter, who displayed it in his office at the Sixth Avenue Baptist Church.[10]

The night before the museum was opened to the public on those sacred grounds, a special ceremony marked the unveiling of the only statue gracing the front of the Civil Rights Institute itself: a sculpture of Birmingham's Reverend Fred Shuttlesworth. A number of former Birmingham colleagues attended the ceremony, including Mayor Arrington. Early on, the mayor himself had suggested that the Shuttlesworth figure be posed in a characteristic fiery preaching stance with a fist bursting through the barriers of segregation. The living icon offered a correction: the hand should be open, reaching out in love and nonviolence, to whites as well as to blacks. An ecstatic Fred Shuttlesworth listened as speakers told once again of his exploits. He looked around and thought that the institute *still* had not gotten it exactly right. He later said that the institute "highlights *the crescendo* of the Birmingham movement more than anything else, the climax when King was invited in." Board member and professional historian Marvin Whiting agreed, lamenting that the sacred ground of the Birmingham Civil Rights Institute was weak in depicting the background of the ACMHR, whose central figure was the fiery minister from Oxmoor.[11]

In 1986, forty-three years after departing his boyhood home, Fred Shuttlesworth returned to St. Matthew AME Church to preach the congregation's annual homecoming service. Beginning slowly and deliberately, the aging minister gradually built up a head of steam, once more stoking "the fire you can't put out." His preaching zeroed in on his audience: "Black folks are getting like some other folks; they don't have a lot of patience in church. They go to football games, stay all night, and sit up in the rain in the football game, but won't go to church through the rain." The fire flared once more as Oxmoor's favorite son moved into another "whoop":

> Devil doesn't mind using your life . . . (Uh huh!)
> So you oughta give God a full life . . . (That's right!)
> Living folks doing dead things . . .
> Reason why the church is dead, we got too many dry bones . . .
> Spirit of God can't breathe on them . . . (Preach it!)
> Am I right? . . . (Amen!)
> Crying when you ought to be shoutin' . . .
> Complainin' when you ought to be praising God . . .
> But Jesus can change things . . . (That's right!)
> And Jesus makes a difference . . .
> Ain't that right? . . . (Amen!)[12]

Notes

Abbreviations

ACMHR	Alabama Christian Movement for Human Rights
BN	*Birmingham News*
BPH	*Birmingham Post-Herald*
BPL	Birmingham Public Library, Department of Archives and Manuscripts
BU	Boston University, Mugar Library
BW	*Birmingham World*
JFKL	John F. Kennedy Library, Boston
MA	*Montgomery Advertiser*
MLKC	Martin Luther King Center for Nonviolent Social Change, Archives, Atlanta
NYT	*New York Times*
SCLC	Southern Christian Leadership Conference

Introduction

1. *Birmingham News* (hereafter referred to as BN), May 18, 1961, 1, quoted in Alabama Christian Movement for Human Rights, *People in Motion* (Louisville, Ky.: Southern Conference Educational Fund, 1966), 12; also see editorial "Welcome, 'Jailbirds,'" BN, June 4, 1988, A15, and accompanying article, A4. This article reports on the school bus incident on the basis of an interview with Ruby Fredericka ("Ricky") Shuttlesworth Bester, October 30, 1988, Cincinnati, Ohio. See also the author's interview with Fred Shuttlesworth, June 4-7, 1990, and with Laverne Revis McWilliams Martin, August 7, 1990. Unless otherwise indicated, interviews cited were conducted by the author. Where possible, citations from these interviews will include references to page numbers in the complete transcript, available in the Department of Archives and Manuscripts, Birmingham Public Library (hereafter referred to as BPL), Birmingham, Alabama. Citations without page numbers indicate that the transcription process for these interviews is incomplete, and references point the reader to audiotape recordings in the possession of the author and the BPL. Eventually, all interviews will be reproduced in transcript form and deposited in the Archives Department of the BPL. A complete list of all interviews conducted by the author is located in the bibliography. (Note: Because my sources are often interviews given after the events or comments under discussion, throughout this book I shall occasionally change verb tenses from past to present, or vice versa, in order to fit more smoothly into the narrative.)

2. Charles Morgan, interview, May 24, 1989, 34; Ed Gardner, interview in Howell

Raines, *My Soul Is Rested: Movement Days in the Deep South Remembered* (New York: G. P. Putnam's Sons, 1977), 122; Martin Luther King Jr., *Why We Can't Wait* (New York: New American Library, 1964), 51–52.

3. James Armstrong, interview, August 9, 1990.

4. Jonathan MacPherson, interview, August 4, 1989, 14, 18; Armstrong, interview; Colonel Stone Johnson, interview, July 31, 1991.

5. On the success of the Birmingham demonstrations, see John Walton Cotman, *Birmingham, JFK, and the Civil Rights Act of 1963: Implications for Elite Theory* (New York: Peter Lang, 1989); Glenn T. Eskew, *But for Birmingham: The Local and National Movements in the Civil Rights Struggle* (Chapel Hill: University of North Carolina Press, 1997); Adam Fairclough, *To Redeem the Soul of America: The Southern Christian Leadership Conference and Martin Luther King Jr.* (Athens: University of Georgia Press, 1987), 134–36.

6. On Birmingham's impact on Kennedy, see Martin Luther King Jr., interview by Berl I. Bernhard, March 9, 1964, Atlanta, Georgia, Oral History Program, John F. Kennedy Library (hereafter cited as JFKL), Boston, Massachusetts, 17–18; Anthony Lewis, "Robert F. Kennedy Interview," in *Robert Kennedy: In His Own Words: The Unpublished Recollections of the Kennedy Years*, ed. Edwin O. Guthman and Jeffrey Shulman (New York: Bantam Books, 1988), 149; Wyatt T. Walker, "The Meaning of Birmingham," *News Illustrated* 1 (May 1964): 1–2; Claude Sitton, interview by Jack Bass, 1974, Southern Oral History Program, Manuscripts Department, University of North Carolina, Chapel Hill, 11.

7. James T. Montgomery, interview, August 4, 1989, 31–32.

8. Joseph E. Lowery, interview, July 29, 1991; J. L. Chestnut, interview, December 27, 1989, 11; Wyatt T. Walker, interview, April 20, 1989, 8.

9. Fred Shuttlesworth, interview by James Mosby, September 1968, Cincinnati, Ohio, Ralph Bunche Oral History Collection, Moorland-Spingarn Research Center, Howard University, 26–28; Fred Shuttlesworth, interview by Joyce Ladner, November 19, 1969, Cincinnati, Ohio, cassette tape recording, Oral History Program, Martin Luther King Jr. Center for Nonviolent Social Change (hereafter cited as MLKC), Atlanta, Georgia; see also transcript of Fred L. Shuttlesworth and Charles Billups v. Eugene T. Connor and Jamie Moore *(Shuttlesworth v. Connor)*, November 22, 1960, Fred L. Shuttlesworth Papers, box 3, MLKC, 31–32. In a 1964 article, Shuttlesworth wrote: "We have been used to police attending mass meetings since 1958, but they came with sirens screaming, lights flashing, fire axes, rushing into buildings hunting 'fires' which were not there—but failing to stampede Negroes or to extinguish the fire that wouldn't go out." See Fred L. Shuttlesworth, "Birmingham Shall Be Free Someday," *Freedomways* 4 (winter 1964): 10. The incident at St. James Baptist Church took place on December 8, 1959, according to testimony in *Shuttlesworth v. Connor*, November 22, 1960, transcript in Shuttlesworth Papers, box 3.

10. On the central elements of African American religion, see James H. Evans Jr., *We*

Have Been Believers: An African-American Systematic Theology (Minneapolis: Fortress Press, 1992), 2; Cornel West, *Prophetic Fragments* (Grand Rapids, Mich.: William B. Eerdmans Publishing, 1988), 6; Cornel West, interview by Bill Moyers, *Bill Moyers, A World of Ideas* 11: Public Opinions from Private Citizens (New York: Doubleday, 1990), 105–6. The distinction between "fiery glad" and "fiery mad" is emphasized in Henry H. Mitchell, *Celebration and Experience in Preaching* (Nashville: Abingdon Press, 1990), 63. This spirituality is an alternative consciousness that resists domination or "an oppositional way of seeing and being in the world that affirms those expressions of black culture that cannot be completely domesticated by the dominant culture and society." See Carlyle Fielding Stewart 111, *Soul Survivors: An African American Spirituality* (Louisville, Ky.: Westminster/John Knox Press, 1997), 5.

1. Alberta

1. Patricia Shuttlesworth Massengill, interview, October 29, 1988, Cincinnati, Ohio, n.p.; Fred Shuttlesworth Jr., interview, January 13, 1989, Cincinnati, Ohio, 15; Clifton Shuttlesworth, interview, February 4, 1989, Philadelphia, Pennsylvania, 43.

2. Fred Shuttlesworth, telephone interview, May 27, 1993; Eugene Shuttlesworth, telephone interview, March 6, 1993; Clifton Shuttlesworth, interview, 3; Eula Mae Mitchell (sister of Fred Shuttlesworth), interview, April 7, 1989, Philadelphia, Pennsylvania (quotation).

3. Eugene Shuttlesworth, interview, March 6, 1993; Fred Shuttlesworth, interview, October 10, 1987, Birmingham, Alabama, 1–2; Cleola Willis, interview, December 28, 1988, Birmingham, Alabama, 17.

4. Fred Shuttlesworth, interview, October 10, 1987, 2–3; Eugene Shuttlesworth, interview, March 6, 1993; Willis, interview, 17. Fred never met his biological father until, as an adult, he lived in Montgomery attending Alabama State College.

5. Carl V. Harris, *Political Power in Birmingham, 1871–1921* (Knoxville: University of Tennessee Press, 1977), 12–19, 32–33; John B. Mathews, *Tennessee Coal and Iron* (Cambridge: Harvard University Press, 1964), 1; George Leighton, "Birmingham: City of Perpetual Promise," *Harper's,* August 1937, 225–42; Henry O. Mayfield, "Memoirs of a Coal Miner," *Freedomways* (winter 1964): 53.

6. Otis Dismuke and Jeff [Robert J.] Norrell, *The Other Side: The Story of Birmingham's Black Community* (Birmingham: Birmingfind, n.d.); Blaine Brownell, "Birmingham, Alabama: New South City in the 1920s," *Journal of Southern History* 38 (February 1972): 21–48; Harris, *Political Power,* 34–35; Harris, *Political Power,* 186–87; Carl V. Harris, "Reforms in Government Control of Negroes in Birmingham, Alabama, 1890–1920," *Journal of Southern History* 38 (November 1972): 570; Robert J. Norrell, "Caste in Steel: Jim Crow Careers in Birmingham, Alabama," *Journal of American History* 73 (December 1986): 693–94; Eugene Shuttlesworth, interview, March 6, 1993; Fred Shuttlesworth, interview, October 10, 1987, 3–4; Lewis W. Jones,

"Fred L. Shuttlesworth, Indigenous Leader," in *Birmingham, Alabama, 1956–1963: The Black Struggle for Civil Rights,* ed. David J. Garrow (Brooklyn: Carlson Publishing Inc., 1989), 117–18.

7. Dismuke and Norrell, *The Other Side;* Eugene Shuttlesworth, telephone interview, May 28, 1993.

8. Fred Shuttlesworth, interview, October 10, 1987, 3; Eugene Shuttlesworth, interview, March 6, 1993; Fred Shuttlesworth, interview, October 27–28, 1988, Cincinnati, Ohio, 5, 7; Jones, "Indigenous Leader," 117.

9. Eugene Shuttlesworth, interview, March 6, 1993; Mitchell, interview; Betty Williams (sister of Fred Shuttlesworth), interview, December 28, 1988, Birmingham, Alabama, 5; Clifton Shuttlesworth, interview, 22–24; Fred Shuttlesworth, interview, October 10, 1987, 1, 4–5, 20; Lewis, "Kennedy Interview," 117; Shuttlesworth, interview by Ladner, November 19, 1969, and March 17, 1970.

10. Wallace E. Chilcoat, telephone interview, April 4, 1993.

11. Eugene Shuttlesworth, interview, March 6, 1993; Fred Shuttlesworth, interview, October 27–28, 1988, 6–7; Fred Shuttlesworth, telephone interview, May 31, 1993; Mitchell, interview.

12. Fred Shuttlesworth, interview, October 27–28, 1988, 6; Fred Shuttlesworth, interview, October 10, 1987, 9; Willis, interview, 3–4; Eugene Shuttlesworth, interview, March 6, 1993.

13. Fred Shuttlesworth, interview, October 27–28, 1988, 10–11; Eugene Shuttlesworth, interview, March 6, 1993.

14. On family violence, see John Hope Franklin, *The Militant South* (Cambridge: Harvard University Press, Belknap Press, 1956), passim; John Shelton Reed, *The Enduring South: Subcultural Persistence in Mass Society* (Chapel Hill: University of North Carolina Press, 1972 [1974]), 45–56; Ted Ownby, *Subduing Satan: Religion, Recreation, and Manhood in the Rural South, 1865–1920* (Chapel Hill: University of North Carolina Press, 1990), 135–36; E. Franklin Frazier, *Black Bourgeoisie: The Rise of a New Middle Class* (New York: Free Press, 1957), 71–78, 112; Richard J. Gelles, *The Violent Home: A Study of Physical Aggression between Husbands and Wives* (Beverly Hills, Calif.: Sage Publications, 1974), 120–30; Richard J. Gelles and Claire Pedrick Cornell, *Intimate Violence in Families,* 2d ed. (Newbury Park, Calif.: Sage Publications, 1990); Robert Hampton, ed., *Black Family Violence: Current Research and Theory* (New York: Lexington Books, 1991); Charles Johnson, *Growing Up in the Black Belt* (New York: Schocken Books, 1967), 72–77. According to Johnson's empirical studies, socioeconomic status in the Black Belt fell as follows: upper class, 6 percent; middle class, 12 percent; lower class (combining upper lower and lower lower), 82 percent.

15. Fred Shuttlesworth, interview, October 10, 1987, 8, 17; Mitchell, interview.

16. Fred Shuttlesworth, interview, October 27–28, 1988, 2–3.

17. Eugene Shuttlesworth, interview, March 6, 1993.

18. Clifton Shuttlesworth, interview, 6. On the contributions of violent marriages to the development of mother-son alliances, see M. Elbow, "Children of Violent Marriages: The Forgotten Victims," *Social Casework* 63 (1982): 468.

19. Fred Shuttlesworth, interview, October 27–28, 1988, 4; Clifton Shuttlesworth, interview, 13–14; Eugene Shuttlesworth, interview, March 6, 1993.

20. Eugene Shuttlesworth, interview, March 6, 1993; Mitchell, interview.

21. Shuttlesworth, interview by Ladner; Fred Shuttlesworth, interview, October 27–28, 1988, 12; Clifton Shuttlesworth, interview, 40.

22. Eugene Shuttlesworth, interview, March 6, 1993; Clifton Shuttlesworth, interview, 5–9; Mitchell, interview.

23. Fred Shuttlesworth, quoted in Willis, interview, 11 (first quotation); Fred Shuttlesworth, "Together Building the Beloved Community" (address given at Xavier University of Louisiana, New Orleans, January 20, 1988), videotape in author's possession (second quotation); Fred Shuttlesworth, interview, October 10, 1987, 5, 10–11; Mitchell, interview (third quotation); Clifton Shuttlesworth, interview, 17.

24. Fred Shuttlesworth, interview, October 10, 1987, 5; Fred Shuttlesworth, interview, October 27–28, 1988, 3; Clifton Shuttlesworth, interview, 8; Williams, interview, 4; Willis, interview, 12; Mitchell, interview. Regarding the "mothering" role in first-born children, see Marie Ferguson Peters, "Parenting in Black Families with Young Children: A Historical Perspective," in *Black Families,* ed. Harriette Pipes McAdoo (Newbury Park, Calif.: Sage Publications, 1988), 234; V. Young, "Family and Childhood in a Southern Negro Community," *American Anthropologist* 72 (April 1970): 269–88.

25. On parental teaching styles, see Peters, "Parenting in Black Families"; R. D. Hess, et al., *The Cognitive Environments of Urban Preschool Children: Report to the Children's Bureau, U.S. Department of Health, Education, and Welfare* (Washington, D.C.: Government Printing Office, 1968); D. Baumrind, "An Exploratory Study of Socialization Effects on Black Children: Some Black-White Comparisons," *Child Development* 43 (1972): 261–67; Wade W. Nobles, "African-American Family Life: An Instrument of Culture," in McAdoo, *Black Families,* 49–50. On punishment and the "authoritarian personality," see Richard J. Gelles, *Family Violence* (Beverly Hills, Calif.: Sage Publications, 1979), 192; see also T. W. Adorno, ed., *The Authoritarian Personality* (New York: Harper, 1950).

26. Willis, interview, 9–10, 16.

27. Fred Shuttlesworth, interview, October 27–28, 1988, 22; Willis, interview, 13–14, 17; Clifton Shuttlesworth, interview, 42.

28. Williams, interview, 3 (quotation); Ruby F. Lassiter, "Child Rearing in Black Families: Child-Abusing Discipline," in *Violence in the Black Family: Correlates and Consequences,* ed. Robert L. Hampton (Lexington, Mass.: Lexington Books, 1987), 46–48.

29. Fred Shuttlesworth, interview, October 10, 1987, 8, 16–18; Clifton Shuttlesworth, interview, 29–34.

30. Fred Shuttlesworth, interview, October 27–28, 1988, 12 (first quotation); Willis, interview, 9–10, 16; Eugene Shuttlesworth, interview, March 6, 1993 (second quotation).

31. Fred Shuttlesworth, interview, October 10, 1987, 13, 20–21; Clifton Shuttlesworth, interview, 29–31; Willis, interview, 5–6 (first quotation); Fred Shuttlesworth, interview, October 27–28, 1988, 19 (second and third quotations).

32. Fred Shuttlesworth, interview, October 10, 1987, 19–22.

33. Ibid., 21–22, 27–28; Fred Shuttlesworth, interview, October 27–31, 1988, 13 (quotation).

34. Clifton Shuttlesworth, interview, 27–28; Mitchell, interview; Williams, interview, 2.

35. Dismuke and Norrell, *The Other Side;* Harris, *Political Power,* 172; Johnson, *Growing Up in the Black Belt,* 103, 107; Zane L. Miller, "Urban Blacks in the South, 1865–1920: The Richmond, Savannah, New Orleans, Louisville, and Birmingham Experience," in *The New Urban History: Quantitative Explorations by American Historians,* ed. Leo F. Schnore (Princeton: Princeton University Press, 1975), 192, based on census data.

36. Jones, "Indigenous Leader," 118; Clifton Shuttlesworth, interview, 20–21; Eugene Shuttlesworth, interview, March 6, 1993; Fred Shuttlesworth, interview, October 10, 1987, 11–12, 15–16 (quotation).

37. Fred Shuttlesworth, interview, October 27–28, 1988, 13–14.

38. Shuttlesworth, interview by Ladner, November 19, 1969, and March 17, 1970; *Cincinnati Enquirer,* October 14, 1980, B1.

39. Fred Shuttlesworth, interview, October 27–28, 1988, 14; Eugene Shuttlesworth, interview, March 6, 1993; Mitchell, interview; Fred Shuttlesworth, interview, October 10, 1987, 18–19; Clifton Shuttlesworth, interview, 18.

40. Fred Shuttlesworth, interview, October 10, 1987, 13–14, 19–20; Eugene Shuttlesworth, interview, March 6, 1993; Willis, interview, 2; Johnson, *Growing Up in the Black Belt,* 173; Fred Shuttlesworth, interview, October 27–28, 1988, 25–26 (quotation).

41. Montgomery, interview, 2–4; Fred Shuttlesworth, interview, October 10, 1987, 14; Shuttlesworth, interview by Ladner.

42. Harris, "Reforms," 568–69, 574, 579–80; Harris, *Political Power,* 186–87.

43. *Message of the Mayor and Annual Reports of the Officers of Birmingham, 1906* (Birmingham: City of Birmingham, 1906), 16–17.

44. Fred Shuttlesworth, interview, October 27–28, 1988, 20–21.

45. Fred Shuttlesworth, interview, October 10, 1987, 5–7; record of arrests and criminal history of Fred Lee Shuttlesworth, October 16, 1963, Police Surveillance Files, Archives Department, BPL. Records include two arrests before Shuttlesworth began

his civil rights activities. The first occasion, on August 4, 1940, for distilling, led to his being placed on two years of probation. The second instance, August 27, 1942, was for violating probation; the record shows no court disposition of this case.

46. Fred Powledge, *Free at Last? The Civil Rights Movement and the People Who Made It* (Boston: Little, Brown, 1991), 79.

2. Ready

1. Many scholars of African and African American religion comment on the cultural-theological emphasis on providence, which in large measure derives from the African philosophical concept of the High God who controls human destiny. Edward P. Wimberly calls this the "eschatological plot" of African American theology in which God is always "working out God's purpose in life on behalf of persons." See Edward P. Wimberly, *African American Pastoral Care* (Nashville: Abingdon Press, 1991), 13. Henry Mitchell, perhaps the foremost authority on African American preaching, has written that "in Black culture the Providence of God is far and away the most popular doctrine" (quoted in a sermon in Richard L. Eslinger, *A New Hearing: Living Options in Homiletic Method* [Nashville: Abingdon Press, 1987], 57). See also Henry Mitchell and Nicholas C. Lewter, *Soul Theology* (San Francisco: Harper and Row, 1986), 14; Albert J. Raboteau, *Slave Religion: The "Invisible Institution" in the Antebellum South* (New York: Oxford University Press, 1979).

2. Jones, "Indigenous Leader," 119. Jones's article is based on a 1960 interview with Shuttlesworth; see also Shuttlesworth, interview by Ladner, November 19, 1969, and March 17, 1970; Fred Shuttlesworth, interview, October 27–28, 1988, 23–29.

3. Ruby Keeler Shuttlesworth's family background is gleaned from the following sources: Fred Shuttlesworth, interview, October 27–28, 1988, 25–29; Shuttlesworth certificate of marriage, Jefferson County Office of Probate, FBI file 100-438794-2, copy in author's possession; Massengill, interview; Fred Shuttlesworth Jr., interview, 8–12; Johnson, interview.

4. Fred Shuttlesworth Jr., interview, 9 (first quotation); Fred Shuttlesworth Jr., interview, 12; Bester, interview (second quotation); Fred Shuttlesworth, interview, October 27–28, 1988, 25–29.

5. Fred Shuttlesworth, interview, October 27–31, 1988, 24–25; Shuttlesworth, interview by Ladner; Fred Shuttlesworth, interview, October 27–31, 1988, 24–25 (quotation).

6. Fred Shuttlesworth, interview, October 10, 1987, 23; Jones, "Indigenous Leader," 119; Fred Shuttlesworth, interview, March 10, 1984, 3; Bester, interview (quotation).

7. James A. Burran, "Urban Racial Violence in the South during World War II: A Comparative Overview," in *From the Old South to the New: Essays on the Transitional South,* ed. Walter J. Fraser Jr. and Winfred B. Moore Jr. (Westport, Conn.: Greenwood Press, 1981), 168; Fred Shuttlesworth, interview, October 27–31, 1988; Jones, "Indigenous Leader," 119; Shuttlesworth, interview by Ladner; Fred Shuttlesworth,

interview, March 10, 1984, 2–7 (quotation); Fred Shuttlesworth, interview, October 10, 1987, 25–26; Fred Shuttlesworth, interview, October 27–31, 1988, 34–35.

8. Fred Shuttlesworth, interview, March 10, 1984, 9–10; Jones, "Indigenous Leader," 121.

9. Both incidents are recounted in Jones, "Indigenous Leader," 121–23.

10. BN, May 28, 1943, 12; BN, May 29, 1943, 2; BN, May 30, 1943, 14; New York Times (hereafter referred to as NYT), May 26, 1943, 25; NYT, June 13, 1943, 34. See also Burran, "Urban Racial Violence," 169–71.

11. Fred Shuttlesworth, interviews, October 10, 1987, 22–24, and October 27–31, 1988, 29.

12. Fred Shuttlesworth, interview, October 10, 1987, 24–25; Fred Shuttlesworth, interview, October 27–31, 1988, 45; Fred Shuttlesworth, interview, March 10, 1984, 5–7.

13. Fred Shuttlesworth, interview, October 27–31, 1988, 45; Fred Shuttlesworth, interview, October 10, 1987, 24–25 (quotation); Fred Shuttlesworth, interview, March 10, 1984, 2.

14. Jones, "Indigenous Leader," 121; Fred Shuttlesworth, interviews, March 10, 1984, 8–9, and October 27–31, 1988, 64–67.

15. Fred Shuttlesworth, interview, March 10, 1984, 64–65.

16. The term *association* is standard among Baptists for an organization of black Baptist churches in a given area, usually a county. As a church polity, an association is comparable to a district (Methodist) or a synod (Presbyterian). The white Baptists of a county generally had a segregated association of their own, in this case called the Mobile Baptist Association; see Malcolm Burroughs, Administrative Assistant, Cedar Grove Preparatory School, interview, Mobile, Alabama, September 16, 1994; Fred Shuttlesworth, interview, March 10, 1984, 7–8.

17. Fred Shuttlesworth, interview, October 27–31, 1988, 53–54 (dispute with Robinson); Fred Shuttlesworth, interview, January 11, 1989, 2–3.

18. Fred Shuttlesworth, interview, October 27–31, 1988, 36–41. On apprenticeships, see Joseph Washington, *Black Religion* (Boston: Beacon Press, 1964), 64–65. Regarding the issue of ordination and gender, black Baptists have traditionally ordained only men, though by the late 1980s practices had slowly begun to change. Still, at the time of this writing, ordained women in African American Baptist churches constitute a very small minority. Most black Baptist ministers continue to oppose women in the ministry and particularly in the pastorate. See C. Eric Lincoln and Lawrence Mamiya, *The Black Church in the African American Experience* (Durham, N.C.: Duke University Press, 1990), ch. 10, and J. Deotis Roberts, *The Prophethood of Black Believers: An African American Political Theology for Ministry* (Louisville, Ky.: Westminster/John Knox Press, 1994), 75–89; Fred Shuttlesworth, interviews, October 27–31, 1988, 36–39, and October 10, 1987, 24–25.

19. Fred Shuttlesworth, interview, January 11, 1989, 1.

20. Fred Shuttlesworth, interview, March 10, 1984, 5–8; Fred Shuttlesworth, interview,

October 27–31, 1988, 51; Fred Shuttlesworth, interview, May 22–25, 1990; Jones, "Indigenous Leader" (quotation), 123.

21. Fred Shuttlesworth, interview, March 10, 1984, 9; Fred Shuttlesworth, interview, October 27–31, 1988, 51 (quotation); Fred Shuttlesworth, interview, March 10, 1984, 11; Jones, "Indigenous Leader," 123.

22. Bester, interview; Willis, interview, 4–5.

23. On the background of Selma and of Dallas County, see Johnson, *Growing Up in the Black Belt*, 49–50, 54; J. L. Chestnut and Julia Cass, *Black in Selma: The Uncommon Life of J. L. Chestnut Jr.* (New York: Anchor Books, 1990), 1–6, 44–49; Chestnut, interview, 1–3.

24. James D. Anderson, *The Education of Blacks in the South, 1860–1935* (Chapel Hill: University of North Carolina Press, 1988), 239–40; Evelyn Brooks Higginbotham, *Righteous Discontent: The Women's Movement in the Black Baptist Church, 1880–1920* (Cambridge: Harvard University Press, 1993), 58 (first quotation); Robert G. Scherer, *Subordination or Liberation? The Development and Conflicting Theories of Black Education in Nineteenth-Century Alabama* (Tuscaloosa: University of Alabama Press, 1977), 97; Charles Octavius Boothe, *The Cyclopedia of the Colored Baptists of Alabama* (Birmingham: Alabama Publishing Company, 1895), 33–34; Scherer, *Subordination or Liberation*, 96–99; Colored Missionary Baptist Convention of Alabama, *Minutes, 1868;* Colored Missionary Baptist Convention of Alabama, *Minutes, 1869*, 21 (quotation). (The name of the state convention of African American Baptists in Alabama is also rendered the Colored Baptist State Convention of Alabama.)

25. Program, Selma University Founder's Day Observance, April 21–22, 1986, 5, citing the Selma University, *Catalogue, 1907–1908;* see also Scherer, *Subordination or Liberation*, 102–6; Selma University, *Catalogue, 1913–1914*, 14–15; Anderson, *Education of Blacks*, 34–35.

26. The name of the school has changed several times: Selma University in 1885; the Alabama Baptist Colored University in 1895; and back to Selma University in 1908. See Selma University, *Catalogue, 1926–1927*, 10; Colored Missionary Baptist Convention of Alabama, *Minutes, 1885*, 7, 13 (Brawley quotations); Higginbotham, *Righteous Discontent*, 62–63, 77, 118–19, 249 (women's convention quotation); Selma University, *Catalogue, 1913–1914*, 14.

27. Selma University, *Catalogue, 1952–1953*, 19–21; Selma University, *Bulletin, 1926–1927*, 13–14; Reverend Terry Lee Lane, interview, Cincinnati, Ohio, January 12, 1989, 10; Reverend Nelson H. Smith, interview, Birmingham, Alabama, December 29, 1988, 2, 7–8.

28. In 1973 theological schools in the United States changed the nomenclature of the Bachelor of Divinity (B.D.) to the Master of Divinity (M.Div.) because it held an undergraduate college degree as a prerequisite; Charles L. Purce, Colored Missionary Baptist Convention of Alabama, *Minutes, 1892*, 38–39; Alvin A. Cleveland Sr. (dean of Religious Studies Division), telephone interview, Selma University, Sep-

tember 16, 1994; Louretta Wimberly (dean of students), telephone interview, Selma University, September 19, 1994, 35; transcript of Fred L. Shuttlesworth, Selma University, copy issued to the author, August 21, 1987. The junior college program in which Shuttlesworth was enrolled is now called an associate of arts (or science) degree.

29. Fred Shuttlesworth, interview, October 27–31, 1988, 56–57.

30. Chestnut, interview, 16–17; Fred Shuttlesworth, interviews, March 10, 1984, 10–11, and October 27–31, 1988, 58–59.

31. Fred Shuttlesworth, interview, October 27–31, 1988, 60–61; Jones, "Indigenous Leader," 124.

32. Mitchell, interview, April 7, 1989.

33. Jones, "Indigenous Leader," 126–27; Fred Shuttlesworth, interview, March 10, 1984, 11.

34. Shuttlesworth was ordained to the Baptist ministry at the Corinthian Baptist Church, Mobile, Alabama, August 10, 1948. Baptists do not ordain until a congregation "calls" a licensed minister as its pastor. Traditionally, Baptist churches "call" their pastors; they do not "hire" them. Such terminology is designed to help avoid the impression of a "hireling" ministry.

35. Jones, "Indigenous Leader," 125; Fred Shuttlesworth, interviews, March 10, 1984, 11–13, and October 27–31, 1988, 71–73; Jones, "Indigenous Leader," 126–27; Fred Shuttlesworth, interview, May 22–25, 1990; Smith, interview, 5.

36. Chestnut, interview, 20–21; Louretta Wimberly, interview, October 5, 1994, 12, 24–25. Wimberly noted that Shuttlesworth was viewed as a "strong biblical preacher" with "a charisma where he could arouse the public."

37. Chestnut recalled his grandmother "indicating that Shuttlesworth had some powerful people importuning her husband and J. D. Pritchard that this was a step up for Shuttlesworth." He identified one of those "powerful people" as W. H. Dinkins, noting that "if he went to them and said, 'Give the boy a shot,' it is more than likely that they would do it." See Chestnut, interview, 10, 20–21; Fred Shuttlesworth, interview, October 27–31, 1988, 72–73; Wimberly, interview, October 5, 1994, 10. Middle-class leaders liked Shuttlesworth's charisma but anticipated that he would "become more polished." Unfortunately, "what they were not able to do was polish the rough stone." Wimberly, interview, October 5, 1994, 27, 30; Shuttlesworth, interview by Ladner, November 19, 1969; Fred Shuttlesworth, interview, October 27–31, 1988, 79–80. Shuttlesworth's Selma address is listed as 614 First Avenue on Shuttlesworth's Selma University and Alabama State College transcripts, copies in author's possession. That this address was the parsonage of the First [African] Baptist church was verified by Louretta Wimberly, telephone conversation, October 3, 1994.

38. Cleveland, interview; Fred Shuttlesworth, interview, March 10, 1984, 13; Chestnut, interview, 6–7. On "class churches" see Roberts, *Prophethood,* 22–24. On respectability, see Higginbotham, *Righteous Discontent,* 185–229.

39. Chestnut, interview, 6–7; Shuttlesworth, interview by Ladner; Jones, "Indigenous Leader," 129–30.

40. Fred Shuttlesworth, interviews, October 27–31, 1988, 75–76, 93, and March 20, 1990.

41. Wimberly, interview, October 5, 1994, 2, 26–28; Chestnut, interview, 4, 25–27.

42. There are many names given to the sermonic genre called "whooping," among them "moaning," "mourning," "tuning" ("getting a tune"), "zooming," "coming on up at the end," and "the climax." More recently, Henry H. Mitchell, who has written extensively on this form, called it "the celebration." See Mitchell, *Celebration and Experience in Preaching*, 12, 61–75; Henry H. Mitchell, *Black Preaching* (Philadelphia: J. B. Lippincott, 1970), 162–77; Albert J. Raboteau, "'A Fire in the Bones': The Afro-American Chanted Sermon," Occasional paper, n.d., copy in author's possession. The term "hacking" for the gasping delivery was used by Wimberly, interview, October 5, 1994, 29. Though uncommon, the expression is not unique to her.

43. Chestnut, interview, 24–25.

44. Fred Shuttlesworth, interview, March 24, 1990; Fred Shuttlesworth, interview, October 27–31, 1988, 72–73.

45. Chestnut, interview, 8–10, 14; Wimberly, interview, October 5, 1994, 36.

46. Reverend Lewis Lloyd Anderson, interview, Selma, Alabama, August 7, 1987, 6. The preference among many blacks, especially in the middle class, for lighter skin is well attested. Advertisements in black newspapers for skin lighteners are evidence of this phenomenon. The negative side of the preference for light skin is the prejudice against it. African American literature has touched on this subject incisively in Wallace Thurman's 1929 novel, *The Blacker the Berry: A Novel of Negro Life* (New York: AMS Press, 1971) and in Shirlee Taylor Haizlip's autobiography, *The Sweeter the Juice* (New York: Simon and Schuster, 1994). Together these two titles make up a well-known saying among African Americans: "The blacker the berry, the sweeter the juice." It should also be noted that conflict in the black community over skin tones has traditionally been a "family quarrel," not often shared with or noticed by whites.

47. E. Franklin Frazier, *The Negro Church in America* (New York: Schocken Books, 1964), and James Melvin Washington, *Frustrated Fellowship: The Black Baptist Quest for Social Power* (Macon, Ga.: Mercer University Press, 1986); see also Lincoln and Mamiya, *Black Church*, 8, 196–235. For the role of women in the black church's public role, see Higginbotham, *Righteous Discontent*, 1–13. On elements of this in First Baptist Church, Selma, see Chestnut, interview, 7–9, and Chestnut and Cass, *Black in Selma*, 24–25; Chestnut, interview, *passim*; Smith, interview, 5; Cleveland, interview.

48. Fred Shuttlesworth, interview, October 27–31, 1988, 75–76.

49. Smith, interview, 5–6; Fred Shuttlesworth, interview, October 27–31, 1988, 71–77, 80.

50. Fred Shuttlesworth, interview, October 27–31, 1988, 71–77, 80.

51. Ibid.

52. Fred Shuttlesworth, interviews, October 27–31, 1988, 79–80; January 11, 1989, 29; and May 22–25, 1990. Louretta Wimberly credited Shuttlesworth's refusal to give up his teaching position as the "last straw" in his relationship with the deacons. Wimberly, interview, October 5, 1994, 5–8.

53. Louretta Wimberly described Shuttlesworth as "fiery," "hot-headed," and "hard-headed," adding that "he was going to tell you what he thought, and he was not going to back down on whatever he said." Wimberly, interview, October 5, 1994, 12, 26–28, 31; Cleveland, interview.

54. Wimberly, interview, September 19, 1994; Wimberly, interview, October 5, 1994, 20 (quotation); Fred Shuttlesworth, interview, May 29–June 1, 1990.

55. The description of the train experience is a composite from Fred Shuttlesworth, interview, October 27–31, 1988, 81–82, 90–92; Shuttlesworth, interview by Ladner; Shuttlesworth, interview by Mosby, 6; and Jones, "Indigenous Leader," 128–29. For interpretations of this and similar experiences, see William James, *The Varieties of Religious Experience* (Cambridge: Harvard University Press, 1985); James Fowler, *Stages of Faith: The Psychology of Human Development and the Quest for Meaning* (San Francisco: Harper and Row, 1981), 285; Wayne Proudfoot, *Religious Experience* (Berkeley: University of California Press, 1985), 188–89, 202; Edward P. Wimberly and Anne E. Wimberly, *Liberation and Human Wholeness* (Nashville: Abingdon Press, 1986), 19; and Frazier, *Negro Church*, 24.

56. In my comparison between the religious experiences of Shuttlesworth and Sojourner Truth, I am greatly indebted to Theophus H. Smith, *Conjuring Culture: Biblical Formations of Black America* (New York: Oxford University Press, 1994), 159–65; Fred Shuttlesworth, interview, October 27–31, 1988, 74.

57. Fred Shuttlesworth, interview, October 27–31, 1988, 70, 82–83.

58. Ibid.

59. J. L. Chestnut, generally a witness sympathetic to Fred Shuttlesworth, nonetheless used the term "fired" to describe Shuttlesworth's departure from First Baptist. He recalled his grandfather recruiting his wife to attend a business meeting, which she usually tried to avoid, to vote against Shuttlesworth. See Chestnut, interview, 22–23. Louretta Wimberly depicted the final decision as a forced termination after Shuttlesworth refused to give up his teaching position. See Wimberly, interview, October 5, 1994, 13.

60. Shuttlesworth, interview by Ladner; Fred Shuttlesworth, interview, October 27–31, 1988, 90–91.

3. Bethel

1. Fred Shuttlesworth, interview, October 27–31, 1988, 98; Fred Shuttlesworth, interview, March 10, 1984, 16–17; Fred Shuttlesworth, interview, October 27–31, 1988, 89–90, 98–101; Jones, "Indigenous Leader," 130–31; Shuttlesworth, interview by Mosby, 8.

2. Daisy Winston, interview, Birmingham, Alabama, July 31, 1987; Nell Irvin Painter, *The Narrative of Hosea Hudson: His Life as a Negro Communist in the South* (Cambridge: Harvard University Press, 1979), 169–78 (quotations).

3. James Roberson, "A Deep Look Into Our Past," in Program for Homecoming and Mortgage Burning, Bethel Baptist Church, August 3, 1980, n.p.; James Roberson, interview, August 2, 1989, Birmingham, Alabama, 15; Martin, interview, August 7, 1990.

4. Fred Shuttlesworth, interview, October 27–31, 1988, 107; Program, 56th Anniversary of Bethel Baptist Church, September 4, 1960, n.p.; Fred Shuttlesworth, interview, October 27–31, 1988; Roberson, interview, 27; Reuben Davis, interview, August 3, 1987, 7; *Birmingham World* (hereafter referred to as *BW*), January 20, 1956, 1.

5. Roberson, interview, 6, 26; Fred Shuttlesworth, interview, October 27–31, 1988, 108 (quotation).

6. Smith, interview, 17–19; Lane, interview, 28–29; Fred Shuttlesworth, interview, October 27–31, 1988. Although this view of the pastorate is presently moderating somewhat in the African American churches, it remains a powerful assumption of many black ministers and theologians. Leaning toward the traditional view are, for example, Beecher Hicks Jr., *Images of the Black Preacher* (Valley Forge, Penn.: Judson Press, 1977), 84–85, and James H. Harris, *Pastoral Theology: A Black Church Perspective* (Minneapolis: Fortress Press, 1991), 81–82. Recent interpreters of African American religion and ministry who question the theological appropriateness of this tradition are Roberts, *Prophethood*, 65–66; Edward P. Wimberly, *Pastoral Care in the Black Church* (Nashville: Abingdon Press, 1979); and Forrest E. Harris Sr., *Ministry for Social Crisis: Theology and Praxis in the Black Church Tradition* (Macon, Ga.: Mercer University Press, 1993), 107–8.

7. Fred Shuttlesworth, interview, October 27–31, 1988, 113–14, 117–20; Julia Rainge, interview, August 6, 1987, Birmingham, Alabama, 18–19.

8. Rainge, interview; Fred Shuttlesworth, interview, May 29–June 1, 1990.

9. Fred Shuttlesworth, interview, October 27–31, 1988, 114–16; Fred Shuttlesworth, interview, May 29–June 1, 1990.

10. Fred Shuttlesworth, interview, October 27–31, 1988, 105; Fred L. Shuttlesworth Jr., interview, 5.

11. Shuttlesworth, interview by Mosby, 11 (registrar quotation); Fred Shuttlesworth, interview, October 27–31, 1988, 110–11; Shuttlesworth, interview by Ladner (Ellens quotation).

12. Fred Shuttlesworth, interview, March 10, 1984, 18; Fred Shuttlesworth, interview, October 27–31, 1988, 110–11.

13. See Jones, "Indigenous Leader," 131–32.

14. Martin Luther King Jr., *Stride toward Freedom: The Montgomery Story* (New York: Harper and Row, 1958), 44; Fred Shuttlesworth, interview, October 10, 1987, 29–30.

15. Richard M. Dalfiume, "The Forgotten Years of the Negro Revolution," *Journal of American History* 55 (1968): 90–106. Regarding NAACP efforts and the Baton Rouge boycott, see Aldon D. Morris, *The Origins of the Civil Rights Movement: Black Communities Organizing for Change* (New York: Free Press, 1984), 17–27; and Richard Kluger, *Simple Justice: The History of Brown v. Board of Education and Black America's Struggle for Equality* (New York: Vintage, 1975).

16. Lola Hendricks, interview, August 3, 1989; Fred Shuttlesworth, interview, October 27–31, 1988, 109–10.

17. Fred Shuttlesworth, interview, March 10, 1984, 18.

18. BW, January 20, 1956, 1; Fred Shuttlesworth, telephone interview, March 20, 1990; Davis, interview, 11; Fred Shuttlesworth, interview, October 27–31, 1988.

19. Fred L. Shuttlesworth, "No Easy Walk, 1961–1963," in *Eyes on the Prize*, ed. Henry Hampton (Boston: Blackside), 1986, 2–4; Fred Shuttlesworth, interview, October 27–31, 1988.

20. Fred Shuttlesworth, interview, October 27–31, 1988, 19–20; Fred L. Shuttlesworth, "Birmingham Revisited," *Ebony*, August 1971, 114; Shuttlesworth, "No Easy Walk" 14–15.

21. Eskew, *But for Birmingham*, 53–61; BN, December 8, 1957, 1; Joe David Brown, "Birmingham, Alabama: A City in Fear," *Saturday Evening Post*, March 2, 1963, 14; *Birmingham Post-Herald* (hereafter referred to as BPH), April 27, 1956, 1; on Bull Connor and police violence, see Eskew, *But for Birmingham*, 95–97; BPH, July 17, 1951; BW, July 17, 1951; and William A. Nunnelley, *Bull Connor* (Tuscaloosa: University of Alabama Press, 1991), 48–50; Fred Shuttlesworth, interview, May 29–June 1, 1990.

22. Eskew, *But for Birmingham*, 95–96, 103–5; Nunnelley, *Bull Connor*.

23. Numan V. Bartley, *The Rise of Massive Resistance: Race and Politics in the South during the 1950s* (Baton Rouge: Louisiana State University Press, 1969); George R. Stewart, "Birmingham's Reaction to the 1954 Desegregation Decision" (master's thesis, Samford University, 1967); *Southern Patriot* 12 (June 1954): 3.

24. Eskew, *But for Birmingham*, 103–4, citing BN, January 5, 1955; Mrs. J. W. Siniard to J. W. Morgan, January 5, 1955, box 21, file 24, James W. "Jimmie" Morgan Papers, Department of Archives, BPL. The two officers and assistant jail warden were all indicted by a federal grand jury for the violation of Charles Patrick's civil rights. See BW, February 25, 1955, 1.

25. Fred Shuttlesworth, interview, May 29–June 1, 1990; BW, January 25, 1955, 1.

26. BW, January 28, 1955, 8; BW, February 18, 1955, 8.

27. See Eskew, *But for Birmingham*, 104–5, citing BW, January 22, 1952; BN, February 17–19, 1952; BPH, January 15, 1953; see also BN editorial of July 3, 1955, reprinted in BW, July 19, 1955, 8; BW, July 29, 1955, 3; Fred Shuttlesworth (Interdenominational Ministerial Association) to the City Commission, July 25, 1955, Albert Boutwell Papers, 12.43, Department of Archives, BPL. See also Morgan Papers, box 18, file 35.

28. *BW*, July 29, 1955, 1; Fred Shuttlesworth, interview, March 24, 1990.

29. *BW*, July 19, 1955, 8; Fred Shuttlesworth, interview, March 24, 1990; see also Jones, "Indigenous Leader," 133.

30. Fred Shuttlesworth to City Commissioners, September 1, 1955, Morgan Papers, box 18, file 35; *BW*, July 29, 1955, 1, 8.

31. *BW*, July 29, 1955, 3; Fred Shuttlesworth, interview, March 24, 1990; *BW*, August 26, 1955, 8. Note: Some sources indicate that there were 4,500, rather than 3,500, signers of this petition. See Fred Shuttlesworth, "An Account of the Alabama Christian Movement for Human Rights," in Jacquelyne Johnson Clarke, "Goals and Techniques in Three Civil Rights Organizations in Alabama" (Ph.D. diss., Ohio State University, 1960), 135; "Shuttlesworth Lives by Faith," *Southern Patriot* 17 (March 1959): 4. These are later sources and possibly subject to inflation due to lapse of memory. I have chosen the more conservative figure of 3,500 on the basis of earlier sources.

32. Fred Shuttlesworth to City Commissioners, September 1, 1955, Morgan Papers, box 18, file 35; *BW*, September 6, 1955, 1; *BW*, 8 (editorial).

33. Fred L. Shuttlesworth, statement to representatives of the U.S. Civil Rights Commission (James W. Davis and Raymond H. Miller), spring 1961, Shuttlesworth Papers, box 4, file 50; Fred Shuttlesworth, interview, March 24, 1990 (response to Clay); Shuttlesworth, "No Easy Walk," 5, and Fred Shuttlesworth, interview, March 24, 1990 (responses to Lindbergh); Jones, "Indigenous Leader," 133; *Southern Patriot* 17 (March 1959): 1, 4; Jones, "Indigenous Leader," 133 (last quotation).

34. *BW*, October 4, 1955, 8; *BW*, October 18, 1955, 8; *BPH*, October 20, 1955, cited in FBI Special Agent in Charge (SAC) Birmingham to director, memorandum, August 17, 1956, FBI file 105-48948-4 (files released under the Freedom of Information Act; copies in author's possession); *BW*, November 4, 1955, 8.

35. Fred Shuttlesworth, interview, March 24, 1990; King, *Stride*, 60–62.

36. Fred Shuttlesworth, interview, May 29–June 1, 1990; Walker, interview, 30.

37. Fred Shuttlesworth, interview, May 22–25, 1990; Shuttlesworth, interview by Ladner.

38. *BW*, January 10, 1956, 1; *BW*, January 20, 1956, 1; *BW*, January 10, 1956, 1; *BW*, January 27, 1956, 1, 8. In a rare lapse of memory, Shuttlesworth has consistently referred to this speech as an Emancipation Day speech, traditionally held in the African American community on January 1. In interviews he has occasionally been unable to say with certainty whether the speech occurred in 1955 or 1956. See Jones, "Indigenous Leader," 134 (based on an interview in 1960), and Fred Shuttlesworth, interview, March 10, 1984, 19. The *Birmingham World* typically covered this event each year, either publicizing the event ahead of time or reporting it afterward and usually both. The paper indicated (*BW*, December 30, 1955, 1) that Emory Jackson served as Emancipation Day speaker for 1956. The paper did, however, give significant pub-

licity to Shuttlesworth's January 22 speech, even indicating that it was his first major speech at an NAACP mass meeting. That Shuttlesworth remembered the event inaccurately as an Emancipation Day address seems to me more plausible than that the paper both would fail to cover an Emancipation Day address *and* that it would mistake his January 22 (NAACP installation) speech as Shuttlesworth's first major address. Moreover, according to the BW, Emancipation Day speakers were the following: 1955, T. J. Jemison; 1956, Emory Jackson; 1957, Martin Luther King Jr.; 1958, W. C. Patton; 1959, several speakers (Shuttlesworth not included); 1960, L. L. Anderson; 1961, J. L. Ware; 1962, L. H. Pitts; 1963, Raymond Harvey. As to Shuttlesworth's appropriation of King's rhetoric, Shuttlesworth heard the December 5, 1955, speech at Holt Street Church in Montgomery in which King said, "But there comes a time that people get tired. . . . We are tired—tired of being segregated and humiliated; tired of being kicked about by the brutal feet of oppression." See King, *Stride*, 61.

39. BW, October 11, 1955, 1; Fred Shuttlesworth, interview, March 24, 1990. Four days after enrolling, on February 7, Lucy was suspended for "causing" a riot. She was expelled on February 29, 1956. See Lerone Bennett Jr., *Before the Mayflower: A History of Black America*, 5th ed. (New York: Penguin Books, 1982), 552; FBI SAC Birmingham to director, memorandum, August 1, 1956, FBI HQ file 105-48948, 1–4.

40. Martin, interview; Fred Shuttlesworth, interview, January 11–12, 1989, 31; Fred Shuttlesworth, interview, January 11–12, 1989, 9–10, 11; "The Old Book for This New Age," a sermon preached at Friendship Baptist Church, Cincinnati, Ohio, 1964, in Shuttlesworth Papers, box 4, folder 37.

41. Phyllis Gooden, interview, Birmingham, Alabama, August 5, 1987; Veronica Chappell Flemmon, interview, Birmingham, Alabama, August 5, 1987; Flemmon, interview. On Shuttlesworth's influence, Flemmon testified: "These are the principles that are still a part of me, that I received from his training and sitting under him for the years that he was my pastor."

42. BW, February 24, 1956, 1; Fred Shuttlesworth, interview, March 10, 1984, 34, 39.

43. Thomas Pickens Brady, *Black Monday* (Winonah, Miss.: Association of Citizens Councils, 1955); John Hope Franklin, *From Slavery to Freedom: A History of Negro Americans*, 5th ed. (New York: Alfred A. Knopf, 1980), 457; George Brown Tindall, *America: A Narrative History*, 2d ed. (New York: W. W. Norton, 1988), 1332; John Patterson, interview by Jack Bass and Walter DeVries, July 12, 1974, Southern Oral History Program, Southern Historical Collection, Manuscripts Department, University of North Carolina, Chapel Hill, 9–10.

44. BW, June 8, 1956, 1; Robert Gaines Corley, "The Quest for Racial Harmony: Race Relations in Birmingham, Alabama, 1947-1963" (Ph.D. diss., University of Virginia, 1979), 125; Fred Shuttlesworth, interview, May 22–25, 1990.

45. Shuttlesworth, interview by Mosby, 12, and Shuttlesworth, "No Easy Walk," 20–21 (deputy incident); Fred Shuttlesworth, interview, October 27–31, 1988; Fred Shuttlesworth, interview, May 22–25, 1990.

46. Shuttlesworth, interview by Mosby, 12; Fred Shuttlesworth, interview, March 10, 1984, 21–23; Anne Braden, "The History That We Made: Birmingham, 1956–1979," *Southern Exposure* 7 (summer 1979): 50.

47. Fred Shuttlesworth, interview, March 10, 1984, 21–23; Fred Shuttlesworth, interview, May 22–25, 1990; Fred L. Shuttlesworth, lecture at the Southern Baptist Theological Seminary, Louisville, Kentucky, November 10, 1978, tape in Audio-Visual Department, Boyce Centennial Library, and in author's possession; Braden, "History That We Made," 50–51; Shuttlesworth, "No Easy Walk," 22–23.

48. *BW*, June 5, 1956, 1; *BW*, June 8, 1956, 1, 7; Lola Hendricks, Alabama Christian Movement for Human Rights (ACMHR) Newsletter, July 1961, Shuttlesworth Papers, box 3, folder 6; Edward Gardner, interview, Birmingham, Alabama, February 28, 1987.

49. Alabama Christian Movement for Human Rights, "People in Motion: The Story of the Birmingham Movement," in *Black Protest: History, Documents, and Analyses,* ed. Joanne Grant (Greenwich, Conn.: Fawcett Books, 1968), 284–85. (Clearly, the use of "movement" rather than "organization" is a misnomer, as this new organization would take on institutional forms, including, for example, officers, committees, and legal incorporation. It was, of course, one of many organizations making up the larger, less definable civil rights "movement." Nevertheless, the group's "Declaration of Principles," written primarily by Shuttlesworth and adopted by the mass meeting, used the term "organization" several times. Finally, this wording illustrates Shuttlesworth's occasional tendency to use words imprecisely.) Shuttlesworth, "Account," 137–38; Shuttlesworth, "No Easy Walk," 25. On the distinction between civil and human rights, Shuttlesworth later commented: "I wouldn't spend a lot of time trying to define it." See Fred Shuttlesworth, interview, May 22–25, 1990; Shuttlesworth, "Account," 138–39; Shuttlesworth, "No Easy Walk," 25; Fred Shuttlesworth, interview, May 22–25, 1990; R. L. Alford, interview, Birmingham, Alabama, August 9, 1990.

50. Shuttlesworth, "Account," 139–40.

51. Shuttlesworth, "No Easy Walk," 22.

52. *BW*, June 8, 1956, 1, citing pastor R. L. Alford. On the significance of the "devotional," see Walter Pitts, *The Old Ship of Zion* (New York: Oxford University Press, 1993); Shuttlesworth, "Account," 136–39.

53. Narrative of the speeches and actions of the meeting are a composite derived from the following sources: Shuttlesworth, "Account," 139–40; *BN*, June 7, 1956; *Washington Post,* June 7, 1956, 24; *BW*, June 8, 1956, 1, 7; SAC FBI Birmingham to director, memorandum, August 17, 1956, FBI HQ file 105-48948; *BN*, June 6, 1956, cited in FBI HQ file 105-8948-A; *Alabama Journal,* June 6, 1956; *Mobile Register,* June 6, 1956; Jones, "Indigenous Leader," 134.

54. *BN*, June 7, 1956; Jones, "Indigenous Leader," 134; Shuttlesworth, "Account," 140; *BN*, June 6, 1956, cited in FBI file 105-48948-A; *BW*, June 8, 1956, 1; Morris, *Origins,* 39,

citing an interview with Shuttlesworth; Abraham L. Woods Jr., interview, Birmingham, Alabama, December 30, 1988, 4–5.

55. Fred Shuttlesworth, interview, May 29–June 1, 1990; Winston, interview.

56. Fred Shuttlesworth Jr., interview, 52–54; Eugene Shuttlesworth, interview, March 6, 1993; Massengill, interview; Fred Shuttlesworth, interview, October 27–31, 1988 (quotation).

57. ACMHR, News Release, June 8, 1956, in Shuttlesworth Scrapbook, personal holdings of Fred Shuttlesworth; BW, June 8, 1956, 7; director, FBI, to SAC Birmingham, memorandum, June 14, 1956, in FBI HQ file 105-48948.

58. BW, July 7, 1956, 8; NYT, June 6, 1956, 1; cf. also King, Stride, 151–52; Fred Shuttlesworth to directors of [Birmingham] Transit Company, July 7, 1956, Morgan Papers, box 27, file 35C; BPH, July 11, 1956, n.p., in SAC FBI Birmingham to director, memorandum, July 11, 1956, FBI HQ file 105-48948; BN, July 10, 1956, in SAC FBI Birmingham to director, memorandum, July 11, 1956, and in director, FBI, to SAC Birmingham, memorandum, July 13, 1956, both in FBI HQ file 105-8948; Daily Worker, July 12, 1956, 2; BN, July 11, 1956; NYT, July 12, 1956, 14; United Press, news release, July 10, 1956, cited in FBI files 105-48948-2, 29, and 105-48948-7, 9; BN, July 18, 1956, cited in FBI HQ file 105-48948-A; letter printed in BN, August 1, 1956; BW, August 1, 1956, 1.

59. Shuttlesworth to City Commission, July 16, 1956, Morgan Papers, box 27, folder 35C; Shuttlesworth to City Commission, July 26, 1956, Morgan Papers, box 24, folder 33B; BN, July 18, 1956, in FBI HQ file 105-48948-A; letter also printed in BN, August 1, 1956; BW, August 1, 1956, 1; BW, August 8, 1956, 1.

60. Shuttlesworth, "Account," 147 (first quotation); BW, August 22, 1956, 1; BN, October 15, 1956; BN, August 20, 22, and 27, 1956; BPH, October 17, 1956; BN, February 1, 1957; Fred Shuttlesworth, interview, March 24, 1990 (second and third quotations).

61. BN, October 16, 1956, 1, 13; BPH, October 17, 1956, in FBI HQ file 105-49948-A; see also Eskew, But for Birmingham, 129–30; Corley, "Quest" (diss.), 73–77.

62. BW, November 10, 1956, 8, and November 17, 1956, 1, 8; NYT, December 21, 1956, 1.

63. Eskew, But for Birmingham, 130–31; Norman W. Walton, "The Walking City: A History of the Montgomery Bus Boycott," in The Walking City: The Montgomery Bus Boycott, 1955–1956, ed. David J. Garrow (Brooklyn: Carlson Publishing Inc., 1989), 3–58; NYT, December 21, 1956, 1; BW, December 1, 1956, 1; Montgomery Advertiser (hereafter MA), December 3–6, 1956; "Institute on Nonviolence and Social Change," program, December 3–9, 1956, Glenn E. Smiley Papers, Fellowship of Reconciliation Peace Collection, Swarthmore College, Swarthmore, Pennsylvania; cf. also David J. Garrow, Bearing the Cross: Martin Luther King Jr. and the Southern Christian Leadership Conference (New York: William Morrow, 1986), 81; Daily Worker, December 6, 1956, 1, cited in FBI file 104-28948-A (speech); Norfolk Journal and Guide, December 15, 1956.

64. MA, December 8, 1956, 1, 2A; Fred Shuttlesworth, interview, May 22–25, 1990.

65. Fred Shuttlesworth, interview, May 22–25, 1990; Shuttlesworth, "No Easy Walk," 9–10; Shuttlesworth, "Account," 149 (telegram); Shuttlesworth, statement to representatives of the U.S. Civil Rights Commission, Shuttlesworth Papers, box 4, file 50; MA, December 21, 1956; NYT, December 21, 1956, 1; BW, December 29, 1956, 1 (letter to James).

66. BN, December 22, 1956; BW, December 26, 1956, 8; Fred Shuttlesworth, interview, October 27–31, 1988; Massengill, interview; NYT, December 24, 1956, 6.

67. Eskew, But for Birmingham, 131, citing BN, December 25, 1956; Fred Shuttlesworth, address at Xavier University, New Orleans, Louisiana, January 20, 1988, audiotape in author's possession; BN, December 25, 1956.

68. Fred Shuttlesworth Jr., interview, 46; see also interviews with Fred Shuttlesworth Jr. and James Roberson in Ellen Levine, ed., Freedom's Children: Young Civil Rights Activists Tell Their Own Stories (New York: G. P. Putnam's Sons, 1993), 9; NYT, December 26, 1956, 1; BW, December 29, 1956, 1; Shuttlesworth, address, Xavier University; Washington Star, December 26, 1956, A1, A5; F. L. Price to Mr. Rosen, memorandum, December 26, 1956, in FBI HQ file 105-48948; Washington Star, December 26, 1956, A1, A5.

69. Fred Shuttlesworth, quoted in the 1961 CBS television special, "Who Speaks for Birmingham," transcript, BW, December 29, 1956, 1; NYT, December 26, 1956, 1; Fred Shuttlesworth, interview, March 10, 1984, 24; Shuttlesworth, address, Xavier University; Fred Shuttlesworth, interview, March 10, 1984; BN, December 28, 1956. The Miami Daily News, December 28, 1956, carried the headline, "Fighting Cleric Leads Segregation Attack." See FBI file 100-135-4-A.

70. Evans, We Have Been Believers, 75; Shuttlesworth, "Account," 152; Fred Shuttlesworth, interview, May 22–25, 1990.

71. Fred Shuttlesworth, interview, October 27–31, 1988; Roberson, interview, 1–2; Vivian Durant, interview, July 30, 1987, 12; James Roberson, in Levine, Freedom's Children, 7–8; Shuttlesworth, "No Easy Walk," 12–13; Fred Shuttlesworth, interview, October 27–31, 1988.

72. Washington Star, December 26, 1956, A1, A5; Washington News, December 26, 1956, 7.

73. Flemmon, interview; on religious awe, see Rudolf Otto, The Idea of the Holy (New York: Oxford University Press, 1958); Roberson, interview, 1–2; Levine, Freedom's Children, 8; Fred Shuttlesworth, interview, October 27–31, 1988; C. T. Vivian, interview, Selma, Alabama, December 27, 1989, 5; Winston, interview.

74. Winston, interview; Shuttlesworth, interview by Mosby, 19; Fred Shuttlesworth, interview, October 27–31, 1988, 112–13; Fred Shuttlesworth, interview, May 22–25, 1990.

75. Fred Shuttlesworth, interview, October 27–31, 1988; "Freedom Need: Civil Rights Leader Talks at Fox Lane," newspaper clipping, n.n., n.d., Shuttlesworth Papers, box 4, file 49.

4. Agitation

1. Shuttlesworth, "No Easy Walk," 12–13; Abraham L. Woods Jr., interview, December 30, 1988, 15.

2. *BW*, January 2, 1957, 8; Shuttlesworth, "Account," 149–50; Shuttlesworth, statement to representatives of the U.S. Civil Rights Commission, Shuttlesworth Papers, box 4, file 50; Fred Shuttlesworth, interview, March 10, 1984, 25–26; *BN*, December 27, 1956; *NYT*, December 27, 1956, 1, 29.

3. Shuttlesworth, "Account," 34; Lane, interview, 40–41; Alabama Christian Movement for Human Rights, "People in Motion," in Shuttlesworth Papers, box 1, folder 17; see also Grant, *Black Protest*, 286.

4. Fred Shuttlesworth, interview, March 10, 1984, 25–26; *Atlanta Journal*, December 26, 1956; MacPherson, interview.

5. *BN*, December 27, 1956; *NYT*, December 27, 1956, 1, 29.

6. *BN*, December 26, 1956 (first quotation); *NYT*, December 27, 1956, 1, 29 (second quotation); *Christian Science Monitor*, December 28, 1956; *BPH*, December 27, 1956 (third quotation); *BW*, December 29, 1956, 1 (fourth quotation).

7. *NYT*, December 28, 1956, 1, 11; *BN*, December 27, 1956.

8. Vivian, interview, 2–3.

9. Shuttlesworth, interview by Mosby, 18; Alabama Christian Movement for Human Rights, "People in Motion," 7.

10. Carter Gaston, interview, Birmingham, Alabama, February 28, 1987, 2; Pinky Shortridge, interview, August 3, 1989, 7; Johnson, interview; Roberson, interview, 5.

11. Corley, "Quest" (diss.), 132. On the parallels between civil rights organizations and the black church, see Fairclough, *To Redeem the Soul*, 11–35; and Morris, *Origins*, 77–99; for the same relationship regarding the Alabama Christian Movement for Human Rights and the church, see Eskew, *But for Birmingham*, 15–16; Alabama Christian Movement for Human Rights, certificate of incorporation, August 16, 1956, William E. Shortridge Papers, in possession of Pinky Shortridge, Birmingham, Alabama, copies in author's files; Shuttlesworth, "Account," 141; Hendricks, interview; Clarke, "Goals and Techniques," 27.

12. Alabama Christian Movement for Human Rights, certificate of incorporation, August 16, 1956, Shortridge Papers; Clarke, "Goals and Techniques," 32, 34, 55, 76, 163–73; Reverend Harold Long, telephone interview, Miami, Florida, April 8, 1989.

13. Fairclough, *To Redeem the Soul*, 32–34; Coretta Scott King, *My Life with Martin Luther King Jr.* (New York: Holt, 1969), 151; *Daily Worker*, January 3, 1957, cited in FBI file 62-101087-A; Garrow, *Bearing the Cross*, 84–86; Southern Leaders Conference on Transportation, "A Statement to the South and the Nation," Martin Luther King Jr. Papers, box 14, MLKC; *Daily Worker*, January 9, 1957, 1, cited in FBI file 44-11127-A.

14. *BW*, January 12, 1957, 1; *BW*, December 29, 1956, 8; *BW*, January 2, 1957, 8; *BW*, January 16, 1957, 8.

15. *NYT*, December 28, 1956, 1, 11; Shuttlesworth, "Account," 149–51; Shuttlesworth, statement to representatives of the Civil Rights Commission, Shuttlesworth Papers, box 4, file 50; Fred Shuttlesworth to city commissioners, January 9, 1957, Morgan Papers, box 24, folder 33A.

16. *BN*, January 15, 1957; *New York Courier*, January 26, 1957, 4; *BW*, March 9, 1957, 1; Fred Shuttlesworth, interview, May 22–25, 1990.

17. Lowery, interview.

18. Fred Shuttlesworth, interview, May 22–25, 1990.

19. *BN*, February 7, 1957, cited in FBI file, n.n.; Fairclough, *To Redeem the Soul*, 32; Garrow, *Bearing the Cross*, 90; *Pittsburgh Courier*, August 17, 1957, cited in FBI file 100-427079-1.

20. *Chattanooga Times*, February 16, 1957.

21. "Birmingham Integration Fight," *Militant*, February 18, 1957, cited in FBI files, n.n.

22. *Chicago Daily Defender*, February 21, 1957; *BN*, February 21, 1957; *BN*, February 1, 1957; *BN*, February 21, 1957, and *BN*, February 23, 1957, all in FBI HQ file 105-48948-A.

23. *BW*, March 9, 1957, 1; *BN*, March 5, 1957; *BW*, March 5, 1957, 1; Shuttlesworth, interview by Mosby, 22.

24. *BN*, March 7, 1957.

25. *BN*, February 19, 1957; *New York Post*, March 4, 1957, cited in FBI file 100-135-4-A; Congressional Quarterly, *Congress and the Nation, 1945–1964* (Washington, D.C.: Congressional Quarterly Service, 1965), 1621.

26. *BW*, March 9, 1957, 1; *BN*, n.d., clipping in Shuttlesworth Papers, box 4, folder 49; *Newsweek*, March 18, 1957, 35; Abraham L. Woods Jr. and Addie Pugh, interview, October 28, 1975, Oral History Collection, Department of History, University of Alabama at Birmingham, 21.

27. See Shuttlesworth, interview by Mosby, 22–23; *BW*, March 9, 1957, 1; *BN*, March 7, 1957; *BN*, n.d., clipping in Shuttlesworth Papers, box 4, folder 49; *Newsweek*, March 18, 1957, 35; *Nashville Tennessean*, March 7, 1957; *Birmingham Mirror*, March 6 and 9, 1957, in Shuttlesworth Papers, box 4, folder 50; *NYT*, March 7, 1957, 15; Shuttlesworth, statement to representatives of the U.S. Civil Rights Commission, Shuttlesworth Papers, box 4, file 50; Fred Shuttlesworth, interview, May 22–25, 1990.

28. *BW*, March 9, 1957, 1.

29. *BN*, March 7, 1957; *BN*, March 12, 1957; *BN*, March 18 and 21, 1957; *Southern Patriot* 15 (March 1957): 4.

30. "Institute on Nonviolence and Social Change," Smiley Papers.

31. *Minneapolis Spokesman*, March 15, 1957, cited in FBI file 61-3176-1911.

32. Fred Shuttlesworth, interview, May 29–June 1, 1990.

33. Winston, interview (first quotation); Flemmon, interview; Alexander L. Brown, telephone interview, February 27, 1993 (second quotation).

34. "The Negro's Hope for the Future," preached in 1964, is in Shuttlesworth Papers, box 4, folder 43.

35. Fred Shuttlesworth, interview, October 27–31, 1988, 67.

36. BN, April 19, 1957; BN, May 8, 1957; Garrow, *Bearing the Cross,* 92–93; BW, May 22, 1957, 1; Thomas R. Peake, *Keeping the Dream Alive: A History of the Southern Christian Leadership Conference from King to the 1980s* (New York: P. Lang, 1987), 49; on the attempted bombing of Temple Beth-El, see Michael C. Nichols, "'Cities Are What Men Make Them': Birmingham, Alabama, Faces the Civil Rights Movement, 1963" (bachelor's thesis, Brown University, 1974), 89; Fred L. Shuttlesworth, "Address at Prayer Pilgrimage," May 17, 1957, Shuttlesworth Papers, box 4.

37. Fred Shuttlesworth, interview, January 11–12, 1989, 39–41; Clarke, "Goals and Techniques," 55.

38. William M. Kunstler, *Deep in My Heart* (New York: Morrow, 1966), 176; Nichols, "Cities," 49–82; Nunnelley, *Bull Connor,* 9–32; T. Eugene Connor, "Communists in Birmingham," *Alabama Local Government* (August 1950): 4.

39. Nichols, "Cities," 73–76.

40. Nunnelley, *Bull Connor,* 57–60; Nichols, "Cities," 75, citing a 1973 interview with Connor's wife and children.

41. Anne Braden, interview, Louisville, Kentucky, October 29, 1988, 18–20.

42. Braden, interview, 9–17; FBI file CI 100-13760; BN, October 5, 1963, 1; Police Surveillance Files, file on Fred L. Shuttlesworth, BPL.

43. Braden, interview, 20–21.

44. Fred L. Shuttlesworth, "A Faith for Difficult and Critical Times," manuscript, Shuttlesworth Papers, box 4, folder 29.

45. Fred Shuttlesworth, interview, October 27–31, 1988; Bester, interview.

46. M. A. Jones to Jamie Moore, reports on mass meetings, Birmingham Police Department, January 23, 1961, 4–5, Eugene "Bull" Connor Papers, box 9, folder 24, BPL; M. A. Jones and J. B. Jones to Jamie Moore, March 28, 1961, Connor Papers, box 9, folder 24, 2.

47. Bester, interview; Massengill, interview.

48. Bester, interview; Fred Shuttlesworth Jr., interview, 24–25; Massengill, interview.

49. Bester, interview; Massengill, interview.

50. Fred Shuttlesworth Jr., interview, 28; Bester, interview; Massengill, interview.

51. Massengill, interview; Fred Shuttlesworth Jr., interview, 34.

52. Fred Shuttlesworth Jr., interview, 31.

53. Massengill, interview; Fred Shuttlesworth Jr., interview, 25, 83.

54. Morris, *Origins,* 71; Oscar W. Adams Jr., interview, Birmingham, Alabama, July 31, 1991, n.p.

55. Fred Shuttlesworth, interview, May 22–25, 1990.

56. Fred Shuttlesworth, quoted in Braden, "History That We Made," 49.

57. Fred Shuttlesworth, interview, May 22–25, 1990; *BN,* August 23, 1957; *BPH,* August 23, 1957; *BW,* September 7, 1957, 1; *BW,* September 11, 1957, 8; *NYT,* August 24, 1957, 34; *BN,* August 29, 1957.

58. *BN,* September 9, 1957.

59. Composite sources on Judge Aaron incident: Ben Allen, quoted in Raines, *My Soul Is Rested,* 153; *BN,* September 4, 1957; *BW,* September 11, 1957, 1; William Bradford Huie, "A Ritual 'Cutting' by the Ku Klux Klan," *True* (1964), copy of article in the David J. Vann Papers, *BPL.* The article is based on trial transcripts and interviews with Aaron; Corley, "Quest" (diss.), 135–37, citing *State of Alabama v. Jesse Mabry* and *State v. Grover A. McCullough,* BPL.

60. FBI File 100-135-4-218; Hendricks, interview; *BW,* September 7, 1957, 1; Fred Shuttlesworth, interview, October 27–31, 1988; *Christian Science Monitor,* September 10, 1957, 5; *BW,* September 11, 1957, 8; *NYT,* September 7, 1957, 10.

61. Kelly Miller Smith, quoted in Will B. Campbell, *Forty Acres and a Goat: A Memoir* (San Francisco: Harper and Row, 1986), 50–51; Levine, *Freedom's Children,* 14, 37–38; Bester, interview; Massengill, interview.

62. Bester, interview.

63. Adams, interview.

64. Edward Gardner, interview, Birmingham, Alabama, August 9, 1990; Abraham L. Woods Jr., interview, December 30, 1988, 10; Armstrong, interview.

65. *BN,* September 9, 1957; Fred Shuttlesworth, interview, February 15, 1995.

66. Bester, interview; Massengill, interview; Levine, *Freedom's Children,* 37–38; for the account of Nathaniel Lee, see *BN,* September 9, 1957.

67. Sources for composite narrative of the mob beating: *BN,* September 9, 1957; *NYT,* September 10, 1957, 1, 25; Shuttlesworth, "Birmingham Revisited," 114, 116; Braden, "History That We Made," 49–50; Fred Shuttlesworth, interview, October 27–31, 1988; Shuttlesworth, interview by Mosby, 24–26; Shuttlesworth, interview by Ladner; Bester, interview; Massengill, interview; Levine, *Freedom's Children,* 37–38.

68. *BN,* September 9, 1957; Fred Shuttlesworth, interviews, March 10, 1984, 28–29; October 27–31, 1988; May 22–25, 1990; and June 4–7, 1990; Braden, "History That We Made," 49–50.

69. *BN,* September 9, 1957; *Richmond Times-Dispatch,* September 10, 1957.

70. *NYT,* September 10, 1957, 1, 25; *BN,* September 9, 1957, 14, quoted in Anne Braden, "The Southern Freedom Movement in Perspective," *Monthly Review* 17 (1965): 80.

71. Abraham L. Woods Jr., interview, December 30, 1988, 10; Armstrong, interview; Roberson, interview, 31–32; Levine, *Freedom's Children,* 39–40; Flemmon, interview.

72. Fred Shuttlesworth Jr., interview, 37, 50–51; Levine, *Freedom's Children*, 39.

73. Montgomery, interview, 10, 12.

74. Braden, "History That We Made," 50; *Christian Science Monitor,* September 10, 1957, 5; BN, September 10, 1957; Fred Shuttlesworth, interviews, March 10, 1984, 28–29, and May 22–25, 1990.

75. Morgan, interview, 7.

76. NYT, September 10, 1957, 1, 25; *Christian Science Monitor,* September 10, 1957; *Time,* September 16, 1957, 27, and September 23, 1957, 17; "Klans and Councils," *New Republic,* September 23, 1957, 27; *Newsweek,* September 23, 1957, 33–34.

77. Walker, interview, 7–8, 16.

78. BW, September 18, 1957, 8.

79. BN, September 10 and 11, 1957; NYT, September 11, 1957, 23.

80. BN, September 10, 1957; MA, September 20, 1957; NYT, September 20, 1957, 17; NYT, October 6, 1957, 37; Shuttlesworth, statement to representatives of the U.S. Civil Rights Commission, Shuttlesworth Papers, box 4, file 50.

81. Fred Shuttlesworth, interview, October 27–31, 1988, n.p.; Minutes of SCLC Executive Board Meeting, October 18, 1957, Atlanta, Georgia, Martin Luther King Jr. Papers, box 48, folder vi.153, Mugar Library, Boston University (hereafter cited as BU); Martin Luther King Jr. to Fred L. Shuttlesworth, December 12, 1957, King Papers, box 71A, folder ix.9.a, BU; BPH, November 9, 1957, cited in FBI file 62-101087-5-A.

82. Quoted in Clarence E. Walker, *A Rock in a Weary Land: The African Methodist Episcopal Church during the Civil War and Reconstruction* (Baton Rouge: Louisiana State University Press, 1982), 42.

83. Fred Shuttlesworth, "Meeting and Matching the Challenge of This Hour," Shuttlesworth Papers, box 4; *Akron Beacon Journal,* November 25, 1957.

84. BN, October 15, 1957, cited in FBI file 62-101087-5-A. Shuttlesworth's agitation aided not only Connor's political career but also Attorney General John Patterson's. In his race-baiting 1958 gubernatorial campaign against George Wallace, Patterson utilized a thirty-minute film of desegregation efforts at Little Rock's Central and Birmingham's Phillips High Schools. After his defeat by Patterson, Wallace reportedly vowed never to be "outniggered" again. See "George Wallace, 1919–1998: A Portrait of Power," *Birmingham News,* September 14, 1998, 8E, special report; and Dan T. Carter, *The Politics of Rage: George Wallace, the Origins of the New Conservatism, and the Transformation of American Politics* (New York: Simon and Schuster, 1995), 96.

5. "Bull" fighting

1. BN, November 4, 1957, cited in Nunnelley, *Bull Connor,* 61; BW, January 1, 1958, 8.

2. Fred Shuttlesworth, interview, March 10, 1984, 30.

3. Johnson, interview (Beverly quotation); Shuttlesworth, "Birmingham Shall Be Free Someday," 10 (Shuttlesworth quotation); Fred Shuttlesworth, interview, May 22–25, 1990; John Cross, interview by Judy Barton, March 23, 1972, Atlanta, Georgia, MLKC, 20.

4. Cross, interview, 21–22; Shuttlesworth, interview by Ladner, November 19, 1969, and March 17, 1970.

5. BW, January 12, 1958, 8; BW, February 1, 1958, 8; BW, February 15, 1958, 1.

6. William E. Shortridge to Emory O. Jackson, March 24, 1958, Shortridge Papers (also printed in BW, March 29, 1958, 8); BN, April 21, 1958; FBI HQ file 105-48948-A; BW, April 30, 1958, 1, 6; BW, May 3, 1958, 1; BW, May 17, 1958, 1; Mobile Register, May 14, 1958; BW, March 22, 1958.

7. BW, June 7, 1958, 1, 8; Fred Shuttlesworth, interview, May 22–25, 1990.

8. Fred Shuttlesworth, interview, May 22–25, 1990 (Shuttlesworth, Connor, and Morgan quotations); Fred Shuttlesworth to City Commission, June 2, 1958, Boutwell Papers, box 12, folder 43 (petition quotations); BW, June 7, 1958, 1, 8; Shuttlesworth, statement to representatives of the U.S. Civil Rights Commission, Shuttlesworth Papers, box 4, file 50.

9. BN, June 4, 1958; BW, June 11, 1958, 1; Fred Shuttlesworth, interview, May 22–25, 1990.

10. Alabama v. Jessie Benjamin Stoner, 10th Jud. Cir. AL, Jefferson County, Div. 6 (1980), testimony by Thomas H. Cook, transcript, 273–84; G. L. Pattie, report on interview with Mr. "S," June 21, 1958, appendix to trial transcript, 566–68; William Hugh Morris (police informant), summary of interview concerning bombing of Bethel Baptist Church, J. B. Stoner File, Police Surveillance Files, BPL.

11. Johnson, interview; Alabama v. Jessie Benjamin Stoner, transcript; Fred Shuttlesworth to Connor, August 9, 1958, FBI HQ file 44-13501; Shuttlesworth, statement to representatives of the U.S. Civil Rights Commission, box 4, file 50, Shuttlesworth Papers.

12. Alabama v. Jessie Benjamin Stoner, testimony by Laverne Revis McWilliams, Colonel Stone Johnson, Fred L. Shuttlesworth, and Mack Roberson, transcript; BW, July 9, 1958, 1; BW, July 12, 1958, 1; Martin, interview, n.p.; "Report on Bombing Attempt, Bethel Baptist Church," July 16, 1958, Bombing Dates File, Police Surveillance Files, Birmingham Police Department, Department of Archives, BPL.

13. Alabama v. Stoner, testimony by Aaron Rosenfeld and Thomas H. Cook, transcript; Martin, interview; "Report on Bombing Attempt, Bethel Baptist Church," Police Surveillance Files, BPL; William Hugh Morris, testimony, J. B. Stoner File, Police Surveillance Files, Birmingham Police Department, BPL.

14. Alabama v. Stoner, testimony by Fred Shuttlesworth, transcript; Shuttlesworth, interview by Ladner.

15. Juanita Parker, statement to Detective T. E. Lindsey, July 8, 1958, J. B. Stoner File; see also Bombing Dates File, Police Surveillance Files, BPL.

16. *Alabama v. Stoner,* police report by G. L. Pattie on meeting with J. B. Stoner and William Hugh Morris, July 14, 1958, 570–74 (appendix).

17. *Alabama v. Stoner,* testimony by J. B. Stoner, 335–38; *Alabama v. Stoner,* testimony by William Hugh Morris, 266.

18. Fred Shuttlesworth, interview, May 22–25, 1990.

19. Fred Shuttlesworth, "President's Address to ACMHR," July 11, 1958, Shuttlesworth Papers, box 1; BW, July 9, 1958, 1.

20. Fred Shuttlesworth, "God in Human Affairs," July 21, 1958, Richmond, California, Shuttlesworth Papers, box 2, folder 24.

21. Martin L. King Jr. to James W. Morgan, July 15, 1958, Boutwell Papers, box 12, folder 43; *Christian Science Monitor,* July 5, 1958, 13; BN, April 28, 1958, and July 1, 1958.

22. BN, July 25, 26, and 27, 1958; MA, July 26, 1958.

23. Shuttlesworth, statement to representatives of the U.S. Civil Rights Commission, Shuttlesworth Papers, box 4, file 50; Fred Shuttlesworth to Connor, August 9, 1958, FBI HQ file 44-13501.

24. BN, August 16, 22, and 28, 1958; *Christian Science Monitor,* August 21, 1958, 13.

25. FBI SAC Birmingham to director, report, August 12, 1958, and Shuttlesworth to Connor, August 9, 1958, FBI HQ file 44-13501; Shuttlesworth to City Commission, August 11, 1958, Morgan Papers, box 29, folders 28-30C (all quotes). The comment to the postal clerk was later reported to an FBI investigator.

26. Nunnelley, *Bull Connor,* 78–79, citing FBI file 100-135-4-365, 1–3.

27. BN, October 14, 1958.

28. BW, October 22, 1958, 1.

29. Ibid., 6.

30. BN, October 17, 1958.

31. *Birmingham v. Shuttlesworth,* Rec. Ct., Birmingham, Disc. No. 23A-B, 24A-B, 25A (October 22, 1958), testimony by Bud Gordon, transcript, October 22, 1958, 17–18, Arthur D. Shores Papers, Archives, Talladega College, Talladega, Alabama.

32. *Birmingham v. Shuttlesworth,* testimony by I. M. Daniel, transcript, October 22, 1958, 5–10, Shores Papers; NYT, October 21, 1958, 27; Shuttlesworth, "Account," 141, 150–51; BN, October 20, 1958; Kunstler, *Deep in My Heart,* 80–81; BN, October 21, 1958.

33. BN, October 22 and 24, 1958 (quotations); NYT, October 22, 1958, 32; BN, October 23, 1958.

34. BN, October 21, 1958.

35. *Birmingham v. Shuttlesworth,* transcript, 1–21; Kunstler, *Deep in My Heart,* 80–82; BN, October 23 and 25, 1958; NYT, October 25, 1958, 44.

36. Alabama Christian Movement for Human Rights, "People in Motion," 8; BN, October 28, 1958; MA, October 28 and 29, 1958; NYT, October 28, 1958, 20; NYT, October 29, 1958, 68.

37. Shuttlesworth, interview by Mosby, 42; *BN*, October 27 and November 19, 1958.

38. *MA*, October 29, 1958; *NYT*, October 30, 1958, 64; *NYT*, November 14, 1958, 1, 17.

39. *Nashville Banner,* November 1, 1958.

40. Lane, interview, 17–20.

41. *BW*, April 29, 1959, 3; Long, telephone interview; Frank Dukes, interview, Birmingham, Alabama, December 28, 1988.

42. Abraham L. Woods Jr., interview, Birmingham, Alabama, June 25, 1991; C. Herbert Oliver, interview, Brooklyn, New York, March 2, 1989, 4–6, passim; Glenn E. Smiley, telephone interview, January 28, 1989; Daphne Sloan, interview, Cincinnati, Ohio, May 30, 1990.

43. Armstrong, interview; Shuttlesworth, interview by Ladner; Fred Shuttlesworth, interview, March 24, 1990.

44. Fred Shuttlesworth, interview, May 22–25, 1990.

45. On disagreement between Joseph H. Jackson and Martin Luther King Jr., see Peter J. Paris, *Black Religious Leaders: Conflict in Unity* (Louisville, Ky.: Westminster/John Knox Press, 1994), 31–48. On the effects of ministerial jealousies in a large congregation, see Joel C. Gregory, *Too Great a Temptation: The Seductive Power of America's Super Church* (Fort Worth, Tex.: Summit Group, 1994); Shuttlesworth, "Account," 146.

46. Paris, *Black Religious Leaders,* 31–48; Sloan, interview.

47. *BW*, November 5, 1958, 1; *Nashville Tennessean,* November 1, 1958.

48. See Fairclough, *To Redeem the Soul,* 43; see also Smiley, telephone interview; *NYT*, November 3, 1958, 72.

49. Shuttlesworth, "Account," 141 (quotation); Fred Shuttlesworth, interview, May 22–25, 1990. On Shuttlesworth's intention not to attempt to duplicate Montgomery, see also an article on Shuttlesworth in early 1959 in *SCEF*'s newspaper, *Southern Patriot,* March 1959, 1, 4.

50. *BN*, October 30 and 31, 1958; *NYT*, October 31, 1958, 59.

51. *BN*, November 13, 1958; Fred Shuttlesworth, interview, May 22–25, 1990. Ruby Shuttlesworth's Chicago speech is summarized in *Pittsburgh Courier* (New York edition), "Birmingham Bus Boycott Gains Momentum, White Press 'Silent,'" cited in *FBI* file 100-429111-A.

52. *Baltimore Afro-American,* November 22, 1958, clipping in Shuttlesworth Papers, box 1, folder 29; *Shuttlesworth v. Connor,* testimony by Samuel Hoskins, transcript, November 22, 1960, Shuttlesworth Papers, box 3, 79–86.

53. *Shuttlesworth v. Connor,* transcript, November 22, 1960, Shuttlesworth Papers, box 3, 25–35.

54. *MA*, November 26, 1958; *Nashville Tennessean,* March 27, 1959; Associated Press, reports, various unnamed newspaper accounts dated approximately November 29–

30, 1958, Smiley Papers; Calvin Woods, interview, Birmingham, Alabama, December 28, 1988, 1–2, 31–33.

55. BN, December 13, 1958; *Nashville Tennessean,* March 27, 1959; BW, December 17, 1958, 1, 6.

56. MA, December 13, 1958; Shuttlesworth, quoted in Southern Conference Educational Fund, "They Challenge Segregation at Its Core," undated pamphlet, 3.

57. Emory O. Jackson, "Right to Protest," BW, November 29, 1958, 8; Fred L. Shuttlesworth to City Commission, December 1, 1958, Shuttlesworth Papers, box 1, folder 5.

58. BN, December 1 and 2, 1958; NYT, December 3, 1958, 46.

59. Glenn E. Smiley, "Birmingham and Its Recent Protest," Smiley Papers.

60. Glenn E. Smiley to Bob Gussner, November 10, 1958, Smiley Papers.

61. Smiley to Gussner, Smiley Papers; Smiley, telephone interview; Fred Shuttlesworth, interview, May 22–25, 1990; BW, December 13, 1958, 1.

62. Smiley, telephone interview.

63. "Connor Links White Cleric, Shuttlesworth," BN, December 21, 1958, 1; Charles R. Lawrence and Alfred Hassler to Mayor James W. Morgan, December 24, 1958, Smiley Papers; Smiley to Gussner, Smiley Papers; Smiley, telephone interview.

64. Fred Shuttlesworth to Glenn Smiley, December 23, 1958, Smiley Papers; Fred Shuttlesworth, interview, May 22–25, 1990.

65. Smiley, telephone interview; see an undated, handwritten copy of Smiley's telegram to Shuttlesworth in Smiley Papers.

66. Walker, interview; Shuttlesworth to Smiley, December 23, 1958, Smiley Papers.

67. Shuttlesworth to Smiley, December 23, 1958, Smiley Papers.

68. Smiley to Gussner, Smiley Papers; Smiley, telephone interview.

69. BW, December 24, 1958, 8; Fred Shuttlesworth, interview, May 22–25, 1990, n.p.

70. Abraham L. Woods Jr., interview, December 30, 1988.

6. Stalemate

1. Fred Shuttlesworth, interview, October 27–31, 1988.

2. MA, January 21, 1959; BPH, January 21, 1959, cited in FBI file 100-135-4-A; *Pittsburgh Courier,* January 3, 1959, 10, cited in FBI file 62-10187-5-A; BN, February 12, 1959; BN, February 13, 1959, cited in FBI file 62-10187-5-62; BN, February 23, 1959, cited in FBI file 44-13490-4-A.

3. Clarke, "Goals and Techniques," 153; Police Report, March 8, 1961, Connor Papers, box 9, folder 24.

4. Shuttlesworth, "Account," 143–46, 153.

5. "Shuttlesworth Hits 'Red' Hunt," *Southern Patriot* 17 (June 1959): 4 (quotations); FBI file SCLC 100-438794-2; BW, April 22, 1959, 1, 6.

6. *Louisville Defender,* May 28, 1959, 1; see also editorial in the same issue.

7. Fred Shuttlesworth, "President's Annual Report, ACMHR," June 5, 1959, Shuttlesworth Papers, box 1, folder 2.

8. CORE, *Newsletter,* July 24, 1959, King Papers, box 3A, folder 1-15, BU.

9. BW, June 6, 1959, 8; BW, June 24, 1959, 6.

10. BPH, June 20, 1959, cited in FBI file 62-101087-5-A; BW, June 24, 1959, 8.

11. BW, June 27, 1959, 8.

12. Trezzvant Anderson, "Birmingham's Big Need," *Pittsburgh Courier,* October 17, 1959, magazine section.

13. BW, January 10, 1959, 8; BW, June 8, 1960, 8.

14. BN, June 15, 1959; Fred Shuttlesworth, interview, October 27–31, 1988.

15. Fred Shuttlesworth, interview, May 29–June 1, 1990.

16. Ibid.

17. Alabama Christian Movement for Human Rights, *They Challenge Segregation At Its Core!* (Birmingham: Southern Conference Educational Fund, 1959), copy in Shuttlesworth Papers, box 1, folder 18.

18. Fairclough, *To Redeem the Soul,* 58.

19. Fred Shuttlesworth, interview, October 27–31, 1988.

20. *Southern Patriot* 17 (March 1959): 1, 4.

21. Shuttlesworth to King, April 24, 1959, King Papers, box 9, BU, cited in Garrow, *Bearing the Cross,* 116.

22. Regarding the beating of Charles Billups, see James M. Lawson Jr., "The Man Who Escaped the Cross," *Fellowship* 25 (November 1959): 10–12; BN, April 24, 1959; Shuttlesworth to King, April 24, 1959, King Papers, box 9, BU, cited in Garrow, *Bearing the Cross,* 116.

23. Shuttlesworth to King, June 15, 1959, King Papers, box 9, BU.

24. "Recommendations Adopted by the Executive Committee and Delegates," October 1, 1959, King Papers, drawer 6, folder 153, BU (first quotation); "President's Recommendations to SCLC Board," September 29–October 1, 1959, King Papers, box 48, folder VI.153, BU; BN, December 8, 1959; "Birmingham, Alabama: South's Toughest City," *Crusader* 1 (November 1959): 4, 6.

25. SCLC, Press Release, December 8, 1959, King Papers, box 71, folder IX.4, BU; Garrow, *Bearing the Cross,* 124.

26. *Southern Patriot* 17 (May 1959): 4; SCEF, Memorandum, April 23, 1959, cited in FBI file 100-438794-2; FBI file 100-438794-2; "Fellowship of Reconciliation Race Relations Work," July 22–24, 1959, Fellowship of Reconciliation Papers, Peace Collection, Swarthmore College, Swarthmore, Pennsylvania.

27. Fred Shuttlesworth, interview, May 22–25, 1990.

28. MA, September 8, 1959; BN, September 8, 1959, cited in FBI file 44-13490-4-A.

29. Shuttlesworth to the Birmingham Board of Education and Superintendent of Education, October 26, 1959, Shortridge Papers; see also Connor Papers, box 1, folder 8; BN, November 4 and 24, 1959.

30. BN, October 20, 1959; BN, October 25, 1959, cited in FBI file 62-10187-5-A; FBI file, SCLC 100-438794-2.

31. Shuttlesworth to Connor, October 26, 1959, Morgan Papers, box 24, folder 30A; also in Shuttlesworth Papers, box 3; BN, October 28, 1959; BN, November 1, 1959, cited in FBI file 157-6-4-72 (Grooms quotation); MA, June 18, 1960; BN, November 18, 1959; BN, June 26, 1960.

32. BN, November 23, 1959; BW, January 2, 1960, 1; *Nashville Tennessean*, November 24, 1959.

33. BN, December 23, 1959; BW, December 12, 1959, 8.

34. BN, December 9, 1959. On fire department harassment at this meeting, see *Shuttlesworth and Billups v. Connor and Moore,* transcript, November 22, 1960, Shuttlesworth Papers, box 3 (quotations); Fred Shuttlesworth, "Birmingham Shall Be Free," 10.

35. BN, December 21, 1959; BW, January 2, 1960, 1, 8; ACMHR, Resolution, December 14, 1959, Shuttlesworth Papers, box 1, folder 19.

36. BN, December 21, 1959.

37. BW, January 2, 1960, 1, 8.

38. Narrative of ACMHR members' testimonies, mass meeting, December 28, 1959, in *Southern Patriot,* "Bus Victory in Alabama," 18 (February 1960): 1, 3; MA, December 14, 1960.

39. *Greensboro Daily News,* February 12, 1960 (first and second quotations); Bob Hughes to Harold Fleming, Southern Regional Council Papers, folder 41.1.1.1.19, BPL; Eskew, *But for Birmingham,* 148; Morris, *Origins,* 201; Garrow, *Bearing the Cross,* 138; Taylor Branch, *Parting the Waters: America in the King Years, 1954–1963* (New York: Simon and Schuster, 1988), 273 (third quotation); Seth Cagin and Philip Dray, *We Are Not Afraid: The Story of Goodman, Schwerner, and Chaney and the Civil Rights Campaign for Mississippi* (New York: Macmillan, 1988), 66.

40. George Wall to Jamie Moore, Report, February 29, 1960, Connor Papers, box 6, folder 14; Branch, *Parting the Waters,* 281–84 (quotation); *Alabama Journal,* February 26, 1960; BN, March 1, 1960; BN, February 26, 1960, 1.

41. Shuttlesworth to Birmingham City Commission, March 1, 1960, Connor Papers, box 6, folder 14.

42. Shuttlesworth, interview by Ladner, November 19, 1969, and March 17, 1970; Powledge, *Free at Last,* 80.

43. For the *Pittsburgh Courier* articles, see Fred L. Shuttlesworth File, Police Surveillance Files, BPL; *National Guardian,* March 21, 1960, copy in Smiley Papers.

Shuttlesworth was a keynote speaker at the March 11, 1960, "Solidarity Rally of the Midwest Conference of Negro Voters, at the Monumental Baptist Church"; see FBI file SCLC 100-438794-2 and 100-438794-64, citing *Chicago Worker,* February 21, 1960, 12, and March 20, 1960, 3. The Mobile rally was a two-day conference on "Nonviolence and Social Change," at the Mt. Zion Baptist Church; see *Mobile Press-Register,* March 20, 1960, cited in FBI file 157-4-61-2.

44. FBI file 44-15627-2; FBI, Memorandum, April 3, 1962, file 44-15668-37; FBI file 44-15668-40; Fred Shuttlesworth, interview, March 10, 1984, 31; BN, April 3, 1960.

45. BN, March 31, 1960; BW, April 2, 1960, 1.

46. BW, April 6, 1960; BN, April 1, 1960; Shuttlesworth, statement to representatives of the U.S. Civil Rights Commission, Shuttlesworth Papers, box 4, file 50 (quotation); Fred Shuttlesworth, statement to FBI special agents, April 20, 1960, FBI file 44-15668-5.

47. Shuttlesworth, statement to FBI special agents, April 20, 1960, FBI file 44-15668-5; FBI file 157-6-4-3.

48. BN, April 2 and 3, 1960; NYT, April 3, 1960, 56.

49. Unnamed newspaper clipping (AP story), April 21, 1960, Shuttlesworth Scrapbook; Martin Luther King Jr. to Fred Shuttlesworth, April 4, 1960, King Papers, box 71A, folder ix.9b, BU.

50. BW, April 9, 1960, 8; Shuttlesworth, statement to representatives of the U.S. Civil Rights Commission, Shuttlesworth Papers, box 4, file 50; Shuttlesworth, statement to FBI special agents, April 22, 1960, FBI file 44-15668-5; BW, April 9, 1960, 1, 8; *Shuttlesworth and Billups v. City of Birmingham,* 67 U.S. Sup. Ct. (1962), copy in FBI file 44-15668-47; *Shuttlesworth v. City of Birmingham,* 373 U.S. 262 (May 20, 1963).

51. NYT, April 12, 1960, 1, 28 (Salisbury quotations); BN, April 14, 1960, 1; NYT, April 15, 1960, 15.

52. Letter to the editor, BN, April 26, 1960.

53. NYT, March 29, 1960, 25.

54. Branch, *Parting the Waters,* 289; Anthony Lewis, *Make No Law: The Sullivan Case and the First Amendment* (New York: Random House, 1991), 11–12, 14.

55. MA, November 2, 1960; *Southern Patriot* 19 (May 1961): 1–3; Branch, *Parting the Waters,* 370–71; Lowery, interview; Fred Shuttlesworth, interview, October 27–31, 1988.

56. MA, November 3, 1960.

57. MA, November 4, 1960; *Time,* March 20, 1964.

58. NYT, January 31, 1961, 14; NYT, February 1, 1961, 33; NYT, February 2, 1961, 17; MA, February 7, 1961.

59. BN, February 5, 1961; MA, February 8, 1961; BN, February 7, 1961; Fred Shuttlesworth, interview, October 27–31, 1988; Eugene Shuttlesworth, interview, March 6, 1993; *Southern Patriot* 19 (May 1961): 1, 3 (quotation).

60. Undated affidavit, copy in scrapbook given to Fred Shuttlesworth in honor of his tenth anniversary as ACMHR president, researched by the author (fall 1988).

61. *NYT*, April 14, 1961, 21; *NYT*, June 27, 1961, 19.

62. *New York Times Co. v. Sullivan*, 376 U.S. 254 (1964); Lewis, *Make No Law*, 103, 157–63 (Brennan quotation); Geoffrey R. Stone, "New York Times Co. v. Sullivan," in *The Oxford Companion to the Supreme Court of the United States*, ed. Kermit L. Hall (New York: Oxford University Press, 1992), 586–87.

63. Fred Shuttlesworth to Governor John Patterson, SCLC, News Release, June 16, 1960, King Papers, BU.

64. *National Guardian*, September 12, 1960, 8, cited in FBI file 44-16274-A; Fred Shuttlesworth Jr., interview, 68–70; Bester, interview; Police Intelligence Report of ACMHR mass meeting, June 27, 1961, Connor Papers, box 9, folder 24.

65. *National Guardian*, September 12, 1960, 8.

66. Ricky Shuttlesworth Bester, in Levine, *Freedom's Children*, 67–68; Fred Shuttlesworth Jr., interview, 70–75; "Delinquency—Alabama Style," *Southern Patriot* 18 (October 1960): 2. See also Fred Shuttlesworth, statement to FBI on arrests, August 17, 1960, cited in FBI file 44-665, and FBI report on arrests, cited in file 44-16274-A.

67. FBI files 157-6-4-30; SI 157-6-4-34; SI 157-6-4-52; Johnson, interview.

68. Jones, "Indigenous Leader," 143–45; FBI report on arrests cited in FBI file 44-16274-A.

69. Johnson, interview; Jones, "Indigenous Leader," 143–45.

70. *MA*, August 18, 1960; *Chattanooga Times*, August 18, 1960; see also unnamed, undated newspaper clipping in Shuttlesworth Papers, box 4; Harold R. Tyler Jr. to J. Edgar Hoover, n.d., cited in FBI file 44-16274-2; FBI director to SAC Birmingham, telex, August 19, 1960, cited in FBI file 44-16274-3.

71. Copies in FBI file 44-16274-11.

72. *BW*, September 3, 1960, 1; *MA*, August 19, 1960; Shuttlesworth to Gadsden mayor and police chief, August 18, 1960, cited in FBI file 44-16274-A.

73. *Southern Patriot* 18 (September 1960): 4.

74. *BN*, September 7, 1960; *BPH*, September 17, 1960; see also report in FBI file 44-16274-A.

75. *BPH*, January 4, 1961, cited in FBI file 44-16274-A; *MA*, November 9, 1961.

76. *BN*, April 15, 1960; *Washington Post*, October 23, 1961.

77. Fred Shuttlesworth, interview, May 29–June 1, 1990; Winston, interview.

78. Fred Shuttlesworth, interview, May 29–June 1, 1990; *BN*, September 8, 1960.

79. *BPH*, November 23, 1960; Fred Shuttlesworth, interview, May 29–June 1, 1990; Adams, interview.

80. Narrative comes from *Reverend F. L. Shuttlesworth and Reverend Charles Billups v. Eugene Connor and Jamie Moore*, transcript, November 22, 1960, copy in Shuttlesworth Papers, box 3.

7. Jailbirds

1. T. G. Harris, "It's a Difficult Thing to Teach a President," *Look,* November 17, 1964, 61–62. Martin Luther King Jr. had attempted to move the Kennedy administration into the civil rights camp by a series of speeches and three annual articles in the *Nation:* "Equality Now" (February 4, 1961, 91–95); "Fumbling on the New Frontier" (March 3, 1962, 190–93); and "Bold Design for a New South" (March 30, 1963, 259–62). In the last of these articles, published on the eve of the Birmingham demonstrations, King wrote that "this new social revolution confronts the Administration with the responsibility to pattern programs in bold designs" (261).

2. Fred Shuttlesworth, interview, March 10, 1984, 33; Police Intelligence Reports, January 23, 1961, Connor Papers, box 9, folder 24; Police Intelligence Reports, September 28, 1961, Connor Papers, box 9, folder 25.

3. Fred L. Shuttlesworth File, Police Surveillance Files, BPL, includes program for the Carnegie Hall event, February 10, 1961; *Chicago Sun Times,* February 11, 1961, cited in FBI file 100-42869-A; *Worker,* March 19, 1961, 3.

4. Minutes of the Administrative Committee, March 8–9, 1961, SCLC Papers, box 36, folder 11, MLKC; Fred Shuttlesworth, interview, May 29–June 1, 1990; Walker, interview, 1–2; Fairclough, *To Redeem the Soul,* 76.

5. Howard K. Smith, "CBS Reports: Who Speaks for Birmingham?" transcript, BPL.

6. Ibid.; Fred Shuttlesworth, interview, October 27–31, 1988.

7. Massengill, interview; Bester, interview.

8. Fred Shuttlesworth, interview, October 27–31, 1988; L. Venchael Booth, interview, Cincinnati, Ohio, June 4, 1990, n.p.

9. Fred L. Shuttlesworth Jr., interview, 20–24.

10. Roberson, interview.

11. See author's interviews with Davis, Durant, Martin, Roberson, and Winston.

12. Ibid.; Fred Shuttlesworth, interview, October 27–31, 1988.

13. Braden, interview.

14. Fred Shuttlesworth, interview, March 24, 1990.

15. Regarding the calling practices of African American Baptist Churches, see Hicks, *Images of the Black Preacher,* 93; "Recommendations to the Revelation Baptist Church, April 16, 1961," Shuttlesworth Papers, box 2.

16. See James Farmer, *Lay Bare the Heart: An Autobiography of the Civil Rights Movement* (New York: Arbor, 1985), 195–99; John Hope Franklin, *From Slavery to Freedom,* 467; Victor S. Navasky, *Kennedy Justice* (New York: Atheneum, 1970), 98.

17. Wyatt Tee Walker, interview by John Britton, October 11, 1967, Moorland-Spingarn Research Center, Howard University, Washington D.C.

18. Police Intelligence Reports, May 11, 1961, Connor Papers, box 9, folder 24; Kunstler, *Deep in My Heart*, 24–25.

19. For Shuttlesworth's testimony in a trial arising from his involvement in the Freedom Rides, Alabama Circuit Court, Judge Wallace Gibson, see BN, November 9, 1961.

20. Fred Shuttlesworth, interview, May 29–June 1, 1990; James Peck, *Freedom Ride* (New York: Simon and Schuster, 1962), 124 (quotation); Farmer, *Lay Bare the Heart*, 202–3; Raines, *My Soul Is Rested*, 99; Cagin and Dray, *We Are Not Afraid*, 110.

21. Fred Shuttlesworth, interview, May 29–June 1, 1990; Fairclough, *To Redeem the Soul*, 77.

22. Shuttlesworth, interview by Mosby, 38; Fred Shuttlesworth, interview, May 29–June 1, 1990; Bester, interview.

23. Peck, *Freedom Ride*, 127 (first and second quotation); Gary Thomas Rowe, quoted in Kenneth O'Reilly, "The FBI and the Civil Rights Movement during the Kennedy Years: From the Freedom Rides to Albany," *Journal of Southern History* 54 (1988): 207 (third quotation); "A Freedom Rider's Story: Incident in Alabama," *New York Post Magazine*, May 15, 1961, 6; Peck to Alfred Hassler, May 27, 1961, Smiley Papers; Kunstler, *Deep in My Heart*, 26; *Washington Post*, May 16, 1961; Howard K. Smith, "CBS Reports: Who Speaks for Birmingham," transcript, BPL, 29–30.

24. David Vann, "The Change from Commission to Mayor-Council Government and the Racial Desegregation Agreements in Birmingham, Alabama, 1961–1963," rev. ed. (paper delivered at the Center for Urban Affairs, University of Alabama at Birmingham, 1988), 9, in Vann Papers, box 12, folder 32; O'Reilly, "The FBI and the Civil Rights Movement," 206–14; Branch, *Parting the Waters*, 420 (Connor quotation); FBI, teletype message, quoted in NYT, February 17, 1980.

25. Shuttlesworth, interview by Mosby, 38–39; Fred Shuttlesworth, interview, May 29–June 1, 1990.

26. MA, May 15, 1961.

27. Flemmon, interview; Fred Shuttlesworth, quoted in "A Great Thing," *Southern Patriot* 19 (June 1961): 4; Branch, *Parting the Waters*, 423.

28. Police Intelligence Report, J. E. LeGrand and M. A. Jones, May 16, 1961, Connor Papers, box 9, folder 24; Fred Shuttlesworth, interview, May 29–June 1, 1990; Shuttlesworth, interview by Ladner, November 19, 1969 and March 17, 1970; Peck, *Freedom Ride*, 124–32.

29. BN, May 15, 1961, 1 (newspaper quotation); BN, May 18, 1961, 11, 19; NYT, May 16, 1961, 1, 26 (YMBC quotation); *Washington Post*, May 5, 1961 (Connor quotation).

30. Fred Shuttlesworth, interview, May 29–June 1, 1990; Shuttlesworth, interview by Mosby, 39–40 (composite of Shuttlesworth-Kennedy conversation); Police Intelligence Report, J. E. LeGrand and M. A. Jones, May 16, 1961, 3, Connor Papers, box 9, folder 24.

31. MA, May 16, 1961 (Peck quotation); Shuttlesworth, interview by Mosby, 40–41

(Shuttlesworth–police officer dialogue); Police Intelligence Report, J. E. LeGrand and M. A. Jones, May 16, 1961, 3, Connor Papers, box 9, folder 24 (attacker quotation).

32. Robert F. Kennedy Papers, General Correspondence, transcript.

33. MA, May 16, 1961; NYT, May 16, 1961, 1, 26 (first quotation); *Washington Post,* May 16, 1961 (second quotation).

34. Peck, *Freedom Ride,* 129–32; James Peck, "Freedom Ride," CORE-lator 89 (May 1961): 1–4; MA, May 16, 1961.

35. Police Intelligence Report, J. E. LeGrand and M. A. Jones, May 16, 1961, 1–3, Connor Papers, box 9, folder 24.

36. Ibid.

37. Fred Shuttlesworth, interview, May 29–June 1, 1990.

38. Diane Nash, telephone interview, March 4, 1989, 1–2; Shuttlesworth, interview by Mosby, 41–42; information also gathered from the opinion of Alabama Court of Appeals' decision on Shuttlesworth's later Freedom Ride case, March 5, 1963, reprinted in BW, March 13, 1963.

39. BW, March 13, 1963; Gardner, interview, August 9, 1990; James Forman, *The Making of Black Revolutionaries* (New York: Macmillan, 1972), 150–52; MA, May 18, 1961, 1; NYT, May 18, 1961, 27.

40. BN, May 18, 1961; MA, May 20, 1961; BW, March 13, 1963; NYT, March 10, 1964, 24; Kunstler, *Deep in My Heart,* 26–27.

41. BN, May 18, 1961, 1.

42. MA, May 19, 1961; NYT, May 20, 1961, 1, 18; John Lewis, quoted in Pat Watters, *Down to Now: Reflections on the Southern Civil Rights Movement* (New York: Random, 1971), 103–4 (quotation); Kunstler, *Deep in My Heart,* 27–28; Powledge, *Free at Last,* 259–60.

43. Fred Shuttlesworth, interview, May 29–June 1, 1990; Powledge, *Free at Last,* 260.

44. Memorandum to Robert F. Kennedy, May 17, 1961, Robert F. Kennedy Papers, General Correspondence; Fred Shuttlesworth, interview, May 29–June 1, 1990; Powledge, *Free at Last,* 280–81 (dialogue a composite from Shuttlesworth interview and Powledge); phone logs, Burke Marshall Papers, box 8, JFKL.

45. Branch, *Parting the Waters,* 439–44; NYT, May 20, 1961, 1; MA, May 20, 1961, 1; Forman, *Making of Black Revolutionaries,* 153; Harris Wofford, *Of Kennedys and Kings* (New York: Farrar, Strauss, and Giroux, 1980), 153–54; Arthur M. Schlesinger Jr., *Robert F. Kennedy and His Times* (Boston: Houghton Mifflin, 1978), 296; Fred Shuttlesworth, interview, May 29–June 1, 1990; Powledge, *Free at Last,* 280–81; Police Surveillance Files, BPL.

46. Forman, *Making of Black Revolutionaries,* 154–55; John Lewis, quoted in Watters, *Down to Now,* 106–7; *Mobile Press Register,* May 21, 1961; eyewitness account of William Orrick, quoted in Navasky, *Kennedy Justice,* 124 (bystander quotation);

Burke Marshall, interview (no. 1), 20–21, Robert F. Kennedy Papers; *Newsweek,* May 29, 1961, 21.

47. Robert F. Kennedy Papers, General Correspondence; unnamed newspaper clipping, Smiley Papers (quotation); Kunstler, *Deep in My Heart,* 29–30.

48. Fred Shuttlesworth, interview, May 29–June 1, 1990; Fred Shuttlesworth, interview, March 10, 1984, 24–25 (quotation).

49. Farmer, *Lay Bare the Heart,* 204–5 (Farmer quotations); James Farmer, telephone interview, May 5, 1993; Henry Hampton and Steve Farmer, eds., *Voices of Freedom: An Oral History of the Civil Rights Movement from the 1950s through the 1980s* (New York: Bantam Books, 1990), 91; Fred Shuttlesworth, interview, May 29–June 1, 1990.

50. John Patterson, interview, Robert F. Kennedy Papers, 38; *Christian Science Monitor,* May 22, 1962, 5; *Louisville Courier-Journal,* May 22, 1961; unnamed newspaper clipping, Smiley Papers (crowd quotation).

51. Walker, interview, 12–14; *Christian Science Monitor,* May 22, 1962, 5; Shuttlesworth, "No Easy Walk."

52. Fred Shuttlesworth, interview, May 29–June 1, 1990; Walker, interview, 12–14 (Shuttlesworth quotation); Farmer, interview; Farmer, *Lay Bare the Heart,* 205 (Farmer quotation); Kunstler, *Deep in My Heart,* 30–31; telephone logs, Robert F. Kennedy Papers, Attorney General's General Correspondence, box 10; Fairclough, *To Redeem the Soul,* 79–80.

53. Walker, interview (first quotation); Police Surveillance Files, Connor Papers, box 9, folder 13, quoted in Branch, *Parting the Waters,* 465 (second quotation).

54. Fairclough, *To Redeem the Soul,* 80–81. Diane Nash believed King was not radical enough, influenced too much by "middle class standards." More radical and less middle class, Shuttlesworth received this criticism to a much smaller degree. See Forman, *Making of Black Revolutionaries,* 148.

55. Nash, telephone interview, 8.

56. SCLC, *Newsletter* 1 (August 1961): 1–3; NYT, May 26, 1961, 20; NYT, May 28, 1, 38; MA, May 29, 1961.

57. MA, May 29, 1961; MA, May 31, 1961.

58. BPH, June 2, 1961; NYT, June 2, 1961, 20; W. W. Self and J. B. Jones to Jamie Moore, June 14, 1961, 3–4, Connor Papers, box 9, folder 24.

59. BN, June 3, 1961; NYT, June 4, 1961, 82; Fred Shuttlesworth, interview, May 29–June 1, 1990 (court quotations); BN, November 8 and 9, 1961; MA, November 8, 1961; BN, January 9, 1962; BN, November 21, 1962.

60. MA, June 3, 1961.

61. *Cincinnati Herald,* June 16, 1961, 5; *Cincinnati Herald,* June 30, 1961, 1.

62. Winston, interview; Durant, interview, 18–20; Davis, interview, 22–24; Reuben Davis to members of Bethel Baptist Church, July 2, 1961, Davis private scrapbook, copy in author's files.

63. "Concluding Service and Friendship Hour" program, Bethel Baptist Church, August 13, 1961, Shuttlesworth Papers, box 1, folder 33; Fred Shuttlesworth, "A Southerner Speaks," *Pittsburgh Courier,* n.d. [sometime between August 6 and 13, 1962], clipping found in Shuttlesworth Papers, box 4, folder 49.

64. Fred Shuttlesworth, "Fifth Annual President's Report," June 5, 1961, Shuttlesworth Papers, box 1, folder 1; *BW,* June 10, 1961, 8.

65. Clarke, "Goals and Techniques," 76; Police Intelligence Report on July 31 mass meeting, August 2, 1961, Connor Papers, box 9, folder 25.

66. Police Intelligence Reports, September 13, 1961, December 6, 1961, and November 13, 1961, Connor Papers, box 9, folder 25; Police Intelligence Report on June 26, 1961, mass meeting, J. E. LeGrand and M. A. Jones to Jamie Moore, June 27, 1961, Connor Papers, box 9, folder 24.

67. *Pittsburgh Courier,* October 7, 1961; James Farmer, telephone interview, May 5, 1993.

68. Branch, *Parting the Waters,* 500–6; SCLC, News Release, September 12, 1961, King Papers, BU; Fred Shuttlesworth, interview, May 22–25, 1990.

69. SCLC, News Release, September 21, 1961, King Papers, BU.

70. *BN,* October 5, 1963, 1; *Southern Patriot* 12 (December 1954): 3; *Southern Patriot* 19 (June 1961): 4; *Southern Patriot* 19 (October 1961), 1, 3.

71. Braden, interview, 50–52.

72. *Houston Chronicle,* September 22, 1961. The court reaffirmed that ruling some six weeks later; see *BN,* November 3, 1961.

73. Police Intelligence Report, M. A. Jones and J. W. Holland to Jamie Moore, October 25, 1961, Connor Papers, box 9, folder 25.

74. *BN,* October 25, 1961; "Declaratory Judgment and Permanent Injunction," U.S. District Court, Birmingham, Alabama, Judge Hobart H. Grooms, November 8, 1961, copy in Shuttlesworth Papers, box 3; *BN,* November 9, 1961; *NYT,* November 10, 1961, 21.

75. *MA,* October 30, 1961; statement by Eugene T. Connor, October 25, 1961, Connor Papers, box 8, folder 14.

76. Police Intelligence Report, J. W. Holland and J. C. Wilson to Jamie Moore, November 14, 1961, Connor Papers, box 9, folder 25.

77. Nunnelley, *Bull Connor,* 112–17; Vann, "Change from Commission," 13; Resolution of the Birmingham Baptist Pastors' Conference, December 18, 1961, and Beulah Burrell to Connor, December 16, 1961, both in Connor Papers, box 8, folder 13; *BN,* December 18, 1961, 1; *BN,* December 19, 1961, 1.

78. Benjamin Muse, "Dangerous Situation in Birmingham," January 11, 1962, Southern Regional Council Papers, 41.1.3.2.8, BPL; Rev. Norman Jimerson to Paul Rilling, January 5, 1962, Southern Regional Council Papers, 41.2.1.3.9, BPL; Jimerson to Rilling, December 27, 1961, Southern Regional Council Papers, 41.1.1.1.23, BPL; *Time,*

December 22, 1961; Charles Morgan Jr., *A Time to Speak* (New York: Harper and Row, 1964), 60.

79. *BW*, January 3, 1962, 1; Eskew, *But for Birmingham*, 196–97.

80. *BN*, January 8, 1962; Police Intelligence Report, W. W. Self and R. R. Long to Jamie Moore, January 15, 1962, Connor Papers, box 12, folder 17 (mass meeting quotation).

81. Wyatt T. Walker to SCLC Board Members, n.d., SCLC Papers, box 36, folder 13; statement to Attorney General Robert Kennedy, n.d., King Papers, box 125, folder 5, MLKC.

82. Statement to Attorney General Robert Kennedy, n.d., King Papers, box 125, folder 5, MLKC; *Southern Patriot* 20 (February 1961): 4; Branch, *Parting the Waters*, 570–71; Burke Marshall to Robert Kennedy, memorandum, January 22, 1962, box 16, Marshall Papers, JFKL; Marshall to King, January 22, 1962, King Papers, box 24, folder 18, BU; Kunstler, *Deep in My Heart*, 82–83.

83. *NYT*, January 17, 1962, 15 (Connor quotation); *NYT*, February 1, 1962, 17; Police Intelligence Report, J. W. Holland and J. E. Lambert, January 19, 1962, Connor Papers, box 10, folder 18. Branch (*Parting the Waters*, 570–71) narrates the incident but errs in seeing these churches as involved with ACMHR. He also mistakes the New Bethel Baptist Church on Thirteenth Avenue and Sipsey Street as Shuttlesworth's Bethel on Twenty-ninth Avenue. Regarding the announcement for the governor's race, see George Osborne, "Boycott in Birmingham," *Nation*, May 5, 1962, 399.

84. *BW*, January 24, 1962, 6; *BN*, January 26, 1962; Fred Shuttlesworth, interview, May 29–June 1, 1990.

85. Martin Luther King Jr., to Robert Kennedy, quoted in *Chicago Daily Defender*, January 30, 1962, 2; King to "Doctor," February 6, 1962, King Papers, box 1, folder 6, MLKC; SCLC Press Release, January 26, 1962, King Papers, box 22, folder 30, MLKC.

86. Woody L. Taylor, "Thousands Urge U.S. to Intervene for Shuttlesworths, *Cleveland Courier*, February 24, 1962, clipping in Shuttlesworth Papers, box 4, folder 49.

87. *BW*, January 31, 1962, 1.

88. Police Intelligence Report, J. E. LeGrand and M. A. Jones to Jamie Moore, January 30, 1962, Connor Papers, box 12, folder 17; W. E. Shortridge to FBI SAC Birmingham, telegram, February 26, 1962, cited in FBI file 157-477-4.

89. Police Intelligence Report, R. R. Long to Jamie Moore, February 20, 1962, Connor Papers, box 12, folder 17 (quotations); Cross, interview by Barton.

90. *Cleveland Courier*, February 17, 1962, 3.

91. Unidentified newspaper clipping, n.d., in Shuttlesworth Papers, box 4, folder 49 (first quotation); Fred Shuttlesworth, interview, May 29–June 1, 1990 (second quotation); *BPH*, February 7, 1962, 1, 2 (third quotation); *BW*, February 10, 1962.

92. *BW*, February 17, 1962 (quotation); *Baltimore Afro-American*, February 24, 1962.

93. *BN*, February 2, 1962; Kunstler, *Deep in My Heart*, 83.

94. *BPH*, February 7, 1962; *MA*, February 15, 1962 (quotation); Kunstler, *Deep in My Heart*, 83–85.

95. *BN*, February 26, 1962.

96. *MA*, February 27, 1962; *MA*, March 1 and 2, 1962; *BN*, March 1, 1962, cited in FBI HQ file 157-417-A; *BN*, March 2, 1962; *BW*, March 7, 1962, 1, 2.

97. Kunstler, *Deep in My Heart*, 84–85 (court quotations); *Jet*, March 22, 1962, 24f.; SCLC, Press Release, March 1, 1962, SCLC Papers, box 125, folder 5; *Baltimore Afro-American*, March 10, 1962, 9; Police Intelligence Report, A. Wallace and C. C. Ray to Jamie Moore, March 7, 1962, Connor Papers, box 12, folder 17 (Walker quotation).

98. Police Intelligence Report, A. Wallace and C. C. Ray to Jamie Moore, March 7, 1962, Connor Papers, box 12, folder 17.

99. Shuttlesworth to Wyatt Walker, February 11, 1962, in SCLC Papers, box 36, folder 8.

100. Ibid.

8. Confrontations

1. Adams, interview; Abraham L. Woods Jr., interview, June 25, 1991; John Drew, interview, Birmingham, Alabama, December 29, 1988, 5–7, 15.

2. Abraham L. Woods Jr., interview, June 25, 1991.

3. Walker, interview, 7–11; Fred Shuttlesworth, interview, May 22–25, 1990.

4. Hendricks, interview; Montgomery, interview, 15–16; Adams, interview; Armstrong, interview.

5. Paul Rilling, interoffice memorandum regarding February 23, 1962 trip to Birmingham, February 28, 1962, Southern Regional Council Papers, 41.1.1.1.24, BPL. Regarding Sidney Smyer and the Council of 100, see Vann, "Change from Commission," 11; Robert Gaines Corley, "The Quest for Racial Harmony: Race Relations in Birmingham, Alabama, 1947–1963," in *Southern Businessmen and Desegregation*, ed. Elizabeth Jacoway and David R. Colburn (Baton Rouge: Louisiana State University Press, 1982), 182–83.

6. Paul Rilling, interoffice memoranda, February 28 and March 5, 1962, Southern Regional Council Papers, 41.1.1.1.24, BPL; Reggie Robinson, Field Report, May 5, 1962, Southern Regional Council Papers, 41.1.1.1.24, BPL.

7. Dukes, interview; "This We Believe," copy in Shuttlesworth Papers, box 3, folder 42.

8. Regarding the formation of the Anti-Injustice Committee and the advice of Lucius H. Pitts, see Corley, "Quest" (diss.), 232, and Garrow, *Bearing the Cross*, 199. Regarding Pitts's private support of the civil rights movement, see Fred Shuttlesworth, interview, May 29–June 1, 1990; Abraham L. Woods Jr., interview, June 25, 1991; Norman Jimerson, interview, Washington, D.C., June 13, 1989, 28.

9. Police Intelligence Report, J. B. Jones and J. C. Wilson to Jamie Moore, January 24,

1962, Connor Papers, box 12, folder 17; Fred Shuttlesworth, interview, May 22–25, 1990; Fred Shuttlesworth, interview, May 29–June 1, 1990.

10. Norman Jimerson to Per Laureen, March 2, 1962, Southern Regional Council Archives, Woodruff Library, Atlanta University Center, Atlanta, Georgia; Eskew, *But for Birmingham,* 198–205; Osborne, "Boycott in Birmingham," 397, 401; Corley, "Quest" (diss.), 233–34; Norman Jimerson, Confidential Report, April 5, 1962, Southern Regional Council Papers, folder 41.1.1.1.24, BPL.

11. Nichols, "Cities," 159–60, based on interview with Frank Dukes, August 1973; Dick Shapiro to Alex Miller, March 30, 1962, Anti-Defamation League Papers, BPL (Pitts quotation).

12. Jimerson, Confidential Report.

13. Nichols, "Cities," 166; *NYT,* April 4, 1962, 1, 24; Jimerson, Confidential Report; Corley, "Quest" (diss.), 324; Osborne, "Boycott in Birmingham," 401; Corley, "Quest" (diss.), 324; *Atlanta Constitution,* April 5, 1962, 1; *NYT,* April 5, 1962, 19.

14. Fred Shuttlesworth, interview, May 29–June 1, 1990; *Cincinnati Enquirer,* October 13, 1965, 4; Jimerson, Confidential Report; *BPH,* April 5 and 6, 1962, cited in FBI HQ file 157-417-A.

15. Police Intelligence Reports, L. H. Kirk to Jamie Moore, April 11, 1962, and M. A. Jones and J. B. Jones to Jamie Moore, April 25, 1962, Connor Papers, box 12, folder 17.

16. "More Race Pressure on Business," *Business Week,* May 12, 1962, 130; Jimerson, Confidential Report; Osborne, "Boycott in Birmingham," 398; *NYT,* November 17, 1962, 10; *Nation,* May 5, 1961; *BN,* April 9, 1995; Nichols, "Cities," 173.

17. Minutes of a Joint Meeting of the SCLC Administrative Committee and New York Administrative Staff, March 9, 1962, SCLC Papers, box 36, folder 11.

18. *BN,* March 9, 1962.

19. *BW,* March 14, 1962, 1; *BW,* March 17, 1962, 1.

20. Police Intelligence Report, J. E. Lambert and J. C. Wilson to Jamie Moore, March 21, 1962, Connor Papers, box 12, folder 17.

21. Kunstler, *Deep in My Heart,* 84–85; Shuttlesworth to Birmingham City Commission, March 19, 1962, Connor Papers, box 12, folder 17.

22. Shortridge, interview.

23. William E. Shortridge to FBI, testimony, May 29, 1962, Shortridge Papers.

24. Fred Shuttlesworth, interview, May 29–June 1, 1990; Garrow, *Bearing the Cross,* 197; Police Intelligence Report, A. Wallace and M. A. Jones to Jamie Moore, June 5, 1962, Connor Papers, box 12, folder 17 (quotation).

25. Braden, interview, 22–24; *Southern Patriot* 20 (May 1962): 1, 3.

26. Fred Shuttlesworth, quoted in Anne Braden, "The White Southerner in the Integration Struggle," *Freedomways* 3 (winter 1963): 19–20.

27. Norman Jimerson to Paul Rilling, April 12, 1962, Southern Regional Council Papers, 41.1.1.1.24, BPL; *Baltimore African American,* April 7, 1962; *BW,* April 21, 1962; *BW,*

April 25, 1962, 1; Braden, interview, 24–25 (quotations); *Southern Patriot* 20 (May 1962): 1, 3.

28. *Southern Patriot* 20 (May 1962): 3.

29. Braden, interview, 27–29.

30. *Newsweek,* May 14, 1962, 30.

31. Police Intelligence Report on the May 21, 1962, mass meeting, May 23, 1962, Connor Papers, box 12, folder 17.

32. Vann, "Change from Commission," 15–19, 23–27.

33. Minutes of the SCLC Board Meeting, May 16, 1962, SCLC Papers; King, *Why We Can't Wait,* 52; "Interview with Martin Luther King Jr.," *Playboy,* January 1965, reprint.

34. BW, June 9, 1962, 1, 8.

35. Police Intelligence Report of June 25 ACMHR Mass Meeting, O. V. Vance and J. E. Lambert to W. J. Haley (acting chief of police), June 27, 1962, 3, Connor Papers, box 12, folder 18.

36. FBI file 100-438794-2; Police Intelligence Report of July 16, 1962, ACMHR Mass Meeting, R. R. Long and J. B. Jones to Jamie Moore, July 20, 1962, 2–3, Connor Papers, box 12, folder 18.

37. FBI files 157-1131-4, 157-417-6, and 157-417-7; Police Intelligence Report of July 30, 1962 ACMHR Mass Meeting, J. C. Wilson and O. C. Ellard to Jamie Moore, August 1, 1962, 4, Connor Papers, box 12, folder 18; FBI file 157-417-9.

38. Police Intelligence Report on September 10, 1962, Mass Meeting, J. E. LeGrand and C. C. Ray to Jamie Moore, September 12, 1962, Connor Papers, box 12, folder 18.

39. David Levering Lewis, *King: A Critical Biography* (New York: Praeger, 1970), 150 (quotation).

40. Fred Shuttlesworth, quoted in Henry Hampton and Steve Fayer, eds., *Voices of Freedom: An Oral History of the Civil Rights Movement from the 1950s through the 1980s* (New York: Bantam, 1990), 125; Martin Luther King Jr., SCLC Newsletter, July 1963, 1–4, SCLC Papers.

41. Shuttlesworth, in Hampton and Fayer, *Voices of Freedom,* 125 (first and second quotations); Fred Shuttlesworth, interview, May 29–June 1, 1990 (third and fourth quotations); Gardner, interview, February 28, 1987.

42. Police Intelligence Report of May 21 Mass Meeting, May 23, 1962, Connor Papers, box 12, folder 17.

43. Norman Jimerson to Paul Rilling, October 3, 1962, and John J. Brewbaker to Leslie W. Dunbar, October 29, 1962, both in Southern Regional Council Papers, 41.1.1.1.25, BPL; Police Intelligence Report, July 25, 1962, Connor Papers, box 12, folder 18; Garrow, *Bearing the Cross,* 220 (quotation); Corley, "Quest" (diss.), 235–37; Fred Shuttlesworth, interview, May 29–June 1, 1990.

44. Corley, "Quest," in Jacoway and Colburn, *Southern Businessmen,* 185–86; Southern

Regional Council Field Report, September 18, 1962, Southern Regional Council Papers, BPL; *Southern Patriot* 20 (November 1962): 1, 3; Jimerson, interview, 33–35. Jimerson identified himself as having been dispatched by Birmingham attorney David J. Vann, operating at Smyer's behest. Jimerson, however, remembered the conversation with Wyatt Tee Walker as occurring in November.

45. *MA*, September 21, 1961, 1.

46. See James H. Cone, *The Spirituals and the Blues: An Interpretation* (New York: Seabury, 1972), 27.

47. Powledge, *Free at Last,* 497–99; Eskew, *But for Birmingham,* 203–4.

48. *Powledge,* Free at Last, 497–99.

49. Ibid.

50. Ibid.

51. Ibid.

52. SCLC Convention, Program, Sept. 25–28, 1962, SCLC Papers; *BN*, September 25, 1962, 26.

53. FBI file 100-438794-1; *NYT*, September 27, 1962, 29.

54. Branch, *Parting the Waters,* 650, citing an interview with Wyatt T. Walker (Shuttlesworth to King); *BN*, September 26, 1962, 13; *MA*, September 26, 1962, 1; *NYT*, September 27, 1962, 29; Branch, *Parting the Waters,* 650; FBI file 100-438794-1 (Shuttlesworth to reporters); *NYT*, September 29, 1962, 6; Garrow, *Bearing the Cross,* 221.

55. Garrow, *Bearing the Cross,* 222; Vincent Harding, "A Beginning in Birmingham," *Reporter* 28 (1963): 14; Powledge, *Free at Last,* 499, based on interview with Shuttlesworth.

56. Fred Shuttlesworth, interviews, May 29–June 1, 1990, and June 4–7, 1990 (meeting with Kennedy); *Baltimore Afro-American,* October 13, 1962.

57. Police Intelligence Report of the October 29, 1962, Mass Meeting, O. C. Ellard and J. C. Wilson to Jamie Moore, October 31, 1962, and Police Intelligence Report of November 5, 1962, Mass Meeting, L. H. Kirk to Jamie Moore, November 7, 1962, Connor Papers, box 12, folder 18 (quotation); Garrow, *Bearing the Cross,* 224–25.

58. *BN*, December 15, 1962; *Jackson Daily News,* December 15, 1962; Police Surveillance Files, Documents on the Bethel Baptist Church Bombing, December 14, 1962, BPL; *Delta Democrat-Times,* December 19, 1962; FBI file 157-417-10; SCEF, News Release, December 17, 1962, SCLC Papers, box 127, folder 11; Branch, *Parting the Waters,* 683–84; *BN*, December 15, 1962, 1 (quotations).

59. *BN*, December 17, 1962; *Delta Democrat-Times,* December 19, 1962; Police Intelligence Report on December 17, 1962, Meeting, M. A. Jones and W. E. Chilcoat to Jamie Moore, December 19, 1995, Connor Papers, box 12, folder 18.

60. Police Intelligence Report on December 17, 1962, Meeting, M. A. Jones and W. E. Chilcoat to Jamie Moore, December 19, 1995, Connor Papers, box 12, folder 18.

61. FBI file 157-417-10.

62. Police Intelligence Report on January 8, 1963, Mass Meeting, L. H. Kirk and J. C. Parsons to Jamie Moore, January 9, 1963, Connor Papers, box 13, folder 2; FBI file 100-358916-288, 1, 2, 5.

63. King, *Why We Can't Wait,* 57.

64. Nichols, "Cities," 275–76, based on 1973 interviews with Wyatt Tee Walker and Ed Gardner (Walker quotation); Garrow, *Bearing the Cross,* 227–29 (Shuttlesworth quotations); H. Whittemore, *Together* (New York: William Morrow, 1971), 56 (Young quotation); Andrew J. Young, "And Birmingham," *Drum Major* 1 (winter 1971): 21–22; Andrew Young, "Dynamics of a Birmingham Movement in the Sixties," in *Nonviolence in the 70s* (Atlanta: Martin Luther King Center, 1972), 9–15; "There's a New World Coming," *Bulletin of the Peace Studies Institute* (August 1971): 7.

65. Garrow, *Bearing the Cross,* 226–27; Young, "Dynamics," 6; Fred Shuttlesworth, interview, June 4–7, 1990; Walker, interview by Britton, 55; John Cross to Ed Gardner and Wyatt Tee Walker, October 29, 1962, SCLC Papers, box 33, folder 15; Branch, *Parting the Waters,* 691 (Shuttlesworth to King); Garrow, *Bearing the Cross,* 229, citing interview with Stanley Levison (King quotation).

66. Morgan, interview, 11 (first quotation); MA, April 4, 1963; Shuttlesworth, quoted in Hampton and Fayer, *Voices of Freedom,* 128.

67. Martin Luther King Jr., quoted in William Robert Miller, *Martin Luther King Jr.: His Life, Martyrdom, and Meaning for the World* (New York: Weybright, 1968), 134; Police Intelligence Report of February 4, 1963, Mass Meeting, W. E. Chilcoat and C. C. Ray to Jamie Moore, February 7, 1963, Connor Papers, box 13, folder 2.

68. Walker, interview, 6–7.

69. Gaston, interview, 13–14; Walker, interview, 6–7, 19–20; Hendricks, interview; Abraham L. Woods Jr., interview, June 25, 1991; Walker, interview by Britton.

70. On the theory that King primarily sought national attention leading to a "federal commitment to the civil rights movement" rather than the full desegregation of Birmingham, historian Glenn Eskew has written: "King's willingness to settle for less than the movement's original objectives . . . suggests that he viewed *his* victory as won. The interests of the local activists no longer concerned the national civil rights leader, who apparently saw an opportunity to claim success while bailing out of Birmingham." See *But for Birmingham,* 292. My narrative differs slightly from Eskew's and holds that he overstates the distinction between national and local goals in the Birmingham movement.

71. Fred Shuttlesworth, interview, June 4–7, 1990.

72. Ibid.

73. Walker, interview by Britton, 30; Shuttlesworth, interview by Mosby, 47–49; Fred Shuttlesworth, interview, June 4–7, 1990.

74. Vann, "Change from Commission," 28; MA, March 6, 1963; BW, March 13, 1963 (quotation); SCEF, News Release, March 13, 1963, Shuttlesworth Papers, box 4.

75. Fairclough, *To Redeem the Soul*, 116; Police Intelligence Report on March 11 and March 18 Mass Meetings, C. R. Jones to Jamie Moore, March 12, 1963, and Wallace Chilcoat and C. R. Jones to Moore, March 18, 1963, Connor Papers, box 13, folder 2; Norman C. Jimerson to Paul Rilling, March 11, 1963, Southern Regional Council Archives, box 67, folder 9, Woodruff Library, Atlanta University Center, Atlanta, Georgia; Special Memorandum to Constituency of the Alabama Christian Movement for Human Rights and All Citizens of Birmingham, Alabama, March 19, 1963, SCLC Papers; Fred Shuttlesworth, interview, June 4–7, 1990.

76. On middle-class criticism of the SCLC demonstrations, see Branch, *Parting the Waters*, 703, and Garrow, *Bearing the Cross*, 238, both of whom base their narrative primarily on interviews with Wyatt T. Walker; on John T. Porter's evaluation of Shuttlesworth, see Garrow, *Bearing the Cross*, 237–38; John Thomas Porter, interview, February 28, 1987, Birmingham, Alabama, 1–4, 7–9, BPL.

77. Fred Shuttlesworth, interview, May 29–June 1, 1990; Porter, interview.

78. Harding, "Beginning in Birmingham," 18; Montgomery, interview, 32–33; Johnson, interview.

79. Rev. Thurman Echols, public lecture, April 4, 1994, Averett College, Danville, Virginia; James Orange, interview, June 21, 1991, Atlanta, Georgia.

80. Harding, "Beginning in Birmingham," 14.

81. Fred Shuttlesworth, interview, June 4–7, 1990; Jimerson, interview, 35.

82. Walker, interview by Britton, 58; Shuttlesworth to Walker and King, March 15, 1963, King Papers, MLKC; Fred Shuttlesworth, interview, June 4–7, 1990.

83. Kunstler, *Deep in My Heart*, 173–75; King, *Why We Can't Wait*, 57–58; Lewis, *King*, 177.

9. Cataclysm

1. Police Intelligence Report, W. E. Chilcoat and C. C. Ray to Jamie Moore, February 7, 1963, Connor Papers, box 13, folder 2.

2. *Washington Post*, April 4, 1963, A2; Vann, "Change from Commission," 29–30; Emma Gelders Sterne, *I Have a Dream* (New York: Knopf, 1965), 185.

3. Alan F. Westin and Barry Mahoney, *The Trial of Martin Luther King* (New York: Crowell, 1974), 65–66, 122 (Connor quotation); Branch, *Parting the Waters*, 708; Fred Shuttlesworth, interview, June 4–7, 1990; "Birmingham Manifesto," Connor Papers, box 13, folder 2; Statement of Birmingham Campaign Aims, April 4, 1963, SCLC Papers; NYT, April 5, 1963, 16.

4. *Washington Post*, April 4, 1963, A2.

5. Gaston, interview, 15–16; *Washington Post*, April 4, 1963, A2; Woods and Pugh, interview, 15–17; MA, April 4, 1963; Abraham L. Woods Jr., interview, June 25, 1991.

6. Police Intelligence Report, R. S. Whitehouse and R. A. Watkins to Jamie Moore, April 5, 1963, Connor Papers, box 13, folder 4.

7. Fred Shuttlesworth, interview, June 4–7, 1990.

8. Orange, interview, June 21, 1991; Brown, telephone interview. As a sixteen-year-old volunteer, Brown served as a "gopher" for movement leaders at these meetings and was thus able to observe some of these discussions.

9. *NYT*, April 6, 1963, 20.

10. Ibid.

11. *BN*, April 3, 1963, 2 (quotations); *BN*, April 4, 1963, 7; Norman Jimerson, Southern Regional Council Quarterly Report, July 16, 1963, Southern Regional Council Papers, *BPL*; Kunstler, *Deep in My Heart*, 179.

12. *BN*, April 5, 1963, 2; *BN*, April 6, 1963, 2; *BW*, April 13, 1963, 1; *BN*, April 6, 1963, 2; *BW*, April 13, 1963, 1; "The South: Poorly Timed Protest," *Time*, April 19, 1963, 30–31; Police Intelligence Report, R. A. Whitehouse and R. A. Watkins to Jamie Moore, April 10, 1963, Connor Papers, box 13, folder 4.

13. *BW*, April 10, 1963, 1; *NYT*, April 7, 1963, 55; Kunstler, *Deep in My Heart*, 79.

14. *BN*, April 6, 1963, 2; *BN*, April 7, 1963; Westin and Mahoney, *Trial of Martin Luther King*, 67.

15. Fred Shuttlesworth, interview, June 4–7, 1990.

16. Police Intelligence Report, R. A. Whitehouse and R. A. Watkins to Jamie Moore, April 10, 1963, Connor Papers, box 13, folder 4; *BW*, April 8, 1963, 2; *NYT*, April 8, 1963, 31; *BN*, April 8, 1963, 2; Fred Shuttlesworth, interview, June 4–7, 1990; Walker and Cotton quoted in Forman, *Making of Black Revolutionaries*, 311–12.

17. King, *Why We Can't Wait*, 64–65; Morris, *Origins*, 263; Fairclough, *To Redeem the Soul*, 118–19; Cross, interview by Barton, 13; Woods and Pugh, interview, 19–20; Jimerson, interview, 23–24; Oliver, interview, 13. Two discrepancies exist among historians and participants regarding the accurate date of the meeting and the nature of King's speech there. Garrow, Fairclough, and Branch all place the meeting as Tuesday, April 3, the first day of demonstrations. They also have King berating the ministers for riding in fine cars but being unwilling to enter the civil rights struggle and concluding, "If you can't stand up with your people, you are not fit to be a preacher" (Cross, interview by Barton). I am following Police Intelligence Report, R. S. Whitehouse and B. A. Allison to Jamie Moore, April 11, 1963, Connor Papers, box 13, folder 4, which reports Shuttlesworth informing a mass meeting crowd on April 9 that 125 ministers had endorsed the movement at a meeting the previous day, Monday, April 8. Eskew (*But for Birmingham*, 229–30) also dates this meeting as April 8. As to the nature of King's speech, Shuttlesworth, Oliver, and Jimerson all indicated that King was much more diplomatic and respectful of the ministers than indicated by Garrow, Fairclough, and Branch. Regarding the April 4 mass meeting, see Police Intelligence Report, R. S. Whitehouse and R. A. Watkins to Jamie Moore, April 5, 1963, Connor Papers, box 13, folder 4.

18. *NYT*, April 9, 1963; Connor, quoted in "Birmingham Commissioner Wears Nickname with Pride," *Westchester Evening News,* April 10, 1963, 1; Garrow, *Bearing the Cross,* 239–41.

19. "Gaston Asks All to Work Together," *BN*, April 10, 1963, 1; *BN*, April 13, 1963, 6; *BW*, April 10, 1963, 1, 8; *BN*, April 19, 1963, 1; Nichols, "Cities," 263, based on an August 1973 interview with Arthur Hanes; Police Intelligence Report, R. S. Whitehouse and B. A. Allison to Jamie Moore, April 11, 1963, Connor Papers, box 13, folder 4.

20. Jimerson, Quarterly Reports, Southern Regional Council Papers, *BPL*; Morgan, *A Time to Speak,* 151–53.

21. Morgan, interview, 16–17; Raines, *My Soul Is Rested,* 196–97; Fred Shuttlesworth, interview, June 4–7, 1990; Powledge, *Free at Last,* 500–501.

22. *BW*, April 10, 1963, 6; *BW*, April 17, 1963, 6; Fred Shuttlesworth, interview, May 22–25, 1990; Fred Shuttlesworth, interview, June 4–7, 1990; Armstrong, interview.

23. Westin and Mahoney, *Trial of Martin Luther King,* 61–62.

24. Ibid., 69–72, 76, 77; Anonymous Police Report, April 10, 1963, Connor Papers, box 13, folder 4.

25. *NYT*, April 12, 1963, 1, 13; Westin and Mahoney, *Trial of Martin Luther King,* 77–78; *ACMHR*, Press Release, April 11, 1963, Marshall Papers, Alabama File—Correspondence, *JFKL*.

26. Statement by Rev. F. L. Shuttlesworth, April 14, 1963, Shuttlesworth Papers, box 1, folder 23. The statement later appeared in the *Cincinnati Herald,* April 19, 1963, 1.

27. Police Intelligence Report, R. S. Whitehouse and R. A. Watkins to Jamie Moore, April 12, 1963, Connor Papers, box 13, folder 4.

28. Ibid.

29. Westin and Mahoney, *Trial of Martin Luther King,* 83–85; Kunstler, *Deep in My Heart,* 185; *NYT*, April 13, 1963, 1, 15.

30. Andrew Young, "Easter Sunday: Parting of the Red Sea," *Atlanta Journal-Constitution,* July 17, 1983, 1C, 14C; Jim Bishop, *The Days of Martin Luther King* (New York: Putnam, 1971), 28.

31. Sterne, *I Have a Dream,* 187; Fred Shuttlesworth, interview, June 4–7, 1990.

32. Resolution by the Revelation Baptist Church, April 14, 1963, *SCLC* Papers, box 5, folder 23.

33. Police Intelligence Report, R. S. Whitehouse and R. A. Watkins to Jamie Moore, April 18, 1963, Connor Papers, box 13, folder 4; *Washington Post,* April 12, 1963, A2; *BPH*, April 13, 1963; Fred Shuttlesworth, interview, June 4–7, 1990; Branch, *Parting the Waters,* 745.

34. *NYT*, April 14, 1963, 1, 46; *BPH*, April 13, 1963, 10; King, *Why We Can't Wait,* 74; *NYT*, April 15, 1963, 1, 14; *Christian Science Monitor,* April 16, 1963, 2 (quotation); *BW*, April 17, 1963, 1, 6; Miller, *Martin Luther King Jr.,* 137.

35. *NYT*, April 15, 1963, 1, 14; *BW*, April 17, 1963, 1, 6. Even the reporters from the *Bir-*

mingham World confused marchers with bystanders, writing that "about 1,500 Negroes attempted an anti-segregation protest march."

36. Westin and Mahoney, *Trial of Martin Luther King,* 90–94.

37. Ibid.

38. Police Intelligence Report on April 15 Mass Meeting, R. S. Whitehouse and R. A. Watkins to Jamie Moore, April 17, 1963, Connor Papers, box 13, folder 4.

39. Ibid.

40. Ibid.; Fred Shuttlesworth, interview, June 4–7, 1990; NYT, April 16, 1963, 1, 17; *Christian Science Monitor,* April 16, 1963, 2 (Marshall quotation); BN, April 14, 1963, 2.

41. Police Intelligence Report on April 15 Mass Meeting, R. S. Whitehouse and R. A. Watkins to Jamie Moore, April 17, 1963, Connor Papers, box 13, folder 4; NYT, April 20, 1963, 12; BPH, April 13, 1963, 10; Kunstler, *Deep in My Heart,* 188; Fred Shuttlesworth, interview, October 27–31, 1988 (dialogue).

42. Norman Jimerson, Quarterly Reports, Southern Regional Council Papers, BPL; Fred Shuttlesworth, interview, October 27–31, 1988; Fred Shuttlesworth, interview, June 4–7, 1990.

43. NYT, April 18, 1963, 21; undated ACMHR-SCLC press release, King Papers, box 1, file 8, MLKC.

44. NYT, April 18, 1963, 21; Fred Shuttlesworth, interview, June 4–7, 1990; Police Intelligence Report on April 26 Mass Meeting, B. A. Allison, R. A. Watkins, and R. S. Whitehouse to Jamie Moore, April 30, 1963, Connor Papers, box 13, folder 4.

45. *Washington Post,* April 18, 1963; FBI HQ file 157-417-A.

46. Fred Shuttlesworth, interview, June 4–7, 1990; Marshall, telephone logs; Wyatt Walker to Burke Marshall, April 16, 1963; Marshall to Walker, April 24, 1963 (quotation); Marshall to Robert F. Kennedy, April 23, 1963, all in Marshall Papers, JFKL; Walker to King and Abernathy, Progress Report, April 20, 1963, King Papers, MLKC.

47. Fred Shuttlesworth, interview, June 4–7, 1990; Police Intelligence Report, R. S. Whitehouse and R. A. Watkins to Jamie Moore, April 21, 1963, Connor Papers, box 13, folder 4.

48. Fred Shuttlesworth, interview, June 4–7, 1990; Kunstler, *Deep in My Heart,* 188; NYT, April 21, 1963, 70; Police Intelligence Report, T. H. Cook to Jamie Moore, May 6, 1963, Connor Papers, box 13, folder 5.

49. Westin and Mahoney, *Trial of Martin Luther King,* 102–6, 121–26, 141–42; Fred Shuttlesworth, interview, June 4–7, 1990 (quotation); NYT, April 23, 1963, 20; NYT, April 25, 1963, 20; NYT, April 27, 1963, 9; *Civil Liberties Review* 3 (December 1976–January 1977): 26. A complete list of the defendants included fifteen African American ministers: Shuttlesworth, King, Abernathy, Walker, Young, James Bevel, A. D. King, Ed Gardner, Abraham Woods Jr., Calvin Woods, J. L. Palmer, J. W. Hayes, N. H. Smith, John T. Porter, and T. L. Fisher.

50. Westin and Mahoney, *Trial of Martin Luther King,* 102–6, 121–26, 141–42 (quotations

of witnesses); *BPH*, April 24, 1963, 1; *BN*, April 23 and 24, 1963, 1; Vann, "Change from Commission," 29–30.

51. Kunstler, *Deep in My Heart*, 189; Police Intelligence Report, B. A. Allison, R. A. Watkins, and R. S. Whitehouse, April 25, 1963, Connor Papers, box 13, folder 4.

52. Branch, *Parting the Waters*, 750–55; Fred Shuttlesworth, interview, June 4–7, 1990.

53. *NYT*, April 26, 1963, 1, 17; *NYT*, April 27, 1963, 12; *BN*, April 25, 1963, 1; *BN*, April 26, 1963, 1; Schlesinger, *Robert F. Kennedy*, 362–65 (Kennedy quotation); Police Intelligence Report, R. S. Whitehouse and B. A. Allison to Jamie Moore, April 29, 1963, Connor Papers, box 13, folder 4 (Shuttlesworth quotation).

54. Boutwell Papers, box 21, folder 23; Police Intelligence Report, B. A. Allison, R. A. Watkins, and R. S. Whitehouse to Jamie Moore, April 30, 1963, Connor Papers, box 13, folder 4.

55. Police Intelligence Report, R. S. Whitehouse to Jamie Moore, April 29, 1963, Connor Papers, box 13, folder 4; Orange, interview; Police Intelligence Report, M. H. House to Jamie Moore, April 30, 1963, Connor Papers, box 13, folder 5; Brown, telephone interview; Woods and Pugh, interview, 25.

56. Oliver, interview, 14; A. G. Gaston, *Green Power: The Successful Way of A. G. Gaston* (Birmingham: Birmingham Publishing Company, 1968), 133 (Gaston's statement originally appeared in the *Birmingham News*); Long, telephone interview.

57. Police Intelligence Report, M. H. House to Jamie Moore, April 30, 1963. An anonymous report to Jamie Moore, May 1, 1963, indicated Shuttlesworth was not in the party of five traveling with King back to Birmingham on the afternoon of May 1. The report indicated he did attend the SCLC board meeting in Memphis. Both reports in Connor Papers, box 13, folder 5. See also Garrow, *Bearing the Cross*, 247.

58. Police Intelligence Report, B. A. Allison to Jamie Moore, May 2, 1963, Connor Papers, box 13, folder 5; Garrow, *Bearing the Cross*, 248.

59. *NYT*, May 3, 1963, 1, 15; *NYT*, May 7, 1963, 33; see also *BN*, May 3, 1963, 2; Fred Shuttlesworth, interview, June 4–7, 1990.

60. Nichols, "Cities," 291, based on interview (White quotation); Fred Shuttlesworth, interview, June 4–7, 1990 (Shuttlesworth quotation); Police Intelligence Report, R. A. Watkins and R. S. Whitehouse, May 3, 1963, Connor Papers, box 13, folder 5 (Shuttlesworth–police officer dialogue); police officer Jack Warren, quoted in Nunnelley, *Bull Connor*, 147 (Connor quotation).

61. Statement by Albert Boutwell, May 2, 1963, Boutwell Papers, box 35, folder 27; *BN*, May 3, 1963; *BPH*, May 4, 1963, 2; *NYT*, May 4, 1963, 8 (Kennedy and Malcolm X quotations); *NYT*, May 11, 1963, 1.

62. Police Intelligence Report, R. A. Watkins, T. M. Cook, and R. S. Whitehouse to Jamie Moore, May 3, 1963, Connor Papers, box 13, folder 5.

63. "Birmingham and Beyond," *New South* 18 (October–November 1963): 17; *BN*, May 3, 1963, 2, 4; *BN*, May 4, 1963; *NYT*, May 4, 1963, 1, 8; *Newsweek*, May 13, 1963, 27–28.

64. "Birmingham and Beyond," *New South* 18 (October–November 1963): 17; BN, May 3, 1963, 2, 4; BN, May 4, 1963; NYT, May 3, 1963, 1 (quotation); NYT, May 4, 1963, 1, 8; *Newsweek,* May 13, 1963, 27–28.

65. David Vann, quoted in Hampton and Fayer, *Voices of Freedom,* 133; Dave Dellinger, "The Negroes of Birmingham," *Liberation* 8 (summer 1963): 21; Stephen C. Rose, "Test for Nonviolence," *Christian Century,* May 29, 1963, 715.

66. Vann, "Change from Commission," 30–33.

67. David Vann, interview, August 7, 1990.

68. Vann, "Change from Commission."

69. Police Intelligence Report, L. H. Bailey, May 4, 1963, Connor Papers, box 13, folder 5; NYT, May 5, 1963, 1, 82; NYT, May 6, 1963, 1; BN, May 4, 1963, 2; BW, May 8, 1963, 1; James Bevel, quoted in Hampton and Fayer, *Voices of Freedom,* 134.

70. NYT, May 6, 1963, 1, 59; BW, May 8, 1963, 1; King, *Why We Can't Wait,* 101; "Interview," *Playboy;* Young, "Easter Sunday," 1C, 14C. Young's narrative inaccurately dates this particular march as Easter Sunday, April 14, 1963.

71. NYT, May 7, 1963, 1, 33; Garrow, *Bearing the Cross,* 252–53; Hampton and Fayer, *Voices of Freedom,* 135–36 (quotation).

72. Fred Shuttlesworth, interview, June 4–7, 1990 (quotation); see also Shuttlesworth interview in Raines, *My Soul Is Rested,* 171; Garrow, *Bearing the Cross,* 253; David Vann, "Outline of Negotiations," n.d., Vann Papers, box 25, folder 24.

73. Fred Shuttlesworth, interview, June 4–7, 1990; Vann, "Outline of Negotiations"; NYT, May 7, 1963, 1, 33; Corley, "Quest" (diss.), 263–65; Garrow, *Bearing the Cross,* 252–53; Fairclough, *To Redeem the Soul,* 127.

74. Len Holt, "Birmingham Demonstration, 1963," in Grant, *Black Protest,* 344–47; BN, May 6, 1963, 2 (quotation); NYT, May 7, 1963, 1, 33; NYT, May 8, 1963, 2; BN, May 7, 1963; Vann, "Outline of Negotiations"; Garrow, *Bearing the Cross,* 246–63.

75. NYT, May 8, 1963, 28.

76. NYT, May 8, 1963, 1; Forman, *Making of Black Revolutionaries,* 314–15; Fred Shuttlesworth, interview, May 29–June 1, 1990.

77. Fred Shuttlesworth, interview, June 4–7, 1990.

78. Holt, "Birmingham Demonstration," 347–49; NYT, May 8, 1963, 1, 28; NYT, May 11, 1963, 1; BN, May 7, 1963, 2; BN, May 8, 1963, 1; Fred Shuttlesworth, interview, June 4–7, 1990; Fred Shuttlesworth, interview, October 27–31, 1988. See also the interview with Birmingham police officer and eyewitness Glenn V. Evans in Raines, *My Soul Is Rested,* 156 (quotation).

79. Shuttlesworth, "Birmingham Revisited," 118 (quotations); Orange, interview.

80. NYT, May 8, 1963, 1, 28; *Pittsburgh Courier,* May 18, 1963, 1.

81. Fred Shuttlesworth, interview, June 4–7, 1990.

82. BN, May 7, 1963, 2; BN, May 8, 1963, 1; BN, May 10, 1963, 2; NYT, May 8, 1963, 29; NYT,

May 9, 1963, 1, 17; *NYT*, May 11, 1963, 9; see also Burke Marshall, interview, John F. Kennedy Oral History Collection, JFKL.

83. *BN*, May 8, 1963, 1; Vann, "Change from Commission," 33–34.

84. Navasky, *Kennedy Justice*, 219; Garrow, *Bearing the Cross*, 255–56 (quotations).

85. Fred Shuttlesworth, interview, May 29–June 1, 1990; Oliver, interview, 9–10.

86. Fred Shuttlesworth, interview, May 29–June 1, 1990, 10; Fred Shuttlesworth, interview, June 4–7, 1990. Interviews years after the events reveal Shuttlesworth's tendency to highlight his agreements with King rather than the points of contention between them. In the years since his assassination, King has taken on a mythical status among African Americans, and thus few participants in the movement criticize him or emphasize their disagreements with him. In interviews Shuttlesworth was at times critical of King but more typically downplayed his differences with him.

87. Fred Shuttlesworth, interview, May 29–June 1, 1990; Fred Shuttlesworth, interview, October 27–31, 1988; Raines, *My Soul Is Rested*, 172–74 (dialogue composite from interviews and Raines); Garrow, *Bearing the Cross*, 256–57.

88. Fred Shuttlesworth, interview, June 4–7, 1990; Branch, *Parting the Waters*, 782–83 (quotation).

89. This interpretation, which contrasts the styles of King and Shuttlesworth as well as their goals for the Birmingham campaign, is perceptively and accurately advanced by Eskew. I agree with this interpretation, although Eskew overplays the degree to which Shuttlesworth was willing to turn over the decisions to King. Shuttlesworth did not make as much a distinction between the local and national civil rights movements as Eskew believes. One should not make too much of this distinction because, as Wyatt Walker later argued, "one hand washes the other," meaning that the local and national were inextricably linked (Walker, interview).

90. Fred Shuttlesworth, interview, June 4–7, 1990.

91. *NYT*, May 9, 1963, 1, 17 (quotation); *BW*, May 11, 1963, 1, 8; *Christian Science Monitor*, May 9, 1963, 1.

92. Andrew Young, *An Easy Burden: The Civil Rights Movement and the Transformation of America* (New York: HarperCollins, 1996), 246–47 (Dolan quotation); Forman, *Making of Black Revolutionaries*, 315; Police Intelligence Report, B. A. Allison and R. A. Watkins to Jamie Moore, May 9, 1963, Connor Papers, box 13, folder 5; *Christian Science Monitor*, May 16, 1963, 6 (Shuttlesworth quotation).

93. *NYT*, May 10 1963, 1, 14; also see Eskew, *But for Birmingham*, 291–92.

94. *NYT*, May 10, 1963, 1, 14; Police Intelligence Report, R. S. Whitehouse to Jamie Moore, May 10, 1963, Connor Papers, box 13, folder 5.

95. *NYT*, May 9, 1963, 1, 17; *NYT*, May 10, 1963, 1, 14.

96. *Cincinnati Post and Times-Star*, May 11, 1963, 2; *NYT*, May 11, 1963, 1, 8 (quotation);

Robert Gutwillig, "Six Days in Alabama," *Mademoiselle* 57 (September 1963): 116–17, 186–93, 202.

97. ACMHR, News Release, May 10, 1963, Boutwell Papers, box 35, folder 27.

98. *NYT*, May 11, 1963, 1, 8.

99. Police Intelligence Report, R. S. Whitehouse to Jamie Moore, May 11, 1963, Connor Papers, box 13, folder 5.

100. Ralph David Abernathy, *And the Walls Came Tumbling Down: An Autobiography* (New York: Harper and Row, 1989), 268. Abernathy's comment, coming late in his life, represents his final conclusion on Shuttlesworth's role in Birmingham and contrasts sharply with the view of Wyatt T. Walker, who said, "We never could have been able to pull Birmingham off if it had not been for his Alabama Christian Movement for Human Rights." See Walker, interview by Britton, 82.

101. On the number of arrests in the protests, see *BN*, May 11, 1963, 2; Eskew, *But for Birmingham*, 296–97.

10. "Actionist"

1. Young, *Easy Burden*, 246–47; Fred Shuttlesworth, interview, June 17, 1991.

2. *NYT*, May 11, 1963, 2 (Connor quotation); *NYT*, May 12, 1963, 1, 53; Rose, "Test for Nonviolence," 714–16; David Cort, "The Voices of Birmingham," *Nation*, July 27, 1963, 46 (Shelton quotation).

3. *NYT*, May 9, 1963, 1, 33; *Christian Science Monitor*, May 9, 1963, 1; Garrow, *Bearing the Cross*, 260–63; "Birmingham and Beyond," 17–23; *BW*, May 15, 1963, 1, 6; *NYT*, May 14, 1963, 1, 26; *NYT*, May 19, 1963, 62.

4. *NYT*, May 14, 1963, 1, 26, 27; *Christian Science Monitor*, May 16, 1963, 6.

5. *St. Louis Post-Dispatch*, May 15, 1963, 10A; *NYT*, May 15, 1963, 1, 26.

6. *NYT*, May 17, 1963, 1; Martin Luther King Jr., Ralph Abernathy, and Fred Shuttlesworth to David Vann, Sidney Smyer, and Burke Marshall, May 17, 1963, SCLC Papers, box 139, folder 7.

7. *Cincinnati Post and Times-Star*, May 18, 1963, 5; *Cincinnati Enquirer*, May 18, 1963, 31; *Cincinnati Herald*, May 24, 1963, 1.

8. *St. Louis Post-Dispatch*, May 29, 1963, 3A; Shuttlesworth Papers, box 3; Shuttlesworth to William Shortridge, June 1, 1963, Shuttlesworth Papers, box 3.

9. Fred Shuttlesworth, "Seventh Annual President's Address," Shuttlesworth Papers, box 1, folder 2.

10. *NYT*, May 19, 1963, 1, 62; Pierre Salinger, "Memorandum of Conversation between President Kennedy and Governor George Wallace," May 18, 1963, President's Office Files, JFK Library.

11. *NYT*, June 12, 1963, 20.

12. *Cincinnati Enquirer,* June 18, 1963, 11; Eskew, *But for Birmingham,* 312; Hugh Davis Graham, *The Civil Rights Era: Origins and Development of National Policy* (New York: Oxford University Press, 1990), 74–83; Arthur M. Schlesinger Jr., *A Thousand Days: John F. Kennedy in the White House* (Boston: Houghton-Mifflin, 1965), 971. For Shuttlesworth's recollection of the meeting with the President and his "But for Birmingham" comment, see his 1964 presidential address to the ACMHR, "The National Civil Rights Crisis and Our Relationship to It," June 5, 1964, Shuttlesworth Papers, box 1, folder 1. Many others have attributed the Kennedy administration's turn toward stronger legislation to the effects of the Birmingham demonstrations. Citing several quotations from Edwin Guthman, Roy Wilkins, and Burke Marshall, Adam Fairclough summarizes the historiographical debate and concludes: "Even allowing for . . . qualifications, history must regard Birmingham as the decisive factor." See *To Redeem the Soul,* 133–35.

13. *Southern Patriot* 21 (June 1963): 4; Braden, interview, 34–37; *Cincinnati Enquirer,* June 9, 1963.

14. Fred Shuttlesworth, interview, March 10, 1984, 38–41.

15. Ibid.; see also Braden, interview, 37–39.

16. Report, June 11, 1963, FBI file 157-417-13; Report, June 19, FBI file, n.n.

17. *NYT,* July 16, 1963, 1, 16; *BN,* October 5, 1963, 1; *BN,* October 6, 1963, D-17; *BN,* October 5, 1963, 1; *Cincinnati Post and Times-Star,* October 5, 1963, 5; *Southern Patriot* 22 (June 1964): 3; *Southern Patriot* 30 (May 1972): 2.

18. *NYT,* July 4, 1963, 38; *Cincinnati Post and Times-Star,* July 4, 1963, 6; Len Holt, *An Act of Conscience* (Boston: Beacon Press, 1965), 200–202.

19. Fred Shuttlesworth, interview, June 4–7, 1990; Garrow, *Bearing the Cross,* 296, 301–20; *NYT,* November 10, 1963, 80; FBI file 157-6-41-1458; Miller, *Martin Luther King Jr.,* 172.

20. Garrow, *Bearing the Cross,* 265–86; Branch, *Parting the Waters,* 846–50, 869–70, 872–83.

21. Garrow, *Bearing the Cross,* 265–86; Branch, *Parting the Waters,* 846–50, 869–70, 872–83.

22. FBI file CI 157-161, August 28, 1963; FBI file 157-6-53-185, June 27, 1963; Miller, *Martin Luther King Jr.,* 161 (quotation).

23. Fred Shuttlesworth, quoted in Haynes Johnson, "Passing the Torch: Rights March Draws Faithful," *Cincinnati Enquirer,* August 24, 1988, A1, A12; Fred Shuttlesworth, interview, June 4–7, 1990.

24. *BN,* September 2, 1963, 1 (Griswold quotation); *MA,* September 4, 1963; J. Wayne Flynt, "The Ethics of Democratic Persuasion and the Birmingham Crisis," *Southern Speech Journal* 35 (1969): 43–44, citing *BPH,* September 4, 1963, *BN,* September 4, 1963, and *BPH,* September 5, 1963 (Stoner quotation).

25. *BN,* September 4, 1963, 1, 10; teletype, September 5, 1963, FBI file 157-4-4-171, 1, 2; Fred Shuttlesworth, interview, June 4–7, 1990.

26. *NYT,* September 6, 1963, 14; *NYT,* September 7, 1963, 9; "Rev. Shuttlesworth Name

on a Birmingham Bullet," *Muhammad Speaks,* September 27, 1963, 6, cited in FBI file 100-438794-64 (quotation); Arthur Shores, interview by Jack Bass, July 17, 1974, Southern Oral History Program, Southern Historical Collection, Manuscript Department, University of North Carolina, Chapel Hill, 3–4.

27. BN, September 7, 1963, 13; "A Call for Calmness and Restraint during the Racial Crisis," copy in Boutwell Papers, box 34, folder 4.

28. Flynt, "Ethics of Democratic Persuasion," 45–46, citing BN, September 14, 1963; NYT, September 13, 1963, 14; NYT, September 14, 1963, 11.

29. Report on Bombing Dates, September 25, 1963, Police Surveillance Files, BPL; Fred Shuttlesworth, interview, June 4–7, 1990.

30. NYT, September 16, 1963, 1, 26; NYT, September 16, 1963, 1, 26; NYT, September 17, 1963, 1, 25.

31. NYT, September 16, 1963, 1, 26; Hampton and Fayer, *Voices of Freedom,* 175–76; Adams, interview.

32. NYT, September 17, 1963, 1, 25; Police Intelligence Report, R. S. Whitehouse and R. A. Watkins to Jamie Moore, September 20, 1963, Hamilton Papers, box 3, folder 40, BPL; telegram to Robert Kennedy, September 16, 1963, Marshall Papers, Alabama File—Correspondence, JFKL.

33. NYT, September 18, 1963, 1, 26; Mary McGrory, "Funeral Fails to Close Void," *Washington Evening Star,* September 19, 1963; Fred Shuttlesworth, interview, June 4–7, 1990.

34. Diane Nash Bevel, Report to SCLC, 9/17-20/63, SCLC Papers, box 141; Fred Shuttlesworth, interview, June 4–7, 1990.

35. Fred Shuttlesworth, interview, June 4–7, 1990.

36. McGrory, "Funeral"; NYT, September 19, 1963, 17; Mary McGrory, "'Big Mules' Shun Problem," *Washington Evening Star,* September 19, 1963, 16.

37. NYT, September 19, 1963, 17.

38. Ibid., 25.

39. Fred Shuttlesworth, interview, June 4–7, 1990.

40. NYT, September 20, 1963, 1, 19; *Public Papers of the Presidents,* John F. Kennedy, 1963, No. 360, 681–82; No. 365, 692–93; No. 372, 702–3 (Washington, D.C.: National Archives and Record Service, Federal Register Division, 1963); NYT, September 23, 1963, 2; Hampton and Fayer, *Voices of Freedom,* 173–74.

41. Royall and Blaik to Lyndon Johnson, December 16, 1963, Marshall Papers, Alabama File—Correspondence, JFKL; *Southern Patriot* 21 (November 1963): 1 (Kunstler quotation); NYT, September 25, 1963, 33; *Baltimore Afro-American,* October 5, 1963, 1; *Christian Science Monitor,* September 30, 1963, 3 (King quotation).

42. Kenneth C. Royall and Earl H. Blaik, "Report to the President of the United States," October 10, 1963, Marshall Papers, Alabama File—Royall-Blaik Mission, JFKL.

43. Ibid.

44. ACMHR, News Release, September 30, 1963, Shuttlesworth Papers, box 1, folder 9; ACMHR, News Release, October 1, 1963, Shuttlesworth Papers, box 1, folder 11; *NYT*, September 29, 1963, 79; Shuttlesworth to Royall and Blaik, October 2, 1963, Hamilton Papers, box 3, folder 40; Shuttlesworth to Boutwell and M. E. Wiggins (president of the city council), October 4, 1963, and copy of telegram, Shuttlesworth to Boutwell, October 8, 1963, both in Boutwell Papers, box 15, folder 41.

45. *Cincinnati Herald,* October 5, 1963, 1, 2. One of those arrested, Klansman Robert E. Chambliss, was eventually convicted of the bombing and the murder of the four girls. After lying dormant for fifteen years the case was pressed by Alabama Attorney General Bill Baxley in 1978. Chambliss received a life sentence and died in prison. Baxley later lost a bid for governor of Alabama, at least partly because of his role in convicting Chambliss. He later spoke of citizens who told him, "I would have voted for you, except for what you did to that old man." See Louis D. Mitchell, "Another Redemption: Baxley in Birmingham," *Crisis* 78 (1978): 311–17.

46. Reports to Director, FBI, from Special Agent in Charge, Cincinnati, October 11 and 12, 1963, FBI file 157-0.

47. George S. Seibels Jr., Report, and Albert Boutwell, Statement, both dated October 22, 1963, in Boutwell Papers, box 15, folder 42; Garrow, *Bearing the Cross,* 302–3; Fred Shuttlesworth, interview, June 4–7, 1990; Shuttlesworth to King, November 7, 1963, King Papers, box 22, folder 1, MLKC.

48. Bayard Rustin to Martin Luther King Jr., memorandum, November 5, 1963, King Papers, box 20, folder 39, MLKC.

49. *Ardmore (Penn.) Main Line Times,* January 30, 1964, and *Philadelphia Inquirer,* February 2, 1964, cited in FBI file 157-1525-2; *Canton Repository,* February 15, 1964.

50. *NYT*, March 10, 1964, 1, 24; *Cincinnati Post and Times-Star,* March 9, 1964, 4; *Militant,* March 19, 1964, cited in FBI HQ file 157-417-A. For fuller discussion of the import of the *Sullivan* decision, see *Time,* March 20, 1964, and Lewis, *Make No Law.*

51. Shuttlesworth to Boutwell, March 12, 1964, Hamilton Papers, box 3, folder 36; Shuttlesworth to Department Stores, March 16, 1964, Hamilton Papers, box 3, folder 42; Shuttlesworth to Boutwell, telegrams, March 21, 1964, Boutwell Papers; ACMHR, News Release, March 19, 1964, Boutwell Papers; Royall-Blaik Interim Report to Robert F. Kennedy, March 12, 1964, Marshall Papers, Alabama File—Royall-Blaik Mission, JFKL; John Herbers, "Birmingham's Progress Slow in Race Relations," *NYT*, May 15, 1964, special report.

52. Shuttlesworth told a *Wall Street Journal* reporter named Tammer that Birmingham would see "more massive efforts than last summer." This conversation is summarized in an unsigned police report, April 20, 1964, Demonstrations File, Police Surveillance Files, BPL. This anonymous report was based on conversations with a similarly unnamed source inside the ACMHR. Subsequent reports identified the ACMHR source as Vice President Ed Gardner but yielded no indication of the identity of the anonymous informant. Although eventually naming Gardner as their ACMHR

source, these reports remained unsigned. Regarding Shuttlesworth's complaints to Gardner, see Anonymous Memo, June 4, 1964, Demonstrations File, Police Surveillance Files, BPL.

53. Anonymous Memo, June 4, 1964, Demonstrations File, Police Surveillance Files, BPL; Gaston to Boutwell, May 2, 1964, Boutwell Papers, box 15, folder 42.

54. Abraham L. Woods Jr., interview, June 25, 1991; Fred Shuttlesworth, interview, June 4–7, 1990.

55. Fred Shuttlesworth, "The National Civil Rights Crisis and Our Relationship to It," Eighth Annual President's Address to the ACMHR, June 5, 1964, Shuttlesworth Papers, box 1, folder 1; *Atlanta Daily World,* June 9, 1964, 2.

56. Anonymous Memo, June 5, 1964, Demonstrations File, Police Surveillance Files, BPL; *NYT,* June 19, 1964, 1, 16 (quotation).

57. *Cincinnati Post and Times-Star,* June 27, 1964, 3; Fred Shuttlesworth, interview, June 4–7, 1990; Vivian, interview, 1–2; Vivian, telephone interview, October 15, 1998.

58. *NYT,* July 3, 1964, 1, 9; Rowland Evans and Robert Novak, "Birmingham—Keeping Our Fingers Crossed," *New Republic,* July 1964, 17–18; Fred Shuttlesworth, interview, June 4–7, 1990.

59. Garrow, *Bearing the Cross,* 354–55, 357, 364; Anonymous Police Report, January 15, 1965, Hamilton Papers, box 4, folder 1; Fred Shuttlesworth, interview, June 4–7, 1990. In the interview Shuttlesworth indicated that his ACMHR board members were also bothered by what they viewed as an affront to their leader. Ed Gardner, who provided information to the Birmingham Police Department's anonymous informant, was, of course, privy to discussions at board meetings and was in a position to hear Shuttlesworth complain about the episode. See Anonymous Police Report, February 16, 1965, Hamilton Papers, box 4, folder 1. In this report, the informant reveals Ed Gardner as his source.

60. Demonstrations File, January 1965, Police Surveillance Files, BPL; *Cincinnati Herald,* February 6, 1965, 1, 8.

61. Fred Shuttlesworth, interview, June 4–7, 1990.

62. *Cincinnati Post and Times-Star,* February 5, 1965.

63. *Cincinnati Enquirer,* February 11, 1965, 24; Anonymous Police Report, February 11, 1965, Hamilton Papers, box 4, folder 1; FBI file 100-106670-24.

64. *Cincinnati Post and Times-Star,* March 9, 1965, 5; Fred Shuttlesworth, Statement to the Press, March 8, 1965, Shuttlesworth Papers, box 4, folder 47.

65. *Cincinnati Herald,* March 13, 1965, 1.

66. Fred Shuttlesworth, interview, May 29–June 1, 1990; Fred Shuttlesworth, interview, June 4–7, 1990; Fairclough, *To Redeem the Soul,* 243–46.

67. Fred Shuttlesworth, interview, June 4–7, 1990; *Cincinnati Enquirer,* March 12, 1965, 1; *Cincinnati Herald,* March 20, 1965, 1, 7; Fred Shuttlesworth, "Address at Sympathy and Memorial March for James Reeb," March 15, 1965, Shuttlesworth Papers, box 4,

folder 42. "Statement Adopted at Birmingham Mass Memorial Service for Jimmy Lee Jackson and Rev. James Reeb," March 16, 1965, and Shuttlesworth to Boutwell, March 17, 1965, both in Boutwell Papers, box 15, folder 41.

68. Fred Shuttlesworth, interview, June 4–7, 1990.

69. *Cincinnati Herald,* May 23, 1964, 7; *Cincinnati Enquirer,* March 9, 1965, 4; *Cincinnati Herald,* March 27, 1965, 1.

70. Shuttlesworth to Trustees of Revelation Baptist Church, June 23, 1965, in Shuttlesworth Papers, box 2, folder 10.

71. Fred Shuttlesworth, interview, October 27–31, 1988.

72. Ibid.; *Cincinnati Post,* August 27, 1965, 7.

73. Fred Shuttlesworth, News Release, August 15, 1965, Shuttlesworth Papers, box 4, folder 10; *Cincinnati Enquirer,* August 16, 1965, 1; *Cincinnati Post and Times-Star,* August 16, 1965, 4.

74. *Cincinnati Herald,* August 21, 1965, 1, 9; *Time,* September 3, 1965, 71 (quotations).

75. *Cincinnati Enquirer,* August 18, 1965, 9; *Cincinnati Enquirer,* August 19, 1965, 5; Mrs. Lovie M. Lowe to Martin Luther King Jr., telegram, SCLC Papers, box 22, folder 13; *Cincinnati Post and Times-Star,* August 17, 1965, 7; *Cincinnati Enquirer,* August 18, 1965, 9.

76. *Cincinnati Post,* August 20, 1965, 32; *Cincinnati Enquirer,* August 20, 1965, 12; *Cincinnati Post,* August 21, 1965, 2; *Cincinnati Enquirer,* August 23, 1965, 25; *Cincinnati Post,* August 23, 1965, 4; Martin Luther King Jr. to Mrs. Lovie M. Lowe, telegram, August 23, 1965, SCLC Papers, box 22, folder 13.

77. Fred Shuttlesworth, News Release, August 24, 1965, Shuttlesworth Papers, box 4; *Cincinnati Enquirer,* August 26, 1965, 10; *Cincinnati Post,* August 27, 1965, 1; *Cincinnati Post,* August 27, 1965, 7 (quotations); *Cincinnati Post,* August 30, 1965, 1; Report of Audit of Revelation Baptist Church Finances, September 28, 1965, Shuttlesworth Papers, box 2, folder 14.

78. Edward Gardner and Georgia Price to Chairmen of Deacon and Trustees Boards of Revelation Baptist Church, October 2, 1965, Boutwell Papers, box 15, folder 41; Shuttlesworth Papers, box 1, folder 6.

79. *Cincinnati Post,* October 8, 1965, 47; News Release, October 8, 1965, Boutwell Papers, box 15, folder 41; *Southern Patriot* 23 (November 1965): 2; *Cincinnati Post,* November 24, 1965, 3; *Cincinnati Enquirer,* October 18, 1965, 18; "Statement by Youth and Young Adults," *Cincinnati Herald,* October 16, 1965, 1; see also Shuttlesworth Papers, box 2, folder 17.

80. *Cincinnati Herald,* November 6, 1965, 1; *Cincinnati Enquirer,* November 5, 1965, 1; *Cincinnati Post,* November 5, 1965, 1; *Cincinnati Herald,* November 13, 1965, 1, 9; *Cincinnati Enquirer,* November 7, 1965, 6A.

81. *Cincinnati Herald,* November 13, 1965, 2.

82. *Cincinnati Enquirer,* December 2, 1965, 4; James Adams, "Shuttlesworth Blames Troubles on Right Wing," *Cincinnati Post,* December 3, 1965, 68; Booth, interview.

83. Florence Livers, Mary Patterson, et al., Statement, December 29, 1965, Shuttlesworth Papers, box 2 (supporters' quotations); Mortgage Burning Day Program, July 28, 1968, Shuttlesworth Papers, box 1, folder 17; Shuttlesworth to Revelation Baptist Church, January 19, 1966, Shuttlesworth Papers, box 2 (Shuttlesworth quotations); *Cincinnati Herald,* January 22, 1966, 1, 8; *Cincinnati Post,* January 10, 1966, 5; NYT, January 11, 1966, 10; *Cincinnati Herald,* January 15, 1966, 1, 8.

84. *Cincinnati Post,* January 17, 1966, 4; *Cincinnati Enquirer,* January 17, 1966, 8; *Cincinnati Herald,* January 22, 1966, 1, 8; Fred Shuttlesworth, "Annual Message to the ACMHR," June 6, 1966, Shuttlesworth Papers, box 1, folder 1; *Cincinnati Herald,* December 24, 1966, 1.

85. NYT, January 5, 1965, 12.

86. *Cincinnati Herald,* June 25, 1966, 2, 7; Fred Shuttlesworth, interview, June 4–7, 1990.

87. *Southern Patriot* 24 (August 1966): 1; Lucinda Robey, Mrs. Dester Brooks, and Edward Gardner, ACMHR News Release, October 20, 1966, Shuttlesworth Papers, box 1, folder 14; *Cincinnati Herald,* October 29, 1966, 1, 8.

88. Report, February 28, 1967, Demonstrations File, Police Surveillance Files, BPL. Although Shuttlesworth later denied any rift with Lowery, evidence suggests a rather significant one. Anonymous police reports derived through Gardner's connections in the police department give ample evidence of Shuttlesworth's sometimes harsh feelings toward Lowery and the intelligentsia who preferred Lowery's leadership style to his own. See Anonymous Police Report, February 28, 1967, Hamilton Papers, box 3, folder 28.

89. Fred Shuttlesworth, "Statewide Civil Rights Leaders Meeting on Law Enforcement," March 13, 1967, Hamilton Papers, box 3, folder 24; Fred Shuttlesworth, "Thirteenth Annual Message to the ACMHR," June 2, 1969, Shuttlesworth Papers, box 1, folder 1.

90. *Cincinnati Herald,* June 25, 1966, 1, 6.

91. *Cincinnati Herald,* July 2, 1966, 1, 3; *Cincinnati Herald,* July 23, 1966, 11; *Cincinnati Enquirer,* July 31, 1966, 6A; *Cincinnati Herald,* August 6, 1966, 1, 9.

92. NYT, June 14, 1967, 1, 34.

93. NYT, June 25, 1967, 1, 34.

94. NYT, June 15, 1967, 1, 34.

95. Fred Shuttlesworth, interview, October 10, 1987, 37–38 (quotations); Booth, interview, n. p.

96. NYT, July 10, 1967. Regarding the "Rabble Rouser Index," it is well known that the FBI kept a close eye on American civil rights leaders, watching carefully for inflammatory rhetoric. A bureau letter dated August 18, 1967, still listed Shuttles-

worth on its "Rabble Rouser Index." Another undated letter appearing in FBI surveillance files shortly thereafter reported: "This individual does not qualify for RRI. The file does not contain any information indicating he has made any speeches or statements that would . . . influence his audience with racial hatred." See FBI file 157-417.

97. Powledge, *Free at Last*, 646–47 (first quotation); *Cincinnati Enquirer*, June 17, 1979, B6 (second quotation); *Cincinnati Enquirer*, June 2, 1979.

98. *Cincinnati Enquirer*, June 28, 1979, B1 (quotation); idem, July 29, 1979, B1; *Cincinnati Enquirer*, October 30, 1979, B1.

99. *Cincinnati Enquirer*, June 20, 1981, D3; *Cincinnati Post*, June 19, 1981, B3; *Cincinnati Post*, June 20, 1981, A7 (quotations).

100. *Cincinnati Post*, June 20, 1981, A7; *Cincinnati Enquirer*, January 26, 1983, A2; Shuttlesworth, "Address on Martin Luther King Jr. Week of Peace," Xavier University, New Orleans, Louisiana, January 20, 1988.

101. "SOC: A Southwide Network of Activists against Racism, War, and Economic Injustice," pamphlet, Southern Organizing Committee Papers, personal collection of Anne Braden, Louisville, Kentucky, copies in author's files.

102. *Cincinnati Enquirer*, May 29, 1982, D1.

103. *Cincinnati Enquirer*, March 13, 1989, A9; *Cincinnati Enquirer*, March 13, 1989, A9; Fred Shuttlesworth, interview, May 22–25, 1990; *Cincinnati Enquirer*, June 18, 1993, B2.

104. Fred Shuttlesworth, interview, October 27–31, 1988; Eugene Shuttlesworth, interview, March 6, 1993.

105. Massengill, interview; Bester, interview.

106. Fred Shuttlesworth, interview, October 27–31, 1988; Eugene Shuttlesworth, interview, March 6, 1993.

107. Fred Shuttlesworth, interview, October 27–31, 1988.

108. Ibid.

109. Harold Bester, interview, January 12, 1989, 11–12; Fred Shuttlesworth, interview, October 27–31, 1988.

110. *Cincinnati Enquirer*, April 29, 1970, cited in FBI file CI 157-3876; Fred Shuttlesworth, interview, October 27–31, 1988; Massengill, interview; *Cincinnati Post*, February 2, 1971; *Cincinnati Enquirer*, February 2, 1971; SCEF, News Release, February 11, 1971, all in clipping file, Schomberg Center for Black Culture, New York, New York.

111. Personal observation of author.

Epilogue

1. The concept of "sacred time" is common in the history of religious methodology. See especially Mircea Eliade, *The Sacred and the Profane: The Nature of Religion*

(New York: Harcourt, Brace and World, 1957), 20–67; and Mircea Eliade, *Myth and Reality* (New York: Harper and Row, 1963), 21–38.

2. *Cincinnati Enquirer,* March 21, 1978, B1.

3. Flip Schulke and Penelope McPhee, *King Remembered* (New York: W. W. Norton, 1986), 254; *Cincinnati Post and Times-Star,* cited in FBI file 17-9342-52; "A Blueprint for Living or a Pattern for Dying," Shuttlesworth Papers, box 4, folder 26.

4. Sample of awards from plaques and citations on the walls of Shuttlesworth's office at the Greater New Light Baptist Church, Cincinnati, Ohio.

5. *Cincinnati Enquirer,* September 23, 1978, D1; *NYT,* June 26, 1978; *BPH,* September 25, 1978; *Cincinnati Enquirer,* September 25, 1978, D2; Report of Conference on Civil Rights and Social Change, University of Alabama at Birmingham, November 15, 1978, cited in *NYT,* November 16, 1978, 20; Vann, "Change from Commission," 41.

6. Author's memory of Shuttlesworth's visit to the Southern Baptist Theological Seminary, November 10, 1978. Audiotape of speech in author's possession and in Audio-Visual Department of Boyce Library, Southern Baptist Theological Seminary, Louisville, Kentucky.

7. Author's memory of Shuttlesworth's activities during a visit to Xavier University of Louisiana, February 20, 1988. Audiotape in author's possession.

8. *BPH,* August 17, 1988, 1; *BPH,* August 17, 1988.

9. Fred L. Shuttlesworth, telephone interview, February 5, 1998; Marvin Whiting, telephone interview, February 5, 1998.

10. Bill J. Leonard, telephone interview, February 5, 1998. Leonard, a former member of Porter's church and dean of the Divinity School, Wake Forest University, reported that Porter told this story in a fall 1998 chapel address at Wake Forest.

11. *Cincinnati Enquirer,* November 10, 1992; *Cincinnati Post,* November 13, 1992, 1A, 6A; Fred Shuttlesworth, telephone interview, February 5, 1998; Whiting, telephone interview.

12. Home videotape, copy in author's possession.

Bibliography

MANUSCRIPT COLLECTIONS

Anti-Defamation League. Papers. Birmingham Public Library.
Boutwell, Albert. Papers. Birmingham Public Library.
Connor, T. Eugene "Bull." Papers. Birmingham Public Library.
Hamilton, William. Papers. Birmingham Public Library.
Kennedy, Robert F. Papers. John Fitzgerald Kennedy Library. Boston.
King, Martin Luther, Jr. Papers. Martin Luther King Jr. Center for Nonviolent Social Change. Atlanta.
——. Papers. Special Collections Department, Mugar Library, Boston University.
Marshall, Burke. Papers. John Fitzgerald Kennedy Library. Boston.
Morgan, James W. "Jimmie." Papers. Birmingham Public Library.
Police Surveillance Files. Birmingham Public Library.
Shores, Arthur D. Papers. Archives. Talladega College, Talladega, Alabama.
Shortridge, William E. Papers. Pinky Shortridge private collection. Birmingham.
Shuttlesworth, Fred L. Papers. Martin Luther King Jr. Center for Nonviolent Social Change. Atlanta.
Smiley, Glenn E. Papers. Fellowship of Reconciliation Peace Collection, Swarthmore College, Pennsylvania.
Southern Christian Leadership Conference. Papers. Martin Luther King Jr. Center for Nonviolent Social Change. Atlanta.
Southern Regional Council. Archives. Woodruff Library, Atlanta University Center.
——. Papers, Birmingham Public Library.
Vann, David. Papers. Birmingham Public Library.

INTERVIEWS

Interviews in Collections

Cross, John. Interview by Judy Barton, March 23, 1972. Oral History Program, Martin Luther King Jr. Center for Nonviolent Social Change, Atlanta.

King, Martin Luther, Jr. Interview by Berl I. Bernhard, March 9, 1964. Oral History Program, John F. Kennedy Library, Boston.

Marshall, Burke. Interview by Anthony Lewis, June 13 and 20, 1964. John F. Kennedy Oral History Collection, John F. Kennedy Library, Boston.

Patterson, John. Interview by Jack Bass and Walter DeVries, July 12, 1974. Southern Oral History Program, Southern History Collection, Manuscript Department, University of North Carolina, Chapel Hill.

———. Interview by John Stewart Montgomery, May 26, 1967. John F. Kennedy Library, Boston.

Shores, Arthur. Interview by Jack Bass, July 17, 1974. Southern Oral History Program, Southern History Collection, Manuscript Department, University of North Carolina, Chapel Hill.

Shuttlesworth, Fred L. Interview by Joyce Ladner, November 19, 1969, and March 17, 1970. Oral History Program, Martin Luther King Jr. Center for Nonviolent Social Change, Atlanta.

———. Interview by James Mosby, September 1968. Ralph Bunche Oral History Collection, Moorland-Spingarn Research Center, Howard University, Washington, D.C.

Sitton, Claude. Interview by Jack Bass, December 11, 1974. Southern Oral History Program, Southern History Collection, Manuscript Department, University of North Carolina, Chapel Hill.

Walker, Wyatt Tee. Interview by John Britton, October 11, 1967. Moorland-Spingarn Research Center, Howard University, Washington, D.C.

Woods, Abraham L., Jr., and Pugh, Addie. Interview, October 28, 1975. Oral History Collection, Department of History, University of Alabama at Birmingham.

Interviews by Author

Adams, Oscar, July 31, 1991

Alford, R. L., August 9, 1990

Anderson, Lewis L., August 7, 1987

Armstrong, James, August 9, 1990

Bester, Ricky Shuttlesworth, October 30, 1988

Booth, L. Venchael, June 4, 1990

Braden, Anne, October 29, 1988

Brown, Alexander, February 27, 1993

Burroughs, Malcolm, September 16, 1994

Chestnut, J. L., December 27, 1989

Chilcoat, Wallace, April 4, 1993

Cleveland, Alvin, September 16, 1994

Davis, Reuben, August 3, 1987

Drew, John, December 29, 1988

Dukes, Frank, December 28, 1988

Durant, Vivian, July 30, 1987

Echols, Thurman, April 4, 1994

Farmer, James, May 5, 1993

Flemmon, Veronica Chappell, August 5, 1987

Gardner, Edward, February 28, 1987; August 9, 1990

Gaston, Carter, February 28, 1987

Gooden, Phyllis, August 5, 1987

Hendricks, Lola, August 3, 1989

Jimerson, Norman, June 13, 1989

Johnson, Colonel Stone, July 31, 1991

Lane, Terry Lee, January 12, 1989

Leonard, Bill, February 5, 1998

Long, Harold, April 8, 1989

Lowery, Joseph, July 29, 1991

MacPherson, Jonathan, August 4, 1989

Martin, Laverne Revis McWilliams, August 7, 1990

Massengill, Patricia Shuttlesworth, October 29, 1988

Mitchell, Eula Mae, April 7, 1989

Montgomery, James, August 4, 1989

Morgan, Charles, May 24, 1989

Nash, Diane, March 4, 1989

Oliver, C. Herbert, March 2, 1989

Orange, James, June 21, 1991

Porter, John T., February 28, 1987

Rainge, Julia, August 6, 1987

Roberson, James, August 2, 1989

Shortridge, Pinky, August 3, 1989

Shuttlesworth, Clifton, February 4, 1989

Shuttlesworth, Eugene, March 6, 1993; May 28, 1993

Shuttlesworth, Fred, March 10, 1984; October 10, 1987; October 27–31, 1988; January 11–12, 1989; March 20, 1990; March 24, 1990; May 22–25, 1990; May 29–June 1, 1990; June 4–7, 1990; June 17, 1991; February 15, 1995; February 5, 1998

Shuttlesworth, Fred, Jr., January 13, 1989

Sloan, Daphne, May 30, 1990

Smiley, Glenn, February 28, 1989

Smith, Nelson H., December 29, 1988

Vann, David, August 7, 1990

Vivian, C. T., December 27, 1989; October 15, 1998

Walker, Wyatt T., April 20, 1989

Whiting, Marvin, February 5, 1998

Williams, Betty, December 28, 1988

Willis, Cleola, December 28, 1988

Wimberly, Louretta, September 19, 1994; October 3, 1994; October 5, 1994

Winston, Daisy, July 31, 1987

Woods, Abraham L., Jr., December 30, 1988; June 25, 1991

Woods, Calvin, December 28, 1988

NEWSPAPERS

Akron Beacon Journal, 1957

Alabama Journal, 1956, 1960

Atlanta Constitution, 1962

Atlanta Daily World, 1964

Atlanta Journal, 1956

Baltimore Afro-American, 1962, 1963

Birmingham News, 1943, 1955–63, 1988

Birmingham Post-Herald, 1951, 1953, 1955, 1956, 1960–63, 1978, 1988

Birmingham World, 1951, 1952, 1955–60, 1962, 1963

Canton Repository, 1964

Chattanooga Times, 1957, 1960

Chicago Daily Defender, 1957, 1962

Christian Science Monitor, 1956–58, 1962, 1963

Cincinnati Enquirer, 1963, 1965, 1966, 1971, 1978–83, 1988, 1989, 1992, 1993

Cincinnati Herald, 1961, 1963–66

Cincinnati Post, 1965, 1966, 1971, 1981, 1992

Cincinnati Post and Times-Star, 1963–65

Cleveland Courier, 1962

Daily Worker, 1956, 1961

Delta Democrat-Times, 1962

Greensboro Daily News, 1960

Houston Chronicle, 1961

Jackson Daily News, 1962

Louisville Courier-Journal, 1961

Louisville Defender, 1959

Mobile Press Register, 1961

Mobile Register, 1956, 1958

Montgomery Advertiser, 1956–63

Nashville Banner, 1958

Nashville Tennessean, 1957–59

National Guardian, 1960

New York Courier, 1957

New York Times, 1943, 1956–58, 1960–67, 1978, 1980

Norfolk Journal and Guide, 1956

Pittsburgh Courier, 1961, 1963

Richmond Times-Dispatch, 1957

St. Louis Post-Dispatch, 1963

Washington News, 1956

Washington Post, 1956, 1961, 1963

Washington Star, 1956

BOOKS, ARTICLES, AND OTHER PUBLICATIONS

Abernathy, Ralph David. *And the Walls Came Tumbling Down: An Autobiography.* New York: Harper and Row, 1989.

Adams, James. "Shuttlesworth Blames Troubles on Right Wing." *Cincinnati Post,* December 3, 1965.

Adorno, T. W., ed. *The Authoritarian Personality.* New York: Harper, 1950.

Alabama Christian Movement for Human Rights. *People in Motion.* Louisville, Ky.: Southern Conference Educational Fund, 1966.

———. "People in Motion: The Story of the Birmingham Movement." In *Black Protest: History, Documents, and Analyses,* edited by Joanne Grant. Greenwich, Conn.: Fawcett Books, 1968.

———. *They Challenge Segregation At Its Core!* Birmingham, Ala.: Southern Conference Educational Fund, 1959.

Anderson, James D. *The Education of Blacks in the South, 1860–1935.* Chapel Hill: University of North Carolina Press, 1988.

Anderson, Trezzvant. "Birmingham's Big Need." *Pittsburgh Courier,* October 17, 1959.

Bartley, Numan V. *The Rise of Massive Resistance: Race and Politics in the South during the 1950s.* Baton Rouge: Louisiana State University Press, 1969.

Baumrind, D. "An Exploratory Study of Socialization Effects on Black Children: Some Black-White Comparison." *Child Development* 43 (1972): 261–67.

Bell, Charles G. "Battle Hymn in Birmingham." *Nation,* May 4, 1963, 370–73.

Bennett, Lerone, Jr. *Before the Mayflower: A History of Black America.* 5th ed. New York: Penguin Books, 1982.

———. *The Negro Mood.* Chicago: Johnson, 1964.

"Birmingham, Alabama: South's Toughest City." *Crusader* 1 (November 1959).

"Birmingham and Beyond." *New South* 18 (October–November 1963).

Bishop, Jim. *The Days of Martin Luther King.* New York: Putnam, 1971.

Bloom, Jack M. *Class, Race, and the Civil Rights Movement.* Bloomington: Indiana University Press, 1984.

Blumberg, Rhoda L. *Civil Rights: The 1960s Freedom Struggle.* Boston: Hall, 1984.

Boothe, Charles Octavius. *The Cyclopedia of the Colored Baptists of Alabama.* Birmingham: Alabama Publishing Company, 1895.

Boylan, James. "Birmingham: Newspapers in a Crisis." *Columbia Journalism Review* (summer 1963): 29–32.

Braden, Anne. "The History That We Made: Birmingham, 1956–1979." *Southern Exposure* 7 (summer 1979): 48–54.

———. "The Southern Freedom Movement in Perspective." *Monthly Review* 17 (1965): 1–93.

———. "The White Southerner in the Integration Struggle." *Freedomways* 3 (winter 1963): 19–27.

Brady, Thomas Pickens. *Black Monday.* Winonah, Miss.: Association of Citizens Councils, 1955.

Branch, Taylor. *Parting the Waters: America in the King Years, 1954–1963.* New York: Simon and Schuster, 1988.

Brown, Joe David. "Birmingham, Alabama: A City in Fear." *Saturday Evening Post,* March 2 1963, 11–19.

Brownell, Blaine A. "Birmingham, Alabama: New South City in the 1920s." *Journal of Southern History* 38 (1972): 21–48.

Burran, James A. "Urban Racial Violence in the South during World War II: A Comparative Overview." In *From the Old South to the New: Essays on the Transitional South,* edited by Walter J. Fraser Jr. and Winfred B. Moore Jr. Westport, Conn.: Greenwood Press, 1981.

Cagin, Seth, and Philip Dray. *We Are Not Afraid: The Story of Goodman, Schwerner, and Chaney and the Civil Rights Campaign for Mississippi.* New York: Macmillan, 1988.

Campbell, Will B. *Forty Acres and a Goat: A Memoir.* San Francisco: Harper and Row, 1986.

Carson, Clayborne. *The Eyes on the Prize Reader.* New York: Penguin Books, 1991.

Carter, Dan T. *The Politics of Rage: George Wallace, the Origins of the New Conservatism, and the Transformation of American Politics.* New York: Simon and Schuster, 1995.

Chestnut, J. L., and Julia Cass. *Black in Selma: The Uncommon Life of J. L. Chestnut Jr.* New York: Anchor Books, 1990.

Childs, John B. *The Political Black Minister: A Study in Afro-American Politics and Religion.* Boston: G. K. Hall, 1980.

Clarke, Jacquelyne Johnson. "Goals and Techniques in Three Civil Rights Organizations in Alabama." Ph.D. diss., Ohio State University, 1960.

Cleghorn, Reese. "Bustling Birmingham." *New Republic,* April 20, 1963.

Cone, James H. *The Spirituals and the Blues: An Interpretation.* New York: Seabury, 1972.

Congressional Quarterly. *Congress and the Nation, 1945–1964.* Washington, D.C.: Congressional Quarterly Service, 1965.

Connor, T. Eugene. "Communists in Birmingham." *Alabama Local Government* (August 1950).

Corley, Robert Gaines. "The Quest for Racial Harmony: Race Relations in Birmingham, Alabama, 1947–1963." In *Southern Businessmen and Desegregation,* edited by Elizabeth Jacoway and David R. Colburn. Baton Rouge: Louisiana State University Press, 1982.

———. "The Quest for Racial Harmony: Race Relations in Birmingham, Alabama, 1947–1963." Ph.D. diss., University of Virginia, 1979.

Cort, David. "The Voices of Birmingham." *Nation*, July 27, 1963, 46–48.

Cotman, John Walton. *Birmingham, JFK, and the Civil Rights Act of 1963: Implications for Elite Theory*. New York: Peter Lang, 1989.

Crain, Robert, and Gerald McWhorter. "Subcommunity Gladiatorial Competition: Civil Rights Leadership as the Competitive Process." *Social Forces* 46 (1967): 8–21.

Dalfiume, Richard M. "The Forgotten Years of the Negro Revolution." *Journal of American History* 55 (1968): 90–106.

Dellinger, Dave. "The Negroes of Birmingham." *Liberation* 8 (summer 1963): 17–21.

Deming, Barbara. "Editor Repo[r]ts Children's Revolution in Alabama." *Liberation* 8 (1963): 5.

———. "Notes after Birmingham." *Liberation* 8 (1963): 13.

Dismuke, Otis, and Jeff [Robert J] Norrell. *The Other Side: The Story of Birmingham's Black Community*. Birmingham: Birmingfind, n.d.

Dorman, Michael. *We Shall Overcome*. New York: Delacorte, 1964.

Elbow, M. "Children of Violent Marriages: The Forgotten Victims." *Social Casework* 63 (1982): 460–69.

Eliade, Mircea. *Myth and Reality*. New York: Harper and Row, 1963.

———. *The Sacred and the Profane: The Nature of Religion*. New York: Harcourt, Brace and World, 1957.

Eskew, Glenn T. "The Alabama Christian Movement and the Birmingham Struggle for Civil Rights, 1956–63." Thesis, University of Georgia, 1987.

———. *But for Birmingham: The Local and National Movements in the Civil Rights Struggle*. Chapel Hill: University of North Carolina Press, 1997.

Eslinger, Richard L. *A New Hearing: Living Options in Homilectic Method*. Nashville: Abingdon Press, 1987.

Evans, James H., Jr. *We Have Been Believers: An African-American Systematic Theology*. Minneapolis: Fortress Press, 1992.

Evans, Rowland, and Robert Novak. "Birmingham: Keeping Our Fingers Crossed." *New Republic*, July 1964.

Fairclough, Adam. "The Preachers and the People." *Journal of Southern History* 52 (1986): 403–40.

———. *To Redeem the Soul of America: The Southern Christian Leadership Conference and Martin Luther King Jr*. Athens: University of Georgia Press, 1987.

Farmer, James. *Lay Bare the Heart: An Autobiography of the Civil Rights Movement*. New York: Arbor, 1985.

Fey, Harold E. "King Demands Negro Policemen: Birmingham." *Christian Century* 80 (1963): 1294.

Flynt, J. Wayne. "The Ethics of Democratic Persuasion and the Birmingham Crisis." *Southern Speech Journal* 35 (1969): 40–53.

Forman, James. *The Making of Black Revolutionaries.* New York: Macmillan, 1972.

Fowler, James. *Stages of Faith: The Psychology of Human Development and the Quest for Meaning.* San Francisco: Harper and Row, 1981.

Franklin, John Hope. *From Slavery to Freedom: A History of Negro Americans.* 5th ed. New York: Alfred A. Knopf, 1980.

———. *The Militant South.* Cambridge: Harvard University Press, Belknap Press, 1956.

Frazier, E. Franklin. *Black Bourgeoisie: The Rise of a New Middle Class.* New York: Free Press, 1957.

———. *The Negro Church in America.* New York: Schocken Books, 1964.

"A Freedom Rider's Story: Incident in Alabama." *New York Post Magazine,* May 15, 1961, 6.

Fulton, Robert B. "Grounds for Hope in Birmingham." *Christian Century,* August 12, 1964, 1012–13.

Garrow, David J. *Bearing the Cross: Martin Luther King Jr. and the Southern Christian Leadership Conference.* New York: William Morrow, 1986.

———, ed. *Birmingham, Alabama, 1956–1963: The Black Struggle for Civil Rights.* Brooklyn: Carlson, 1989.

Gaston, Arthur G. *Green Power: The Successful Way of A. G. Gaston.* Birmingham: Birmingham Publishing Co., 1968.

Gavins, Raymond. *The Perils and Prospects of Black Southern Leadership: Gordon Blaine Hancock, 1884–1970.* Durham: Duke University Press, 1977.

Gelles, Richard J. *Family Violence.* Beverly Hills, Calif.: Sage Publications, 1979.

———. *The Violent Home: A Study of Physical Aggression between Husbands and Wives.* Beverly Hills, Calif.: Sage Publications, 1974.

Gelles, Richard J., and Claire Pedrick Cornell. *Intimate Violence in Families.* 2d ed. Newbury Park, Calif.: Sage Publications, 1990.

Good, Paul. "Birmingham Two Years Later." *Reporter* 33 (1965): 21–27.

Graham, Hugh Davis. *The Civil Rights Era: Origins and Development of National Policy.* New York: Oxford University Press, 1990.

Grant, Joanne, ed. *Black Protest: History, Documents, and Analyses.* Greenwich, Conn.: Faucett, 1968.

Gregory, Joel C. *Too Great a Temptation: The Seductive Power of America's Super Church*. Fort Worth, Tex.: Summit Group, 1994.

Grigsby, Marshall C. "The Public Roles of the Black Churches: Education as a Political Problem." *Criterion* 14 (1975).

Guthman, Edwin. *We Band of Brothers*. New York: Harper and Row, 1964.

Gutwillig, Robert. "Six Days in Alabama." *Mademoiselle* 57 (September 1963).

Haizlip, Shirlee Taylor. *The Sweeter the Juice*. New York: Simon and Schuster, 1994.

Hamilton, Charles V. *The Black Preacher in America*. New York: Morrow, 1972.

Hampton, Henry, and Steve Fayer, eds. *Voices of Freedom: An Oral History of the Civil Rights Movement from the 1950s through the 1980s*. New York: Bantam Books, 1990.

Hampton, Robert, ed. *Black Family Violence: Current Research and Theory*. New York: Lexington Books, 1991.

Harding, Vincent. "A Beginning in Birmingham." *Reporter* 28 (1963): 13–19.

Hardy, Alister. *The Spiritual Nature of Man: A Study of Contemporary Religious Experience*. Oxford: Clarendon Press, 1979.

Harris, Carl V. *Political Power in Birmingham, 1871–1921*. Knoxville: University of Tennessee Press, 1977.

———. "Reforms in Government Control of Negroes in Birmingham, Alabama, 1890–1920." *Journal of Southern History* 38 (1972): 567–600.

Harris, Forrest E., Sr. *Ministry for Social Crisis: Theology and Praxis in the Black Church Tradition*. Macon, Ga.: Mercer University Press, 1993.

Harris, James H. *Black Ministers and Laity in the Urban Church*. Lanham, Md.: University Press of America, 1987.

———. *Pastoral Theology: A Black Church Perspective*. Minneapolis: Fortress Press, 1991.

Hess, R. D., et al. *The Cognitive Environments of Urban Preschool Children: Report to the Children's Bureau, U.S. Department of Health, Education, and Welfare*. Washington, D.C.: Government Printing Office, 1968.

Hicks, H. Beecher, Jr. *Images of the Black Preacher*. Valley Forge, Penn.: Judson Press, 1977.

Higginbotham, Evelyn Brooks. *Righteous Discontent: The Women's Movement in the Black Baptist Church, 1880–1920*. Cambridge: Harvard University Press, 1993.

Holt, Len. *An Act of Conscience*. Boston: Beacon Press, 1965.

———. "Birmingham Demonstration, 1963." In *Black Protest: History, Docu-*

ments, and Analyses, edited by Joanne Grant. Greenwich, Conn.: Faucett, 1968.

"Interview with Martin Luther King Jr." *Playboy,* January 1965. Reprint.

Jacoway, Elizabeth, and David R. Calburn, eds. *Southern Businessmen and Desegregation.* Baton Rouge: Louisiana State University Press, 1982.

James, William. *The Varieties of Religious Experience.* Cambridge: Harvard University Press, 1985.

Johnson, Charles S. *Growing Up in the Black Belt.* New York: Schocken, 1967.

Jones, Lewis W. "Fred L. Shuttlesworth, Indigenous Leader." In *Birmingham, Alabama, 1956–1963: The Black Struggle for Civil Rights,* edited by David J. Garrow. Brooklyn: Carlson, 1989.

Killian, Lewis, and Charles Smith. "Negro Protest Leaders in a Southern Community." *Social Forces* 38 (1960): 253–57.

King, Coretta Scott. *My Life With Martin Luther King Jr.* New York: Holt, 1969.

King, Martin Luther, Jr. *Stride toward Freedom: The Montgomery Story.* New York: Harper and Row, 1958.

——. *The Trumpet of Conscience.* New York: Harper and Row, 1968.

——. *Why We Can't Wait.* New York: New American Library, 1964.

"Klans and Councils." *New Republic,* September 23, 1957.

Klibaner, Irwin. "The Travail of Southern Radicals: The Southern Conference Educational Fund, 1946–1976." *Journal of Southern History* 49 (1983): 179–202.

Kluger, Richard. *Simple Justice: The History of Brown v. Board of Education and Black America's Struggle for Equality.* New York: Vintage, 1975.

Kunstler, William M. *Deep in My Heart.* New York: Morrow, 1966.

Ladd, Everett C., Jr. *Negro Political Leadership in the South.* New York: Atheneum, 1969.

Lassiter, Ruby F. "Child Rearing in Black Families: Child-Abusing Discipline." In *Violence in the Black Family: Correlates and Consequences,* edited by Robert L. Hampton. Lexington, Mass.: Lexington Books, 1987.

Lawson, James M. "The Man Who Escaped the Cross." *Fellowship* 25 (November 1959): 10–12.

Leighton, George R. "Birmingham: City of Perpetual Promise." *Harper's,* August 1937, 225–42.

Levine, Ellen, ed. *Freedom's Children: Young Civil Rights Activists Tell Their Own Stories.* New York: G. P. Putnam's Sons, 1993.

Lewis, Anthony. *Make No Law: The Sullivan Case and the First Amendment.* New York: Random House, 1991.

———. "Robert F. Kennedy Interview." In *Robert Kennedy: In His Own Words: The Unpublished Recollections of the Kennedy Years,* edited by Edwin O. Guthman and Jeffrey Shulman. New York: Bantam Books, 1988.

Lewis, David Levering. *King: A Critical Biography.* New York: Praeger, 1970.

Lincoln, C. Eric. "Key Man in the South: The Negro Minister." *New York Times Magazine,* July 12, 1964, 20.

Lincoln, C. Eric, and Lawrence Mamiya. *The Black Church and the African American Experience.* Durham: Duke University Press, 1990.

Manis, Andrew Michael. *Southern Civil Religions in Conflict: Black and White Baptists and Civil Rights, 1947–1957.* Athens: University of Georgia Press, 1987.

Marable, Manning. *Race, Reform and Rebellion: The Second Reconstruction in Black America.* Jackson: University Press of Mississippi, 1984.

Massey, Floyd, Jr., and Samuel B. McKinney. *Church Administration in the Black Perspective.* Valley Forge, Penn.: Judson Press, 1976.

Mayfield, Henry O. "Memoirs of a Coal Miner." *Freedomways* (winter 1964): 53.

Mays, Benjamin E., and Joseph Nicholson. *The Negro's Church.* New York: Institute of Social and Religious Research, 1933.

McGraw, James R. "An Interview with Andrew J. Young." *Christianity and Crisis* 27 (1968): 324–30.

McGrory, Mary. "'Big Mules' Shun Problem." *Washington Evening Star,* September 19, 1963.

———. "Funeral Fails to Close Void." *Washington Evening Star,* September 19, 1963.

McMillan, George. "The Birmingham Church Bomber." *Saturday Evening Post,* June 6, 1964, 11–19.

Meier, August. *Negro Thought in America, 1880–1915.* Ann Arbor: University of Michigan Press, 1966.

Message of the Mayor and Annual Reports of the Officers of Birmingham, 1906. Birmingham: City of Birmingham, 1906.

Miller, William R. *Martin Luther King Jr.: His Life, Martyrdom, and Meaning for the World.* New York: Weybright, 1968.

Miller, Zane L. "Urban Blacks in the South, 1865–1920: The Richmond, Savannah, New Orleans, Louisville, and Birmingham Experience." In *The New Urban History: Quantitative Explorations by American Historians,* edited by Leo F. Schnore. Princeton: Princeton University Press, 1975.

Mitchell, Henry H. *Black Preaching.* Philadelphia: J. B. Lippincott, 1970.

———. *Celebration and Experience in Preaching.* Nashville: Abingdon Press, 1990.

Mitchell, Henry, and Nicholas C. Lewter. *Soul Theology.* San Francisco: Harper and Row, 1986.

Mitchell, Louis D. "Another Redemption: Baxley in Birmingham." *Crisis* 78 (1978): 311–17.

Moore, Geraldine. *Behind the Ebony Mask: What American Negroes Really Think.* Birmingham: Southern University Press, 1961.

"More Race Pressure on Business." *Business Week,* May 12, 1962.

Morgan, Charles Jr. *A Time to Speak.* New York: Harper and Row, 1964.

———. "Who Is Guilty in Birmingham." *Christian Century,* October 2, 1963, 1195–96.

Morris, Aldon D. *The Origins of the Civil Rights Movement: Black Communities Organizing for Change.* New York: Free Press, 1984.

Myrdal, Gunnar. *An American Dilemma: The Negro Problem and Modern Democracy.* New York: Harper and Brothers, 1944.

Nash, Diane. "Inside the Sit-ins and Freedom Rides: Testimony of a Southern Student." In *The New Negro,* edited by Mathew H. Ahmann. Notre Dame, Ind.: Fides Publishers, 1961.

Navasky, Victor S. *Kennedy Justice.* New York: Atheneum, 1970.

Nelsen, Harold A. "Leadership and Change in an Evolutionary Movement." *Social Forces* 49 (1971): 343–71.

Nelson, Hart M., and Anne K. Nelsen. *The Black Church in America.* New York: Basic, 1971.

Nichols, Michael C. "'Cities Are What Men Make Them': Birmingham, Alabama, Faces the Civil Rights Movement, 1963." Thesis, Brown University, 1974.

Nobles, Wade W. "African-American Family Life: An Instrument of Culture." In *Black Families,* edited by Harriette Pipes McAdoo. 2d ed. Newbury Park, Calif.: Sage Publications, 1988.

Norrell, Robert J. "Caste in Steel: Jim Crow Careers in Birmingham, Alabama." *Journal of American History* 73 (1986): 669–94.

———. *The New Patrida: The Story of Birmingham's Greeks.* Birmingham: Birmingham Public Library, n.d.

———. *The Other Side: The Story of Birmingham's Blacks.* Birmingham: Birmingham Public Library, n.d.

——. *Reaping the Whirlwind: The Civil Rights Movement in Tuskegee.* New York: Knopf, 1985.

Nunnelley, William A. *Bull Connor.* Tuscaloosa: University of Alabama Press, 1991.

O'Reilly, Kenneth. "The FBI and the Civil Rights Movement during the Kennedy Years: From the Freedom Rides to Albany." *Journal of Southern History* 54 (1988): 201–32.

Osborne, George R. "Boycott in Birmingham." *Nation,* May 5, 1962, 397–401.

Otto, Rudolf. *The Idea of the Holy.* New York: Oxford University Press, 1958.

Ownby, Ted. *Subduing Satan: Religion, Recreation, and Manhood in the Rural South, 1865–1920.* Chapel Hill: University of North Carolina Press, 1990.

Painter, Irvin. *The Narrative of Hosea Hudson: His Life as a Negro Communist in the South.* Cambridge: Harvard University Press, 1979.

Paris, Peter J. *Black Religious Leaders: Conflict in Unity.* Louisville, Ky.: Westminster/John Knox Press, 1994.

Peake, Thomas R. *Keeping the Dream Alive: A History of the Southern Christian Leadership Conference from King to the 1980s.* New York: P. Lang, 1987.

Peck, James. *Freedom Ride.* New York: Simon and Schuster, 1962.

——. "Freedom Ride." CORE-lator 89 (May 1961): 1–4.

Peters, Marie Ferguson. "Parenting in Black Families with Young Children: A Historical Perspective." In *Black Families,* edited by Harriette Pipes McAdoo. 2d ed. Newbury Park, Calif.: Sage, 1988.

Pitts, Walter. *The Old Ship of Zion.* New York: Oxford University Press, 1993.

Powledge, Fred. *Free at Last? The Civil Rights Movement and the People Who Made It.* Boston: Little, Brown, 1991.

Proudfoot, Wayne. *Religious Experience.* Berkeley: University of California Press, 1985.

Raboteau, Albert J. *Slave Religion: The "Invisible Institution" in the Antebellum South.* New York: Oxford University Press, 1979.

Raines, Howell. "The Birmingham Bombing Twenty Years Later: The Case That Won't Close." *New York Times Magazine,* July 24, 1983, 12.

——. *My Soul Is Rested: Movement Days in the Deep South Remembered.* New York: G. P. Putnam's Sons, 1977.

Reed, John Shelton. *The Enduring South: Subcultural Persistence in Mass Society.* Chapel Hill: University of North Carolina Press, 1974.

Roberts, J. Deotis. *The Prophethood of Black Believers: An African American Political Theology for Ministry.* Louisville, Ky.: Westminster/John Knox Press, 1994.

Rogers, Kim L. "Oral History and the History of the Civil Rights Movement." *Journal of American History* 75 (1988): 567–76.

Rose, Stephen C. "Epitaph for an Era." *Christianity and Crisis* 10 (June 1963): 103–10.

———. "Test for Nonviolence." *Christian Century,* May 29, 1963.

Rovere, Richard. "Letter from Washington." *New Yorker,* June 1, 1963, 100–8.

Rowe, Gary Thomas, Jr. *My Undercover Years with the Ku Klux Klan.* New York: Bantam Books, 1976.

Rustin, Bayard. *Down the Line: The Collected Writings of Bayard Rustin.* Chicago: Quadrangle, 1971.

———. "The Meaning of Birmingham." *Liberation* 8 (1963): 7.

Scherer, Robert G. *Subordination or Liberation? The Development and Conflicting Theories of Black Education in Nineteenth-Century Alabama.* Tuscaloosa: University of Alabama Press, 1977.

Schlesinger, Arthur M., Jr. *Robert F. Kennedy and His Times.* Boston: Houghton Mifflin, 1978.

———. *A Thousand Days: John F. Kennedy in the White House.* Boston: Houghton-Mifflin, 1965.

Schulke, Flip, and Penelope McPhee. *King Remembered.* New York: W. W. Norton, 1986.

Shannon, William V. "The Crisis in Birmingham." *Commonwealth* 78 (1963): 238–39.

Shea, John. *Religious Experiencing: William James and Ernest Gendlin.* Lanham, Md.: University Press of America, 1987.

Shuttlesworth, Fred L. "An Account of the Alabama Christian Movement for Human Rights." In "Goals and Techniques in Three Civil Rights Organizations in Alabama," Appendix B, by Jacquelyne Johnson Clarke. Ph.D. diss., Ohio State University, 1960.

———. "Birmingham Revisited." *Ebony,* August 1971, 114–118.

———. "Birmingham Shall Be Free Some Day." *Freedomways* 4 (winter 1964): 16–19.

———. "No Easy Walk, 1961–1963." In *Eyes on the Prize,* edited by Henry Hampton. Boston: Blackside, 1986.

———. "Together Building the Beloved Community." Address given at Xavier University of Louisiana, New Orleans, January 20, 1988.

Sitkoff, Harvard. *The Struggle For Black Equality, 1954–1980.* New York: Hill and Wray, 1981.

Smith, Theophus H. *Conjuring Culture: Biblical Formations of Black America.* New York: Oxford University Press, 1994.

Snell, William R. "The Ku Klux Klan in Jefferson County, Alabama." Thesis, Samford University, 1967.

Sobel, Lester A., ed. *Civil Rights, 1960–1966.* New York: Facts on File, 1967.

Sterne, Emma G. *I Have a Dream.* New York: Knopf, 1965.

Stewart, Carlyle Fielding, III. *Soul Survivors: An African American Spirituality.* Louisville, Ky.: Westminster/John Knox Press, 1997.

Stewart, George R. "Birmingham's Reaction to the 1954 Desegregation Decision." Thesis, Samford University, 1967.

Stone, Geoffrey R. "New York Times Co. v. Sullivan." In *The Oxford Companion to the Supreme Court of the United States,* edited by Kermit L. Hall. New York: Oxford University Press, 1992.

"There's a New World Coming." *Bulletin of the Peace Studies Institute* (August 1971).

Thurman, Wallace. *The Blacker the Berry: A Novel of Negro Life.* New York: AMS Press, 1971.

Tindall, George Brown. *America: A Narrative History.* 2d ed. New York: W. W. North, 1988.

Vann, David. "The Change from Commission to Mayor-Council Government and the Racial Desegregation Agreements in Birmingham, Alabama, 1961–1963." Rev. ed. Paper delivered at the Center for Urban Affairs, University of Alabama at Birmingham, 1988.

Vowels, Robert C. "Atlanta Negro Business and the New Black Bourgeoisie." *Atlanta Historical Bulletin* 21 (1977): 48–63.

Walker, Clarence E. *A Rock in a Weary Land: The African Methodist Episcopal Church during the Civil War and Reconstruction.* Baton Rouge: Louisiana State University Press, 1982.

Walker, Jack. "The Functions of Disunity: Negro Leadership in a Southern City." *Journal of Negro Education* 32 (1963): 227–36.

Walker, Wyatt T. "The Meaning of Birmingham." *News Illustrated* 1 (May 1964): 1–2.

Walton, Norman W. "The Walking City: A History of the Montgomery Bus Boycott." In *The Walking City: The Montgomery Bus Boycott, 1955–1956,* edited by David J. Garrow. Brooklyn: Carlson Publishing, 1989.

Warren, Richard L. "Birmingham: Brinkmanship in Race Relations." *Christian Century,* May 30, 1962, 689–90.

Washington, James Melvin. *Frustrated Fellowship: The Black Baptist Quest for Social Power.* Macon, Ga.: Mercer University Press, 1986.

———, ed. *A Testament of Hope: The Essential Writings of Martin Luther King Jr.* San Francisco: Harper and Row, 1986.

Washington, Joseph R. *Black Religion.* Boston: Beacon, 1964.

———, ed. *Black Religion and Public Policy: Ethical and Historical Perspectives.* Philadelphia: Symposium at the University of Pennsylvania, 1978.

Watters, Pat. *Down to Now: Reflections on the Southern Civil Rights Movement.* New York: Random, 1971.

West, Cornel. *Prophetic Fragments.* Grand Rapids, Mich.: William B. Eerdmans Publishing, 1988.

Westin, Alan F., and Barry Mahoney. *The Trial of Martin Luther King.* New York: Crowell, 1974.

Whittemore, H. *Together.* New York: William Morrow, 1971.

Wimberly, Edward P. *African American Pastoral Care.* Nashville: Abingdon Press, 1991.

———. *Pastoral Care in the Black Church.* Nashville: Abingdon Press, 1979.

Wimberly, Edward P., and Anne E. Wimberly. *Liberation and Human Wholeness.* Nashville: Abingdon Press, 1986.

Wofford, Harris. *Of Kennedys and Kings.* New York: Farrar, Strauss, and Giroux, 1980.

Young, Andrew J. "And Birmingham." *Drum Major* 1 (winter 1971).

———. "The Day We Went to Jail in Birmingham." *Friends* 3 (February 1964): 3–11.

———. "Dynamics of a Birmingham Movement in the Sixties." In *Nonviolence in the 70s,* 9–15. Atlanta: Martin Luther King Center, 1972.

———. "Easter Sunday: Parting of the Red Sea." *Atlanta Journal-Constitution,* July 17, 1983.

———. *An Easy Burden: The Civil Rights Movement and the Transformation of America.* New York: HarperCollins, 1996.

Young, V. "Family and Childhood in a Southern Negro Community." *American Anthropologist* 72 (April 1970): 269–88.

Index

rights activities, 78, 79; begins ministry at Bethel Baptist Church, 69, 71; begins ministry at Everdale Baptist Church, 51; begins ministry at First Baptist Church (Selma), 54; begins ministry at Greater New Light Baptist Church, 427; begins ministry at Mount Zion Baptist Church (Potter Station, Alabama), 52; begins ministry at Revelation Baptist Church, 281–82; "betrayal" by Glenn E. Smiley, 195–200; biblicism of, 42–43, 90; birth of, 12; and black leadership, 86–87, 89, 213–19; on bombings, 113, 177–78, 407; challenges Connor to debate, 227; charisma of, 66–67, 71, 72, 111, 124, 134; childhood of, 15–34; children arrested in Gadsden, Alabama, 246–52; civic activities (at Bethel), 74–76; "combative spirituality," 8, 9, 24, 448–49 (n. 9); confrontational personality of, 7, 8, 42, 56, 64, 66, 67, 300, 392; considers offer of Revelation Baptist Church, 256–61; contact with Kennedy administration, 268, 270, 273–74, 278, 393, 396; courage of, 113, 123, 339; criticism of, 195–200; "devilishness" of, 28; as disciplinarian of his children, 142–44; discusses Sixteenth Street Church bombing with President Kennedy, 407; divorce of, 436–39; early career choices of, 27; early community concerns, 74–76, 78–79; early education of, 28–32; early jobs, 32; efforts toward hiring black police, 82–83, 85, 164; as father, 144; fired by First Baptist Church (Selma), 66, 458 (n. 59); first sermon of, 40–41; and the founding of the sclc, 119–20; and Freedom Rides, 263–80; as grandfather, 439; as icon of the civil rights

movement, 390, 440–44; injured by fire hose, 378–79; integrates bus terminal, 125–28; on integration, 160–61; involvement with the Southern Organizing Committee for Economic and Social Justice (soc), 434; licensed to preach, 40; as male chauvinist, 436; marital difficulties, 3, 215–16, 224–25, 257, 260, 436–39; marriage, 35–36; and Martin Luther King Jr., 89, 221–24, 286–87, 343, 381–83, 392, 417, 419, 496 (n. 86); meeting with downtown merchants, 322–25; militancy, 121, 122, 123; ministerial activities of, 56, 71–72, 78, 90, 129, 130; ministerial calling of, 28; on ministers, 105–6, 317, 351; and naming of "F. L. Shuttlesworth Drive," 1; ordained to the ministry, 51; pastors of, 26; personal style of, 4, 456 (n. 37); philosophy of history of, 77; possible assassination attempts of, 173, 318–19, 398, 402; preaching of, 40–41, 43, 51, 52, 56–58, 72, 73, 77, 90, 131–34, 140–41, 445; protests presence of detectives, 193–94; and Ralph Abernathy, 231–32; rejects moratorium on demonstrations (1963), 381–85; relationship with stepfather, 16–19; religious experience of, 27–28, 44, 63–65, 67, 108–9, 151–52, 378; resignation from acmhr presidency, 428, 429; as role model, 90–91; rumored run for Birmingham City Commission, 161; on schoolchildren as demonstrators, 366; and the Selma campaign, 418–21; on southern whites, 129; speaks at March on Washington, 401; stops school bus, 1–2; studies at Cedar Grove Academy, 41–43; studies at Selma University, 44, 49–51; sues Connor and Moore over detectives,

About the Author

Andrew M. Manis is the author of *Southern Civil Religions in Conflict: Black and White Baptists and Civil Rights, 1947–1957*. He is currently the editor of Religion and Southern Studies at Mercer University Press. He also serves as adjunct professor at Mercer University and at Wesleyan College, Macon, Georgia.